D1823099

Archaeological Science: Theories, Models and Techniques

Archaeological Science: Theories, Models and Techniques

Edited by
Levi Johnston

Published by States Academic Press,
109 South 5th Street,
Brooklyn, NY 11249, USA

ISBN: 978-1-63989-058-3

Cataloging-in-Publication Data

Archaeological science : theories, models and techniques / edited by Levi Johnston.
p. cm.
Includes bibliographical references and index.
ISBN 978-1-63989-058-3
1. Archaeology. 2. History. 3. Antiquities. 4. Archaeology and history.
5. Historic sites. I. Johnston, Levi.
CC72 .R43 2022
930.1--dc23

For information on all States Academic Press publications
visit our website at www.statesacademicpress.com

Contents

Preface

This book has been a concerted effort by a group of academicians, researchers and scientists, who have contributed their research works for the realization of the book. This book has materialized in the wake of emerging advancements and innovations in this field. Therefore, the need of the hour was to compile all the required researches and disseminate the knowledge to a broad spectrum of people comprising of students, researchers and specialists of the field.

Archaeological science or archaeometry is the development and application of scientific techniques to the analysis of archaeological data. It includes the study of human prehistory and history. Physical, chemical and biological analysis of the collected data has been embraced by the field to understand the date, origin, manufacture and use of artifacts along with their ancestry. Dating techniques like radio-carbon dating and artifact studies are two methods of archaeological science which provide information about human culture, origin, relative chronologies, past landscape, flora and fauna and spatial variations in soil and sediments. The topics covered in this book offer the readers new insights in the field of archaeological science. The readers would gain knowledge that would broaden their perspective about archaeological science. This book attempts to assist those with a goal of delving into the field of archaeological science.

At the end of the preface, I would like to thank the authors for their brilliant chapters and the publisher for guiding us all-through the making of the book till its final stage. Also, I would like to thank my family for providing the support and encouragement throughout my academic career and research projects.

Editor

1

ANALYSIS AND INTERPRETATION OF NEOLITHIC PERIOD FOOTPRINTS FROM BARCIN HÖYÜK, TURKEY

Derya Atamtürk[1], Rana Özbal[2], Fokke Gerritsen[3], and İzzet Duyar[1]

[1]*İstanbul University, Faculty of Letters, Department of Anthropology, Ordu Caddesi 6, 34134 Laleli/İstanbul, Turkey*
[2]*Koç University, Department of Archaeology and History of Art, Rumelifeneri Yolu, 34450 Sarıyer/İstanbul, Turkey*
[3]*Netherlands Institute in Turkey, İstiklal Caddesi 181, Merkez Han, 34433 Beyoğlu/İstanbul, Turkey*

Corresponding Author: Rana Özbal (rozbal@ku.edu.tr)

ABSTRACT

Presented here are a pair of preserved footprints discovered in 2014 at the site of Barcın Höyük, a Neolithic site located in northwestern Turkey. Found within the entrance of Structure 2a, the footprints date to approximately 6400 cal. BC. Footprints are rarely discovered in prehistoric settlements, adding significance to their study and to the conditions that led to their formation and ultimate preservation. This article provides anthropological estimations for the individuals who left the footprints and discusses the possibility of symbolism using contextual information and ethnographic and archaeological parallels. The measurements and analyses confirm that the footprints are the bare left and right foot of a single individual and provide clues about the biological profile of the individual. The footprint of the right foot produces various measurements such as footprint length, breadth and heel breadth. When compared with known standards, the print appears likely to be of an adult male 169.9 cm tall (with a 16.78 CI at 95% ranging from 153.1-186.66 cm) and weighing 71.9 kg (with a 31.14 kg CI at 95% ranging from 40.76 - 103.04 kg).

KEYWORDS: Barcın Höyük, Neolithic, footprints, sex determination, stature estimation, body weight estimation

1. INTRODUCTION

The analysis of footprints provides scientists working in various areas with new information. For instance, footprints provide the opportunity to determine the biological profile of the individual(s) who made them (Atamtürk 2010; Atamtürk and Duyar 2008; Jasuja et al. 1993; Robbins 1986). Prehistoric footprints allow us to determine the physical characteristics of ancient people and, in evolutionary cases, may even enable insights into the locomotor biomechanics of hominins and the evolution of the foot structure (Bennett and Morse 2014; Mietto et al. 2003; Webb et al. 2006).

Carved, painted and incised footprints are often considered sacred and the literature on their symbolism is wide ranging (Bertilsson 2013; Bradley 1997; Brown 1990; Dunbabin 1990; Hasan 1993; Ludowyk 2013; Takacs 2007; Thomas 2008; van Pelt and Staring 2017). Impressed footprints, on the other hand, may have an equally high ritual standing but they also carry the possibility of being unintentionally produced. Artwork depicting footprints carries symbolic connotations because it is often considered a sign either of an invisible deity or a revered holy person. Bertilsson (2013) and Bradley (1997) demonstrate that incised footprints are a cosmological pictogram cross-regionally in prehistoric rock art. In Ancient Egypt, priests graffitied their footprints and sometimes their names and titles onto temple roofs, often with an accompanying text stating that they would "remain forever in the presence of their god" (van Pelt and Staring 2017). Located at the entrance of the 8th Century BC Neo-Hittite temple of Ain 'Dara, the giant 1 meter long carved footprints likely carry ritual significance as their location suggests (Thomas 2008). Footprint engravings likewise continue through the Graeco-Roman Period, like those known from Kızıldağ in the Konya Plain of Central Anatolia, and have been interpreted as either a way to record the location of partakers in religious ceremonies (Rojas and Sergueenkova 2014) or the pilgrimage of the disciples of Craterus (Dunbabin 1990). In either case, footprints are associated with considerable symbolism (Takacs 2007). Hasan (1993) demonstrates how veneration of footprints transcends into Islam and explores the ritual of Qadam Rasul honoring the footprint of the prophet, and its antecedents in both Christianity and Judaism. Likewise, stylized footprints of the Buddha often incised in stone are revered across many Buddhist countries (Brown 1990; Ludowyk 2013).

Impressed footprints, on the other hand, are often simply preserved because of favorable natural and geological conditions. Such footprints show the mold of the foot by becoming fossilized in ash layers or the like. The most well-known is, of course, the 3.5-million-year-old Laetoli footprints from Tanzania providing important insights on foot morphology and the evolutionary development of the foot. Turkey, too, specifically the Kula Demirköprü Region houses over 200 fossilized Pleistocene footprints dating to approximately 26,000 B.P. and belonging to at least three different individuals (Kayan 1992; Ozansoy 1969; Westaway et al. 2006). Other examples like those from Willandra Lakes, Australia (Webb et al. 2006), Roccamonfina, Italy (Mietto et al. 2003), Koobi Fora and Ileret in Kenya (Dingwall et al. 2013, Roberts and Berger 1997), Jaguar Cave, Tennessee (Willey et al. 2005) Lake Managuq, Nicaragua (Brinton 1887), Namib Sand Sea, Namibia (Morse et al. 2013) and Pompeii, Italy (Mastrolorenzo et al. 2006) are also the result of accidental preservation situations. Many of these footprints have been studied in terms of stratigraphy, taphonomy and approximate dates (Scaillet et al. 2008; Grün et al. 2011; Bennett and Morse 2014). Fossilized footprints may make it possible to determine the foot structure and locomotion form as well (Tuttle 2008; Morse et al. 2013; Bennett and Morse 2014). In addition, the discovery of foot imprints prompts in some cases an interest in biological profiles including stature, body weight and gender of the individuals who left the prints, using forensic calculations and estimations (Capecchi 1984; D'Août et al. 2010; Dingwall et al. 2013; Mieto et al. 2003; Tuttle 2008; Webb et al. 2006; White and Suwa 1987).

More difficult to answer is whether strategically placed foot imprints carried symbolic meanings such as incised and etched footprints may have had. In other words, could an imprint of a foot be made specifically for a symbolic purpose? This question is addressed for the Barcın Höyük footprints by discussing whether they were implanted accidentally or deliberately and by placing the footprints in their archaeological context.

2. THE BARCIN HÖYÜK FOOTPRINTS

Preserving both the two dimensional and the three dimensional impressions of the foot, the footprints discovered at the settlement of Barcın Höyük were made by pressing the sole of the foot onto a soft surface. Discovered in 2014, they date to approximately to 6400 cal. BC. Barcın Höyük is located in NW Anatolia (Fig. 1) and at present represents the earliest farming settlement in the region (Gerritsen et al. 2013a, 2013b; Gerritsen and Özbal 2016; Özbal and Gerritsen 2015). Though practiced in Central and Southeast Anatolia already for over a millennium, the spread of farming and animal husbandry to western Anatolia and from there to Europe did not take place before 6700 cal. BC (Düring 2013; Schoop 2005; Weninger et al. 2014). Barcın Höyük must therefore be viewed as a pioneer settlement and represents the first farming groups that left these core areas to explore new horizons. The footprint was not discovered in the earliest level of occupation dating to 6600-6500 cal. BC but to Phase VId1, which represents the occupational phase immediately thereafter. Excavated structures in this phase were aligned linearly in a row. From the four aligned structures, it appears that larger structures ranging in size around 23 m^2 and smaller structures about half the size were placed alternatingly (Fig. 2). Both of the smaller structures 21 and 2a were burnt, allowing for good preservation of interior characteristics which in both cases included plastered wood and loam platforms and *in situ* finds. The footprints were discovered near the entrance zone of Structure 2a, positioned as if exiting the structure.

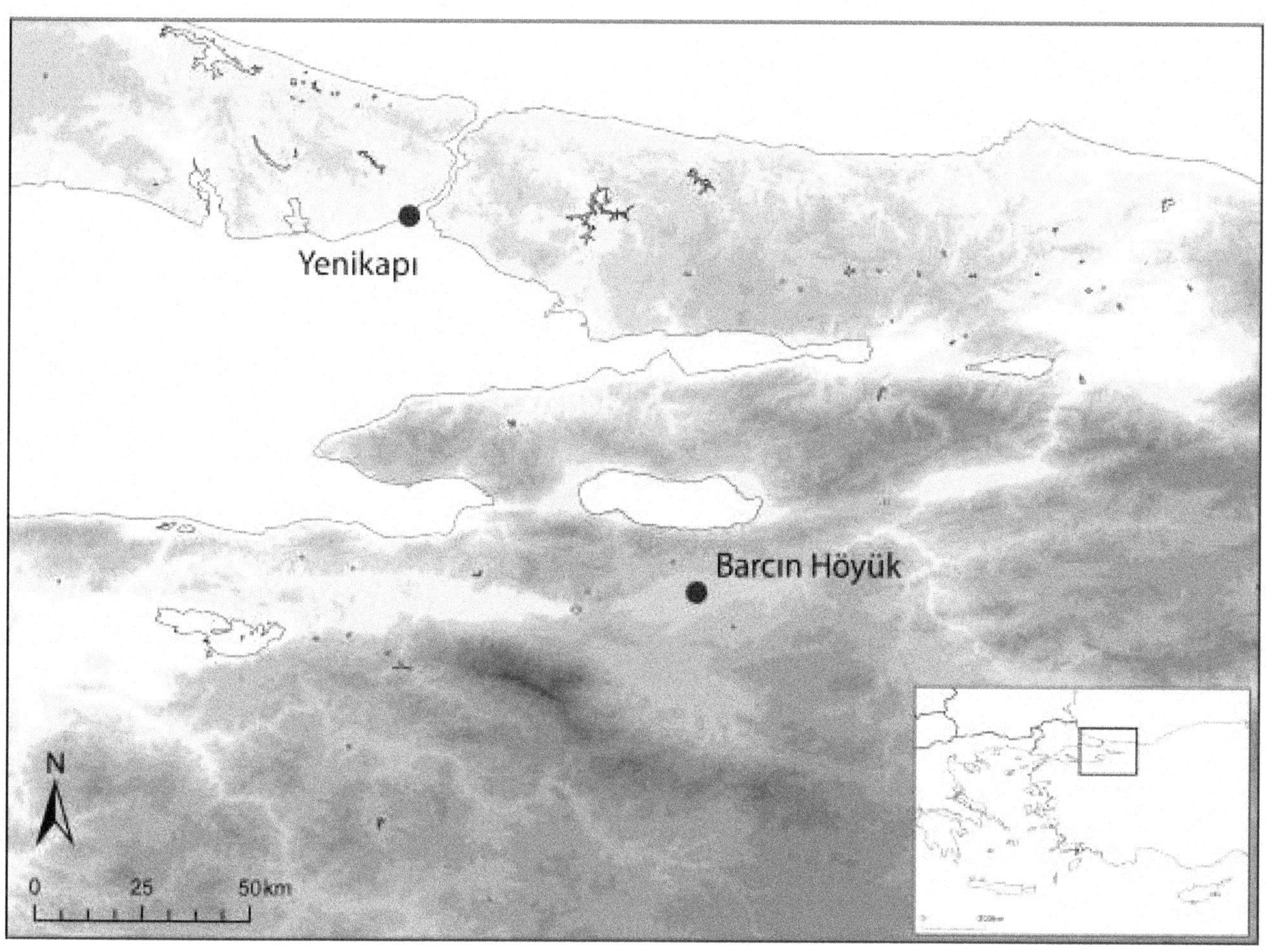

Figure 1 : Map showing the location of Barcın Höyük and Yenikapı both mentioned in the text

It is worth noting that this is the second set of footprints found dating to the seventh millennium from the Marmara region. Excavations at the site of Yenikapı in İstanbul yielded over 2000 footprints, some barefooted and others wearing some sort of footgear (Kızıltan and Polat 2013:118). Those from Barcın are a few centuries older and unlike those from Yenikapı, come from an indoor context (Özbal and Gerritsen 2015). Perhaps more significant may be the circumstances of their production; while those from Yenikapı represent accidentally preserved prints by inhabitants walking about in every which way, those from Barcın may carry other connotations.

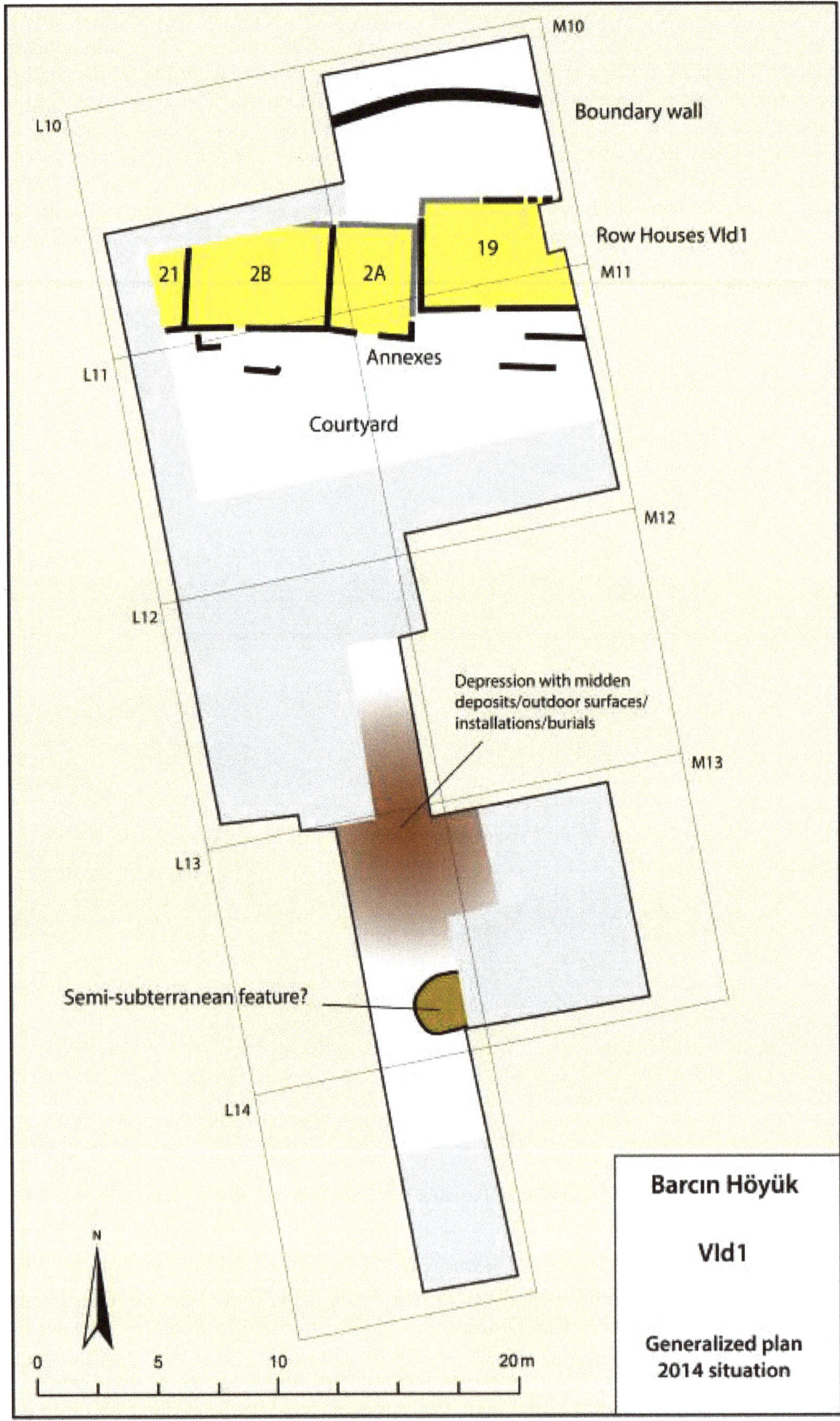

Figure 2: Schematic plan of Barcın Höyük Level VId1 showing structure 2a

Figure 3: Photo of both footprints at Barcın Höyük

The conditions of preservation of the Barcın Höyük footprints are noteworthy. They were impressed within a freshly plastered floor in the room (Fig, 3). The plaster was made of loam with straw mixed in. However, thereafter another layer of floor plaster had been placed on top, hiding them from view. The burning of the structure caused the uppermost plaster layers of the floor to be fire-hardened and as a consequence, preserved the footprints. Following excavation, the footprint was consolidated, removed in a single piece, placed in a wooden box specifically made for the feature, and transported to the local museum. A silicon mold and a plaster replica of the footprint were made of the footprint, enabling later study of the feature. One factor that complicated the removal of the footprint was the discovery of a cattle skull located immediately beneath the plaster under the left footprint. The resistence from underneath prevented the left footprint, located about half a foot's length in front of the right footprint, from forming a deep impression and resulted in a shallow and superficial print. Measurements taken, as explained below, comfirm that both prints belonged to the same individual. Even though the left footprint remains shallow, the right foot was firmly sunken into the clay which enabled an impression that showed all five toes, the heel and the arch (Fig. 4).

3. MATERIALS AND METHODS

Depending on the condition of the ground, footprints in soft surfaces are classified as "positive" footprints and footprints left on a hard surface are classified as "negative" footprints. While the right footprint at Barcın Höyük made by stepping into the wet freshly plastered floor must be classified as a "positive footprint" (Figure 4 and Figure 5), the other one, which faced the resistance of the animal skull below is, consequently, a negative footprint, impressed into hard ground. All the contours and lines were clearly visible and well-maintained in the print of the right foot as it plunged into freshly applied plaster although such delineations were much less clear in the left one. Nonetheless, measurements and calculations and morphological observations, indicate that the two Barcın footprints, most probably, belong to the same individual.

Figure 4: Photo of the right footprint

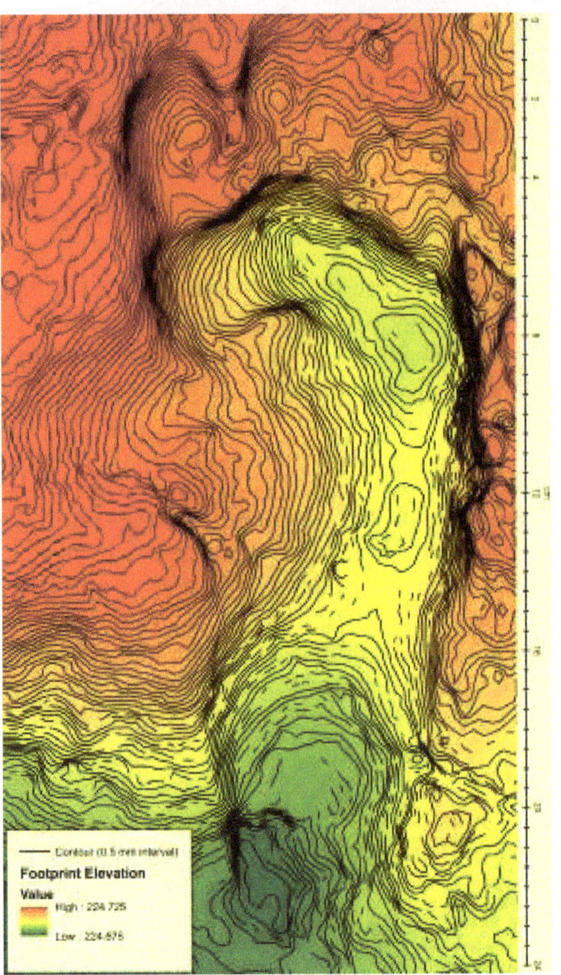

Figure 5: An elevation diagram of the right footprint

It is well-known that footprints differ significantly from the actual foot size of the individual who made the imprint. Some studies examine this difference; Dingwall et al. (2013), for example, state that the footprint length could vary approximately 1.7-14.5% from the actual foot length such that the footprint length on average may be as much as 10% smaller than the actual length of the foot. Atamtürk (2003), likewise, put forward that the difference between the actual length of the foot and the size of its corresponding print could differ by about 2 cm in length and about 1 cm in breadth. Consequently, in order to minimize the error rate, in this article, the footprint size rather than actual foot size has been taken into consideration.

Generally, when determining an individual's gender, stature and body weight, the footprints' length, breadth and the heel breadth measurements are collectively taken into consideration (Abledu et al. 2015; Hemy et al. 2013; Ukoha et al. 2013). Because the right footprint found at Barcın Höyük was so clear, anthropometric measurements were taken from the right footprint. The sizes have been obtained in the following manner (Laskowski and Kyle 1988):*Footprint length* (FPL) is measured as the direct maximum distance from the most posterior point of the heel to the tip of longest toe.

Footprint breadth (FPB) is the linear distance between the points of maximum lateral obtrusion of the fifth foot bone and the most medial point of the first toe of the foot.

Footprint heel breadth (FPHB) is the distance between the uppermost lateral obtrusive points of the heel.

These measurements given in Table 1 provide the biological profile of the footprint's owner determined using these values. To minimize the error margin, calculations are based on equations deriving from right foot measurement values.

Table 1: The measurement values for the Barcın Höyük right footprint in mm

	Right footprint
Footprint length (FPL)	245
Footprint breadth (FPB)	97
Footprint heel breadth (FPHB)	66

4. ANALYSES AND EVALUATION

Although less well preserved, the measurements indicate that the left foot belongs to the same person. Because foot size grows synchronically with the other parts of the body until the end of puberty (Liu et al. 1998), the size of a footprint can only be useful in determining the age of pre-adults Based on cross-cultural ethnographic analogies (Atamtürk 2010; Hemy et al. 2013; Krishan 2008), our measurements indicate that the Barcın Höyük footprints belong to an adult individual, completely grown. Nonetheless, whether this person was a young or middle-aged adult or elderly individual cannot be ascertained.

4.1. ESTIMATION OF SEX

While experiments to determine whether the pressure exerted on the ground differs in the footprints of males and females have yielded inconclusive results (Putti et al. 2010), sex identification can, in fact, be made by measuring the absolute and proportional dimensions of a footprint (Atamtürk 2010; Fessler et al. 2005; Wunderlich and Cavanagh 2001; Krishan 2008).

Table 2: Comparison of anthropometric figures from a range of different populations

	Barcın Höyük	Turkey (Atamtürk 2010)		Australia (Hemy et al. 2013)		India (Krishan 2008)
Variable	Male	Males	Females	Males	Females	Males
Footprint length (mm)	24.5	24.99±1.22	22.77±1,04	25.48±1.33	23.01±1.17	24.13±3.26
Footprint breadth (mm)	9.7	10.03±0.62	9.21±0,67	9.95±0.63	8.97±0.57	8.69±1.90
Footprint heel breadth (mm)	6.6	6.20±0.53	5.76±0,58	5.59±0.46	5.06±0.46	4.92±1.39

Our study of the Barcın Höyük footprints uses the anthropometric dimensions obtained from different populations and discriminant functions obtained from these measurements to identify sex. While genetic factors help to determine the form of the general structure of the foot, many studies emphasize the importance of environmental factors in the shaping of the foot. Consequently, one notes particular differences in foot measurements and forms across different communities (Anıl et al. 1997; Rocke and Davila 1972; Rutishauser 1968). Data from the three aforementioned studies have been applied (Table 2). The measurements of the Barcın Höyük footprints have been compared to the sizes of adult individuals living in Turkey (Atamtürk 2010; 254 males and 262 females), in Western Australia (Hemy et al. 2013; 90 males and 110 females) and in Northern India (Krishan 2008; 1040 males). Measurements indicate that the length, breadth and heel size of the Barcın footprint equates more closely with male individuals' measurements in the studied populations.

In addition to the abovementioned studies, the Barcın footprint's measurements were compared to the right footprints of 126 Ghanaian males and females varying in age from 18-30 years as a further step in the sex determination of the Barcın footprints' owner (Abledu et al. 2015; Table 3). The table indicates that all the three equations targeted to determine the sex of the individual fall within the range of an adult male.

Table 3: Regression equations used for sex estimation

Researchers	Equations	Estimated sex
Atamtürk (2010)	0.847 x Footprint length - 20.155 = 187.36 (mid-point 23.78)	Male
	1.553 x Footprint breadth - 14.829 = 135.812 (mid-point 9.55)	Male
	1.768 x Footprint heel breadth - 10.533 = 106.155 (mid-point 5.96)	Male
Hemy et al. (2013)	(0.606 x Footprint length + (0.533 x Footprint breadth) - 19.544 = 0.473 (section point - 0.130)	Male
Abledu et al. (2015)	0.828 x Footprint length - 20.205 = 0,081 (section point - 0.057)	Male

4.2. ESTIMATION OF STATURE

There are many studies addressing body height estimation from bare foot length (Atamtürk and Duyar 2008; Giles and Vallandigham 1991; Martin and Saller 1957; Robbins 1986; Rutishauser 1968; Saxena 1984). However, height estimation studies using only the right foot was considered in the Barcın case in order to reduce the estimation error (Atamtürk and Duyar 2008; Krishan 2008; Ukoha et al. 2013). Given that the Barcın footprint likely belonged to a male individual, only male regression equations of bare footprint length were used.

While studies unanimously agree that measurements taken from long bones give better results in the estimation of stature (Duyar and Pelin 2003; Sjøvold 2000; Trotter and Gleser 1952, 1958), foot size too can likewise be used to successfully estimate stature (Atamtürk and Duyar 2008). The stature of the individual who left the Barcin footprint was calculated using the regression equations developed in three different studies based on maximum footprint length. The first study is based on the sizes taken from 127 males living in Turkey (Atamtürk and Duyar 2008), the second, on the foot sizes of 100 males ages 18-30 from Nigeria (Ukoha et al. 2013) and the third on 50 adult males living in Northern India (Krishan 2008). The research estimates deriving from these studies suggests that the Barcın footprint was left by an adult male between 169.9-173.2 cm tall, as indicated in Table 4. Despite the genetic distance between the modern and ancient Anatolian populations this study uses the equations derived by Atamtürk and Duyar (2008) and assumes an estimated stature of 169.88 cm given that the other equations values derive from geographically distant studies. With a SEE (standard error of the estimate) of 8.56 cm, the stature of the individual who left the footprint based on a 95% confidence interval (confidence interval, CI 95% = 16.78 cm) would hence range between 153.1 and 186.66 cm.

Table 4: Estimated stature of the Barcın Höyük footprint using different height calculation equations.

Researcher	Equations	Estimated stature (cm)
Atamtürk (2003)	5.014 × Footprint length + 47.041 ± 8.557	169.88
Ukoha ve ark. (2013)	3.080 × Footprint length + 95.042 ± 4.842	170.50
Krishan (2008)	3.510 × Footprint length + 87.214 ± 2.16	173.21

Anthropological analyses of Barcın Höyük human skeletons were carried out by Alpaslan-Roodenberg (Alpaslan-Roodenberg et al. 2013). In the stated study, the stature was estimated using the Trotter and Gleser (1952, 1958) equation of the left radius length of four elderly individuals (3 females, 1 male). While the females in Barcın Höyük varied between 146.8–159.21 cm tall; the single male was found to be 166.5 ± 4.66 cm. The stature of the Barcın Höyük male footprint owner is 3.5 cm taller than the other male whose stature was calculated from his radius bone.

At this stage, we must seek the meaning of these stature estimates for the Barcın community in terms of the Anatolian prehistoric past. Angel (1984) carried out one of the most comprehensive evaluations on this subject. According to this researcher, studies carried out on skeletons from the Eastern Mediterranean region, the average stature value of males in the Late Paleolithic period is 177.1 cm. This value decreases to 172.5 cm in the Mesolithic period, to 169.6 cm in the Early Neolithic period and to 167.3 cm in the Late Neolithic period. There is an obvious decrease in the average stature in the time slice from the Late Paleolithic period to the Late Neolithic period. Since the Barcın Höyük footprint belongs to an adult male 169.9 cm tall, his calculated height complies with the biological profile put forward by Angel.

4.3. ESTIMATION OF BODY WEIGHT

There are also studies estimating body weight from foot size. Studies have shown a certain correlation between foot width and body weight (Atamtürk 2003; Atamtürk and Duyar 2008; Robbins 1986). Using this information, the width of the Barcın Höyük footprint (the footprint metatarsal width and the footprint heel width) were used to estimate body weight.

Table 5: Body weight estimations calculated based on provided equations

Researcher	Equations	Body weight estimation (kg)
Atamtürk (2003)	7.60 × Footprint breadth - 1.830 ± 15.370	71.89
	5.23 × Footprint heel breadth + 41.957 ± 11.845	76.48
Krishan (2008)	2.86 × Footprint breadth + 37.63 ± 3.51	65.37
	3.94 × Footprint heel breadth + 39.55 ± 3.74	65.55

The results are presented in Table 5. As shown, the body weight values calculated using Atamtürk and Duyar are much higher than the values based on comparisons with values from northern India. Table 5 shows that footprint metatarsal width yields better results than the footprint heel width (Atamtürk and Duyar 2008). Accordingly, it can be assumed that the body weight of the owner of the Barcın footprint was 71.89 kg. Because of the study's SEE (standard error of the estimate), the value of the equation is 15.37 kg, the body weight of the individual who left the footprint estimated with a 95% confidence interval (CI 95% = 31.14 kg) ranges between 40.75 – 103.03 kg.

4.4. FOOTPRINTS AND SHOE USAGE

As described above, the footprints were made with bare feet. While this could indicate that there was no shoe usage in that period or that shoe use was not widespread, this is not likely. Since the indirect (anatomical) proof of shoe usage extends up to the Upper Paleolithic period in the Eurasia region (Trinkaus 2005; Trinkaus and Shang 2008), one assumes that shoe or sandal usage was widespread in Anatolia in the Neolithic period. Likewise, about 2080 footprints dating to ca. 6200 BC were found in Late Neolithic layers of the not too distant Yenikapı excavations (Kızıltan and Polat 2013). In the vast majority of these footprints, one finds clear signs of shoe usage and bare footprints constitute only a small part of the total footprints found. Consequently, it seems likely that the owner of the Barcın footprints followed a no-shoes-indoors custom, or because the symbolic message he wanted to convey through the footprints required bare feet.

5. FOOTPRINT POSITION AND SYMBOLIC MEANING

In addition to their anthropological weight and height estimates, the footprints may offer further evidence regarding symbolism and purpose and there may be additional reasons to consider these footprints as the products of an intentional, symbolically-charged act. This includes, first of all, the fact that the footprints were a result of standing and not walking; these prints were not haphazardly placed here in midstride as the indivial accidentally walked on the fresh plaster as he exited the building. Moreover, in addition to the smaller than usual stride length, the fact that the footprints were formed by firmly pressing the sole of the foot into the ground and with the distribution of the body weight fully between the heel, metatarsus, foot and toe bones further supports this idea of intentionality and, hence, potential symbolic significance (Bennett and Morse 2014; Robbins 1986).

Secondly, worth mentioning here is their spatial location because at least the left foot, as stated above, was positioned immediately above a buried cattle skull (Özbal and Gerritsen 2014, 2015). In the Neolithic of Anatolia, the use of bucrania within structural complexes are often equated with ritual significance (Russel 2012). At the contemporaneous site of Çatalhöyük, located in Central Anatolia, the most elaborate houses were decorated with bucrania which were placed in association with platforms and are assumed to have endowed the spaces with a ritual character (Mellaart 1967). Though the bucranium discovered at Barcın Höyük was hidden from sight, it could still have been placed in this location to provide the space with some symbolic attributes. Foundation deposits are a known phenomenon for sanctifying spaces (Tsuneki 2002). Nevertheless, with the exception of goat bucrania located on the floor to the east of the entrance, this small structure seems to lack other obvious clues for ritual symbolism (Özbal and Gerritsen 2015).

Furthermore, their positioning near the entrance area of structure 2a may also carry symbolic significance. The practice of placing footprints into doorways resembles historical cases of footprint engravings in religious settings such as those found in the Ain 'Dara temple in Syria. Footprints may have been imprinted here perhaps with the idea of marking for posterity the presence of the deity represented (Thomas 2008). Together these lines of data and the fact that the footprints were made with bare feet immediately after the floor had been renewed makes accidental walking on a moist floor unlikely and may suggest that the replastering of the floor atop the bucranium marked a time of symbolic renewal.

ACKNOWLEDGEMENTS

The Barcın Höyük Excavations were directed by Fokke Gerritsen and Rana Özbal with permission from the Turkish Ministry of Culture and Tourism, under the auspices of the Netherlands Institute in Turkey, with funding from the Netherlands Organization for Scientific Research (NWO) and the National Geographic Society. The excavators would like to thank conservator Evren Kıvançer and Prof. Hadi Özbal for conserving the footprints and Piet Gerrits for his help with Figure 5.

REFERENCES

Abledu, J.K., Abledu, G.K., Offei E.B., Antwi, E.M. (2015) Determination of sex from footprint dimensions in a Ghanaian population. *Plos One* Vol. 10, e0139891. doi:10.1371/journal.pone.0139891.

Alpaslan Roodenberg, M.S., Gerritsen, F.A., Özbal, R. (2013) Neolithic burials from Barcın Höyük: the 2007-2012 excavation seasons. *Anatolica*, 39, 1-19.

Angel, J.L. (1984) Health as a crucial factor in the changes from hunting to developed farming in the Eastern Mediterranean. In: *Paleopathology at the Origins of Agriculture*. Cohen, M.N., Armelagos, G.J. (eds.) Orlando, Academic Press, pp. 51-73.

Anıl, A., Peker, T., Turgut, H.B., Ulukent, S.C. (1997) An examination of the relationship between foot length, foot breadth, ball, girth, height and weight of Turkish university students aged between 17 and 25. *Anthropol Anz* Vol. 55, No: 1, pp. 79-87.

Atamtürk, D. (2003) Ayak ve ayak ölçülerinden boy uzunluğu ve vücut ağırlığının tahmini üzerine adli antropolojik bir araştırma. Unpublished MA Thesis, Department of Anthropology, Institute of Social Sciences, Hacettepe University, Ankara.

Atamtürk, D. (2010) Estimation of sex from the dimensions of foot, footprints and shoe. *Anthropol Anz* Vol, 68, No. 1, pp. 21-29.

Atamtürk, D., Duyar, İ. (2008) Age-related factors in the relationship between foot measurements and living stature and body weight. *J Forensic Sci* Vol. 53, No: 6, pp. 1296-1300.

Bennett, M.R., Morse, S.A. (2014) *Human Footprints: Fossilised Locomotion*? London, Springer.

Bertilsson, U. (2013) Divine footprints. Traces of cosmological archetypes and prehistoric religion on the rock faces. In *Art as Source of History*, E. Anati, Capo di Ponte, Edizione del Centro, pp. 163-172.

Bradley, R. (1997) Death by water: boats and footprints in the rock art of western Sweden. *Oxford Journal of Archaeology* Vol. 16, No. 3, pp. 315-324.

Brinton, D.G. (1887) On an ancient human footprint from Nicaragua. *Proc Am Philos Soc* Vol. 24. Pp. 437-444.

Brown, R.L. (1990) God on earth: the walking Buddha in the art of South and Southeast Asia. *Artibus Asiae* Vol. 50.1, No. 2, pp. 73-107.

Capecchi ,V. (1984) Reflections on the footprints of the hominids found at Laetoli. *Anthropol Anz* Vol. 42, No. 2, pp. 81-86.

D'août, K., et al. (2010). Experimentally generated footprints in sand: analysis and consequences for the interpretation of fossil and forensic footprints. *Am J Phys Anthropol* Vol. 141, No. 4, pp. 515-525.

Dingwall, H.L., Hatala, K.G., Wunderlich, R.E., Richmond, B.G. (2013) Hominin stature, body mass, and walking speed estimates based on 1.5 million-year-old fossil footprints at Ileret, Kenya. *J Hum Evol* Vol, 64, pp. 556-568.

Dunbabin, K. (1990) Ipsa deae vestigia... Footprints divine and human on Graeco-Roman monuments. *J Roman Archaeol* Vol. 3, pp. 85-109.

Düring, Bleda S. (2013). Breaking the bond: Investigating the Neolithic expansion in Asia Minor in the seventh millennium BC. *Journal of World Prehistory* Vol. 26, No. 2, pp. 75-100.

Duyar İ, Pelin C. (2003) Body height estimation based on tibia length in different stature groups. *Am J Phys Anthropol* Vol. 122. No. 1, pp. 23-27.

Fessler, D.M.T., Haley, K.J., Lal, R.D. (2005) Sexual dimorphism in foot length proportionate to stature. *Ann Hum Biol* Vol. 32. No. 1, pp. 44-59.

Gerritsen, F., Özbal, R., Thissen L. (2013a). Barcın Höyük. The beginnings of farming in the Marmara region, In *The Neolithic in Turkey. New Excavations and New Research. Vol. 5.* M. Özdoğan, N. Başgelen, P. Kuniholm, (ed.) İstanbul, Arkeoloji ve Sanat Yayınları, pp. 93-112.

Gerritsen, F., Özbal R, Thissen L. (2013b) The Earliest Neolithic Levels at Barcın Höyük, Northwestern Turkey. *Anatolica* Vol. 39, pp. 53-92.

Gerritsen, F., Özbal, R. Barcın Höyük and the pre-Fikirtepe Neolithization of the Eastern Marmara Region. *Anatolian Metal VII, Der Anschnitt Beiheft,* Vol. 8, pp. 211-220.

Grün R., Spooner N., Magee J., Thorne A., Simpson J., Yan G., and Mortimer G. (2011) Stratigraphy and chronology of the WLH 50 human remains, Willandra Lakes World Heritage Area, Australia. *J Hum Evol* Vol. 60, pp. 597-604.

Hasan, P. (1993) The Footprint of the prophet. *Muqarnas* Vol. 10, pp. 335-343.

Hemy N., Flavel A., Ishak N., Franklin D. (2013) Sex estimation using anthropometry of feet and footprints in a Western Australian population. *Forensic Sci Int* Vol. 231, No. 402, pp. e1-e6.

Weninger, B., Clare, L. Gerritsen, F., Horejs, B., Krauß, R., Özbal, R., Rohling, E. (2014) Neolithisation and Rapid Climate Change (6600-6000 cal BC) in the Aegean and Southeast Europe, *Documenta Praehistorica* Vol. 41, pp. 1-31

Jasuja OPM. (1993) Estimation of stature from footstep length. *Forensic Sci Int* Vol. 61, pp. 181-185.

Kayan İ. (1992) Demirköprü baraj gölü batı kıyısında Çakallar volkanizması ve fosil insan ayak izleri. *Ege Coğrafya Dergisi* Vol. 6, pp. 1-32.

Kızıltan, Z. and Polat, M.A. (2013) The Neolithic at Yenikapı, Marmaray Metro Project Rescue Excavations. In *The Neolithic in Turkey. New Excavations and New Research. Vol. 5.* M. Özdoğan, N. Başgelen, P. Kuniholm, (ed.) İstanbul, Arkeoloji ve Sanat Yayınları, pp. 113-165.

Krishan K. (2008) Estimation of stature from footprint and foot outline dimensions in Gujjars of North India. *Forensic Sci Int* Vol. 175, pp. 93-101.

Laskowski E., Kyle V.L. (1988) Barefoot impressions: A preliminary study of identification characteristics and population frequency of their morphological features. *J Forensic Sci* Vol. 33, No .2, pp. 378-388.

Liu KM, Shinoda K, Akiyoshi T, Watanabe H. (1998) Longitudinal analysis of adolescent growth of foot length and stature of children living in Ogi area of Japan: a 12 years data. *Z Morphol Anthropol* 82(1):87-101.

Ludowyk, E.F.C. (2013). *The footprint of the Buddha*. New York, Routledge.

Martin R., and Saller K. (*1957*). *Lehrbuch der Anthropologie*. Stuttgart, Gustav Fischer Verlag.

Mastrolorenzo G., Petrone P., Pappalardo L., Sheridan M.F. (2006) The Avellino 3780-yr-B.P. catastrophe as a worst-case scenario for a future eruption at Vesuvius. *Proc Natl Acad Sci*, Vol. 103, pp. 4366–4370.

Mellaart, J. (1967) *Çatal Hüyük: A Neolithic Town in Anatolia*. London, Thames and Hudson.

Ozansoy F. (1969) Türkiye Pleistosen fosil insan ayak izleri. *Maden Tetkik ve Arama Enstitüsü Dergisi,* Vol. 72, pp. 204-208.

Özbal R. and Gerritsen F. (2014) Barcın Höyük'te Neolitik ayak izi. *Aktüel Arkeoloji,* Vol. 42, pp. 26-27.

Özbal, R. and Gerritsen F. (2015) Barcın Höyük: The 2014 Season in Perspective, In *The Archaeology of Anatolia: Recent Discoveries 2011-2014,* S. Steadman and G. McMahon (ed.). Cambridge, Cambridge Scholars Publishing, pp. 26-45.

Özbal R, Gerritsen F. (2016) The Barcın Höyük Excavations in 2013 and 2014. *Annual Report Netherlands Institute for the Near East, Leiden Netherlands Institute in Turkey, Istanbul.* Vol. 2016, pp. 11-15.

Mietto P., Avanzini M., Rolandi G. (2003). Human footprints in Pleistocene volcanic ash. *Nature* Vol. 422, No.6928, pp, 133-133.

Morse S.A., Bennett M.R., Liutkus-Pierce C., Thackeray F., McClymont J., Savage R., Crompton R.H. (2013) Holocene Footprints in Namibia: The Influence of Substrate on Footprint Variability. *Am J Phys Anthropol* Vol, 151, pp. 265–279.

Putti A.B., Arnold G.P., Abboud R.J. (2010) Foot pressure differences in men and women. *Foot Ankle Surg* Vol. 16, pp. 21-24.

Robbins M.L. (1986) Estimating height and weight from size of foot prints. *J Forensic Sci* Vol. 31, No: 1, pp. 143-152.

Roberts, D., Berger, L.R., 1997. Last Interglacial (c. 117 kyr) human footprints from South Africa. *S. Afr. J. Sci.* Vol. 93, pp, 349-350.

Roche A.F., Davila G.H. (1972) Late adolescent growth in stature. *Pediatrics,* Vol. 50, No. 6, pp. 874-880.

Rojas, F., and Sergueenkova, V. (2014) Traces of Tarhuntas: Greek, Roman, and Byzantine Interaction with Hittite Monuments. *Journal of Mediterranean Archaeology* Vol. 27, No. 2, pp. 135-160.

Rutishauser I.H. (1968) Prediction of height from foot length: use of measurement in field surveys. *Arch Dis Child* Vol. 43, pp. 310-313.

Russell, N. (2012) *Social Zooarchaeology: Humans and Animals in Prehistory*. New York, Cambridge University Press.

Scaillet S., Vita-Scaillet G., Guillou H. (2008) Oldest human footprints dated by Ar/Ar. *Earth Planet Sci Lett* Vol. 275, pp. 320–325.

Schoop, U.D. (2005) The late escape of the Neolithic from the central Anatolian plain. In *How did farming reach Europe.* C. Lichter (ed.), Istanbul, Byzas, pp. 41-58.

Sjøvold T. (2000) Stature estimation from the skeleton. In: *Encyclopedia of Forensic Sciences.* J. Siegel, P. Saukko, G. Knupfer (ed.) London, Academic Press, pp. 276–284.

Takacs S. (2007). Divine and human feet: records of pilgrims honouring Isis. In: *Pilgrimage in Graeco-Roman and Early Christian Antiquity: Seeing the Gods.* J. Elsner and I. Rutherford (ed.) Oxford, Oxford University Press, pp. 353-369.

Thomas P.B. (2008). The riddle of Ishtar's shoes: The religious significance of the footprints at Ain Dara from a comparative perspective. *J Relig Hist* Vol. 32, No. 3, pp. 303-319.

Trinkaus E. 2005. Anatomical evidence for the antiquity of human footwear use. *J Archaeol Sci* Vol. 32, pp. 1515-1526.

Trinkaus E, Shang H. 2008. Anatomical evidence for the antiquity of human footwear: Tianyuan and Sungir. *J Archaeol Sci* Vol. 35, pp. 1928-1933.

Trotter M, Gleser G. (1952) Estimation of stature from long bones of American whites and Negroes. *Am J Phys Anthropol* Vol. 10, pp. 463-514.

Trotter M, Gleser G.C. (1958) A re-evaluation of estimation of stature based on measurement of stature taken during life and of long bones after death. *Am J Phys Anthropol* Vol. 16, pp. 79-123.

Tsuneki A. (2002) A Neolithic Foundation Deposit At Tell 'Ain El-Kerkh. In *Magic Practices and Ritual in The Near Eastern Neolithic*, H.G.K. Gebel, B.D. Hermansen and C. Hoffman Jensen (ed.), Berlin, Ex Oriente, pp. 133-143

Tuttle RH. (2008) Footprint clues in hominid evolution and forensics: lessons and limitations. *Ichnos* Vol. 15, pp. 158-165.

Ukoha U.U., Egwu O.A., Ezeani M,C,, Anyabolu A,E,, Ejimofor O,C., Nzeako H.C,, et al. (2013) Estimation of stature using footprints in an adult student population in Nigeria. *IJBAR* Vol. 4, pp. 827-833.

van Pelt, W.P. and N.T.B. Staring (2016) Interpreting graffiti in the Saqqara New Kingdom necropolis as expressions of popular customs and beliefs. *British Museum studies in ancient Egypt and Sudan*, forthcoming.

Webb S., Cupper M.L., Robins R. (2006) Pleistocene human footprints from the Willandra Lakes, Southeastern Australia. *J Hum Evol* Vol. 50, pp. 405-413.

Westaway R., Guillou H., Yurtmen S., Beck A., Bridgland D, Demir T, Scaillet S, Rowbotham G. (2006) Late Cenozoic uplift of Western Turkey: improved dating of the Kula Quaternary volcanic field and numerical modeling of the Gediz river terrace staircase. *Global Planet Change* Vol. 51, pp. 131–171.

White T.D. and Suwa G. (1987) Hominid footprints at Laetoli: facts and interpretations. *Am J Phys Anthropol* Vol. 72, pp. 485-514.

Willey P., Stolen J., Crothers G., Watson P.J. (2005) Preservation of prehistoric footprints in Jaguar Cave, Tennessee. *J Cave Karst Stud*, Vol. 67, No. 1, pp. 61-68.

Wunderlich R.B. and Cavanagh P.R. (2001) Gender differences in adult foot shape: implications for shoe design. *Med Sci Sports Exerc* Vol. 33, No. 4, pp. 605-611.

2

MORPHOLOGY OF ANCIENT POTTERIES USING X-RAY DIFFRACTION ANALYSIS AND X-RAY FLUORESCENCE IN SISTAN PLAIN, EASTERN IRAN

Vahid Pourzarghan[1], Hossein Sarhaddi-Dadian[2], Zuliskandar Ramli[3]

[1]*Department of Restoration, Faculty of Art and Architecture, University of Zabol, Iran*
[2]*Archaeological Research Center, University of Zabol, Iran*
[3]*Institute of the Malay World and Civilization, the National University of Malaysia*

Corresponding author: Vahid Pourzarghan (vahidpourzarghan@gmail.com)

ABSTRACT

Sistan plain, located in the north of Sistan and Baluchestan province, is one of the most significant cultural area in eastern Iran. This region is located between south Asia (Indus valley) and Western Asia (Mesopotamia) and also has been a connector between cultures of Central Asia and South of Persian Gulf area. Sistan was the main area to connecting between west and south Asia. Much of the cultural items found in the site under exploration were huge bulk of diverse pottery. Most pieces of pottery found in the Sistan plain were of the pottery belonging to Shahr-e Sukhteh, and its villages dating back to the third millennium BC, Dahan-e Gholaman of the Achaemenid period 550 BC and a large number of sites belonging to the Islamic period, which vary in term of the colour ranging from buff, gray, black and red and in terms of thickness. This study aims to determine the morphological relations of the pottery of Sistan plain using semi-quantitative X-ray diffraction (XRD) and X-ray fluorescence (XRF) methods. In this regard, 52 pieces of pottery from prehistoric, historic and Islamic eras, which were collected from archaeological surveys, were analysed. The samples were gathered from Gerdi domain, Dahaneh Gholaman, Shahr-e Sukhteh, south of the Hamoun Lake, Rostam castle and around the Shileh River. The instrumentation and cluster analysis of pottery sherds indicated that the prehistoric pottery pieces of Sistan plain have a different composition compared with that of Sistan area. Moreover, the glazed pottery pieces of the Islamic era are different from those of Sistan plain in terms of their chemical and have silica compounds, gypsum and aluminosilicate, which indicates the continuity of local technology, production and trade in Sistan to the Islamic period. In addition, the composition and structure of pottery in this region accounts for the high level of skills and knowledge of potters, who made a variety of pottery pieces with diverse applications in the local communities, which continued from prehistory to the Islamic era in this plain.

KEYWORDS: Sistan plain, Prehistoric pottery, Historical period, Islamic pottery, XRD, XRF, Local manufacturing

1. INTRODUCTION

Sistan area is located in the eastern Iran and in northern Sistan and Baluchestan province. It has an area of 8114 square kilometres. This region from the Bronze Age has had a significant role in the development of human civilization and heritage of this Iranian region (Moradi et al, 2014; Sarhaddi-Dadian et al 2015a; Sarhaddi-dadian et al, 2017a). Shahr-e Sukhteh, Dahaneh Gholaman, Khajeh Mount, the first settlement in the region were dating back to the late fourth millennium BC, which coincided with the history of urbanization in Central Asia. This era prolonged to the second millennium BC, (Sajjadi, 2008; 307, Tosi 1983; 73-125) (many sites have been discovered in Sistan and Share-Sukhteh is only one of significant sites of the region) (Vidale and Tosi 1996; 251-269; Biscione 1987; 394) (each of these regions has a lot of ceramic sherds which are diverse in terms of colour, era, ornaments and technical features. The main feature of the Bronze Age pottery is the application of geometrical, plant ornaments as well as drawing animals inside and outside of the piece with black and ochre colour to the buff pottery or those with decorated with light gray slime (Tosi, 1983; 136-139, Salvatori Andvidale, 1997). There is no evidence of such type of pottery since the Bronze era, about 3200 years BC, to the Achaemenid Empire, 550 AD. The next era which is the historic period of Sistan plain which began from 550 BC and continued to 550 AD included the periods of the Achaemenid, Parthian and Sassanid empires (Chavalas, 1999; 88). The important feature of the pottery of this era was its simplicity and the absence of any type of interior or exterior decoration and the ornamentation is generally carvel lines in the form of reputed grooved Sistani pottery. The other feature of these pottery pieces is the thick or thinner glaze and sometimes in red colour (Mehrafarin and Musavi, 2011; 240-58). Studies indicate that no pottery piece has been found in this region between the late Sassanid era (16th century) and the 13th century AD. Many new sites were discovered following this era in Sistan, from which large pieces of pottery were recovered. Pottery of this period is different than the two previous eras, which is simultaneous with middle Islamic era. This type of pottery pieces is decorated in different colours. The dominant colour glazes of this era are decorated green, gray-blue, milky and black and special decorations like under glaze motif or glaze or black colour glazes (niello) as well as geometrical decoration in the form of wide-mouthed bowls with flat base. The paste colour of pottery is light buff in the Islamic era (Mousavi and Atai 2010). Six pottery variation belonging to the areas of the Shileh River, Gerdi Castle, south of Rostam Castle, Shahre-sukhteh, south of Hamoun Lake, and Dahaneh Gholaman were systematically examined (Sarhadi-Daddian, 2013). Nine hundred pieces of pottery were selected from the region, and most of them belong to the pre- and historic eras. The pottery pieces of the historic period were mainly red and buff in terms of paste colour while the pottery of the prehistoric era generally was buff, gray, red black. Previous studies indicate that the red and gray pottery was less common in the Sistan region: however, the use of this type of pottery was prevalent, especially in Balochestan and marginal areas of India. The samples of this type of pottery were common as the burial pottery among other pottery pieces in the graveyard of Shahre-Sukhteh (Moradi et al, 2013a). The origin of the raw material of pottery— whether it is imported— can be determined by comparing the main and secondary elements according to instrumental analyses. Therefore, this study aims to determine whether all the pottery gathered from different regions of Sistan with a close relation are manufactured in local workshops or are cultural remote communications. The Documentation of the origin of the pottery is very vital for archaeologists and archeometrist as they contribute to investigate local civilization and culture in the manufacture of pottery and commercial activities in connection with other communities cultural activities (See Papageorgiou and Liritzis 2007).

2. MATERIALS AND METHOD

In The pottery of Sharhe-sukhteh found in the site and its surrounding Tape-Aghmari around like hills 3 Km to the south of Shahre-Sukhteh (Tosi, 1934; 34) and the other, which is Biyaban river 25 kilometers south of Shahre-Sukhteh, are the clear sample of ancient pottery workshops in the third millennium BC, are (Tosi, 1983; 42. Vidale & Tosi, 1996; 252). Fifty-eight factors from the wide prehistoric area of Sistan, i.e., Shahreh-sukhteh, and in total 186 images were identified according to the table of Sheppard (Tosi, 1983; 136-9. Salvatori and Vidale, 1997,27). XRF semi-quantitative analysis was conducted to identify the local origin of pottery (Sarhadi-Dadian et. al., 2015b). Scientific analysis conducted on Shahreh-Sukhteh reveals that some segments of red and buff pottery are imported goods and have a large content of lead. (Moradi et al, 2013). Example: Two pieces of the Islamic pottery are covered with plant motif and is decorated glaze. These two samples are decorated with enamels. Sample 1/332 is decorated with plant motifs in blue while Sample 8 / 369ZR are decorated with brown, blue and red plant motifs. The origin of these two pieces of pottery is not clear and is not local which probably belongs to the Safavid era. (Lane, 1947; Lane, 1948). Conducting combined analysis is one of the most crucial methods to determine the chemical composition of ancient relics such as pottery, mortar, ancinet metals, brick and glass (Bieber et al, 1976. Brokmans et al, 2008. Marghusian et al, 2009;l Wong et al, 2010; Zuliskandar et al, 2013a; 2013b; Bater. 2010). Other historic sites of the plain include Dahaneh Gholaman, Gerdi domain, Shile Rhiver, the south of Hamoun Lake, and Rostam castle, on which little quantitative analysis has been done (Sarhad-daddian et al, 2017b). Given the geographical location of Sistan region which had many impacts on the trade between mentioned zones as well as central Asia and Arabians located south of the Persian Gulf from prehistoric times has been the focus of attention from pre-historic era because of its location among eastern civilizations such as India, Pakistan as well as eastern civilizations such as Elam, Mesopotamia. High traveling in the region has caused the art and civilization to restore; pottery is one of the arts that requires demanding is research. It is an issue that attracts the attention of archeologists and archeometrists

3. RESEARCH METHOD

This study employs an empirical analytic library research method on the basis of field and laboratory studies. After collecting data and samples from six sites, including Shahr-e Sukhteh, Dahaneh Gholaman, the south of Hamoun Lake, Shileh River, Rostam Castle and explorations into Sistan, 52 samples of pottery were collected that includes pottery of gray, red and buff color. To investigate the source of crude pottery, 2 clay samples were also taken from the soil mines in Sistan plain to be tested in the laboratory; one sample was taken from one meter and the other sample was taken from 4 meters below ground level. Since the pottery from various eras was dispersed, first, we put them into three categories according to the prehistoric, historical and Islamic eras, and presented the characteristics and type of decoration in each era. Next, the instrumental analysis of samples was performed using the XRD and XRF elemental analysis. The results and data were investigated using hierarchical cluster analysis (HCA) and Ntsys ver2.1 software based on Nei and Li similarity matrix and Upgma method. Finally, the data shows that the pottery of prehistoric communities to the Islamic era forms the culture in Sistan where the pottery is recognized as a product with specific applications which are found in local areas of the hills or sites discussed here.

4. MATERIALS AND METHODS

This section includes the introduction of samples, sampling and sample preparation process and the equipment used for analysis methods.

4.1 Samples

This study investigates and performs XRF and XRD semi-quantitative analysis on 52 pieces of pottery recovered from six sites in Sistan plain in order to find the connection between these sites and the raw material used in the production of this ancient relic (Table 1).

Table 1: Gross observation of pottery collected from Sistan

Number	Shape	Paste color	Body color	Chamotte	Pattern color	Done	Type	Era
18264-1	Jar	Buff	Buff	Aeolian sand	____	On a wheel	Standard	II-III
18261-2	Jar	Buff	Buff	Aeolian sand	Dark brown	On a wheel	Standard	II-III
18267-3	Jar	Buff	Buff	Fine gravel	____	On a wheel	Coarse	II-III
18273-4	Jar	Buff	Buff	Aeolian sand	Brown	On a wheel	Standard	II-III
18262-5	Jar	Brick	Brick	Fine gravel	____	On a wheel	Coarse	II-III
18263-6	Jar	Buff	Buff	Fine gravel	____	On a wheel	Standard	II-III
18269-7	Bowl	Buff	Buff	Aeolian sand. Fine gravel	Brown	On a wheel	Standard	II-III
18268-8	Bowl	Buff	Buff	Aeolian sand	Brown	On a wheel	Standard	II-III
18259-9	Bowl	Gray	Gray	Aeolian sand	____	On a wheel	fine	II-III
18265-10	Bowl	Gray	Gray	Aeolian sand	Black	On a wheel	Fine	II-III
18270-11	Bowl	Buff	Buff	Aeolian sand	Light brown	On a wheel	Standard	II-III
18260-12	Cup	Buff	Buff	Fine sand	Dark brown	On a wheel	Fine	II-III
18266-13	Bowl	Red	Red	Aeolian sand	____	On a wheel	Fine	II-III
18272-14	Glass shaped	Buff	Buff	Aeolian sand. Fine gravel	____	On a wheel	Standard	II-III
18271-15	Jar	Red	Red	Aeolian sand	____	On a wheel	Standard	II-III
QH6-1	Bowl	Red	Red	Aeolian sand	____	On a wheel	Standard	Historical
QH29-2	Cup	Red	Red	Aeolian sand	____	On a wheel	Standard	Historical
QH20-3	Bowl	Red	Red	Straw and grass	____	On a wheel	Coarse	Historical
QH6-1	Bowl	Red	Red	Aeolian sand	____	On a wheel	Fine	Historical
QH8-15	Jar	Red	Red	Straw and grass	____	On a wheel	Standard	Historical
QH17-11	Cup	Red	Red	Aeolian sand	____	On a wheel	Fine	Historical

QH18-13	Bowl	Red	Red	Aeolian sand	____	On a wheel	Fine	Historical
QH2-14	Bowl	Red	Red	Aeolian sand	____	On a wheel	Fine	Historical
QH3-8	Bowl	Red	Red	Straw and grass	____	On a wheel	Fine	Historical
QH23-9	Bowl	Red	Red	Straw and grass	____	On a wheel	Coarse	Historical
QH26-5	Bowl	Red	Red	Straw and grass	____	On a wheel	Coarse	Historical
QH29-2	Bowl	Red	Red	Straw and grass	____	On a wheel	Standard	Historical
QH32-4	Jar	Red	Red	Aeolian sand and fine gravel	____	On a wheel	Coarse	Historical
QH34-7	Jar	Red	Red	Aeolian sand	____	On a wheel	Standard	Historical
QH38-12	Bowl	Red	Red	Straw and sand	____	On a wheel	Standard	Historical
Ghulam-1	Jar	Red	Red	Aeolian sand	____	On a wheel	Standard	Historical
ZR332/3	Bowl	White	White	____	White and blue glaze	On a wheel	Standard	Islamic
ZR028/1	Jar	Red	Red	Aeolian sand	Black	On a wheel	Standard	II-III
ZR087/6	Jar	Buff	Buff	Aeolian sand	Engraved decorations	On a wheel	Standard	II-III
ZR077/2	Jar	Buff	Buff	Aeolian sand	____	On a wheel	Standard	Historical
ZR078/8	Bowl	Buff	Buff	Aeolian sand	____	On a wheel	Standard	Historical
ZR079/5	Bowl	Buff	Buff	Aeolian sand	____	On a wheel	Fine	Historical
ZR080/4	Bowl	Buff	Buff	Aeolian sand and fine gravel	____	On a wheel	Coarse	Historical
ZR081/2	Jar	Buff	Buff	Aeolian sand	____	On a wheel	Coarse	Historical
ZR083/4	Bowl	Gray	Gray	Aeolian sand	Burnished	On a wheel	Standard	Historical
ZR084/3	Bowl	Buff	Buff	Aeolian sand	____	On a wheel	Coarse	Historical
ZR086/3	Bowl	Red	Red	Aeolian sand	____	On a wheel	Standard	Historical
ZR247/4	Bowl	Red	Red	Aeolian sand	____	On a wheel	Standard	Historical
ZR088/3	Bowl	Buff	Buff	Aeolian sand and fine gravel	Embossed	On a wheel	Coarse	Historical
ZR089/2	Bowl	Buff	Buff	Aeolian sand	____	On a wheel	Standard	Historical
ZR253/1	Bowl	Gray	Gray	Aeolian sand	Black	On a wheel	Standard	II-III
ZR253/4	Bowl	Red	Red	Aeolian sand	____	On a wheel	Standard	historical
ZR093/2	Bowl	Buff	Buff	Aeolian sand	____	On a wheel	Standard	Historical
ZR094/1	Bowl	Red	Red	Aeolian sand and fine gravel	____	On a wheel	Coarse	Historical
ZR271/5	Jar	Red	Red	Aeolian sand and fine gravel	____	On a wheel	Coarse	Historical
ZR369/8	Bowl	White	White	____	White and blue glaze	On a wheel	Fine	Islamic
ZR061/4	Bowl	Buff	Buff	Aeolian sand and fine gravel	____	On a wheel	Coarse	Historical

We have collected 52 pieces of pottery in Sistan plain belonging to different era. Moreover, to investigate the clay used by potters, two clay samples as raw materials were selected from two different areas to be tested in laboratory, hence comparing the pottery. One sample was taken from a depth of 4 meters in the vicinity of Shahre Sukhteh (about 10 gr) and the other was taken from 3 kilometers to the south of the site of Shahre Sukhteh (about 10 gr) where the people of Sistan still use this clay to make pottery and bricks (Fig.1).

We have divided the pottery into three categories according to the prehistoric, historical and Islamic eras. The 18 pieces of pottery belonging to the prehistoric era were collected from the area of Shahre Sukhteh and the surrounding hills, including the samples with the numbers 253/1, 18259/9, 18265/10, 028/1, 18266/13, 18271/15, 087/6, 18260/12, 18261/2, 18262/6, 18263/6, 18264/1, 18267/3, 18268/8, 18269/7, 18270/11, 18272/14, 18273/4, a collection which statistically includes buff, red and gray pieces of pottery in terms of priority. These pieces have been done on a wheel and in most cases had buff-colored clay paste (Fig.2). Buff pottery is common in Sistan and the paste has different tones ranging from absolutely buff to green. Statistically speaking, the gray pottery has second order dispersion and the red one has third order dispersion (Tosi 1983b; 132). Unfortunately, according to the surveys and data, there is no evidence of Iron Age in Sistan and it is still unknown to us. The evidence may have been covered by sediments that had been carried by the Hirmand River in Sistan plain over thousands of years. The historical era has begun in the Dahaneh Gholaman site. The diversity of the pottery indicates the benefits and usefulness of these relics in the past, and according to the shape, the skilled potter defined a particular usage for it.

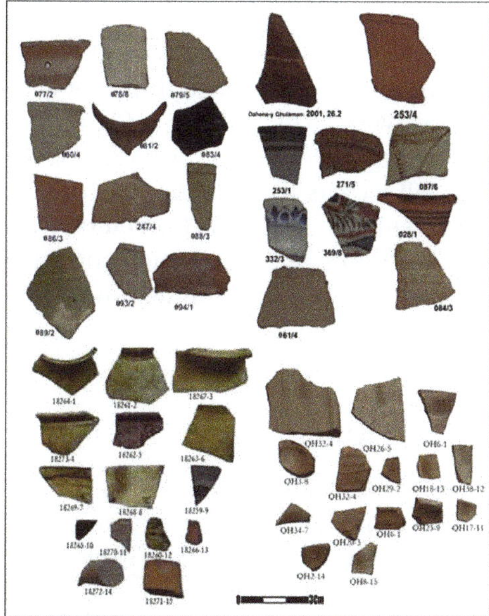

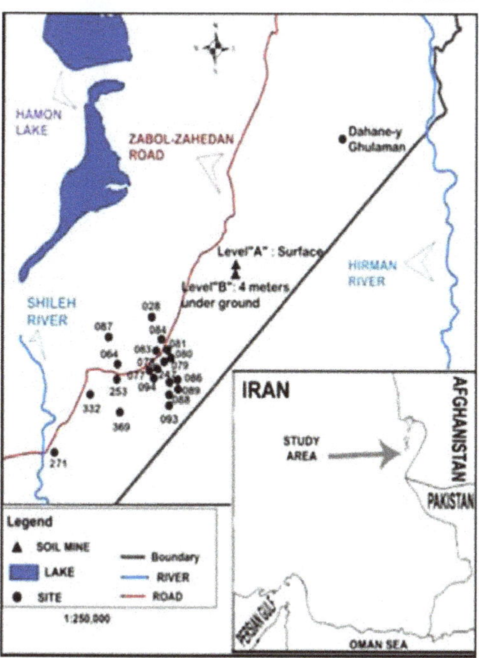

Figure 1: Sistan plain map site locations and representative sherds (Sarhaddi-dadian et al., 2015b ; 2017b)

Since most historical sites that have been investigated in this study belong to the historical era, thirty pieces of pottery selected for chemical studies were taken from the historical sites, the most important of which includes Dahaneh Gholaman, Gerdi domain, Shileh River, the south of Hamoun Lake and Rostam castle. The collection belonging to that era with the numbers: 061/4, 077/2, 078/8, 079/5, 080/4, 081/2, 083/4, 084/3, 086/3, 247/4, 088/3, 089/2, 093/2, 094/1, 253/4, 271/5 and excavated from Shileh River, Rostam castle, the south of Hamoun Lake and Gerdi domain were simple (Fig. 2). The other historical pieces excavated from Dahaneh Gholaman historical site include: Gholaman 2/26 / 2001, QH1/6, QH2/29, QH3/20, QH6/1, QH8/15, QH17/11, QH18/13, QH19/10, QH20/3, QH23/9, QH26/5, QH29/2, QH32/4, QH34/7, QH38/12 which (Figure 2) belong to the Achaemenid empire. (Sarhadi-daddian, 2013). These pieces are devoid of any decorative motif. They have the paste colors of buff, light red and red and mineral fillers and chopped herbs. It seems that the use of horizontal grooves in decoration started from the Achaemenid period and developed in later periods. The pieces found in Dahaneh Gholaman site have all simple human motifs and these decorative motifs are observed on the outside surface of the cups that have the same size of rim and body (Genito, 1990; 588-601).

The pottery belonging to the Partian era has significant difference in terms of form and style with the Achaemenid era. Most of the pieces are simple and usually covered with buff, bright, red and dark slip. Pottery with burnished decoration (Mehrafarin et al., 2013) is one of the most common motifs in the Partian era in Sistan (Haerinck, 1980; 43-45; Mehrafarin and Mousavi, 2011; 240-258). According to the archaeological studies, there are few Sasanian settlements in southern Sistan and there is not enough evidence related to these parts. The pottery belonging to the Sassanid period has the same properties as the Partian era. This era is also characterized with unglazed ceramics and the dominant color of the pottery is red as before. The pottery is mostly simple, covered with a thick layer of slip. It is decorated with grooves on the surface. The other ones are decorated with stamped patterns, and geometric and plant motifs (Mehrafarin and Mousavi; 2010; 256-272) The Islamic era pottery have been identified in the site 332 with the number 3 and in the site 369 with the number 8. Islamic era pottery is different from other pottery in Sistan. The pottery is glazed like the pottery of other parts of Iran; therefore, the classification includes both the glazed and unglazed patterned pottery (Mousavi and Ataie, 2010; 302-321). The mineral fillers and the patterns of zig-zag lines and small circles are used. Painted and glazed pieces belonging to the Safavid era have been found in sites 332/3 and 369/8 that are decorated with red, brown and blue patterns on a milky background and are transparently glazed (Lane, 1947. Lane, 1948. p 1032) A special type of pottery that was mentioned has patterns under a blue glaze and geometric and plant motifs that are comparable to the pottery belonging to the 6th -13th century AD in southern Sistan. (Golombek, 2003; 53-270. Sconlon, 1948).

4.2 Analysis and Sampling Methods

For the characterization of the shards and clay samples, analytical instruments used included X-Ray Diffraction SIEMENS D5000 Diffractometer and XRF Spectrometer Philips Model PW1480. X-ray fluorescence spectrometry (XRF) is employed as a non-destructive analytical method widely used to determine the elemental composition of materials. (Ferretti, 2000; Milazzo, 2004). For the analysis, in order to determine the chemical composition of the pottery, each sample of weight 0.7 g was pulverized, heated up at a temperature of 105°C for one hour and mixed until homogenous with the flux powder, a type of Spectroflux 110 (product of Johnson & Mathey). These mixtures were baked for one hour in a furnace with a temperature of 1100°C. The homogenous molten material was molded in a container and cooled gradually into pieces of fused glass with a thickness of 2 mm and a diameter of 32 mm. The samples were of 1:10 dilution. Press pallet samples were prepared by mixing 1.0 g of samples together with 6.0 g of boric acid powder; then, a pressure of 20 psi (137.895 kPa) was applied using hydraulic pressure equipment. The samples of fused pallets and pressed pallets were analyzed by wavelength-dispersive X-Ray Fluorescence (WD-XRF). A Philips PW1480 sequential spectrometer fitted with a rhodium-anode X-Ray tube (3kW 60kV) was used for the analysis of major and trace elements. The spectrometers were controlled using Philips X40 application software package version 3.2 and 4.01 running under the DEC VMS operating system.

5. RESULTS AND DISCUSSION

5.1 X-ray diffraction analysis

X-ray diffraction analysis (XRD) was conducted on 33 pieces of pottery and the two soil samples to determine minerals of the samples (Table 2).

Table 1 a: The results of XRD analyzes on Sistan plain pottery

	ZR 332/3	ZR 028/1	ZR 087/6	ZR 077/2	ZR 078/8	ZR 080/4	ZR 079/5	ZR 081/2	ZR 083/4	ZR 086/3	ZR 084/3
QTZ	+	+	+	+	+	+	+	+	+	+	+
PLQ	+	+	+	+	-	-	+	+	+	+	-
GYP	+	-	-	-	-	-	-	-	-	-	-
DIP	-	-	+	+	+	+	-	+	+	+	+
AND	-	-	-	-	-	-	+	-	-	-	-
LAB	-	-	-	-	-	-	-	-	+	-	-
HEM	-	+	-	-	-	-	-	-	-	-	-
DIK	-	+	-	-	-	-	-	-	-	-	-

Table 1 b: The results of XRD analysis Sistan plain pottery

	LS-1	LS-2	18259-9	18260-12	18270-11	18273-4	ZR 247/4	ZR 088/3	ZR 089/2	ZR 253/2	ZR 093/2
QTZ	+	+	+	+	+	+	+	+	+	+	+
PLQ	+	+	+	+	+	+	+	+	+	+	+
DIP	-	-	-	-	-	-	+	+	+	+	+
GYP	-		+	+	+	+	-	-	-	-	-
DOL	+	+	-	-	-	-	-	-	-	-	-
Ca	+	+	-	-	-	-	-	-	-	-	-
ClF	+	+	-	-	-	-	-	-	-	-	-
MUS	+	+	-	-	-	-	-	-	-	-	-
CHAM	+	+	-	-	-	-	-	-	-	-	-
AND	-	-	-	-	-	-	+	-	-	+	-
TEPH	-	-	-	-	-	-	-	+	-	-	-
PYR	-	-	-	-	-	-	-	-	-	+	-

Table 1c: The results of XRD analysis on Sistan plain pottery

	Gh-1	QH 2-29	QH 8-15	QH 20-3	QH 23-9	QH 26-5	QH 29-2	ZR 094/1	ZR 271/5	ZR 369/8	ZR 061/4
QTZ	+	+	+	+	+	+	+	+	+	+	+
PLQ	+	-	-	+	+	-	+	+	+	+	-
DOL	-	+	+	+	+	+	+	+	-	-	+
DIP	+	-	-	-	-	-	-	-	+	-	-
GYP	-	-	-	-	-	-	-	-	-	+	-
HEM	-	-	-	-	-	-	-	+	-	-	-

PLQ: Plagioklaz
DIP: Diopside Ca(Mg, Al)(Si, Al)2O6
LAB: Labradorite Ca0.65Na0.35(Al1.65Si2.35O8)
TEPH: Tephrite (Mg, Fe,Al, Ti)(Ca, Fe, Na, Mg)(Si,Al)2O6
PYR: Pyrocene (Mg0.998Fe0.002)(Ca0.999Fe0.028)(Si2O6)
CLF: Clinochlore-1MIIb, ferroan, (Mg,Fe)6(Si,Al)4O10(OH)8
CHAM: Chamosite (Mg5.036Fe4.964)Al2.724(Si5.70Al2.30O20)(OH)16
AND: Andesine Na0.622Ca0.368Al1.29Si2.71O8
DIK: DickiteAl2Si2O5(OH)4(HCONH2)

QTZ:Quartz, syn SiO2
GYP:Gypsum CaSO4.2H2O
MUS:Muscovite, KAl2Si3AlO10
Ca:Calcite, CaCO3
DOL:Dolomite CaMg(CO3)2
HEM:Haematite Fe2O3
GH-1: Gholaman
LS: Local Soil

XRD analysis on the pieces of prehistoric pottery indicates that these parts include minerals such as quartz, albite, dickite, hematite and is diopside. Two pottery pieces belong to the Islamic period (ZR 3/332, ZR 8/369) which have color motif and glaze on the surface, and the data is indicative of quartz, gypsum and calcium (sodium Aluminosilicates). Sample ZR3 / 332 according to XRF analyses have a high level of quartz, which as the remained mineral substance suggest the high temperature of firing near the 1000°C. The historic pottery piece also implies the presence of the phases of quartz, diopside, plagioclases in the form of anorthite, albite, andesine, labradorite and lower amounts of minerals such as palladium, gunite and gypsum in these pieces while cuprite has only one of the pieces. Sample of analyzed clay include the phases of quartz, calcite, clinochlore, muscovite, dolomite, Chamosite and plagioclase. Clay samples were supplied from older units that had been used for pottery and bricks.

The diopside only exists in pottery pieces while it is not found in clay samples. Prehistoric pottery has diopside while most of the historic pieces of pottery have diopside. This mineral substance is found in ultramafic igneous rocks (i.e., kimberlite and peridotite), as well as rich diopside agite. Moreover, this is common in mafic rocks such as basalt and andesite. Diopside is also formed in a variety of metamorphic rocks while being in contact with developed metamorphic skarn created from dolomite with high silica. Regarding the remaining diopside in the pottery pieces, it is suggested that diopside mineral substances in the pottery pieces may come from dolomitic present in clay.

5.2 X-Ray fluorescence analysis

Table 3 shows the main elements of the recovered pottery pieces from several ancient sites in Sistan plain, which have a homogeneous composition (Table 3).

Table 3: The main constituent elements of Sistan plain pottery by Dry Weight%

Sample	Major Elements (%)										
	Na2O	Mg O	A12O3	SiO2	P2O5	SO3	K2O	CaO	TiO2	MnO	Fe2O3	SrO
QH1-6	1.7	3.8	15.3	64.5	1.2	0.67	1.2	5.6	0.38	0.65	5.4	0.079
QH2-29	1.1	4.6	15.1	60.4	2.1	0.58	1.7	5.8	0.49	0.086	7.9	0.073
QH3-20	0.98	4.4	13.2	63.5	1.6	0.37	1.6	5.9	0.50	0.078	7.8	0.068
QH6-1	1.4	4.2	14.3	61.7	1.0	-	1.1	7.3	0.53	0.087	8.2	0.052
QH8-15	-	4.3	13.4	62.0	1.2	-	1.5	7.2	0.58	0.094	9.5	0.080
QH17-11	-	4.1	13.9	62.4	2.2	-	1.6	5.9	0.63	0.075	8.8	0.075
QH18-13	1.2	4.7	14.2	60.4	1.7	-	1.5	5.6	0.60	0.098	9.8	0.061
QH19-10	2.4	4.9	12.9	66.6	0.84	-	1.4	4.5	0.37	0.058	5.8	0.071
QH20-3	3.1	4.6	10.8	65.4	1.9	0.034	1.7	4.8	0.54	0.060	6.7	0.13
QH23-9	1.4	4.6	15.9	62.1	0.77	-	1.5	4.7	0.50	0.077	8.3	0.072
QH26-5	1.7	6.6	13.8	60.1	0.93	0.026	1.3	7.7	0.46	0.077	7.2	0.058
QH29-2	2.8	6.3	14.3	57.2	1.7	0.52	1.5	5.5	0.58	0.091	9.3	0.073
QH32-4	2.8	5.3	17.6	57.3	1.3	0.49	1.5	4.6	0.50	0.079	8.3	0.081
QH34-7	2.3	5.1	15.7	54.9	5.5	0.62	1.8	5.6	0.47	0.091	7.8	0.095
QH38-12	2.2	6.3	15.5	56.8	1.4	-	1.6	5.7	0.56	0.12	9.3	0.68
18259-9	1.43	4.43	17.84	55.55	0.21	0.42	3.44	5.79	0.81	0.10	8.71	0.06
18260-12	3.04	6.84	12.57	50.88	0.12	0.50	1.80	12.62	0.53	0.10	5.57	0.10
18261-2	2.34	5.46	13.69	51.78	0.13	1.72	2.33	10.99	0.60	0.11	6.01	0.067
18262-5	4.73	5.87	11.25	51.27	1.39	1.05	2.65	10.40	0.44	0.09	4.97	0.11
18263-6	3.86	5.46	11.25	49.30	0.23	0.85	2.47	12.07	0.49	0.09	4.97	0.059
18264-1	2.77	7.67	10.63	49.69	0.17	2.80	2.37	12.71	0.47	0.09	4.81	0.096
18265-10	1.42	4.66	16.58	60.39	0.13	0.15	3.21	2.40	0.82	0.09	8.84	0.016
18266-13	1.82	3.74	16.60	53.14	0.15	0.34	3.42	5.00	0.73	0.09	7.22	0.057
18267-3	2.75	7.03	12.59	52.89	0.16	0.73	1.96	12.75	0.54	0.12	5.56	0.10
18268-8	2.21	5.46	12.36	52.86	0.14	2.00	2.63	11.34	0.52	0.10	5.35	0.092
18269-7	2.77	9.87	10.58	52.30	0.11	1.33	2.14	11.62	0.46	0.09	5.05	0.083
18270-11	2.25	6.00	13.29	51.34	0.30	0.73	2.74	12.36	0.58	0.11	6.10	0.065
18271-15	2.61	3.33	15.26	62.64	0.60	0.17	2.71	1.55	0.75	0.66	6.79	0.063
18272-14	3.23	5.09	10.51	47.36	0.18	2.98	3.09	12.69	0.51	0.08	4.78	0.061
18273-4	2.98	6.07	12.24	49.57	0.27	0.72	2.43	11.85	0.56	0.10	5.64	0.16
ZR 332/3	4.85	0.93	3.13	77.56	0.09	-	1.32	1.52	0.11	0.02	0.48	0.021
ZR 028/11	1.34	4.84	16.73	56.32	0.14	-	3.02	4.10	0.77	0.09	7.64	0.030
ZR 087/6	2.19	5.07	15.08	52.04	0.20	-	2.55	9.78	0.67	0.12	6.52	0.041
ZR 077/2	2.01	6.10	15.43	52.37	0.12	-	2.58	9.07	0.64	0.10	6.31	0.042
ZR 078/8	2.16	5.02	13.16	43.98	0.41	-	2.27	13.64	0.58	0.14	6.04	0.090
ZR 079/5	3.12	7.04	14.59	48.75	0.23	-	1.20	12.28	0.63	0.11	6.00	0.040
ZR 080/4	2.56	6.68	12.55	54.76	0.31	-	2.09	10.04	0.52	0.10	5.12	0.051
ZR 081/2	2.28	4.99	14.76	50.45	0.91	-	2.62	7.90	0.64	0.10	6.60	0.10
ZR 083/4	1.41	4.29	15.34	50.59	0.31	-	3.20	8.77	0.69	0.11	7.38	0.035

ZR 084/3	1.82	5.49	15.34	48.83	0.31	-	2.39	12.81	0.71	0.13	6.42	0.042
ZR 086/3	2.43	4.93	15.22	55.18	0.26	-	3.19	6.68	0.62	0.11	6.10	0.043
ZR 247/4	2.32	5.34	15.95	54.68	0.25	-	2.47	8.71	0.10	0.61	6.35	0.051
ZR 088/3	2.53	5.48	12.79	53.98	0.16	-	1.90	11.78	0.58	0.09	5.16	0.059
ZR 089/2	2.86	5.27	14.33	47.93	0.18	-	1.81	11.57	0.66	0.11	6.32	0.041
ZR 253/1	2.02	5.79	16.75	53.15	0.13	-	2.74	8.53	0.66	0.12	6.87	0.041
ZR 253/4	1.32	4.67	14.96	49.67	0.18	-	2.93	11.22	0.72	0.13	6.76	0.052
ZR 093/2	1.98	5.02	15.79	53.59	0.42	-	2.81	9.18	0.61	0.11	6.28	0.052
ZR 094/11	2.01	6.92	13.46	43.36	0.18	-	2.13	11.20	0.50	0.10	5.20	0.070
ZR 271/5	2.26	4.73	14.60	53.51	0.15	-	2.31	9.43	0.67	0.13	6.21	0.031
ZR 369/8	5.47	1.18	3.88	78.98	0.09	-	1.46	2.23	0.12	0.02	0.79	0.032
ZR 061/4	2.52	7.17	11.66	45.49	0.33	-	1.56	12.92	0.53	0.09	5.06	0.11
Gh-1	2.01	4.90	14.67	57	1.38	-	1.5	4.8	0.75	0.091	7.07	0.032
Clay-LS-1	0.87	4.57	13.14	45.56	0.15	-	2.60	12.94	0.78	0.13	6.95	0.032
Clay-LS-2	0.88	4.74	13.03	45.47	0.14	-	2.57	13.80	0.72	0.13	6.45	0.033

Excluding two pieces of pottery which belong to the Islamic period, the dry weight percent of silica for the layers of prehistoric and historic pottery pieces is approximately from 43 to 65.4 and aluminum content of is 10 to 17. Except for 18271-4, 18256-10, 18259-9, which are probably non-native pottery of the region (Sarhadi-Dadian et. al, 2015b; 2017b) the calcium amount is 4 to 13 calcium and iron ranges approximately from 5 to 5.9. Alkali elements such as magnesium, sodium and potassium percent with dry weight of approximately 4 to 9.87, 1 to 4.73 and 1.20 to 3.25 respectively are shown in 1 the XRF data table.

Two samples of pottery recovered from the Islamic sites show different data, in which the range of dry weight silica is much higher 77-79% and calcium much lower 2.23-2.48%, a very low level of magnesium 0.03-1.185% and high sodium 4.85-5.47%, which is compared with other historic and prehistoric pottery. Sample ZR 8-369% has a small amount of 0.79% iron which has been compared with other samples. The average P2O5 percentage indicates that these containers were not used for organic material. Because of the high percentage of lime in pottery pieces, data shows that Sistan pottery is mainly manufactured by the calcareous clay as the main source for pottery. This data indicated the high level of lead in one of samples of Shahreh-Sukhteh (Sarhaddi-Dadian, 2013). Lead, as one of the dyeing factors, were added by potters to the old clay, and the archaeological studies suggest that lead was used as dyeing element in old social communication in the valley of India (Caleb, 1991). No lead element was detected in the prehistoric and historic pottery pieces. Therefore, there is no lead in historic and prehistoric eras and strengthens our claim that none of these two pieces of pottery belong to Sistan area.

5.3 Dispersion and Hierarchical Cluster Analysis

The Fig. 3 presents the percent values of SiO_2 and CaO in Excel to determine the dispersion of pottery.

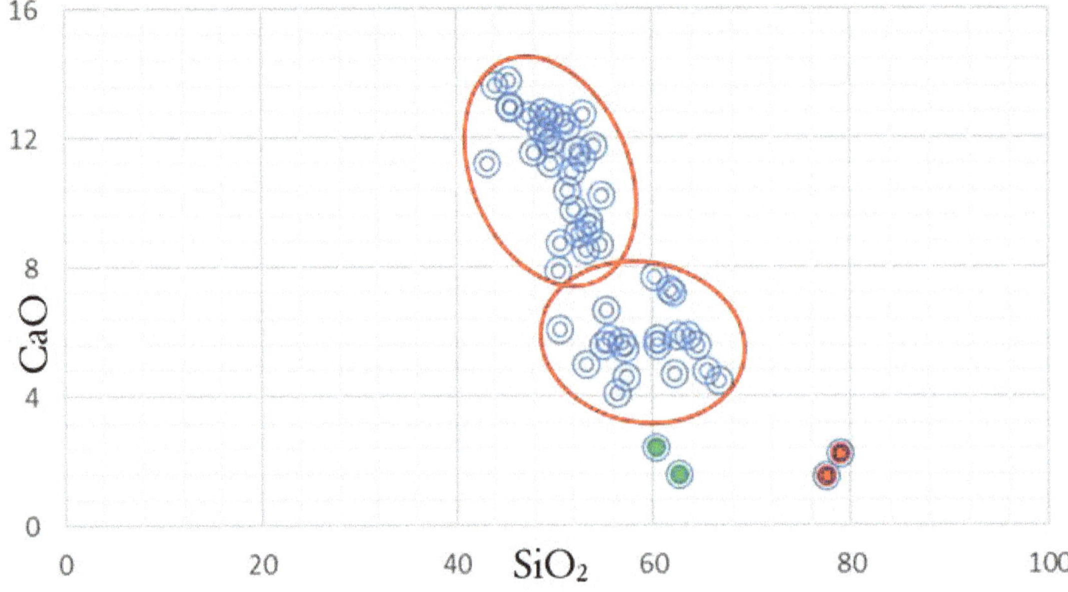

Figure 3: The graph presenting the dispersion of calcium oxide and silicon dioxide

The graph clearly indicates that the two pieces of pottery belonging to the Islamic era with numbers ZR3/332 and ZR 8/369 have different chemical composition that have been compared with the other pottery analyzed and indicated in red color at the bottom right of the graph. Both samples include a very high percentage of silica, sodium, low aluminum, calcium, iron and potassium. Therefore, compared with the other samples, it is suggested that the two samples have been imported from other parts or abroad. Two pieces of pottery marked in green on the graph also have a long association with the two other areas and probably with the imported pottery. The two red spots in the graph indicate the association of the pottery belonging to the prehistoric and historical eras in Sistan plain.

In Fig. 4, a dendrogram of HCA is drawn in terms of SiO_2 and CaO. Here the pottery pieces are classified into three categories A, B and C. In A category, the hierarchical cluster analysis includes the pottery with similar shapes. It is more likely that the pieces in this category are from nearby and related sites compared with the other two categories and it has a coefficient of above 5 which indicates that the pieces are likely to be local. Although group B, which contains the highest rate of the pieces, is believed to be the site for local pieces, it includes a combination of both imported pottery and pottery with its raw material brought from the surrounding areas since the coefficient is significantly below 5. Group C is also presented as containing the imported pottery in the diagram.

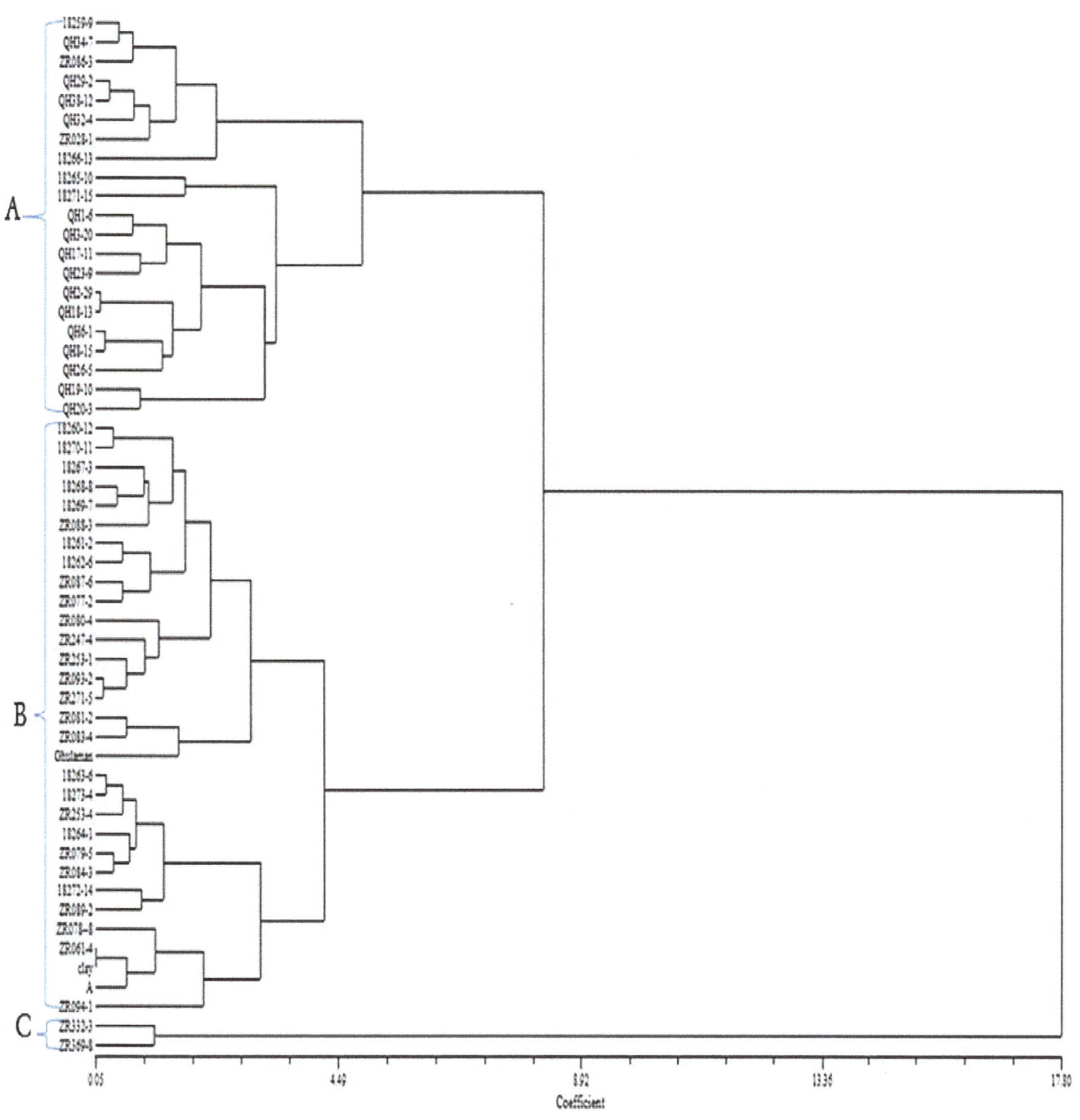

Figure 4: A dendrogram of HCA in terms of SiO_2 and CaO of the tested pieces

5. CONCLUSION

The results of the analysis show that most pieces of pottery found during the archaeological investigations in Sistan are indicative of similarity in the material used suggesting that these pieces are local. The XRD and XRF analysis data show that the two pieces of glazed pottery ZR 332-3 and ZR 369-8 recovered from two different sites have different chemical composition. Both pieces were compared with the other pieces and the high percentage of silicon in these pieces may be due to the glaze used; therefore, regarding the composition material, we recommended that these two pieces do not belong to this category and probably does not belong to Sistan. The piece of pottery entitled ZR 028-1 from the prehistoric era has a different composition compared with the other pieces. ZR 028-1 sample has a lower level of calcium and a higher level of potassium compared with the other pieces belonging to the historical and prehistoric era. Moreover, the XRD analysis determined the mineral substances of the pieces. The raw materials were distanced from the furnaces and they were probably at a distance of 6 to 10 km from the location of the raw materials. The analysis of the pieces found in Sistan shows that there used to be commercial activities in Sistan since the prehistoric era and these activities has continued to the Islamic era. The results also show that the local community had skills and specific knowledge in the field of making pottery from the prehistoric to the historical era in Sistan. The data are applicable in the field of archaeology and archaeometry and the association of this type of cultural item with important sites such as Shahdad and Espidezh can be examined. The pottery morphology of these areas helps us realize the cultural and commercial association of these civilizations.

ACKNOWLEDGMENT

This research was conducted using the UOZ-GR-9517-36 grants and researchers would like to express their gratitude to the University of Zabol for the research grants awarded.

REFERENCES

Bater, M. (2010): Structural Studied of Fresco Pigments of Period Parti in Kuh-E Khwaja of Sistan. *Iranian Journal of Crystallography & Mineralogy* 18, no. 3

Bieber, A. M. Jr., D.W. Brooks, G. Harbottle, and E.V. Sayre. (1976): Application of multivariate techniques to analytical data on Aegean ceramics, *Archaeometry*, 18: 59–74.

Biscione, R. (1987): The Elusive Phase 2 of Shahr-I Sokhta Sequence. *South Asian Archaeology* (1987): 391-409.

Broekmans, T., A. Adriaens, and E. Pantos, 2008, Insights into the production technology of north Mesopotamian Bronze Age pottery, *Applied Physics A*, 90: 35–42

Chavalas, M. W. (1999): Ancient Persia from 550 BC to 650 AD. *History: Reviews of New Books* 27, no. 2:88-88.

Ferretti, M. 2000, x-ray fluorescent application for the study and conservation of cultural heritage, in Radiation in Art and Archaeometry(eds D.C. Creagh and D.A. Bradly), Elsevier, Amesterdam, pp 285-296.

Genito, B. (1990): The Most Frequent Tyoes at Dahan-E Gholaman (Sistan) and Their Spatial Variability. *South Asian Archaeology*, 588-601,

Golombek, L. (2003): The Safavid Ceramic Industry at Kirman. *Iran* 41: 253-70.

Haerinck, E. 1980. Twinspouted vessels and their distribution in the Near East from the Achaemenian to the Sasanian periods. *Iran* **18**: 43-54.

Lane, A (1947): Early Islamic Pottery. The Bernard Rackham Collection. Bernard Rackham was Keeper of the Department of Ceramics at the Victoria and Albert Museum from 1914 to 1938. The Bernard Rackham Collection consists of 68 books from his private library, some of which contain loose archive material such as letters and associated personal papers. The collection was given to Cardiff School of Art and Design as a series of donations from Bernard Rackham's family over a six year period from 2002 to 2008.

Lane, A. (1948): Late Islamic Pottey Persian, Syria, Egypt, Turkey. London: Faber and Faber.

Marghussian, A.K., H. Fazeli and H. Sarpoolaky, 2009. Chemical-mineralogical analyses and microstructural studies of prehistoric pottery from Rahmatabad, south-west Iran. Archaeometry, 51(5): 733-747. Piperno, M. and M.

Mehrafarin, R., M.S. Rustaee, and J. Moghadam. (2013): Sofale Daghdar, Sofale Shakhese dore Ashkani dar Sistan Iran" [The Burnishe Pottery, the Distinctive Pottery of Partian period in Sistan, Iran], *Iranian Journal of Archaeological Studies*, 4:6,120-105.

Mehrafarin, R., and S.R.M. Haji (2010): In Search of Ram Shahrestan the Capital of the Sistan Province in the Sassanid Era. *Central Asiatic journal* 54, no. 2: 256-72.

Mehrafarin, R., Musavi Hadji, S.R. and Feyz, S.A (2011): A Study of the Ceramics of East Iran during the Later Parthian Era with Special Reference to Tapa Gowri. *Central Asiatic journal* 55, no. 2: 240-58.

Milazzo, M., Radiation application in art and archaeometry. x-ray fluorescence application to archaeometry. possibility of obtaining non-destructive quantitative analysis, nuclear instruments and methods in physice Research B, 213, 683-692.

Moradi, H., Sarhaddi-Dadian, H. & Rahman, N. H. S. N. A. (2014): Development and Decline of the Bampur Valley, Based on the New Archaeological Evidence from Prehistoric Period. *Iranian Studies*, 47, no 2: 263-287.

Moradi, H., Sarhaddi-Dadian, H., Zuliskandar R., AND Nik Hassan Shuhaimi Nik Abdul Rahman. 2013a: Compositional Analysis of the Pottery Shards of Shahr-I Sokhta, South Eastern Iran. *Research Journal of Applied Sciences, Engineering and Technology* 6(4), 654-659.

Mousavi Haji, S. A., & Atai, M. 2010. The Study of a Collection of Potteries Samples from Sistan Ed. Zahedan: The Organization of Cultural Heritage, Handicrafts and Tourism of Sistan and Baluchesan.

Ramli, Z., N.H.S.N.A. Rahman and A.L. Samian. (2011): X-ray fluorescent analysis on Indo-Pacific glass beads from Sungai Mas archaeological sites, Kedah, Malaysia. *J. Radioanalytical Nuclear Chem.*, 227: 741-747

Papageorgiou.I and Liritzis.I (2007) Multivariate mixture of normals with unknown number of components. An application to cluster Neolithic ceramics from the Aegean and Asia Minor. *Archaeometry*, 49, 4, 795-813.

Sajjadi, SMS, M. Casanova, L. Costantini, and KO Lorentz. (2008): Sistan and Baluchistan Project: Short Reports on the Tenth Campaign of Excavations at Shahr-I SokhtaIran: *journal of the British Institute of Persian Studies* 46: 307.

Salvatori, S., and M. Vidale. (1997): Shahr-I Sukhta 1975-1978: Central Quarters Excavations, Preliminary Report. Roma: *Istituto* Italiano per l'Africa e l'Oriente.

Sarhaddi-Dadian, H., Zohre Oveisi-Keikha, Vahid Purzarghan, (2017a) Introducing Troglodyte Architecture at Chabahar City in South-east of Iran, *International Journal of Archaeology*. Vol. 5, No. 1, 1-5. doi: 10.11648/j.ija.20170501.11

Sarhaddi-Dadian, H., Moradi, H,. Zuliskandar, R., and V. Purzarghan. (2017b): X-Ray Fluorescence Analysis of the Pottery Shards from Dahan-e Ghulaman, the Achaemenid Site in Sistan, East of Iran. *Interdisciplinaria Archaeologica* 8(1): Online First

Sarhaddi-Dadian, H., Morad, H., Soltani, M. (2015a): Preliminary Study of Rock Art at Negaran Valley in Baluchistan, Iran. *Rock Art Research* 32, no. 2: 8-11

Sarhaddi-Dadian, H., Zuliskandar, R., Nik Hassan Shuham, N. A. R., Mehrafarin, R. (2015b): X-Ray Diffraction and X-Ray Fluorescence Analysis of Pottery Shards from New Archaeological Survey in South Region of Sistan, *Mediterranean,Archaeology and Archaeometry*, Vol 15(3), 45-56

Sarhaddi-Dadian, H. (2013): Archaeology of Sistan, Iran during the Achaemenian Empire (from 550 BC to 331 BC). National University of Malaysia, Ph.D Thesis.

Scanlon, G.T. (1948): Mamluk Pottery: More Evidence from Fustat, In: Muqarnas Ii: An Animal on Islamic Art and Architecture, Oleg Grabar (Ed). . New Haven Yale University Press.

Sheikhakbari, S. Sarhaddi-Dadian, H., Amirhajloo, S., & Daneshi, A. (2015). Comparative Study of Pottery Industry in Zeh-Klout Historical Period in Roudbar-Kerman with Its Neighbouring Cultures Based on the New Archaeological Evidences. *International Journal of Archaeology*, 3(3), 22-32.

Tosi, M. (1983a): Excavations at Shahr-I Sokhta 1969-70. Prehistoric Sistan 1: 73-125.Tosi, M (1983b) Prehistoric Sistan. IsMEO, Vidale, M., and Tosi. M (1996): The Development of Wheel Throwing at Shahr-I Sokhta Slow and Fast Revolutions Towards Statehood. *East and West* 46, no. 3/4: 251-69.

Wong, E.H, C.A. Petrie, & H. Fazeli. (2010): Cheshmeh Ali ware: a petrographic and geochemical study of a transitional halcolithic period ceramic industry on the northern central plateau of Iran. *Iran XLVII*: 11-26

Vidale, M., & Tosi, M. (1996). The development of wheel throwing at Shahr-i Sokhta slow and fast revolutions towards statehood. *East and West*, 46(3-4):, 251-269.

Zuliskandar R and Nik Hassan Shuhaimi Nik Abdul Rahman. (2013): Composition Analysis of Ancient Bricks, Candi Bukit Kechil, BUjang Valley, Kedah. *Research Journal of Applied Sciences, Engineering and Technology* 6(5): 924-930

3

ARCHAEOMETRIC INVESTIGATION ON RED SLIP OF URARTIAN POTTERY

Atilla Batmaz[1] and İlker Özkan[2]

[1]Ege University, Department of Archaeology, 35100, Bornova, Izmir, Turkey
[2] Dokuz Eylül University, Torbalı Vocational School, Industrial Glass and Ceramics Department, Torbalı, Izmir, Turkey

Corresponding author: İlker Özkan (ilker.ozkan@deu.edu.tr)

ABSTRACT

The primary objective of the present work is to make a comparison between the red glossy slip of Urartian pottery (commonly known as Urartian red polished ware) and local clays by conducting a variety of examinations. As a result of these investigations, the authors will suggest the most likely clay sources for ceramics and the slip that may have been used by the Urartian potters. Four samples from Ayanis Fortress have been characterised from the chemical, mineralogical, morphological and petrographic points of view. Scanning electron microscopy, optical microscope, X-ray diffraction, energy dispersive spectrometry, chemical analysis and colour measurement investigations have been carried out on the ceramic body and red glossy slip to determine their characteristics and technological features. In addition, three local clays were characterised by chemical, mineralogical and petrographic analyses. Test pieces made from local raw material were fired in a traditional updraft mud-brick kiln in order to better understand the paste and red-slip-making processes of Urartu. The results obtained from the different analyses demonstrate significant similarities between ceramic samples and fired clay test pieces. It may be concluded that it is possible these local clays were used in production of Urartian red glossy ceramics.

KEYWORDS: Urartian red glossy ware, archaeometric investigation on pottery, experimental archaeology, local clay sources

1. INTRODUCTION

The Urartian Kingdom was one of the most predominant kingdoms in the Near East between 9th-7th century B.C. (Çilingiroğlu, 1997). Its territory extended from Eastern Turkey to Northwestern Iran and Transcaucasia and incorporated high mountain fortresses and highlands during the Middle Iron Age. The highlands incorporate various landscapes, and for months of every year their valleys, highlands and roads are covered with snow. Almost all information we have about Urartian culture so far has come from archaeological excavations on the kingdom's fortresses and graveyards. Although the culture is best known for its metalworking technology and skills, a group of ceramics, referred to as red polished ware, which were produced by copying metal vessels (Kroll and Zahlhaas, 1976, 85; Van Loon, 1966, 32), is also a fruitful area of study for archaeologists. This group of pottery is an indicator of the Urartian presence and is unearthed in almost all Urartian fortresses. The fact that the pottery is found in small quantities in fortresses when compared with other ware groups reflects that is demanding to make, and its elegant appearance, with its shiny red surface, leads us to believe that the ware may have been produced under the control of ruling elites and reserved for their own use. The common forms are mostly tableware, composed of jugs, plates, bowls, and goblets, but most famous is the one-handled trefoil jug. The body generally has light brown-red colours and low-density inclusions. The glossy surface has diverse red tones due to different firing environments, slip compositions and/or locations of the pots relative to one another in the kiln.

The common characteristic and indicator of the pottery is its red and glossy slip. Although it is generally believed that the glossiness came from the highly manual polishing process using tools such as stone, bone or metal, in some cases, the slip composition and firing methods must have been decisive in obtaining the desired red colour and glossy finish. In fact, there is various contemporary or non-contemporary similar class of red slipped and glossy pottery traditions in the Mediterranean from Neolithic to Roman times with their refined ferruginous clay suspensions on the surface of the ceramic body such as Red Lustrous Ware in Late Bronze Age (Knappett et. al., 2005) or Roman Terra Sigillata (Picon et. al., 1971, 1975; Tite et. al., 1982). However, our preliminary observations indicate that the surface treatments of red slipped glossy Urartian pottery bears some specifications.

The key element or method used to obtain the desired brightness is not yet certain, but several suggestions have been made. S. Kroll (1970) noted that the slip has a glaze-like, glossy finish and suggested that this resulted from quartz crystals, while E. Akça (Akça et. al., 2010) mentioned that the slip contains a "completely and extensively vitrified matrix and was probably produced from low-melting hydrous mica." Alternatively, S. Kapur (Kapur et. al., 1991) suggested for Hatti ceramics that developed firing technologies using basaltic raw materials could yield highly vitrified ceramics. Lastly, H. Kapmeyer (2005) thinks that elements in the slip such as lithium or boron, which melt in low temperatures, act as fluxes and thus may be responsible for the vitrified surface.

Although some studies on the characterisation of the Urartian red glossy ceramics based on experimenting with different techniques have been reported in the literature (Kleinmann, 1976; Speakman et al., 2004; Kapmeyer, 2005; Erdem et al., 2008; Akça et al., 2010), detailed study of the production technology by comparing local clays has not until now been undertaken. B. Kleinmann (1976, 64 ff.) focused on the mineralogical aspects of the pottery from Bastam, E. Akça et al. (2010, 233 ff.) performed some chemical and morphological analysis (ICP-AES and SEM) of several sherds from sites in Eastern Turkey such as Aznavurtepe (Ağrı), Çavuştepe (Van) and Van Fortress (Van). Kapmeyer (2005, 313 ff.) conducted a number of analyses such as SEM, EDX and REM to answer questions related to how the glossy surface of the ceramic was produced, what the chemical composition of the core and the slip were, and whether these factors were uniform throughout the Urartian territories. A very few analyses have also been undertaken on the clay of the ceramics. Speakman et al. (2004, 119 ff.) did neutron activation analysis (NAA) on the Urartian Pottery from Eastern Anatolia and detected mobility from region to region. Erdem et al. (2008, 2486 ff.) tried to characterise the Iron Age pottery from Eastern Turkey through the use of laser-induced breakdown spectroscopy. The present work was motivated by the fact that no comprehensive analysis and experimentation on local clays has previously been carried out in the area of understanding the production technology of red glossy slip of the Urartian pottery and identifying the clay sources that might have been used by the makers. In order to fill this gap in the literature, the present study is designed to: (i) determine the characteristics of the Urartian ceramics, their slips and local clays obtained from the Van and Bitlis region (ii) compare the characteristics of the two. The results will also enable us to comprehend better the qualities and composition of local clays used in pottery manufacturing.

2. MATERIAL AND METHODS

In the present work we would like to place extra emphasis on the material from Ayanis Fortress, from which we selected four representative Urartian pottery samples to examine, coded as S1, S2, S3 and S4 (Table 1, Figure 1, Figure 2). Ayanis Fortress is thought to have been one of the most important cultic and administrative centres of the kingdom in the seventh century BC. It was established by the Urartian king Rusa II (685–653 BC) on a rocky hill on the eastern shore of Lake Van, across from the volcanic mountain, Süphan(Çilingiroğlu 2013). The investigations suggested that the Ayanis fortress was dated to 673/2 B.C. (Çilingiroğlu, 2013; 2016), and it must have collapsed before 653 BC, likely as a consequence of an earthquake (Çilingiroğlu 2002: 484–488; Çilingiroğlu 2011: 339, 346). All the samples selected are red slipped glossy ceramics and some of their characteristics are described in Table 1.

In addition, three clay samples local to the related region were studied (Figure 3). These are a) green clay (2 Y 7/3 pale yellow), which is called Van Light due to its colour (VL), b) brown clay (10 YR 5/3 brown), which is called Van Dark (VD), derived from Van, and c) red soil (2.5 YR 4/6 red), which is called Bitlis Soil (BS) (locally called Avusku) and is obtained from Bitlis, Eastern Turkey (Figure 4). According to the ethnological data obtained from potters in the Bardakçı Village (Van), the ideal firing temperature of VL is 900–1000°C. It takes on white tones at 1050°C, and becomes brick reddish at 850°C. In the village, VD is mostly mixed with green clay to produce cookware (locally called *güveç*). It reaches the ideal red colour at 600–700°C. The colour turns yellow at 800°C and the clay starts to deform at 900°C.

Table 1. Description of the samples on the basis of form, colour, firing, production and matrix characteristics.

Sample	Description
S1	Bowl (Inverted rim), reddish-orange fabric, red slipped (10 R 4/8), well fired, wheel made, poorly sorted, vitrified matrix texture, low grain/matrix ratio, low porosity with isolated pores.
S2	Jar (groove-rimmed), reddish-brown fabric, red slipped (10 R 4/8), medium fired, wheel made, poorly sorted, vitrified matrix texture, low grain/matrix ratio, low porosity with isolated pores.
S3	Bowl (ring base), yellow-brown fabric, red slipped (10 R 4/6), very well fired, wheel made, moderately sorted, vitrified matrix texture, low-medium grain/matrix ratio, low porosity with isolated pores.
S4	Jug (trefoil), yellow-brown, red slipped (10 R 4/6), very well fired, wheel made, poorly sorted, vitrified matrix texture, low-medium grain/matrix ratio, low porosity with isolated pores.

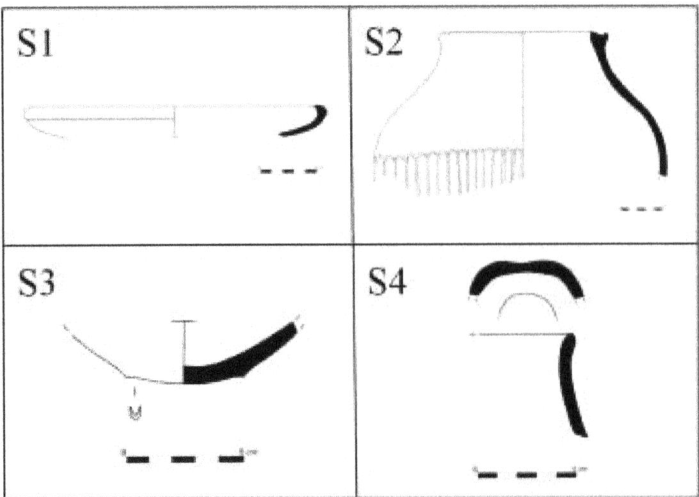

Figure 1. Drawings of the examined potsherds.

Figure 2. Representative images of ceramic sample coded S2 (a) Obverse (b) Reverse and (c) Section.

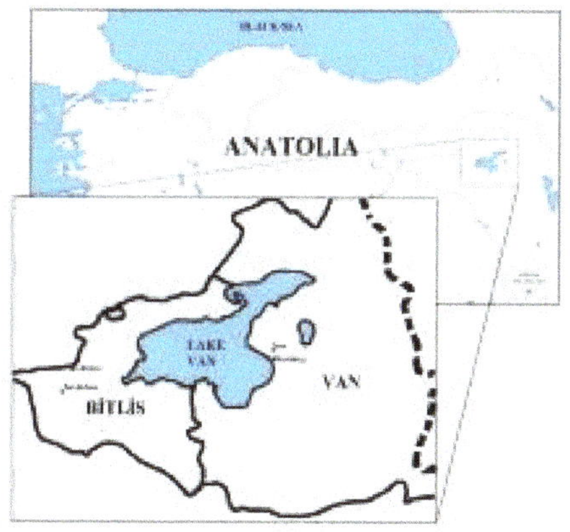

Figure 3. Sampling areas.

Figure 4. Analysed soil samples from Van and Bitlis.

Chemical analyses were conducted on the clay samples and the glossy surface layer of the Urartian samples. Their chemical compositions were analysed using ICP-MS at Bureau Veritas Mineral Laboratories, Canada. The major and minor oxides (SiO_2, Al_2O_3, Fe_2O_3, MgO, CaO, Na_2O, K_2O, TiO_2, P_2O_5, MnO, Cr_2O_3) and trace elements (Ba, Ni, Sr, Zr, Y, Zr, Nb, Sc) were determined. The results with minimum detection limits (MDL) are given in Table 2. The test pieces taken from the clay samples were fired at 800°C, 850°C and 900°C. The phases present in the bodies of the ceramic samples, glossy surface layers and fired clay samples were identified by X-ray diffraction (XRD) using a Rigaku Model diffractometer with monochromatic Cu Kα radiation. XRD patterns were obtained by scanning 3 to 90°, with a goniometer speed of 2°/min, operating at 40 kV and 36 mA. The microstructures of the samples were investigated under a JEOL-JSM 6060 Scanning Electron Microscope (SEM) and an optical microscope. The SEM worked under an acceleration potential of 20 kV, with a 40 µm spot size and a 100 c/s live time for EDS analyses. Chemical compositions of the particular regions from the investigated cross sections were determined by an energy dispersive X-ray spectrometer, EDS (IXRF System 500) attached to the SEM. Colour measurements of the samples were performed using a portable colorimeter 3NH (model NH-310) as well as a Munsell soil chart (2000 edition) of the type frequently employed by archaeologists to determine the colours of ceramics and soil.

Slipped test pieces (Figure 5), measuring 4x4 cm and made of green (VL) and brown clays (VD) from Van, coded 1A and 1B, were fired at 1050 °C in Bardakçı Village, where traditional pottery making is being continued by only one active workshop. The aim was to obtain the most accurate and comparable outputs. As Bitlis soil has not enough plasticity for shaping a vessel, it was merely used for the slip.

Figure 5. Photographs of test pieces fired at 1050 °C.

Firing was performed in the totally traditional way in the mud-brick updraft kiln of potter Osman Eşme. The kiln was composed of two chambers: a combustion chamber in its lower section, and a pottery alcove on the top. The ceramics are laid on a perforated platform so that the fire can properly reach the upper section.

Thin section analysis was performed on four Urartian ceramics and two clay test pieces (1A and 1B). Thin sections were obtained by fixing the sherds on glass lamellae and then reducing their total thickness to 30 µm by chafing. Prepared sections were examined under the optical microscope through the use of plain and polarised light. Table 2 lists all the analyzed samples.

Table 2. List of the all analyzed samples and analyses performed. (CA: Chemical Analysis, OM: Optical Microscope, XRD: X-Ray Diffraction, SEM: Scanning Electron Microscope, EDS: Energy Dispersive Spectrometry, CM: Colour Measurement).

Sample code	Description	CA	OM	XRD	SEM	EDS	CM
S1	Ceramic sample from a bowl.		X	X	X	X	X
S2	Ceramic sample. A part from a jar.		X	X	X	X	X
S3	Ceramic sample. A part from a bowl.		X	X	X	X	X
S4	Ceramic sample. A part from a jug.		X	X	X	X	X
GSL	Glossy surface layer of the pottery samples.	X	X	X	X	X	X
VL	Green clay that is called Van Light due to its color.	X		X			
VL	Fired at 800°C			X			X
VL	Fired at 850°C			X			X
VL	Fired at 900°C			X			X
VD	Brown clay that is called Van Dark due to its color.	X		X			
VD	Fired at 800°C			X			X
VD	Fired at 850°C			X			X
VD	Fired at 900°C			X			X
BS	Bitlis soil.	X		X			
BS	Fired at 800°C			X			X
BS	Fired at 850°C			X			X
BS	Fired at 900°C			X			X
1A	Test piece made of VL clay.		X				
1B	Test piece made of VD clay.		X				

3. RESULTS AND DISCUSSION

Chemical compositions of the clay samples and glossy surface layers (GSL) are shown in Table 3. It should be reminded that the burial environment of archaeological ceramics may modify the chemical composition of their bodies. In particular, solutions migrating from the soil to buried samples can deposit extraneous matter on the ceramic body (Antonelli et al., 2014). The clay samples and surface layers consist mainly of SiO_2 and Al_2O_3, which correspond to about 50-68% of the total due to the presence of clay minerals and quartz. In addition, all the samples consist of a significant amount of iron oxide, which accounts for the reddish colour after firing. VL and VD have higher CaO content than BS due to the presence of calcareous materials. Na_2O and K_2O quantities are in the moderate ranges that are indicators of the presence of illite and feldspathic minerals. The similarity between BS and GSL is clearly seen in terms of major oxides and some trace elements.

Table 3. Chemical analyses results (MDL: Minimum Detection Limit, VL: Van Light Clay, Van Dark Clay, BS: Bitlis Soil, GSL: Glossy Surface Layer).

Element or element oxide concentration	Unit	MDL	Sample Code			
			VL	VD	BS	GSL
SiO_2	(%)	0.01	49.70	38.21	47.90	46.21
Al_2O_3	(%)	0.01	12.00	11.92	20.73	20.30
Fe_2O_3	(%)	0.04	6.46	7.09	11.49	10.54
MgO	(%)	0.01	5.07	4.85	1.37	1.37
CaO	(%)	0.01	8.91	14.44	0.51	2.60
Na_2O	(%)	0.01	1.86	1.19	0.32	1.46
K_2O	(%)	0.01	1.99	2.04	1.93	3.36
TiO_2	(%)	0.01	0.80	0.91	1.60	1.81
P_2O_5	(%)	0.01	0.17	0.22	0.25	0.17
MnO	(%)	0.01	0.08	0.12	0.21	0.17
Cr_2O_3	(%)	0.002	0.040	0.027	0.041	0.021
Ba	ppm	5	212	282	341	884
Ni	ppm	20	206	99	187	195
Sr	ppm	2	256	587	77	289
Zr	ppm	5	154	135	268	541
Y	ppm	3	23	21	35	120
Nb	ppm	5	16	19	27	37
Sc	ppm	1	15	19	23	17
LOI	ppm	-5.1	12.7	18.7	13.4	-

The results of XRD analyses of the bodies, glossy slip of the potsherds, clays and clays fired at elevated temperatures are given in Table 4, respectively. Quartz, illite, albite, hematite, diopside/augite, chlorite, calcite, dolomite and microcline phases were identified from the XRD spectra of the samples. Glossy surface layers and bodies have similar phases except microcline phase.

Representative SEM and optical microscopic cross section images of bodies and glossy surface layers and the corresponding EDS spectra taken from the glossy surface layers and bodies are given in Figure 6-9. For all samples, the bodies have porosities in their structure, whereas surface layers are more compact. The bodies have isolated pores in the clay matrix.

The optical microscopic images of the GSL on all samples revealed an average thickness of about 0.125 mm; a very compact structure with no voids and a greater degree of sintering compared to the body. This indicates that the slips were applied to body surfaces in a form of suspension in order to make a uniform slip layer. Also, it can easily be seen that the colour of the GSL on all samples is different from the colour of the body. These data clearly indicate that finer clay, with colorant and fluxes, was used in the production of the GSL than was utilised for the body. Additionally, no cracks were observed on the GSL of the samples, which shows there was no mismatch between the thermal expansion coefficients of the bodies and the glossy slip.

Table 4. XRD results of the samples.

Sample	Minerals/Phases
S1-Body	Quartz, illite, albite, hematite, diopside/augite
S2-Body	Quartz, illite, albite, hematite, diopside/augite
S3-Body	Quartz, illite, albite, hematite, diopside/augite
S4-Body	Quartz, illite, albite, diopside/augite
S1-Glossy Surface Layer	Quartz, illite, hematite, diopside/augite, albite, microcline
S2-Glossy Surface Layer	Quartz, illite, hematite, diopside/augite, albite, microcline
S3-Glossy Surface Layer	Quartz, illite, hematite, diopside/augite, albite, microcline
S4-Glossy Surface Layer	Quartz, illite, hematite, diopside/augite, albite, microcline
BS	Quartz, illite, kaolinite, albite, hematite, chlorite, dolomite
VL	Quartz, illite, kaolinite, albite, hematite, chlorite, calcite
VD	Quartz, illite, kaolinite, albite, hematite, chlorite, calcite
VL (fired at 800°C)	Quartz, illite, calcite, hematite, albite
VL (fired at 850°C)	Quartz, illite, hematite, albite
VL (fired at 900°C)	Quartz, illite, hematite, albite
VD (fired at 800°C)	Quartz, illite, albite, hematite
VD (fired at 850°C)	Quartz, illite, albite, hematite

VD (fired at 900°C)	Quartz, illite, albite, hematite
BS (fired at 800°C)	Quartz, illite, albite, hematite
BS (fired at 850°C)	Quartz, illite, albite, hematite
BS (fired at 900°C)	Quartz, illite, albite, hematite

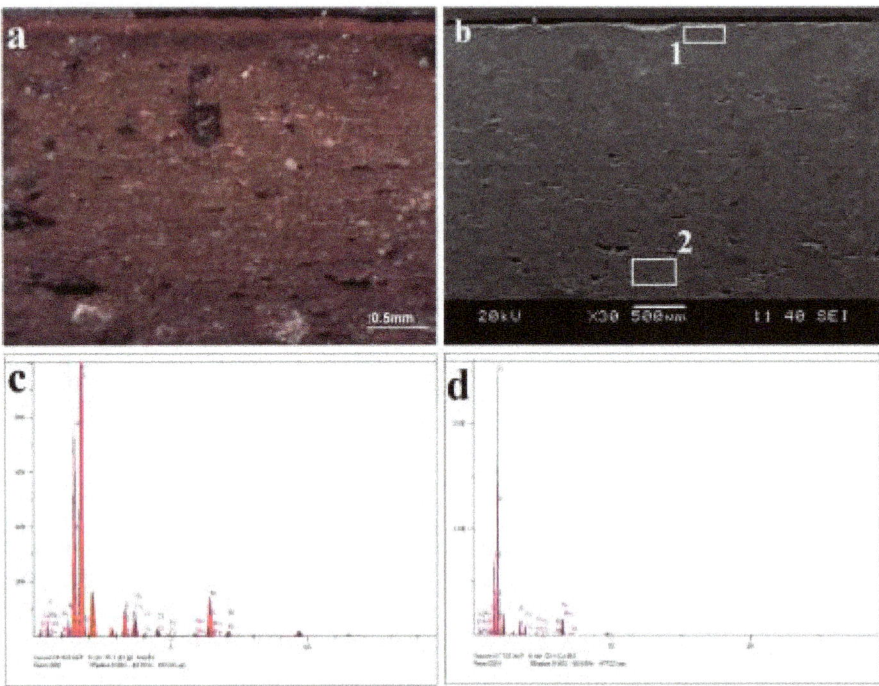

Figure 6. Cross sectional (a) optical and (b) SEM micrographs of S1, EDS spectra of (c) area 1 and (d) area 2.

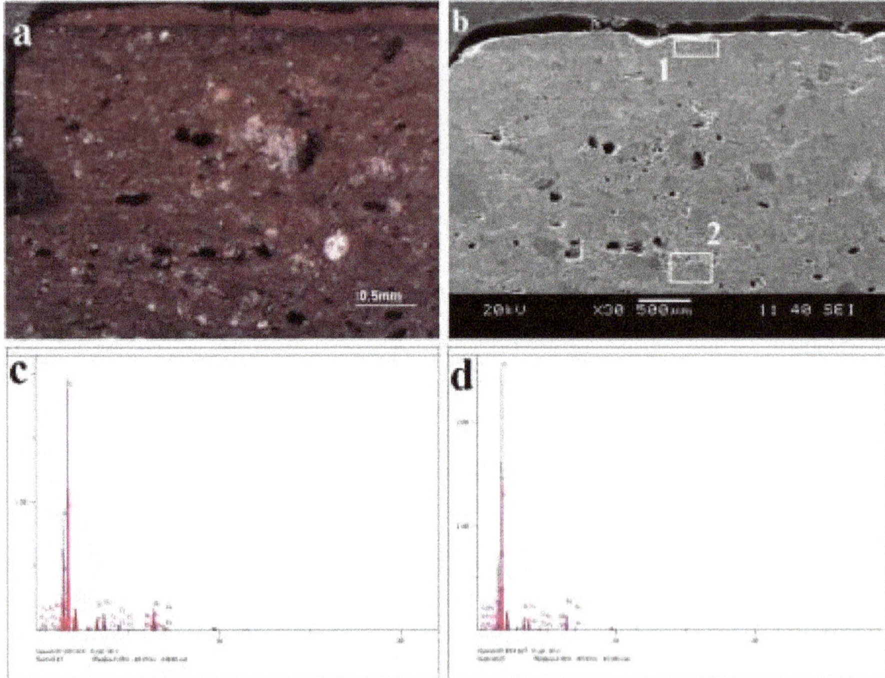

Figure 7. Cross sectional (a) optical and (b) SEM micrographs of S2, EDS spectra of (c) area 1 and (d) area 2.

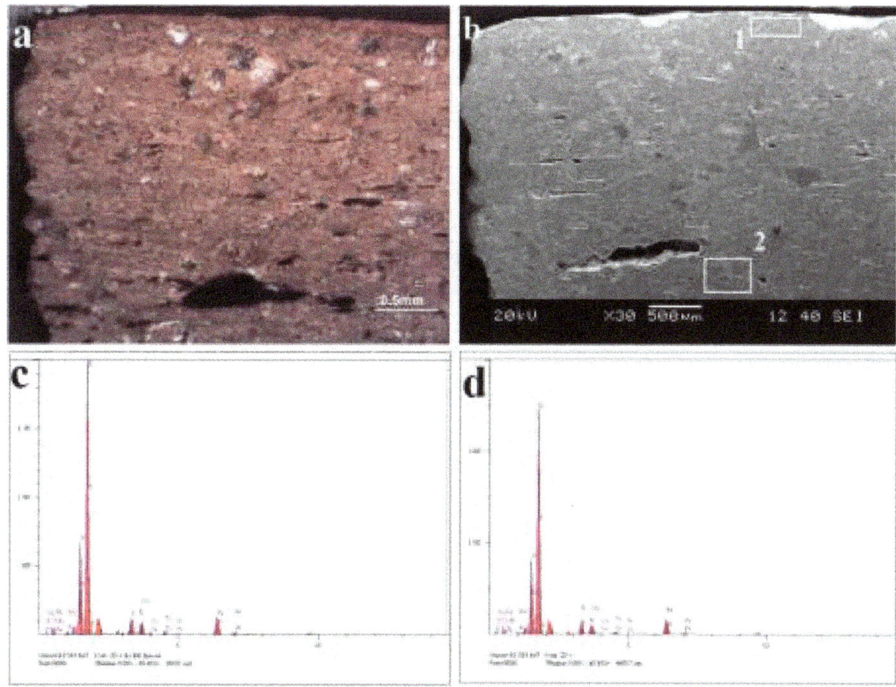

Figure 8. Cross sectional (a) optical and (b) SEM micrographs of S3, EDS spectra of (c) area 1 and (d) area 2.

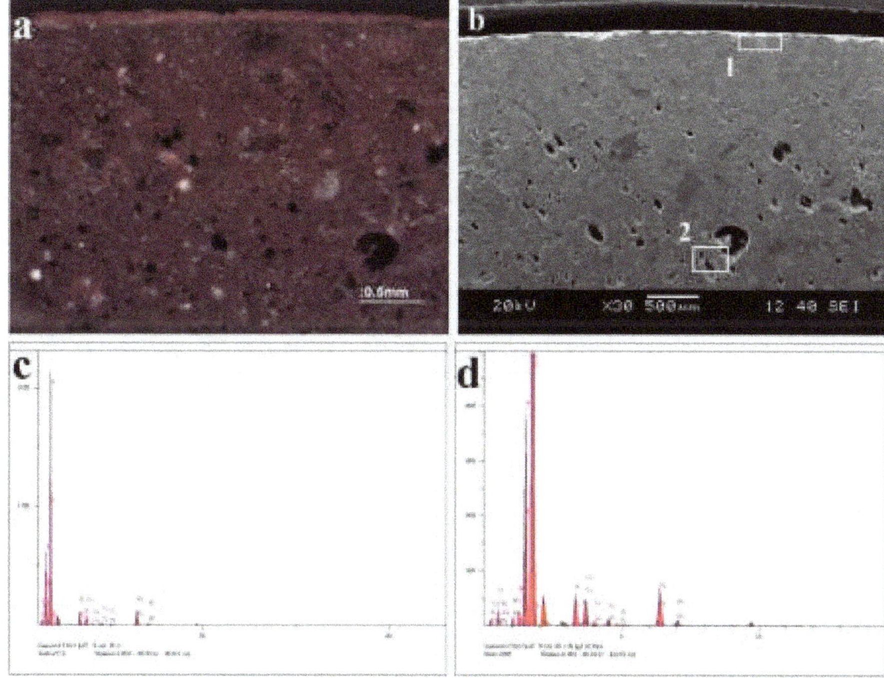

Figure 9. Cross sectional (a) optical and (b) SEM micrographs of S4, EDS spectra of (c) area 1 and (d) area 2.

Table 5 lists the semi-quantitative EDS analysis results in terms of elements and oxides. Elemental compositions of the body and GSL are important for evaluating the production technology used in the ceramic samples under investigation. Both the body and GSL have similar elemental components, but in different ratios (Table 5). According to these data, iron oxide seems to be the major colorant of the GSL. The amount of iron (originating from hematite) varies between 7.894 and 10.319 wt.% for bodies and from 8.027 to 9.367 wt.% for the slip. These results are compatible with Kapmeyer's study on the Urartian ceramics from Bastam Fortress at Iran and Toprakkale Fortress at Van. According to Kapmeyer, the iron content of the Toprakkale ceramics varies between 9.55 and 13.77 wt.% for slip and 10.83 and 13.50 wt.% for bodies. On the other hand, the iron content of Bastam ceramics reaches as high as 22.90 wt%. The iron content of slip is higher than for the bodies; therefore, it is reasonable to think that additional iron-bearing minerals were used to obtain the colour of the GSL. Also, the Na and K values of the slip are higher than for the bodies. This indicates that Na- and K-bearing minerals (such as Na_2CO_3 and K_2CO_3) were used as deflocculants during the preparation of the suspension for the surface application.

Table 5. Semi-quantitative EDS analysis results taken from the body and GSL of the investigated samples in terms of (a) elements and (b) oxides.

(a)	Elements (wt.%)								
	Na	Mg	Al	Si	K	Ca	Ti	Fe	O
Figure 6b- GSL	0.838	0.890	9.578	27.723	3.134	2.337	0.737	8.194	46.568
Figure 6b- Body	0.776	0.875	8.442	29.065	3.405	1.959	0.746	7.894	46.838
Figure 7b- GSL	0.680	0.961	9.216	27.834	3.279	2.262	0.830	8.416	46.522
Figure 7b- Body	0.677	0.888	9.196	27.845	3.260	2.538	0.862	8.223	46.512
Figure 8b- GSL	0.824	0.782	8.871	28.671	2.797	2.472	0.668	8.027	46.839
Figure 8b- Body	0.482	0.736	10.632	25.025	2.423	2.676	1.339	10.319	45.827
Figure 9b- GSL	0.653	0.937	9.187	27.272	3.255	1.857	0.784	9.367	46.279
Figure 9b- Body	0.517	0.991	10.019	26.753	3.017	1.829	0.845	9.078	46.372

(b)	Oxides (wt.%)							
	Na_2O	MgO	Al_2O_3	SiO_2	K_2O	CaO	TiO_2	Fe_2O_3
Figure 6b- GSL	1.129	1.476	18.096	59.308	3.775	3.270	1.229	11.716
Figure 6b- Body	1.046	1.451	15.951	62.179	4.101	2.741	1.245	11.286
Figure 7b- GSL	0.917	1.593	17.413	59.545	3.950	3.165	1.384	12.033
Figure 7b- Body	0.913	1.472	17.375	59.569	3.926	3.551	1.437	11.756
Figure 8b- GSL	1.110	1.296	16.761	61.336	3.369	3.459	1.114	11.477
Figure 8b- Body	0.649	1.220	20.089	53.536	2.919	3.744	2.234	14.753
Figure 9b- GSL	0.881	1.554	17.358	58.342	3.921	2.599	1.308	13.393
Figure 9b- Body	0.697	1.643	18.931	57.232	3.634	2.559	1.409	12.979

Thin section analysis reveals that plagioclase and feldspar grains are very common in the examined samples (Figure 10). Both large and small grains of feldspar were observed on all pottery samples and also on traditionally prepared and fired test piece 1B. Sample 1A is very poor in rock and mineral grains; only a large feldspar grain was detected on that sample. The feldspar grains observed in thin section analyses are not sharp edged, suggesting that feldspar grains were not grinded and added to the bodies, but rather occurred in the original clay source.

The shapes and distribution of the particles dispersed throughout the matrix are similar for all pottery samples. This similarity shows that a particular clay source was likely to have been chosen for the production of these ceramics and/or similar raw material preparation processes were used. Volcanic rock fragments were identified in samples S3 and 1B, indicating a possible raw material source.

Although the thickness of the thin section can change the colour to some extent, matrix colour is mainly an indicator of the firing atmosphere. Red indicates oxidative firing conditions. As a result of oxidation, hematite minerals are seen in the structure. It was observed that samples S2 and S1 have a red-brown colour, while samples S4 and S3 are yellowish-orange. Sample 1A is in shades of yellow and the colour of 1B is red-brown.

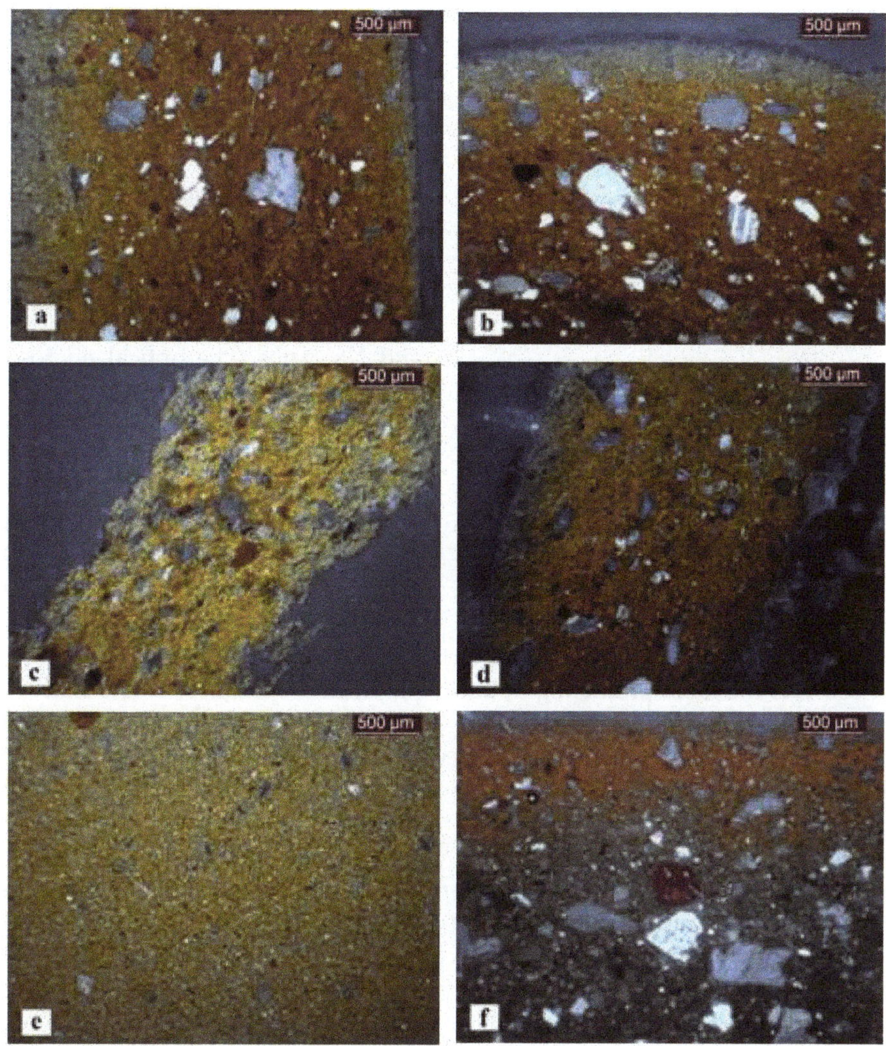

Figure 10. Optical microscopy images from thin sections of (a) S1, (b) S2, (c) S3, (d) S4, (e) 1A and (f)1B.

Table 6. Colour measurement values.

Sample Code		Chromatic Coordinates		
		L	a	b
S1	Body	45.99	18.24	23.20
	Glossy Surface Layer	42.35	26.50	26.11
S2	Body	47.49	18.6	22.92
	Glossy Surface Layer	40.19	26.81	24.52
S3	Body	46.12	16.99	23.15
	Glossy Surface Layer	32.87	24.68	18.99
S4	Body	44.89	21.24	25.26
	Glossy Surface Layer	36.71	28.11	23.87
VL clay	800°C	51.21	16.93	27.89
	850°C	53.56	19.90	31.12
	900°C	55.05	21.63	32.21
VD clay	800°C	49.69	19.06	25.98
	850°C	49.18	20.85	25.47
	900°C	52.36	21.60	25.13
BS clay	800°C	32.21	28.12	26.94
	850°C	36.41	28.32	29.78
	900°C	39.70	25.16	28.11

Table 6 shows the colour measurements of four pottery sherds and three local soil samples fired at different temperatures. Colour values were evaluated by 'L', 'a', and 'b' values along the chromatic coordinates ('L' value indicates the lightness scale, where 0 is black and 100 is white; 'a' value indicates the red–green scale, where positive values are red, negative values are green and 0 is neutral; 'b' value indicates the blue–yellow scale, where positive values are yellow, negative values are blue and 0 is neutral).

'L' values of the bodies are higher than for glossy slip, so the colours of the bodies are lighter than those of the surfaces. On the other hand, higher 'a' values of glossy slip indicate that slip have a stronger reddish colour than bodies; this may have been intensified by using additional iron-bearing minerals. The 'L' and 'a' values of the fired clay samples increased with higher temperatures. When the 'a' value is taken into account, it can easily be seen that VD clay fired at 850°C is the most promising option for production of the body. In addition, 'L' and 'a' values of BS clay fired at 850°C fit the values for glossy surface layers.

The characterization studies give clues to the production technology of Urartian red glossy ceramics. The presence and absence of some mineralogical/phase contents in the samples constitutes very important data for estimating firing temperatures. Illite was the only clay mineral identified in body and slip. Illite mica structure breaks down at 900–1000°C. Quartz and feldspars can persist up to 1000°C. In addition, diopside/augite may be generated at 800–900°C. During heating decomposition and phase transformation, processes take place. The calcite peaks that can be seen in unfired samples disappeared in the fired samples due to thermal decomposition. Dolomite has the decomposition with two stages that begins at around 650°C and continues up to 900°C. Therefore dolomite peaks are not observed for the fired samples of BS. Although the illite structure breaks down at 900–1000°C, it was observed that the intensity of illite peaks becomes lower as the temperature increases. Hence the BS clay sample has high Fe_2O_3 content (Table 3); hematite peaks with higher intensity are seen at all temperatures. Thus it is reasonable to think that the firing temperature was probably not over 900°C. All the samples contain hematite, which is evidence that all the ceramics are fired in oxidative condition. The diopside/augite phase was identified in the samples. This phase may be generated at 800–900°C. Porosities in the body of the ceramic samples reveal that the ceramics were unlikely to have been fired at higher temperatures. Furthermore, the colour values of the local clays fired at 850°C are very close to the colour values of the bodies. Kapmeyer indicated that the surface gloss disappeared and dullness increased when clay was fired at 900°C (Kapmeyer, 2005). Similarly, test pieces 1A and 1B fired at 1050°C justified this conclusion with their dullness. When these data are taken into account, the firing temperature of the Urartian glossy red ceramics should not be higher than 850°C.

Elemental composition of the glossy surface layers indicated that those layers contained higher Fe, K and Na ratios. The optical microscopy images suggest that the thicknesses of the surface layers are not uniform (Figure 6-9). In addition, the colours of these layers are reddish and darker than the bodies. The glossy surface layers are observed not only on open wide surfaces, but also on inner curved surfaces. As mentioned in Kapmeyer's study (2005), some spiralling signs and bumps were observed on the surface layers. These observations suggest that polishing was not applied; a suspension was probably prepared and spread over the body. Minerals such as Na_2CO_3 and K_2CO_3 are used as defflocculant to suspend the solid particles in the liquid. In addition, oxides of Na and K act like flux in the batch, helping to form the sintered and glossy slip. This also explains the higher Na and K ratios.

During the cross sectional observations, there were black regions (black cores) in the bodies of some samples (Figure 2c). This indicates the presence of carbonaceous materials in the utilised clay. During firing, air is needed for combustion of materials containing carbon. It needs to penetrate the interior, and this takes time. Also, a sintered glossy surface layer decelerates the penetration of air and stops the decarbonisation. As a result, black deposits form in the bodies.

The comparison results between pottery and raw materials give useful data. The colour analyses indicated that the local clays VL and VD are significant candidates for the clays used to produce the bodies of the ceramics. Thin section analyses also confirm this view. The fired VL clay sample has a similar microstructure to S4 and S3. The fired VD clay sample has similar microstructure to S2 and S1. When the red slip is taken into account, the chemical compositions of GSL and BS are very similar in terms of both major oxides and some trace elements (Table 3). This strong similarity gives rise to the thought that BS may have been used for the surfaces. Additionally, due to its high Fe_2O_3 and very low CaO content, with suitable additives BS clay might have been used for the suspension that forms the red slip when it is applied over the body.

The Bitlis region, from where BS was obtained, is situated on the western and southwestern shores of Lake Van, in the lake basin. This region, which was an integral part of the Urartian kingdom, was also an important state centre. As regards geomorphology, Bitlis province and its districts are rich in iron ore as seen on the metallogenic map of General Directorate of Mineral Research and Exploration (MTA) (Figure 11). It can be deduced that the clay from the region is suitable for making pottery, as the towns of Günkırı and Kavakbaşı in Bitlis continue to produce pottery in traditional ways. Moreover, BS has long been used for slip in the production of traditional pots in those towns (Figure 12). Therefore, it is quite reasonable to think that the Urartians may also have used BS, which is rich in iron and very suitable for making slip, with its very thin grain and soluble structure.

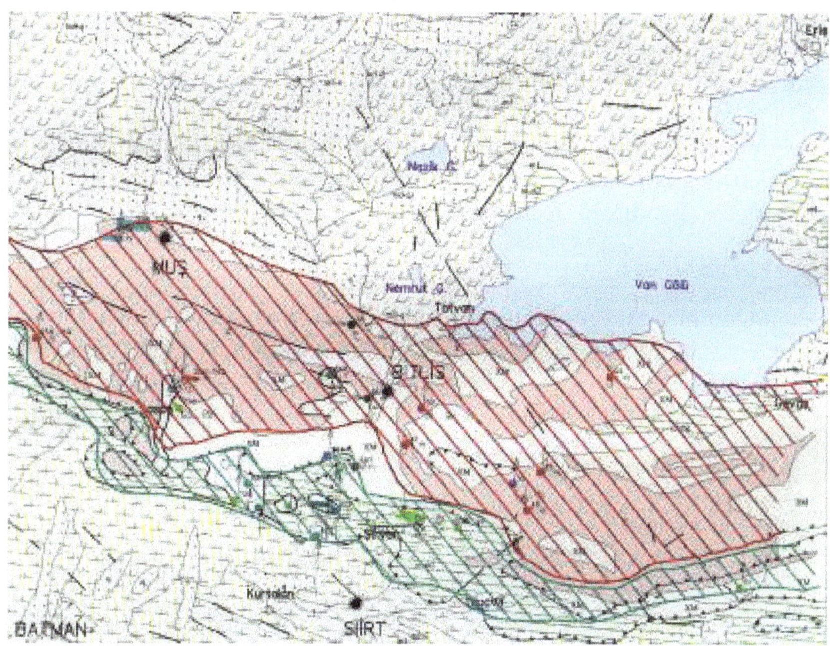

Figure 11. Metallogenic map of the around Lake Van. Iron is located in areas coloured red (adopted from MTA). The map was retrieved from http://www.mta.gov.tr/v2.0/haritalar/maden_haritalari/metal/28.html, on 06/05/2016.

It has been determined that raw material is usually located in the range of 1-7 km from the workshops that manufacture pottery (see, for detail, Arnold, 1989, 50).

The distance between Van, the centre of the kingdom, and the towns of Bitlis from where BS procured is 125 km as the crow flies. Although such a distance could be thought quite considerable, there are two reasons why it would not have been an insurmountable problem for the Urartian Kingdom: the first is that as stated above the Bitlis region was not only within the domination area of the kingdom but also one of the important Urartian province which possessed slip soil rich in iron for red slipped glossy Urartian pottery; the second is that the amount of soil to be obtained would not have to be produce the pottery itself, but only the slip. The total amount of soil required for the slip would be much less for transportation and would not be a great challenge for a powerful kingdom with organised labour and state resources.

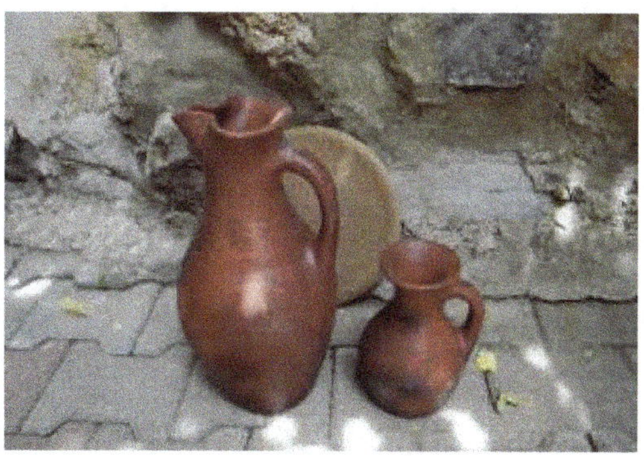

Figure 12. Jugs from Kavakbaşı village slipped with BS (Avusku)

4. CONCLUSIONS

In this study, four representative Urartian pottery samples from Ayanis Fortress and three clay samples from the local region were characterised using chemical, mineralogical, morphological and petrographic analyses.

The phases obtained through XRD analyses revealed that the firing temperature of the pottery samples is unlikely to have been over 900°C and that an oxidation atmosphere was probably formed during firing. The optical microscopic images of the glossy slip obtained from all samples indicated that a very compact and uniform structure, with a larger degree of sintering compared to the body, was formed over the vessels. The difference between the colours of these layers and of the bodies clearly indicates that finer clay, with colorant and fluxes, was used in the production of the GSL than for the bodies. The higher content of Fe, Na and K elements obtained from EDS analyses also supports this finding.

Petrographic data obtained from thin section analyses reveal the similarities between the pottery samples and the test pieces produced from local clays. Samples S1 and S2 showed similarity to 1B while Samples S3 and S4 showed similarity to 1A. It is reasonable to think that these clays were used as raw material for the bodies. Chemical analyses and colour measurements show a strong relationship between GSL and BS.

To conclude, the results of the experiments described here add significant details to our knowledge of the production technology of red slipped glossy Urartian pottery. Promising data obtained from different analyses reveals significant similarities between ceramic samples and fired clay test pieces. It may be concluded that the local clays could have been used in production of Urartian ceramics with red glossy slip.

ACKNOWLEDGEMENTS

We are grateful to Altan Çilingiroğlu and Mehmet Işıklı, who allowed us to study the Ayanis materials. We would also like to thank Hannelore Kapmeyer for her valuable comments and advice. We are in debt to local potter Osman Eşme, who provided information on local clays and allowed us to use his workshop and kiln. Our special thanks go to Abby Robinson for her carefully reading and copyediting article's English.

REFERENCES

Akça, E., Arocena, J., Kılıç, S., Dingil, M., and Kapur, S. (2010) Preliminary chemical and micromorphological observations on Urartu (800–600 B.C.) ceramics, Eastern Turkey. *Geoarchaeology*, Vol.25, No.2, pp.233–244.

Antonelli, F., Ermeti, A. L., Lazzarini, L., Verita, M. and Raffaelli, G. (2014) Archaeometric contribution to the characterization of renaissance Majolica from Urbino and a comparison with Coeval Majolica from Pesaro (The Marches, Central Italy), *Archaeometry*, Vol.56, No.5, pp.784–804.

Arnold, D. E. (1989) *Ceramic Theory and Cultural Process*. Cambridge, Cambridge University Press.

Çilingiroğlu,A. (1997) *Urartu Tarihi ve Sanatı*. Izmir, Yaşar Eğitim ve Kültür Vakfı.

Çilingiroğlu, A. (2002) The reign of Rusa II: towards the end of the Urartian Kingdom, in R. Aslan, S. Blum, G. Kastl, F. Schweizer ve D. Thumm (Eds), *Festschrift für Manfred Korfmann, Mauer Schau Band 1*, Bernhard Albert Greiner, pp. 483–489.

Çilingiroğlu, A. (2011) Ayanis Kalesi, K. Köroğlu ve E. Konyar (Eds), *Urartu: Doğuda Değişim/Urartu: Transformation in the East*, İstanbul, YKY, pp. 336–359.

Çilingiroğlu, A. (2013) The Urartian city and citadel of Ayanis: an example of interdependence, in S. Redford and N. Ergin (eds.) *Cities and Citadels in Turkey: From the Iron Age to the Seljuks, Ancient Near Eastern Studies Supplement 40*, Leuven: Peeters, pp.81-96.

Çilingiroğlu, A. (2016) Did weapons dedicated to the Urartian god of Haldi help to save the Ayanis fortress, in M. Egg, A. Naso and R. Rollinger (eds.) *Waffen für die Götter, Waffenweihungen in Archäologie und Geschichte*, Akten de in ternationalen Tagung am Institut für Archäologien der Leopold-Franzens-Universität, Innsbruck, 6-8. März 2013, Mainz: Verlag des Römisch-Germanischen Zentralmuseums, pp. 17-26.

Erdem, A. Ü., Çilingiroğlu, A., Giakoumaki, A., Castanys, M., Kartsonaki, E., Fotakis, C. and Anglos, D. (2008) Characterization of Iron Age pottery from eastern Turkey by laser- induced breakdown spectroscopy (LIBS), *Journal of Archaeological Science*, Vol.35, pp.2486–2494.

Kapmeyer, H. (2005) Zur Herstellung urartäischer Palastkeramik, Archäologische Mitteilungen aus Iran und Turan, Band 35-36 (2003-2004), pp.313–333.

Kapur, S., Sakarya, N., and FitzPatrick, E.A. (1991) Mineralogy and micromorphology of Chalcolithic and Early Bronze Age İkiztepe ceramics. *Geoarchaeology*,Vol.7, pp.327–337.

Kleinmann, B. (1976) *Mineralogische untersuchungen an urartäischer keramik, Urartu: Ein wiederentdeckter Rivale Assyriens, Katalog der Ausstellung*, München, pp.64–66.

Knappett, C., Kilikoglou, V., Steele, V. and Stern, B. (2005) The circulation and consumption of red lustrous wheelmade Ware: petrographic, chemical and residue analysis. *Anatolian Studies*, Vol.55, pp.25–59.

Kroll, S. (1970), Die Keramik aus der Ausgabung Bastam 1969, *Archäologische Mitteilungen aus Iran, Neue Folge Band 3*, pp.67–92.

Kroll, S.-Zahlhaas G. (1976) Katalog: Der Ausgestellten Funde. In H.J. Kellner (ed.),*Urartu. Ein wiederentdeckt Rivale Assyriens. Katalog der Ausstellung München 8. Sept.-5 Denz. 1976 Ausstellungskataloge der Prähistorichen Staatssammlung München, Band 2*, pp.68–86.

Picon, M., Vichy, M. and Meille, E. (1971) Composition of the Lezoux, Lyon and Arezzo Samian Ware. *Archaeometry*, Vol.13, No.2, pp.191–208.

Picon, M., Carre C., Cordoliani M. L., Vichy M., Hernandez J. A. and Mignard J. L. (1975) Composition of the La Graufesenque, Banassac and Montans Terra Sigillata. *Archaeometry*, Vol.17, No.2, pp.191–199.

Speakman, R.J., Stone, E.C., Glascock, M.D, Çilingiroğlu, A., Zimansky, P. and Neff, H. (2004) Neutron activation analysis of Urartian pottery from Eastern Anatolia. *Journal of Radioanalytical and Nuclear Chemisty*, Vol.262, No.1, pp.119–127.

Tite M. S., Bimson M., and Freestone I. C. (1982) An examination of the high gloss surface finishes on Greek Attic and Roman Samian Wares. *Archaeometry*, Vol.24, No.2, pp.117–126.

van Loon, M. N. (1966) *Urartian Art, Its Distinctive Traits in the Light of New Excavations*. İstanbul, Nederlands historisch-archaeologisch instituut.

4

POTTERY PRODUCTION DURING "ROMANIZATION" OF SICILY: AN ARCHAEOMETRIC STUDY OF PLAIN TABLE-WARE CLASSES FROM ANCIENT AKRAI (SICILY)

G. Barone[1,*], R. Chowaniec[2], M. Fituła[2], P. Mazzoleni[1], L. Mirabella[1], S. Raneri[1]

[1]University of Catania, Department of Biological, Geological and Environmental Sciences, C.so Italia 57, 95129 Catania, Italy
[2]University of Warsaw, Institute of Archeology, Krakowskie Przedmiescie 26/28, PL 00-927, Warsaw, Poland

Corresponding author: Germana Barone (gbarone@unict.it)

ABSTRACT

In this paper, petrographic, mineralogical and chemical analyses have been performed on plain table-ware fragments discovered in the ancient town of Akrai (modern Palazzolo Acreide, Syracuse, Sicily) and dated between the Hellenistic and the Late Roman periods (4th-5th/6thcentury A.D.). The project is developed in the context of the archeological debate on the cultural and political process occurred in Sicily since the 3rdcentury B.C. and known in archaeological literature as *Romanization*. In this framework, a gradually substitution of Greek-Hellenistic materials with the Roman ones has occurred in Sicilian colonies and the city of Akrai was deepened involved in this process. As the sensitiveness of material culture to cultural and social changes, the archaeometric investigation has been focused on provenance and technological manufacture aspects of table-ware production, in order to delineate the eventually changes took place in the area during the investigated period. The comparison of obtained data with numerous references local groups of ceramics allows to identify different highly specialized local productions, drawing-back the commercial movements of potteries in Sicily during Roman Age.

KEYWORDS: Akrai (Palazzolo Acreide), archaeometry, pottery, plain table-ware

1. INTRODUCTION

1.1 *Archeological framework*

Ancient Akrai (in Latin Acrae, Agris, Acrenses), located near the modern town Palazzolo Acreide (Syracuse, Sicily, Fig. 1(a,b)), occupied one of the plateaus of the Hyblaean Mountains, called Acremonte. The city was founded in 664 B.C. as a subcolony of Syracuse and was remaining under the influence of metropolis, equally in politics, economy and culture up to the fall of Syracuse in 212 B.C. Afterward, Akrai was listed among *stipendiariae civitates* as a self-supporting and tax-paying town, yet obviously dependent on Rome (civitas decumana).

Since the Roman conquest of Syracuse in 214-212 B.C., the political, administration and culture state and the conditions of the Greek colonies in Sicily have to be changed. A gradual vanishing of the Hellenistic elements and its substitution with the Roman ones took place in a long-lasting cultural process, known in the archaeological literature as Romanization. Gradually, Rome introduced its own life model, but the organization of the first provinces delivered many difficulties. The Romans were faced with something that went beyond their experience and their approaches to solving problems (Wilson, 1988); the old Greek urban centres had, in fact, their own infrastructure and model of civic administration, and the inhabitants of Sicily, who were different culturally and ethnically from the Romans, were not very loyal to them. This situation forced the Romans to adopt a moderate assimilation instead of power solutions, thanks to which the culture of the conquered people made a lasting impression on the culture of the victors; therefore, it wasn't lost, becoming a permanent element of the new order. Thanks to these long-term multidimensional relations and arrangements, in the course of which the Romans demonstrated a growing interest in shaping life on the island, a specific mix of languages, legal systems, culture, architecture and religion was created (Alcock, 1989; Buscemi, 2007; Dearden, 2004; Hollegaard et al., 1995;Wilson, 1990).

The archeological excavations within the ancient Greek colony of Akrai conducted on behalf of the Archeological Mission of University of Warsaw, in deep cooperation with Superintendence for Cultural Heritage of Syracuse, began in 2011. The research is still continued and is focused on exploring the history of the Greek-Roman urban centre after the fall of Syracuse in 212 B.C. as well as the material culture of its inhabitants.

The archaeological excavations of the town of Akrai brought many interesting observations about the Romanization process, allowing to better understand the changes that involved Sicilian colonies during this period. Doubtlessly, Akrai took new political realities, even if its character and role after the conquest of Syracuse by Romans is still widely debated (Chowaniec, 2013; Więcek*et al.*, 2014).

The first stage of archaeological works was focused on exploring and documenting the Late Roman and Byzantine strata, in which architectural remains, built with re-used blocks and architectural elements from earlier foundations, have been found. These discovered levels were only remains of a secondary use of a Late Hellenistic and Early Roman residential complex and were filled with strongly intermingled, heterogeneous archaeological material, represented mainly by artifacts dated from the 4thto the 6thcenturies A.D. (Chowaniec, 2014; Chowaniec, 2015b). On the basis of archaeological evidences, it possible to suppose that the town functioned continuously as far as the Late Antiquity, when the structural changes have been done; in fact, no urban long-term abandonment can be observed. A change in the arrangement of the Hellenistic-Roman town has been registered in the last decades of 4thcentury A.D. and has been testified by a modification of the arteries from the original town grid, by a less intense inflow of the coins and by a quite heedless Late Roman architectural remains, which more or less duplicated the earlier Hellenistic-Roman foundations (Fig. 1(c)).

1.2 *Fine and plain table-wares from Akrai*

The archaeological excavations of Akrai delivered a vast amount of potteries, mainly represented by splendid examples of thin-walled ceramic (*i.e.*, Hellenistic thin-walled bowls, terra sigillata), amphorae and storage vessels (*i.e.*, dolia, pithoi, etc.) (Chowaniec *et al.*, 2014; Chowaniec, 2015a).

Among them, several fragments of table-wares have been found; this category of pottery can be divided into two groups: fine table-ware and plain table-ware. Fine table-ware is mainly represented by terra sigillata italica, usually considered the symbol of the Romanization process. It is a ceramic class characterized by glossy red slipped surface, with thin walls, stamps and relief decorations, whose production begun around the half of 1stcentury B.C. at Arretium (modern Arezzo), in northern Tuscany, and spread out in the Mediterranean area during the next centuries, also beyond the Italy geographic limits (e.g.in Gallic provinces; see Picon et al., 1975; Maggetti and Kupfer, 1978). In Sicily the finds of terra sigillata italica are mainly focused in coastal areas, in the principal economic centers-ports (i.e. Messina, Catania, Syracuse, Tyndaris, Thermae Himeraeae, Palermo, Marsala, Agrigento), even if examples of shards have been found also in the interior centers (i.e. Morgantina, Centuripe, Troina, Monte Iato, Megara Hyblaea, Camarina (Malfitana, 2004)). About 130 fragments of this class of pottery were discovered also in Akrai.

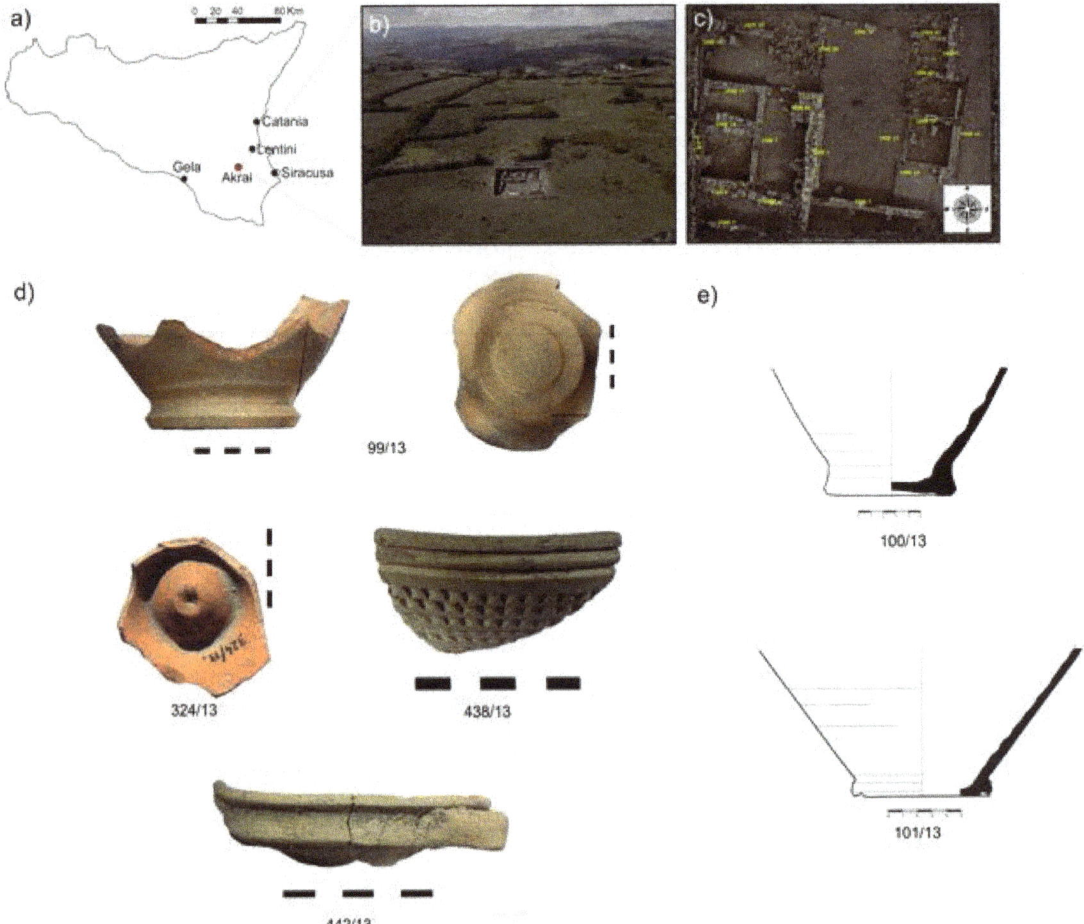

Figure 1. (a) Geographical localization of the site of Akrai (Palazzolo Acreide, prov. Syracuse), (b) aerial view with excavated area, (c) picture of Trench I with architectural structures found (USM#) and (d) pictures and (e) drawing of representative examples of plain table-ware from Akrai (photo and drawing by Wicenciak U., Krakowian J. and Wójcik K)

The fine table-ware found in Sicily is partially diagnosed and widely discussed in scientific and archeological literature (Polito, 2000; Malfitana, 2004; Olcese, 2011-2012), while the study of plain table-ware is neglected and not commonly published. This is a critical and vast gap in our knowledge about Antiquity, because such pottery class was the most widespread and commonly used in ancient time, being also a substantial part of the Ancient Mediterranean frame (Hayes, 1997). Therefore, the better knowledge of this class of material could support us in the interpretation about the presence/absence of specific pottery types in particular regions of Sicily. Moreover, in the case of Akrai, an in-depth investigation of plain table-wares could allow us in recognizing workshops, commercial interests, possible trade routes, habits of the households and finally drawing-back relevant changes in complex culture contexts, characterized by different cultural phases.

In general, the identification of provenance and technological features of plain table-ware class is difficult in view of the fine grain of the clay paste, often high depurated and without inclusions. For this reason, the knowledge of aspects as manufacture process, aesthetics and role of the pottery in the society can be achieved only by archaeometric analyses, including comparison with a great number of ceramics and reference raw materials with certain provenance. In this sense, the presence in scientific literature of reference ceramics and clay sediments supplies a fundamental issue in the fine pottery researches.

For aforementioned, this work is focused on the archaeometric characterization of a selection of representative samples of plain table-ware obtained during the 2013 excavation season at Akrai (totally, 1161 fragments of fine table-ware and 1413 fragments plain table-ware have been excavated, representing about 58% of all the pottery fragments found in this year), with the aim to characterize samples in term of both technology and manufacture, and identify the provenance of the studied artifacts, trying to delineate the commercial movements that have involved the site during Roman Age.

2. MATERIALS AND METHODS

2.1 Materials

Generally, the plain table-ware class includes vessels intended for serving and consuming food and for meal preparation. The plain table-wares founded in Akrai present a huge diversity in shape and chronology, even if the large typologically variety is represented by undecorated fragments. Among the pottery shards, the following shapes have been distinguished: table amphorae, jugs, basins, bowls, lekanai, craters, unguentaria and lids (Młynarczyk, 2015).

For the present study, a totally of 47 specimens supposed to be related to a local production and mainly dated between the Hellenistic and the Late Roman periods (4th–5th/6th century A.D.) have been selected for archaeometric analyses.

The selection of the fragments was performed while the macroscopic analysis, that allow the identification of several macro-fabriques, including fine and plain table-ware fragments recovered in the framework of the 2013 archaeological excavation season (Młynarczyk 2015); the plain table-wares represent mainly three macro-fabriques, namely fabrique F1 (red to orange clay, cream to greenish wash: Munsell Index 5 YR 6/6, 2.5 YR 6/6; very dense clay paste, clean or exhibiting some small to medium-size white grits and some small black grits, often with white wash), fabrique F3 (brownish to reddish break/surface: M.I. 2.5 YR 6/6 - 5 YR 6/6; rather dense clay paste with some small black and white grits) and fabrique F10 (red to orange clay: M. I. 10R 5/8; coarse grain clay paste with medium-size black grits and some small white ones). In consideration of the large amount of pottery fragments excavated in the site and the identification of the aforementioned archeological typologies and macro-fabriques, the selection criteria has been based on the representatively of the samples in term of shape, chronology and archaeological fabriques (Table 1; Figure 1(d, e)); moreover, all samples represent diagnostic fragment parts of potteries (rim/base/handle).

2.2 Methods

All studied samples have been analyzed by petrographic, mineralogical and chemical analyses (see Table1).

In detail, petrographic characterization of samples has been obtained by Whitbread classification (Whitbread, 1995). Moreover, X-ray diffraction analysis (XRD) have been performed on all samples in order to obtain mineralogical composition; analysis have been carried out through a SIEMENS D5000 with Cu-Kα radiation and an Ni filter. Randomly oriented powders were scanned from 2° to 45° 2θ, with a 0.02° 2θ step size and a counting time of 2s per step. The tube current and the voltage were 30 mA and 40 kV, respectively. Finally chemical composition of studied samples have been obtained by X-ray fluorescence analysis (XRF) performed by using a Philips PW 2404/00 on powder-pressed pellets of ceramic. Further details are reported on previous papers (Barone *et al.*, 2014; Barone *et al.*,2012).

Chemical data have been treated with statistical methods according to Aitchison (1986) by using CoDaPack (Thio-Henestrosa and Martin Fernandez, 2005), a compositional software that implements the basic methods of analysis of compositional data based on log-ratios. In addition, chemical results and chemical data of reference materials have been treated with a statistical and computational method proposed by Tukey (1977) by using software STATISTICA (Hill and Lewicki, 2007).

Table 1. Synthetic chart of studied materials with indications on samples IDs, shape, archeological fabrique, provenance, dating of stratigraphic units (US), surface and bulk color determined by Munsell color chart (Munsell Color Chart, 2000; M.I. = Munsell Index) and analyses performed are reported.

Sample ID	Class	Shape and fragment	Archeological fabrique	Provenance	US dating	M.I. (Munsell Index)
324/13	Plain-table ware	Jug; bottom part	Fabrique 1	Trench I; US 3	III-II B.C. - VII A.D.	**Surface:**2,5 YR 5/8
						Bulk:2,5 YR 5/8
326/13	Plain-table ware	Jug; bottom part	Fabrique 1	Trench I; US 3	III-II B.C. - VII A.D.	**Surface:**5YR 5/8
						Bulk:2,5 YR 5/8
327/13	Plain-table ware	Basin; rim	Fabrique 1	Trench I; US 3	III-II B.C. - VII A.D.	**Surface:**5 YR 6/4
						Bulk:GLEY1 6/5G
328/13	Plain-table ware	Basin; rim	Fabrique 1	Trench I; US 3	III-II B.C. - VII A.D.	**Surface:**2,5 YR 6/8
						Bulk:2,5 YR 5/6
329/13	Plain-table ware	Basin; rim	Fabrique 1	Trench I; US 3	III-II B.C. - VII A.D.	**Surface:**5 YR 6/6
						Bulk:2,5 YR 4/8
331/13	Plain-table ware	Lekane; rim	Fabrique 3	Trench I; US 3	III-II B.C. - VII A.D.	**Surface:**5 YR 6/8
						Bulk:10 YR 6/6
332/13	Plain-table ware	Jug; bottom part	Fabrique 3	Trench I; US 3	III-II B.C. - VII A.D.	**Surface:**5 YR 6/6
						Bulk:5 YR 6/8

333/13	Plain-table ware	Jug; bottom part	Fabrique 3	Trench I; US 3	III-II B.C. - VII A.D.	**Surface:**5 YR 6/8 **Bulk:**5 YR 5/8
336/13	Plain-table ware	Big basin; rim	Fabrique 3	Trench I; US 3	III-II B.C. - VII A.D.	**Surface:**7,5 YR 7/6 **Bulk:**10 YR 7/4
529/13	Plain-table ware	Big basin; bottom part	Fabrique 1	Trench I; US 3	III-II B.C. - VII A.D.	**Surface:**5 YR 6/6 **Bulk:**7,5 YR 6/6
99/13	Plain-table ware	Jug; bottom part	Fabrique 1	Trench I; US 4	III-II B.C. - V A.D.	**Surface:**5 YR 6/6 **Bulk:**2,5 YR 5/8
100/13	Plain-table ware	Jug; bottom part	Fabrique 1	Trench I; US 4	III-II B.C. - V A.D.	**Surface:**5 YR 5/6 **Bulk:**5 YR 5/6
101/13	Plain-table ware	Jug; bottom part	Fabrique 1	Trench I; US 4	III-II B.C. - V A.D.	**Surface:**5 YR 6/4 **Bulk:**5 YR 5/6
102/13	Plain-table ware	Jug; bottom part	Fabrique 1	Trench I; US 4	III-II B.C. - V A.D.	**Surface:**2,5 YR 6/6 **Bulk:**2,5 YR 5/8
113/13	Plain-table ware	Big basin; bottom part	Fabrique 1	Trench I; US 4	III-II B.C. - V A.D.	**Surface:**2,5 YR 6/6 **Bulk:**10 YR 6/3
114/13	Plain-table ware	Big basin; bottom part	Fabrique 1	Trench I; US 4	III-II B.C. - V A.D.	**Surface:** 5 YR 5/6 **Bulk:** 7,5 YR 6/6
339/13	Plain-table ware	Pithos; bottom part	Fabrique 10	Trench I; US 4	III-II B.C. - V A.D.	**Surface:** 7,5 YR 6/6 **Bulk:** 7,5 YR 6/6
342/13	Plain-table ware	Basin; rim	Fabrique 10	Trench I; US 4	III-II B.C. - V A.D.	**Surface:**5 YR 6/8 **Bulk:**10 YR 6/2
349/13	Plain-table ware	Krater; rim	Fabrique 1	Trench I; US 4	III-II B.C. - V A.D.	**Surface:** 5 YR 6/6 **Bulk:** 5 YR 6/6
351/13	Plain-table ware	Lekane; rim	Fabrique 3	Trench I; US 4	III-II B.C. - V A.D.	**Surface:**2,5 YR 6/6 **Bulk:**5 YR 5/8
353/13	Plain-table ware	Lekane; rim	Fabrique 3	Trench I; US 4	III-II B.C. - V A.D.	**Surface:**5 YR 6/6 **Bulk:**7,5 YR 6/6
355/13	Plain-table ware	Basin; rim	Fabrique 1	Trench I; US 4	III-II B.C. - V A.D.	**Surface:** 5 YR 7/4 **Bulk:** 5 YR 5/6
374/13	Plain-table ware	Lid	Fabrique 3	Trench I; US 4	III-II B.C. - V A.D.	**Surface:** 5 YR 6/6 **Bulk:** 5 YR 5/6
375/13	Plain-table ware	Lid	Fabrique 3	Trench I; US 4	III-II B.C. - V A.D.	**Surface:** 5 YR 7/4 **Bulk:** 7,5 YR 5/6
377/13	Plain-table ware	Lid; handle	Fabrique 1	Trench I; US 4	III-II B.C. - V A.D.	**Surface:**2,5 Y 7/3 **Bulk:**2,5 YR 5/8 - GLEY1 5N
378/13	Plain-table ware	Jug; rim	Fabrique 1	Trench I; US 4	III-II B.C. - V A.D.	**Surface:**5 YR 7/4 -2,5 Y 7/3 **Bulk:**2,5 YR 5/8
383/13	Plain-table ware	Jug; rim	Fabrique 1	Trench I; US 4	III-II B.C. - V A.D.	**Surface:**2,5 Y 8/2 **Bulk:**2,5 YR 5/8
386/13	Plain-table ware	Jug; bottom part	Fabrique 1	Trench I; US 4	III-II B.C. - V A.D.	**Surface:**10 YR 5/2 **Bulk:**5 YR 5/8
387/13	Plain-table ware	Jug; bottom part	Fabrique 1	Trench I; US 4	III-II B.C. - V A.D.	**Surface:**5 YR 6/6 **Bulk:**5 YR 5/6
388/13	Plain-table ware	Jug; bottom part	Fabrique 1	Trench I; US 4	III-II B.C. - V A.D.	**Surface:**10 YR 4/2 **Bulk:**5 YR 4/6
392/13	Plain-table ware	Jug; rim	Fabrique 1	Trench I; US 4	III-II B.C. - V A.D.	**Surface:**2,5 Y 7/3 **Bulk:**2,5 YR 5/8
393/13	Plain-table ware	Basin; rim	Fabrique 1	Trench I; US 4	III-II B.C. - V A.D.	**Surface:**2,5 Y 7/2 **Bulk:**2,5 YR 5/6
394/13	Plain-table ware	Basin; rim	Fabrique 1	Trench I; US 4	III-II B.C. - V A.D.	**Surface:**10 YR 6/4 **Bulk:**2,5 YR 5/6
400/13	Plain-table ware	Jug; rim	Fabrique 1	Trench I; US 4	III-II B.C. - V A.D.	**Surface:**5 YR 7/6 **Bulk:**5 YR 5/6
424/13	Plain-table ware	Bottle; rim	Fabrique 1	Trench I; US 4	III-II B.C. - V A.D.	**Surface:**2,5 Y 8/2 **Bulk:**2,5 YR 5/8
435/13	Plain-table ware	Basin; rim	Fabrique 1	Trench I; US 4	III-II B.C. - V A.D.	**Surface:**2,5 Y 8/2 **Bulk:**2,5 YR 6/6 -10 YR 5/1
436/13	Plain-table ware	Basin; rim	Fabrique 1	Trench I; US 4	III-II B.C. - V A.D.	**Surface:** 2,5 Y 7/2 **Bulk:** 2,5 YR 5/8
437/13	Plain-table ware	Basin; rim	Fabrique 1	Trench I; US 4	III-II B.C. - V A.D.	**Surface:** 2,5 Y 7/2 **Bulk:** 2,5 YR 5/8
438/13	Plain-table ware	Basin; rim	Fabrique 1	Trench I; US 4	III-II B.C. - V A.D.	**Surface:** 2,5 Y 7/4

						Bulk: 5 YR 5/8
444/13	Plain-table ware	Bowl; rim	Fabrique 1	Trench I; US 4	III-II B.C. - V A.D.	**Surface:** 5 YR 7/4 **Bulk:** 5 YR 5/6
301/13	Plain-table ware	Jug; bottom part	Fabrique 1	Trench I; US 7	III-II B.C. – half V A.D.	**Surface:** 2,5 Y 7/3 **Bulk:** 2,5 Y 7/4
305/13	Plain-table ware	Jug; bottom part	Fabrique 1	Trench I; US 7	III-II B.C. – half V A.D.	**Surface:**10 YR 8/4 **Bulk:** 5 YR 7/6
306/13	Plain-table ware	Jug; bottom part	Fabrique 1	Trench I; US 7	III-II B.C. – half V A.D.	**Surface:** 2,5 YR 5/6 **Bulk:** 7,5 YR 5/4
293/13	Plain-table ware	Dish; rim	Fabrique 10	Trench I; US 8	III-II B.C. – half V A.D.	**Surface:** 7,5 YR 5/4 **Bulk:** 2,5 YR 5/6
284/13	Plain-table ware	Basin; rim	Fabrique 1	Trench I; US 10a	I B.C. – half V A.D.	**Surface:** 10 YR 6/3 **Bulk:**5 YR 5/6
285/13	Plain-table ware	Krater; rim	Fabrique 1	Trench I; US 10a	I B.C. – half V A.D.	**Surface:**2,5 Y 8/3 **Bulk:**2,5 YR 5/8
550/13	Plain-table ware	Pithos; rim	Fabrique 10	Trench I; US 10a	I B.C. – half V A.D.	**Surface:** 2,5 Y 7/3 **Bulk:** 2,5 YR5/8

3. RESULTS

Thin section analysis allows to identify four petrographic fabrics on the basis of groundmass features (Fig.2); noteworthy is that for each petrographic group slight variations in term of inclusions have been recognized.

The first petrographic group, namely Fabric 1 (specimens 113/13 (Figure 2(a)), 327/13, 332/13, 339/13, 387/13, 388/13 (Fig. 2(b)), comprises basin and jug fragments with a medium grain size. The groundmass, quite homogeneous, is micaceous and exhibits also fine grained quartz (< 0.1 mm). Additionally, it is characterized by a medium-high birefringence and reddish-brown colour. The vughy microstructure consists in sub-rounded vughs and rare vesicles, exhibiting a spatial distribution from double spaced to open, without a preferential orientation. Finally, inclusions (inclusion: groundmass ratio 30:70) are mainly represented by dominant volcanic rocks fragments, common plagioclase and pyroxene, with unimodal grain size distribution. Noteworthy is the presence of magmatic biotite in sample 339/13.

The most numerous class is represented by fine-grained specimens with homogeneous, micaceous and fossil-rich groundmass, fine quartz and carbonatic fragments sub-angular in shape and sub-millimetric in dimension (< 0.1 mm) (Fabric 2). Groundmass exhibits an high birefringence and a reddish colour. The vughy microstructure consists in sub-rounded vughs, channels and vesicles with spatial distribution from open to double spaced and a slightly preferential orientation of channels. The majority of samples are characterized by absence of inclusions (99/13, 100/13, 101/13, 102/13 (Figure 2(c)), 331/13, 355/13, 375/13, 377/13, 383/13, 393/13, 438/13, 349/13, 394/13, 400/13, 424/13, 435/13, 436/13, 437/13, 444/13). However, in some cases, scarce volcanic inclusions (114/13, 284/13, 285/13, 324/13, 351/13, 374/13, 392/13), zeolites (293/13 (Figure 2(d)), 550/13), volcanic glass (306/13, 326/13, 329/13) and chamotte (378/13) have been observed. Finally, secondary calcite has been observed, especially in samples 331/13, 438/13, 349/13, 394/13, 400/13, 435/13.

Fabric 3 comprises fine-grained samples characterized by carbonate, fossiliferous and poorly micaceous groundmass, and absence of inclusions (specimens 328/13; 333/13 (Figure 2(e)); 336/13; 353/13; 386/13; 529/13). Groundmass is quite homogeneous, with abundant fine quartz (<0.1 mm), medium-high birefringence and yellowish-brown colour. The vughy (sub-spherical voids) microstructure is characterized by sub-rounded vughs and rare vescicles, with a spatial distribution from open to double spaced and a slight preferential orientation of vescicles (in samples 328/13 and 529/13).

Finally, a fine-grained fabric characterized by carbonate groundmass has been distinguished (Fabric 4: specimens 301/13, 305/13, 342/13). It is characterized by a vughy microstructure with dominant rounded vughs and rare vescicles, exhibiting a spatial distribution from single to double spaced. The homogeneous and fossil-rich groundmass is characterized by a light brown color and low birefringence in samples 301/13 (Figure 2(f)) and 305/13. Only in sample 342/12, a medium-high birefringence and the presence of inclusions (inclusion:groundmass ratio 40:60) consisting in fine grain quartz and dominant volcanoclastic fragments have been recognized.

Information on groundmass optical activity can be useful to obtain preliminary information on firing temperature in archaeological ceramics (Barbera *et al.*, 2013). In this sense, the thin section analysis of studied potteries highlights for all petrographic fabrics a medium-high groundmass birefringence, attesting firing temperature in a medium range (850-900 °C). Moreover, the fine grain texture observed in all samples, both in term of matrix and inclusions (when present) suggests the use of high depurated clay sediments for the manufacture of this ceramic class.

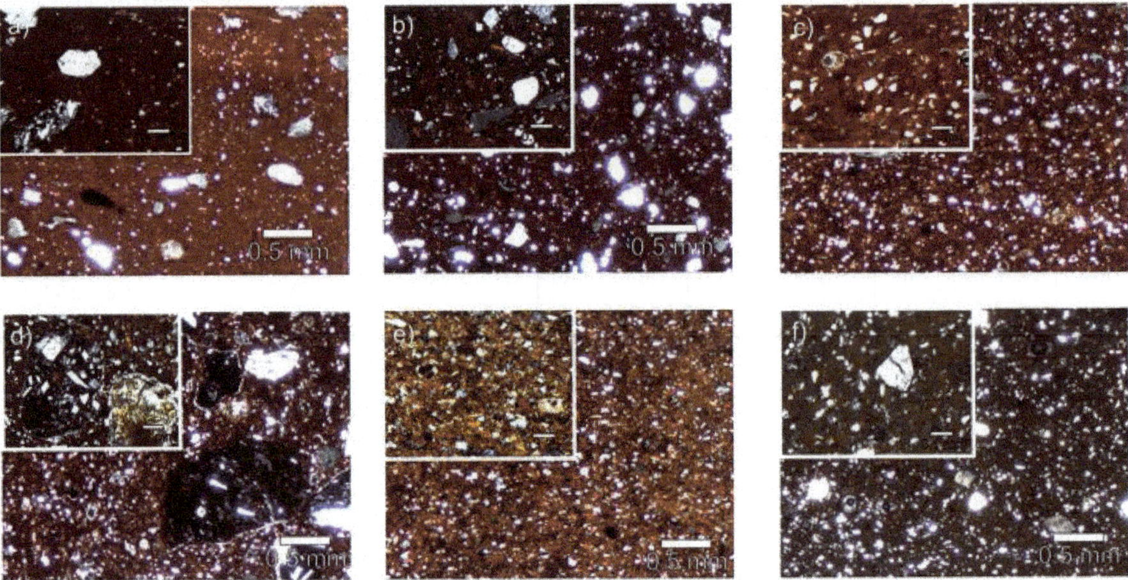

Figure 2. Microscopic pictures of studied samples representative of each petrographic fabric identified. (a, b) Fabric 1 (samples 113/13 and 388/13); (c, d) Fabric 2 (samples 102/13 and 293/13); (e) Fabric 3 (sample 333/13); (f) Fabric 4 (sample 301/13).

In order to confirm the hypotheses suggested by petrographic features and determine the firing temperature on the basis of mineralogical composition, XRD analyses have been performed. In fact, reactions in the matrix during firing bring to modifications of the original mineralogical association of the groundmass (mainly clay minerals and calcite) and to the formation of cryptocrystalline new phases (*i.e.*, anorthite, diopside, wollastonite and gehlenite) (Maggetti, 1982; Riccardi *et al.*, 1999; Cultrone *et al.*, 2001), indicative in many cases of the temperature achieved. The mineralogical associations of all the studied potteries are reported in Table 2 together with information on birefringence of the groundmass. The use of Ca-rich sediments (CaO> 6%; see chemical composition in Table 3) allows the presence of gehlenite, anorthite and/or diopside in almost all samples; therefore, on the whole, medium-high temperature (in a range of T_{max}~ 850 -900°C) can be hypothesized for all studied specimens. Exceptions are represented only by two samples belonging to Fabric 4 (301/13 and 305/13), in which the absence of birefringence and the absence of newly formed minerals has to be correlated whit lower temperatures. Finally, noteworthy is the coexistence, in some cases, of newly formed minerals and calcite, especially in samples characterized by fossil-rich groundmass (see Fabric 3), explainable only considering the presence of secondary calcite due to circulation of Ca-rich solutions in burial conditions (Cultrone *et al.*, 2014).

Table 2. Petrographic and mineralogical data of the studied samples. Bir. = Birefringence: +++ = high; ++ = medium; + = low or absent birefringence; Qtz = Quartz; Cal = Calcite; Gh = gehlenite; An = Anorthite; Di = diopside; Hem = Hematite; CM = Clay Minerals. The number of (+) is related to the mineralogical phase abundance: +++= abundant; ++= present; += scarce/rare; - = absent; tr= trace

			Sample ID	*Bir.*	*Qtz*	*Cal*	*Gh*	*An*	*Di*	*Hem*	*CM*
FABRIC 1	micaceous groundmass, medium grain size and quartz	with volcanic inclusions	113/13	+++	+++	tr	+	++	tr	+	+
			327/13	++	+++	-	-	+++	+	-	+
			332/13	+++	+++	-	+	++	-	+	+
			387/13	++	+++	tr	tr	++	-	tr	+
			388/13	++	+++	tr	tr	++	-	tr	+
		with magmatic biotite	339/13	+++	+++	+	tr	++	++	tr	++
FABRIC 2	micaceous and fossil-rich groundmass and fine quartz	Without inclusions	99/13	+++	+++	+	-	+	-	tr	+

			100/13	+++	+++	++	tr	+	-	-	+
			101/13	+++	+++	tr	+	++	tr	+	+
			102/13	+++	+++	tr	tr	+	-	tr	+
			331/13	++	+++	++	tr	tr	-	tr	+
			349/13	++	+++	tr	+	++	++	tr	+
			355/13	+++	+++	+	tr	+	-	tr	+
			375/13	+++	+++	+	tr	+	-	-	+
			377/13	+++	+++	tr	+	++	+	+	+
			378/13	++	+++	+	+	+	+	+	+
			383/13	++	+++	+	+	+	tr	tr	+
			393/13	++	+++	+	+	++	tr	tr	+
			394/13	++	+++	tr	tr	++	tr	tr	+
			400/13	++	+++	+	tr	+	tr	-	+
			424/13	++	+++	+	+	+	-	tr	+
			435/13	++	+++	tr	+	++	++	+	+
			437/13	++	+++	tr	+	+	+	tr	+
			436/13	++	+++	tr	-	+	tr	tr	+
			438/13	+++	+++	++	-	+	-	-	+
			444/13	++	+++	+	tr	++	tr	tr	+
		with scarce volcanic inclusions	114/13	++	+++	++	tr	++	-	tr	+
			284/13	+++	+++	+	tr	++	+	tr	+
			285/13	+++	+++	tr	tr	tr	-	tr	+
			324/13	++	+++	+	+	++	+	+	+
			351/13	+++	+++	++	tr	+	tr	tr	+
			374/13	++	+++	++	-	+	-	tr	++
			392/13	++	+++	tr	+	++	-	+	+
			293/13	+	+++	+	-	++	+	tr	+
			550/13	+	+++	+	-	+	tr	tr	+
		with volcanicglass	306/13	++	+++	tr	+	+	+	tr	+
			326/13	++	+++	+	+	+	-	tr	+
			329/13	++	+++	+	tr	tr	-	tr	+
FABRIC 3	fossiliferous and poorly micaceous groundmass and absence of inclusions		328/13	+++	+++	+	+	++	-	+	+
			333/13	+++	+++	+	-	+	-	-	+
			336/13	+++	+++	+++	-	tr	-	tr	++
			353/13	+	+++	++	-	tr	-	-	+
			386/13	++	+++	tr	+	++	tr	-	+
			529/13	+++	+++	+++	-	tr	-	tr	+
FABRIC 5	carbonate groundmass	without inclusion and rich in foraminifera	305/13	-	++	+++	-	-	-	-	++
		with absent micromass optical activity	301/13	-	+++	tr	tr	+	+	-	+
		with volcanic inclusions	342/13	+++	+++	++	-	++	+	tr	++

Even if petrographic and mineralogical data help to supply useful information on manufacture technology (*i.e.*, firing temperature and features of clay sediments), information on provenance can be obtained only by chemical analysis, due to the fine grain size of studied materials, often exhibiting absence of inclusions. For aforementioned, XRF data (Table 3) have been used to investigate eventually significant variation in chemical composition. Most of samples show a quite compositional homogeneity, as inferred by the inspection of triangular and binary diagrams shown in Figure 3. In detail, the CaO-SiO_2-Al_2O_3 diagram (Figure 3(a)) indicates the use of Ca-rich clays for the manufacture of almost all analysed samples, mainly plotted in the stability fields of anorthite and wollastonite as potential newly formed minerals in high firing temperature conditions. The similarity in chemical composition has been also highlighted by trends shown in binary diagrams (Figure 3(b)); in fact, referring to major elements, comparable abundances can be observed for all analysed samples. Small variations are detectable in SiO_2, CaO, MgO, Fe_2O_3 levels; in detail, samples belonging to Fabric 1 exhibit the lower abundance of CaO, respect to the all analysed set, overall characterized by average CaO contents of about 15 wt%; the higher contents have been detected in samples 336/13, 529/13 (Fabric 3) and 305/13 (Fabric 4), as evidenced also by mineralogical data. Additionally, really low levels in Fe_2O_3 can be observed for sample 306/13 (Fabric 2). Regarding minor elements, also in this case an homogeneity in chemical composition can be assessed; noteworthy is the high contents of Rb in sample 339/13 (Fabric 1), and the really high level of Co in sample 306/13 (Fabric 2).

3. DISCUSSION

As suggested by the petrographic analysis, among the plain table-ware class artifacts, three main groups can be identified on the basis of groundmass features, namely (i) micaceous, (ii) fossiliferous and (iii) a combination of them, with slightly variation due to the presence/absence of inclusions.

In this sense, the variation in term of inclusions can be attributed to technical expedient finalised to realize different ceramic shape and/or typology.

In facts, shapes as basins, bowls, lids, dishes, kraters and pithoi are mainly made with highly purified clay pastes and without inclusions, while for the manufacture of the larger dimension vessels, as big basins and jugs, the use of volcanic inclusions has be observed. Therefore, an high technical specialized manufacture can be hypothesized.

Referring to provenance issues, the manufacture features determined throughout thin section and mineralogical analyses (*e.g.* groundmass composition, use of highly depurated clays, medium-high firing temperature and presence, in some petrographic fabrics, of volcanic inclusions) suggest several similarities with some local fine well-known ceramic workshops active in Sicily during Hellenistic and Roman Age, namely Syracuse, Gela, Lentini and Catania ones.

In fact, the Syracuse Hellenistic-Roman fine pottery production was characterized by micaceous and fossiliferous groundmass and inclusions formed mainly by fine quartz; the used clay pastes were more or less purified through the removal of the sandy-to-coarse silty granulometric fraction (Barone *et al.*, 2014). Gela fine potteries production was characterized by fine micaceous and fossil-rich groundmass and low amount of inclusions consisting in dominant quartz and rare feldspars (Aquilia *et al.*, 2012).

The Catania production (Barone *et al.*, 2005) showed a matrix with common mica and fine-grained aplastic inclusions predominantly formed by quartz, common volcanic rock fragments and rare feldspar. Finally, the Lentini potteries were characterized by an homogeneous matrix with low optical activity and fine-grained aplastic inclusions mainly formed by mono- and polycrystalline quartz, rare feldspar and volcanic rock fragments (Barone *et al.*, 2005).

For the aforementioned, with the aim to determine provenance of studied samples and characterize raw materials, chemical results have been compared with reference ceramics and clays from Syracuse, Gela, Catania and Lentini (Barone *et al.*, 2005; Aquilia*et al.*, 2012; Barone *et al.*, 2014). In detail, a principal component analysis (PCA) has been carried out using major (SiO_2, TiO_2, Al_2O_3, Fe_2O_3, MgO, CaO, K_2O) and trace elements (Sr, V, Cr, Ni, Rb, Y, Zr, La, Ce) data.

The obtained first three principal components (PC) explain the 68.9% of the total variance. For the evaluation of provenance, data treatment has been performed by using bivariate boxplot namely bagplot (Rousseeuw *et al.*, 2012). It's composed by a bag containing the 50% of data points (darker area), a fence that separates inliers from outliers (line) and a loop (lighter area) in which are plotted liers that are outside the bag but inside the fence. The white square inside the bag represent the depth median, namely the point with the highest density of probability.

Table 3. Chemical data of studied samples grouped on the basis of petrographic fabrics. Major elements are reported in wt%, minor elements are in ppm. The chemical data reported have been recalculated to 100% on volatile-free basis.

Sample ID	Fabric	SiO_2	TiO_2	Al_2O_3	Fe_2O_3	MnO	MgO	CaO	Na_2O	K_2O	P_2O_5	Sr	V	Cr	Co	Ni	Zn	Rb	Y	Zr	Nb	Ba	La	Ce	Pb	Th
327/13	**Fabric 1**	58.31	1.05	17.69	7.08	0.12	2.92	8.52	1.09	2.93	0.30	353	152	127	14	54	121	122	32	203	24	344	51	101	20	12
332/13	**Fabric 1**	63.57	0.91	15.63	6.28	0.09	2.33	7.54	0.74	2.51	0.39	275	113	112	10	51	115	82	18	160	10	361	39	101	18	11
113/13	**Fabric 1**	60.04	0.99	17.23	6.69	0.12	2.91	7.89	0.79	2.97	0.37	289	147	124	13	58	118	108	22	158	14	330	50	99	19	10
387/13	**Fabric 1**	63.57	0.91	15.52	6.48	0.11	2.55	7.19	0.81	2.47	0.39	330	115	108	12	51	113	97	30	238	18	323	46	92	27	11
388/13	**Fabric 1**	62.99	0.93	15.81	6.51	0.11	2.53	7.60	0.72	2.51	0.29	342	120	112	12	52	110	107	31	239	20	373	44	107	22	13
339/13	**Fabric 1**	55.89	0.70	15.92	4.52	0.10	3.33	13.99	0.97	4.36	0.23	633	94	107	12	67	91	177	24	160	13	776	47	100	36	18
331/13	**Fabric 2**	56.20	0.71	13.05	4.31	0.05	1.78	21.32	0.43	1.75	0.41	338	95	76	8	41	73	69	28	279	16	383	30	54	19	11
99/13	**Fabric 2**	61.67	0.87	14.65	5.36	0.07	2.04	12.10	0.59	2.31	0.36	280	104	95	6	39	105	79	19	199	9	356	38	79	15	10
100/13	**Fabric 2**	60.48	0.88	15.51	5.67	0.06	1.94	12.51	0.42	2.15	0.37	406	109	97	7	40	107	92	28	219	16	401	38	96	25	10
101/13	**Fabric 2**	60.12	0.92	15.36	5.71	0.07	2.18	12.01	0.69	2.36	0.56	378	112	104	12	43	100	106	32	272	19	350	39	95	21	14
102/13	**Fabric 2**	59.93	0.85	14.32	5.21	0.07	1.89	14.46	0.62	2.23	0.44	313	93	88	7	39	90	76	20	208	10	391	36	73	18	10
349/13	**Fabric 2**	57.97	0.89	14.45	5.92	0.07	2.25	15.09	0.96	2.01	0.39	372	117	104	11	47	97	85	30	283	20	325	34	90	32	9
355/13	**Fabric 2**	59.99	0.81	13.88	5.05	0.08	1.89	15.22	0.58	2.07	0.44	296	108	85	12	37	87	70	22	227	8	348	29	78	18	9
375/13	**Fabric 2**	60.85	0.90	15.03	5.70	0.07	1.85	12.46	0.52	2.24	0.38	351	132	99	6	40	90	98	29	254	17	363	36	104	23	13
377/13	**Fabric 2**	60.82	0.93	15.22	5.61	0.07	1.97	11.56	0.77	2.66	0.41	208	127	104	8	43	87	52	14	118	1	333	46	63	7	15
378/13	**Fabric 2**	60.17	0.90	15.11	5.60	0.07	2.09	12.46	0.72	2.40	0.49	374	114	103	10	42	101	96	30	238	17	345	41	104	22	13
383/13	**Fabric 2**	59.61	0.91	15.34	5.47	0.06	2.16	12.80	0.59	2.58	0.47	327	127	105	9	43	100	89	22	196	11	316	43	103	33	12
393/13	**Fabric 2**	59.63	0.88	14.94	5.49	0.07	2.16	13.18	0.75	2.35	0.54	382	111	96	6	39	101	102	33	279	20	344	36	77	22	14
394/13	**Fabric 2**	59.41	0.92	14.85	5.66	0.09	2.15	13.61	0.65	2.10	0.55	357	104	95	9	44	98	91	31	294	19	390	44	108	21	14
400/13	**Fabric 2**	60.07	0.85	14.42	5.23	0.07	2.06	14.33	0.51	2.17	0.30	340	119	96	8	40	89	87	29	265	16	333	31	94	19	11
424/13	**Fabric 2**	60.70	0.87	14.50	5.43	0.06	2.25	13.03	0.57	2.25	0.34	332	107	95	7	38	94	82	22	224	13	332	41	86	26	10
435/13	**Fabric 2**	59.48	0.96	15.80	5.88	0.07	2.42	11.82	0.58	2.58	0.40	356	131	118	12	51	103	90	22	185	12	337	46	99	19	9
436/13	**Fabric 2**	59.50	0.90	15.37	5.57	0.08	2.24	12.97	0.60	2.34	0.44	377	114	101	6	43	101	101	31	257	19	325	37	82	21	10
437/13	**Fabric 2**	59.37	0.90	15.18	5.47	0.06	2.14	13.10	0.72	2.53	0.52	356	114	103	10	41	102	91	25	220	15	352	41	79	20	11
438/13	**Fabric 2**	59.44	0.82	15.14	5.02	0.06	2.16	14.96	0.36	1.79	0.26	276	91	91	7	38	85	52	14	140	5	368	31	63	12	7

444/13	Fabric 2	59.37	0.93	15.55	5.60	0.06	2.21	12.94	0.50	2.42	0.42	342	137	109	9	44	100	95	24	196	15	373	54	73	20	13
324/13	Fabric 2	60.71	0.92	14.69	5.83	0.07	1.93	12.41	0.73	2.25	0.45	381	114	104	9	40	96	90	30	271	18	465	44	102	21	11
114/13	Fabric 2	58.35	0.76	13.57	4.54	0.06	1.99	17.05	0.71	1.91	1.05	232	92	82	4	46	72	28	9	77		363	33	74	8	13
351/13	Fabric 2	60.67	0.84	14.64	5.25	0.06	2.02	13.25	0.54	2.06	0.67	376	99	90	10	36	100	83	27	252	14	436	37	85	24	9
374/13	Fabric 2	60.70	0.85	15.60	5.60	0.07	1.82	12.62	0.36	1.91	0.46	357	103	90	7	38	111	88	28	239	16	377	41	67	35	11
392/13	Fabric 2	58.24	0.93	15.71	5.63	0.08	2.27	13.33	0.62	2.61	0.58	404	114	104	11	44	100	99	31	241	19	353	44	86	24	11
284/13	Fabric 2	56.82	0.83	14.21	5.35	0.06	2.61	15.90	1.15	2.33	0.73	473	91	99	8	39	98	94	30	235	17	296	43	90	16	11
285/13	Fabric 2	58.19	0.97	15.93	5.99	0.08	2.15	12.79	1.01	2.54	0.36	510	139	97	11	42	97	99	30	236	21	356	45	88	24	14
293/13	Fabric 2	59.93	1.11	14.56	7.03	0.10	2.64	10.41	1.28	2.09	0.85	572	147	114	19	56	84	80	29	249	18	593	47	97	2184	30
550/13	Fabric 2	56.69	1.16	15.51	6.91	0.11	2.91	12.33	1.66	2.26	0.45	666	139	90	13	47	95	76	32	258	34	522	53	126	24	12
326/13	Fabric 2	60.21	1.04	15.16	6.21	0.08	2.57	11.31	0.52	2.52	0.36	364	119	124	12	54	102	99	31	260	19	341	42	102	21	12
329/13	Fabric 2	59.42	1.04	15.30	6.33	0.08	2.53	11.98	0.47	2.54	0.32	318	126	127	10	58	101	98	31	257	19	360	42	81	19	12
306/13	Fabric 2	62.30	0.94	16.16	0.31	0.07	2.49	14.51	0.61	2.07	0.54	282	103	93	65	37	75	71	26	249	15	438	39	81	18	9
328/13	Fabric 3	54.93	0.98	15.64	5.51	0.08	3.05	16.05	0.62	2.53	0.60	654	116	124	7	56	97	98	33	205	23	347	43	101	20	12
333/13	Fabric 3	62.60	0.84	14.64	5.25	0.06	1.61	12.18	0.42	1.94	0.47	372	97	86	8	37	93	79	23	261	13	450	40	84	31	9
336/13	Fabric 3	49.51	0.68	13.51	3.37	0.04	2.01	28.93	0.26	1.42	0.27	347	64	69	6	34	83	47	16	130	8	382	27	57	11	5
529/13	Fabric 3	51.46	0.75	13.62	4.22	0.06	2.11	24.93	0.35	1.91	0.59	422	83	91	7	39	83	74	26	184	15	369	41	74	14	10
353/13	Fabric 3	59.64	0.75	14.08	4.74	0.05	1.72	16.59	0.39	1.62	0.42	350	88	81	8	35	101	65	25	236	12	453	33	73	20	9
386/13	Fabric 3	60.69	0.91	15.12	5.68	0.07	2.12	11.95	0.70	2.31	0.44	340	124	106	10	42	101	93	25	238	13	365	47	78	20	10
301/13	Fabric 4	66.13	0.68	11.23	4.60	0.07	2.02	11.98	0.73	2.09	0.47	428	83	77	5	34	76	70	20	257	9	368	39	82	13	10
305/13	Fabric 4	41.31	0.60	14.62	3.44	0.05	1.88	35.42	0.25	1.94	0.50	924	68	82	13	57	78	54	20	67	9	292	41	74	27	5
342/13	Fabric 4	57.07	0.97	16.48	6.11	0.07	2.10	13.17	0.92	2.68	0.45	756	132	90	15	49	110	95	31	199	22	438	59	88	22	12

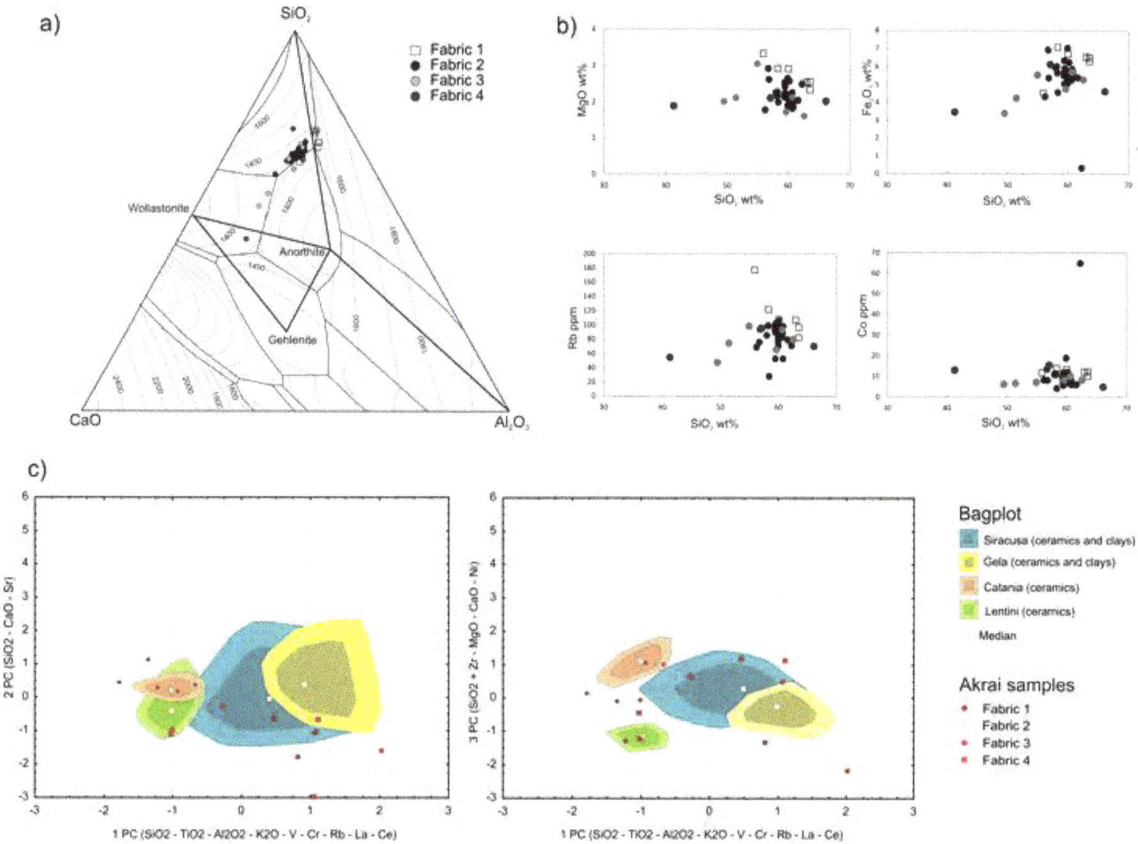

Figure 3. (a) SiO_2–CaO–Al_2O_3ternarydiagram. (b) Binary diagrams of MgO (wt%), Fe_2O_3 (wt%), Rb (ppm) and Co (ppm) vs. SiO_2 (wt%). (c) Bag plots of the reference datasets (Siracusa, Gela, Catania and Lentini) and studied samples from Akrai distinguished on the basis of petrographic fabrics identified.

An inspection of the bag-plots reported in Figure 3(c) highlights the formation of clusters in good accordance with petrographic groups. In detail, a good correspondence between Fabrics 2 and 3 (*e.g.*, small vessels, fine wares, micaceous, fossil-rich groundmass and mainly without inclusions) and Hellenistic and Roman fine ceramic production from Syracuse can be established. Noteworthy is that the diagrams show an overlapping between Syracuse and Gela ceramics and clays, so that for samples plotted in this field no certainly attribution can be supplied.

Samples with volcanic inclusions (typologically classified as big basins and jugs and mainly belonging to Fabric 1 with some samples of Fabric 2) are plotted in the areas of Catania and Lentini ceramic productions, according to petrographic features of reference data. Finally, for samples of Fabric 4, characterized by high CaO levels and fossil-rich groundmass, no correspondence has been found, excepting for 342/13 specimen with volcanic inclusions, plotted in Catania production cluster.

4. CONCLUSIONS

The archaeometric investigation carried out on plain table-ware samples from the ancient city of Akrai allow to obtain information on the technology and provenance of pottery productions. In spite of a slight heterogeneity in term of inclusions, the whole of petrographic, mineralogical and chemical data highlights a quite homogeneity of all the studied materials. As far as the technological point of view, the use of high depurated clay sediments and the medium-high firing temperature esteemed (in the range of 850-900 °C) suggest a good technological level of the production, with a clear differentiation of manufacture among the different typology of vessels. In fact, samples typologically classified as vessels devoted to serving and consuming food are mainly included in petrographic fabrics characterized by absence of inclusions, micaceous and fossiliferous groundmass and highly depurated clays; otherwise, bigger shapes used for holding liquids, such as jugs and basins, are characterized by the presence of volcanic inclusions and a slightly coarser grain clay paste. On the basis of the comparison with reference data, these two main categories can be also attributed to different Sicilian workshop centres, namely the Hellenistic and Roman fine ceramic production from Syracuse (Fabric 2 and 3 samples), and Catania and Lentini productions (Fabric 1 and some specimens of Fabric 2), respectively.

Therefore, the plain table-wares from Akrai can be defined as a rather regional than local manufacture and a Sicilian provenance can be assessed, without a substantial change of artifacts supplying over the stratigraphic range investigated. In fact, the different pottery productions are equally testified along the stratigraphic units explored during the archeological excavation, dated back from the 3rdcentury B.C. to 5thcentury A.D.. It seems to be very important to stress that plain table-wares present in Akrai could be described as a good quality products, regardless of the period of production.

It could be also observed that the pottery production centres were continued their manufacture and, most probably, did not change the technology and materials when the Romans appeared on the island.

Generally, the Sicilian case could be considered an excellent example of mixing of experiences of different people and blending of culture and manufacture, also in pottery production, while the centuries.

In conclusion, considering the start point of the research, *i.e.* the use of material culture to monitor cultural and political changes in ancient cities, the obtained results highlight how beside the political and economical changes that have interested the town of Akrai during the Romanization process, a continuity in commercial exchanges has been maintained over the time. So far the archaeological together with the archaeometric studies have testified that no abandonment of town and urban decline after 212 B.C. has been occurred, as well as the continuation of life and vigorous development of trade exchanges.

The continuation of this research is very important and should bring the knowledge not only about the preferences in local products or imported pottery, but also about the economy of the ancient town in Hellenistic and Roman periods.

ACKNOWLEDGEMENTS

The archaeological excavations at Akrai have been financed by Polish National Centre of Science (nr UMO-2011/03/B/HS3/00567) and have been carried out thanks to the cooperation between the Superintendence of Cultural Heritage of Syracuse, authorized by Dr. Beatrice Basile and Dr. Rosa Lanteri, and University of Warsaw, Poland. From the ceramological stand point the assemblage of plain table-ware is systematically and carefully studied by Prof. Jolanta Młynarczyk and Dr Krzysztof Domżalski.

REFERENCES

Aitchison, J. (1986)*The statistics analysis of compositional data London*, UK, Chapman and Hall.

Alcock, S.E. (1989) Archaeology and Imperialism. Roman Expansion and the Greek City, *Journal of Mediterranean Archaeology*, vol. 2/1, pp. 87–135.

Aquilia, E., Barone, G., Mazzoleni, P. and Ingoglia, C. (2012) Petrographic and chemical characterisation of fine ware from three Archaic and Hellenistic kilns in Gela, Sicily, *Journal of Cultural Heritage*, vol. 13, pp. 442–447.

Barbera, G., Barone, G., Crupi, V., Longo, F., Maisano, G., Majolino, D., Mazzoleni, P., Teixeira, J. and Venuti, V. (2013) Small angle neutron scattering study of ancient pottery from Syracuse (Sicily, Southern Italy), *Journal Archaeological Science*, vol. 40, pp. 983-991.

Barone, G., Lo Giudice, A., Mazzoleni, P. and Pezzino, A. (2005) Chemical characterization and statistical multivariate analysis of ancient pottery from Messina, Catania, Lentini and Siracusa (Sicily), *Archaeometry*, vol. 47(4), pp. 745-762.

Barone, G., Mazzoleni, P., Spagnolo, G. and Aquilia, E. (2012) The Transport Amphorae of Gela: A Multidisciplinary Study on Provenance and Technological Aspects, *Journal of Archaeological Sciences*, vol. 39, pp. 11-22.

Barone, G., Mazzoleni, P., Aquilia, A. and Barbera, G. (2014) The Hellenistic and Roman Syracuse (Sicily) fine pottery production explored by chemical and petrographic analysis, *Archaeometry*, vol. 56(1), pp. 70-87.

Buscemi, F. (2007) Architettura e romanizzazione nella Sicilia di età imperiale gli anfiteatri, *Archivio Storico Siracusano*, vol.III XXI, pp. 7–53.

Chowaniec, R. (2013) Ancient Akrai in the light of new researches. Non-invasive researches in PalazzoloAcreide, south-eastern Sicily, *SOMA 2012 Identity and Connectivity, Proceedings of the 16thSymposium on Mediterranean Archaeology*, L. Bombardieri, A. D'Agostino, G. Guarducci, V. Orsi and S. Valentini, Oxford, pp. 965–971,.

Chowaniec, R. (2014)PalazzoloAcreide, Sicily, Italy. Excavations in 2013, *Światowit fasc. A. Mediterranean and Non-European Archaeology*,vol. XI (LII), fasc. A.

Chowaniec, R. (2015a) The Sicilian world after the Punic Wars: the Greek colony in a new reality, *Interdisciplinary Perspectives on Colonisation, Maritime Interaction and European Cultural Integration*, H. Glørstad, L. Melheim and Z. Glørstad, Sheffield.

Chowaniec, R. (2015b) Comments on the history and topography of Akrai/Acrae in the light of new research, *Unveiling the past of an ancient town. Akrai/Acrea in south-eastern Sicily*, R. Chowaniec,Warsaw,pp. 43-78.

Cultrone, G., Rodriguez-Navarro, C., Sebastian, E., Cazalla, O. and De la Torre, M. J. (2001) Carbonate and silicate phase reactions during ceramic firing, *European Journal of Mineralogy*, vol. 13, pp. 621–634.

Cultrone, G., Molina, E. and Arizzi, A. (2014) The combined use of petrographic, chemical and physical techniques to define the technological features of Iberian ceramics from the Canto Tortoso area (Granada, Spain), *Ceramics International*, vol. 40, pp. 10803–10816

Dearden, C. (2004) Sicily and Rome. The Greek context for roman drama, *Mediterranean Archaeology*, vol. 17, pp. 121–130.

Hayes, H.W. (1997) *Handbook of Mediterranean Roman Pottery*, London, UK.

Hill, T. and Lewicki, P. (2007)*Statistics: Methods and Applications*, StatSoft, Tulsa, Oklaoma, USA.

Hollegaard, O.C., A. Rathje, C. Trier and C. Winther (1995)*The Roman domus of the Early Empire. A Case Study: Sicily in Ancient Sicily*, T. Fischer-Hansen, Danish Studies in Classical Archaeology. ActaHyperborea6, pp. 209–261.

Kiiskinen, H. (2013)*Production and Trade of Etrurian Terra Sigillata Pottery in Roman Etruria and beyond between c. 50 BC and c.150 CE*, University of Turku, Turku.

Maggetti, M. and Küpfer, T. (1978) Composition of the terra sigillata from La Péniche (Vidy/Lausanne, Switzerland), *Archaeometry*, vol. 20(2), pp. 183–188.

Maggetti, M. (1982)*Phase analysis and its significance for technology and origin, in Archeological Ceramics*, J.S. Olin, A.D. Franklin, Smithsonian Inst. Press, Washington, pp.121–133

Malfitana, D. (2004) Italian Sigillata Imported in Sicily: the evidence of stamps, in Early Italian Sigillata. The chronological framework and trade patterns. *Proceedings of the First International Conference ROCT-Congress Leuven*, J. Poblome, P. Talloen, R. Brulet and M. Waelkens, Leuven-Paris, pp. 295-323.

Młynarczyk, J. (2015)Plain Table Ware from Akrai. Preliminary approach, *Unveiling the past of an ancient town. Akrai/Acrea in south-eastern Sicily*, R. Chowaniec, Warsaw, pp. 295-310.

Munsell Color (2000)*Munsell soil color chart*, Gretag, Macbeth, New Windsor.

Olcese, G. (2011-2012) *Atlante dei siti di produzione ceramica (Toscana, Lazio, Campania e Sicilia) con le tabelle dei principali relitti del Mediterraneo occidentale con carichi dall'Italia centro meridionale (Immensa Aequora 2)*, Edizioni Quasar, Roma.

Picon, M., Carre, C., Cordoliani, M.L., Vichy, M., HernandezAndj, J.A. and Mignard, L. (1975)Composition of the La Graufesenque, BanassacandMontansterra sigillata, *Archaeometry*, vol. 17(2), pp. 191–199.

Polito, A. (2000) La circolazione della sigillata liscia in Sicilia, *Quaderni di Messina*, vol. 1(2), pp. 65-102.

Riccardi, M.P., Messiga, B. and Duminuco, P. (1999) An approach to the dynamics of clay firing, *Applied Clay Science*, vol. 15, pp. 393–409.

Rousseeuw, P.J., Ruts, I. and Tukey, J.W. (1999) The Bagplot: A Bivariate Boxplot, *The American Statistician*, vol. 53(4), pp. 382-387.

Thió-Henestrosa, S. and Martín-Fernández, J. A. (2005) Dealing with compositional data: the freeware CoDaPack, *Mathematical Geology*, vol. 37, pp. 773-793.

Tukey, J. W. (1977)*Exploratory data analysis*. Reading, MA, Addison-Wesley.

Whitbread, I. K. (1995)*Greek transport amphorae: a petrological and archaeological study*, Fitch Laboratory Occasional Paper, 4, British School at Athens, Athens.

Więcek, T., Chowaniec, R. and Guzzardi, L. (2014) Greek Akrai and Roman Acrae. New numismatic evidence. Polish-Italian archaeological excavations 2011-2012, *Archeologia*, vol. 62-63, pp. 19–30.

Wilson, R.J.A. (1988) Towns of Sicily during the Roman Empire, *Aufstieg und Niedergang der römischen Welt (eds. H. Temporini), vol. II. Prinzipat. B. 11. Politische Geschichte (Provinzen und Randvölker: Sizilien und Sardinien; Italien und Rom; Allgemeines). 1. Teilband: Sizilien und Sardinien*, Berlin-New York: Walter de Gruyter., pp. 90–204.

Wilson, R.J.A. (1990)*Sicily under the Roman Empire: The Archaeology of a Roman Province*, 36 B.C.–A.D. 535. Warminster.

5

PHYSICOCHEMICAL PROPERTIES OF GLASS TESSERAE IN ROMAN TERRACE HOUSE FROM ANCIENT ANTANDROS (BASE GLASS, OPACIFIERS AND COLORANTS)

Zisan Kaplan*, Basak Ipekoglu and Hasan Boke

Department of Architectural Restoration, İzmir Institute of Technology

Corresponding author: Zisan Kaplan (kzisan@hotmail.com)

ABSTRACT

In this study, material characteristics of glass mosaic tesserae from Antandros ancient city, western Turkey, were investigated. The main objective of this study was to determine the compositional group of the glass tesserae. Their color, mineralogical, chemical and microstructural characteristics were determined using colorimeter, x-ray diffraction, x-ray fluorescence and scanning electron microscope. The results show that all the Antandros glasses were produced by using coastal sand as Levantine I glasses and exhibit similar compositions with natron type glasses (Roman type glasses), except for lower natron levels. Lower natron levels indicate that Antandros mosaic glass may have been produced in 7th century AD or natron may have been provided from a new flux source due to the shortage of Egyptian mineral soda or due to economic reasons glass manufacturers succeeded to produce same glass with low flux addition. Antandros glass tesserae were all opacified with antimony oxides and colored with transition metal oxides which are common used in Roman Period.

KEYWORDS: Roman, Mosaic, Glass tesserae, Natron glass, Opacifiers, Colorants.

1. INTRODUCTION

Glass was first produced in Mesopotamia around 2500 BC and was developed through to the Roman Period. In the Roman Period, a base glass batch consisted of sand as the source of silica and natron (soda) as flux. Silica and calcium carbonate containing sand was preferred and natron was used from the early-mid 1st millennium BC to the 9th century AD before the plant ash was used. It was obtained from the Wadi Natrun in Northern Egypt (Bimson and Freestone, 1988; Brill and Cahill, 1988; Lilyquist et al., 1993; Sayre and Smith, 1961). In the Roman Period glasses, had quite high Na_2O contents (16-20%). The drop-in soda contents start from the Late-Roman/Byzantine Period onwards. From the early Islamic Period, plant ash was used as alkaline flux in the glass batch instead of natron because of availability (Henderson, 1985). The glass was first produced in primary production centres, which were located near the sand and natron sources in Egypt (Sayre and Smith, 1961). The produced base glass was then distributed to secondary (local) glass workshops where additives (opacifiers and colorants) were introduced and glass was worked into a final product (Freestone et al., 2002).

During secondary production, glass was opacified using calcium or lead antimonate from about 1500 BC until antimony sources were depleted at the end of the Roman Period (Fiori et al., 2003). Opacification relies on two processes; addition of ex situ synthesized crystals to the raw glass or addition of raw compounds that lead to in situ crystallization of opacifying crystals in the glass melt (Lahlil et al., 2010b; Verita, 2000). Glass was colored by chromophore elements and opacifiers as coloring agent. Cobalt and copper oxides were used to obtain blue, green, purple and red colors in ancient glasses (Mirti et al., 2002; Newton and Davison, 1989). Iron oxide presented as natural traces in the sand however, it was also added intentionally to obtain different colors. Manganese oxide gives purple color to the glass and it was used as a de-colorant and combined with iron and cobalt to produce black and brown colors.

Throughout history, glass has been used as beads, bottles, vessels, windowpanes, and mosaic tesserae. Most of the studies concerning ancient glass compositions are about glasses that were originated from Hellenistic to Late Byzantine Period and they reported the origin and production technologies of glass and its raw materials, colorants and opacifiers (Arletti et al., 2006b; Brill, 1968; Fiori, 2015; Freestone, 1987; Henderson, 1988; Möncke et al., 2014; Rehren and Freestone, 2015; Sayre and Smith, 1961; Schibille, 2011; Shortland and Tite, 2000; Silvestri et al., 2011; Turner, 1956). In Turkey, there are few studies concerning glass compositions. Brill (1999), investigated early glass compositions and prepared a catalogue including glass compositions from Sardis in western Anatolia and Aphrodisias in southwestern Anatolia. Uhlir et al., (2006), investigated compositions of glass objects from the Late Hellenistic to Late Byzantine period at Terrace House I, Ephesus in western Anatolia. Schibille, (2011), provided chemical and technological data of Byzantine glass production, and collected chemical data from Pergamon in northwestern Anatolia. Schibille et al., (2012), also determined the origin, and production technology of Byzantine glass tesserae from Sagalasos, in southwestern Anatolia. Rehren et al., (2015), reports compositional data of Roman glass from Pergamon Turkey.

In addition, Lauwers et al., (2007) studied local glass workshops in Anatolia. They determined the local glass workshops that built during the late Roman and Byzantine Periods in Turkey according to previous studies (Figure 1).

Although there are only a few studies concerning glass compositions in Turkey, there is still a lack of analytical data concerning the production technology and compositions of mosaic glass tesserae from Anatolia. This study presents the chemical data of glass tesserae found during excavations of Antandros Ancient City, Turkey. The aim of the study is to determine the compositional groups of the mosaic glass to contribute to the analytical data of the ancient glasses found in Turkey.

2. ARCHEOLOGICAL BACKGROUND

Antandros was located on the top and western slopes of Dervent Hill (Kaletaşı Hill), at an altitude of 215 m, descending steeply down to Adramyttion (Edremit) Gulf in western Turkey (Figure 1). Antandros was an imported city of the ancient Torad Region, it was a harbour city and famous for its dockyards. Strabo, 2000, mentions a harbour in Antandros, called Aspaneus where timber was exported. The city dates back from late 6th century BC to Byzantine Period. After Arab invasions in 6th century AD, a new settlement was established in Antandros and the city became a Bishopric Centre (Quien M. Le, 1958). It was completely abandoned in 14th century. In 1989, the area was zoned for housing and graves (Necropolis) were found and salvage excavations were started in 1991 (Yalman, 1993). In 2001, archaeological excavations started and a Roman Terrace House, with its bath complex was found.

Figure 1. Late Roman and Byzantine Periods secondary glass production sites in Anatolia and Location of Antandros

Terrace House was built in early 4th century AD and it was used until the 6th -7th centuries AD. The House was similar to Roman Terraced House typology due to its rows of spaces on one side of the portico (Smith, 1997). The house was oriented from east to west. It has a rectangular plan and an adjacent bath complex at the south east of the house (Figure 2). There were a portico and a *kriptoportico* (upper portico). The portico was located on the sea side of the house with 32.90×4.30 m dimensions and its floor was covered with well-preserved mosaics. There were six rooms at the north and a *latrine* (toilet) to the east of the portico. Two of the six adjacent rooms were *triclinia* used in summer and winter (welcoming spaces) and one room decorated with well-preserved floor mosaics (Figure 1).

Figure 2. Plan of the Terrace House and the spaces covered with mosaics

On the south-east corner of the portico there is a stair reaching to the bath with circular steps. Spatial characteristics of the bath were altered due to usage changes and deformations in the past (Polat et al., 2007). *Apodyterium* (dressing room-space 7) is situated at the west of the bath, it has a rectangular form with 11.63×3.40 m dimensions. Floor of the *apodyterium* is covered with mosaics and the on walls there are remains of wall paintings (Figure 2). *Tepidarium* (warm space-space 8), is situated at the south of *apodyterium,* it has rectangular form with 6.20×4.15 m dimensions. There is an opening between *apodyterium* and *tepidarium* to provide connection. Mortar traces of *sectile* mosaics are observed on the floor of *tepidarium*. Two *natationes* (pool) situated at the west of the *tepidarium* and they are in square form with

2×2.30 m. *Calidarium* (hot space-space 9) is situated at the east of the *apodyterium,* it has rectangular form with 3.5×4.15 m dimensions. At the south of the *calidarium* there is an *alveus* (hot water pool). Floor of the *calidarium* was elevated due to the renewing of the hypocaust system. *Praefurnium* (furnace-space 10) of the bath is situated north of the *calidarium,* it has a square form with 1.95×2.90 m dimensions which was converted into a furnace. There is another space (space 11) situated at the north of the *apodyterium,* it has rectangular form with 5.30 m width (Polat, 2002; Polat et al., 2007; Polat and Polat, 2005).

In Roman times, the size of the house, style, decoration of the house was related with the social class of the owner. The most important rooms were decorated with mosaic pavements. Mosaic patterns were designed according to the function of the space. Mosaic pavements give clues to the date, technique, craftsmen, and the use of the room and the function of the house.

3. MATERIALS AND METHODS

In this study, eighteen opaque colored glass tesserae were chosen from broken mosaics of the *portico* and *kriptoportico* of the terrace house. Samples were labelled with the first one or two letters of their colors. (Table 1). The tesserae contain yellow, green, cyan, turquoise, blue, light brown, dark red, black and white colors. All tesserae are opaque except one semi-opaque blue and one semi-opaque white tesserae. They were all preserved with minor surface pitting and corrosion. All the analysis was carried out after weathering layers were removed and samples were washed with distilled water and dried at 60°C in an oven. Color measurements were done with washed samples. For the X-Ray Fluorescence (XRF) and X-ray Diffraction analysis (XRD), small fragments were taken from each tesserae and ground into fine powder. For Scanning Electron Microscope Analysis (SEM), small sections were cut and left uncoated.

Table 1. Glass tesserae samples

Name	Transparency	Photo	Name	Transparency	Photo	Name	Transparency	Photo
Y	Opaque	0 1cm	T1	Opaque	0 1cm	Bv-O	Opaque	0 1cm
Lg	Opaque	0 1cm	T2	Opaque	0 1cm	Bv-So	Semi-Opaque	0 1cm
Dg1	Opaque	0 1cm	Dt	Opaque	0 1cm	Lbr	Opaque	0 1cm
Dg2	Opaque	0 1cm	C1	Opaque	0 1cm	W	Semi-Opaque	0 1cm
G1	Opaque	0 1cm	C2	Opaque	0 1cm	Dr	Opaque	0 1cm
G2	Opaque	0 1cm	Lb	Opaque	0 1cm	B	Opaque	0 1cm

In the experimental stage of this study, colors of the tesserae were identified by using a colorimetric measurement instrument (Avantes) by Avasoft 6.2. Measurements were conducted on homogenous flat and smooth surface with 4mm diameter spot size, D65 daylight illuminant and 10° observer. Results are expressed by colorimetric coordinates (L, a, b, C, h, X, Y, Z) in the CIEL *a*b color space system based on Commission Internationale de I' Eclairage colors. The L*, a* and b* values were converted into RGB values with an online "Color Calculator" program (www.easyrgb.com) and expressed on the coordinate system with CIELab (L*a*b) color sphere using Microsoft Office Excel 2012 and Adobe Photoshop CS4 software. In this color system L* is the lightness factor (L*=0 black; L*=100 white), a* is the value between green and red (-a*= green; +a*=red), and b* is the value between blue and yellow (-b*=blue; +b*=yellow) (CIE).

Major and minor elements of tesserae were identified by XRF (Ali and Abd-allah, 2015; Arinat et al., 2014). Analysis were carried out on powdered samples using a Spectro IQ-II on melt tablets with 0.01% detection limit. Powdered samples were dried at 105°C and calcinated at 1000°C, then they were diluted with lithium tetra borate by Materials Research Center in Izmir Institute of Technology.

X-Ray diffraction analysis were performed on powdered samples to determine the crystalline phases with Philips X-Pert Pro X-Ray Diffactrometer. The spectra were collected at 40 kV and 40mA from 5° to 60° with 2θ and processed by using Philips X-Pert Pro Software.

Microstructural characteristics of glass tesserae were determined using Philips XL 30S FEG scanning Electron Microscope (SEM) equipped with X-Ray Energy Dispersive System (EDS) located at the Izmir Institute of Technology Center for Materials Research, Turkey. Backscattered images (BSE) were taken at 15-20 kV accelerating voltage with a beam size from 2μm to 500μm.

In general, mosaic glass tesserae show compositional homogeneity, such as bands or mineral inclusions besides the opacifiers and colorants. For this reason, analysis was carried out on both SEM-EDS to match the micro texture with the chemical composition. For more precise elemental compositional data XRF analysis were carried out. In addition, to identify the crystal shape of opacifiers SEM-EDS analysis were done.

4. RESULTS AND DISCUSSION

Surface colour properties of the glass tesserae were determined and expressed using colorimetric coordinates (L*, a*, b*, C*, h, X, Y, Z) in the CIEL*a*b* colour space system. Colours were determined, to the high and low positions of positive and negative values of *a and b* values of CIEL*a*b* colour space system, as black, red, brown, yellow, green, blue, cyan, turquoise, white and their shades (Figure 3).

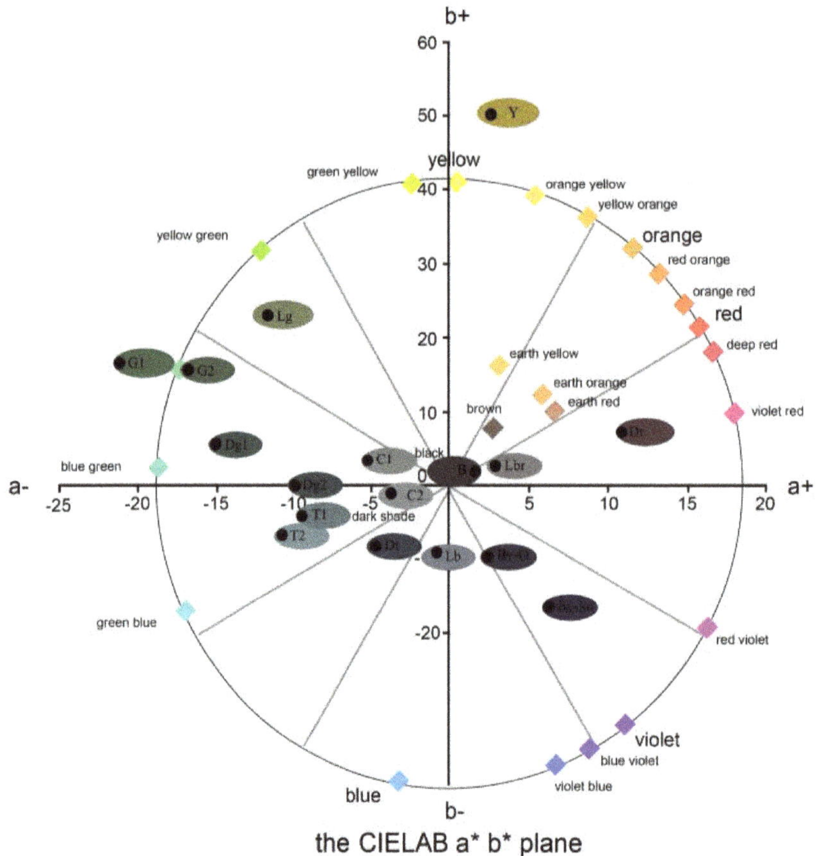

*Figure 3. Colours of the samples in CIELa*b* color space*

Only the green, blue and turquoise glasses have different shades of color. Green glasses are two green, light green and two dark green. Blue glasses are one light blue and two dark blue. Turquoise glasses are one light turquoise, one turquoise and one dark turquoise. The L*, a*, b*, C and h values and coloring agents of the tesserae are given in Table 2.

High positive b*values and low positive a* values correspond to yellow glass containing high lead and low antimony contents. Green samples have variable positive b* values and low negative a* values that are distinguished by both high lead and high copper contents. A significant number of tesserae have variable negative b* and a* values that have high antimony and low lead contents these are cyan, turquoise and blue samples. Dark red sample has distinctive high positive a* and b* values that are distinguished with high iron content. Brown and black samples have weak positive b* and a* values ~1, whereas brown contains high antimony and black contains high Fe_2O_3 (Table 2).

Table 2. Colorimetric coordinates, opacifiers and colorants of the glass tesserae.

Name-Colour	Colorimetric Coordinates					Elements							Opacifier	Colorant
	L	a	b	C	h	Sb_2O_5	ZnO	CoO	MnO	CuO	PbO	Fe_2O_3		
Y Yellow	64.73	2.6	50.21	50.28	87.03	1.02%	0.03%	0.01%	0.40%	0.49%	19.3%	0.85%	Pb-antimony ($Pb_2Sb_2O_7$)	PbO
Lg Light Green	57.95	-11.69	23.03	25.83	116.92	0.83%	0.03%	0.01%	0.42%	0.88%	22.6%	1.02%		PbO+ CuO
Dg1 Dark Green	37.03	-15.01	5.63	16.04	159.43	0.64%	0.38%	0.01%	0.73%	2.65%	6.61%	0.80%		
Dg2 Dark Green	35.49	-9.95	0.06	9.95	179.65	0.58%	0.04%	_	0.46%	1.80%	16.2%	0.71%		
G1 Green	43.57	-21.19	16.54	26.88	142.03	0.86%	0.03%	0.01%	0.50%	2.39%	18.9%	0.85%		
G2 Green	43.73	-16.81	15.71	10.59	136.93	0.77%	0.03%	_	0.48%	1.70%	17.4%	0.82%		
T1 Turquoise	51.13	-9.5	-4.18	10.38	203.77	3.46%	0.03%	_	0.50%	3.25%	0.06%	0.69%	Ca-antimony ($CaSb_2O_6$)	CuO+ CoO
T2 Turquoise	60.12	-10.77	-6.69	12.68	211.86	3.44%	0.02%	_	0.39%	0.74%	0.09%	0.49%		
Dt Dark Turquoise	29.76	-4.79	-8.26	9.55	239.91	1.41%	0.02%	_	0.49%	2.56%	0.13%	0.57%		
C1 Cyan	59.89	-5.32	3.34	6.28	147.92	4.07%	0.01%	_	0.49%	0.35%	0.29%	0.79%		
C2 Cyan	62.45	-3.74	-1.1	3.9	196.47	4.22%	_	0.01%	0.50%	0.30%	0.35%	0.75%		
Lb Light Blue	54.16	-0.81	-1.71	1.89	244.57	3.26%	_	0.02%	0.46%	0.07%	0.27%	0.59%		CoO
Bv-O Dark Blue	23.47	2.36	-9.68	9.96	283.72	4.27%	_	0.11%	0.36%	0.16%	0.18%	1.11%		
Bv-So Dark Blue	17.64	6.21	-16.46	17.59	290.66	2.03%	_	0.07%	0.41%	0.10%	0.04%	0.85%		
Lbr Light Brown	57.34	2.9	2.72	3.98	43.2	3.10%	_	_	2.38%	0.04%	0.05%	0.54%		MnO
W White	80.21	1.69	8.25	8.42	78.46	1.68%	0.01%	_	0.07%	0.02%	0.19	0.44%		Ca-antimony
B Black	30.32	1.64	1.87	2.48	48.84	_	_	_	0.05%	_	_	5.61%	--	Fe_2O_3
Dr Dark Red	35.77	10.81	7.18	12.97	33.6	0.59%	0.02%	_	0.65%	1.07%	2.00%	3.81%	Iron oxides, copper oxides	CuO. Fe_2O_3

Table 3. Major elements of glass tesserae by XRF in wt % of the oxides

Sample[1] / Elements	Y	Lg	Dg1	Dg2	G1	G2	T1	T2	Dt	C1	C2	Lb	Bv-O	Bv-SO	Lbr	W	B	Dr
SiO_2	59.18±0.07	56.05± 0.07	66.27± 0.08	60.78±0.07	58.37± 0.07	59.29± 0.07	69.08± 0.08	71.95± 0.08	71.57± 0.08	69.99± 0.08	70.22± 0.05	72.05± 0.08	69.78± 0.08	72.51±0.08	69.90± 0.08	76.21± 0.08	65.96± 0.05	68.55± 0.08
Na_2O	6.27± 0.08	5.90± 0.08	6.70± 0.073	6.25± 0.076	5.67± 0.075	6.18± 0.077	6.83± 0.07	7.75± 0.074	7.49± 0.072	7.39± 0.073	7.61± 0.074	8.08± 0.075	6.98± 0.07	8.50± 0.075	7.66± 0.075	8.35± 0.075	10.51± 0.08	7.07± 0.073
CaO	6.81± 0.027	6.73± 0.028	9.17± 0.027	7.38± 0.027	6.69± 0.027	7.51± 0.028	8.76± 0.026	7.96± 0.025	8.92± 0.025	8.22± 0.028	7.97± 0.028	7.61± 0.026	9.59± 0.027	8.64± 0.025	9.05± 0.026	6.92± 0.022	7.39± 0.015	9.06± 0.025
Al_2O_3	2.31± 0.016	2.14± 0.016	2.57± 0.015	2.26± 0.015	2.21± 0.015	2.30± 0.016	2.56± 0.015	2.41± 0.014	2.50± 0.015	2.76± 0.015	2.49± 0.015	2.38± 0.014	2.77± 0.015	2.45± 0.014	2.51± 0.014	2.14± 0.014	3.13± 0.016	2.81± 0.015
MgO	0.99± 0.017	0.98± 0.018	1.11± 0.016	1.01± 0.017	0.94± 0.017	0.99± 0.017	1.12± 0.015	1.15± 0.015	1.15± 0.015	1.25± 0.015	1.19± 0.015	1.17± 0.015	1.17± 0.015	1.17± 0.014	1.18± 0.015	1.13± 0.014	2.22± 0.027	1.20± 0.015
K_2O	0.33± 0.013	0.26± 0.014	0.57± 0.011	0.37± 0.013	0.30± 0.013	0.35± 0.013	0.62± 0.01	0.56± 0.01	0.59± 0.01	0.62± 0.011	0.57± 0.011	0.84± 0.0092	0.51± 0.0099	0.69± 0.011	0.67± 0.01	0.43± 0.0099	0.49± 0.0078	0.64± 0.011
P_2O_5	0.48± 0.0061	0.51± 0.0064	0.34± 0.0046	0.42± 0.0055	0.46± 0.058	0.43± 0.0057	0.23± 0.0039	0.23± 0.0039	0.23± 0.0039	0.27± 0.004	0.26± 0.004	0.25± 0.0039	0.23± 0.0038	0.24± 0.0039	0.28± 0.0039	0.17± 0.0038	0.16± 0.0018	0.31± 0.004
SO_3	–	–	0.28± 0.0087	–	–	–	0.98± 0.0037	0.97± 0.0036	0.47± 0.0027	1.22± 0.004	1.17± 0.004	0.92± 0.0039	1.05± 0.004	0.65± 0.003	0.75± 0.0032	0.50± 0.0027	0.23± 0.0009	0.37± 0.0048
Cl	0.69± 0.002	0.65± 0.0021	0.85± 0.0017	0.75± 0.0019	0.64± 0.019	0.77± 0.002	0.98± 0.0017	1.03± 0.002	1.09± 0.002	0.99± 0.0017	0.98± 0.0017	1.04± 0.002	0.74± 0.0014	0.95± 0.0017	0.99± 0.0017	1.11± 0.002	0.55± 0.0011	0.97± 0.0017
TiO_2	0.10± 0.0044	0.11± 0.0044	0.12± 0.0037	0.12± 0.0041	0.11± 0.042	0.13± 0.0042	0.14± 0.0041	0.12± 0.004	0.12± 0.0039	0.13± 0.0043	0.11± 0.0042	0.09± 0.0042	0.12± 0.0039	0.14± 0.0039	0.12± 0.0041	0.12± 0.0039	0.08± 0.0017	0.14± 0.0037
MnO	0.40± 0.0073	0.42± 0.0078	0.73± 0.0069	0.46± 0.0069	0.50± 0.072	0.48± 0.0077	0.50± 0.0059	0.39± 0.0053	0.49± 0.0058	0.49± 0.0061	0.50± 0.006	0.46± 0.0055	0.36± 0.0053	0.41± 0.0051	2.38± 0.011	0.07± 0.0038	0.05± 0.0029	0.65± 0.0069
Fe_2O_3	0.85± 0.0065	1.02± 0.007	0.80± 0.0057	0.71± 0.0058	0.85± 0.0065	0.82± 0.0064	0.69± 0.0052	0.49± 0.0042	0.57± 0.0047	0.79± 0.0055	0.75± 0.0053	0.59± 0.0046	1.11± 0.006	0.85± 0.0053	0.54± 0.0053	0.44± 0.0038	5.61± 0.009	3.81± 0.012
SrO	0.12± 0.0018	0.08± 0.002	0.07± 0.001	0.13± 0.0016	0.07± 0.0017	0.10± 0.0017	0.08± 0.00066	0.09± 0.00063	0.09± 0.00073	0.11± 0.00064	0.12± 0.00067	0.12± 0.00065	0.07± 0.00063	0.12± 0.00059	0.08± 0.0007	0.05± 0.00062	0.05± 0.00033	0.10± 0.0012
CuO	0.49± 0.0041	0.88± 0.0054	2.65± 0.007	1.80± 0.007	2.39± 0.008	1.70± 0.006	3.25± 0.007	0.74± 0.0033	2.56± 0.006	0.35± 0.0028	0.30± 0.0026	0.07± 0.0019	0.16± 0.0021	0.10± 0.0018	0.04± 0.0017	0.02± 0.0014	–	1.07± 0.005
SnO_2	0.08± 0.0038	0.12± 0.0049	0.04± 0.0019	0.20± 0.0045	0.20± 0.0049	0.12± 0.0042	0.39± 0.0035	0.09± 0.0025	0.44± 0.0048	0.07± 0.0018	0.07± 0.002	0.03± 0.0013	0.02± 0.00098	–	0.02± 0.0012	–	–	0.10± 0.0044
Sb_2O_5	1.02± 0.006	0.83± 0.0056	0.64± 0.0046	0.58± 0.0042	0.86± 0.0051	0.77± 0.0049	3.46± 0.008	3.44± 0.009	1.41± 0.006	4.07± 0.008	4.22± 0.009	3.26± 0.008	4.27± 0.009	2.03± 0.007	3.10± 0.008	1.68± 0.006	–	0.59± 0.0085
Ta_2O_5	0.47± 0.013	0.50± 0.018	–	0.44± 0.021	–	0.46± 0.021	–	0.23± 0.011	–	–	0.45± 0.0085	0.43± 0.0057	0.35± 0.0066	0.36± 0.0056	0.33± 0.0049	0.30± 0.0043	–	–
CoO	0.01± 0.0018	0.01± 0.0019	0.01± 0.001	–	0.01± 0.0013	–	–	0.02± 0.0021	0.00326± 0.00079	–	0.01± 0.0011	0.02± 0.0014	0.11± 0.0023	0.07± 0.0019	–	–	–	–
PbO	19.31± 0.03	22.66± 0.03	6.61± 0.013	16.27± 0.03	18.95± 0.03	17.48± 0.03	0.06± 0.0019	0.09± 0.014	0.13± 0.0017	0.29± 0.0038	0.35± 0.004	0.27± 0.0021	0.18± 0.0021	0.04± 0.0011	0.05± 0.0011	0.19± 0.0018	–	2.00± 0.007
Total[2]	99.90%	99.90%	99.55%	99.93%	99.25%	99.92%	99.73%	99.66%	99.81%	98.96%	99.29%	99.62%	99.56%	99.88%	99.67%	99.84%	96.41%	99.41%

[1] Sample: Sample names as the first one or two letter of their colours, [2]Other Oxides: Ba, Te, Mo, V_2O_5, I, Br, Nb_2O_5,

4.1. Base Glass

Elemental composition of each sample was identified with XRF analysis. Results show that glass tesserae are soda lime silica and lead glasses composed of SiO_2 (56.05%-76.21%), Na_2O (5.67%-10.51%) and CaO (6.69%-9.59%) (Table 3). Lead glasses contain higher amounts of PbO (n.d-22.66%) in yellow and green samples, which is a peculiar glass characteristic, responsible for the strong colours and lower melting point of the glass batch (Vandini et al., 2006).

Analysed tesserae from Antandros show low MgO (0.94%-1.25%) and low K_2O (0.26%-0.84%) (Figure 4) which indicates that the glass tesserae are natron type glass (Brill, 1999). Another fact that indicates the use of natron is the considerable amounts of Cl (0.55%-1.11%) and SO_3 (0.23%-1.22%) which exist as deposits in sodium carbonates (Silvestri et al., 2012b). Furthermore lower (< 0.15%) P_2O_5 contents (0.16%-0.51%) also indicate the use of natron (Sayre and Smith, 1961).

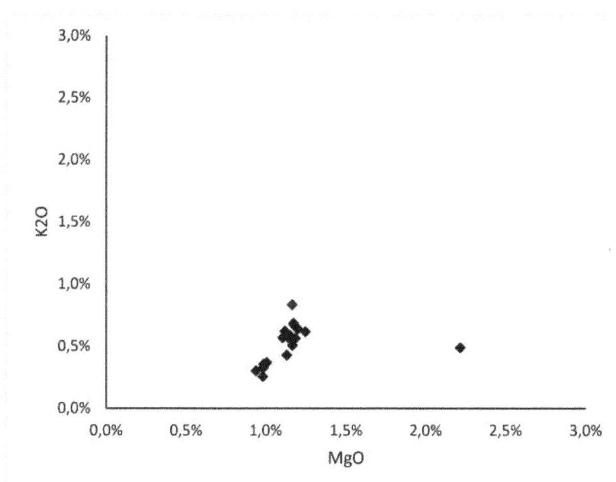

Figure 4. K_2O% versus MgO% diagram of glass tesserae.

Based on magnesium and potassium levels, of analysed Antandros tesserae are natron based glasses, however, the detected Na_2O levels are lower than natron glasses as determined in literature (12-20%) (Table 4) except black tesserae (B) (10.51%).

Therefore, a comparison with similar studies related with glass tesserae was done to clarify the glass production period and the compositional group. In Table 4 concentrations of SiO_2, Na_2O, CaO, Al_2O_3, MgO, K_2O and MnO were compared since they are diagnostic for compositional groups. In Table 4, analysed glasses show similar concentrations with previous studies except for Na_2O. In addition, analysed tesserae were compared with Roman blue-green glasses by Jackson et al., 1991 and glass groups identified by Freestone, 2006, from Levant to Egypt between 4th to 8th centuries (Table 5). They are all natron based glasses and exhibit different major and minor oxides due to impurities in the sand and flux. Also, glasses were compared with Early Islamic plant ash glasses (Freestone et al., 2002; Gratuze and Barrandon, 1990; Silvestri et al., 2012b; Tite et al., 2007).

Another comparison was made with Byzantine mosaic glass that was identified by Vandini et al., 2006 and Arinat et al., 2014. The analyzed tesserae exhibit similar compositions to that Late Byzantine glass from Dafni in Greece, in Late Byzantine, 11th century A.D and 6th to 7th century A.D glass mosaic tesserae from the Cross church in Jerash in northern Jordan which contains lower levels of natron (5-13%).

In comparison, it is shown that glass tesserae exhibit similar compositions with natron type glasses (Roman type glasses), except for lower natron levels. It can be suggested that Antandros mosaic glass may have been produced in 7th century AD. Another suggestion is that, natron may have been provided from a new flux source due to the shortage of Egyptian mineral soda or due to economic reasons glass manufacturers succeeded to produce same glass with low flux addition.

In literature, Pergamon (4th-14th century AD) and Aphrodisias (5th -7th century AD) glasses contained different alkali and alkali earth materials such as boron, lithium and strontium which indicates a different flux source in western Anatolia surrounding Pergamon (Brill, 1988; Schibille, 2011). Another comparison was made on CaO and Al_2O_3 contents as they reflect the silica source. CaO (6.81% to 9.59%) and Al_2O_3 (2.14% to 3.13%) contents are compared in Figure 5 with reference data obtained by Freestone with Wadi Natrun, Egytp II, Bet Eli'ezer, Levantine I and HIMT glasses from Mediterranean Area (4th -9th A.D) to evaluate the possible origin of the glass. According to Figure 5, the sand used in the manufacture of Antandros glasses show similar concentrations with Levantine I glass (Freestone, 2005). However, black tesserae show different characteristics from Levantine I group glasses.

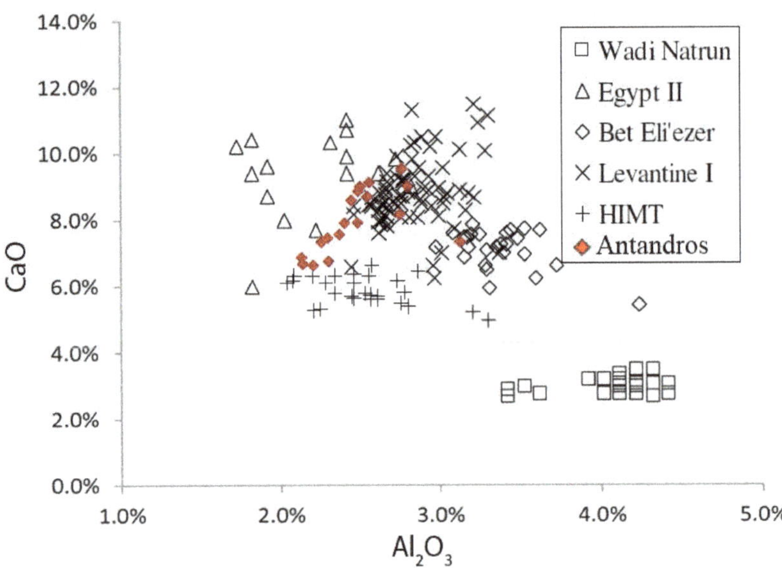

Figure 5. CaO% versus Al_2O_3% diagram of glass tesserae. Source: (data except Antandros from Freestone, 2005)

Besides alumina, iron oxides and titanium oxides are important to define the different sand sources. In Figure 6, Fe_2O_3 versus Al_2O_3 graph, data are compared with five glass groups (Freestone et al., 2002) and Antandros glasses show similarities with Levantine I group. In this graph, black and red tesserae are similar with the high iron magnesia titanium (HIMT) group glasses due to their higher iron contents.

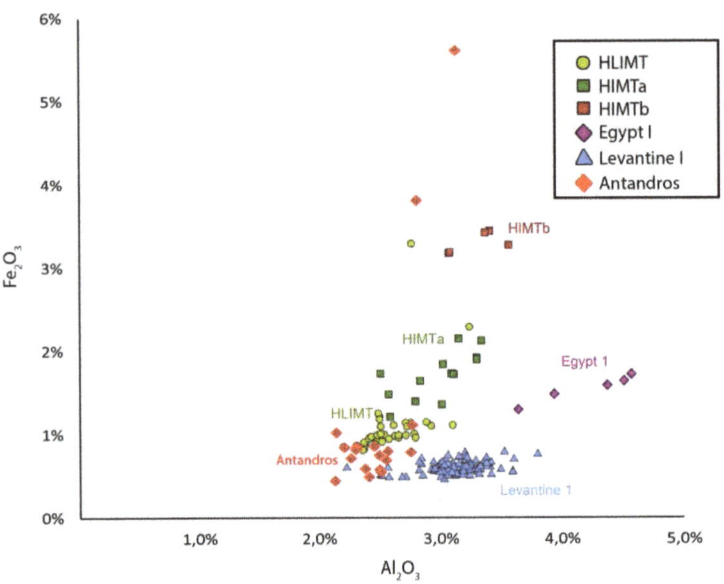

Figure 6. Fe_2O_3 % versus Al_2O_3% diagram of glass tesserae. Source: (data except Antandros from Ceglia et al., 2015)

The TiO_2 levels (0.08%-0.14%) indicate that glasses were produced by the same silica sources. When analyzed tesserae were compared with TiO_2 levels of Levantine glasses, it can be suggested that glasses were produced with the sand from Levantine coast due to their low TiO_2 levels (Foy, 2000; Freestone et al., 2015).

Strontium levels also indicate the source of the sand as either coastal or inland sands. Strontium concentrations are derived from the shell fragments in the sand (Freestone, 2005; Freestone et al., 2003; Silvestri et al., 2008; Wedepohl and Baumann, 2000; Werf et al., 2009). Analyzed tesserae have high amounts of SrO (0.05%-0.13%) that indicates the use of coastal sand in the glass manufacture except for black tesserae.

These results suggest that all the Antandros glasses were produced by using coastal sand as Levantine I glasses (Freestone, 2005) except black tesserae. Black tesserae may have been produced with a different sand and natron source.

Table 4. Comparison of chemical compositions of glasses with similar studies

	Glass tesserae										Glass	
	XRF	SEM/EDS	EPMA	EMPA	WDS-EPMA	SEM/EDS	ICP-MS	EPMA	EDS-WDS	ICP	EPMA	EPMA
	2017	(Paynter et al., 2015)	(Schibille et al., 2012)	(Silvestri et al., 2011)	(Arletti et al., 2011a)	(Croveri et al., 2010)	(Werf et al., 2009)	(Arletti et al., 2006b)	(Mass J. L et al., 2002)	(Costagliola et al., 2000)	(Schibille, 2011)	(Rehren et al., 2015)
	Antandros 4th AD	West Clac-ton, 2nd AD	Sagalassos 6th AD	Padova Italy (6th AD)	Florence Baptistery 4th -5th AD	Enna Italy, 3rd -4th AD	Herculane-um Italy 1st AD	Pompeii	Amorium	Florence Italy	Pergamon	Pergamon
SiO_2	56.05-76.21	53.69-69.30	45.02-71.23	63.8-70.4	40.07-64.21	58.66-68.35	55.00-68.07	46.35-98.65	52.8-69.4	43.38-98.25	65.85-73.49	65.0-73.1
Na_2O	**5.67-10.51**	**13.30-19.13**	**12-20.55**	**13.3-18.7**	**1.78-14.39**	**16.65-20.76**	**7.95-19.76**	**0.08-18.23**	**13.0-19.2**	**nd-18.00**	**14.51-18.57**	**14.8-18.9**
CaO	6.69-9.59	4.80-7.68	4.45-7.83	5.2-9.1	4.42-10.60	4.82-7.44	2.82-10.97	0.02-14.30	6.6-10.7	0.07-18.30	6.24-9.10	5.3-8.6
Al_2O_3	2.14-3.31	1.82-2.58	1.64-3.28	1.79-2.51	0.55-2.84	0.92-2.17	1.05-3.04	0.01-2.81	2.1-3.0	0.45-4.77	1.78-3.13	1.68-2.59
MgO	0.94-2.22	0.34-2.79	0.42-1.42	0.41-1.28	0.74-4.24	0.74-2.56	0.25-2.12	0.01-1.01	0.5-2.7	0.14-3.23	0.38-0.95	0.32-0.68
K_2O	0.26-0.84	0.54-2.11	0.28-1.71	0.39-0.79	0.68-25.37	0.61-1.50	0.49-4.13	nd-0.9	0.5-1.6	nd-5.05	0.44-0.78	0.37-1.11
FeO	0.44-5.61	0.52-1.69	0.40-7.67	0.31-1.25	0.24-2.05	0.47-2.10	0.53-3.01	nd-0.92	0.38-5.4	0.17-2.39	0.29-2.85	0.22-1.39
MnO	0.05-2.38	<0.1-0.93	0.04-1.75	<0.05-2.00	0.05-2.6	nd-1.05	0.07-1.22	nd-5.44	0.03-2.6	nd-2.65	nd-3.66	nd-1.43

EMPA: Electron microprobe analysis

Table 5. Comparison of Antandros glasses with glass composition groups

		Roman	Late Roman	Byzantine	Early Islamic	Early Islamic
		Blue-green	**HIMT**	**Levantine I**	**Levantine II**	**Plant ash**
	Antandros	(Jackson et al., 1991)	(Freestone et al., 2002)	(Freestone and Gorin-Rosen, 1999)	(Freestone, 2000)	**Freestone&Leslie (unpublished)**
	4th AD	1-3rd A. D	4-5th A. D	6-7th A. D	7-8th A. D	10-13th A. D
SiO_2	56.05-76.21	na	65.80	69.30	74.90	70.50
Na_2O	**5.67-10.51**	**18.40**	**18.00**	**15.60**	**12.10**	**12.50**
CaO	6.69-9.59	6.43	5.99	9.17	7.16	8.55
Al_2O_3	2.14-3.31	2.33	2,69	3.03	3.32	1.06
MgO	0.94-2.22	0.55	0.94	0.59	0.63	2.72
K_2O	0.26-0.84	0.69	0.46	0.63	0,46	1.89
MnO	0.05-2.38	0.26	1.51	<0.1	<0.1	1.00
FeO	0.44-5.61	0.6	2.18	0.45	0.52	0.40

Source: Freestone and Hughes, 2006

4.2. Opacifiers and Colorants

Opacifiers of the glasses were determined by XRD analysis. Shapes, sizes and distribution of the opacifiers were determined by SEM analysis. Abundance of crystals were calculated using XRF results. Antimony based opacifiers were detected.

Considerable amounts of antimony in glass compositions (0.59-4.27 %) were determined, except black sample. The XRD analysis and BSE images confirmed that small crystals were dispersed in the glassy matrix with different shapes and sizes.

Lead antimonate crystals (yellow-$Pb_2Sb_2O_7$) were identified in yellow and green tesserae (Figure 7). They are both densely and homogenously dispersed in yellow and green glass.

The amount of $Pb_2Sb_2O_7$ crystals dispersed in the matrix is approximately 1.38% to 2.43%. The size of crystals varies between 0.3 µm-1.2 µm. Lead antimony was determined with euhedral and tiny acicular in yellow and tiny acicular shapes in green samples as they were produced by ex situ crystallization (Figure 8). Similar observations had been obtained by Lahlil et al., 2008; Schibille et al., 2012; Silvestri et al., 2012b.

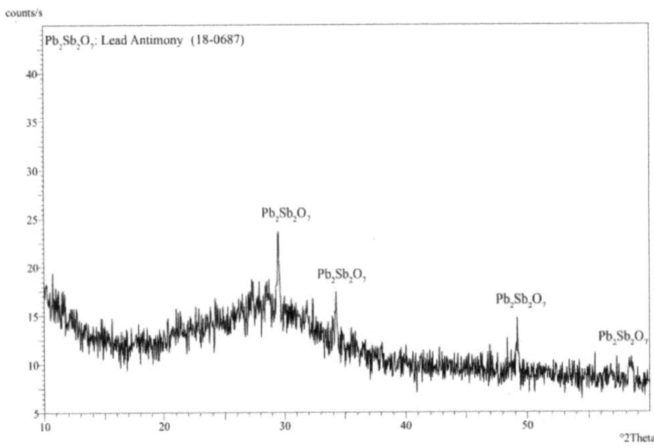

Figure 7. XRD pattern of yellow tesserae

Figure 8. BSE images of Pb antimonate crystals as hexagonal in yellow (left) and tiny acicular in green (right)

Calcium antimonate crystal (white-$CaSb_2O_6$) were identified in turquoise, blue, cyan, white and brown tesserae. The BSE images of blue, turquoise, dark turquoise, and cyan samples shows different density of Ca antimony crystals than semi opaque white and blue samples. They are densely and homogenously well dispersed in the glassy matrix. They have euhedral (hexagonal) shapes which indicates that the glass was opacified with in situ crystallization by adding roasted stibnite to the glass melt (Figure 9) (Schibille et al., 2012).

Total amount of dispersed crystals in the matrix is approximately 3.64% to 4.95%. The size of crystals varies between 0.1 µm- 1 µm. In the XRD analysis, $CaSb_2O_6$ diffraction patterns confirm the crystals in BSE images (Figure 10).

In BSE images of semi-opaque white tesserae, a few Ca-antimony crystals were determined dispersed in the matrix which is less than the other tesserae. In semi, opaque blue tesserae, the glassy matrix contains a few Ca antimony crystals similar with the white glass. The number of particles per unit volume indicates different opacity degrees in Ca antimony glasses. Therefore, it can be suggested that Pb antimony is a more effective opacifier than the Ca antimony.

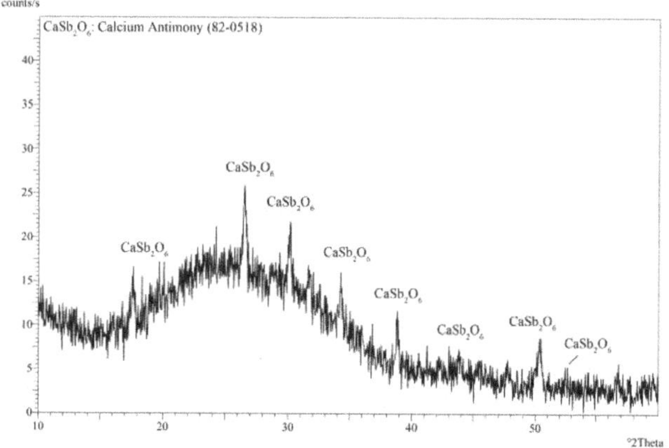

Figure 9. XRD pattern of light brown tesserae

***Figure 10.** BSE images of Ca antimonate crystals as hexagonal in blue (a), cyan (b), dark turquoise (c), and turquoise (d).*

Colorants of the glasses were determined by XRF analysis (Table 3). All analyzed tesserae were colored by transition metal compounds. The colorants are cobalt, copper, manganese and iron that are typical of the Roman Period (Henderson, 1991; Lahlil et al., 2010a, 2010b, 2008; Werf et al., 2009). They dissolve in the glass melt in varying oxidation states or precipitate as metals by redox reactions giving color to the glass (Möncke et al., 2014).

Green color of the Lg, Dg1, Dg2, G1 and G2 tesserae were obtained by adding $Pb_2Sb_2O_7$ (yellow) to the transparent blue glasses. Based on the theory of color, the addition of yellow to blue modifies the color towards greenish hues, in opaque glass this effect can be obtained by introducing yellow crystals in a transparent blue glass. CuO (0.88-2.65 wt %) were also responsible for the greenish hues of the glasses with $Pb_2Sb_2O_7$ (Arletti et al., 2006a; Croveri et al., 2010). Therefore the variability of green tonality is certainly due to the abundance of copper oxide and contribution of bindheimite (yellow lead antimonite) crystals in varying amounts (Werf et al., 2009). The source of copper might be tin bronze due to the presence of tin oxide in the chemical composition of the green tesserae due to weight percent ratio of tin to copper as approximately 0.1 (Brill, 1988; Brun et al., 1991; Freestone, 1987; Gedzevičiute et al., 2009; Henderson, 1985; Werf et al., 2009).

As in green tesserae, yellow tesserae (Yt) contain higher PbO content, however contain lower amount of CuO than green tesserae. Higher amount of PbO in the form of lead antimonite, responsible for the yellow color, was detected in XRF, XRD analysis and SEM-BSE images. The use of lead antimonate crystals are noted as both opacifying and coloring agent for yellow and green tesserae in Roman and Byzantine Period (Croveri et al., 2010; Schibille et al., 2012; Werf et al., 2009).

White tessera contains Sb_2O_5 (1.68%) and low amounts of transition metal oxides, which are responsible for the intense colors. The Sb_2O_5 levels are lower than the other opaque glasses due to its semi opaque appearance. In recent studies, it has been indicated that white Roman and Byzantine glass tesserae were obtained using $CaSb_2O_6$ (~0.5%) (Schibille et al., 2012; Werf et al., 2009).

Turquoise and cyan tesserae (T1, T2, Dt, C1, C2) contain high amounts of CuO (3.25%, 0.74%, 2.56%, 0.35%, 0.30%) and lower CoO (nd, 0.02%, 0.003%, nd, 0.01%) respectively. In a soda lime silica glass, cobalt and copper ions both give blue color to the glass. Copper gives a greenish hue, whereas cobalt gives a deep blue color. Cobalt has higher absorption coefficient than the copper ions, therefore a few ppm of cobalt ions is enough to give bluish hue to the glass (Brill, 1999; Fiori and Macchiarola, 1998; Freestone and Bimson, 1995; Licenziati and Calligaro, 2015; Mirti et al., 2002; Nenna, 1999). The amount of copper and cobalt ions are directly related to the green and blue hue of the glass color. Different shades of turquoise and cyan can be obtained by introducing variable amounts of Ca-antimony that whiten and brighten up the color. This can be seen in the analyzed light turquoise tesserae (T1 and T2), that exhibit higher contents of Sb_2O_5 (3.46%, 3.44%) than the dark turquoise (Dt) (1.41%). Regarding the cyan tesserae (C1, C2), they exhibit higher amounts of Sb_2O_5 (4.07%, 4.22%) levels than the light turquoise samples. In turquoise and cyan tesserae, relative percentages of SnO_2 and CuO may be dependent on the use of a tin bronze as the copper source similar with yellow and green tesserae. In recent studies, the use of copper has been noted in Roman glasses to obtain blue-green colors (Arletti et al., 2011b; Croveri et al., 2010; Verita, 2000; Werf et al., 2009).

Blue tesserae (Lb, Bv-O, Bv-So) exhibit slightly higher cobalt levels (0.02%, 0.11%, 0.07%) responsible for the blue color of the glass. According to literature, cobalt is associated with copper, arsenic, iron or nickel, however any element related with the cobalt source was determined in the analysis (Arletti et al., 2006b; Fiori and Vandini, 2004; Henderson, 2000; Silvestri et al., 2012a). In addition, for the cobalt source an iron rich ore may have been used due to the higher iron levels of the blue glasses.

Dark red tessera contains high amounts of CuO (1.07%), Fe_2O_3 (3.81%), PbO (2.00%) and SnO_2 (0.1%). Iron and the copper ions are responsible for the red color of the glass. Iron is the most utilized colorant agent of the glass which is naturally found in the sand as an impurity. High iron content of the red glass suggests that it was intentionally added as a reducing agent for the copper (Brill, 1988). Copper gives bright red color of the glass as cuprite (CuO_2) which is a typical characteristic of the red glasses Freestone, 1987. Considerable amounts of tin indicates that copper was not added in the form of copper metal, it was added as bronze scale which dissolves easily (Brill and Cahill, 1988).

However, dark red tesserae contain much lower amounts of copper than ancient bright red colored tesserae also in the microstructural analysis there are no cuprite minerals. Consequently, it can be suggested that lower copper ions are responsible for the brownish red color and higher iron levels are responsible for the dark color of the Antandros dark red tesserae.

Black glass tesserae contain higher Fe_2O_3 (3.81%) and MnO (0.05%) and do not contain other transition metal oxides or Sb_2O_5. Ancient black glasses were produced by intentional addition of iron and manganese oxides to the glass batch without addition of other coloring agents (Henderson, 1985; Mass J. L et al., 2002). There were two types of black glasses with respect to their iron concentrations. If black glass contains low amounts of iron oxides (1-2% Fe_2O_3) this type of glass was produced in the Early Roman period, whereas if they contained high amounts of iron oxides (4-10% Fe_2O_3), they are produced after 150 AD. In addition, considering antimony concentrations of the glass, Levantine group glasses are contain antimony, however, Egyptian glasses do not contain antimony (Van Der Linden et al., 2009). Thus, black glass exhibits a different compositional characteristic from other analyzed glass tesserae and may have been produced in a different period.

Light brown tesserae contain significant amounts of MnO (2.38%) and Sb_2O_5 (3.10%) which give the light brownish color to the glass. Manganese has been used as a colorant and a decolorizer and also as an oxidizer of iron ions which is balancing the greenish brown color of the raw glass (Fiori, 2015; Silvestri et al., 2012b; Vandini et al., 2006). Higher magnesium levels give an orange color to the glass (Möncke et al., 2014). Therefore, high amounts of Sb_2O_5 balance the orange color and provide a brownish color.

5. CONCLUSION

Antandros mosaic glass tesserae contradict historical Roman glass regarding the natron levels as fluxing agent which were traded from the Wadi Natrun in Egypt. Glasses were produced in a limited number of primary glass production centres with pure soda coming from the Wadi Natrun in Egypt and the sand was obtained locally. Later the produced glass batches were exported to secondary glass production centres where the glasses were turned into final products. In Roman Period, before the depletion of natron sources, glasses were produced with pure soda and contained higher amounts of natron. Although, Antandros glasses exhibited similar characteristics to Roman glasses, they have lower natron levels. This is supporting two production possibilities in the production of Antandros glasses. First, natron might have been provided from another or a new source due to the shortage of natron in Wadi Natrun. Second, glass manufacturers succeeded in producing glass with low flux addition due to economic reasons. Regarding the silica sources, in the production of Antandros tesserae, coastal sand was used from Palestine coast similar with Levantine I group glasses except for black tesserae.

Glasses were all opacified with antimony oxides and coloured with transition metal oxides. These are typical characteristics of Roman period except black tesserae which do not contain antimony oxides. The amount of the colorants and their abundance effects the hue and brightness of the glass. In addition, composition of the glass influences the effects of the colorants especially the amount of opacifiers influence the effect of the colorants. Furthermore, colorimetric coordinates of the glasses are in accordance with the chemical composition of the Antandros glasses. Antandros glasses were most probably produced in a nearby local production centre in Assos ancient city. Besides lower natron levels, all the analysed glasses were soda lime silica glasses that show similar compositions of Roman antimony-decoloured glasses except black one. Black tesserae exhibit a different production technology and raw materials. It may have been produced at a different production period. Analytical data of glass from Anatolia and potential silica sources in the region are insufficient thus more analytical studies need to be conducted.

ACKNOWLEDGEMENTS

I would like to thank the Prof. Dr. Gürcan Polat and the archaeological excavation team of Antandros for providing samples and researchers of the Centre for Materials Research at the Izmir Institute of Technology for XRD, XRF, TGA and SEM-EDS analyses for the experimental stage of this study.

REFERENCES

Ali, N., Abd-allah, R., 2015. the Authentication and Characterization of Glass Objects Excavated From Tell Es-Sukhnah , Jordan 15, 39–50.

Arinat, M., Shiyyab, A., Abd-Allah, R., 2014. Byzantine glass mosaics excavated from the "cross church", Jerash, Jordan: An archaeometrical investigation. Mediterr. Archaeol. Archaeom. 14, 43–53.

Arletti, R., Conte, S., Vandini, M., Fiori, C., Bracci, S., Bacci, M., Porcinai, S., 2011a. Florence Baptistery: Chemical and Mineralogical Investigation of Glass Mosaic Tesserae. J. Archaeol. Sci. 38, 79–88. doi:10.1016/j.jas.2010.08.012

Arletti, R., Dalconi, M.C., Quartieri, S., Triscari, M., Vezzalini, G., 2006a. Roman Coloured and Opaque Glass: a Chemical and Spectroscopic Study. Appl. Phys. A 83, 239–245. doi:10.1007/s00339-006-3515-2

Arletti, R., Quartieri, S., Vezzalini, G., 2006b. Glass mosaic tesserae from Pompeii: An archeometrical investigation. Period. di Mineral. 75, 25–38.

Arletti, R., Vezzalini, G., Fiori, C., Vandini, M., 2011b. Mosaic Glass From St Peter'S, Rome: Manufacturing Techniques and Raw Materials Employed in Late 16Th-Century Italian Opaque Glass. Archaeometry 53, 364–386. doi:10.1111/j.1475-4754.2010.00538.x

Bimson, M., Freestone, I.C., 1988. Some Egyptian Glasses Dated by Royal Inscription. J. Glass Stud. 30, 11–15.

Brill, R.H., 1999. Chemical Analyses of Early Glasses.

Brill, R.H., 1988. Scientific investigations of the Jalame glass and related finds. Excav. Jalame site a Glas. Fact. late Rom. Palest. 257–295.

Brill, R.H., 1968. The Scientific Investigation of Ancient Glasses.

Brill, R.H., Cahill, N.D., 1988. A Red Opaque Glass From Sardis and Some Thoughts on Red Opaques In General. J. Glass Stud. 30, 16–27.

Brun, N., Mazerolles, L., Pernot, M., 1991. Microstructure of Opaque Red Glass Containing Copper. J. Mater. Sci. Lett. 10, 1418–1420. doi:10.1007/BF00735696

Ceglia, A., Cosyns, P., Nys, K., Terryn, H., Thienpont, H., Meulebroeck, W., 2015. Late antique glass distribution and consumption in Cyprus: a chemical study. J. Archaeol. Sci. 61, 213–222. doi:10.1016/j.jas.2015.06.009

Costagliola, P., Baldi, G., Cipriani, C., 2000. Mineralogical and Chemical Characterisation of the Medicean Glass Mosaic Tesserae and Mortars of the Grotta del Buontalenti, Giardino di Boboli, Florence. J. Cult. Herit. 1, 287–299.

Croveri, P., Fragalà, I., Ciliberto, E., 2010. Analysis of Glass Tesserae from the Mosaics of the "Villa del Casale" near Piazza Armerina (Enna, Italy). Chemical Composition, State of Preservation and Production Technology. Appl. Phys. A 100, 927–935. doi:10.1007/s00339-010-5670-8

Fiori, C., 2015. Production technology of Byzantine red mosaic glasses. Ceram. Int. 41, 3152–3157. doi:10.1016/j.ceramint.2014.10.160

Fiori, C., Macchiarola, M., 1998. Studio e confronti fra la composizione chimica di vetri del II-I sec. A.C. Provenienti da delos (grecia) e vetri provenienti dalla capitanata (fg): Herdonia, I-II sec. D.c., arpi e ascoli satriano, II sec. A.c. Atti 2e Giornate Naz. di Stud. AIHV - Com. Naz. Ital. 139–146.

Fiori, C., Vandini, M., 2004. Chemical composition of glass and its raw materials: chronological and geographical development in the first millennium A. D., When Glass Matters. Studies in the History of Science and Art from Graeco-Roman Antiquity to Early Modern Era. Leo S. Olschki, Florence.

Fiori, C., Vandini, M., Mazzotti, V., 2003. Colore e Tecnologia Degli Smalti Musivi dei Riquadri di Giustiniano e Teodora Nella Basilica di San Vitale a Ravenna. Ceramurgia 33, 135–154.

Foy, D., 2000. Technologie, géographie, économie: les ateliers de verriers primaires et secondaires en Occident. Esquisse d'une évolution de l'Antiquité au Moyen Âge. La route du verre. Ateliers primaires Second. du Second millénaire avond J.C. au Moyen Age 147–170.

Freestone, I., 1987. Composition and Microstructure of Early Opaque Red Glass. Early Vitr. Mater. 56, 173–191.

Freestone, I.C., 2006. Glass production in Late Antiquity and the Early Islamic period: a geochemical perspective. Geomaterials Cult. Herit. 257, 201–216. doi:10.1144/GSL.SP.2006.257.01.16

Freestone, I.C., 2005. The provenance of ancient glass through compositional analysis. Mater. Res. Soc. Symp. Proc. 852, 1–14. doi:10.1557/PROC-852-OO8.1

Freestone, I.C., 2000. Nature [14, 17]. 1–17.

Freestone, I.C., Bimson, M., 1995. Early Venetian Enamelling on Glass: Technology and Origins. MRS Proc. doi:10.1557/PROC-352-415

Freestone, I.C., Gorin-Rosen, Y., 1999. The great glass slab at Bet She'arim, Israel: an early islamic glassmaking experiment. J. Glass Stud. 41, 105–116.

Freestone, I.C., Hughes, M.J., 2006. The origins of the Jarrow glass. Wearmouth Jarrow Monast. Sites Vol. 2 2, 147–155.

Freestone, I.C., Jackson-Tal, R.E., Taxel, I., Tal, O., 2015. Glass production at an Early Islamic workshop in Tel Aviv. J. Archaeol. Sci. 62, 45–54. doi:10.1016/j.jas.2015.07.003

Freestone, I.C., Leslie, K.A., Thirlwall, M., Gorin-Rosen, Y., 2003. Strontium Isotopes in the Investigation of Early Glass Production: Byzantine and Early Islamic Glass from the Near East. Archaeometry 45, 19–32.

Freestone, I.C., Ponting, M., Hughes, M.J., 2002. The origins of Byzantine glass from Maroni Petrera, Cyprus. Archaeometry 44, 257–272. doi:10.1111/1475-4754.t01-1-00058

Gedzevičiute, V., Welter, N., Schüssler, U., Weiss, C., 2009. Chemical composition and colouring agents of Roman mosaic and millefiori glass, studied by electron microprobe analysis and Raman microspectroscopy. Archaeol. Anthropol. Sci. 1, 15–29. doi:10.1007/s12520-009-0005-4

Gratuze, B., Barrandon, J.N., 1990. Islamic glass weights and stamps: analysis using nuclear techniques. Archaeometry 32, 155–162.

Henderson, J., 2000. The Science and Archaeology of Materials: An Investigation of Inorganic Materials.

Routledge, London.

Henderson, J., 1991. Chemical Characterization Of Roman Glass Vessels, Enamels And Tesserae In Vandiver. Mater. Issues Art Archaeol. 2, 601–720.

Henderson, J., 1988. Electron Probe Microanalysis of Mixed-Alkali Glasses. Archaeometry 30, 77–91.

Henderson, J., 1985. The Raw Materials of Early Glass Production. Oxford J. Archaeol. 4, 267–292. doi:10.1111/j.1468-0092.1985.tb00248.x

Jackson, C.M., Hunter, J.R., Warren, S.E., Cool, H.E.M., 1991. The analysis of blue-green glass and glassy waste from two Romano-British glass working sites. Archaeometry 90, 295–304.

Lahlil, S., Biron, I., Cotte, M., Susini, J., 2010a. New Insight on the in Situ Crystallization of Calcium Antimonate Opacified Glass During the Roman Period. Appl. Phys. A 100, 683–692. doi:10.1007/s00339-010-5650-z

Lahlil, S., Biron, I., Cotte, M., Susini, J., Menguy, N., 2010b. Synthesis of Calcium Antimonate Nano-Crystals by the 18th Dynasty Egyptian Glassmakers. Appl. Phys. A Mater. Sci. Process. 98, 1–8.

Lahlil, S., Biron, I., Galoisy, L., Morin, G., 2008. Rediscovering ancient glass technologies through the examination of opacifier crystals. Appl. Phys. A 92, 109–116. doi:10.1007/s00339-008-4456-8

Lauwers, V., Degryse, P., Waelkens, M., 2007. Evidence for Anatolian Glassworking in Antiquity: the Case of Sagalassos (Southwestern Turkey). J. Glass Stud.

Licenziati, F., Calligaro, T., 2015. Study of mosaic glass tesserae from Delos, Greece using a combination of portable µ-Raman and X-ray fluorescence spectrometry. J. Archaeol. Sci. Reports. doi:10.1016/j.jasrep.2015.10.017

Lilyquist, C., Brill, R., Wypsyski M. T, 1993. Studies in Ancient Egyptian Glass. The Metropolitan Museum of Art, New York.

Mass J. L, Wypsyski M. T, Stone R. E, 2002. Malkata and Lisht Glassmaking Technologies: Towards a Specific Link Between Second Millenium BC Metallurgists and Glassmakers. Archaeometry 1, 67–82.

Mirti, P., Davit, P., Gulmini, M., 2002. Colourants and Opacifiers in Seventh and Eighth Century Glass Investigated by Spectroscopic Techniques. Anal. Bioanal. Chem. Chem. 372, 221–229. doi:10.1007/s00216-001-1183-9

Möncke, D., Papageorgiou, M., Winterstein-Beckmann, A., Zacharias, N., 2014. Roman Glasses Coloured by Dissolved Transition Metal Ions: Redox-Reactions, Optical Spectroscopy and Ligand Field Theory. J. Archaeol. Sci. 46, 23–36. doi:10.1016/j.jas.2014.03.007

Nenna, M.D., 1999. Exploration archéologique de Délos Fascicule XXXVII Les verres. Ecole française d'Athènes diff. de Boccard, Athènes Paris.

Newton, R., Davison, S., 1989. Conservation of Glass. Butterworth Heinemann, Oxford.

Paynter, S., Kearns, T., Cool, H., Chenery, S., 2015. Roman coloured glass in the Western provinces: The glass cakes and tesserae from West Clacton in England. J. Archaeol. Sci. 62, 66–81. doi:10.1016/j.jas.2015.07.006

Polat, G., 2002. Antandros 2001 Yılı Kazıları, 24. Kazı Sonuçları Toplantısı, Cilt 2. Ankara.

Polat, G., Polat, Y., 2005. Antandros 2003-2004 Yılı Kazıları, 27. Kazı Sonuçları Toplantısı, Cilt 2,. Ankara.

Polat, G., Polat, Y., Yağız, K., 2007. Antandros 2005 Yılı Kazıları, 28. Kazı Sonuçları Toplantısı - II. Cilt. Ankara.

Quien M. Le, 1958. Oriens christianus 1. Graz.

Rehren, T., Connolly, P., Schibille, N., Schwarzer, H., 2015. Changes in glass consumption in Pergamon (Turkey) from Hellenistic to late Byzantine and Islamic times. J. Archaeol. Sci. 55, 266–279. doi:10.1016/j.jas.2014.12.025

Rehren, T., Freestone, I.C., 2015. Ancient glass: from kaleidoscope to crystal ball. J. Archaeol. Sci. 56, 233–241. doi:10.1016/j.jas.2015.02.021

Sayre E. V, Smith R. W, 1961. Compositional Categories of Ancient Glass. Am. Assoc. Adv. Sci. 133, 1824–1826.

Schibille, N., 2011. Late Byzantine mineral soda high alumina glasses from Asia Minor: a new primary glass production group. PLoS One 6, e18970. doi:10.1371/journal.pone.0018970

Schibille, N., Degryse, P., Corremans, M., Specht, C.G., 2012. Chemical Characterisation of Glass Mosaic Tesserae from Sixth-Century Sagalassos (south-west Turkey): Chronology and Production Techniques. J. Archaeol. Sci. 39, 1480–1492. doi:10.1016/j.jas.2012.01.020

Shortland, A.J., Tite, M.S., 2000. Raw Materials of Glass From Amarna and Implications for The Origins Of Egyptian Glass. Archaeometry 1, 141–151.

Silvestri, A., Molin, G., Salviulo, G., 2008. The colourless glass of Iulia Felix. J. Archaeol. Sci. 35, 331–341. doi:10.1016/j.jas.2007.03.010

Silvestri, A., Tonietto, S., D'Acapito, F., Molin, G., 2012a. The Role of Copper on Colour of Palaeo-Christian Glass Mosaic Tesserae: An XAS study. J. Cult. Herit. 13, 137–144. doi:10.1016/j.culher.2011.08.002

Silvestri, A., Tonietto, S., Molin, G., 2011. The palaeo-Christian glass mosaic of St. Prosdocimus (Padova, Italy): archaeometric characterisation of "gold" tesserae. J. Archaeol. Sci. 38, 3402–3414. doi:10.1016/j.jas.2011.07.027

Silvestri, A., Tonietto, S., Molin, G., Guerriero, P., 2012b. The Palaeo-Christian Glass Mosaic of St. Prosdocimus (Padova, Italy): Archaeometric Characterisation of Tesserae with Antimony- or Phosphorus-Based Opacifiers. J. Archaeol. Sci. 39, 2177–2190. doi:10.1016/j.jas.2012.03.012

Smith J.T, 1997. Roman Villas. A Study in Social Structure, London and New York: Routledge. doi:10.1017/CBO9781107415324.004

Strabo, 2000. Geographika, Arkeoloji Sanat Yayınları. İstanbul. doi:10.1017/CBO9781107415324.004

Tite, M., Pradell, T., Shortland, A.J., 2007. Discovery, Production and Use of Tin-Based Opacifiers in Glasses, Enamels and Glazes From the Late Iron Age Onwards: a Reassessment. Archaeometry 0, 071024000902001–??? doi:10.1111/j.1475-4754.2007.00339.x

Turner, W.E.S., 1956. Studies in Ancient Glasses and Glassmaking Processes: Raw Materials and Melting Processes. part V.

Uhlir, K., Melcher, M., Czurda-Ruth, B., Schreiner, M., Krinzinger, F., 2006. Scientific investigations on ancient glasses from Hanghaus I in Ephesos/Turkey using SEM/EDX and μ-XRF. Proc. 36th Int. Symp. Archaeom. May 2nd - 6th, 2006, Quebec City, Canada 6–11.

Van Der Linden, V., Cosyns, P., Schalm, O., Cagno, S., Nys, K., Janssens, K., Nowak, A., Wagner, B., Bulska, E., 2009. Deeply coloured and black glass in the northern provinces of the Roman empire: Differences and similarities in chemical composition before and after AD 150. Archaeometry 51, 822–844. doi:10.1111/j.1475-4754.2008.00434.x

Vandini, M., Fiori, C., Cametti, R., 2006. Classification and Technology of Byzantine Mosaic Glass. Ann. Chim. 96, 587–599.

Verita, M., 2000. Technology and Deterioration of Vitreous Mosaic Tesserae. Rev. Conserv. 1, 65–76.

Wedepohl, K.H., Baumann, A., 2000. The use of marine molluskan shells for Roman glass and local raw glass production in the Eifel area (Western Germany). Naturwissenschaften 87, 129–132.

Werf, I., Mangone, A., Giannossa, L.C., Traini, A., Laviano, R., Coralini, A., Sabbatini, L., 2009. Archaeometric Investigation of Roman Tesserae from Herculaneum (Italy) by the Combined Use of Complementary Micro-Destructive Analytical Techniques. J. Archaeol. Sci. 36, 2625–2634. doi:10.1016/j.jas.2009.07.015

Yalman, B., 1993. Antandros Nekropolisi Kurtarma Kazısı, III. Müze Kurtarma Kazlar Semineri. Ankara.

6

ARCHAEOMETRIC CHARACTERIZATION OF THE CERAMICS FROM TWO CELTIBERIAN HILLFORTS: PRELIMINARY RESULTS

Álvaro Sánchez-Climent[1], Carlos J. Sánchez-Jiménez[2], Francisco J. Poblete[3] and María L. Cerdeño[1]

[1]*Departamento de Prehistoria. Facultad de Geografía e Historia. Universidad Complutense de Madrid. 28040. Madrid. Spain.*
[2]*Área de Mineralogía y Cristalografía. Departamento de Química-Física. Facultad de Ciencias y Tecnologías Químicas. Universidad de Castilla-La Mancha. 13071. Ciudad Real. Spain.*
[3]*Departamento de Química-Física. Facultad de Ciencias y Tecnologías Químicas. Universidad de Castilla-La Mancha. 13071. Ciudad Real. Spain.*

Corresponding author: Dr. Álvaro Sánchez-Climent: alvsan12@ucm.es

ABSTRACT

In this work, we present the preliminary results of the archaeometric analysis of several ceramic and clay samples from two Celtiberian hillforts of the Iron Age from the Spanish Central Plateau: El Ceremeño and its cemetery (Early and Middle Iron Age) and the oppidum of Los Rodiles (Late Iron Age) including La Rodriga, a potter's workshop contemporary to Los Rodiles. Clay samples were collected from all sites in order to carry out a provenance analysis and to determine if the ceramic production of the proposed archaeological sites was local or foreign. Mineralogical analysis was performed by Thin-Layer Petrography (TLP) and X-Ray Diffraction (XRD), whereas chemical analysis was done by X-Ray Fluorescence: Semi-quantitative (XRF) and Trace Elemental analysis (XRF-t). Moreover, to complete the study a thermal analysis was carried out by a dilatometer (DLT). Although the number of samples evaluated was limited, in all the studied cases, the analyzed pottery was clearly found to be made with the clay from the surroundings of the archaeological sites.

KEYWORDS: Celtiberian Culture, Iron Age, ceramic production, provenance analysis

1. INTRODUCTION

Archaeometric analysis of ceramics has benefited from the development and application of chemical, structural and micro-structural techniques, exceeding the capabilities of the morphological description of the artefacts. Despite the interest in these techniques, the Spanish archaeological community did not employ archaeometric analysis until mid-nineties, when the I Iberian Congress of Archaeometry (Capel, 1999) was organized. More recently, the number of researchers in this field has significantly increased, especially the based in ceramics (Montero et al. 2007; Cordero et al. 2006; García Heras, 2003a, etc.).

In several areas of the inner Iberian Peninsula, where historical Celtiberia was located, García Heras started to carry out structural analysis of ceramics that were considered ground-breaking. García Heras characterized ceramics from the sites of *Numantia* (1999a; 1999b and 2003), *Segontia Lanka* (2003b), Castilterreño (1994 and 2003b) and El Palomar de Aragoncillo (González et al. 1999). Moreover, he analysed several other materials from these sites, including glass (García Heras et al. 2003; García Heras, 2008, etc.). Following these initial studies, few projects have investigated the structural properties of ceramics in this region, including the Celtiberian potter's workshop (Igea et al. 2008 and Saiz et al. 2010) and some archaeological sites of the Celtiberia from the Spanish Central Plateau such as La Coronilla, La Yunta, El Torrejón, etc. (Sánchez Climent, 2015). The interesting findings of these studies motivated us to continue on this research line.

Recently published previous studies have applied characterization technologies to prehistoric pottery with the aim to reinterpret the significance of the ceramic provenance in the Neolithic from the Mondego Plateau in Portugal by Jorge et al. (2013), and the case of the Neolithic ceramics from the Central Plateau of Iran (Marghussian et al. 2017). In the last publication the same techniques were used to stablish a gradual evolution of the pottery from the Sialk I to Sialk II periods due to relative similarity of compositions and homogenous structures, and also the presence of high-temperature phases demonstrated a high specialization in the fabrication of the ceramics. Relevant work that is usual practice in archaeometry from earlier times to later antiquity is the recent ones from the central and other side of Mediterranean (Zeinab Javanshah, 2018; Nagwa. S. Abdel Rahim, 2016).

In the case of the Iron Age, the work from colleagues of the University of Salamanca is very interesting. They studied the Second Iron Age ceramic from the north-western of the Iberian Peninsula (Reyes De Soto et al. 2014), whose results showed differences between local and foreign ceramics related to the origin of the raw materials. The work of Krueger and Brand herm (2016) about archaeometry and chronology of the Early Iron Age pottery from the south-western Iberia is also of interest. In other parts of Europe, it is important to highlight the archaeometric characterization of the ceramics from Oropos (Mazarakis & Vlachou 2014). In this work, the authors carried out archaeometric analysis to several ceramic samples from the archaeological site to determine the local or the Euobean production.

The aim of this work was to carry out a provenance analysis of ceramics from two Celtiberian archaeological hillforts: El Ceremeño (and some ceramic samples from its cemetery) and Los Rodiles. Furthermore, we have collected some clay samples from the surroundings of the hillforts and from La Rodriga potter's workshop, an archaeological site with the same chronology to Los Rodiles. In order to perform this study, common analysis techniques have been used such as X-Ray Diffraction and Thin-Layer Petrography for mineralogical analysis, and X-Ray Fluorescence (Semi-quantitative and Traces) for the chemical study. To complete this archaeometric characterization, we used a dilatometer to determine firing temperatures.

2. METHODOLOGY: SAMPLES AND TECHNIQUES

The archaeometric studies presented in this work were applied to 17 ceramic samples from three Celtiberian archaeological sites of Guadalajara (Spain) (Fig. 1): El Ceremeño hillfort, its cemetery in Herrería, and Los Rodiles oppidum. Furthermore, some clay samples were collected from the surroundings of the mentioned sites and from La Rodriga potter's workshop (Fuentelsaz) that is contemporary to Los Rodiles site. Mineralogical, thermal and chemical analysis were carried out using the most popular techniques for the ceramic characterization. Because the techniques used in this work are destructive, it was not possible to analyse every sample by all listed methods. Table 1 shows the techniques used for each sample, together with the chronology, the archaeological site and the description of the sample.

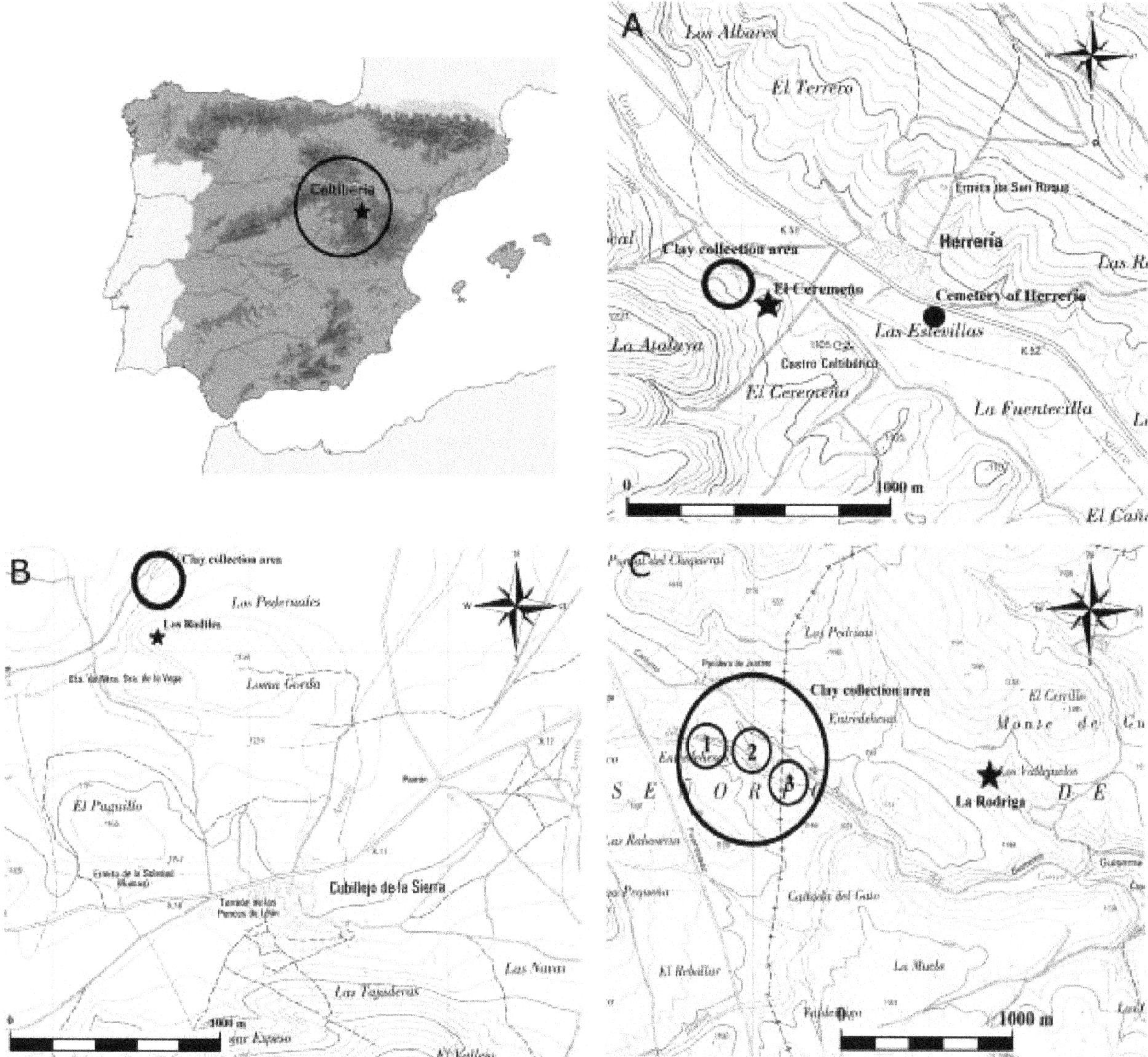

Figure 1. Location of the archaeological sites and clay collection areas in Celtiberia (Spain): (A) El Ceremeño and its cemetery Herrería, (B) Los Rodiles and (C) La Rodriga potter's workshop.

Table 1: Summary of the characteristics of the analysed samples and techniques used.

Id	Sample	Site	Chronology	Description	Technique*
1	CEI-VivA-1	El Cerameño I	VII-VI BC	Handmade	XRD, XRF, XRF-t and DLT
2	CEI-VivA-2	El Cerameño I	VII-VI BC	Handmade	XRD
3	CE92-I-VivB-UE9-sector 1/2	El Cerameño I	VII-VI BC	Wheel	XRD, XRF and XRF-t
4	CE92-II-UE4-VivIII	El Cerameño II	V BC	Wheel	XRD, XRF and XRF-t
5	CE92-UE28-VivIII (1)	El Cerameño II	V BC	Wheel	XRD, XRF and XRF-t
6	CE92-UE28-VivIII (2)	El Cerameño II	V BC	Wheel	XRD, XRF and XRF-t
7	NMO05-15b-N1-P3	Herrería III	VII-VI BC	Handmade	XRD and DLT
8	HRRIII-T353A	Herrería III	VII-VI BC	Handmade	XRD
9	NMO02-24sup-1632	Herrería IV	V-IV BC	Handmade	XRD, XFR, XFR-t and DLT
10	RO09-31e-4014	Los Rodiles I	III-½II BC	Handmade	TLP
11	RO09-31e-4023	Los Rodiles I	III-½II BC	Wheel	TLP

12	RO09-31f-4014	Los Rodiles I	III-½II BC	Wheel	XRD and DLT
13	RO09-27G-1205	Los Rodiles II	½II-I BC	Wheel	TLP
14	RO09-27G-1206	Los Rodiles II	½II-I BC	Wheel	TLP
15	RO09-31f-4020	Los Rodiles II	½II-I BC	Roman	TLP
16	RO09-3F-2002-1	Los Rodiles II	½II-I BC	Wheel	XRD, XRF, XRF-t and DLT
17	RO09-3F-2002-2	Los Rodiles II	½II-I BC	Wheel	XRD, XRF, XRF-t and DLT
18	El Cеremeño clay sample	El Ceremeño	---	Red	XRD, XRF, XRF-t
19	Los Rodiles clay sample	Los Rodiles	---	Red-brown	XRD, XRF, XRF-t
20	La Rodriga clay sample (x3)	La Rodriga	---	Grey	XRD, XRF, XRF-t

*XRD: X-Ray Diffraction; XRF: X-Ray Fluorescence (semi-quantitative); XRF-t: X-Ray Fluorescence (trace elements); DLT: Dilatometry; TLP: Thin-Layer Petrography.

2.1. *Mineralogical analysis*

Two techniques were used for the mineralogical analysis: X-Ray Diffraction (XRD) and Thin-Layer Petrography (TLP).

The mineralogical characterization by XRD consisted of the analysis of crystalline particles from the diffraction of the X-Ray according to Bragg's Law. It was carried out in IRICA by using a diffractometer (Philips X'Pert MPD) in which the angular range was set between 3 and 75° with increases of 0.05°. The sample was introduced in the instrument after being ground with an agate mortar for 10 minutes. The final diameter of the sample particles ranged between 50 and 100 µm. For the provenance analysis, all the clay samples were measured in loose clay format. The quantitative mineralogical composition of the samples analysed by XRD is shown in Table S1. This analysis was carried out using a reflectance powder method. The reflective factors have been taken from some specialist authors such as Schultz (1964) and Barahona (1974).

The analysis by TLP was performed in the HSC (Human Science Complex) of the University of Toronto. The samples were cut using pliers, placed in sample cups, and heated up to 50 °C in a drying oven until the samples were completely dry. Afterwards, an EpoFix epoxy was added to the cup and, immediately, the cup was placed again in the drying oven for 2 minutes. The samples were transferred to a vacuum chamber and the air inside the epoxy was removed through several vacuum cycles at 800 mbar. The samples were then heated in the oven at 35 °C for 24 hours and removed from the sample cups. A razor blade was used to cut the sample with the epoxy and, after optimization, it was placed between two glass slides using UV curing glue (Loctite 358 Adhesive IDH No.135414). A polarizing transmitted light microscope (Nikon Photolab 2 POL) was used to analyse the sample. In Fig. S1 some examples of the observations with the microscope are presented.

2.2. *Thermal analysis*

As ceramics are being manufactured, the clay undergoes some changes in its structure during the firing process. For example, there is a dilatation process of the mineral particles. If the changes in the dilatation are measured, it is possible to know the temperature at which the ceramics was baked. In this work, a dilatometer (Misura ODHT 1400 50) located in the AITEMIN Technological Centre (Toledo, Spain) was used. This equipment measures the length variation as a function of temperature for a ceramic sample. The only preparation of the sample required was to have it cut in a cylindrical shape to fit in the instrument. Diagrams like the ones shown in Fig. S2 were obtained with this technique.

2.3. *Chemical analysis*

An X-Ray Fluorescence spectrometer (Philips MagiX PRO) located in IRICA (Instituto Regional de Investigación Científica Aplicada, University of Castilla-La Mancha, Spain) was used to analyse the chemical composition of the ceramic and the clay samples. A pre-treatment of the sample was carried out before the analysis with the spectrometer. First, it was ground to a diameter less than 53 µm (36 µm for the trace analysis). Then, 2 ml of a solution of n-butyl methacrylate in acetone (5%) were added to 8 g of the ground sample and they were well mixed then left to dry until the solvent was evaporated. Boric acid was added to the sample and a tablet 4-mm width was made with the mixture using a 200kN press during 30 s. This tablet was finally introduced in the instrument. Two kind of measurements were done: semi-quantitative (XRF) and trace analysis (XRF-t). The first made possible to detect the oxides of all the possible elements, giving a result in percentage (%). The second analysis only detected 27 programmed elements and the results were given in parts per million (ppm).

A basic statistical analysis was performed to compare the chemical composition of the different samples. The elemental information obtained by XRF

(Table S2) and XRF-t (Table S3) for each ceramic sample was divided by the same elemental information for the clay. The closer the result of the ratio is to 1, the more similar the composition of that element is for the two samples. Finally, for each ceramic sample, an average was done considering the results of the division carried out for each element. Again, if the ratio is close to 1, the ceramic sample will share more chemical features with the clay, and there will be higher probability that the ceramics were made using that clay.

3. RESULTS AND DISCUSSION

3.1. *El Cerameño and its cemetery*

El Cerameño (Herrería, Guadalajara) is a small hillfort located on a hilltop near to Saúco River (Fig. 1-A). Two very well differenced occupational levels have been documented: Cerameño I (Early Iron Age, 7th-6th centuries cal. BC) and Cerameño II (Middle Iron Age, 5th century cal. BC). Due to the obtained archaeological information, this archaeological site is considered to be one of the most significant Celtiberian sites in the recent years (Fig. 2), becoming a representative site of the Celtic Hispania in the recently opened remodelled Spanish National Archaeological Museum. From the point of view of the ceramic materials, it is important to emphasize that the majority of the ceramics from the first occupational level (Cerameño I) were handmade. Ceramics produced using a wheel were in minority proportion, considered to be imported ceramic from the Eastern Iberian culture (Cerdeño and Juez, 2002: 77-78). On the other hand, in the second occupational level (Cerameño II), the amount of handmade ceramic decreased whereas wheel ceramic became the principal ceramic production in the hillfort.

The land surrounding the site is very clayey, specifically ferruginous, with clays of good quality and suitable for ceramic production. Six ceramic samples were collected from the site (2 handmade and 4 wheel) from the two occupational levels (Table 1). In addition to this, a clay sample (sample 18) was collected from the surroundings of the hillfort to determine the mineralogical and chemical similarities to the selected ceramics. The appearance of the clay was reddish, very rich in iron oxides and composed by small and hard blocks. Furthermore, some ceramic samples were gathered from the Herrería cemetery, very close to El Cerameño, because its occupational levels III and IV were contemporary to the two levels of the hillfort. The main goal of the analysis was to determine if the origin of the ceramics was local or foreign for El Cerameño and its cemetery.

Figure 2. Aerial picture of El Cerameño hillfort.

When the samples were mineralogically analysed by XRD (Fig. 3-A), it was found that all of them contained illite. This mineral is a phyllosilicate (or laminar), very similar to muscovite, and it was found to be abundant in all samples, except in sample 5, in which there were only traces of this material. It is interesting to point out that, in the diffractogram, the peak that corresponded to illite was shifted in samples 5 and 6 of Cerameño II and sample 3 of Cerameño I. This is related with the granulometry, i.e. the grind made to the clay in the ceramic production. In this particular case, the shift indicates that it was much depurated, in agreement with the clay used in wheel ceramics.

The most remarkable feature of the clay sample (sample 18) is the presence of kaolinite. This is a two-layer phyllosilicate clay mineral that was not found in any ceramic sample. This might question if the ceramics had the same mineralogical origin than the clay. However, kaolinite disappears at temperatures higher than 550ºC which is its thermal deshydroxylation point (the dilatometry shows the firing temperature in all of the ceramic samples are over 700ºC). For that reason, according to the XRD, the ceramics reached this thermal deshydroxylation point of the kaolinite during the firing process, what would explain the absence of this mineral in the ceramic samples despite its presence in the clay. However, the melting point of illite is circ. 900ºC (the thermal deshydroxylation point of the illite is at 700ºC, but the mineral maintains the crystalline structure), so its presence in El Cerемеño ceramics indicate that the firing process was carried out between 550 and 900ºC. This is supported by the dilatogram of sample 1 (Fig. S2), in which the measured firing temperature was between 850 and 875ºC.

The samples from the cemetery of Herrería were also analysed (Table 1). The diffractogram (Fig. 3-B) showed again that the ceramics and the clay were very similar. It must be pointed out that samples 8 and 9, in contrast with the clay, did not present illite, because during the firing process the temperature was higher than 900ºC. On the other hand, in the diffractogram of sample 7 there was a clear peak corresponding to that mineral. As can be seen in the dilatometry results (see Fig. S2), it is confirmed that firing temperature for sample 9 was between 1000 and 1050ºC, whereas for sample 7, it was between 700 and 750ºC, explaining the presence of illite in this sample. Sample 7 also contained calcite and dolomite, which are two minerals that were not found in the rest of the ceramic samples. There are two hypotheses that can explain this: either the ceramic was not produced from the analysed clay (sample 18), or these minerals were secondary depositions, considering that clay and ceramic are mineralogically similar enough.

From the mineralogical point of view, all the samples are similar as confirmed by the diffractograms. This similarity between the samples might indicate that the ceramics were made with clay from the surroundings of the hillfort, and that El Ceremeño was a local ceramics producer. However, since quartz, feldspar, and phyllosilicates are very abundant in nature, they do not fully confirm that the ceramics were made with that clay. To confirm this, it was necessary to perform the chemical analysis by XRF and XRF-t proposed in this work.

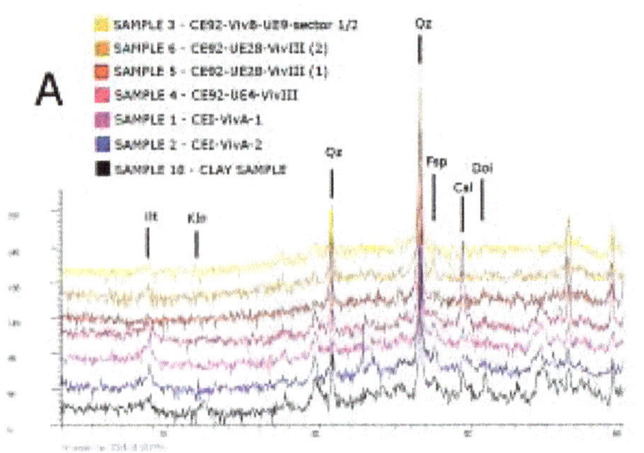

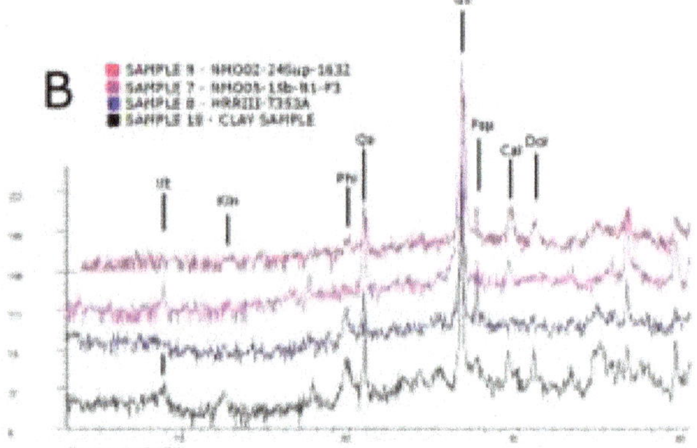

Figure 3. XRD diffractograms showing the comparison between the clay and the ceramics from (A) El Ceremeño and (B) the cemetery of Herrería.

Chemical Analysis by XRF and XRF-t was carried out to evaluate the similarities between the selected samples. From pre-stablished chemical elements detected by the instrument, it was possible to know the chemical composition of the samples. The XRD study showed several similarities between ceramics and clay from the mineralogical point of view. In this section, the chemical analysis can confirm these aspects.

It is very important to take into account that the chemical composition in nature is not homogenous, i.e. the percentage of each element found in all the samples will not be exactly the same. Ceramics can suffer some alterations in the composition during the fabrication process: when tempers are added, due to washing and firing processes, and even if different clays are mixed. Clay can also suffer contamination (due to farming), runoff, etc. that could modify its chemical composition. Therefore, the accuracy when comparing ceramics and clay is not so important. We only have to take into account what elements were similar in amount and in which proportion they were close.

Trace elements analysis

The results obtained by this technique following the statistical analysis (see Methodology section) are shown in Table 2. The only element with a ratio significantly greater than 1 was cesium, Cs, with a ratio greater than 2 in samples 3 and 6, and greater than 3 in samples 1 and 9. This indicated that the ceramics contained more Cs than the clay, but this does not necessarily mean that the clay was not used to make those ceramics, as it is discussed below. All the ceramic samples showed similar proportions of Cs (see Table S3), suggesting that they shared the same origin and fabrication process.

For other chemical elements, the calculated ratios were close to 1, except for some elements, such as, barium, (Ba), lead, (Pb), thorium, (Th), tungsten, (W), and cerium, (Ce). Sample 9, the cemetery ceramic sample, was the most chemically different sample. In this particular case, there was a high ratio, over 3, of Ce and neodymium, Nd. Only the average of ratios could indicate the degree of similarity between the ceramics and the clay. As we can observe in Table 2, the determined averages were very similar between all the ceramics. The average in all the hillfort samples was between 1.2 and 1.3, except for sample 9 (Herrería IV) that was 1.6, being slightly different.

In summary, the resulting averages obtained by XRF-t indicated that the ceramics of El Cerameño and Herrería have high possibilities of coming from El Cerameño clay (or some other similar clay from the surroundings). As we have seen, the only sample that deviated from the expected ratio of 1 was the ceramic from the cemetery. However, its average (1.6) is not significantly different from the other hillfort samples to consider a foreign production, which is the reason why, although numerically it has a higher ratio, it could also be considered as a local ceramic.

Table 2. Comparison ratios between the results obtained by XRF-t for the ceramics from El Cerameño and Herrería and the clay from the hillforts surroundings.

Sample	1	3	4	5	6	9
Sc	0.97	1.30	1.02	1.02	0.92	1.42
V	1.02	0.80	0.93	0.77	0.76	0.84
Cr	1.10	0.92	1.15	0.84	0.68	0.80
Co	1.31	0.66	1.13	0.76	0.12	0.94
Ni	1.03	0.39	1.17	0.45	0.17	0.66
Cu	1.81	0.73	1.65	0.71	0.51	0.73
Zn	1.61	0.63	1.88	0.80	0.54	0.69
Ga	1.22	1.73	0.99	1.39	1.50	1.48
As	1.40	0.70	0.94	0.63	0.57	0.47
Rb	1.38	1.32	1.16	1.06	1.35	1.43
Sr	0.59	0.19	0.24	0.24	0.18	0.11
Y	1.13	1.06	1.20	1.82	1	2.54
Zr	0.87	1.51	1.12	1.87	1.79	1.29
Nb	1.06	1.50	1.06	1.52	1.33	1.39
Mo	0.90	---	0.81	0.45	---	---
Sn	---	---	---	---	---	---
Cs	3.04	2.51	1.64	1.90	2.45	3.41
Ba	1.85	1.04	2.15	0.83	0.81	0.53
La	1.17	1.15	0.98	1.46	2.02	2.60
Ce	0.98	0.94	0.90	1.42	1.63	3.10
Hf	1	1.86	1.37	2.11	2.48	1.57
Ta	---	---	---	---	---	---
W	1.16	2.20	1.04	2.64	2.48	3.16
Pb	2.55	2.52	2.16	2.55	4.14	2.38
Th	1.18	2.13	1.57	2.18	2.56	2.11
U	1.75	1.66	1.95	1.70	1.91	2.20
Nd	0.97	0.70	0.88	1.67	1	3.76
AVERAGE	**1.32**	**1.26**	**1.24**	**1.31**	**1.37**	**1.65**

Semi-quantitative analysis

The results of the XRF Semi-quantitative showed that, almost all the ceramic samples had a similar ratio between the concentration in the ceramic and the clay, ranging between 0.1 and 3.0 (Table 3). It is very significant that for Na_2O in sample 1 and CaO in sample 4, the ratio was higher than 2.0, which is far from our ideal ratio of 1. Surprisingly, CaO in the rest of samples showed a ratio much lower than 1. It is also noteworthy that MgO and SO_2 showed ratios always below 0.6 in all the samples.

Like in the Trace Elements analysis, the most interesting result is the average of the ratios for the different elements, which ultimately indicates if the ceramics and the clay were similar or not. Based on the Trace Elements results, sample 4 (with a ratio of 0.98) was the most likely ceramic to be made from the analysed clay. The other ceramics varied slightly from our ideal ratio of 1, with low probabilities of coming from the clay. Samples 3, 5, 6 and 9 presented ratios higher than 0.7, but sample 1, the handmade ceramic, showed an average of 1.23. It is interesting that this value was very similar to that obtained by XRF-t, which suggests that its origin was from the analysed clay or from the surrounding area.

Table 3. Comparison ratios between the results obtained by XRF for the ceramics from El Ceremeño and Herrería and the clay from the hillforts surroundings.

Sample	1	3	4	5	6	9
Na_2O	2.96	1.25	0.65	0.79	1.44	1.17
MgO	0.59	0.17	0.42	0.16	0.17	0.17
Al_2O_3	0.81	1.51	1.05	1.39	1.64	1.57
SiO_2	1.03	1.09	0.92	1.29	1.27	1.23
P_2O_5	2.49	0.48	1.43	0.66	0.62	0.59
SO_3	0.43	0.13	0.46	0.21	0.57	0.14
K_2O	1.18	0.54	0.69	0.49	0.60	0.70
CaO	0.64	0.19	2.39	0.48	0.16	0.16
TiO_2	0.98	1.15	1.04	1.41	1.04	1.28
Fe_2O_3	1.13	0.58	0.70	0.64	0.44	0.68
AVERAGE	**1.23**	**0.71**	**0.98**	**0.75**	**0.80**	**0.78**

We can conclude from the chemical analysis of the ceramics and the clay from El Ceremeño and its cemetery that all the ceramics were locally produced, since the average ratios are close to our ideal value of 1. The mineralogical composition was also very similar when the ceramics and the clay were compared, which corroborated the hypothesis that they had a local origin.

Previous studies discussed the presence of the wheel ceramic in the first stages of the Iron Age in the Spanish Central Plateau, because this type of ceramic was considered a very novel artefact that could indicate that there were contacts between Celtiberi and the Iberian people from the Levant (Cerdeño y Juez, 2002: 77-78). Therefore, until now, the wheel ceramic was considered to be imported, whereas the handmade ceramics were thought to be locally produced. Since we observed a great similarity in the composition between the handmade and the wheel made ceramics from El Ceremeño I, we can conclude that all these ceramics were produced using the clay from the surroundings of El Ceremeño, either in the hillfort, or in an unknown potter's workshop close to the hillfort. This hypothesis is confirmed when the ceramics from El Ceremeño I and El Ceremeño II were compared and found to be similar, since the latter had always been considered to be locally made. The same conclusion can be deduced with the ceramics from the cemetery. Since these samples were mineralogically similar, we believe that they could have been produced using clay from the surroundings.

The present study showed, for the first time, that the ceramics from El Ceremeño I were made with local clay. This analysis would indicate that the potter's wheel arrived to the Spanish Central Plateau between the 7th and 6th centuries BC. Although in this work it was possible to establish some hypothesis about the origin of the production of the ceramics, it has to be pointed out that the number of samples used in this work was limited, so more analysis should be done in the future with a greater number of samples of ceramics and clays. This work can be considered as the key for further studies related to this hypothesis.

3.2. *Los Rodiles*

The Celtiberian Los Rodiles *oppidum* is a good example of the final stages of the Celtiberian culture (Fig. 4) at Late Iron Age. Similarly to the previous study, the ceramic characterization was focused on the mineralogical and chemical analysis of some ceramic samples from the two occupational levels (see Table 1): Rodiles I (3rd-½2nd centuries cal. BC) and Rodiles II (½2nd-1st centuries cal. BC). Due to the size of this archaeological site, we aimed to determine if the *oppidum* was a ceramic production centre. For this reason, we collected a clay sample from the riverbank near the site (see Fig. 1-B). The appearance of this clay was very similar to the clay from El Ceremeño, with a reddish colour typical of ferruginous clays.

Clay from La Rodriga potter's workshop (Fuentelsaz, Guadalajara) was also collected since it is located 15 km from the site and it is dated between 3rd-2nd centuries BC (Arenas, 1991-92: 225), similar chronology to Los Rodiles archaeological site. This clay had a very good quality and it was ideal for the ceramic production. The clay was sedimentary, originated in the Jurassic and Cretaceous, and composed by dolomites, loams and limestone. In fact, it was completely different from Los Rodiles clay. The clay from La Rodriga was grey coloured since it contained more calcium carbonate. Clay was collected from three different points in a location known as Fuente de Rodriga (Fig. 1-C), that is 800 m from the potter's workshop. Some ceramics were found in this site, and they were studied from a mineralogical and chemical point of view (Igea et al. 2008). These authors reported great compositional similarities between the samples, showing that it was possible that they share the same origin. In the present work, we compared the ceramics of Los Rodiles with the clays collected near the archaeological site and in the potter's workshop to determine if there was any correspondence between the samples.

Figure 4. Aerial picture of Los Rodiles.

The results obtained in the mineralogical analysis by TLP and XRD were very interesting. The ceramic samples from Los Rodiles presented mineralogical similarities with the two clays analysed: from the site and from the potter's workshop. All of them contained minerals typically found in nature, such as quartz and muscovite.

Unlike XRD, using TLP is possible to observe non crystalline elements or the porosity of the ceramic paste. In that sense, it is interesting to highlight that sample 10 from Rodiles I was found to contain, other abundant minerals such as quartz and phyllosilicates, grog and basalt as tempers, and that the ceramic had great porosity. The presence of porosity and tempers may be have been intentional because a very porous ceramic creates a humid environment that is ideal for storage. In the case of sample 10, since it was handmade ceramic, it was probably used for cooking purposes. This was corroborated by the fact that it contained abundant tempers that reduced the thermal shock when the ceramic was placed in the kiln.

The rest of samples, which were wheel made, were analysed either by TLP (see Fig. S1), or XRD (see Table S1). The results obtained by both techniques showed negligible differences in the mineral composition. All these samples presented high levels of quartz, calcites (micrites), feldspars and silicates (muscovite and illite). In particular illite was found to be very abundant in all the samples. It is worth noting that in samples 12 and 16, the peak corresponding to illite in XRD was shifted when compared to the other samples (Fig. 3). The presence of this particular mineral indicated that the firing temperature was always below 950ºC. This was confirmed by the dilatometry assays on samples 12, 16 and 17 that showed a temperature range between 800 and 900ºC (see Fig. S2).

When the ceramics from Los Rodiles were compared with the clay from the surroundings of the site (Fig. 4-A), no kaolinite was observed in any sample. There are two hypothesis that can explain this: (1) the clay used to produce these ceramics was from Los Rodiles surroundings, or (2) the ceramics contained kaolinite initially but it disappeared when the temperature in the kiln reached the melting point of this mineral (550 ºC), a condition confirmed by dilatometry.

The ceramics were also compared to the three samples of clay from La Rodriga (see Fig. 4-B). In the diffractogram, a good similarity was observed between this clay and the clay from Los Rodiles: both presented high levels of quartz and feldspar. In La Rodriga clay samples, the major component was calcite and dolomite, although sample 20-2, which was collected at the riverbank, presented more carbonate than the other samples. Lower amounts of illite and phyllosilicate were observed in these clay samples than in the ceramics. Sample 20-1 presented kaolinite, which was negligible in the other clay samples.

From the mineralogical point of view, the ceramics presented significant similarities to Los Rodiles clay and the clay from the potter's workshop. However, this was not enough evidence to confidently state that the ceramics were locally produced, so we decided to conduct the chemical analysis to confirm the origin of these ceramics and to distinguish the provenance of the clay in the ceramic production.

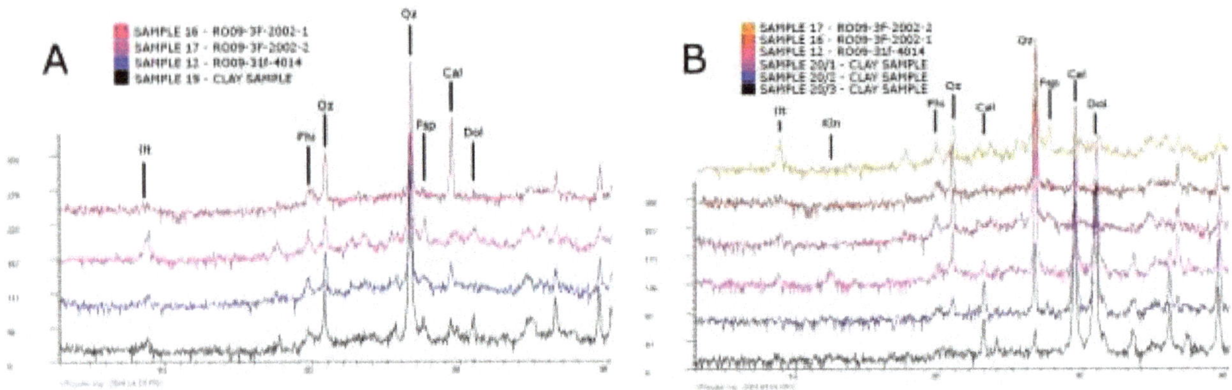

Figure 4. XRD diffractograms showing the comparison between the ceramics from Los Rodiles and the clay from (A) the hillfort surroundings and (B) La Rodriga potter's workshop.

In the chemical study of Los Rodiles samples, we applied the same statistical method used for El Cеremeño (see methodology): the ratio between the elemental results for the ceramics and the results for the different clays was determined, an average was reported, and then used to determine the degree of similarity between the samples.

Trace Elements

The ratios obtained when the ceramics were compared with the four available clays are presented in Table 4. In this table, a better agreement (i.e. the ratios are closer to 1) is observed when the ceramics are compared to Los Rodiles clay (sample 19). In this case for most of the elements, the ratio was around 1, except for rubidium, (Rb), Cs, zirconium, (Zr), W, Pb and Th, for which the ratio was higher than 2 in sample 16, and between 1.2 and 1.6 in sample 17. Gallium, (Ga), was also an exception since its ratio was approximately 2.4 in both samples.

When the ceramics were compared to La Rodriga clay, the ratio of each element was always further from 1, indicating less similarity between the samples. Better agreement was found when the samples were compared to clay 20-1, for which the ratios were closer to 1 for sample 16. The only two elements for which the ratios were much higher than 1 were Cs and barium, (Ba).

The resulting averages showed that the ratio between the ceramics and Los Rodiles clay was close to 1: 1.6 for sample 16 and 1.7 sample 17. This indicated that these samples were similar to Los Rodiles clay. On the other hand, the ratios from La Rodriga clays were further from 1. Sample 20/2 was the most similar to the ceramics, although its ratio was much higher than the result for Los Rodiles. The two other clays from La Rodriga, samples 20/1 and 20/3, presented final averages above 3.5 and 5, respectively. In summary, the results obtained by XRF-t suggest that the ceramics have a higher probability of being locally produced than coming from La Rodriga potter's workshop.

Table 4. Comparison ratios between the results obtained by XRF-t for the ceramics from Los Rodiles and the clay from different sources (Los Rodiles surroundings and La Rodriga potter's workshop).

Sample	16	17	16	17	16	17	16	17
Clay	Clay sample 19		Clay sample 20/1		Clay sample 20/2		Clay Sample 20/3	
Sc	1.44	1.74	2.27	2.74	1.17	1.41	3.40	4.11
V	1.40	2.25	4.05	6.51	1.93	3.10	5.56	8.92
Cr	1.12	1.74	2.82	4.38	2.13	3.32	3.11	4.83
Co	1.01	0.61	2.29	1.38	0.90	0.54	1.56	0.94
Ni	1.04	1.94	2.65	4.93	1.30	2.43	3.64	6.79
Cu	1.31	3.52	2.62	7.05	1.09	5.13	1.05	2.82
Zn	1.44	1.54	1.45	1.55	1.78	1.90	2.03	2.17
Ga	2.38	2.45	5.4	5.55	2.89	2.97	7.59	7.81
As	0.88	1.72	1.88	3.68	1.43	2.80	1.67	3.26
Rb	2.33	1.20	6.46	3.34	4.05	2.09	10.26	5.31
Sr	0.81	0.63	1.14	0.88	1.64	1.27	1.05	0.82
Y	1.79	1.17	3.20	2.09	1.68	1.10	5.22	3.40
Zr	2.52	1.65	5.33	3.5	1.76	1.16	14.48	9.51
Nb	2.01	1.62	2.97	2.40	2.11	1.71	3.76	3.05
Mo	0.5	3	0.6	3.6	0.75	4.5	0.27	1.63
Sn	---	---	---	---	---	---	---	---
Cs	0.79	0.87	---	---	4.17	4.58	---	---
Ba	1.57	6.10	5.82	22.55	4.28	16.57	8.14	31.51
La	1.62	1.36	5.82	4.84	1.89	1.59	6.25	5.25
Ce	1.53	1.01	5.37	3.57	2.08	1.38	6.39	4.25
Hf	2.02	1.25	4.57	2.84	1.58	0.98	6.69	4.15
Ta	---	---	14.5	2	---	---	9.66	1.33
W	2.73	1.46	1.64	0.88	2.73	1.46	10.25	5.5
Pb	2.01	1.44	0.67	0.48	1.53	1.09	0.87	0.62
Th	2.70	2.07	6.17	4.75	2.08	1.60	---	---
U	1.60	1.25	3.21	2.50	1.8	1.4	4.5	3.5
Nd	1.22	0.71	3.44	2.01	1.74	1.02	3.24	1.89
AVERAGE	**1.59**	**1.77**	**3.85**	**4**	**2.05**	**2.68**	**5.03**	**5.14**

Semi-quantitative

The analysis by XRF corroborated the results obtained by XRF-t (see Table 5). Similar to the results of trace elements analysis, the chemical composition of the ceramics is similar to Los Rodiles clay. The ratios for most of the elements remained around 1 only for the clay sample 19.

The same ceramic samples showed a lesser degree of similarity when compared to La Rodriga clay, as few compounds had a ratio close to 1. Some examples with ratios far from the ideal value 1 are Fe_2O_3 in sample 17 compared to clay 20/1 and 20/3, with values above 4, and Al_2O_3 and SiO_2 in samples 16 and 17 compared to clay samples 20/1 and 20/3, especially in the latter clay. For clay sample 20/2, ratios are closer to 1, but still far from this ideal value.

By considering at the averages obtained (last row in Table 5), it is concluded that the ceramics were more likely made with Los Rodiles clay (average = 0.9-1.1) than the clays from La Rodriga (average = 1.5-4.4), although sample 20/2 showed some similarities.

Table 5. Comparison ratios between the results obtained by XRF for the ceramics from Los Rodiles and the clay from different sources (Los Rodiles surroundings and La Rodriga potter's workshop).

Sample	16	17	16	17	16	17	16	17
Clay	Clay sample 19		Clay sample 20/1		Clay sample 20/2		Clay Sample 20/3	
Na_2O	1.12	0.94	2.53	2.12	2.02	1.7	2.31	1.94
MgO	0.52	0.53	0.35	0.36	0.32	0.33	0.31	0.32
Al_2O_3	1.56	1.55	4.16	4.13	1.90	1.89	5.70	5.66
SiO_2	0.95	0.8	4.66	3.90	2.15	1.80	9.22	7.73
P_2O_5	0.85	2.76	0.86	2.79	1.35	4.37	2.03	6.56
SO_3	0.17	0.20	0.10	0.12	0.3	0.34	0.006	0.007
K_2O	1.09	0.62	6.16	2.96	3.89	1.87	9.87	4.74
CaO	0.47	0.62	0.05	0.06	0.07	0.10	0.04	0.06
TiO_2	1.70	1.39	3.60	2.94	1.79	1.46	8.62	7.05
Fe_2O_3	1.01	1.92	3.95	7.51	1.43	2.72	5.45	10.34
AVERAGE	**0.94**	**1.12**	**2.64**	**2.69**	**1.52**	**1.66**	**4.35**	**4.44**

The obtained results suggested that the selected ceramics were more likely made of the clay from Los Rodiles surroundings due to the similarities observed for samples 16 and 17 from both the mineralogical and the chemical analysis perspectives. Although the results by XRF for sample 20/2 that showed possible similarities with the ceramics, the XRF-t analysis confirmed that it was very unlikely that the ceramics were made using clay from the potter's workshop area. According to the obtained results, the size and the magnitude of Los Rodiles, it is possible that the *oppidum* was a ceramic production centre.

All the ceramic samples from Los Rodiles were very interesting, but we would like to highlight two of them: the handmade ceramic (sample 10) that revealed exciting technological information as reported above, and the Roman black-glazed ceramic (sample 15) that presented a mineralogical composition very similar to rest of the analysed ceramics that were Celtiberian. This may confirm that black-glazed ceramic was really a local production (showing all the same origin), being an interesting case of imitation of Roman production.

4. CONCLUSIONS

The samples analysed in this work established provisional conclusions about the origin of the ceramic production in the evaluated archaeological sites. The diffractograms made it possible to observe great mineralogical similarities between the ceramics and the clays from the surroundings. Due to the crystalline elements of the ceramics samples and clays are very common in nature, the most relevant results were obtained by XRF and XRD.

The chemical composition varied among the samples, which was useful in determining the origin of the ceramics. The chemical composition showed significant differences between La Rodriga clay and the clays from El Ceremeño and Los Rodiles (these two were found to be mineralogically and chemically very similar). These differences were clearly observed in their appearance since clays from El Ceremeño and Los Rodiles were reddish coloured because of their high level of iron oxides, whereas La Rodriga clay was grey coloured due to the presence of calcium carbonate. For the ceramics, all of them were found to be similar in composition and to have a local origin, as they were made with clays from the surroundings and distributed later to different hillforts. This fact was most evident in the case of Los Rodiles.

El Ceremeño site and its cemetery were the most interesting examples of ceramics that were closely related to the clay of the surroundings. In both occupational levels, we found a compositional correspondence between handmade and wheel made ceramics. This, together with the similarities with the clay, indicated that the potter's wheel should have arrived in the Spanish Central Plateau earlier than researchers previously suspected, i.e. in the Early Iron Age (7th-6th centuries BC).

Moreover, this work shows for the first time that ceramics were produced imitating Iberian ceramics which confirmed the exchange of craft techniques or, according to Miller, "cross-crafts" (Miller, 2007: 237). The same can be said for the black-glazed ceramic found in Los Rodiles, which showed a similar mineralogical composition than the other ceramics found in the site.

Other relevant information obtained in this work was the related to the technological purposes of the ceramics, such as the handmade ceramic of Los Rodiles (sample 10). This sample showed the intentional addition of tempers to the clay that could be related to its thermal shock resistance. This fact confirmed its use as cooking pottery.

As shown above, the results obtained in this work were interesting and they encourage us to work in this direction in the future by analysing a greater number of samples. This will make it possible to confirm the hypotheses presented in this work with greater confidence. With this study we intended to improve the characterization studies of the Celtiberian ceramics that until now were not well studied.

ACKNOWLEDGEMENTS

This work could not be possible without the collaboration of several colleagues and friends. We would like to thank Prof. Heather M.-L. Miller and Dr. Greg Braun from the Anthropology Department at University of Toronto (Canada) for their assistance during the preparation of the TLP of some ceramic samples from Los Rodiles. We want also to thank Jorge Velasco from AITEMIN Technological Centre of Toledo (Spain) for the DLT applied to several ceramic samples. Also we would like to thank Carlos Cabanillas, laboratory technician at Instituto Regional de Investigación Científica Aplicada (IRICA) of University of Castilla-La Mancha (Spain) for his assistance during the analysis by XRD and XRF. Finally, we appreciate the collaboration of María Antiñolo and Katie Badali for their assistance in the elaboration and English translation of the paper.

REFERENCES

Barahona-Fernández, E. (1974) *Arcillas de ladrillería de la Provincia de Granada: evaluación de algunos ensayos de materias primas.* Granada: Servicio de Publicaciones de la Universidad de Granada. Doctoral Thesis.

Capel, J. (1999) Arqueometría y Arqueología. *I Congreso Nacional de Arqueometría.* Granada: Universidad de Granada.

Cordero, T., García San Juan, L., Hurtado, V., Martín, J.M., Polvorinos del Río, A. and Taylor, R. (2006) La arqueometría de materiales cerámicos. Una evaluación de la experiencia andaluza. *Trabajos de Prehistoria,* 63 (1), pp. 9-35.

Cerdeño, M.L., Sagardoy, T., Chordá, M. and Gamo, E. (2008) Fortificaciones celtibéricas frente a Roma: el *oppidum* de Los Rodiles (Cubillejo de la Sierra, Guadalajara). *Complutum,* 19, pp. 173-189.

Cerdeño, M.L. and Juez, P. (2002) *El castro celtibérico de El Ceremeño (Herrería, Guadalajara).* Teruel: Monografías Arqueológicas del SAET, 8, p. 183.

García-Heras, M. (1994) El yacimiento celtibérico de Izana (Soria): un modelo de producción cerámica. *Zephyrus, XLVII,* pp. 133-155.

García-Heras, M. (1999a) Estudios arqueométricos sobre materiales cerámicos de la Edad del Hierro. *Boletín de la Sociedad Española de Cerámica y Vidrio, 38 (4),* pp. 289-295.

García-Heras, M. (1999b) Primeros resultados de la caracterización arqueométrica de la cerámica numantina del s. I a.C. *Caesaragusta, 73,* pp. 59-66.

García-Heras, M. (2003a) Malos tiempos para la lírica. ¿Hay todavía un futuro para la Arqueología Científica en la universidad española? *Complutum,* 14, pp. 7-18.

García-Heras, M. (2003b): *Caracterización Arqueométrica de la Producción Cerámica Numantina.* Madrid: Universidad Complutense de Madrid.

González, M., González, M.C., García, M. and Arenas, J.A. (1999) La caracterización de los materiales cerámicos del yacimiento celtibérico de 'El Palomar' (Aragoncillo, Guadalajara) in Capel, J. (coord.) *Arqueometría y Arqueología.* Granada: Universidad de Granada.

Igea, J.; Lapuente, P., Saiz, M.E., Burillo, F., Bastida, J. and Pérez-Arantegui, J. (2008) Estudio arqueométrico de cerámicas procedentes de cinco alfares celtibéricos del sistema ibérico central. *Boetín de la Sociedad Española de Cerámica y Vidrio. 47 (1),* pp. 44-55.

Jorge, A., Dias. M.I. and Day, P.M. (2013) Plain Pottery and Social Landsacpes: Reinterpreting the Significance of Ceramic Provenance in Neolithic. *Archaeometry,* 55 (5), pp. 825-851.

Krueger, M. and Brandherm, D. (2016) Early Iron Age Pottery in South-Western Iberia: Archaeometry and Chronology in Delfino, D., Piccardo, P. and Baptista, J.C. (eds.) *Networks of Trade in Raw Materials and Technological Innovations in Prehistory and Protohistory: An Archaeometric Approach. Proceedings of the XVII UISPP World Congress (1-7 September 2014, Burgos, Spain). Vol. 12/Session B34. Oxford: Archaeopress,* pp. 95-103.

Marghussian, A.K., Coningham, R.A.E. and Fazeli, H. (2017) The Evolution of Pottery Production during the Late Neolithic Period at Sialk on the Kashan Plain, Central Plateau of Iran. *Archaometry,* 59 (2), pp. 222-238.

Mazarakis, A. and Vlachou, V. (2014) Archaeometric Analysis of Early Iron Age Pottery Samples from Oropos: Local or Euboean Production? in Kerschner, M. and Lemos, I.S. (eds.) *Archaeometric Analyses of Euboean and Euboean Related Pottery: New Results and Their Interpretations.* Vienna: Österreichisches Archäologisches Institut Wien, pp. 95-107.

Miller, H. M.-L. (2007) *Archaeological Approaches to Technology.* San Diego: Elsevier.

Montero, I., García Heras, M. and López-Romero, E. (2007) Arqueometría: cambios y tendencias actuales. *Trabajos de Prehistoria,* vol. 64 (1), pp. 23-40.

Nagwa. S. Abdel Rahim (2016) Analytical study and conservation of archaeological terra sigillata ware from roman period, Tripoli, Libya. *SCIENTIFIC CULTURE,* Vol. 2, No 2, pp. 19-27 (DOI: 10.5281/zenodo.44896)

De Soto, M.R., De Soto, I.S. and Garcia, R. (2014) Archaeometrical Study of Second Iron Age Ceramics from the Northwestern of the Iberian Peninsula. *Mediterranean Archaeology and Archaeometry (MAA),* vol. 14 (1), pp. 143-153.

Rovira, S. Montero, I. and Gómez, P. (2002) Metalurgia celtibérica en el poblado de El Ceremeño (Guadalajara) in Cerdeño, M.L. and Juez, P. *El Castro Celtibérico de El Ceremeño (Herrería, Guadalajara).* Teruel: Monografías arqueológicas del SAET.

Sáiz, M.E., Burillo, F., Igea, J., Lapuente, P. and Pérez-Arantegui, J. (2009) Caracterización de los materiales cerámicos de alfares de época celtibérica del Sistema Ibérico Central in Saiz, M.E., López, R., Cano, M.A., Calvo, J.C. (coords.) Actas VIII Congreso Ibérico de Arqueometría. Teruel: SAET, 37-48.

Sánchez-Climent, A. (2015) *La cerámica celtibérica meseteña: tipología, metodología e interpretación cultural.* Madrid: University Complutense of Madrid. Unpublished Doctoral Thesis.

Schultz, L.G. (1964) Quantitative Interpretation of Mineralogical Composition from X-Ray and Chemical Data for the Pierre Shale, US Geological Survey, Professional Paper 391-C. Washington: United States Government Printing Office, p. 31.

Zeinab Javanshah (2018) Chemical and mineralogical analysis for provenancing of the Bronze Age pottery from shahr-i-sokhta, south eastern Iran. *SCIENTIFIC CULTURE,* Vol. 4, No 1, pp. 83-92 *(DOI: 10.5281/zenodo.1048247)*

SUPLEMENTARY INFORMATION

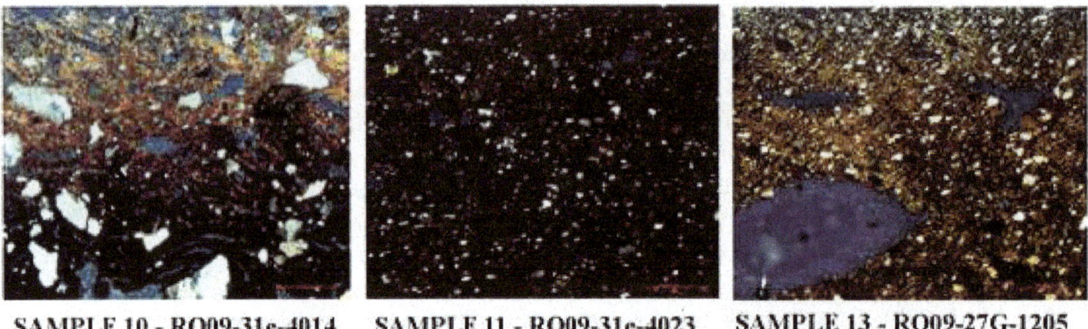

SAMPLE 10 - RO09-31e-4014 SAMPLE 11 - RO09-31e-4023 SAMPLE 13 - RO09-27G-1205

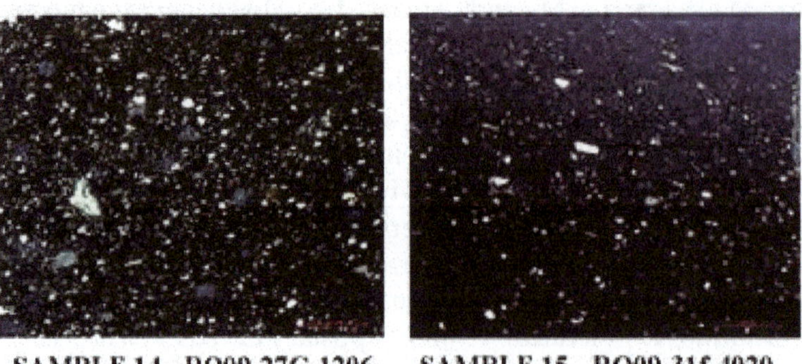

SAMPLE 14 - RO09-27G-1206 SAMPLE 15 - RO09-31f-4020

Figure S1. Pictures obtained by TLP. Samples from Los Rodiles hillfort.

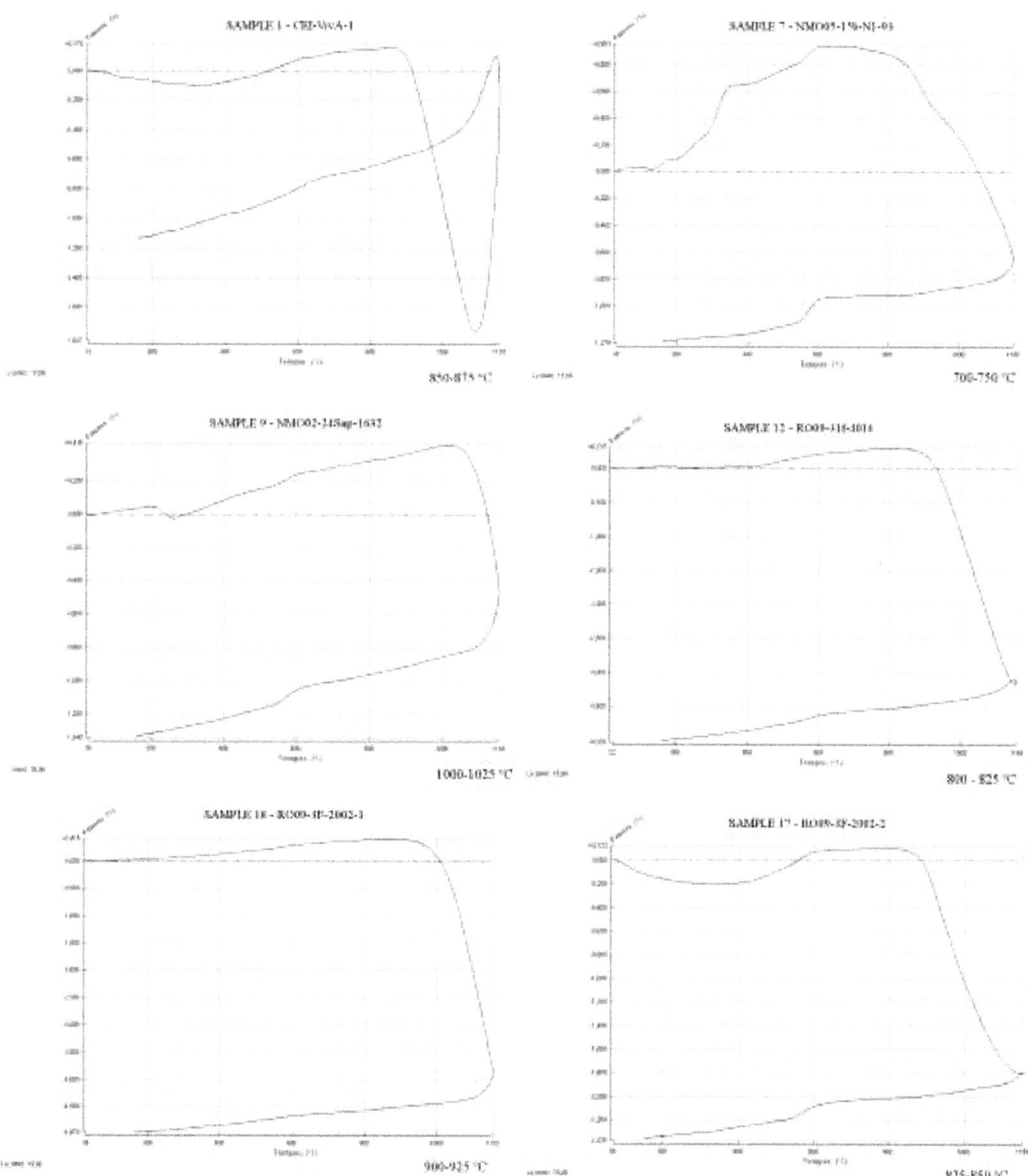

Figure S2. Pictures obtained by DLT. Samples from Los Rodiles hillfort.

Table S1. Mineralogical composition obtained by XRD (expressed in %).

Sample	Qz	Fsp	Calc	Dol	Hem	Phyllos	Ilt	Kln
1	8	7	traces	---	---	85	X	---
2	8	7	---	---	---	85	X	---
3	100	traces	---	---	---	traces	X	---
4	100	traces	---	---	---	traces	X	---
5	100	traces	---	---	---	traces	X	---
6	100	traces	---	---	---	traces	X	---
7	7	10	8	10	---	65	X	---
8	8	7	traces	---	---	80	X	---
9	75	---	25	---	---	traces	X	---
12	10	8	7	---	---	75	X	---
16	10	10	---	---	---	80	X	---
17	10	5	15	---	---	70	X	---
18	<5	<5	<5	traces	---	90	X	X
19	8	traces	15	22	traces	54	X	X
20/1	7	traces	35	50	traces	54	X	X
20/2	7	---	40	53	traces	traces	X	X
20/3	5	<5	18	17	6	50	X	X

Qz: quartz; Fsp: feldspar; Calc: calcite; Dol: dolomite; Hem: hematite; Phyllos: phyllosilicates; Ilt: illite; Kln: kaolinite.

Table S2. Chemical composition of mayor elements (expressed in % oxide).

Sample	1	3	4	5	6	9	16	17	18	19	20/1	20/2	20/3
Na_2O	< 0.5	< 0.5	< 0.5	< 0.5	< 0.5	< 0.5	< 0.5	< 0.5	< 0.5	< 0.5	< 0.5	< 0.5	< 0.5
MgO	2.8	0.83	2	0.7	0.8	0.8	1	1	4.7	2	3	3.2	3.3
Al_2O_3	13.6	25.3	17.5	23.3	27.3	26.3	21.1	21	16.6	13.5	5	11.1	3.7
SiO_2	50.7	53.6	45.2	63.1	62.1	60.4	62	52	48.8	65	13.3	28.8	6.7
P_2O_5	< 0.5	< 0.5	< 0.5	< 0.5	< 0.5	< 0.5	< 0.5	< 0.5	< 0.5	< 0.5	< 0.5	< 0.5	< 0.5
SO_3	< 0.5	< 0.5	< 0.5	< 0.5	< 0.5	< 0.5	< 0.5	< 0.5	< 0.5	< 0.5	< 0.5	< 0.5	6.7
K_2O	5.4	2.4	3.1	2.2	2.7	3.2	4.6	2.2	4.5	4.2	0.7	1.1	0.4
CaO	2.9	0.8	10.9	2.1	0.7	0.7	1.7	2.3	4.5	3.8	34.1	22.8	39.1
TiO_2	0.8	0.9	0.9	1.2	0.9	1.1	0.8	0.7	0.8	0.5	< 0.5	< 0.5	< 0.5
Fe_2O_3	7.4	3.8	4.6	4.2	2.9	4.4	3.9	7.4	6.5	3.8	0.9	2.7	0.7
LOI	8.7	11.4	14.4	2.4	1.8	2.3	3.9	11.8	12.4	6	41.6	29.2	45.3

Table S3. Chemical composition of trace elements (expressed in ppm).

Sample	Error	1	3	4	5	6	9	16	17	18	19	20/1	20/2	20/3
Sc	± 0.00017	17.1	22.8	18	17.9	16.1	24.9	14.3	17.3	17.5	9.9	6.3	12.2	4.2
V	± 0.00086	115.6	90.9	106.2	87.9	86.6	96.1	84	134.8	113.3	59.7	20.7	43.4	15.1
Cr	± 0.00053	80.2	66.8	83.9	61.1	49.6	58.3	55.4	86	72.6	49.2	19.6	25.9	17.8
Co	± 0.00011	17.3	8.8	15	10.1	1.6	12.5	7.8	4.7	13.2	7.7	3.4	8.6	5
Ni	± 0.00164	48.4	18.6	54.5	21.1	7.9	31	17.5	32.6	46.6	16.8	6.6	13.4	4.8
Cu	± 0.00046	41.4	16.6	37.4	16.1	11.6	16.5	18.9	50.8	22.6	14.4	7.2	9.9	18
Zn	± 0.00086	87.3	34.5	101.7	43.3	29.5	37.8	42	44.8	54.1	29	28.8	23.5	20.6
Ga	± 0.00036	24.4	34.6	19.8	27.8	30	29.6	24.3	25	19.9	10.2	4.5	8.4	3.2
As	± 0.00037	28	14.1	18.7	12.7	11.5	9.5	16.2	31.7	19.9	18.4	8.6	11.3	9.7
Rb	± 0.00048	150.6	143.8	126.6	115.8	147.6	155.9	176.6	91.4	108.7	75.8	27.3	43.6	17.2
Sr	± 0.00246	314.3	100.1	127	127.4	94.6	60.7	136	105.6	525.5	166.5	119.3	82.8	128.8
Y	± 0.00021	29.5	27.6	31.2	47.2	26	65.8	28.2	18.4	25.9	15.7	8.8	16.7	5.4
Zr	± 0.00112	158.9	274	203.7	338.7	325.1	233.6	286.8	188.3	180.9	113.7	53.8	162.1	19.8
Nb	± 0.00055	18.6	26.3	18.7	26.7	23.4	24.4	21.1	17.1	17.5	10.5	7.1	10	5.6
Mo	± 0.00006	1	n.d.	0.9	0.5	n.d.	n.d.	0.3	1.8	1.1	0.6	0.5	0.4	1.1
Sn	± 0.00012	1.1	6.1	n.d.	5.3	7.5	4.6	2.6	0.4	n.d.	n.d.	n.d.	n.d.	n.d.
Cs	± 0.00049	18.9	15.6	10.2	11.8	15.2	21.2	12.1	13.3	6.2	15.2	n.d.	2.9	n.d.
Ba	± 0.00147	1043.7	587.5	1216.2	472.6	456.6	299.6	563.7	218.1	563.6	357.3	96.7	131.6	69.2
La	± 0.00127	52.7	51.8	44.2	65.9	91.3	117.3	50.7	42.6	45	31.3	8.8	26.8	8.1
Ce	± 0.00146	81.7	78.4	75.2	118.3	136.4	258.6	81.2	54	83.3	53	15.1	39	12.7
Hf	± 0.00011	4.5	8.4	6.2	9.5	11.2	7.1	8.7	5.4	4.5	4.3	1.9	5.5	1.3
Ta	± 0.00015	0.1	3.4	2.1	3.2	2.8	3.1	2.9	0.4	n.d.	n.d.	0.2	n.d.	0.3
W	±0.00037	2.9	5.5	2.6	6.6	6.2	7.9	4.1	2.2	2.5	1.5	2.5	1.5	0.4
Pb	± 1.65604	29.9	29.5	25.3	29.9	48.5	27.9	25.6	18.3	11.7	12.7	37.8	16.7	29.2
Th	± 0.00018	11.1	20.1	14.8	20.5	24.1	19.9	17.3	13.3	9.4	6.4	2.8	8.3	n.d.
U	± 0.00013	4.2	4	4.7	4.1	4.6	5.3	4.5	3.5	2.4	2.8	1.4	2.5	1
Nd	± 0.00072	36.2	26.2	32.8	62.3	37.4	140.2	33.4	19.5	37.2	27.2	9.7	19.1	10.3

n.d. Not detected

7

ENTANGLED WORLDS: MATERIALITY, ARCHAEOMETRY AND MEDITERRANEAN-ATLANTIC IDENTITIES IN WESTERN IBERIA

Javier Rodriguez-Corral

School of Archaeology, University of Oxford, UK

Corresponding author: Javier Rodriguez-Corral (javier.rodriguezcorral@arch.ox.ac.uk)

ABSTRACT

The aim of this paper is to gain insights into the mechanisms by which new socio-materialities were co-created in western Iberia as a result of encounters between people of Atlantic and Mediterranean cultural and technological backgrounds during the Late Bronze Age (1400/1200-700 BC). Particular emphasis is placed on the landscapes where socio-cultural encounters took place and where material images, artefacts and technologies were hybridised, integrated or recreated. To do this, typology and archaeometry information is taken into consideration. The material evidence analysed comprises specific objects such as gold items, bronze axes, statue-menhirs and stelae, which sheds light on the ways in which the social identity of the Atlantic people shifted or was altered through these encounters, and to what extent the people adopted and adapted socio-material practices within a shared cultural milieu.

KEYWORDS: connectivity, atlactic-mediterranean interactions, colonial and pre-colonial encounters, trade, gift and commodities economies, Bronze Age.

1. INTRODUCTION

The last few years have seen a growing trend in the field of archaeology with attention focuses on the concept of materiality in order to help formulate new perspectives on social connectivity and identity (Gosden 2004; Van Dommelen and Knapp 2010). From this viewpoint the underpinnings of connectivity reside in the encounters of both people and objects in a specific context, as a result of their movements and relationships. Objects may be exchanged and transformed as they are circulated among people, thus co-creating new social and material relations. Connectivity, therefore, functions as a mechanism that serves to establish, bolster or modify trans-regional and local identities.

People and objects are mutually entangled (Gosden 2004: 36). Different socio-material practices (Chapman 2000; Knappett 2006; Glambe 2007) enable individuals to have a social impact on different scales of interaction (local, regional, or interregional contexts), even when not physically present. Accumulation processes (such as grouping objects in deposits) and enchainment processes (by which social groups were held together or established relationships in networks spread over the distance) were two of these socio-materially determined practices of interaction. Artefacts and material forms are commonly conceptualised as constituent parts in the creation of human identity, or regarded as components of an extended sense of personhood (Strathern 1990: 178). In this particular context, objects, or object fragments, moved across the landscape, allowing interaction networks to be sustained across time and space. Thus, social agency was not restricted to the physical presence of individuals, but was also articulated through these artefacts, even at some distance in time and place.

The concept of hybridisation (Knapp 2008: 57-61) is useful for exploring contexts of interaction such as these, as it allows us to move away from a top-down perspective of acculturation by linking the creation of a mixed or altered material culture to the actions and choices of social agents within a contact situation, as an expression of their identity. It is through this notion of hybridisation that cultural encounters can be explored as an interactive process in which diverse social agents actively created new social situations, adopting and adapting new practices and new material forms within a shared cultural milieu (Gosden 2004).

This paper explores issues of materiality, mobility and identity in the study of interactions between Mediterranean and Atlantic backgrounds during the Late Bronze Age, focusing, more specifically, on processes of connectivity linking Southern (the transition area to the Atlantic façade for Mediterranean agents) and Northwestern Iberia (the Atlantic area furthest away from the Mediterranean Sea with archaeological evidence of the Mediterranean presence). The purpose of this research is to gain insights into the mechanisms by which new socio-materialities were co-create in Western Iberia as a result of encounters between people of Atlantic and Mediterranean cultural and technological backgrounds. Particular emphasis is placed on the landscapes where socio-cultural encounters took place and where objects were hybridised, integrated, or recreated. The material evidence analyzed includes specific objects, such as goldwork, bronze axes, statue-menhirs or stelae that permits the better understanding of the ways in which the social identity of Atlantic people changed or was altered through these encounters during this period.

2. HYBRIDISATION AND MATERIAL CONNECTIONS IN GOLDWORK

In this section, understanding of the material connections between the Mediterranean world and the Atlantic communities of the western Iberia will be explored. Attention will be focused on specific gold artefacts of this period and the material culture involved in the development of identities will be analysed, which involved the development of identities from the mid-second millennium BC and played a part in co-creating landscapes of connectivity **(Fig. 1).**

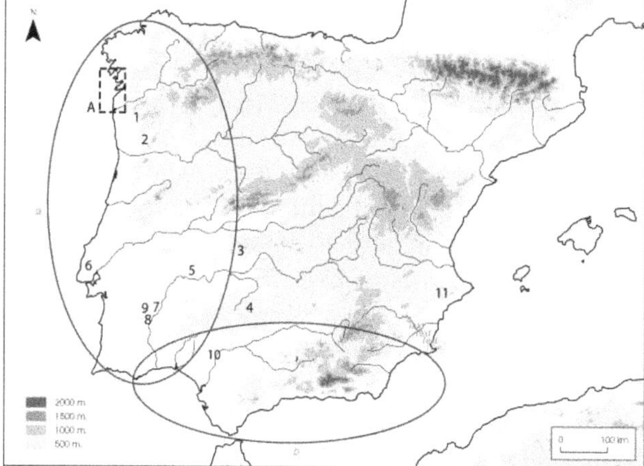

Figure 1. Map of deposits that are mentioned in this article: 1. Baião (Porto), 2. Cantonha (Guimarães), 3. Berzocana (Cáceres), 4. Bélmez (Cordoba), 5. Sagrajas (Badajoz), 6. Sintra (Lisbon), 7. Herdade do Alamo (Beja), 8. Baleizão (Alentejo), 9. Portel (Évora), 10. El Carambolo (Sevilla), 11. Villlena (Alicante). Area A: Northwestern region with Phoenician presence. Circle-a: Atlantic background and circle-b: Mediterranean background.

In many Mediterranean regions, an increased demand for metals such as gold and tin, as well as their concentration in mostly marginal areas, encouraged interaction among social groups from different regions and backgrounds during the Late Bronze Age (Bradley, 2013). This period witnessed the development and intensification of interaction processes (movement of persons, objects, knowledge and social values), and linking processes (regional and trans-regional political alliances), aimed at building exchange and interaction networks. One of the consequences of these processes was the emergence of a shared cultural milieu in regions beyond the Mediterranean borders. New metal artefacts were adopted and/or adapted to permit their integration into hybrid socio-material practices linked to the construction of identities in these new contexts of interaction.

These practices are evidenced particularly in the gold metallurgy of western Iberia. Specifically, three types of supra-regional material connections denote the adoption and adaptation of objects that defined processes of connectivity during the Late Bronze Age: (1) deposits combining Atlantic and Mediterranean objects, (2) hybrid artifacts created from objects or object fragments belonging to different technological domains, both Atlantic and Mediterranean, and (3) objects of Atlantic typology manufactured with Mediterranean technology.

The first type of material connection corresponds to the placement of Mediterranean and Atlantic objects in the same hoard or deposit, in Western and Southern areas of Iberia. Three specific deposits can well exemplify this type of material connection: Berzocana, in the province of Cáceres, Spain; Bélmez, in the province of Córdoba, Spain; and Baleizâo, in the district of Beja, Portugal. The first one contains two gold torcs belonging to the Atlantic technological domain, as well as an omphalos bowl from the Eastern Mediterranean one (Perea 2005: 100). The Bélmez deposit holds an Atlantic torc and a combination of miscellaneous gold objects of Mediterranean origin (Perea and Armbruster 2008: 516). The Baleizâo deposit consists of a torc, a bangle, an ingot, several axes, six measuring weights, glass paste and filigree wire. In the latter case, apart from the association of Atlantic and Mediterranean objects, it is interesting to note the presence of an ingot and of weight sets, which seems to link the group of objects to trading activities, as is the case for a large number of deposits in the north of Portugal where both types of elements are common (Torres 2008: 64-67; Vilaça 2008a, 2008b; Senna-Martinez et al. 2011).

Additionally, artefacts manufactured with Atlantic technology circulated in western Mediterranean exchange networks: the deposit of Villena (Ruiz-Galvez 1998; Perea 2008), in the province of Alicante (Spain) is a good example of this. However, while this deposit, located in eastern Spain, has the largest number of artefacts made with Atlantic technology, it also contains Mediterranean objects.

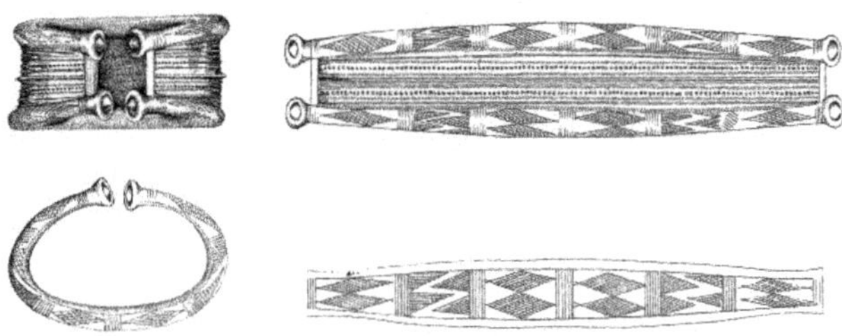

Figure 2. Bangle of Cantonha, Guimarães (Portugal). After Silvia, 1986.

The second type of material connection encountered consists of objects made from two or more pieces belonging to two specific Atlantic technological domains (which Perea and Armbruster define as the Sagrajas/Berzonaca typology and the Villena/Estremoz typology), and to the Mediterranean technological domain. The production of these hybrid objects shows two important facts. First, the merging of objects or parts of objects manufactured with different kind of Atlantic technologies. Second, that these artefacts were made not only from old Atlantic objects, but they also incorporated new elements such as filigree, welding or decorative motifs such as bells, all of which were typical of the Mediterranean typology and technology (Perea 2005: 99-100; Perea and Armbruster 2008: 516-517). And thirdly, these objects were created in the last phase of the Atlantic Late Bronze Age, when the Mediterranean and Atlantic encounters were more intensive. Examples of this hybridisation include the Bangle of Sintra and the Bangle of Cantonha **(Fig. 2)**. While the first was found in central Portugal (Armbruster 1995), the second appeared in Northwestern Iberia (López 1951; Silva 1986), in the mineral-rich Atlantic region farthest from the Mediterranean. The location of both pieces suggests that the same hybridisation phenomena took place simultaneously in the North and in the Central Atlantic façade of Iberia during the Late Bronze Age, or perhaps that hybrid objects whose formal characteristics denote a strong connectivity were widely circulated in both regions.

These hybridisation processes have diverse explanations, which are often difficult to establish. Artefacts may have been repurposed after losing their original associations (Fontijn 2008). Additionally, the different constituent parts of hybrid objects may have had separate or dissimilar histories, in which case they could have been reassembled in a new context and reconfigured into a new object —a new identity—in consonance with a new situation of contact. Regarding Late Bronze contexts, as noted above, new identities emerged in this period through the metonymic and metaphorical qualities of material objects. The grouping of objects to establish a new materiality, which agglutinated and incorporated different spatial and temporal domains might have stemmed from the existence of a relational component in the development of personhood and identity during the Late Bronze Age (Bruck 2006: 297). Nevertheless, this hybridisation should be understood as the result of the growing interaction between individuals from different backgrounds creating different contact situations; i.e. a shared cultural milieu.

Finally, the third type of Atlantic-Mediterranean connection is seen in the Atlantic items which were made using only Mediterranean technology. According to Armbruster and Parreira (1993: 78- 83), they may be an imitation of athletic types "which has been observed but not assimilated". While, from a morphological and typological viewpoint, these artefacts belong in their entirety to the Atlantic domain, from a technological viewpoint they must be ascribed to the Mediterranean domain. An interesting example of this type of Atlantic-Mediterranean connection can be found in the deposit of Herdade de Álamo, in Beja, Portugal, which is located in the same area as the Baleizão deposit mentioned above (**fig. 3**). The two torcs that comprise this deposit are typologically equals to torcs belonging to the Sagrajas and Berzocana types, characteristic products of Atlantic Iberian metalwork -such as those found in the Late Bronze Age deposits of Sagrajas and Penela, in Spain, or Portel, in Portugal, etc. However, as Perea (1995: 76; see also Perea and Armbruster 2008: 515-517) has pointed out, they were manufactured using only Mediterranean technology, denoted by their hollow rings and the use of welding and filigree workmanship. This type of objects is proof of the existence of direct, personal contacts, and of the establishment of relationships between local and Mediterranean elites. Moreover, the Mediterranean-Atlantic hybridisation fostered by these processes of interaction and knowledge transmission has implications beyond the production of objects themselves. Although these torcs maintained an Atlantic visual appearance, the sensory experience of these artefacts must have presented differences, such as weight, sounds, hardness, etc.

The deposit of Herdade de Álamo also provides additional information that allows us to relate these gold works to the Late Bronze Age iconography. Apart from the two torcs already mentioned, the hoard also contained a necklace featuring a schematic representation of a human figure, analogous to those depicted in the warrior stelae of the Southwest. The representation of Mediterranean iconographic elements in these stelae strengthens the case for a link between the necklace of the Álamo deposit and the individuals represented in these stelae and the entire deposit, by extension, as noted by Perea and Armbruster (2008: 516).

Figure 3. Deposit of Herdade do Alamo, Beja (portugal). Photo: Barbara Armbruster

At the end of the Late Bronze Age and beginning of the early Iron Age (eighth to sixth centuries BC), the hybridisation processes and the resulting artefacts gave way to hoards containing Mediterranean artefacts, such as La Aliseda, in the province of Jaén, Spain; Sines, in the region of Alentejo, Portugal; and Baiao, in the Douro Valley, Portugal. Located in Northwestern Iberia, the latter contained a trousseau comprising a necklace and two pairs of earrings (Silva, 1986). Although the technology, typology and iconography of these pieces of jewelry are fully Mediterranean: more concretely, they are Phoenician. Their finding in this region allows the deposit to be understood as part of the exchange of presents (gift economy) that allowed individuals from different backgrounds to build trust and loyalty. The notions of host and guest were essential and inherent to the creation of exchange networks of this kind, given that without them the establishment of peaceful and friendly relations, as well as the reception and exchange of non-local goods, became a risky and unregulated endeavour (Strathern and Stewart 2005: 235). Given their finding at great distance from where they originated—whether the Mediterranean region or the South of Iberia—the objects of the Baiao deposit should be interpreted as belonging to the trousseaus of Tartessian or Phoenician women who married into the local elites (Ruiz-Gálvez 1992: 238). The institution of marriage is indeed one of the earliest forms of social contract (Sahlins 1972: 222) used to establish a relationship structure that ensured the peaceful unfolding of connectivity (mobility, interaction and exchange).

The different types of material connections evidenced in the gold metallurgy of the Late Bronze Age embody, at different levels (production, circulation, accumulation, etc), linked processes (Chapman 2000) in the construction of identities among the individuals or the elites of the Atlantic region, within a context of connectivity to the Mediterranean world.

3. CONNECTING PEOPLE: AXES AS EXCHANGE ITEMS

Aside from prestige items made from precious metals, such as those already discussed, raw materials including metals could also have figured among the items that the elites exchanged during the Late Bronze Age. The palstave axes typical of the Northwestern Atlantic seaboard supports this argument, showing hybridisation similar to that of the gold objects. While the palstaves are a type of axe characteristic of many European Atlantic regions, the distribution of the types founded in Northwest and West of Iberia (30D, 31C, 34a; 35a, 35C, Monteagudo, 1977) shows more connections with the South of Iberia than with other European western regions. In other words, their distribution reveals interactions with Mediterranean backgrounds, rather than interactions with Atlantic backgrounds.

Axes were part of a category of objects that was distributed in landscapes of mobility, such as the Douro River and Támega River basins, and the coastal areas of the Northwestern Atlantic seaboard (Monteagudo 1977). Palstaves, therefore, belonged to the same geographical core of the deposits that was discussed, plus that of other material forms such as statue-menhirs and stelae which will be explored in the next section. These palstaves were not manufactured for use as axes. Firstly, owing to their chemical composition, they were too soft to have been functional, and secondly, because in many cases they came with their casting mold. An alternative interpretation of these objects suggests that should be regarded as ingots. Following this hypothesis, it has been argued that the weight of these axes corresponded to weight measurement models that were in use in the Mediterranean region (Galán and Ruíz-Gálvez 1996, Galán 2005: 471). Palstaves, therefore, must have been valued principally as exchange items, not as metal tools, given that their use was not advisable because of their high lead content. Although their circulation through trade cannot be completely ruled out, the demarcation between exchanges of gifts and commercial activity during the Late Bronze Age remains nebulous (Pare 2013); furthermore, in economies based on reciprocity, raw materials could have been considered valuable gifts. From a systemic viewpoint, these objects may be regarded as endowed with power, in the sense that they were used in the building of mediated relationships.

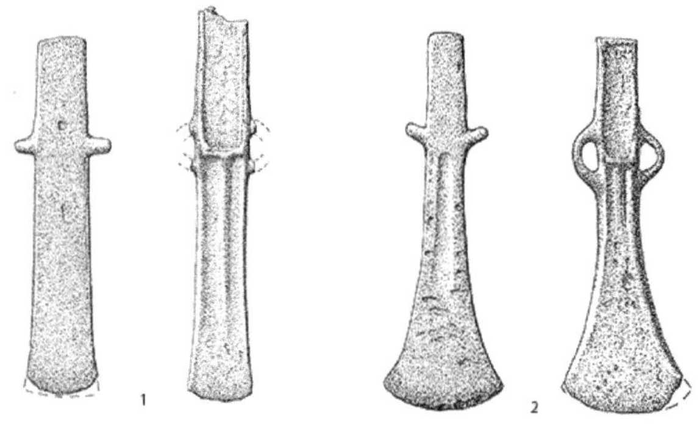

Figure 4. Isomorphism between palstaves and trunnion axes in (1) the Atlantic network (840 and 1224, in: Monteagudo, 1977) and (2) the North plateau network (863 and 1263, in: Monteagudo, 1977).

Thus, the distribution of palstaves took place in a context of gift economies where the reciprocity was the foundation of sociability, the negotiation of identities, and the establishment of regional and supra-regional ties. The types of axes mentioned above circulated from Galicia and the north of Portugal towards the south of the Tajo basin since the beginning of the Late Bronze Age. Simultaneously, the trunnion axe (from a Mediterranean background) circulated from the south toward the northwest (Martin, 1999: 59-61; see also Díaz-Andreu, 1988). Both models of axes then shared networks of interaction. It was during this process that the Atlantic axes arrived in Italy or islands such as the Balearics and Sardinia, while the Mediterranean axes reached the Northwest of Iberia (Giardino, 1995).

The circulation of Palstaves and Trunnion axes encouraged not only the co-presence of both in deposits, but also processes of hybridisation between them with similarity to way to the gold objects. This phenomenon can be compared to what occurred in the western and northern plateau of Iberia - zone where trunnion axes arrived from the Mediterranean shores of Iberia. While both models (palstaves and Trunnion axes) show narrow bodies with almost parallel edges in the Atlantic network, their bodies are more stylised and their edges expand distally in the northern plateau (**Fig. 4**). Additionally, the existence of axes with loops and trunnions reveals another example of hybridisation. Such isomorphism and intermingling between trunnion axes and palstaves can only be explained by material convergences inside particular networks of interaction. Their co-presence in two different exchange networks made it possible for them to adopt a 'family resemblance' in each area. The axes must have been appreciated as elements of value for exchange and to create relations between people. If this was so, then the different levels of connectivity between palstaves and trunnion axes must have been the result of the materialisation of these relationships. While the movement of the axes shows a bi-directional type of connectivity between the Northwest and the South, their isomorphism and hybridisation seem to instantiate moments of integration between social agents in the context of supraregional interactions.

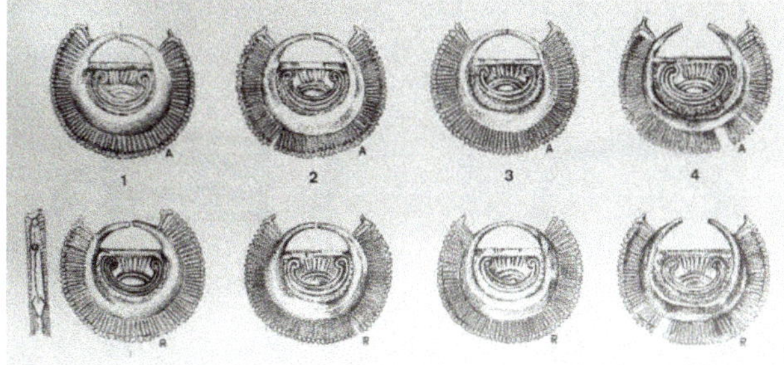

Figure 5. Gold earring with Phoenician decoration from the deposit of Baião. *After Silva, 1986.*

However, the situation appears to change at the end of the Late Bronze Age, from the eight century BC onwards. Henceforth, the circulation of palstaves stopped flowing from the Northwest to South of Iberia. Instead, they began to be withdrawn from circulation, which resulted in their accumulation in deposits on the Northwestern Atlantic coast (Galán 2005). Significantly, these deposits (Samieira, Hio, Estea, Alcabre, etc.) are located in strategic areas—such as Rias Baixas, in the region of Galicia, Spain, and Northern Portugal—which are an integral part of the new "seascapes of interaction" that appeared from the eighth century BC onwards, linking the local communities to the Phoenician agents (González-Ruibal, 2004). This transformation of relationships can be understood in the context of the displacement of the exchange networks which characterised systems of reciprocity among the elites of the Late Bronze Age (gift economies) by an emerging more commercial system fostered by the opening of the Atlantic sea route by the Phoenicians.

The late deposits with completely Mediterranean items such as Baião hoard mentioned above seem to reflect the end of the relationship between the Mediterranean and Atlantic backgrounds through and elite economy **(fig. 5).** The emergence of these items from eight century BC on was due to the need for the Phoenician to work in alliances with local communities. However, the interactions between Mediterranean and local agents henceforth are based on trade rather than on the gift. The new commercial maritime route established by the Phoenicians, focused more on transporting commodities, and could not assimilate the old items of the Late Bronze Age gift economies such as the palstaves. The replacement of the old model of Atlantic-Mediterranean interaction arouse as new ways of relating and building identities were taking shape, and therefore can be understood as part of a trend that implied new ways of understanding exchange processes. This new context sheds light on the withdrawal from circulation of palstaves, and their concomitant accumulation in coastal deposits located within the new geography of maritime interaction. The overlap between these two realities is materialized in the Alcabre Peninsula in Vigo, a small archaeological area in the Spanish Northwest. An axe hoard from the Late Bronze Age was found on this small strip of land just a few meters away from a Phoenician baetylic temple (built in the Early Iron Age) where hundreds of Mediterranean pottery sherds were found (González-Ruibal, 2006) - their study is currently in progress **(Fig. 6).**

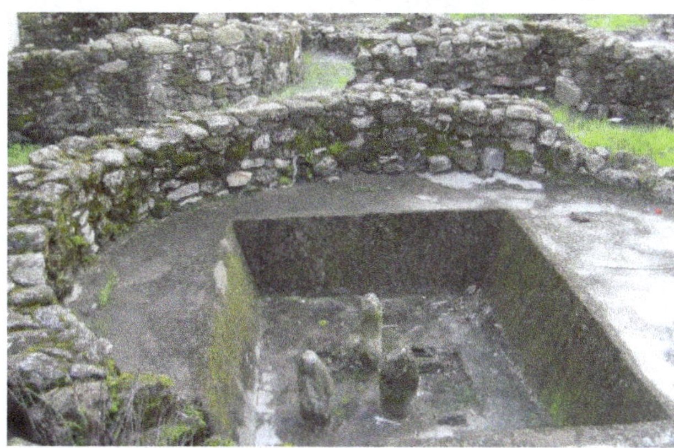

Figure 6. Phoenician betyls in Punta do Muiño, Vigo (Spain)

4. STONE PEOPLE IN LANDSCAPES OF MOBILITY

In addition to the gold items and axes circulating during the Late Bronze Age, other material forms such as statues-menhir and stelae also built the landscape **(Fig. 7)**. The statue-menhirs are standing stone engraved with minimalistic human traits, weapons and insignias which were integrated in the landscape from 1400/1200 BC onwards. They were distributed mainly in Northwestern Iberia, in the region nestled between the valleys of the Douro and Minho rivers. The latest findings, however, indicate that their area of distribution extended to the south of the province of Beira Alta, Portugal, and to the Spanish provinces of Salamanca and Cáceres.

In general, statue-menhirs were distributed in areas of transit and mobility. While their largest numbers are concentrated along the Douro and Tâmega rivers, recently discovered examples in Beira Alta and in the province of Salamanca confirm the recurrence of this typology of standing stone in other areas (Vilaça 2011). The location of statue-menhirs suggests a close association with river landscapes (Faiões, Chaves, Bouça, Muiño de San Pedro, or Nave), as well as with transit zones that later became Roman roads (Marco, Muiño de San Pedro, Vilar de Santos, Tameirón or Ataudes) (Vilaça 2011; Comendador *et al.*, 2011). Additionally, the standing stones of Tremedal de Tiermes, Valdefuentes de Sangusín (Salamanca, Spain) and Segura de Toro (Cáceres, Spain) are located in the vicinity of the natural route along which the Roman Via de la Plata later ran, connecting the west of the Iberian Peninsula from north to south. This distribution pattern suggests that statue-menhirs had a significant role in the construction of the landscapes of mobility that connected Northwestern and Southern Iberia during prehistoric times.

Figure 7. Statue-menhir of Marco at an area of communication between the Northwest and the southern areas.

The location in transit areas of statue-menhirs and other materials forms, such as stelae from the Extremadura region, also points to the existence of a consistent association between these types of artefacts and areas rich in minerals including gold and tin (Senna-Martinez 2011: 293). This link suggests that mineral wealth fostered an intense interaction between local and foreign communities, especially during the Late Bronze Age (Alvés and Reis 2011: 164), a time when a gold and bronze-based material culture became a key element in the negotiation of identity among the elites.

In this context, the role traditionally ascribed to these monoliths in order to explain their location in transit areas has been that of territorial or road markers. The same interpretation has been put forward for the stelae found in the Southwest of the Iberian Peninsula (Ruiz-Gálvez and Galán 1991; Galán 1993; Jorge 1995). However, the type of association between statue-menhirs and transit areas allows us to qualify this interpretation. A GIS-enabled analysis of the location of statue-menhirs vis-à-vis the flow of mobility in the valleys of the Douro and Támega rivers demonstrates that, while statue-menhirs were located near transit areas, they were not completely visible from those areas where mobility took place (Fábrega *et al.* 2011: 317) **(Fig. 8)**. The distribution of statue-menhirs adjacent to transit areas yet often beyond travelers' line-of-sight suggests that these standing stones may have constituted places of special significance established by individuals with ties to the area of transit.

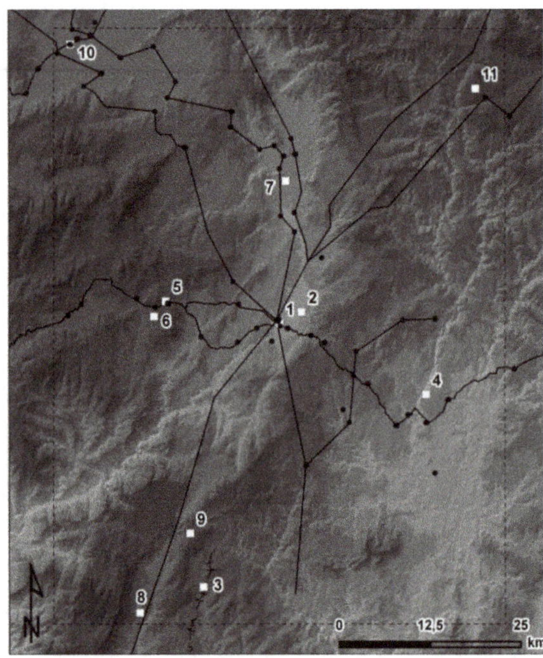

Figure. 8. Relationship between statue-menhir and mobility areas in northwestern Iberia. 1. Chaves, 2. Faioes, 3. Marco, 4. Bouca, 5. Tojais, 6. Cruz de Cepos, 7. Muiño de San Pedro, 8. Samarda, 9. Guilhado, 10. Vilar de Santos, 11. Tameiron. (Fábrega et al. 2011)

The sites created by the placement of statue-menhirs did not necessarily correspond to a logic that sought to organize time and space—as like road markers—but may have simply resulted from the presence of people in transit through the area over time. As Díaz-Guardamino (2006: 21-23) has stated, the signaling function of statue-menhirs was more often used to designate sites intended for the celebration of commemoration rituals (e.g. the deceased), than to mark transit routes and territorial boundaries. This interpretation has also been applied to Southwestern stelae (Celestino 2001: 279). However, our understanding of statue-menhirs should extend beyond their simple signaling function and should include their enabling role in the construction of place in the Heideggerian sense of the term, given that they transformed (monumentalised) the spaces where they were erected, helping to create a specific landscape and sense of place that was perhaps linked to a funerary function or functioned as a locus of memory for the people who traversed the landscape for concrete purposes.

This framework allows us to better grasp the materiality and semiotic significance of statue-menhirs. Using different sculptural techniques and minimalistic representations, these standing stones were the materialisation of the (social rather than physical) body of a very specific type of individual bearing weapons and insignias, within the context of a landscape of mobility. The performative materiality of these artifacts eliminate many features (movement, stance, gestures, and so forth), focusing on the iconography. Similarly to the southwest stelae of the of the peninsula, statue-menhirs do not appear to reflect specific individuals' biographies or characteristics, beyond a generic relationship with weapons and insignias. The representation of human faces was very schematic, with features engraved on the stone. In some cases, these features were limited to the eyes, nose and mouth (Nave 2, Longroiva or Valdefuentes de Sanguisín); in others, additional anatomical elements were included—such as the ears—to delineate the contours of the face (Ermida, Muiño de San Pedro or San Joao de Ver). Nevertheless, in others, the facial representation is reduced to the minimum expression, and only one feature serves to denote the whole face, e.g. the eyes, as in the statue-menhir of Boulhosa (Díaz-Guardamino 2010: 137-138). The facial features engraved on statue-menhirs served only to anthropomorphise the monolith, and different physiognomic elements were chosen depending on each case. The remaining iconographic elements, however, were more standardised, and represented both weapons and a type of insignia or symbol that Spanish scholars have dubbed the sub-rectangular motif. The semiotic interpretation of these combined elements has a clear contextual meaning.

Robb (2009: 174) has recently stated out, in the history of the representation of the human body, the use of schematic and minimalistic depictions "has often been associated with the promotion of a simplified and powerful message." In the case of statue-menhirs, the protagonists are weapons and the symbols overlaid on them. The simplified representation of the human body enabled statue-menhirs to embody a concise, strategic enunciation of the message its creators wished to convey. This economy of representation is coherent with the supra-regional landscapes of mobility and interaction that the statue-menhirs belonged to. Whatever these material forms lost in terms of detail and nuance, they gained in immediacy and inter-contextual and supra-regional compressibility. The aforementioned elements involved in the construction of identity and power—for individuals whose sense of self was built around the use of weapons and metalwork trade—operated within a "semiotic ideology" (Keane 2003) that, in the context of the landscapes of mobility to which they belonged, only required the association of the stone body with the objects depicted on its surface to convey meaning.

In short, our understanding of this set of elements and interpretive evidence can be summarised as follows: Iberian statue-menhirs (1) were associated with mineral-rich areas and should be interpreted as part of landscapes of mobility and connectivity processes; (2) were endowed with the ability not only to represent, but also to create places, in the Heideggerian sense; (3) were inscribed mainly in a Late Bronze Age chronological timeframe, although they may have appeared earlier; and (4) were embedded in a context in which the production of metal objects played an active role in the construction of identities.

5. MOBILITY, IDEOLOGY AND SUPRA-REGIONAL SYMBOLISM

The material images in stone reveal an evolution that is akin to hybridisation found in gold artefacts. The technology and typology of the Atlantic metallurgy remained practically unchanged from the Chalcolithic period to the Late Bronze Age, subsequently growing more complex and hybridising with Mediterranean technology, which resulted in products accordant to their historical context of production and use. Statue-menhirs underwent a similar process: These material forms mingled a series of connections across time and space that reflected the social and identity transformations in which they were embedded as Mediterranean-Atlantic encounters increased.

A material connection with the past is evidenced in the morphology, size, and location of the statue-menhirs in the landscape. As Alves and Reis has pointed out, they "seem to have inherited the monumental and commemorative character of megalithic menhirs" (2011: 176). In fact, a number of statues-menhir (Chaves, Bouça or Muiño de San Pedro) resulted from the re-use of ancient phallic menhirs (Jorge and Jorge 1983; Bettercourt 2005). The emergence of statues-menhirs -they either are new monuments or recycled phallic menhirs-may be related to the transformation of the models of interaction and connectivity and, consequently, to a change in the strategies used by people to create power and identity during the Late Bronze Age. During this period, as noted by Jorge (1999: 122), mounds ceased to be used as places of negotiation, to the detriment of the spaces created by statue-menhirs, both through their inscribing power (monumentalization of space through materiality and iconography) and their incorporation power (as a site for ritual action)

(Connerton 1989). In this context, phallic menhirs became obsolete, or lost their cultural and social meaning, and in the process of being reimagined and recycled, some were anthropomorphised and equipped with weapons and symbols.

Accordingly, statue-menhirs appear to be related to two historical circumstances. The first is the development and consolidation of copper metallurgy from the Early/Middle Bronze Age onwards, in addition to the bronze metallurgy especially during the Late Bronze Age, although there is evidence of its production prior to this period. The engraving of weapons on these monuments, as noted by Bettencourt (2005: 171), denotes the "prestige that was associated with metallurgy" in that moment. The second historical fact is the emergence of strong supra-regional interactions as a result of obtaining raw material and interchanging prestige goods. This can also be evidenced by the aforementioned carving of sub-rectangular motifs on the surface of statue-menhirs (**Fig. 9**). In this respect, the material symbol allows us to link these monuments to processes of interaction throughout the Western Iberia (bidirectional interaction between the Northwest and the South of Iberia), revealing ultimately an intermingling of Atlantic and Mediterranean backgrounds.

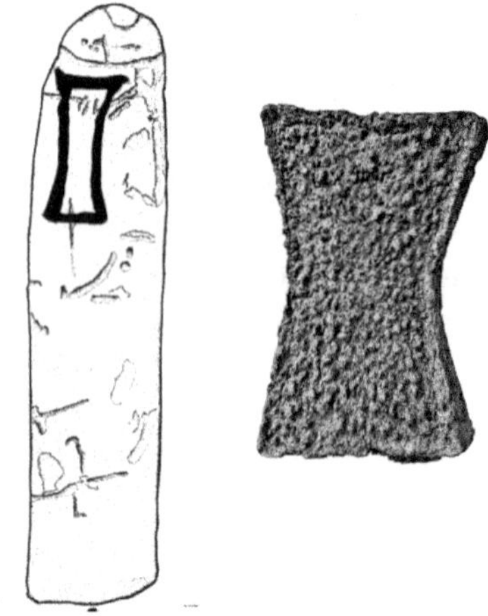

Figure 9. Comparation between a sub-rectangular motif depicted on the Statue-menhir of Bouça (left) and the ox-hide ingot from Zakros, Creta (Heraklion Archaeological Museum) (right).

While the emphasis on symbolism of these motifs only allows us to interpret them as visual codes reflecting power dynamics (Almagro-Gorbea 1993: 126; Jorge and Jorge 1993: 41; López Plaza et al. 1996: 298; Vilaça et al. 2001: 76; Bettencourt, 2005), a relational interpretation can shed light on other aspects they embody, such as actual connections (the motif as index), and similarity linkages (the motif as icon) (Preucel 2006). Viewed as indices, their presence in the landscape directs our attention to the people who produced these material forms, whose existence is evidenced by the very materiality of the artefacts. The distribution of these monuments not only reveals people using the same kind of self-representation (the statue-menhir) in different regions, but also shows people shearing the same kind of material symbols (the sub-rectangular motif) throughout different regions. In other words, they provide material evidence of supra-regional strong connections throughout the Atlantic region (Díaz-Gaurdamino 2011: 78). The material symbol is depicted in the Northwest of Iberia (Douro-Miño region), Beira Alta and inland Beira Baixa (Portugal) and the province of Salamanca (Spain). Thus, if these monoliths are regarded as "people of stone" who shared supra-regional symbols of power, then the identity of the individuals who they materialised encompassed those regions, or in any event, linked them to the act of moving across different zones of interactions from the Northwest to the South of Iberia. Therefore, the people who used this material symbol shared a particular cultural milieu within a context of connectivity that extended beyond logic of local identities.

Likewise, the sub-rectangular motif can be approached as an icon. Generic associations between the sub-rectangular motif and real objects have been put forward in an attempt to identify their meaning. Besides their broad interpretation as an emblem of power, these decorative elements have been associated alternatively with ceremonial robes or stoles (Jorge and Jorge 1993: 39), kardiophilax-type breastplates (Almagro-Gorbea 1993: 126) and weapon belts (Lopez *et al.* 1996) or breastplates used to protect warriors' vital organs (Díaz-Guardamino 2010). The fact that these motifs are commonly found at the front of the statue-menhirs suggests, however, that the interpretation of them as breastplates may be the most accurate. Authors such as Vilaça *et al.* (2001: 78) and Rodriguez-Corral (2015) have noted the iconic resemblance of the so-called sub-rectangular motif and the ox-hide form of many artefacts found in the Mediterranean. In this respect, depictions of oxhide ingots in no-Mediterranean areas have been proposed by other authors. According to Celestino (2001), the ox-hide motif may be depicted on a number of warrior stelae from southwestern Iberia such as Cerro Muriano I, Cortejada and Capilla III. Likewise, representations of oxhide ingots in Scandinavian rock art, such as those on the panel Boglosa and panel Kville, have also been recently suggested by Ling and Stos-Gale (2015). In all these cases, a detailed examination shows that the sides of the depictions are concave, forming a shape typical of oxhide ingots. Thus, they show a high degree of similarity with ingots found along the Mediterranean.

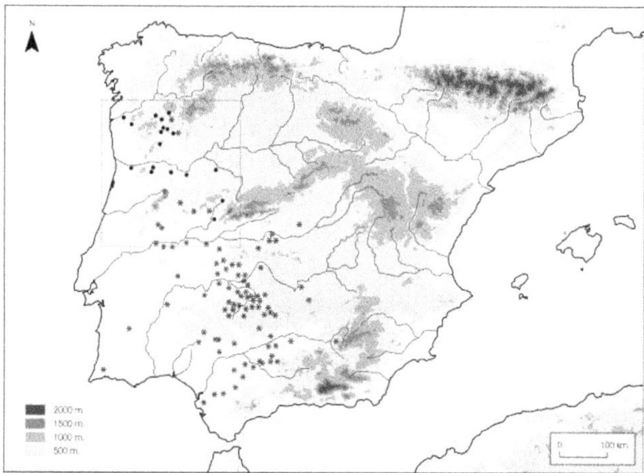

Figure10. Map of interaction between the northwest statue-menhir (dots) and southern steles (asterisks)

The oxhide motif is a *representamen* (Pierce 1998: 203) that was materialised across different media, places, contexts, and times. Over a very broad time range (from the fourteenth century BC until the fifth century BC), the formal quality "oxhide" has assumed different forms (ingots, urns, breastplates, altars, pendants, etc.), has been documented in different contexts (shipwrecks, temples, stelae, paintings, sculptures, etc.), has been distributed in different geographies (from Egypt and Cyprus to the Iberian Peninsula). Therefore, the meaning of the motif could be entangled with different contexts of social value and authority, giving rise to what Keane (2003) has called "the openness of iconicity". Despite this, although the biography of this icon could be diverse and the meaning may have varied according to the context, must be directly linked to the Mediterranean dynamics related to interchange, sacredness and rituality. If the interpretation of the sub-rectangular motif as ox-hide is correct, then this link reveals interactions with Mediterranean backgrounds in the Northwestern Iberia (Duero/Minho region).

6. MATERIAL ENCOUNTERS IN THE LANDSCAPE: STATUE-MENHIRS AND WARRIOR STELAE

A number of material connections show clear links between statue-menhirs and stelae, revealing shared material identities between elites from the Northwest and the South of Iberia **(Fig. 10).** Some can be found in the weapons with which these people of stone were represented. Statue-menhirs such as those of Chaves and Ataúdes illustrate these processes well. In the first case, for example, the statue-menhirs of Chaves **(Fig. 11)** share with the Alentejo stela of Gomes Aires -found in Beja along with a Late Bronze Age warrior stela with writing (Almagro Bosch, 1966: 120) - the same long, rectangular figure, in an identical position, that has been interpreted as a sword hanging from a belt. Moreover, the same dagger depicted in the statue-menhir of Chaves appears in the warrior stelae of Tres Arroyos (Alburquerque, Badajoz). Indeed, this iconographic connection is far from exceptional, inasmuch as it was common in the intermediate regions that tied the Northwest and South of Iberia (Beira Baja, Beira Alta, Badajoz and Cáceres), where this type of sword was frequently represented (Brandherm, 2007).

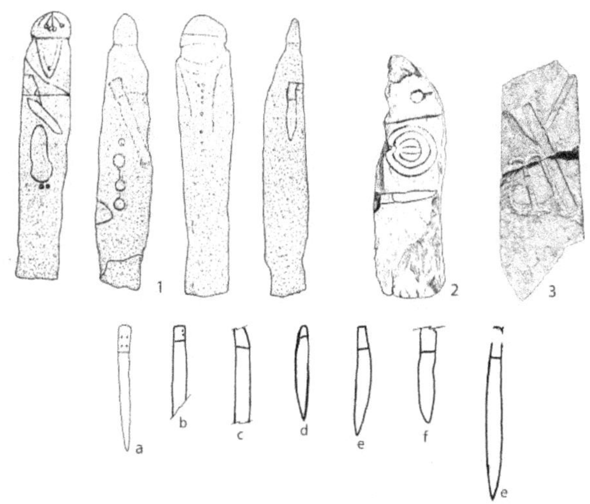

Figure 11. Statue-menhir of Chaves; 2. Warrior stela of Tres Arroyos; 3. Alentejo stela of Gomes Aires; 4. Other depicts of swords on southwestern stela: a. Eiras; b y d. El Manjar de los Puercos, c. Salvatierra de Santiago; e. El Oreganal I; f. Tres Arroyos; g. Los Herraderos

Additionally, the statue-menhir of Ataúdes (Guarda) and the stela of Mouriços (Beja) provide another iconic connection between materialities from the northwest and south of the Iberian Atlantic, since exactly the same sword tip is represented in both monuments, **(fig. 12)**. The first is a Northwestern statue-menhir with the sub-rectangular emblem, while the second one has been traditionally considered a Alentejo stela. However, this is not clear since the latter was found broken, probably due to re-use within a necropolis of the first Iron Age (Ourique, Beja). For this reason and the fact that it shares the same tip with Ataúdes, it may actually be a statue-menhir (Diaz-Guardamino, 2010). However, both hypotheses allow a material connection to be made: while the first interpretation argues an iconography shared between 'Alentejo' stelae (the southwest) and statue-menhirs (the northwest), the second would imply the presence of a statue-menhir directly in the south of Iberia.

In addition, representation of elements of clothing also provide substantial information about the processes of interaction. Some statue-menhirs, such as Ermida, Nave 2 or Millarón, share the fishbone pattern decoration with various metal objects that circulated during the Late Bronze Age in the Atlantic-Mediterranean networks (Taramelli, 1921; Vilaça, 2004). The statue-menhir of São João de Ver (Aveiro), which is dated to eight-seven century BC, is represented with a Mediterranean style helmet (Queiroga, 2003: 85). Other statue-menhirs, for their part, share clothing elements with Late Bronze Age stelae from the south of Iberia. The monuments such as Nave 2, Faiões or Alto de Escrita are represented with the same belts and necklaces to those of the warrior stelae and so-called pebble stelae of the southwest (Celestino, 2001). Likewise, these necklaces find good parallels in both Mediterranean - i.e. necklaces of the Balearic Islands (Delibes and Fernandez-Miranda 1988: 122) - and Atlantic archaeological records - i.e. the necklaces of Sintra (Armbruster, 1995). It is worth noting that Atlantic ancient pieces were reused and combined in this latter necklace to create a final Mediterranean-style product.

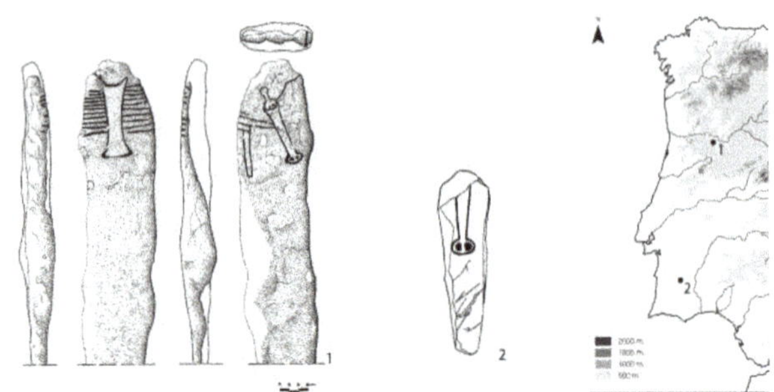

Figure 12. The statue-menhir of Ataúdes (after Vilaça et al. 2001) and the stela de Mouriços (after Díaz-Guardamino 2010).

The group of stelae of San Marinho (Castelo Branco) (Celestino, 2001), localised in Beira Baixa, also provides evidence about connectivity. It is composed of three monuments found on the slope of a Late Bronze Age hillfort - a large number of artefacts such as palstaves, trunnion axe or Mediterranean gold objects decorated with fishbone pattern have been found in this settlement and surrounding areas. Piece number 1 is a stela in which two individuals with horns appear - or with a horned helmet. Piece number 2 is a reused menhir in which a hunting scene, an elbow fibula and a mirror were depicted. Monument number 3 reveals two material connections. On the one hand, the monument has the logic of a statue-menhir and a stela at the same time. While the human figure that is represented on the front seems to indicate that the monolith could function as a support for the image -namely, as a stela -, the belt and kilt engraved under the image seem to use the monolith itself as a representation of the human body. On the other hand, the human figure is represented by the sub-rectangular motif, meaning firstly, stela and statue-menhirs became hybridised and, secondly, the sub-rectangular emblem come to transcend the world of statue-menhirs in regions of transition between the northwest and the south.

Additionally, the supraregional north-south connections are also detected conversely by the presence of material indicators of southern elites such as the warrior stelae in the Northwestern area itself (**fig. 13**).

Figure 13. Southern stela of warrior founded in the Northwest of Iberia. After Alves et al. 2011.

Pedra de Atalaia (Guarda) is found in the north sector of the Serra de Estrala, in the Beira Alta (Vilaça *et al.* 2011). Further north, on the western edge of the Chaves mass (Vila Real), the stela of Tojais is found (Vilaça *et al.*, 2001). Its location is relevant for three reasons. Firstly, it was found in the north of Portugal in a region rich in tin, where in ancient times there was an important exploitation not only of this mineral but also of gold. This fact enforces the vinculation of the warrior stelae with networks of access to mineral resources (Senna-Martínez 2011: 293). Secondly, the Tojáis stela share the landscape with the statue-menhir of Cruz de Cepos (Alves and Reis, 2011), both situated in the border passage. Thirdly, arriving from the south, this highland landscape is the last point that needs to be overcome before descending towards the flood plain of Támega, the traditional area of communication and catchment of southern artefacts (González-Ruibal, 2006-2007).

Finally, Pedra Alta (Castrelo do Val, Ourense) is situated in the extreme north of this flood plain, which is home to a great number of statue-menhirs (**fig. 14**). On its surface, there are engravings of a sword, a v-notch shield and a cart (Reboreda and Nieto 2012). The cart, far from being exceptional in the northwest, may also be present in the art-rock of this region, taking into account the undeniable similarity existing between some of the denominated shield shapes and inscribed carts in the warrior stelae (**fig. 15**).

Figure 14. Hybrid monument of Pedra Alta. Photo: F. J. Torres Goberna.

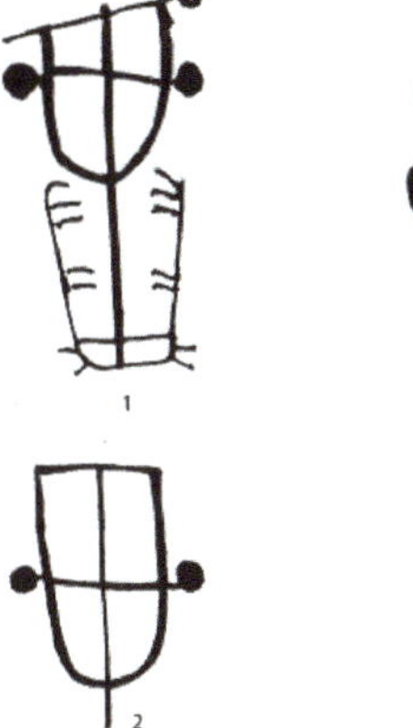
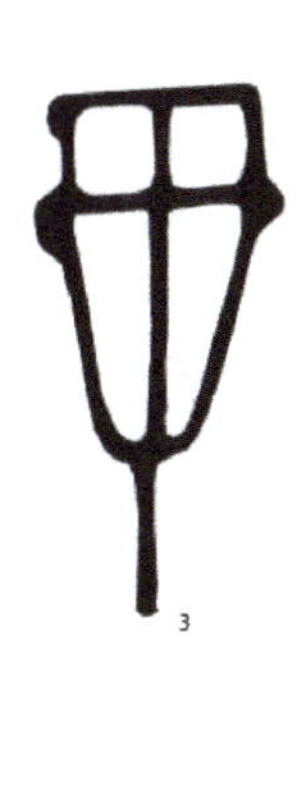

Figure 15. Engravings of carts on warrior stela (1-2) and the armed rock of Agua da Laxe, Gondomar, Pontevedra (3).

In any case, the monument of Pedra Alta seems to instantiate a hybrid form between the iconography of the warrior stela -where are depicted Mediterranean elements such carts (Celestino, 2008)- and the anthropomorphic character of the statue-menhirs. A similar case is found in La Barranca del Águila monument (Talavera) (Celestino, 2001: 355), situated in the intermediate area of communication that joins the northwest with the south of Iberia. It is also a statue-menhir which reflects the iconographic characteristics of the warrior stelae, with no evidence of previous engravings. Possibly, these hybrid monuments are expressing either the prestige that the southwest panoply (with a Mediterranean background) acquires for the elites represented in the statue-menhirs or the adoption of the new way of representation by elites with the southwest panoply. Nonetheless, they seem to be instantiating a well-established shared milieu between elites.

7. TOWARDS AN ARCHAEOMETRY OF THE CONNECTIVITY IN WESTERN IBERIA

The same geographical distribution of the material forms analysed above and of the tin and gold ores shows how the mobility of the elites was closely linked to these mineral resources **(fig.16)**. Accordingly, it is important to understand that the copper and tin sources have a different geographical location. Whereas in the western region of Iberia copper shows a more general dispersion, although mainly focuses in the southern region, the concentration of the tin is only located in the northwestern region. Thereby, in the context of the circulation and consumption of bronze during the Late Bronze Age, this dualistic distribution seems to encourage the dynamics of interaction and exchange between both regions, giving rise to the emergence of supraregional elites involved in the control, exploitation and distribution of minerals needed to produces bronzes.

While the exploitation of copper resources in Iberia is widely accepted, it has traditionally been more difficult to ascertain the exploitation of tin resources. Nonetheless, evidence of tin exploration come from sites such as the settlement of Cerro de Logrosan (Caceres, Spain) (Rovira, 2002) and the mine of S. Martinho (Orgens, Viseu) (Correia *et al.*, 1979). In the latter, a bronze dagger of the 'Porto de Mos' type was found at the bottom of the rubble which filled its shaft, proving its original opening and posterior infilling during the Late Bronze Age, probably for cassiterite exploration (Gomes *et al.* 2013). In addition, a recent study by optical microscopy, micro-EDXRF, SEM-EDS and XRD of metal artefacts from the site of Baiões (Viseu, Portugal) has also suggested the exploration of tin resources during the Late Bronze Age, indicating that metalworking and smelting could have been a commonplace activity in this area (Figueiredo *et al.*, 2010).

Although in Europe many publications on archaeometrical issues use lead isotope ratios, in western Iberia such studies are scarce. Recently, however, this situation seems to have changed. Regarding skeletal remains, the acidity of the soil in much of western Iberia makes archeometric studies difficult, and whenever this has been possible, the results have usually not been conclusive. Nevertheless, it is worth noting recent research which has used the strontium isotope ratios (87Sr/86Sr) in dental enamel of 55 humans in the center Portugal. That has allowed the distinguishing of migrant individuals from seven burial populations of the Late Neolithic and the Bronze Age (3500-1800 BC). Based on this calculation, nine percent (5 out of 55) of the total surveyed population have been considered as migrants, the majority of which come from the cave burial of Cova da Moura (Lisbon), marking this site as socially distinct. This would correspond with known exchange patterns and suggests, as noted by Waterman *et al.* (2014), that both people and items were moving between different areas in West Iberia since the early stages of the Bronze Age.

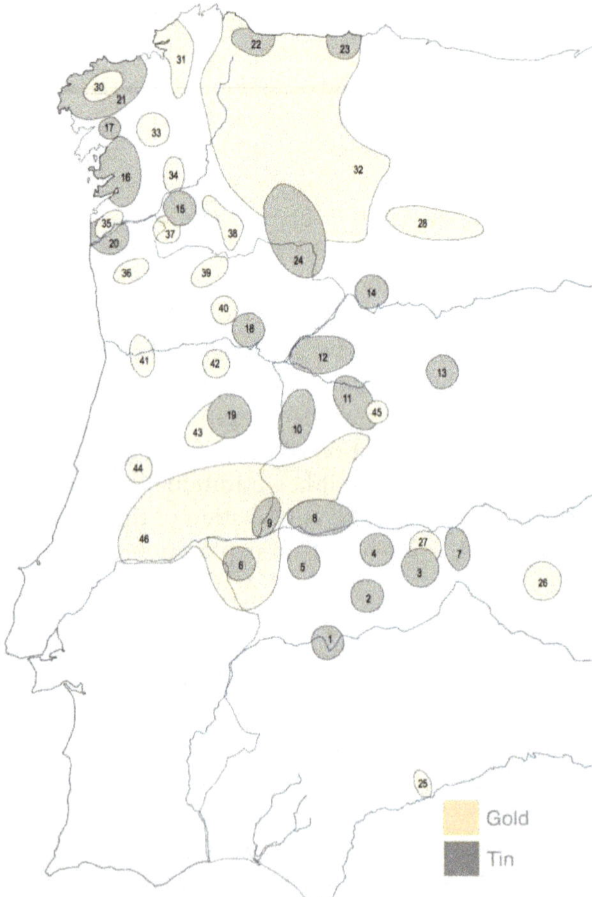

Figure 16. Distribution map of gold and tin ores in western Iberia. Tin ores distribute along the same territory as statue-menhir and stelae.

Metal provenance has always been a central and complex issue in the investigation of the Bronze Age. Elemental composition analyses of metal artefacts were conducted in western Iberia under the framework of the SAM project, however, despite the high number of artefacts under study, it was impossible to determine direct relationships between those artefacts and particular ores (Junghans *et al.*, 1960; 1968; 1974). This could be a result of the geochemical variability of ore deposits and the fractioning of some trace elements during metallurgical processes from ore to metal, as noted by Gomes *et al.* (2013: 662). Nevertheless, the principal technique to obtain information about the provenance and trade routes of archaeological metal artefacts is the analysis of the lead isotopic composition by ICP-MS. It is based on the different distributions of the four stable lead isotopes present in the materials that were used in the manufacturing of artefacts. The traces of lead with specific isotope ratios do not change during their production, remaining identical in the manufactured artefacts. Therefore, in principle, lead isotopic composition can be directly associated to particular mineral ores.

Lead isotope and elemental analysis has recently provided evidence that western Iberian mines supplied metal at a suprarregional scale and, more specifically, from northern Europe. The data suggest that this metal was not supplied directly from western Iberia to northern European regions, but rather the movement of metal between both areas took place through the western Mediterranean networks. There are at least two elements to suggest that the western Mediterranean worked as a proxy between western Iberia and northern Europe. On the one hand, the archaeological data discussed in this paper suggest that the interaction/exchange extended from northwest Iberia to south Iberia and *vice versa* - or at the very least had to be the main network of interaction according to the geographical distribution of the statue-menhirs and warrior stelae as well as axes and deposits of gold items. On the other hand, the archaeometry analysis also provides remarkable evidence that the northwestern European regions accessed the metal resources of western Iberia through a network of contacts that included regions such as southern, southeastern and northeastern Iberia as well as islands such as Sardinia.

These processes of interaction and circulation of metals between the Atlantic and northern regions of Europe through the western Mediterranean were increased as the Bronze Age continued. A number of artefacts from Swedish locations, which were analysed by MC-ICP-MS lead isotope and EPMA, provide significant insights in this regard. The results demonstrate that the lead isotope compositions of theses copper-based items are considerably different from the Scandinavian ores and, therefore, the copper used to produce them was imported (Ling *et al.* 2013). The analytical data of two shaft-hole axes founded at Ödsmål (Bohuslän) (1700-1500 cal. BC) were compared with radiogenetic copper mines from different European regions. The study shows the same lead isotope composition between one of the shaft-holes and the copper ores from El Aramo (Asturias) in northwestern Iberia - a place with a strong evidence of mining activity during the second Millennium BC (Blas *et al.* 2015). Likewise, according to the author of this investigation, the lead isotope compositions of these two axes "lie on the mixing lines of copper ores from the Portuguese part of the Ossa Morena Zone". The authors conclude that the "axes have a close compositional and isotopical consistency with the copper ores from the western and northwestern region of the Iberian Peninsula" (Ling *et al.* 2014: 122).

The Isotopic characteristics of items dated to 1500-1300 cal. BC – for example, a lance head (Ånimskog), a palstave (Östra Ämtervik) and a metal from a crucible (Grimeton) – and dated to 1300-1100 cal. BC – such as a flange-hilted sword (Östra Hoby), a tanged sword (Sunne) and a copper rod (Tillinge) – also match the characteristics of ores from southeastern Iberia. The copper rod is consistent isotopically with the ores from Ossa Morena (Beja-Badajoz) in western Iberia and from Los Pedroches in southeastern Iberia. However, the geochemistry makes it impossible to exclude either of them, as noted by Ling et al. (2014: 122). Furthermore, items from the Grava deposit (Varmland), for example, the hilt-plated sword (1100-950/900 cal. BC), the arm ring (1100-950/900 cal. BC) and the fragment of a bronze lure (950/900-750/700 cal. BC), are consistent isotopically with the ores from south and southeastern Iberia and Bronze Age copper-based artefacts from Spain. They have similar lead isotope and trace element compositions with 0.2% each of As, Sb and Ni (Ling *et al.* 2014: 122).

Finally, two v-notched shields founded in Västergötland (Sunnersberg) provide remarkable evidence of material connections between western Iberia and northern European regions. According to the authors (Ling *et al.* 2014: 125), their composition is analogous in their trace element signature, particularly by the presence of cobalt and antimony in the same order of magnitude and a somewhat higher arsenic concentration. In summary, the shields have lead isotope compositions consistent with copper ores from southwestern Iberia (Beja-Badajoz) in the central area, which connects the northwest to the south of Iberia, and where the warrior stelae with depicted v-notched shields are distributed. In addition, findings of Baltic amber at Late Bronze Age sites in the same region must not be neglected (Murillo-Barosso, 2012). Similarly to other copper rich zones in Europe such as North Tyrol, Sardinia or Cyprus, the presence of Baltic amber can be explained as result of interaction between western Iberian and northern European communities.

A number of studies have been carried out on bronze artefacts, which mainly focused on the alloy composition determination and microstructural characterisation in order to explore the metallurgical technological evolution in west Iberia during the Later Prehistory. In this type of studies, technological innovation is used as a proxy to understand the cultural changes encouraged by the interaction between agents from Atlantic and Mediterranean backgrounds. In a Micro-EDXRF analyses on artefacts from Quinta do Almaraz (Almada, Western Coast of Portugal) concerning bronze artefacts with diverse typologies, chronologies and lead contents, the use of Mediterranean technology could be established (Velerio *et al.* 2012). The study demonstrates that the metallurgy at the settlement was very different from the local technology of the Late Bronze Age. The relatively high content of iron in the composition of artefacts, which is the result of an initial smelting of the raw materials under a strong reduction atmosphere, is characteristic of the fully Mediterranean backgrounds. In addition, the low content of tin in the composition of the bronzes seems to suggest a different process to obtain metal objects. However, there is also evidence of the adoption of innovations by the indigenous cultures, above all, at the end of the Bronze Late Age. As noted by the authors of this investigation, the "complexity of social interactions is quite evident in certain indigenous typologies that were apparently produced using Mediterranean technology, such as Acebuchal or double-spring fibulae" (Velerio *et al.* 2012: 81). Accordingly, this type of artefact seems to be a regional production made by metallurgists working in a context of hybridity.

Archaeometric analysis carried out in the Late Bronze Age archaeological site of Figueiredo das Donas, located in the core of the interaction area studied, also show evidence of Atlantic-Mediterranean hybridisation in a context of local metalwork production. According to the EDXRF and the micro-EDXRF analyses, all metal objects from this site were made of a binary bronze with traces of Pb, As and Sb. It is worth to mention the exceptional character of the nails under study, without parallels in other regions of Iberia. Their large size shows that they were used in heavy structures. In this regard, it has been suggested that they could have been shieldnails as those depicted in warrior stelae (Figueiredo *et al.*, 2011: 1206). Similar to other bronzes from the region, this alloy composition suggests that they were regional productions. However, X-ray digital radiography analysis, associated with detailed visual observations, indicates that the production of the nails involved joining the head to the pin by the casting-on technique. As the authors themselves note, the use of the casting-on technique can be assumed as evidence of the assimilation of "innovative technological solutions by the local metallurgists", due to the various spheres of interactions that were taking place "among the Mediterranean and Atlantic cultural axes" during the Late Bronze Age (Figueiredo *et al*, 2011:1210).

Finally, the study of the artefacts from the site of Fraga dos Corvos also provides remarkable information. This site is located in Trás-os-Montes, a region where a number of statues-menhir and stelae appear. The material culture of this site allows us to better understand the Atlantic-Mediterranean interactions in northwestern Iberia. This is due not only to the Mediterranean items found there, but also to the archaeometric analysis, which shed some light on the mixture of both technological backgrounds. In this respect, a set of metallic items from Fraga dos Corvos were subjected to EDXRF analyses. Artefacts such as tartessian belt hook fragments seem to consist of an unalloyed copper with various impurities (Sn, Pb, As, Sb, Ni and Fe). According to Valério *et al.* (2012), the typological features of most of the assemblage and the higher Fe content indicates a new and more efficient smelting process incorporated by local communities as a result of their interactions with Mediterranean agents. In this regard, according to Senna-Martinez (2011a: 145-146), the manufacture of this type of items, which are made of copper, could be related to the ability of gilding techniques. The technique implies that the piece to be gilded is made of copper and not of bronze. This type of artefacts also appears in the Baiões/Santa Luzia cultural group where there is evidence of the use of gilding by thermo-diffusion technique, a technology originating in Eastern Mediterranean areas (Figueiredo *et al.*, 2010b). Likewise, as noted by Senna-Martinez, the finding of a Bencarrón type fibula and a cauldron handle made of 'unalloyed' copper […], from the site of Almaraz, above mentioned, concurs with "the idea that prestige and ornamental items could be produced in copper in contexts where indigenous and orientalising metallurgical traditions mix" (Senna-Martinez, 2012: 257).

8. ENDPOINT…

The deposit of Carambolo (Camas, Seville) located in southern Iberia is an interesting endpoint for the line of argument adopted in this article. In contrast to the other deposits of gold objects discussed above, it was found in a specific archaeological context: a sanctuary and center of power with several oxhide shaped altars whose foundation appears to have been established during the Late Bronze Age (1020-810 BC) (Fernández et al. 2007: 103-104). The presence of artisans from both the Atlantic and the Mediterranean technological domains have been documented by typology and archaeometry studies (topographic examination using a Scanning Electron Microscope (SEM), and microanalytical study using Energy Dispersive X-ray Spectroscopy (EDS) in order to establish the elemental composition of the alloys) (Perea and Armbruster 2008; Perea and Hunt-Ortíz 2010; Bandera *et al.* 2010).

Two types of gold items have been dealt with above: those made with hybrid Mediterranean and Atlantic technologies (Late Bronze Age) and those that are fully Mediterranean, Phoenician (Early Iron Age). It is interesting to note that both types appeared together in the same deposit concealed under ground. An oxhide shaped gold breastplate, two bangle bracelets, several ornamental plaques and a seal-bead necklace was found as part of a hoard kept in a ceramic urn. Although traditional views have regarded this deposit as the homogenous gathering of Tartessian technology (Carriazo 1980: 222), recent archaeometric and morpho-typological studies have shown its heterogeneous and hybrid character (Perea and Armbruster 1998; Ontalba *et al.* 2002; Bandera *et al.* 2010). These artefacts reveal two different temporalities in connection with the Atlantic-Mediterranean interactions. The first one is embodied by the set of breastplates, bangles and plaques manufactured with hybrid technology. From a technological and ornamental viewpoint, these pieces are characteristic of the Atlantic technology, as evidenced in elements such as the cylindrical structures, the arrangement of the decoration in clusters, the semicircular shapes, and the spiked strips obtained using the lost-wax casting technique. However, as in the case of the gold pieces, their production also made use of Mediterranean technology: some of the spikes are hollow and decorated with typical Mediterranean motifs, such as rosettes (Bandera et al. 2010: 303). This hybridisation confirms the collaboration between workshops belonging to both technological domains during the Late Bronze Age, as demonstrated by Perea and Armbruster (2008; see also Bandera et al. 2010). In other words, the manufacturing methods, as well as the aesthetic and symbolic characteristics of the pieces of the Carambolo deposit, along with the rest of artefacts discussed above, stand as evidence of the interaction between people of Atlantic and Mediterranean extraction. The coming together of individuals from different cultural backgrounds encouraged the exchange of ideas, giving rise to different ways of doing things, which caused new items to be added to the material culture, leading to the creation of a new socio-material reality.

The second temporality revealed in the deposit emerges through the seal-bead necklace manufactured with Mediterranean technology and featuring a decorative scheme of eastern Mediterranean origin— more specifically, from the Phoenician world of the eighth and sixth centuries BC which also produced the treasure of Baião (Támega), in Northwestern Iberia. While the ox-hide-shaped breastplates and the bangles denote connectivity and hybridisation in the Late Bronze Age (similar to the other gold objects discussed in previous sections), the Phoenician necklace indicates a moment when the artefacts were concealed in a deposit (Perea and Armbruster 2008: 519). Interestingly, the ox-hide-shaped breastplate and the bangles (the objects that embody a model of connectivity characteristic of the Late Bronze Age) were buried under the floor of the sanctuary sometime between the eighth and the sixth centuries BC. Thus, the breastplates were removed from circulation coinciding with the Phoenician colonisation of the Portuguese coast and with the opening of the Atlantic sea route to Northwestern Iberia by Phoenician vessels, a development that probably diminished the movement of people and goods over the land route that connected this region with Southern Iberia during the Late Bronze Age. Therefore, both the concealment of the breastplates and the rising importance of the sea route may be seen as embedded in the previously mentioned transitional context that saw a reciprocity-based model of exchange among elites (to which statue-menhirs belong) to give way to another model of exchange controlled by a merchant class based in the ports of Gadir and Onuba, and to a network of colonies and factories located on the Atlantic coast (Arruda 2002).

9. CONCLUSION

This article has focused on cultural contact between the Northwest and the South of Iberia and, by extension, Atlantic and Mediterranean backgrounds it the West of Iberia. These encounters resulted in the exchange of goods, the swapping of ideas and technologies and the learning of new ways of doing things. This adoption of new and foreign items, technologies and ideas meant that not only were assumed, but were also redefined and put to new uses and practices in a myriad of ways.

It has been sought to show the intermingling of relations amongst the people from different regions who procured raw materials in Western Iberia, those who commissioned the finished object, partners in exchange networks and the individuals who used these objects. It became clear that the agency of the object –as well as the people behind its production– was crucial to maintaining these complex networks. People (elites) and objects (gifts) that made and used were irrevocably entwined. Artefacts such as the bracelet of Cantonha or the bangle of Sintra helped to unite different people and cultural backgrounds in a shared cultural milieu. Gift exchange has long been recognised as one of the fundamental logics the Late Bronze Age. In this regard, gifting is far more than a mere economic transaction; instead, gift exchange encourages "appropriation of objects as part of one's *personalia*" (Gell 1986: 112).

The study of the statue-menhirs and stelae of the Late Bronze Age allows us to link them to the elites of Northwestern and Southwestern Iberia respectively. The distribution of these material images in mineral-rich transit areas, where these objects were circulated and the technologies were mixed, make them a form of stone people in motion and connection. Likewise, as is the case with the gold items and bronze axes, the hybridization of both types of monuments (statue-menhirs and stela) reveals strong relations between people from two cultural backgrounds, adopting a mixture of Atlantic and Mediterranean features. The movement of artefacts in the landscape, the hybridisation in a technological and typological level and the shared traits in the iconography were not just a consequence of exchange between groups from different regions or backgrounds, but also a consequence of the emergence of supra-regional elite identities. All in all, the intention here has been to show how during the Late Bronze Age people, their identity and their social relations were totally entangled with the hybrid and suprarregional material world they inhabited.

REFERENCES

Almagro Basch, M. (1966) Las estelas decoradas del Suroeste Peninsular. Madrid, Consejo Superior de Investigaciones Científicas.

Almagro-Gorbea, M. (1993) Les Steles Anthropomorphes de la Péninsule Ibérique. In Les représentations humaines du Néolithique à L`age du Fer. Éditions du Comité des Travaux Historiques et Scientifiques, J. Briard and A. Duval (eds.) Paris, Comité des travaux historiques et scientifiques. pp. 123-139.

Alves, L. B. and Reis, M. (2011) Memoriais de pedra, símbolos de identidade: duas novas peças escultóricas de Cervos (Montalegre, Vila Real). In Vilaça, R. (ed.), Estelas e estátuas-menir: Da Pré à Protohistoria, Sabugal, Museu do Sabugal, pp. 187-216.

Armbruster, B. (1995) O Bracelete de Cantonha. In A Idade do Bronze em Portugal: discusos de Poder, Jorge, S.O. (ed.), Lisboa, Museu Nacional de Arqueología, pp. 104-105.

Armbruster, B. and Parreira, R. (1993) Inventário do Museu Nacional de Arqueologia: Colecção de Ourivesaria. Do Calcolítico à Idade do Bronze, Lisbon, Instituto Português de Museus.

Arruda, A.M. (2002) Los fenicios en Portugal. Fenicios e indígenas en el centro y sur de Portugal (siglos VIII-VI a.C.), Barcelona, Cuadernos de Arqueología Mediterránea 5-6.

Bandera Romero, M.L. de la, Gómez Tubío, B., Ontalba Salamanca, M.A., Respaldiza, M.A. and Ortega Feliu, I. (2010) El tesoro de El Carambolo: técnica, simbología y poder. In El Carambolo. 50 años de un Tesoro, Bandera Romero, M.L. de la and Ferrer Albelda E. (eds.), Sevilla, Servicio de Publicaciones de la Universidad de Sevilla, pp. 297-334.

Bettencourt, A. (2005) A estatuaria. In Arte e Cultura de Galicia e Norte de Portugal Hidalgo Cuñarro, J. M. (ed.), Vigo, Nova Galicia Edicións, pp. 166-177.

Blas Cortina, M.A. de and Rodríguez del Cueto, F. (2015) La cuestión campaniforme en el Cantábrico central y las minas de cobre prehistóricas de la Sierra del Aramo, CuPAUAM, 41, pp. 165-179.

Bradley, R. (2013) Hoards and the deposition of metalwork. In The Oxford Handbook of the European Bronze Age, Harding, A. and Fokkens, H. (eds.), Oxford, Oxford University Press, pp. 121-139.

Brandherm, D. (2007) Las Espadas del Bronce Final en la Península Ibérica y Baleares, Stuttgart, Franz Steiner Verlag.

Bruck, J. (2006) Fragmentation, personhood and the social construction of technology in Middle and Late Bronze Age Britain. Cambridge Archaeological Journal 16 (2), pp. 297–315.

Carriazo, J. (1980) Protohistoria de Sevilla. En el vértice de Tartesos, Sevilla, Ediciones Guadalquivir.

Celestino Pérez, S. (2001) Estelas de guerrero y estelas diademadas. La precolonización y formación del mundo tartésico, Barcelona, Bellaterra.

Celestino, S. (2008) La precolonización a través de los símbolos. In Celestino, S. Rafael, N. and Armada, X.L. (eds.), Contacto cultural entre el Mediterráneo y el Atlántico (siglos XII-VIII a.n.e.). La precolonización a debate (Madrid, Consejo Superior de Investigaciones Científicas), pp. 107-126.

Chapman, J. C. (2000) Fragmentation in Archaeology. People, Places and Broken objects in the prehistoric of South-eastern Europe, London: Routledge.

Comendador Rey, B.; Rodríguez Muñoz, V. and Manteiga Brea, A. (2011) A estatua-menhir do Tameirón no contexto dos resultados de intervención arqueolóxica no Monte Urdiñeira e o seu contorno (A Gudiña-Riós, Ourense). In Estelas e estátuas-menir: Da Pré à Protohistoria, Vilaça, R. (ed.), Sabugal, Museu do Sabugal, 217-244.

Connerton, P. (1989) How societies remember, Cambridge, Cambridge University Press.

Correia, A., Silva, C.T., Vaz, J.I. (1979), Catálogo da Coleção Arqueológica Dr. Jose´ Coelho, Beira Alta, 38, pp. 605–638.

Costas Goberna, F. J. and Peña Santos, A. (2006) Los barcos de los Petroglifos de Oia. Los tesoros del hechicero y una nueva embarcación. Glaucopis 12, pp 277-94.

Delibes de Castro, G; Fernández-Miranda, M. (1988), Armas y utensilios de Bronce en la Prehistoria de las islas Baleares. Series: Studia archaeologica, Valladolid, Universidad de Valladolid, vol. 78.

Díaz-Andreu, M. (1988) El análisis discriminante en la clasificación tipológica: aplicación a las hachas de talón de la Península Ibérica. Boletín del Seminario de Arte y Arqueología de Valladolid, vol. LIV, pp. 25-64.

Díaz-Guardamino Uribe, M. (2006) Materialidad y acción social: el caso de las estelas decoradas y estatuas-menhir durante la Prehistoria peninsular. In Actas del VIII Congresso Internacional de Estelas Funerárias (Lisboa 2005). O Arqueólogo Português. Suplemento 3 (Lisbon), pp. 15-33.

Díaz-Guadarmino Uribe, M. (2010) Las estelas decoradas en la Prehistoria de la Península Ibérica. Tesis Doctoral inédita. Universidad Complutense de Madrid.

Díaz-Guardamino Uribe, M. (2011) Iconografía, lugares y relaciones sociales: reflexiones en torno a las estelas y estatuas-menhir atribuidas a la Edad del Bronce en la Península Ibérica. In Estelas e Estátuas-menhires da Pré à Proto-história, Vilaça, R. (ed.), Sabugal, Câmara Municipal do Sabugal, 63-88.

Fábrega Álvarez, P. Fonte, J. and González García, F. J. (2011) Las sendas de la memoria. Sentido, espacio y reutilización de las estatuas-menhir en el noroeste de la Península Ibérica. Trabajos de Prehistoria 68 (2), pp. 313-330.

Figueiredo, E., Silva, R.J.C., Senna-Martinez, J.C., Fátima Araújo, M., Braz Fernandes, F.M. and Inês Vaz, J.L. (2010a) Smelting and recycling evidences from the Late Bronze Age habitat site of Baiões (Viseu, Portugal), Journal of Archaeological Science, 37, pp. 1623–1634.

Figueiredo, E., Silva, R.J.C., Araújo, M.F. and Senna-Martinez, J.C. (2010b) Identification of ancient gilding technology and Late Bronze Age metallurgy by EDXRF, Micro-EDXRF, SEM-EDS and metallographic techniques. *Microchimica Acta.* 168, p. 283-291.

Figueiredo, E., Araujo M.F., Silva R.J.C., Senna-Martinez J.C. and Ines Vaz, J.L. (2011) Characterisation of Late Bronze Age large size shield nails by EDXRF, micro-EDXRF and X-ray digital radiography, Applied Radiation and Isotopes 69, pp. 1205–1211.

Fernández Flores, A. and Rodríguez Azogue, A. (2007) Tartessos desvelado. La colonización fenicia del Suroeste peninsular y el origen y ocaso de Tartessos, Córdoba, Almuzara.

Fontijn, D. R. (2008) Everything in it's right place? On selective deposition, landscape and the construction of identity in later prehistory. Prehistoric Europe, Theory and Practice, A. Jones (ed.), Oxford, Blackwell, pp. 86-106.

Galán Domingo, E. (1993) Estelas, paisaje y territorio en el Bronce Final del Suroeste de la Península Ibérica. Madrid, Complutum 3.

Galán Domingo, E. (2005) Evolución, adpatación y resitencia. En torno a las formas de intercambio de las comunidades atlánticas en contacto con el mundo orientalizante. In El periodo orientalizante. Actas III simposio internacional de arqueología mediterránea de Mérida: protohistoria del mediterráneo occidental, Celestino Pérez, S. and Jiménez Ávila, J. (eds.), Madrid, Anejos de Archivo Español de Arqueología, XXXV, pp. 467-475.

Galán Domingo, E. and Ruiz-Gálvez, M. (1996) Divisa, dinero y moneda. Aproximación a los patrones metrológicos prehistóricos peninsulares. In Querol, M.A. and Chapa, T. (eds.), Homenaje al profesor Manuel Fernández-Miranda, Madrid, Complutum extra 6, pp. 191-215.

Gamble, C. (2007) Origins and Revolutions: Human Identity in Earliest Prehistory, Cambridge, Cambridge University Press.

Giardino, C. (1995) Il Mediterraneo occidentale fra XIV ed VII secolo a.C.: cerchie minerarie e metallurgiche, Oxford, British Archaeological Reports.

Gell, A. (1998), Art and Agency, Oxford, Oxford University Press.

Gomes, S.S., Figueiredo, E., Araújo, M.F, Lopes, F. and Senna-Martinez, J.C. (2013) Isotopic lead characterization of archaeological bronzes from Fraga dos Corvos (N. Portugal), vol. 4, special issue, pp. 661-672.

González-Ruibal, A. (2004) Facing two seas: Mediterranean and Atlantic contacts in the north- west of Iberia in the first millennium BC. Oxford Journal of Arhcaeology 23(3), pp 287-317.

González Ruibal, A. (2006) "Past the last outpost: Punic merchants in the Atlantic Ocean (5th-1st centuries BC). Journal of Mediterranean Archaeology, 19(1), pp, 121-150.

González-Ruibal, A. (2006-2007) Galaicos. Poder y comunidad en el Noroeste de la Península Ibérica (1200 a.C. - 50 d. C.), Brigantium, Vol. 18-19.

Gosden, Ch. (2004) Archaeology and Colonialism, Cambridge, Cambridge University Press.

Jorge, S. O. (1999) Stelen und Menhirstatuen der Bronzezeit auf der Iberischen Halbinsel: Diskurse der Macht. In Götter und Helden der Bronzezeit. Ostfildern, Europa im zeitalter des Odysseus, pp. 114-122.

Jorge, V.O. and Jorge, S.O. (1983) Nótula preliminar sobre uma nova estátua-menir do Norte de Portugal. Arqueologia, 7, pp. 44-47.

Jorge, V.O. and Jorge, S.O. (1993) Statues-menhirs et stèles du nord du Portugal. In Les representations humaines du Néolithique à L´Age du Fer. Actes du 115e congrès national des sociétés savantes. Avignon (1990), Briard, J. and Duval, A. (eds.), Paris, Comité des travaux historiques et scientifiques, pp. 29-44.

Junghans, S.; Sangmeister, S.; Schröder, M. (1960) Metallanalysen kupferzeitlicher und frühbronzezeitlicher Bondenfunde aus Europa, Studien zu den Anfängen der Metallurgie, vol. I, Berlin, Gerb. Mann Verlag, p. 220.

Junghans, S.; Sangmeister, S.; Schröder, M. (1960) Kupfer und Bronze in der frühen Metallzeit Europas, Studien zu den Anfängen der Metallurgie, vols. II-III, Berlin, Gerb. Mann Verlag, p. 315.

Junghans, S.; Sangmeister, S.; Schröder, M. (1974) Kupfer und Bronze in der frühen Metallzeit Europas, Studien zu den Anfängen der Metallurgie, vols. II-IV, Berlin, Gerb. Mann Verlag, p. 406.

Knapp, B. (2008) Prehistory and protohistory Cyprus: identity, insularity, and Connectivity, Oxford, Oxford University Press.

Keane, W. (2003) Semiotics and the Social Analysis of Material Things. Language and Communication 23 (2-3), pp. 409-425.

Knappett, C. (2011) An Archaeology of Interaction: Network Perspectives on Material Culture and Society, Oxford, Oxford University Press.

Ling, J., Hjärthner-Holdar, E., Grandin, L., Billström, K., Persson, P.-O. (2013) Moving metals or indigenous mining? Provenancing Scandinavian Bronze Age artefacts by lead isotopes and trace elements, Journal of Archaeological Science 40 (1), pp. 291-304.

Ling, J.; Stos-Galeb, Z.; Grandinc, L.; Billströmd, K.; Hjärthner-Holdarc, E.; Persson, P-O. (2014) Moving metals II: provenancing Scandinavian Bronze Age artefacts bylead isotope and elemental analyses, Journal of Archaeological Science 41 (2014), pp. 106-132.

Ling, J. and Stos-Gale, Z. (2015) Representations of oxhide ingots in Scandinavian rock art: the sketchbook of a Bronze Age traveller, Antiquity, 89, pp. 191-209.

López Cuevillas, F. (1951) La Joyas Castreñas, Madrid, Instituto de Arqueología y Prehisotria Rodrigo Caro.

López Plaza, S.; Sevillano SanJosé, M.C.; Grande del Brío, R. (1996) Estatua-menhir de Tremedal de Tormes (Salamanca). *Zephyrus*, 49, pp. 295-303

Martín Bravo, A.M. (1999) Los orígenes de la Lusitania. El I Milenio a.C. en la alta Extremadura, Madrid, Real academia de la Historia.

Monteagudo, L. (1977) Die Beile aufder Iberischen Halbinsel, München, Prähistorische Bronzefunde IX.

Murillo-Barosso, M., Martinón-Torres, M., 2012. Amber sources and trade in the prehistory of the Iberian Peninsula, European Journal of Archaeology 15 (2), pp. 187-216

Ontalba, M. A., Gómez, B., Fernández, F., Respaldiza, M.A. and Bandera, M.L. de la 2002: Análisis del Tesoro de El Carambolo mediante un equipo portátil de fluorescencia de rayos X. In Roldán. C. (ed.): Ponencias del IV Congreso Nacional de Arqueometría. ICMUV (Valencia), 176- 181.

Pare, Ch. (2013) Weighing, commodification and money. In Harding, A. and Fokkens, H. (eds.), The Oxford Handbook of the European Bronze Age (Oxford), 508-523.

Peirce, C. S. (1998 [1932]) The essential Peirce: selected philosophical writings 2 Bloomington, Indiana University Press.

Perea, A. (1995) La metalurgia del oro en la fachada atlántica penin- sular durante el Bronce Final: interacciones tecnológicas. Ritos de paso y puntos de paso. La Ría de Huelva en el mundo del Bronce Final europeo, M. Ruíz-Gálvez (ed.). Complutum, extra 5, pp. 69-78

Perea, A. (2005) Mecanismos identitarios y de construcción de poder en la transición bronce-Hierro. *Trabajos de Prehistoria,* 62 (2), pp. 91-103.

Perea, A. and Hunt-Ortíz, M. (2010) New finds from an old treasure. The archaeometric study of new gold objects from the Phoenician sanctuary of El Carambolo (Camas, Seville, Spain), Archeosciences, vol. 33, 2009, pp. 1-5.

Perea, A. y Armbruster, B. (1998) Cambio tecnológico y contacto entre Atlántico y Mediterráneo: el depósito de El Carambolo (Sevilla) Trabajos de Prehistoria 55 (1), pp. 121-138.

Perea, A. y Armbruster, B. (2008) Tradición, cambio y ruptura generacional. La producción orfebre de la fachada atlántica durante la transición Bronce-Hierro de la Península Ibérica. In Contacto cultural entre el Mediterráneo y el Atlántico (siglos XII-VIII a.n.e.). La precolonización a debate, Celestino, S. Rafel, N. and Armada X. L. (eds.), Madrid, Consejo Superior de Investigaciones Científicas, pp. 509-522.

Preucel, R. W. (2006) Archaeological semiotics, Oxford, Oxford University Press.

Queiroga, F.M.V.R. (2003) War and Castros: New Perspectives in the Iron Age of Northwestern Portugal. Oxford, British Archaeological Reports International Series 1198.

Reboreda Carreira, A.; Nieto Muñiz, E.B. (2012) *A estela de Castrelo do Val. Peza do mes, octubre 2012*, Ourense, Museo arqueolóxico provincial de Ourense.

Robb, J. (2009) People of Stone: stelae, personhood, and society in prehistoric Europe. Journal Archaeological Method Theory 16, pp. 162-183.

Rodríguez-Corral, J. (2015) Las estatuas-menhir noroccidentales en contexto: conectividad y conexiones materiales durante el Bronce Tardío/Final, *Complutum,* 2015, Vol. 26 (1), pp. 153-172.

Rovira, S. (2002) Metallurgy and Society in Prehistoric Spain, in Metals and Society, Ottaway, B.S. and Wagner, E.C. (eds.), British Archaeological Reports, Oxford, pp. 5–20.

Ruiz-Gálvez, M.L. (1992) La novia vendida: orfebrería, herencia y agricultura en la Protohistoria de la Península Ibérica. Spal 1, pp. 219-252.

Ruiz-Gálvez, M.L. (1998) La Europa Atlántica en la Edad del Bronce. Un viaje a las raíces de Europa Occidental, Barcelona, Critica.

Ruiz-Gálvez, M.L. y Galán, E. (1991) Las estelas del Suroeste como hitos de vías ganaderas y rutas comerciales. Trabajos de Prehistoria 48: pp. 257-273.

Sahlins, M. (1972) Stone Age Economics. London, Routledge.

Senna-Martinez, J. C. (2011) La 'conexión lusitana': contactos orientalizantes y búsqueda de estaño y oro en el Centro-Norte portugués. In Gadir y el Círculo del Estrecho revisados. Propuestas de la arqueología desde un enfoque social, Domínguez Pérez, J.C. (ed.), Cádiz, Consejería de Innovación, Ciencia y Empresa de la Junta de Andalucía, pp. 285-296.

Senna-Martinez, J.C., Figueiredo, E. and Araújo, M.F. (2011) Metallurgy and Society in 'Baioes/Santa Luzia' Culture Group: results of the metal bronze project. In Primer Congreso Internacional Povoamento e Exploração de Recursos Mineiros na Europa Atlântica Ocidental Martins, C.B., Bettercourt, A., Martins, J.I.F.P and Carvalho, J. (eds.), Braga, Universidade do Minho, pp. 405-420.

Senna-Martinez, J.C., reprezas, J., Luís E., figueiredo, E., Lopes, F., Gomes, S.S., Araújo, F. and Silva, R.J (2012), Metal Artefacts of Mediterranean Affiliation from Fraga dos Corvos Habitat Site (Eastern Trás-os-Montes, Portugal): A First Appraisal, O Arqueólogo Português, Série V, 2, 2012, pp. 241-263.

Silva, A. C. F. (1986) A Cultura Castreja no Noroeste de Portugal, Paços de Ferreira, Museu Arqueológico da Citânia de Sanfins.

Strathern, M. (1990) The Gender of the Gift, Cambridge, Cambridge University Press.

Strathern, A. and Steward P. J. 2005: Ceremonial exchange. In A Handbook of Economic Anthropology, Carrier, J. G. (ed.), Bloomington, Indiana University Press, pp. 230-245.

Torres Ortiz, M. (2008) Los "tiempos" de la precolonización. In Contacto cultural entre el Mediterráneo y el Atlántico (siglos XII-VIII a.n.e.). La precolonización a debate. Celestino, S., Rafel, N. and Armada, X.L. (eds.), Madrid, Consejo Superior de Investigaciones Científicas, pp. 59-92.

Valério, P., Silva, R.J.C., Araújo, M.F., Soares, A.M.M. and Barros, L. (2012) A multianalytical approach to study the Phoenician bronze technology in the Iberian Peninsula. A view from Quinta do Almaraz, Materials Characterization, 67, pp. 74-82.

Van Dommelen, P and Knapp, B. (2010) Material Connections in the Ancient Mediterranean: Mobility, Materiality and Identity, London, Routledge.

Vilaça, R. (2008a) A través das Beiras: Pré-História e Proto-História, Coimbra, Faculdade de Letras da Universidade de Coimbra.

Vilaça, R. (2008b) Reflexões em torno da 'presença mediterrânea' no Centro do território português, na charneira do Bronze para o Ferro. In Contacto cultural entre el Mediterráneo y el Atlántico (siglos XII-VIII a.n.e.). La precolonización a debate, S. Celestino, Rafael, N. and Armada, X. L. (eds.), Madrid, Consejo Superior de Investigaciones Científicas, pp. 371-402.

Vilaça, R. (ed.) (2011) Estelas e Estátuas-menhires da Pré à Proto-história, Sabugal, Câmara Municipal do Sabugal.

Vilaça, R., Cruz, D. J., Santos, A. T. and Marques, J. N. (2001) A estátua-menir de 'Ataúdes' (Figueira de Castelo Rodrigo, Guarda) no seu contexto regional. Estudos Pré-Históricos 9, pp. 69-82.

Vilaça, R.; Osório, M.; Santos, A.T. (2011) Nova peça insculturada da região raiana do Sabugal (Beira Interior, Portugal): uma primeira abordagem. Estelas e Estátuas-menhires da Pré à Proto-história, Vilaça, R. (ed.), Sabugal, Câmara Municipal do Sabugal, pp. 343-367.

Waterman, A. J., David W. P., Silva, A.M. and Thomas, J.T. (2014) In search of homelands: Using strontium isotopes to identify biological markers of mobility in late prehistoric Portugal. *Journal of Archaeological Science,* 42, pp. 119–127.

8

PO-PU-RE: WORKSHOPS, USE AND ARCHAEOMETRIC ANALYSIS IN PRE-ROMAN CENTRAL EASTERN MEDITERRANEAN

Kalaitzaki, A[1], Vafiadou, A[1], Frony, A.[1], Reese, D.S.[2], Drivaliari, A[3], Liritzis, I[4,5]

[1]*Dept. of Mediterranean Studies, University of the Aegean, Rhodes, Greece*
[2]*Peabody Museum of Natural History, Yale University, New Haven, U.S.A.*
[3]*Lab of Environmental Archaeology, Dept. of Mediterranean Studies, University of the Aegean, Rhodes, Greece*
[4] *Collaborative Innovation Center on Yellow River Civilization of Henan Province & Key Research Institute of Yellow River Civilization and Sustainable Development, Henan University, China*

[5]*Dept. of Mediterranean Studies, Lab of Archaeometry, University of the Aegean, 1 Demokratias Str., Rhodes 85132, Greece*

Corresponding author: I Liritzis (liritzis@rhodes.aegean.gr)

ABSTRACT

Po-pu-re (porphyra) denotes the deep red/ purple colour delivered from sea shells extraction and processing of five species and conversion to dye has been practice in ancient world, especially in the Mediterranean Sea. Archaeological excavations have shown that murex was used in Greece and in other areas, such as Egypt, Israel, Turkey, Italy, Spain and generally throughout the Mediterranean basin. The colour of murex was priceless and used in wall-paintings and textiles. Many fabrics have been found in Crete, Egypt and Israel. Considering the ancient texts, including those of Plutarch, Pliny, Aristotle, Herodotus and Xenokrates, it has been shown that its identification can be advanced by studying chemical production of purple-dye, while using spectroscopy and chemical analysis the basic chemistry, the dibromoindigotin (DBI), is identified. The present report reviews major murex producing workshops in the Mediterranean and archaeometrical analyses that identify this marine shell.

KEYWORDS: Po-pu-re, Porphyra, Murex, Bolinus brandaris, Hexaplex trunculus, Stramonita haemastoma, purple-dye production, Mediterranean, Textile, Workshops, Tyrian purple, Royal purple, Spectroscopy, Chromatography

1. INTRODUCTION

Po-pu-re, the vocalized word to denote purple, the Greek word πορφύρα (porphyra), which used by Myceneans and found Linear B tablets, for deep red to purple color, produced by marine shells murex species. Invertebrates are the largest animal group that exceeds one million species worldwide. Gastropods belong to the family of invertebrates. Specifically, is one of the five classes of the *Phylum Mollusca*. Their name *gastropods* are complex and comes from the ancient Greek word γάστρος = "abdomen" + πόδια = "feet" (belly + feet) from the apparent picture of moving a part of their body, which, in reality, is fleshy leg. The first official recording and description of gastropods taxonomic designation is in 1795. The murex species: *Bolinus brandaris, Hexaplex trunculus, Stramonia haemastoma* belong to this category (Cooksey, 2001a) (Figure 1.1). Most murex species live in the sea, and have a gland that excretes a dye, the purple (Radwin and D'Attilio, 1986). Each kind of shell give us a percentage of colour, such us: red, blue, purple, yellow, etc (Table 1.1).

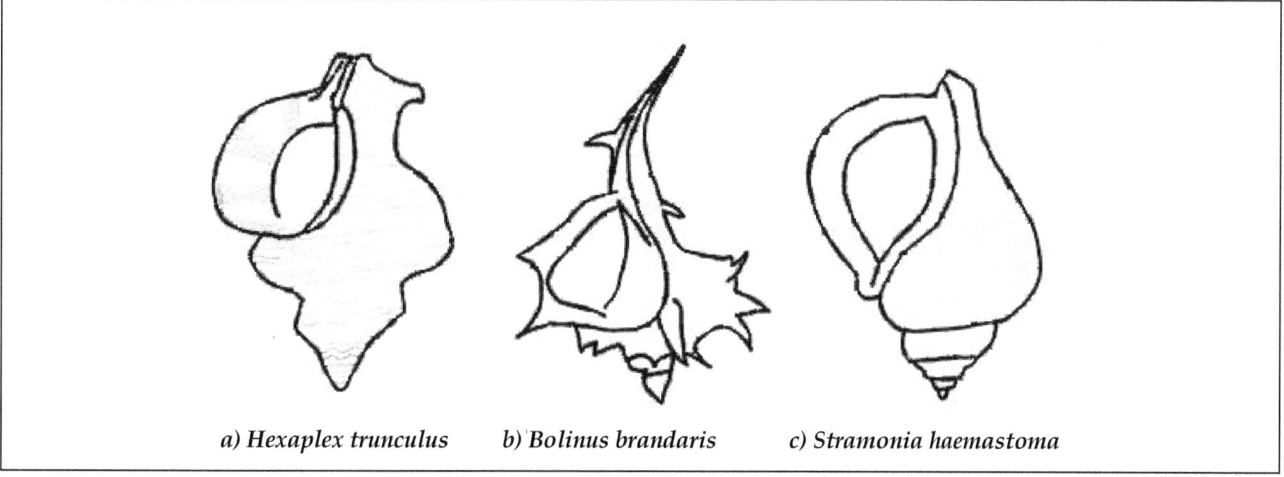

Figure 1.1 Two representative schimatic drawings of Murex species (a, b) and a marine gastropod mollusc of rapaninae subfamily (c): a) Hexaplex trunculus, b) Bolinus brandaris, c) Stramonia haemastoma (drawing by A.K)

Table 1.1 Percentage of colour in different kinds of shells as measured by HPLC peak areas at 288 nm, sample description and references. The archaeological samples analysis was made by improved HPLC, while samples where treated with DMSO at 80° C for 15′. IND: Blue colour INR : Red colour MBI: 6-Monobromoindigo 6′MBI: 6′-Monobromoindirubin 6MBIR: 6-Monobromoindirubin DBI: 6,6′ Dibromoindigo DBIR : 6,6′ Dibromoindirubin (based on Karapanagiotis et al, 2013).

	Region	Solvent	IND (blue)	INR (light purple)	MBI (purple)	6′MBIR (red)	6MBIR (light red)	DBI (Dark red)	DBIR (red)	Other	Sample	Reference
Hexaplex trunculus												
1	Carthage	DMSO	62.6	1.2	31.9	0.2	0.3	3.7	0.1		Carthaginian sample	Karapanagiotis et al., 2013
2	Croatia	DMSO	48.1	4.3	36.3	2.0	1.4	6.8	1.1		Croatian sample	Karapanagiotis et al., 2013
3	Tunisia	DMSO	34.9	0.4	49.4	0.3	0.3	14.3	0.4		Tunisian-red	Karapanagiotis et al., 2013
4	Tunisia	DMSO	53.5	1.5	39.0	0.3	0.7	4.8	0.2		Tunisian-blue	Karapanagiotis et al., 2013
5	Tarragona	Pyridine	56.0	0.0	37.0			7.0	0.0		Sample was stained cotton (not vat)	Wouters, 1992
6	Tarragona	Pyridine	53.0	14.0	33.0			0.0	0.0		Sample was dyed wool (vat)	Wouters, 1992
7	Akhziv	DMF	4.05	0.0	17.79			60.0	18.16		Data were collected at 600nm and converted to 288nm	Koren, 1995, 2008a
8	Saronikos	DMF	30.2	3.19	26.2	5.9	8.2	13.6	8.9			Karapanagiotis et.al, 2006, 2013

9	Akhziv	DMSO	0.35	2.17	7.36	0.0	0.73	67.89	23.68	0.0		Koren, 2008a
10	Spain	DMSO	38.91		39.49	1.14	1.84	4.06	9.90	1.46		Koren, 2008a
11	France	DMSO	5.77	2.17	34.81	4.24	2.57	37.53	8.48	4.23	Data were collected at 298nm	Nowik et.al, 2011
12	Hermione	DMF	21.9	5.3	25.6	1.2	4.0	15.6	2.5	24.0	Data were collected at 283nm	Karapanagiotis et al., 2013
Bolinus Brandaris												
1	Tarragona	Pyri-dine	0.0	0.0	0.0			85.0	15.0		Sample was stained cotton (not vat)	Wouters, 1992
2	Tarragona	Pyri-dine	0.0	0.0	6.0			81.0	13.0		Sample was dyed wool (vat)	Wouters, 1992
3	Saronikos	DMF	Trace	0.0	1.6	0.0	0.0	97.2	1.2			Karapanagiotis et.al, 2006, 2013
4	Flumicino	DMSO	0.0	0.0	0.85	0.0	0.0	59.27	2.35	37.53		Koren, 2008a
5	Thera	DMSO	2.0	0.5	1.8	0.2	0.2	79.0	16.3			Mantzouris and Karapanagiotis, 2014
Stramonita Haemastoma												
1	Tarragona	Pyri-dine	0.0	0.0	3.0			91.0	6.0		Sample was stained cotton (not vat)	Wouters, 1992
2	Tarragona	Pyri-dine	Trace	0.0	3.0			91.0	6.0		Sample was dyed wool (vat)	Wouters, 1992
3	Israel	DMSO	0.0	0.0	0.66	0.0	0.0	65.44	10.46	23.45		Koren, 2008a
4	Hermione	DMF	30.3	0.0	3.8	0.0	0.0	31.0	1.9	32.9	Data were collected at 283nm	Karapanagiotis et al., 2013

The colour of murex was priceless and symbolized the wealth. The purple fabric, with its indelible characteristic deep red color was equivalent to the value of silver. It was synonymous to the absolute luxury and opulence. In Roman time, there was a law forbidding ordinary to wear purple clothes (Rolfe, 1913).

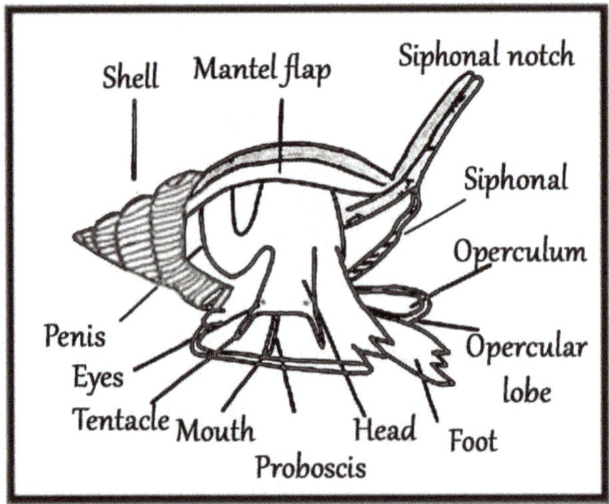

Figure 1.2 Parts of a Murex (drawing by A.K)

Each shell gave only a drop of dye, since the 12,000 shells of *Bolinus,* could produce a few grams of purple able to dye a single fabric (Figure 1.2). The dye was not suitable only for clothes but also for wall-painting and even for cosmetic face pigment.

We do not know much about painting techniques and working methods of the painters. There was a tendency to keep secret the knowledge of profession. It was a profession taught by others with practical application probably changed a bit with the appearance of the first books. The dyeing techniques practically did not change until the late 19th century, when rapid changes in the textile industry demanded improvements in procedures paints.

Figure 1.3 Painting of Heracles and murexby Peter Paul Rubens, Musée Bonnat, Bayonne (Börnchen, 2009)

However, there are many reports about porphyra. Some of those that have survived during the centuries are mentioned in: Linear B, Homer, Aristotle, Herodotus, Aeschylus, Pindar, Simonides of Keos, Plato, Xenophon, Plutarch, Aelian, Pliny the Elder, Xenocrates, Oribasius.

According to tradition, the dog of Hercules (Fig. 1.3) bit a murex and its mouth was discolored red (Protopapas and Gatsos, 2003). Perhaps the same happened to people, since the shells were part of their diet. From the beginning purple it was supposed to be the noble colour and the symbol of Kings. According to mythology, when Perseus emerged from the water, his divine lineage was recognized by Zeus because he wore a purple mantle (*Simonides 31:13D 371 P*). Also, Theseus, when required by Minos to prove his divine origin, he sank into the sea and when he emerged he was wearing a purple garment, given by Amphitrite (*Bacchylides, Lithyramvoi* 17,112). Similarly, Jason had a purple robe given by Athena. Even Apollo presented wreathed with Parnassian laurel and his robe of Tyrian purple swept the ground (Bulfinch, 2009).

Figure 1.4 Tablet in Linear B indicating po-pu-re (Stieglitz, 1994)

Linear B tablets (KNCH976) recorded the purple as (po-pu-re) (Chadwick, 1958; Piteros et al, 1982; Stieglitz, 1994) and certify the earliest-Greek identity of the word, while excluding any relationship with the Eastern peoples, as the name of porphyra during the Phoenician times called "po-ni-ki-ja"(Cardon, 2007) (Figure 1.4).

However, from the shell dozens of Greek epithets are known, such as: πορφυρένιος (porfyrenios-purple), πορφυρίτης (porphyrite), Πορφυρογέννητος (Porphyrogennetus-prince born in the room of porfyra/purple), purple, πορφυρόχρωμος (porfyrochromos-of purple colour), etc.

Figure 1.5 Hexaplex Trunculus from excavation of Antikythera, 2013, Hellenistic period (Permission by A.Tsaravopoulos)

Pliny (*Historia NaturalisIX, 125-136*) mentioned that it was mostly fished in the spring and for the fishing and use as a bait of bivalves. The wicker baskets are called "κύρτοι"(cyrtoi) from their convex shape, of pliable branches from sparto, which is a perennial broom and grows wild over much of the Mediterranean, from rushes or willow(Figure 1.5).

The 15th B.C. Minoans on Crete may have passed the art of processing murex to Phoenicians of the Levant. However, during the 17th century, Minoans and later Phoenicians made purple dye by extracting a liquid from glands of the murex. Each gland yielded only a drop or two of a yellowish substance which darkened when exposed to sun and air. Processing required a slow simmering over about two weeks usually in lead or tin pans, as other metals discolored the dye (Rystedt et al., 2010). At the same time mounds of crushed shells lie piled around ancient dye works, such as, at Tyre and Sidon, Syria, Ugarit and the Gulf coast of the Arabian Peninsula (Reese, 2010; Scott, 2006). The indelible dye of purple was so valuable that during classic period its value was equal to its weight in silver. Phoenicians developed a flourishing sea trade until the late fourth century BC, when the Phoenician cities in corporate into the Greek empire.

Many references are made in ancient sources. The Homeric epics often refer to *aliporfyra* (= marine porphyra). Homer uses this term to distinguish it from plant porphyra, which had markedly less value (*Homer, Odyssey* 6.53). Garments made for heroes such as Agamemnon with royal purple mantle, or Odysseus and Achilles, who appear to use purple covers for their tents. In the 8thc. B.C., Iliad and Odyssey reports of purple include: Andromache and Helen, for example, nip purple fabrics. Even Agamemnon, Odysseus and Telemachus were noted as having purple-dye fabric. Hector's ashes were placed in purple-dye fabric(*Iliad:* C 125 to 128, H 221, Q 796. *Odyssey*, S 115, S 351, 226 h).

Generally, the purple colour indicated prestige and status and therefore only kings and priests had it. Purple was even mentioned in Pindar and Simonides (*13D, 371P*), while in Aeschylus' *Agamemnon* even purple carpets are noted. Extensive reference to purple is made by Plato, too. Also, Assyrians recorded two kinds of purple colours the *Argamannu*, which is the red colour and the *Takiltu*, which is the violet colour (in Plato *Critias* 120b and *Timaeus* 67c).

Plutarch (*The Parallel Lives*, 36) said that Alexander the Great, when he captured Susa in Iran, was impressed by the purple textile he found, originally produced at Hermione in Greece. Specifically he records:

"On making himself master of Susa, Alexander came into possession of forty thousand talents of coined money in the palace, and of untold furniture and wealth besides. Among this they say was found five thousand talents' weight of purple from Hermione, which, although it had been stored there for a hundred and ninety years, still kept its colours fresh and lively. The reason for this, they say, is that honey was used in the purple dyes, and white olive oil in the white dyes; for these substances, after the like space of time, are seen to have a brilliancy that is pure and lustrous".

Xenokrates (*On abstinence from animal food*, C'XXII) wrote that the best murex are the toughest ones. On the other hand, Oribasius (Oreivas.Λογ. D jf) argues that in order to obtain a sweeter taste they have to be boiled two or three times in clear water (Raeder, 1926).

The Roman historian Pliny the Elder, (*Historia Naturalis* IX, 124 - 142) left us one of the few references of the murex fishing method, in antiquity. He argues, therefore, that the ancient fishermen tied half-dead mussels and tossed them into the sea until murex attach to them. Then, the sailors quickly reel in the bait together with the murex.

The information recorded by ancient authors for approximately 2,700 years history of purple raises many questions. This is because the ancient writers who have dealt with the matter were not experts in textile dyes, about which there was an intended disclosure. The later writers who refer to purple quote earlier suppositions and oversimplifications. Today, archaeological excavations and surveys have given clues to many questions.

Vitruvius (*Ten Books, VII, XIII*) narrates about this:

"I would like to talk about the purple color, which goes far beyond all the colors which have been mentioned up to now and as to the accuracy and the amazing result. We have a shell from which the purple color can be obtained and which is excellent as well as anything on the nature in the eyes a careful observer, because it does not have the same shades in all parts, but these will vary depending on the course of the sun"

Also, Aristotle mentioned that Aegean production and use of purple-dye was extensive in many regions such as Crete, Rhodes, Kos, Amorgos, Nisyros (which was the ancient name Porphyris), Chios and the west coast of Asia Minor, Troy, Peloponnese, Cythera Laconia, Corinth and Hermione (Reese, 1980).

During the 17th century, Cyprus and later Tyre and Sidon in Phoenicia were famous centers of purple-dye production with the Phoenicians to dominate the Mediterranean, creating other centers in Egypt and Sicily (Orna, 2013).

Generally, purple was processed throughout the Mediterranean. Historical and archaeological evidences prove that Israel had had the art of purple and then Poulouzatoi (Philistines), who fled to Palestine and Syria in the 12th century BC during the decline of Late Bronze Age cultures in SE Mediterranean and the Middle East, when the Dorians invaded Crete, managed to acquire the knowledge of purple-dye production. Use of shell purple is met in later times in Byzantine period, e.g. Constantine's surname, *Porphyrogenitus*, that is, born in the Purple Chamber of the Imperial Palace in Constantinople, as befitted legitimate children of reigning emperors. The indisputable relationship with Byzantium purple illustrated by the fact that this term appears in Byzantine hymnology, which praised the Mother of God (*Troparion* D'):

"More exalted than the heavens, O immaculate Maid, rejoice, as the one who carried earth's Foundation painlessly in your womb. Rejoice, O murex who dyed in your own virgin blood, the divine purple robe, worn by the King of angelic hosts.Glory"

It is known that the development of shell purple depends on:

- ✓ light
- ✓ temperature
- ✓ salinity
- ✓ availability of nutrients

(Lobban et al., 1985)

Today, however, the technique is known broadly that resembles that of the natural purple dye, since in antiquity were unique dye reduction, with the same precursor compound the indoxyl, which turns into indigotin (dye compound guinea) (Wouters and Verhecken, 1991) and 6,6'-dibromo indigotine,[1] which is a dye compound of purple. The compound for murex is indoxyl. Indoxyl and free radicals give less electrons. This process causes dimerization, from which indigotine is produced. A simulated ex-

[1]For more information about 6,6'-dibromo indigotine see next chapter

periment for the production of shell dye has been made by Koren (2005a). The steps of this experiment includes, a) crushing the shell, b) reduced colour solution, c) resultant colour (Fig.1.6).

Figure 1.6 Method of dyeing fabric and final grading of purple colour (Koren, 2005a)

For the production of purple colour the shell was crushed to extract the living species, which is embossed to an alkaline solution. The air oxidation of the dye makes changes from green to purple colour (Koren, 2005a). An early short review on Tyrian purple is made by Cooksey (2013).

2. EXCAVATED WORKSHOPS OF MUREX IN THE CENTRAL AND EASTERN MEDITERRANEAN

In the last two centuries, frequent archaeological excavations have been made in the Central and Eastern Mediterranean and in recent years in most of them production of purple-dye is revealed (Fig. 2.1, Table 2.1).

Below the discovery of purple dye shells is presented, either in inscriptions or in excavation per site as a brief summary highlighting major prints.

Table 2.1:The workshops of purple dye in the Mediterranean

	Workshop	Reference
1	Agios Georgios, Athens	Lolos, 1990; Reese 2015b
2	Mitrou, Central Greece	Kramer-Hajos and O'Neill, 2008
3	Voulida (Zaltsa), Central Greece	Jackson, 1917; Sideris, 2014
4	Corinthia, Central Greece	Ruscillo, 2005; Reese 2000, 2015b
5	Hermione, Argolid, Peloponnese	Reinhold, 1970; Reese, 2010
6	Iklaina, Peloponnese	Ruscillo, 2005
7	Paulopetri, Peloponnese	Kardara, 1974
8	Kythera	Protopapas and Gatsos, 2003; Reese, 1987, 2015a
9	Yaros, Cyclades	Gounaris, 2005
10	Kythnos, Cyclades	Reese, 2000, 2015b
11	Delos, Cyclades	Reese, 2000, 2015b
12	Amorgos, Cyclades	Reese, 2000
13	Lesbos, western Aegean	Lowe, 2004; Reese 2000
14	Chios, western Aegean	Volonakis, 1990
15	Samos, western Aegean	Volonakis, 1990
16	Agathonisi, Dodecanese, Aegean	Volonakis, 1990
17	Kos, Dodecanese, Aegean	Volonakis, 1990
18	Nisyros, Dodecanese, Aegean	Reese, 2000
19	Chalkis, Dodecanese, Aegean	Lowe, 2004
20	Rhodes, Dodecanese, Aegean	Lowe, 2004
21	Khania, Crete	Shaw and Shaw, 2006; Reese,1987,2015a
22	Pefka, Crete	Apostolakou, 2009; Zimi and Tzachili, 2012; Betancourt et al., 2012
23	Mallia, Crete	Müller, 1991; Reese, 1987, 2015a
24	Papadiokampos, Crete	Sofianou and Brogan, 2010
25	Paleokastro, Crete	Reese, 1987, 2015b; Carannante, 2006
26	Itanos, Crete	Carannante, 2006; Reese, 2015a
27	Koufonissi, island south of Crete	Papadakis, 1983; Ridout-Sharpe, 1998;Reese, 2015a
28	Chrissi, Crete	Apostolakou et al., 2010, 2012
29	Makrigialos, Crete	Shaw and Shaw, 2006; Reese,1987, 2015a
30	Kommos, Crete	Shaw and Shaw, 2006; Ruscillo, 2006; Reese, 2000, 2015b
31	Monastiraki, Crete	Carannante, 2006; Reese, 2015a
32	Istanbul, Turkey	Çakırlar and Becks, 2009
33	Daskyleion, Turkey	İren 2012, 2013
34	Troy, Turkey	Çakırlar and Becks, 2009; Reese 2010
35	Pergamon, Turkey	Çakırlar and Becks, 2009
36	Ephesus, Turkey	Çakırlar and Becks, 2009
37	Miletus, Turkey	Çakırlar and Becks, 2009
38	Hierapolis, Turkey	Çakırlar and Becks, 2009
39	Hala Sultan Tekke, Cyprus	Belgiorno, 2004; Reese, 2010, 2015b
40	Minet el Beidha, Syria	Parri, 1932; Reese,2010,2015b
41	Byblos, Lebanon	Parri, 1932; Reese, 2015b
42	Sarepta, Lebanon	Parri, 1932; Pritchard, 1978; Reese, 2010, 2015b

43	Sidon, Lebanon	Parri, 1932; Reese, 2010, 2015b
44	Tyre, Lebanon	Astour,1965; Reese, 2010,2015b
45	Tel Akko,Israel	Reese, 2010
46	Tel Mor,Israel	Parri,1932; Reese 2007, 2010, 2015b
47	Tobruk, Libya	Parri, 1932; Reese 2015b
48	Sidi Khrebish Bengazi, Libya	Lloyd, 1978; Reese 1980, 2015b
49	Leptcis Magna, Libya	Reese, 2015b
50	Sabraphfa, Libya	Reese 2015b
51	Mennix, Tunisia	Reese, 2015b
52	Dar Essafi,Tunisia	Picard, 1956; Reese 1980, 2015b
53	Carthage, Tunisia	Picard, 1956; Reese, 2015b
54	Agrigento, Sicily, Italy	Forbes, 1956
55	Palermo, Sicily, Italy	Bruin, 1970
56	Torre, Italy	Forbes, 1956
57	Venise, Italy	Bruin, 1970
58	Ancona, Italy	Bruin, 1970
59	Monte Circeo-Latina, Italy	Blanc, 1958; Reese,2005
60	Aquilea, Italy	Bruin, 1970
61	Coppa Nevigata-Apulia, Italy	Minniti, 1999; Reese, 2005
62	Matya, Italy	Forbes, 1956; Reese, 2005
63	Taranto, Italy	Macheboeuf, 2004; Reese 2005, 2015b
64	Otranto, Italy	Bruin, 1970

Figure 2.1 Workshops of purple in the Mediterranean revealed by archaeological excavations

Thessaloniki (40.65°N, 22.9°E)

The term purple-dyeris attested in at least twoin-scriptions from Thessaloniki and Philippi. The inscribed stele from Thessaloniki, which is now in the Archaeological Museum of Istanbul (Mendel, 1914), bear a Hero - rider on top, and dates to the late 2nd century AD (Nigdelis, 2010). At the bottom of the column, the inscription is dedicated to a purple-dyer Menippos Severos by members of the battalion (IG, X.2.1, 291). The inscription reads as follows (Pilhofer, 1995) (Fig. 2.2).

"The Guild of purple-dyers whose workshops were on the eighteenth street dedicates it to the memory of Menippos Severos, son of Amicon, who came from Thyatira."

The inscription shows that purple-dyers had business relations in Roman Thessaloniki and that there was more than one workshop in the city, and that some people derive from Asia Minor.

The second inscription (697/M580) was from the city of Philippi, which was discovered in 1872.The inscription reads (Pilhofer, 1995):

"The city honored, among of purpledyer, Antiochus, son of Lycus native of Thyateira as a local benefactor".

Figure 2.2 Drawing of an inscribed funerary stele from Thessaloniki, referring to Menippos the purple dyer from Thyateira, Istanbul Archaeological Museum. (Mendel, 1914).

In Macedonia, the evidence for the use of murex, for colouring fabrics and wall-paintings, have a long history from the Bronze Age to the Roman period. The evidence from excavations at Toumba Thessaloniki (Veropoulidou et.al., 2008) and Aghios Mamas in Chalkidiki (Becker, 2001) of Bronze Age indicate small production of purple for the needs of the local community. This is supported by archaeological evidence dating from the Iron Age and includes crushed murex of Toumba Thessaloniki (Veropoulidou, 2011) and Methoni in Pieria (Veropoulidou, 2012).

From the Archaic to the Hellenistic period, fragments of murex have been found in Northern Greece. The use of purple as a symbol of the upper class is shown by the finds in the tomb of Vergina late 6th century (Faklaris, 1998), Aghios Mamas in Halkidiki (Moschonisiotou, 1989). Also, purple-dye workshop in Thessaloniki on the south side of the Roman Agora was revealed (Vitti, 1996). The workshop dates between the 2nd / 1st century BC and 1st century AD, (Karaberi and Christodoulidou, 1998). This workshop was part of a large complex next to the ceramic and metallurgical workshops, probably intended for dyeing.

Hermione (37°23'07"N, 23°14'50"E)

The region of Hermione in the Argolid was famous for purple-dye it was the most expensive dye of antiquity. In ancient times, Hermione was an important production center of purple-dye and textile. Many ancient authors such as Aristotle and Plutarch, noted that Hermione was a centre for purple-dye. The paint ("flower", according toAristotle (*History of Animals*, V15)is found in shells, in which the gland was removed with suitable instantaneous breaking careful picking the shell and the living organism. For the dyeing of a cloak, a large amount of shells is required. The maintenance of painting could be done with the help of honey in sealed jars.

The fermentation of dye embossed lasted several days to complete the resulting white compound form soluble salt. As to the nature of the hair, as Plato says in the book of *Politia* D: «*You know, I said, that dyers, when they want to dye wool for making the true sea-purple, begin by selecting their white colour first; this they prepare and dress with much care and efforts, in order that the white ground may take the purple hue in full perfection. Whatever is dyed in this manner becomes a fast colour, and no washing either with lye or without it can take away the bloom. But, when the ground has not been duly prepared, you will have noticed how poor is the look either of purple or of any other colour*».

Followed by exposure to the sun and the air, so as to cause oxidation and white compound be retranslated to 6,6 '-dibromoindigotin and give the purple colour. Followed by washing in a good brine bath, vinegar, etc.,in order to remove the unpleasant smell and colour to acquire splend our and strength (Strabo, XVI 2,23).

It should be noted that murex-dye fabric had great resistance to washing and light Experts noticed that the ancient painters were aware that mixing different types of shells (in "flower" of course) in certain proportions and proper way of preparing the reducing bath was what gave the variety of colours in purple and delicious tones and nuances. Moreover, the repetition of dunking in the same tub - bucket or different with other kind of shell was assumed. The shades of purple that had great appreciation was dark red, like clotted blood, known as the purple of Tyre, and that coloured amethyst, which was dyed in the workshops at Hermione.

The ancient workshops of murex dyeing were located at the eastern edge of the modern city of Hermione, in Bisti (37°23'03"N, 23°15'24"E), which in antiquity was called "Poseidion." So, the bad smell from dyeing was blown out to sea. At the end of the 6th century BC a temple of Poseidon or Athena was built in the middle of the cape. The current location was a "square" great temple and probably the priests of the temple had the control and management of workshop. The research indicates that the people of workshop took the porphyra and followed the same process for the production of the purple colour.

In the 5th century B.C., walls were built around Hermione and had as a binder broken shells instead of gravel. Also, 18% of the binder was broken shells, which means that more than 250 tones were used in building the ancient wall at least 10 million shells.Also with shells built areas through the side of the wall and the use of broken shells as a binder also continued later.

The reports indicate that the dyeing workshops must have been at the side of the modern windmill. They should begin to work at least the 6th century BC and continued until the 6th century AD. During the 1000-plus years of operation in Hermione hundreds of millions of shells were used.

The extraction of the dye from the shells was in the workshop of porpfura, where is the central workshop. Piles of broken shells indicate the position of the workshop. The on-the-spot examination in the region give the impression that workshop should be located at the eastern end of the cape.

The workshops paint needed rain water and thus storage cisterns. In Bisti, there are several, most female figures carved in the rock. Also, the facilities were necessary to present chemical containers, such as caustic soda or potash, soaps, etc. Standard dyed yarn as samples and mixing utensils, scales etc. was considered self-evident. The existence of these, justify the findings and quirky utensils found at the Rauhi at Isthmia, where excavations were made in large amounts of dyes.

The number of shells collected in Bisti reached several thousand a day, which gave 10-20 kg murex purple-dye (Elsner and Spanier, 1985). Therefore, should be specific repository. Surveillance was obvious and rigorous, and economic significance for the city great. This explains the peak of the city by building the walls, temples, etc. The management of such great wealth required people who knew the internal and external markets, since the bulk of the dye was exported. If operated about 1000 years with an average use of 10.000 shells per day, then during this operation three billion shells were processed!

Returning to the text of Plutarch for purple of Hermione found by Alexander at Susa, it is not clear if it was found 5000 fabric dyed with murex, which had been stored before 190 years, using local fresh honey. Also, he noted oil used to create white purple which is incomprehensible if it is cloth (Jameson et al., 1994). Plutarch, who lived in the 1st century AD, certainly reads somewhere this information about events that took place four centuries earlier, and probably did not realize the problem of purple dye being white. In chemical terms, however, it seems that in Susa it was found purple-dye rather than fabrics.

It is known that concentrated alkaline solutions, create a sensation resembling of oil. Therefore, this is probably the white oil, as Plutarch said. If the coating weight was 5000 talents, it is 130,000 kg. This means that at that time in Hermione processing for export was over 100 million shells. Whether workshops capable for dealing per day a few thousand shells, it makes apparent that the coatings must have been worked intensively for 50 years or so.

The Persian emperor Darius I (522-486 BC) reaches its greatest prosperity and glory with the center of vast state Susa, until overwhelming of Alexander the Great in 330 BC by Darius III. The workshops of Hermione gave the purple-dyeing to the Persians for at least two centuries and reaping huge revenues and giving great prosperity to the city by building walls, temples etc. Cyrus the Great was one of the biggest personalities and he was under control of all the workshops of purple-dyeing in Phoenicia. After the annexation of Asia Minor in the 6th century BC all the facilities of purple dyeing used purple imported from a hostile country and especially from Hermione.

On-site collection of shells, chiefly found in Hermione and removing purple-glands, found that their hands painted a purple and violetcolor, close to amethyst. Similar color was a simple dyeing process directly from the "flower" in white cotton fabric. On the other hand, shells of Tyre, which found in the sea of Hermione, but in a small percentage, excretes red color.

Experts believe that the color complexion was impressive. This was the main reason for its production during reign of Cyrus and Darius. Today there is no recollection of the famous Hermione purple-dyers only the piles of broken shells, scattered around the Cape of ancient workshop, witnessing the ancient grandeur and glory of the city.

Chania (35° 30′ 40″ N , 24° 1′ 45″E)

In 2002, during a rescue excavation at Kydonia region (35°30′52″N, 24°00′48″E) remains of the Hellenistic and Roman periods came to light.

In the eastern section of the plot, murex processing installation was found.The remains of the installation comprise of two circular ovens built of rough stones. They are 1.82 and 1.45m in diameter and their sides are preserved to a height of 0.60-0.70m.There is a large round stone in the middle of its oven presumably for the deposition of vessels in which murex shells boiled. A layer of ash and intense traces of burning were located in front of the ovens. The third oven was destroyed by a modern pit (Tsingou, 2009).

Rhodes (36°11'42"N, 27°56'49"E)

The ancient Rhodes stated between the positions of the Aegean producing murex-dye. Indications for treatment of murex on the island have been since prehistoric times. Porphyra, which was found strewn on the floor substrate of the Late Bronze IA settlement in Trianta is a good testimony to similar activity of the inhabitants of this region.

The presence of crushed murex in thickness up to 0.50 m in excavations of the city of Rhodes found in the early 1970s testifies to the presence of a workshop of purple-dyeing. Workshopsarelocated in several places in the city. Foundries within the area of the Temple of Diagoridon road (36°26'27"N, 28°12'54.5"E), workshop glass beads in the southern part of the city, but also in artisanal zones near the edges of the city, such as ceramic workshops in the large port on the side northeastern fortifications, all inside the fortified walls.

The Hellenistic city of Rhodes was not the only place on the island which developed crafts. There are two other metallurgical workshops in Ialyssos, and potteries making amphorae in the area of Ialyssos and Charaki and other areas on the island.

In southern fortifications of Rhodes there has been identified litharge plant (Kakavogiannis, 1984). In the same area outside the walls, a part of murex workshop has been found. A large amount of shells, which is visible today, has been found in landscaped archaeological site and dated to the early 3rd century BC.

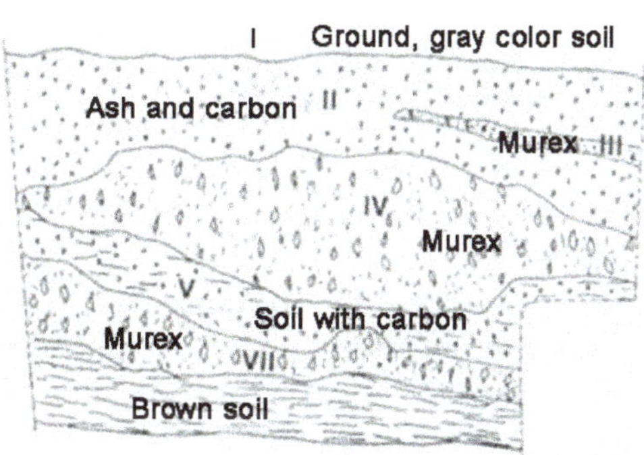

Figure 2.3 Stratigraphy in eastern section east of the southern area (Kakavogiannis, 1984)

Very close to the shambles of the defense system of Hellenistic Rhodes and out of town, just south of wall (built after the earthquake of 227 BC) workshopwas found in 1979 for processing murex dyes. The location of the workshop on the outskirts of the city, in the space between the wall of the city and necropolis meet the demands of the time for such an establishment. One of the main characteristics of workshop was the distance from residential areas, because of the bad smell, which exposed during the dyeing process (Kakavogiannis, 1984).

Characteristic is the image of historical stratigraphy in eastern cheek on the southern part of the murex workshop, the east exterior wall of the southern area (Fig. 2.3). Stratigraphy features seven layers. The presence of two successive layers of murex and the combustion layer below this is indicative of the activity on site.The layer II, under a surface of gray colour soil (layer I), was mainly ash and carbon, located at the southern end of which is inserted a thin layer of murex (layer III). It was a thicker (layer IV) with murex. The next layer V contained soil with carbon, while the latter layer murex grazed her on brown soil.

In accordance with the data of the excavation, it should be noted that the area took place all the work on the production dye, but the next stage of the dye. The complex, located outside the city, covered all the basic tasks for the production of murex dye.

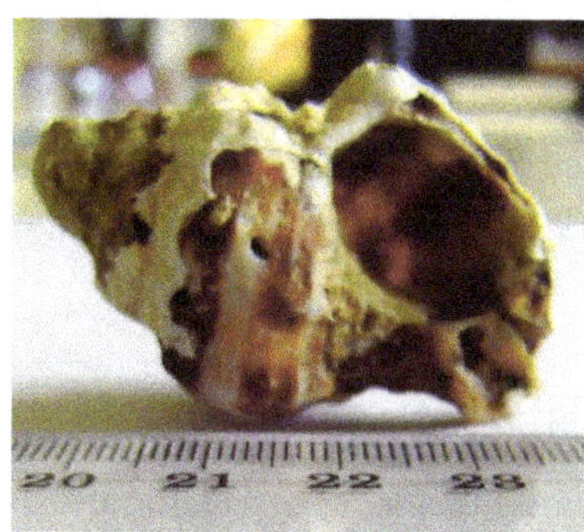

Figure 2.4 Hexaples found in Psaropoula area of Rhodes

The crushing shells was the wider open space with the remains of the rampart. In the southern area with temperatures of south tanks made probably stages of boiling for the production of pigment. In this case, should have been space outdoor. The found eleven coins over and near the steps of the laboratory of Rhodes is a possible indication of trade era of porphyra (Fig. 2.4).

Agathonisi (37.46°, 26.96°)

The archaeological site Kastraki in the Island includes a fortress in the inaccessible area in the northern part of the island on a rocky hillside at height of 34m above sea level. Kastraki preserves impressive fortification walls, projecting between dense shrubby vegetation and enclose the west, north and south side of the rocky hill. Southwest saved this rectangular and carvings of ancient dockyards, whose relics are below the sea level. These building materials related to fortification, probably the port of the ancient city of Tragaia. The construction of the fort in the northern part of the island is not unexpected, since that the position is of strategic importance to the marine control strait between Miletus and Samos and channel from Kos to Samos. During the Hellenistic period Miletus in order to protect the territorial integrity of the marine area of the Aegean Sea from the thriving piracy Cretans and goblets resorted necessarily the equipment and military installation Guard at Miletus islands as Lipsi, Arki, the Pharmakonisi, Leros and Patmos. The archaeological site identified during the surface surveys of 2001 - 2005 yields many movable finds mostly sherds of Hellenistic and Early Roman periods and household items such as sanders, grinders, and mortars (Triantafyllidis, 2015).

Unexpected was the discovery near the southeastern edge of the southern fortification wall section workshop facilities which are likely related to the production of pigments and dyes, dating from late Hellenistic and Early times (1st century BC-1st century AD) . The associated tanks seem to be connected through the system of overflow and inside them there are numerous marine shells, some of which were found in a stone trough in the southwestern corner of the tank. Though there were no masses of purple dye, however from the field of tanks and around this coming from sections pigments such as ocher, yellow, red and white.

Antikyra, Phokis

A plethora of murex trunculus and brandaris is found in Antikyra area (Pelatia and Boulis sites) in classical to Roman times. Ancient historian-traveller Pausanias (X, 37, 3) reports on this (see, Sideris, 2014). In 2016 season in Kastrouli late Helladic settlement from Tomb A and the commingled layer of bones, soil and small finds comes also a very tiny seashell fragment of a gastropod mollusk, which, on the basis of its physical characteristics,it has been tentatively identified with murex *Hexaplex trunculus*. This edible marine gastropod, which is common in the entire Mediterranean, is abundant in the Corinthian gulf and was used in Antiquity also for the production of a blue-purple dye, documented in the ancient sources for Boulis, a site in the easternmost edge of the gulf of Antikyra (Sideris 2014). Its presence in the secondary burial is rather unusual (Sideris et al 2017).

3. WORKSHOP OF PURPLE IN THE MEDITERRANEAN

TURKEY

Troy (39°57'27"N 26°14'20"E)

Initial excavations of Schliemann in the 1880s and all the recent excavations at Troy have demonstrated the use of *Hexaples* for the production of purple dye (Figure 3.1). These data have been collected by Çakırlar and Becks (2009) and Reese (2015b).

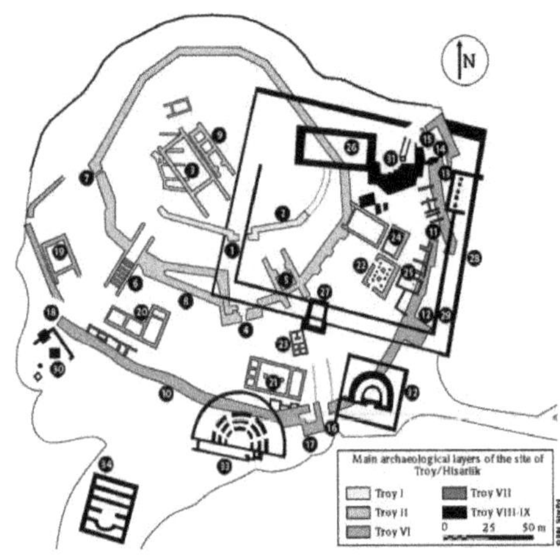

Figure 3.1 The nine layers of Troy (Tobin, 2011)

Uluburun (Kaş) wreck (36°7'43"N 29°41'9"E)

The shipwreck in the region of Kaş (Uluburun) (Fig. 3.2) produceda large quantity of murex. The Uluburun operculae were a by-product a shell purple-dye industry (Reese, 2010, 2015b).

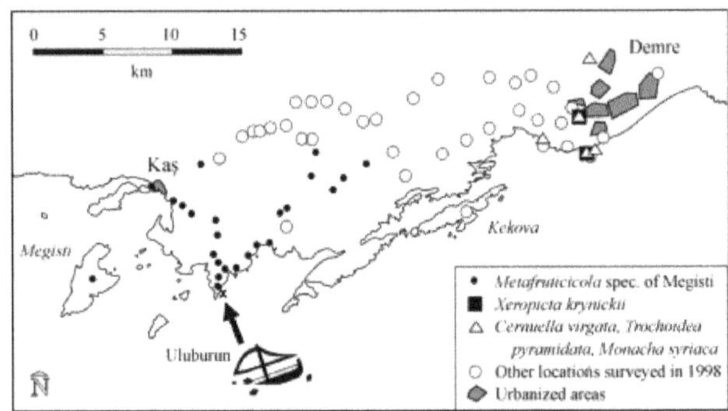

Figure 3.2 Uluburun (Welter-Schultes, 2008)

EGYPT

Bates 'Island (Marsa Matruh, White, 1987) (31°21'13"N, 27°14'16"E)

In Late Bronze Age and Roman small offshore island near the border with Libya, produced 2,352 murex. In Bates' Island (Marsa Matruh) identified two types of Murex dyed in Coptic textiles (Pfister, 1951;Walton, 1985;Reese, 2002, 2010). A purple painted Egyptian woolen cloak of the 3rd century AD is derived from Bolinus (Wouters, 1992). The second fabric for 3rd/4th century AD in Philadelphia was derived from Hexaples (Michel et.al, 1992b).

The two Coptic textiles in Flemish collections have been analyzed: the first fabric, imported from Persia or Mesopotamia the 8th-9th century A.D. (Wouters, 1993) [using Bolinus] and the second, an Egyptian production of the 5th or 6th century A.D. (Wouters, 1993) [possibly using Hexaples].

LEBANON

From Beirut, there is no shell evidence, only a Greek inscription of the 5th-6th century A.D. honouring a dyer of purple (Reese,2010). In Lebanon the production points of shell purple are located at Sidon (Parri, 1932; Reese, 2010, 2015b), Sarepta (Parri, 1932; Reese, 2010, 2015b) and Tyre (Astour, 1965;Reese, 2010, 2015b).

Sidon (33°33'49"N, 35°22'07"E)

Figure 3.4 Crushed Hexaples found in Sidon (de Saulcy, 1864)

In early 1863 de Saulcy found a huge amount of broken Hexaples (de Saulcy, 1864). Shortly afterwards, in 1864, nearby, the French physician Gaillardot discovered broken Hexaples and Bolinus in very good condition (Gaillardot, 1865, 1873).

An article of 1874 (Anonymous, 1874), based on publications of de Saulcy and Gaillardot, erroneously reported separately in Bolinus and Stramonita. This mislead writers like Born (1937) and Ziderman (1987, 1990). Lortet (1883) reported that in the region of Sidon found large quantities of broken Hexaples hundred feet long and several feet thick. A portion of this large set found was recorded as 120 meters long and 7.8 meters high (Forbes, 1956).

Also, Cooke (1909) visited the area. Huge number of Hexaples was also observed during the excavations 1914-1920 (Cardon, 2003). Jensens claimed that the crafts of Sidon used mainly Hexaples and the same kind found in old walls of the space, the south gate, and south of the area (Jensen 1963; Jensen and Jensen 1965; Reese, 2010) (Figure 3.4).

Tyre (33°16'20"N, 35°12'11"E)

Hexaples were found in 1793 and 1811 by Lord Valentin. While in 1839-1840 along the coast, the Irishman Wilde (1839, 1844) found round depressions of broken *Hexaples*.

Chehab (1965) identified a Roman crushed murex through the craft district of the city and a Byzantine workshop. Jidejian (1969) report that the shell is from Tyre and dates from the 1st century A.D.

Therefore, it is worth noting that the Bolinus depicted on the coins of Tyre from 112 AD and later (Jackson, 1916; Reese, 2010). There is written evidence for the imperial purple production during the reign of Diocletian (Eusebius, *Ecclesiastical History*. VII, 32), and in 383 AD production became a state monopoly (*Codex Justinianus* IV. 40.1).

SYRIA

Minet el-Beidha (35°36'03"N, 35°47'05"E)

Piles of murex found in the area ofMinet el-Beidha (Figure 3.5), and the port of Ras Shamra, dating to the 15th to 13th century BC (Schaeffer 1929, 1951). Local production of purple fabric are mentioned in Ugaritic texts in the first half of the 14th century BC and confirmed by excavation at Ras Shamra in 1933 and 1937 (Thureau-Dangin, 1934; Schaeffer, 1951; Reinhold, 1970; Reese,2010).

Figure 3.5 Complete Bolinus found in the region of Minet el-Beidha (Schaeffer, 1929)

Tell Rifa'at (36°28'23"N, 37°05'47"E)

Figure 3.6 Crushed Hexaples found at Tell Rifa'at (Biggs, 1967)

In the Orontes River in the hinterland of Syria, over 100 km from the Mediterranean coast, a large pile of shells *Hexaples* (Figure 3.6) was found, which was crushed in anHellenistic house (Biggs, 1967; Reese, 2010).

ISRAEL

According to archeological elements, the areas of Israel such as Tell Akko, Tell Abu Hawam, Tell Keisan, Tel Shiqmona, Tel Megadim, Tel Dor, Yavneh Yam, Tell Mikhmoret, Tel Mevorakh, Tel Mor, Apollonia Arsuf, were workshops of purple-dye (Fig.3.7).

During the Archaic period (800 BC - 480 BC) many areas involved in dyeing fabrics (Koren, 2005b) in purple color or the processing shell or processing minerals. Below analyzed the areas where identified species of Murex after archaeological excavations (Fig. 3.7).

Figure 3.7 Areas of Israel,Tell Akko, Tell Abu Hawam, Tell Keisan , Tel Shiqmona, Tel Megadim, Tel Dor, Yavneh Yam, Tell Mikhmoret,Tel Mevorakh, Tel Mor, Apollonia Arsuf (Google Earth).

Tell Akko

In 1980 in northern Israel, large quantities of shells were found. The three species found in layers of purple excavation and furnaces, that demonstrate the use and production of purple (Dothan, 1981;Raban 1983;Karmon and Spanier, 1987). Crushed shells in thick layers dating from the 13th to the 12th century BC (Karmon and Spanier, 1987; Reese, 2010) were found and in nearby buildings quite a large number of broken and intact shells (including the three species of shells) were found and dated to the Persian and Hellenistic periods (Karmon and Spanier 1987, 1988).

Tell Abu Hawam

This area is located north of Mount Carmel 1.5 miles from the sea. In 2001, the excavation revealed large quantities of broken shells of the species *Hexaples*. The 155 shells produce 0.5 liters of pigment. An estimate of the minimum volume of 40,000 liters is estimated for breaking 12,400 shells (Baruch et al, 2005; Reese, 2010).

Tell Keisan (Puech, 1980)

This site is currently about seven kilometers from the coast. Samples of purple color found inside a large bowl of Iron Age I date (11th century BC) and examined, proved to be shell purple. In the same area, they found small amounts of *Hexaples* and Bolinus (Reese, 2010).

Tel Shiqmona

Large quantities of shell species *Hexaples* and Bolinus found in Tel Shiqmona in fieldwork (Karmon and Spanier, 1987, 1988). Broken shells of three species found outside the archaeological field, about half a mile south and crafts indicate that could be used for the production of purple dye (Karmon and Spanier 1987, 1988). Also, a number of sherds of Iron Age II (9th-8th century) contained purple spots, indicating the specie of *Murex* (Karmon and Spanier 1987; Cardon, 2003; Reese, 2010).

Tel Megadim

Excavations in 1967-1969 by M. Broshi on the coast found numerous Bolinus and *Hexaples*from the Persian layers (5th century BC). The 1968 excavation unearthed 56 Bolinus and two Hexaples (Reese, 2010).

Tel Dor

In Tel Dor in the laboratory area there was a thick layer of crushed thousands Hexaples. Among others, two in Hellenistic period (layer IV) and some whole shells as well. (Karmon and Spanier, 1987; Stern, 1994; Reese, 2010).

Yavneh Yam

This coastal area is full of many broken *Hexaples, Bolinus* shellsfrom the Hellenistic and Roman period (Reese, 2010).

Tell Mikhmoret

From the excavations of 1982-1984, Stiglitz wrote, "*We found many shells kind murex. I believe it is from the Byzantine era. The shells were mixed in Persian, Hellenistic and Byzantine period*" (Porath et al., 1993; Reese 2010).

Tel Mevorakh

This region showed numerous shells, including the *Hexaplex*, and a sea-shell of the 4thto 3rdcentury BC (Stern, 1978; Reese 2010).

Tel Mor

There are samples of murex from the Canaanite period, according to Raban (1981) and Reese (2007, 2010). They refer to an old report of Dothan (1960) that date the material, but it is more likely that the shells for purple-dye purposes are dated to the Hellenistic period.

Apollonia Arsuf

At this site there were found shells dating from the Persian and Hellenistic period (Karmon, 1999; Reese 2010).

TUNISIA

Carthage (36°51'29"N 10°19'51"E)

Although there have been many excavations in Carthage, only those made from 1982 to 1989 show a large percentage of murex (Reese, 2015b). There has been found a total of 2084 shells of which 1666 or 80% were used for the production of purple color. British, Danish and German excavations confirm the number of shells used for purple-dye production. The other 20% was used for consumption (Zaouali, 1994).

4. METHODS, SAMPLES AND CASE STUDIES

4.1 Murex shell molecular analysis

Several analytical methods have been applied to identify and study the chromophore components of murex shells that produce tyrian purple, such as 3D fluorescence spectrometry (Shimoyama and Noda, 1994), NMR (nuclear magnetic resonance) spectrometry (Clark and Cooksey, 1997, 1999; Voss, 2000; Voss and Schramm, 2000; Cooksey, 2001a, 2001b; Cooksey and Withnall, 2001; Hoffman et al., 2010), MS (mass spectrometry) (McGovern and Michel, 1990; McGovern et al., 1990; Michel et al., 1992a; Withnall et al., 1993; Gibbs et al., 1995; Clark et al., 1996; Clark and Cooksey, 1997; Voss and Schramm, 2000; Benkendorff et al., 2001; Cooksey, 2001a, 2001b; Cooksey and Withnall, 2001; Andreotti et al., 2004; Papanastasiou, 2005; Surowiec et al, 2012), Raman spectrometry (Withnall et al., 1993; Tatsch and Schrader, 1995; Clark and Cooksey, 1999; Cooksey, 2001a, 2001b; Ajiki et al., 2012), IR (infrared) spectrometry (Baker, 1974; McGovern and Michel, 1985; Voss and Gerlach, 1989; Tatsch and Schrader, 1995; Clark and Cooksey, 1997, 1999; Cooksey, 2001a, 2001b), PIXE (particle induced x-ray emission) and ESCA (electron spectroscopy for chemical analysis) (McGovern and Michel, 1984, 1985), Visible Spectrophotometry (Saltzman, 1978, 1986, 1992; Shen et al., 1991; Withnall et al., 1993; Serrano-Andrés and Roos, 1997; Daniels, 1989; Koren, 1993; Miliani et al., 1998; Cooksey, 2001b; Nowik et al., 2011), TLC (thin-layer chromatography)(Cooksey, 1995; Cooksey and Withnall, 2001; Hiyoshi and Fujise, 1992), GC (gas chromatography) (Benkendorff et al., 2001), and HPLC (high-performance liquid chromatography) (Wouters and Verhecken, 1991; Wouters, 1992; Koren, 1994a, 1995, 2006; Clark and Cooksey, 1997; Cooksey, 2001a; Cooksey and Withnall, 2001; Withnall et al., 2003; Karapanagiotis et al., 2006; Nowik et al., 2011; Mantzouris and Karapanagiotis, 2014; Vasileiadou et al., 2016).

Murex shells, produce three main colour components: the isatinoids group, comprised of three chromophores, isatin (IS), 4-bromoisatin (4BIS), 6-bromoisatin (6BIS), which generates the yellow colour; the indigoids group, comprised of three chromophores, indigo (IND), 6-monobromoindigo (MBI), 6,6-Dobromoindigo (DBI) which generates blue and purple colours and the indirubinoids group, comprised of four chromophores, indirubin (INR), 6-monobromoindirubin (6MBIR), 6'-monobromoindirubin (6'MBIR), 6,6-dibromoindirubin (DBIR), which generates that red colour (Koren, 2006).

4.2 Case Studies

The basic dating method used is radiocarbon and the analysis is made by various chromatography techniques. Methods use in earlier times and/or rare use of methods include: Thin Layer Chromatography (TLC), Liquid Chromatography with Atmospheric Pressure Chemical Ionization-Mass Spectroscopy (LC-APCI-MS),Nuclear Magnetic Resonance Spectroscopy(NMR), Mass Spectrometry(MS), Proton-Induced X-ray Emission (PIXE), Ultraviolet /Visible spectroscopy (UV/Vis), Electron Spectroscopic Chemical Analysis (ESCA), Fourier Transform Ion Cyclotron Resonance Mass Spectrometry (FTICRMS) and Microchemical tests (MCT). Modern spectroscopy applied includes: High Pulsed Liquid Chromatography (HPLC), High Performance Liquid Chromatography Photodiode Array Detector (HPLC-PDA), High Performance Liquid Chromatography-Diode Array Detector (HPLC-DAD), X-Ray Florescence XRF, Environmental Scanning Electron Microscopy coupled with X-Ray microanalysis (ESEM-EDX), Infrared Spectroscopy (IR), Fourier Transform Infrared Spectroscopy (FTIR), Raman Spectroscopy (Raman).

A useful bibliography on papers regarding tyrian purple is given online (http://www.chriscooksey.demon.co.uk/tyrian/cjcbiblio.html)

Table 4.1 Samples of murex dye or pigment analyzed per region and technique applied (Karapanagiotis et al, 2013 enriched).

a/a	Location	Date	Object/Samples	Technique	References
1	Trianda, Rhodes, Greece	17thc.BC (or earlier)	Pigment	HPLC-DAD, Raman, FTIR	Karapanagiotis et al 2011, 2013
2	Akrotiri, Thera,Greece	17thc.BC (or earlier)	Lump of pigment and wall paintings	XRD, XRF,HPLC-DAD LC-APCI-MS, RAMAN,FTIR	Karapanagiotis et al, 2011, 2013 E. Aloupi, et al. 1990, 2000 Karapanagiotis et al., in press. Karapanagiotis, 2006 Sotiropoulou and Karapanagiotis, 2006 van Elslande, et al., 2008
3	Kerameikos, Athens, Greece	430-400 BC	textile	ESEM-EDX, RAMAN	Margariti et al 2013
4	Cave of Koroneia, Central Greece	6th-2nd c. BC	Astragalos made of sheep knucklebone	ESEM-EDX	Colombini et al., 2004
5	Chania, Crete, Greece	ca 300 BC	Hellenistic figurines	FTIR, XRF	Maravelaki-Kalaitzaki and Kallithrakas-Kontos, 2003
6	Tomb of Phillip II, Vergina, Macedonia, Greece	336BC	Casket fabric	FTIR, MCT	Hofenk de Graaff, 2004
7	Tomb III at Agios Athanasios, Macedonia, Greece	Last quarter of the 4thc.BC	Wall painting	XRF, HPLC-DAD	Karydas, 2006; Andreotti, et al., 2006
8	Tomb of the palmettes, Mieza, Macedonia, Greece	First half of the 3rd c. BC	Wall paintings	HPLC-DAD	Andreotti, et al., 2006
9	Strozzacapponi, Perugia, Italy	2nd -1st centuries BCE	textile	HPLC-DAD	Gleba and Vanden Berghe, 2014
10	Daskyleion, Turkey	5th c. B.C.	Painted surface of a kline, textile fragment	SEM-EDX, FTIR, HPLC	Papliaka et al., 2015
11	Sarepta, Lebanon	13thc.BC	Pottery sherds with purple deposits	PIXE,ESCA,FTIR,MCT	McGovern and Michel, 1984, 1985
12	Tel Shiqmona,Israel	9th /8thc.BC	Sherds	IR	Karmon, and Spanier, 1988
13	Masada, Israel	1st c. BC	Fabric excavated at the western-Herodonian palace	HPLC-DAD, HPLC-PDA, UV/Vis	Koren, 1997, 2005b Clementi, et al., 2016
14	Tel Keisan, Israel	11th c. BC	Vessel	MCT	Karmon, and Spanier, 1987
15	Tel Kabri, Israel	7th c. BC	Pigment potsherd	HPLC-DAD	Koren, 1995
16	Bible Lands Museum, Jerusalem, Israel	486/485 BC	Outer surface of Darius I stone jar	HPLC-DAD	Koren, 2008a
17	Royal tomb complex within the palace Qatna, Tell Mishrife, Syria	Late Bronze Age	Several sediment samples of decayed fabrics; fossilised-woollentextiles	FTICRMS, HPLC-DAD, NMR	James et al., 2007, 2009
17	Enkomi, Cyprus	75 and 30 BC	Two textiles	TLC, UV/Vis	Daniels 1985, 1987

The analysis by the above methods has shown that the basic component of purple which is bromine (Br) and the three colors of seashell murex (isatinoids, indirubinoids, indigoids).

The methods used are briefly discussed below.

5. ANALYTICAL METHODS

Radiocarbon dating

Suitable for dating samples usually consist of organic materials found in archaeological sites, such as charcoal, wood, seeds, shells, cloth and other plant residues, and human and animal bones (Damon,

1989). It has not been used often in murex. But a characteristic application is by van Strydonck et al, (2012) from Balearic Islands, Spain.

Spectro UV-VIS and RAMAN

Early spectrum analysis for murex recognition started with spectrophotometry UV-VIS spectra, (Koren, 1993), while recently it has been overwhelmed by Raman Spectroscopy which is widely used to solve various problems of chemical, associated with the structure, kinetics, identification, quantitative analysis of various compounds, and in murex in particular (fig. 4.1). Raman has the advantage over uv/vis of suppressing of fluorescence radiation in textiles. For example, analysis with micro - spectroscopy Raman identified the main component dye, 6,6 '-dibromoindigotine, and part of the inorganic pigment was rich in CaCO3 (as calcite and aragonite)(Chryssikopoulou et al., 2001; Withnall et al., 1992).

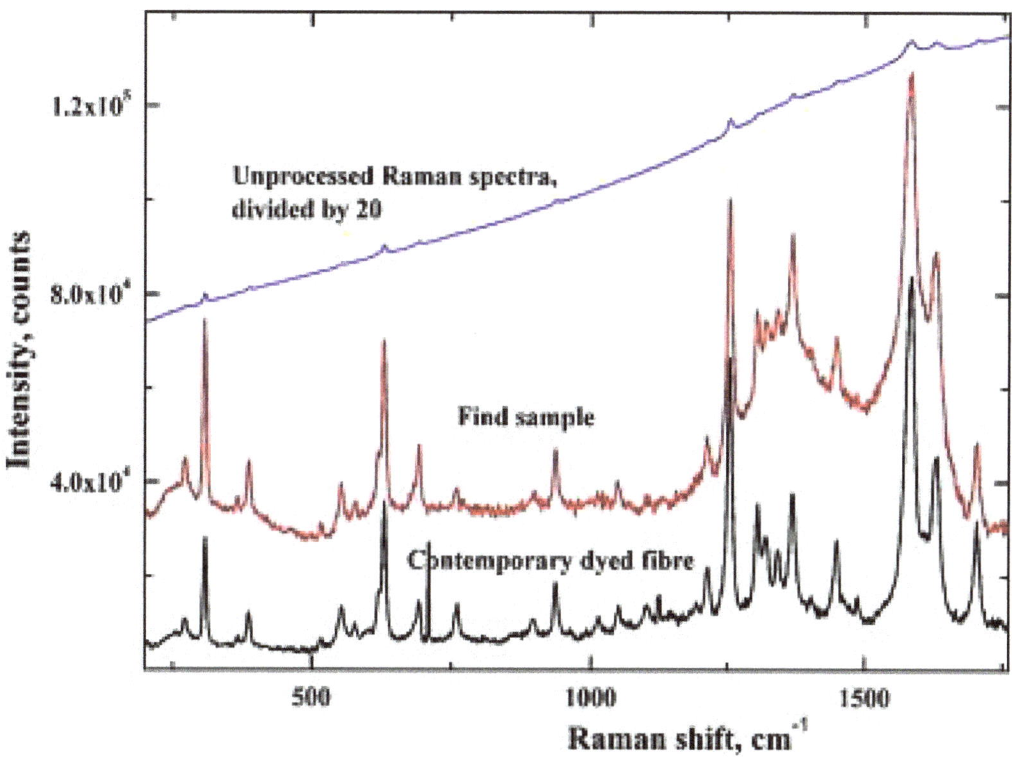

Fig. 4.1 Raman spectra of the excavated textile (red line) and modern fibre (black line) (Margariti et al., 2013)

XRF

The technique of fluorescent X-ray analysis method is a sample based on the X-ray fluorescence and exploits the fact that the energies of the photons emitted by an excited atom is characteristic for the type of atom and may lead to determination of the chemical substance. In murex, high bromine content that implies 6,6-dibromoindigotine.

An earlier use of PIXE has been reported in literature (Table 4.1).

XRD

Analysis of the samples by X-ray diffraction (XRD) provides the mineralogical contect of the analysed solid material. The X-ray spectroscopy describes the interaction of radiation with matter based on diffraction of monochromatic X-ray radiation with a certain wavelength from respective crystal lattice. Aragonite has been detected in this case. In fact, the content of purple that is bromine (6,6 '-dibromoindigotine) and is associated with the presence of aragonite ($CaCO_3$) from the crashed shell and its content, is an indicator of Murex shell from which the pigment derives from (e.g. in Akrotiri by Aloupi et al. 2000).

HPLC (-PDA and -DAD)

Chromatographic spectroscopies were conducted in parallel to the painted surface samples and in samples of a substance to form fine purplish powder (Figure 4.3). Samples were discovered in the area ofAkrotiri, the assay results confirm the similar nature of all samples (Karapanagiotis et al., in press). Characteristic absorption peaks of a standard tyrian purple sample are presented in Fig. 4.2 (Koren, 2008b). Earlier use of TLC has been reported (Table 4.1).

It was found of interest to perform a cluster analysis of different percentages of colors of murex from various origins that may be identified by similar preparation techniques and origin and type of murex (see Table 1, Section 1 and Karapanatiotis et al., 2013) (Fig. 4.3). Here the clusters differentiate type and preparation of murex as appear for T1, T2, T3, T4, T5, T10, T12, separate little locus for T7, T9, for B1, B2,B5, H3 (Spain, Greece, Israel), then B3, H1, H2 (Greece, Spain), then a larger group of AK1, Tri, AK3, AK2, Dar1, Ra, the the sole B4 and H4 (Italy, Greece) and outliers T11, T6, T8 expected as derived from far away sites (France, Greece, Eastern Spain), while the Akrotiri, Trianda at Rhodes and Darius stone are similar. Though of different murex species the preparation produced same pigment i.e chemical compounds.

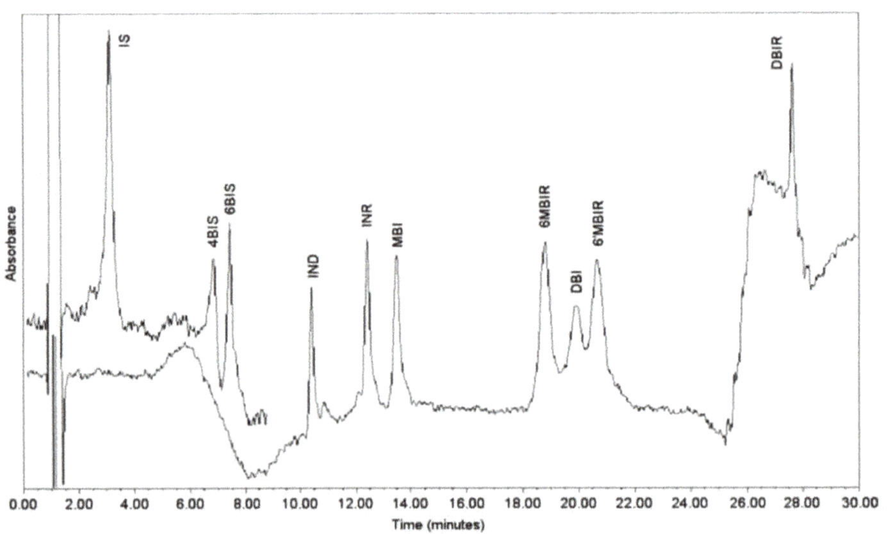

Figure 4.2 HPLC-PDA analysis of standard tyrian purple dyes visualized at 400nm for the isatinoids (top: isatin (IS), 4-bromoisatin (4BIS), and 6-bromoisatin (6BIS)) and at 594nm for the indigoids and the indirubinoids (bottom: indigo (IND), indirubin (INR), 6-monobromoindigo (MBI), 6-monobromoindirubin (6MBIR), 6,6'-dibromoindigo (DBI), 6'-monobromoindirubin (6'MBIR), and 6,6'-dibromoindirubin (DBIR)) (Koren, 2008b)

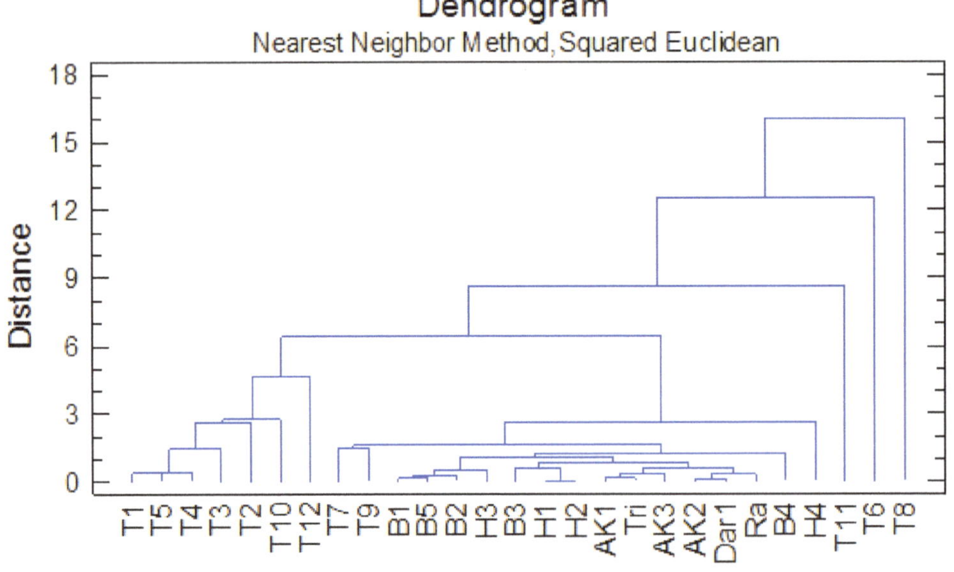

Figure 4.3 Cluster analysis of samples from Table 1 from Chapter 1. T: Hexaplex Trunculus: T1(Carthage, Tunis), T2(Croatia), T3(Tunis), T4(Tunis), T5(Tarragona), T6(Tarragona), T7(Akhziv, Israel/Jordan), T8(Saronikos, Greece), T9(Akhziv), T10(Spain), T11(France) T12(Hermione, Greece), B: Bolinus Brandaris: B1(Tarragona, Spain), B2(Tarragona), B3(Saronikos), B4(Fiumicino), B5(Thera), H: Stramonita Haemastoma: H1(Tarragona), H2(Tarragona), H3(Israel), H4(Hermione), and the archaeological samples Ak1, Ak2, Ak3 (Akrotiri, Thera), Ra(Raos, Thera), Tri(Trianta, Rhodes) and Dar1(Darius stone jar). (Data based on data by Koren, 2008a; Karapanagiotis et al 2013; Mantzouris and Karapanagiotis, 2014).

FTIR

FTIR spectrometers (Fourier Transform Infrared Spectrometer) are widely used in organic synthesis, polymer science, petrochemical engineering, pharmaceutical industry and food analysis. In addition, since FTIR spectrometers can be hyphenated to chromatography, the mechanism of chemical reactions and the detection of unstable substances can be investigated with such instruments. The measurement of the degree of absorption helps to identify minerals and chemical elements, in the case of Tyrian purple presence of bromine (6,6 '-dibromoindigotine) (Fig. 4.4 Karapanagiotis et al., in press).

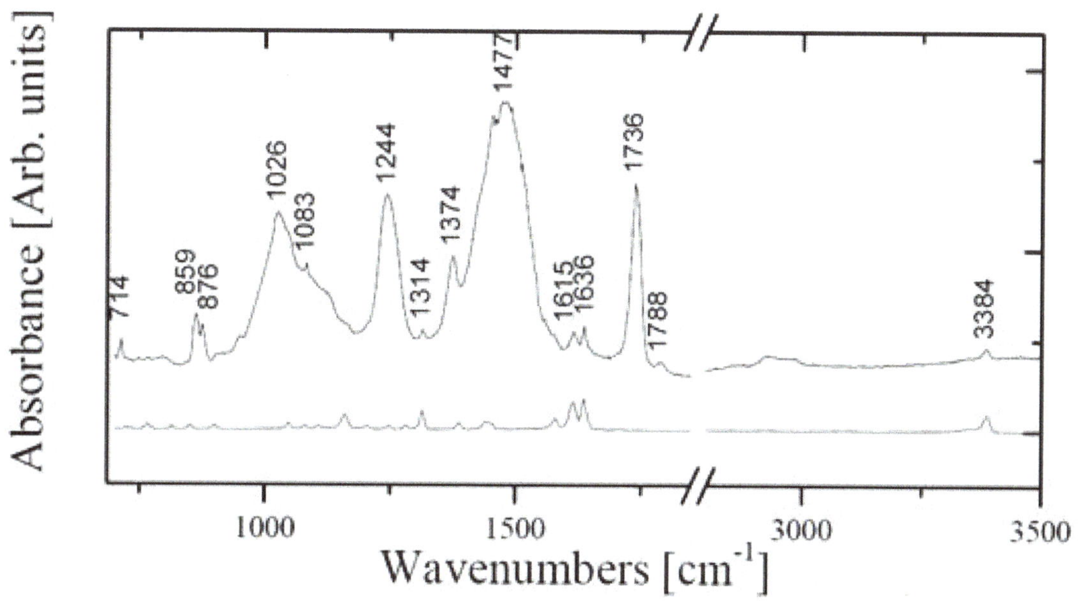

Fig. 4.4 (Lower) FTIR spectrum of apigment sample from Akrotiri, Thera (Late Bronze Age), from the fresco painting "Mistress of Animals and Saffron Gatherer" (Xesté 3, room 3a, First floor, Northwall), containing the purple paint details and the referencesubstance (upper) 6,6'-dibromoindigotin. Bands attributed to 6,6'-dibromoindigotin, aragonite (andpartially to calcite) as well as the consolidant used by the restorers can be identified (Karapanagiotis et al., in press).

Optical Microscope

Optical microscopy was applied to a textile excavated in Kerameikos, Athens, Greece (fig. 4.5) (Margariti et al., 2013). There was identified a decoration with purple colored wefts.

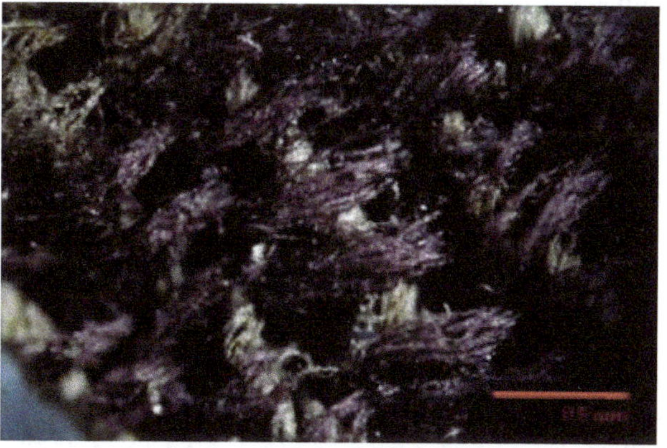

Figure 4.5 Image from Optical Microscope on a fragment of textile from the excavation site in Kerameikos, Athens, Greece (430-400BC). Identification of the decoration with purple wefts is apparent (Margariti et al., 2013).

SEM-EDX

SEM microscopy is a non-destructive technique which will allow us to investigate the structure and the decay of sensitive samples without any additional alterations, such as fibers. In combination with the EDX method and the SEM can provide us with a qualitative and quantitative data analysis. This method allows a fast and non-destructive chemical analysis with spatial resolution in the micrometer regime. The detection of bromine will reveal the presence of murex (Fig. 4.6).

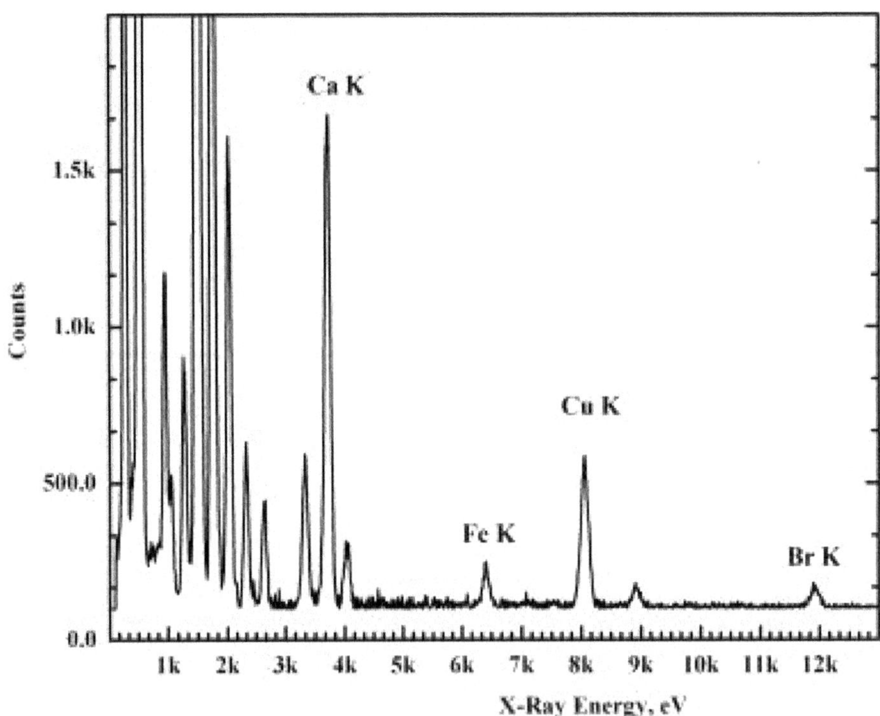

Figure 4.6 EDX spectra of a purple textile excavated in Kerameikos, Athens, Greece (430-400BC) (Margariti et al., 2013).

6. METHODS OF PRODUCTION AND THE CHEMISTRY OF TYRIAN PURPLE

Ways of production of Tyrian purple has been reviewed by Wolk and Frimer, (2010); including significant works such as Cooksey, (2001a) and Imming et al., (2001). Initial attempts in using alkali chemical reagents at dibromoindigotin (DBI) for obtaining corresponding color has been made by Michel and McGovern (1990) shown in brief steps below:

DBI + NaOH + 90°C + 1h — Deep Purple
DBI + $K2CO_3$ +90°C +2 h — Purple
DBI + $K2CO_3$ +90°C +1 h — Light Purple

In experiments performed with different solutions in urine Ph that give the same colors is as below:

DBI with pH 9 + 50-60°C +1 h — Light Violet
DBI with pH 8.6-8.8 +60-70, or 90°C +1 h — Light Violet

In another experiment for blue, brown and pink:
Deionized water+ IND + CaO + Na_2CO_3 • H_2O + 45°C + 6 days — Light Blue
DBI + Deionized water +CaO + Na_2CO_3 • H_2O + 45°C +6 days — Pink
Deionized water + CaO + Na_2CO_3 • H_2O + 45°C + 6 days — Light brown

A follow up has been reviewed by Ziderman et al., (2004); Son et al., (2004); Cooksey and Sinclair, (2005); Koren, (2012); Lavinda et al., (2013); Ramig et al., (2015), among others.

Overall, the murex has been given special attention throughout the last 5,000 years at least in Mediterranean region, but the World as well, and reconstructing trade routes along the orient and occident, from China to Europe, are of particular interest. In fact, among the more unlikely 'matchmaking' arranged by human ingeniousness is the one between the Chinese domesticated silk moth, *Bombyx mori*, and the Mediterranean marine snails, *murex*, of the Muricidae family. The sea snails produce a pigment that, when brought together with silk, led to the world's longest-lasting fashion statement, while in China and elsewhere used it as traditional medicine (Benkendorff et al., 2015).

7. CONCLUSION

Purple is a pigment, which is created by the sea-shell family gastropods. In antiquity, the essence of the animal was used to paint the people of nobility their clothes, so it was considered a "royal" color. Indeed, several ancient sources record the sea-shell of murex while its use of purple is recorded in Linear B tablets, the Homeric epics, by Aristotle, etc. The purple dye testified for the first time in Minoan Crete from the 17th century BC, and since used mainly in the SE Mediterranean. The workshops that were processing the shell to get purple, covered almost the entire Mediterranean mainly the easrern part. The technique of dye was made in several stages with complex processes.

The hues of the dyed fabrics vary from blue-green to blue for indigo, blue to violet for 6-bromoindigo, and violet blue to purple for 6,6′ -dibromoindigo, as determined by reflectance measurements. Many of the dyed fabrics change color markedly with application of gentle heat.

Purple is evocative in its preparation, engages in the colors of the rainbow and raises the royal purple color through malodorous sulfur fumes. It is unpredictable, also in hue, as the air and the sun determine the final tone. Moreover, is surprisingly stable through centuries of given gloss. With all these elements, purple retains almost magical properties and has been used throughout the World as dye and edible for medical purposes. The magnificence of silk and woolen veil, the simple brilliance of parchments and frescos through this color of an inaccessible sophistication compared to modern synthetic dyes, as well as, its multi-color knowledge with the overall elegance, is worthy of attention in our cultural space.

A plethora of scientific methods have been applied to identify this organic pigment in ancient materials. Spectroscopic, chromatographic, microscopic techniques are often used with success and have recognized the chemical substance.

ACKNOWLEDGEMENTS

We thank Assoc. Prof. I. Karapanagiotis and an anonymous referee for useful comments. This is part of a major project of Eastern Mediterranean - China Cultural Contacts led by Ioannis Liritzis as PI of Chinese National Social Science Fund's "Great Site and Capital Civilization's Research of He Luo (Yellow river and Luo river) and Three Generations (Xia, Shang and Zhou Dynasties)" Phased Results (Project Approval: 13 & ZD100).

REFERENCES

Ajiki, H., Pozzi, F., Huang, L., Massa, L., Leona, M., Lombardi, JR. (2012) Raman spectrum of monobromoindigo, *Journal of Raman Spectroscopy*, 43, 4, 520-525

Aloupi, E., Maniatis, Y., Paradellis, T., Karalygiannacopoulou, L. (1990) Analysis of a Purple Material Found at Akrotiri in D. Hardy & C. A. Renfrew (eds.), *Thera and the Aegean World III*, I, London: The Thera foundation, 488-490.

Aloupi, E., Karydas, A.G., Paradellis, T. (2000) Pigment analysis of wall paintings and ceramics from Greece and Cyprus, *X-Ray Spectrom*. 29, 18–24.

Andreotti, A., Bonaduce, I., Colombini, M.P., Ribechini, E. (2004). Characterization of natural indigo and shellfish purple by mass spectrometric techniques. *Rapid Comm. Mass Spectrom.*, 18, 1213-1220.

Andreotti, A., Carmignani, A., Colombini, M.P., Modugno, F. (2006) Characterization of paint organic materials in wall decorations of Macedonian tombs, in: H. Brecoulaki, National Hellenic Research Foundation (Eds.), La peinture funeraire de Macedoine, Emplois et Fonctions de la CouleurIVe-IIe s. av. J. -C, Vol II: Planches & Tableaux, Appendix IV, Athens.

Anonymous, (1874) Eine Purpurfabrik im alten Phoenicien. *Globus*, 26, 37-238

Apostolakou, S. (2009) a workshop for dyeing wool at Pefka near Pacheia Ammos. Kentro, The Newsletter of INSTAP Study Center for East Crete 11 (Fall), 1-2

Apostolakou, S., Betancourt, P.P., Brogan, T.M. (2010) Recent excavations at Pacheia Ammos and Chrissi Island: A preliminary report. In M. Andrianakis and I. Tzachili (eds) Archaeological work in Crete I. Proceedings of the 1st Meeting, Rethymnon, 28-30 November 2008. Rethymnon, *Faculty of Letters Publications*, University of Crete, 143-154

Apostolakou, S., Borgan T.M., Betancourt, P.P. (2012) The Minoan settlement on Chryssi and its Murex Industry. In M.L. Nosch and R. Laffineur (eds) Kosmos: Jewellwry, Adornment and Textiles in the Aegean Bronze Age. Proceedings of the 13th International Aegean Conference, University of Copenhagen, Danish National Research Foundation' s Centre for Textile Research, 21-26 April 2010. Aegaeum 33. Leuven and Liege: Peeters, 179-182 + pls. XXXVIII-XXXIX

Aristotle, *History of Animals*, V15

Astour, M.C. (1965) *The origin of the terms Cannan, Phoenicians and Purple*, *Journal of Near Eastern Studies* 2, 346-350.

Bacchylides, Lithyramvoi 17,112 (http://www.perseus.tufts.edu/hopper/text?doc=Perseus%3Atext%3A1999.01.0064%3Abook%3DDith%3Apoem%3D17).

Baker, J.T. (1974) Tyrian purple. Ancient dye, a modern problem, *Endeavour*, 33, 11-17.

Baruch, I., Artzy, M., Heller, J., Balensi, J., Herrera, M.D. (2005) The molluscfauna from the Late Bronze and Iron Age strata of Tell Abu Hawam. In: D.E. Bar-Yosef Mayer (ed), *Archaeomalacology, Molluscs in former environments of humanbehaviour* (Proceedings of the 9th Conference of the International Council of Archaeozoology, Durham, August 2002). Oxford: Oxbow Books, 132-147.

Becker, C. (2001) Did the people in Ayios Mamasproduce purple-dye during the Middle Bronze Age? Considerations on the Prehistoric production of purple dye in the Mediterranean". In: Buitenhuis, H. and Prummel, W. (Eds), *Animals and Man in the Past*, Groningen: Archaeological Research and Consultancy -Publicatie 41, 122-134.

Belgiorno, M.R. (2004) Cyprus, Advanced Country since 2000 BC. In: Belgiorno, M.R. (Ed.): Pyrgos-Mavroraki. Advanced Technology in Bronze Age Cyprus. *Nicosia Archaeological Museum*, Nicosia, 9–37

Benkendorff, K., Bremner, J.B., Davis, A.R. (2001) Indole derivatives from the egg masses of Muricid molluscs. *Molecules*, 6, 70-78.

Betancourt, P.P., Apostolakou, V., Brogan, T. M. (2012) The Workshop for Making Dyes at Pefka, Crete. In M.L. Nosch and R. Laffineur (eds) Kosmos: Jewellwry, Adornment and Textiles in the Aegean Bronze Age. Proceedings of the 13th International Aegean Conference, University of Copenhagen, Danish National Research Foundation' s Centre for Textile Research, 21-26 April 2010. Aegaeum 33. Leuven and Liege: Peeters, 183-186

Biggs, H.E.J. (1967) Notes on Mollusca. In M.V. Seton-Williams, The Excavations at Tell Rifa'at, 1964. Second Preliminary Report. *Les Annales Archéologiques Arabes Syriennes* 17(1-2), 77-78.

Benkendorff, K, Rudd, R, Bijayalakshmi Devi Nongmaithem, Liu, L, Edwards, V, Avila, C and Abbott, C.A (2015) Are the Traditional Medical Uses of Muricidae Molluscs Substantiated by Their Pharmacological Properties and Bioactive Compounds? *Marine Drugs,* 13(8): 5237–5275.

Blanc, A.C (1958) Residui di manifattura di porpora a Leptis Magna ed al Monte Circero. In Batroccini, R. (ed), *Il Porto Romano di Leptis Magna.* Rome, *Bolletino del Centro Studi per la Storia dell' Architettura Suplemento* 13,187-210

Born, W. (1937) Purple in Classical Antiquity. *Ciba Review* 4, 111-117.

Börnchen, M. (2009) *Farben bereichern unser Leben: Tierische und pflanzliche Farbstoffe,* Universitäts bibliothek der Freien Universität Berlin, Ausstellungsführer der Universitätsbibliothek der Freien Universität Berlin 48, 59-60.

Bruin, F. (1970) Royal Purple and the Dye Industries of the Mycenaeans and Phoenicians. In M. Mollat (ed), Sociétés et Compagnes de Commerce en Orient et dansL'Océan Indien (Actes du Huitième Colloque International d'Histoire Maritime (Beyrouth - 5-10 Septembre 1966). Paris: Bibliothèque Générale de l'École Pratique des Hautes Études, VIe Section, 73-90.

Bulfinch, T. (2009) The *Age of fable: Capter IVMidas–Baucis and Philemon,* Seven Treasures, United States of America,43.

Çakırlar, C., Becks, R. (2009) 'Murex' Dye Production at Troia: Assessment of Archaeomalacological Data from Old and New Excavations. *Studia Troica* 18,87-103.

Carannante, A. (2006) I resti di molluschi marini dal complesso protopalaziale di Monastiraki, Compagne de studio 2002-2003.In A. Kanta and M.Marazzi, (eds), *Monastiraki* I.Naples: University of Naples,107-111 (Italian, English summary).

Cardon, D. (2003) *Le monde des teintures naturelles.* Belin: Paris.

Cardon, D. (2007) *Natural Dyes-Sources, Tradition, Technology and Science,* Archetype Publications Ltd, London,83.

Chadwick, J. (1958) *The Decipherment of Linear B,* Second Edition 1990, Cambridge, UP.

Chehab, M. (1965) Chronique. Bulletin du Musee de Beyrouth 18, 112-114.

Chryssikopoulou, E., Sotiropoulou, S., Andrikopoulos, K. S. (2001) The evidence for purple brush strokes in the wall paintings of Akrotiri. In: *Colours in Antiquity: Towards an Archaeology of Seeing, 10-13/9/2001.* Edinburgh.

Clark, R.J.H., Cooksey C.J. (1997) Bromoindirubins: the synthesis and properties of minor components of Tyrian purple and the composition of the colorant from Nucella lapillus. *J. Soc. Dyers Colour.,* 113, 316-321.

Clark, R.J.H., Cooksey C.J. (1999) Monobromo-indigos: a new general synthesis, the characterization of all four isomers and an investigation into the purple colour of 6,6'-dibromoindigo. *New J. Chem.,* 1999, 323-328.

Clark, R.J.H., Cooksey, C.J., Daniels, M.A.M., Withnall, R. (1996) Indigo - red white and blue, *Educ.Chem.*, 16-19.

Clementi, C., Nowik, W., Romani, A., Cardon, D., Trojanowicz, M., Davantes, A., Chaminade, P. (2016), Towards a semiquantitative non-invasive characterisation of Tyrian purple dye composition: Convergence of UV-Visible reflectance spectroscopy and fast-high temperature-high performance liquid chromatography with photodiode array detection, *Analytica Chimica Acta* 926, 17-27

Colombini, M.P., Carmignani, A., Modugno, F., Frezzato, F., Olchini, A., Brecoulaki, H., Vassilopoulou, V., Karkanas, P. (2004) Integrated analytical techniques for the study of ancient Greek polychromy, *Talanta*, 63, 839–848

Cooke, A.H. (1909) On the shell mound at Sidon. *Proceedings of the Malacological Society of London* 8, 341.

Cooksey, C.J. (1995) TLC of the Indigoid Colorants in Shellfish Purple, *Dyes in History and Archaeology*, 14, 70-77

Cooksey, C.J., Withnall, R. (2001) Chemical studies on Nucella lapillus. *Dyes Hist. Archaeol.*, 16/17, 91-96.

Cooksey, C.J. (2001a) Tyrian purple: 6,6'-Dibromoindigo and related compounds, *Molecules*, 6 (9), 736–769.

Cooksey, C.J. (2001b) The synthesis and properties of 6-bromoindigo: Indigo blue or Tyrian purple? The effect of physical state on the colours of indigo and bromoindigos. *Dyes Hist. Archaeol.*, 16/17, 97-104.

Cooksey, C.J., Sinclair, R.S. (2005) Colour variations in Tyrian purple dyeing. *Dyes Hist. Archaeol*, 20, 127-135.

Cooksey C, (2013) Tyrian purple: The first four thousand years, *Science Progress*, 96(2), 171-186

Damon, P.E. (1989) Radiocarbon dating of the Shroud of Turin, *Nature*, 337 (6208), 611-15.

Daniels, V. (1985) Dye analysis of two fragments from Enkomi, Dyes in History and Archaeology, 4, 15-18

Daniels, V. (1987) Further work on the dye analysis of textile fragments from Enkomi, *Dyes in History and Archaeology*, 6, 3-7

Daniels, V. (1989). Appendix 1. Analysis of the dyes. In Granger-Taylor, H., Jenkins, I.D. and Wild, J.P., From rags to riches: two textile fragments from Cyprus. Cyprus and the East Mediterranean in the Iron Age. Proceedings of the 7th British Museum Classical Colloquium, April 1988 (V. Tatton-Brown, ed): British Museum, London, 153-154.

Diocletian, Eusebius, *Ecclesiastical History*. VII, 32

Diocletian, *Codex Justinianus* IV. 40.1

Dothan, M. (1960) Tell Mor (Tell Kheidar). *Israel Exploration Journal* 10, 123-125.

Dothan, M. (1981) Akko, 1980. *Israel Exploration Journal* 41/1-2, 110-112.

van Elslande, E., Lecomte, S., Le Ho, A.S. (2008) Micro-Raman spectroscopy (MRS) and surface-enhanced Raman scattering (SERS) on organic colourants in archaeological pigments, *J. Raman Spectrosc.*, 39, 1001–1006

Elsner, O., Spanier, E.(1985)The dyeing with murex extracts .An unusual dyeing method of wool to the Biblical sky blue. *Proceedings of the 7th International Wool Textile Research Conference*, Tokyo V, 118-130

Faklaris, P. (1998) Workshops on the Acropolis of Vergina. *In Ancient Greek Technology*. 1st International Conference, September 1997. Proceedings. Society for Macedonian Studies, Thessaloniki, Thessaloniki: *Publications Technical Museum of Thessaloniki*, 193-200 (In Greek).

Forbes, R.J. (1956) *Studies in Ancient Technology* IV. Leiden: E.J. Brill.

Gaillardot, C. (1865) Lettre au Dr. Mougeot. *Annales de la Société d'Emulation des Vosges* 9.

Gaillardot, C. (1873) Les kjoekkenmoeddings et les debris de fabriques de pourpre. *Bulletins de la Société d'Anthropologie de Paris*, 2eme serie, 8, 750-759.

Gibbs, P.J., Jordan, G.J., Sedden, K.R., Cooksey, C.J., Brovenko, N.M., Tiomkin, E.N., Petrosyan, Y.A. (1995) The in situ identification of indigo on ancient papers, *Eur. Mass Spectrom.*, 1, 417-421.

Gleba, M., Vanden Berghe, I. (2014) Textiles from Strozzacapponi (Perugia/Corciano), New evidence of purple production in pre-Roman Italy, in C. Alfaro, M. Tellenbach y J. Ortiz, (eds). Production and Trade of Textiles and Dyes in the Roman Empire and Neighbouring Regions, Actas del IV Symposium Internacional sobre Textiles y Tintes del Mediterráneo en el mundo antiguo (Valencia, 5 al 6 de noviembre, 2010), Universitat de València, 167-234

Gounaris, A. (2005) "Yaros", In A. Vlachopoulos (ed.), *Archaeology and the Aegean Islands*, Athens: Melissa, 220-221

Hiyoshi, Y., Fujise, Y. (1992) Tyrian purple. As a learning tool for natural product chemistry. *Kagaku Kyoiku*, 40, 390-393.

Hofenk de Graaff, J.H. (2004) The Colourful Past, Abegg-Stiftung and Archetype Publications Ltd., Riggisberg and London, 2004.

Hoffman, R.C., Zilber, R.C., Hoffman, R.E. (2010) NMR spectroscopic study of the Murex trunculus dyeing process, *Magnetic Resonance in Chemistry*, 48(11), 892-895

Homer's *Iliad*: C 125 to 128, The 221, Z 796. (http://classics.mit.edu/Homer/iliad.html)

Homer's *Odyssey*, S 115, S 351, h 226 (http://classics.mit.edu/Homer/odyssey.html)

İren, K. (2012) Dascyleum. A multicultural society in the shadow of Persia. *Current World Archaeology*, 54, 49–51.

İren, K. (2013) *Daskyleion*. In: Bagnall RS, Brodersen K, Champion CB, Erskine A, Huebner SR (eds) *The encyclopedia of ancient history*, 1st ed, Wiley-Blackwell, 1930–31.

Imming, P, Zentgraf, M., Imhof, I. (2001) An improved synthetic procedure for 6.6′ - dibromoindigo (Tyrian purple), *Synthetic Communications*, 31 (23), 3721-3727.

Jackson, J.W. (1916) The Geographical Distribution of the Shell-Purple Industry. *Memoirs of the Manchester Philosophical Society* 60(7), 1-29.

Jackson, J.W. (1917) The geographical distribution of the shell-purple industry. *In* J.W. Jackson (ed.). *Shells as evidence of the migrations of early culture*. University of Manchester. 1-29

James, M.A., Anna, J., Mukherjee, A.J., Robertson, F., Crump, M.P., Pfälzner, P., Evershed, R.P. (2007) Recovery of Tyrian Purple from anthropogenic sediments from a bronze age Syrian royal tomb, Poster 23rd International Meeting on Organic Geochemistry September (Torquay, Devon, United Kingdom).

James, M.A., Reifarth, N., Mukherjee, A.J. Crump, M.P. Gates, P.J. Sandor, P., Robertson, F., Pfälzner, P., Evershed, R.P. (2009) High prestige royal purple dyed textiles from the bronze age royal tomb at Qatna, Syria, *Antiquity*, 83, 1109–1118.

Jameson, M.H, Runnels, C.N, Van Andel, T.M. (1994) *A Greek Countryside, The southern Argolid from Prehistory to the Present Day*, Stanford, Stanford University Press, 316

Jensen, L.B. (1963) Royal Purple of Tyre. *Journal of Near Eastern Studies* 22, 104-118.

Jensen, L.B., Jensen, F. (1965) *The Story of Royal Purple*. Privately published, Sarasota, Florida.

Jidejian, N. (1969) *Tyre through the Ages*. Beirut: Dar el-Mashreq Publishers.

Kakavogiannis, E. (1984) Production lead from litharge in Hellenistic Rhodes, *Arch. Annals Ath.* 17, 134 (In Greek).

Karaberi, M., Christodoulidou, E. (1998) Galerius Palace: "Area D" and South Stoa, *Archaeological work of Macedonia-Thrace*, Thessaloniki 12, 103-112.

Karapanagiotis, I. (2006) Identification of indigoid natural dyestuffs used in art objects by HPLC coupled to APCI-MS, *American Laboratory*, 38, 36–40.

Karapanagiotis, I., de Villemereuil, V., Magiatis, P., Polychronopoulos, P., Vougogiannopoulou, K., Skaltsounis, A.L. (2006) Identification of the coloring constituents of four natural indigoid dyes, *Journal of Liquid Chromatography and Related Technologies* 29,1491-1502.

Karapanagiotis, I., Sotiropoulou, S., Valianou, L. (2011) Identification of Tyrian purple in Aegean Bronze age pigments, *Dyes Hist. Archaeol.* 30, Derby, UK October 12–15, Book of abstracts, 14.

Karapanagiotis, I., Mantzouris, D., Cooksey, C., Mubarak, M. S., Tsiamyrtzis, P. (2013) An improved HPLC method coupled to PCA for the identification of Tyrian purple in archaeological and historical samples, *Microchemical Journal*, 110, 70-80.

Karapanagiotis, I., Sotiropoulou, S., Chryssikopoulou, E., Magiatis, P., Andrikopoulos, K.S., Chryssoulakis, Y., (in press), Sous presse - Investigation of Tyrian Purple occurring in historical Wall Paintings of Thera. *Dyes in History and Archaeology*, 23.

Kardara, C. (1974) Painting and paints inantiquity, *Hesperia 42*,447-453.

Karmon, N. (1999) Muricid Shells of the Persian and Hellenistic Periods. In I. Roll and O. Tal (edi), *Apollonia-Arsuf, Final Report of the Excavations* I *The Persian and Hellenistic Periods*. Emery and Claire Yass Publications in Archaeology, Monograph Series No. 16. Tel Aviv: Tel Aviv University, 269-280.

Karmon, N., Spanier, E. (1987) Archaeological Evidence of the Purple Dye Industry from Israel. In E. Spanier (ed), *The Royal Purple and the Biblical Blue, Argaman and Tekhelet. The Study of Chief Rabbi Dr. Isaac Herzog on the Dye Industries in Ancient Israel and Recent Scientific Contributions*. Jerusalem: Keter Publishing House Jerusalem Ltd., 147-158.

Karmon, N., Spanier, E. (1988) Remains of a Purple Dye Industry at Tel Shiqmona. *Israel Exploration Journal*, 38(3), 184-186.

Karydas, A.G. (2006) In situ XRF analyses of wall-painting pigments on ancient funeral Macedonian monument, in: H. Brecoulaki, National Hellenic Research Foundation (Eds.), La peinture funeraire de

Macedoine, Emplois et Fonctions de la Couleur IVe-IIe s. av. J. -C, Vol II: Planches & Tableaux, Appendix IV, Athens.

Koren, Z.C. (1993) 'The colors and dyes on ancient textiles in Israel', *in Colors from Nature: Natural Colors in Ancient Times,* C. Sorek and E. Ayalon (eds), Tel-Aviv: Eretz Israel Museum, 15–31, 47–65.

Koren, Z.C. (1994a). HPLC analysis of the natural scale insect, madder and indigoid dyes. J. Soc. Dyers Colour., 110,273-277.

Koren, Z. C. (1995) High-performance liquid chromatographic analysis of an ancient Tyrian Purple Dyeing at from Israel, *Israel Journal Chemistry* 35, 117-1241.

Koren, Z.C. (1997). The Unprecedented Discovery Of The Royal Purple Dye On The Two Thousand Year-Old Royal Masada Textile. *American Institute for Conservation, The Textile Specialty Group Postprints,* Volume 7, 23-34.

Koren, Z.C. (2005a) 'The First Optimal All-Murex All-Natural Purple Dyeing in the Eastern Mediterranean in a Millennium and a Half', *Dyes in History and Archaeology* 20, 136–149, Colour Plates 15.1–15.5

Koren, Z C. (2005b) Chromatographic Analyses of Selected Historic Dyeings from Ancient Israel In Janaway and Wyeth (eds.) *Scientific Analysis of Ancient and Historic Textiles*: Informing, Preservation, Display and Interpretation, London: Archetype Publications,194-201.

Koren, Z.C. (2006) HPLC-PDA analysis of brominated indirubinoid, indigoid, and isatinoid dyes. In Meijer, L., Guyard, N., Skaltsounis, L. and Eisenbrand, G. (eds.) *Indirubin, the red shade of indigo.* Life in Progress Editions, Roscoff, France, Ch. 5, 45-53.

Koren, Z.C. (2008a), Archaeo-chemical analysis of Royal Purple on a Darius I stone jar, *Microchim, Acta* 162, 381-392.

Koren, Z.C. (2008b) A New HPLC-PDA Method for the Analysis of Tyrian Purple Components', *Dyes in History and Archaeology,* 21, 26–35

Koren, Z.C. (2012) Chromatographic and colorimetric characterizations of brominatedindigoid dyeings. *Dyes Pigments,* 5 (3), 491-501.

Kramer-Hajos, M., K. O"Neill. (2008). The Bronze Age Site of Mitrou in East Lokris: Finds from the 1988–1989 Surface Survey. *Hesperia* 77(2): 163-270

Lavinda, O., Mironova, I., Karimi, S., Pozzi, F., Samson, J., Ajiki, H., Massa, L., Ramig, K. (2013) Singular thermochromic effects in dyeings with Indigo, 6-Bromoindigo, and 6,6'-Dibromoindigo, *Dyes and Pigments,* 96(2), 581-589.

Lloyd, J.A. (1978) *Excavation at Sidi Khrebish, Benghazi.* Vol I. Tripoli: Department of Antiquities.

Lobban, C. S, Harisson, P. J, Duncan, M. J. (1985) *The Physiological Ecology of Seaweeds,* Cambridge: Cambridge University Press.

Lolos, Y. (1990) Heinrich and Sofia Schliemann in the Straits of Salamis, Collective summaries of presentations in the 'Proceedings of the International Conference on Schliemann' in Korres G.S (ed), 14-22 April Athens.

Lortet, L. (1883) *La Syrie d'aujourd'hui.* Paris: Hachette.

Lowe, B. (2004) The industrial exploitation of Murex: Purple dye production in the Western Mediterranean. In L. Cleland and K. Stears (eds*) Colour in the Ancient Mediterranean World,* 46-48. BAR International Series 1267, Oxford.

Macheboeuf, C. (2004) Fabrication et commerce de la porpure en Italie et Sicile dans I' Antiquite romaine. *In Metodi ed approchi archeologici: l' industria ed il commercio nell ' Italia antica,* BAR-IS 1262, Oxford, 25-37

Mantzouris, D., Karapanagiotis, I. (2014) Identification of indirubin and monobromoindirubins in *Murex brandaris, Dyes and Pigments,* 104, 194-196

Maravelaki-Kalaitzaki, P., Kallithrakas-Kontos, N. (2003) Pigment and terracotta analyses of Hellenistic figurines in Crete, Anal. Chim. Acta 497, 209–225

Margariti, C., Protopapas, S., Allen, N., Vishnyakov, V. (2013) Identification of purple dye from molluscs on an excavated textile by non-destructive analytical techniques, Dyes and Pigments, 96, 3, 774–780

Mendel, G. (1914) *Catalogue des sculpturesgrecques, romaines et byzanti nes.* Vol. III. Constantinople: Musée Impérial, 16

McGovern, P.E., Michel, R.H. (1984) Royal purple and the pre-Phoenician dye industry of Lebanon, *MASCA J.,* 3(3), 67-70

McGovern, P.E., Michel, R.H. (1985) Royal purple dye: tracing the chemical origins of the industry, *Anal. Chem.,* 57, 1514A–1522A.

McGovern, P.E., Michel, R.H. (1990) Royal Purple dye: the chemical reconstruction of the ancient Mediterranean industry, *Accounts of Chemical Research*, 23(5), 152-158

McGovern, P.E., Lazar, J., Michel, R.H. (1990) The analysis of indigoid dyes by mass spectrometry. *J. Soc. Dyers Colour.*, 106, 22-25.

Michel, R.H., McGovern, P.E (1990), The Chemical processing of Royal Purple Dye: Ancient Descriptions as elucidated by modern science, PartII, *Archeomaterials,* 4, 97-104

Michel, R.H., Lazar J., McGovern, P.E., (1992a) The chemical composition of the indigoid dyes derived from the hypobranchial glandular secretions of *Murex* molluscs. *Journal of the Society of Dyers and Colourists,* 108, 145-150.

Michel, R.H., Lazar, J., McGovern, P.E. (1992b) Indigoid Dyes in Peruvian and Coptic Textiles of the University Museum of Archaeology and Anthropology. *Archaeomaterials* 6 (1), 69-83

Miliani, C., Romani, A., Favaro, G.A. (1998) Spectrophotometric and fluorimetric study of someanthraquinoid and indigoid colorants used in artistic paintings, *Spectrochim. Acta Ser A, 54,* 581-588.

Minniti, C. (1999) L'utilizzatione dei molluschi nett'eta del Bronzo di Coppa Nevigata.In A.Gravina, (ed.) 19th Convegno Nazionole *sulla Preistoria –Protostoria e Storia della Daunia*, San Severo 1998, 177-198.

Moschonisiotou, S. (1989) *Cemetery in Ag. Mamas, The Archaeological Work in Macedonia and Thrace 3*, 351-356, [In Greek]

Müller, S. (1991) Prospection de la plaine de Malia. *BCH* 115(2): 742-749

Nigdelis, P. (2010) Voluntary Associations in RomanThessalonike: In Search of Identity and Supportin a Cosmopolitan Society. In: L. Nasrallah, C. Bakirtzis & S.J. Friesen (eds.), *From Roman toEarly Christian Thessalonike. Studies in Religionand Archaeology*. Harvard Theological Studies 64. Cambridge, Massachusetts: Harvard Divinity School, 13-47.

Nowik, W., Marcinowska, R., Kusyk, K., Cardon, D., Trojanowicz, M. (2011) High performance liquid chromatography of slightly soluble brominated indigoids from Tyrian Purple, *Journal of Chromatography,* A 1218, 1244-1252.

Oribasius, Oreivas. *Λογ. D jf.*

Orna, M.V. (2013) *The Chemical History of Colour*, New York: Springer.

Papadakis, N. (1983) Koufonisi: "Delos Island" of the Libic sea, Archaeology, 6, 58-65 [In Greek]

Papanastasiou, M. (2005) The use of high performance liquid chromatography – atmospheric pressure photoionization mass spectrometry for the analysis of Murex trunculus and Purpura haemastoma species. Dyes in History and Archaeology, 24th meeting, Liverpool.

Papliaka, E.Z., Konstanta, A., Karapanagiotis, I., Karadag, R. Akyol, AA, Mantzouris, D. Tsiamyrtzis, P. (2015) FTIR imaging and HPLC reveal ancient painting and dyeing techniques of molluskan purple, *Archaeological and Anthropological Sciences*, DOI 10.1007/s12520-015-0270-3

Parri, W. (1932) Relitti di manifatture di porpora a Tobruk. *Rivista delle Colonie Italiana* 6: 720-723.

Pfister, R. (1951) *Textiles de Halabiyeh.* Paris:Geuthner.

Picard, G. (1956) *Le Monde de Carthage,* Paris: Editions Correa.

Pilhofer, P. (1995) Philippi, Band I, Die erste christliche Gemeinde Europas, J.C.B. Mohr, Tübingen.

Piteros, Chr., Olivier, J.-P., Melena, J.L. (1982) Les Inscriptions en Linéaire B des Nodules de Thèbes La Fouille, les Documents, les Possibilités d'Interprétation, *BCH* 114, 103-184.

Plato, *Politia D, Critias* 120b, *Timaeus* 67c

Pliny, *Historia Naturalis,* IX

Plutarch, *The Parallel Lives*, 36

Porath, Y., Paley, S.M., Stieglitz, R.R. (1993) Tel Mikhmoret. In E. Stern (ed), *The New Encyclopedia of Archaeological Excavations in the Holy Land.* Jerusalem: Israel Exploration Society - Carta, 1043-1046.

Pritchard, J. B. (1978) Recovering Sarepta, a Phoenician city: excavations at Sarafand, Lebanon, 1969-1974, by the University Museum of the University of Pennsylvania. Princeton, N.J.: Princeton University Press.

Protopapas, S., Gatsos, V. (2003) The famous ancient purple of Hermione and its technology, *Archaeology and Arts,* vol. 89, 87-92 (In Greek)

Puech, É. (1980) Céramiques des niveaux 9c à 11. In J. Briend and J. -B. Humbert, *Tell Keisan (1971-1976): une cité phènicienne en Galilée.* Orbis Biblicus et Orientalis, Series Archaeologica 1. Fribourg: Éditions Universitaires, 216-234.

Raban, A. (1981) Some Archaeological Evidence for Ancient Maritime Activities at Dor. *Sefunim* 6, 15-26.

Raban, A. (1983) The Biblical Port of Akko on Israel's Coast. *Archaeology* 36(1), 60-61.

Radwin, G. E, D'Attilio, A. (1986) Murex Shells of the world. *An illustrated guide to the Muricidae*, Stanford University Press, USA, 284

Raeder, J. (ed.) (1926), Oribasii Synopsis ad Eusthatiumet libriad Eunapium. Corpus Medicorum Graecorum VI. 3, Leipzig, p. 317-318.

Ramig, K., Lavinda, O., Szalda, D. J., Mironova, I., Karimi, S., Pozzi, F., Shah, N., Samson, J., Ajiki, H., Massa, L., Mantzouris, D., Karapanagiotis, I., Cooksey, C, (2015) The nature of thermochromic effects in dyeings with indigo, 6-bromoindigo, and 6,6'-dibromoindigo, components of Tyrian purple, *Dyes and Pigments*, 117, 37-48

Reese, D.S. (1980) Industrial Exploitation of Murex Shells: Purple dye and Lime Production at Sidi Khrebish, Benghazi (Berenice). *Libyan Studies* 11, (1979-1980), 79-93.

Reese, D. S. (1987) Palaikastro Shells and Bronze Age Purple-Dye Production in the Mediterranean Basin, *Annals of the British School of Archaeology*, 82, 201–206.

Reese, D.S. (2000) Iron Age Shell Purple-Dye Production in the Aegean. In J.W. Shaw and M.C. Shaw (edt), Kommos IV *The Greek Sanctuary*, Princeton: Princeton University Press, 643-645.

Reese, D.S. (2002) Marine Invertebrates. In D.S. Reese and M.J. Rose, Organic Remains from the Island and Adjacent Areas. In D. White, Marsa Matruh II The Objects. *Prehistory Monographs 2*. Philadelphia: *INSTAP* Academic Press, 95-104

Reese, D.S. (2005) Whale Bones and Shell Puple-dye at Motya (Western Sicily, Italy), Oxford, *Journal of Archaeology* 24(2),107-114.

Reese, D.S. (2007) Marine Shells. In T.J. Barako, *Tel Mor - The Moshe Dothan Excavations, 1959-1960*. IAA Reports 32. Jerusalem: Israel Antiquities Authority, 233-238.

Reese, D.S. (2010) Shells from Sarepta (Lebanon) and East Mediterranean Purple-dye Production, *Mediterranean Archaeology and Archaeometry* 10, no. 1, 113-41

Reese, D.S. (2015a) «The Invertebrates», J.A. Mac Gillivray & L.H. Sackett eds., *Palaikastro Building 1*. BSA Suppl. Vol. London, 489-521 (in proof).

Reese, D.S. (2015b) Smelly shelly studies: Reflections on 35 year of pursuing purple, oral presentation at-Lecce Conference International Workshop, May 26-28 2013, Treasures from sea, Oxford Volume (abstract book).

Reinhold, M. (1970) *History of Purple as a Status Symbol in Antiquity*. Collection Latomus, vol. 116. Brussels: Latomus, Revue d'Études Latines.

Ridout-Sharpe, J. S. (1998) Past and present: Shell collecting on Kouphonisi, Conchologist's Newsletter 144, 915–923.

Rolfe, J.C. (1913) *Suetonius*: *The Lives of the Twelve Caesars*, London: Heinemann.

Ruscillo, D. (2005), Reconstructing Murex Royal Purple and Biblical Blue in the Aegean, in D.E. Bar-Yosef Mayer (ed.), *Archaeomalacology. Molluscs in Former Environments of Human Behaviour*, Proceedings of the 9th Conference of the International Council of Archaeozoology, Durham, August 2002, Oxford Book, 99-106.

Ruscillo, D.(2006) "Faunal Remains and Murex Dye Production," in J. W. and M. C. Shaw (eds.), Kommos V: *The Monumental Buildings at Kommos*,Princeton, 776-840.

Rystedt, E., Faegersten, F., Wallensten, J., Östenberg, I. (2010), Tankemönster: en festskrift till Eva Rystedt, Lunt: Fanni Faegersten, 84.

Saltzman, M. (1978) The identification of dyes in archaeological and ethnographic textiles. Archaeological Chemistry II (G.F. Carter, ed), Advances in Chemistry Series, No. 171: *American Chemical Society*, Washington D.C., 172-185.

Saltzman, M. (1986) Analysis of dyes in museum textiles or, you can't tell a dye by its color. *Textile Conservation Symposium* in Honor of Pat Reeves (C.C. McLean and P. Connell, eds): Los Angeles County Museum of Art, Los Angeles, 27-39.

Saltzman, M. (1992) Identifying dyes in textiles. *Am. Sci.*, 80, 474-481.

de Saulcy, F. (1864) Lettre sur la purpre phénicienne. *Revue Archéologique* 9, 218-219.

Schaeffer, C.F.A. (1929) Les Fouilles de Minet al-Beida et de Ras Shamra (Campagne du printempe 1928): Rapport sommaire. Syria 10, 285-297.

Schaeffer C.F.A. (1951) *Une industrie d'Ugarit, la pourpre*. Les Annales Archéologiques de Syrie 1, 188-192.

Scott, P. (2006) "Millennia of Murex", *Saudi Aramco World*, Volume 57, Number 4.

Serrano-Andrés, L., Roos, B.O. (1997) A theoretical study of the indigoid dyes and their chromophore, *Chem.-Eur. J.*, *3*, 717-725.

Shaw, J.W, Shaw, M.C. (2006), Faunal remains and Murex dye production, Princeton, 776-840

Shen, B., Olbrich-Stock, M., Posdorfer, J., Schindler, R.N. (1991) An Optical and Spectroelectrochemical Investigation of Indigo Carmine, *Z. Phys. Chem.*, *173*, 251-255.

Shimoyama, S., Noda Y. (1994) Non-destructive three dimensional fluorescence technique. *Dyes Hist. Archaeol.*, 12, 50-61.

Sideris, A. (2014*) Antikyra: History and archaeology*, Municipality of Distomo-Arachova, Antikyra, Greece (in Greek), with english summary.

Sideris, A, Levy, T and Liritzis, I (2017) New excavations and finds in the Mycenaean site of Kastrouli, Phokis, *Mediterranean Archaeology & Archaeometry*, Vol.17, No.1 (in press).

Simonides 31 (13D 371 P)

Sofianou, C., Brogan T.M. (2010) Minoan settlement Papadiokampos Sitia,excavation of House B1in 2008. In Andrianakis M and Tzachili I. (eds), *Archaeological Project Crete1*,proceedings of conference,28-30 November 2008,Rethumno, 134-142.

Son Y-A, Hong J-P, Kim T-K. (2004) An approach to the dyeing of polyester fiber using indigo and its extended wash fastness properties. Dyes Pigments, 61, 263-272.

Sotiropoulou, S., Karapanagiotis, I. (2006) Conchylian purple investigation in prehistoric wall paintings of the Aegean area, in: L. Meijer, N. Guyard, A.-L. Skaltsounis, G. Eisenbrand (Eds.), Indirubin, *The Red Shade of Indigo,* Life in Progress Editions, Roscoff, pp. 71–78

Stern, E. (1978) *Excavations at Tel Mevorakh (1973-1976)* I *From the Iron Age to the Roman Period*. QEDEM 9. Jerusalem: Institute of Archaeology, Hebrew University.

Stern, E. (1994) *Dor - Ruler of the Seas: Twelve Years of Excavation at the Israelite-Phoenician Harbor Town on the Carmel Coast.* Jerusalem: Israel Exploration Society.

Stieglitz, R. (1994) The Minoan Origins of Tyrian Purple, *Biblical Archaeologist* 57(1), 46-54.

Strabo, XVI 2,23

van Strydonck, M., Boudin, M., Ramis, D. (2012) Direct 14C-dating of Roman and late antique purple dye sites by murex shells, Archaeosciences, *Revue d' Archeometrie,* 36, 15-22.

Surowiec, I., Nowik, W., Moritz, T. (2012) Mass spectrometric identification of new minor indigoids in shellfish purple dye from *Hexaplex trunculus, Dyes and Pigments*, 94(2), 363-369

Tatsch, E., Schrader, B. (1995) Near-Infrared Fourier Transform Raman Spectroscopy of Indigoids, *J. Raman Spectr.*, *26*, 467-473.

Thureau-Dangin, F. (1934) Un comptoir de laine pourpre à Ugarit d'après une tablette de Ras-Shamra. *Syria* 15, 137-146.

Tobin, J. (2011) *From Troy to Constantinople: Cities and Societies of Ancient Turkey,* Recorded Books, LLC.

Triantafyllidis, P. (2015) Archaeological Researches on Milesian Agathonisi in the Dodecanese, Greece Recent Studies on the Archaeology of Anatolia Edited by Ergün Laflı, Sami Patacı, Archaeopress, *British Archaeological Reports, International Series 2750*, 95-104.

Tsingou, A. (2009) Khania (Kydonia). A Tour to Sites of Ancient Memory, Ministry of Culture and Tourism – 25th Ephorate of Prehistoric and Classical Antiquities, 200

Vasileiadou, A., Karapanagiotis, I., Zotou, A. (2016) Determination of Tyrian purple by high performance liquidchromatography with diode array detection, *Journal of Chromatography* A, 1448, 67–72

Veropoulidou, R., Andreou, S., Kotsakis, K. (2008) Small scale purple-dye production in the Bronze Age of Northern Greece: The evidence from the Thessalonike Toumba. In C. Alfaro & L. Karali (eds.), *Vestidos, Textiles y Tintes. Estudios sobrela produccion de bienes de consume en la Antigüedad. Actas del II Symposium Internationalsobre Textiles y Tintes del Mediterráneo en elmundo antiguo (Atenas, 24 al 26 de noviembre,2005). Purpureae Vestes II.* Valencia: Universitat de València, 171-179.

Veropoulidou, R., (2011) *Spondylus gaederopus* tools and meals in Central Greece from the 3rdto the 1st millennium BCE. In M. Nikolaidou &F. Ifantidis (eds.), *Spondylus in Prehistory: New Data and Approaches – Contributions to the Archaeology of Shell Technologies*. BAR International Series 2216. Oxford: Archaeopress.*160*

Veropoulidou, R. (2012) The Tyrian Purple, a "royal" dye. In P. Adam-Veleni and E. Stefani (eds.),*Greeks and Phoenicians at the MediterraneanCrossroads.* Exhibition Catalogue (20/12/2011-20/09/2012). Thessaloniki: Archaeological Museum of Thessaloniki (publ. no. 15), 103-105.

Vitruvius (*Ten Books, VII, XIII*)

Vitti, M.(1996) *Planning evolution of Thessaloniki since its inception as Galerius* Athens: Archaeological Society (vol. 160) (In Greek).

Volonakis, I. (1990) *The Islands Agathonisi and Arkei of the Dodecanese and monuments,* Patmian pages, sheet number 26.1990,18-23 and Figures sheet 27.1990,20-22

Voss G., (2000). The analysis of indigoid dyes as leuco forms by NMR spectroscopy. *J. Soc. Dyers Colour.*, 116, 80-90.

Voss, G., Gerlach, H. (1989) Regioselektiver Brom/Lithium-Austauschbei 2,5-Dibrom-1-nitrobenzol. Eineein-facheSynthese von 4-Brom-2-nitrobenzaldehyde und 6,6'-Dibromindigo, *Chem. Ber., 122*, 1199-1201.

Voss, G., Schramm W. (2000). Selectively C-deuterated indigotins. Helv. Chim. Acta, 83, 2884-2892.

Walton, P. (1985) Shellfish purple in a Coptic textile. *Dyes on Historical and Archaeological Textiles* 4, 33-34.

Welter-Schulters, F. W. (2008) Bronze Age Shipwreck Snails from Turkey: First Direct Evidence for Oversea Carriage of Land Snails in Antiquity,*Journal of Molluscan Studies*, 74, (1), 79-87.

White, D. (1987) Excavations on Bates's Island, Marsa Matruh: Second Preliminary Report. *JARCE*, 26, 87-126.

Wilde, W.R. (1839) On the Purple Dye of Tyre. *Transactions of the Royal Irish Academy* I, 293-295.

Wilde, W.R. (1844) *Narrative of a Voyage to Madeira, Teneriffe, and along the Shores of the Mediterranean* II. Dublin: William Curry.

Withnall, R., Clark, R. J.H., Cooksey, C.J., Daniels, M.A.M, (1992) Non-destructive in situ Identification of Indigo/Woad and Shellfish Purple by Raman Microscopy and Visible Reflectance Spectroscopy. *Dyes in History and Archaeology*, 11, 19-24.

Withnall, R., Clark, R.J.H., Cooksey, C.J., Daniels, M.A.M. (1993) Non-destructive, in situ identification of indigo/woad and shellfish purple by Raman microscopy and visible reflectance spectroscopy, *Dyes Hist. Archaeol., 11*, 19-24.

Withnall, R., Patel, D., Cooksey, C.J., Naegel, L. (2003) Chemical studies of the purple dye of Purpura pansa. Dyes Hist. Archaeol., 19, 109-117.

Wolk, JL, Frimer, AA (2010) Preparation of Tyrian Purple (6,6'-Dibromoindigo): Past and Present, *Molecules*, 15, 5473-5508

Wouters, J., Verhecken, A. (1991) *High-performance liquid chromatography of blue and purple indigoid natural dyes, Coloration Technology* (Journal of the Society of Dyers and Colourists), Vol. 107, Issue 7-8, 266–269.

Wouters, J. (1992) Anew method for the analysis of blue and purple dyes in textiles. *Dyes in History and Archaeology*, 10, 17-21.

Wouters, J. (1993) Dye analysis of Coptic textiles. In A. De Moor (ed), *Coptic Textiles*.Publicaties van let Provinciaal Archaeological Museum van Zuid-oost-Vlaanderean - Site Velzche, 53-64.

Xenokrates, *On abstinence from animal food*, C'XXII

Zaouali, J. (1994) Marine and Land Molluscs. In H.R. Hurst, *Excavation at Carthage*, The British Mission II/I The Circular Harbour, North Side. The Site and Finds other than Pottery. The British Academy, Oxford, Oxford University Press, 320-324

Ziderman, I.I. (1987) First Identification of Authentic Těkēlet. *Bulletin of the American Schools of Oriental Research*, 265, 25-33.

Ziderman, I.I. (1990) Seashells and Ancient Purple Dyeing. *Biblical Archaeologist* 53(2), 98-101.

Ziderman, I.I., Wallert, A., Hoffman, R., Ozery, Y. (2004) Bathochromic effect of heating 6-bromoindigotin to 60°C. 23rd Dyes in history and archaeology meeting, Montpellier.

Zimi, E, Tzachili, I. (2012) *Textiles and Dress in Greece and the Roman East: A Technological and Social Approach*,Athens, Ta Pragmata Publications.

ARCHAEOMETRICAL AND TYPOLOGICAL ANALYSIS OF 17TH CENTURY GLASS PRODUCTION IN SA GERRERIA WORKSHOP (MAJORCA, SPAIN)

D. Albero Santacreu and M. À. Capellà Galmés

Department of Historical Sciences and Arts Theory, University of the Balearic Islands (Spain), Ramon Llull, Campus UIB, Ctra. Valldemossa km 7.5 s/n 07122 Palma, Spain

Corresponding author: Daniel Albero Santacreu (d.albero@uib.es)

ABSTRACT

In this article, we conduct a study of 104 samples (pieces, technological elements, lumps and frit remains) recovered from the 17th century glass workshop of Sa Gerreria (Majorca, Spain). A SEM-EDS analysis of the chemical composition of 104 samples and the analysis of distinct groupings obtained from a statistical treatment of the data using principle components analysis (PCA) have revealed the type of production developed in the workshop, at both the qualitative and the quantitative levels. On the one hand, this study has contributed interesting information regarding the characteristics of local production, particularly little known aspects such as the types of pieces manufactured and their diverse colourations and decorations. On the other hand, this study has allowed us to identify, for the first time through the study of the materials themselves, the existence of a group of typologically consistent samples that does not match the composition of the products made in this workshop and are most likely related to objects of an imported nature. In conclusion, this study has allowed us to develop a more in-depth understanding of the Island of Majorca's role in peripheral production, exchange networks, and the circulation of knowledge regarding the recipes and techniques used by the Sa Gerreria workshop and their relationship with production contexts closely linked to Barcelona and the territories that composed the ancient Crown of Aragon. This understanding has been developed for the first time from a new perspective that is not exclusively documentary.

KEYWORDS: Technology, History of Glass, SEM-EDS, Knowledge transmission, Trade.

1. INTRODUCTION

The quality and variety of forms of glass produced in 16th and 17th century Spain are largely due to the production of Catalonian workshops (e.g. Barcelona, Mataró) and workshops in other territories of the ancient Crown of Aragon. In these zones, the most innovative glassmakers fused the particularities of a rich local tradition with new technologies, typologies, and styles that originated on the Venetian island of Murano in the middle of the 16th century (Domènech, 1999; Rodríguez García, 1985). This process is similar to that which occurred in other European cities and is part of the phenomenon that specialized historiography has designated *à la façon de Venise* (Newman, 1977: 112). Some of the most significant techniques spread from Barcelona to other cities and peripheral zones through the trade of objects and the circulation of glass artisans (Camiade and Fontaine, 2006; Capellà, 2015). Being situated in a strategic enclave on the routes of the Western Mediterranean, the City of Majorca actively participated in these technical and cultural exchanges. For several years during the beginning of the 17th century, Domingo Barovier and his son, members of one of the most important families of master glassmakers of Murano, taught glassmakers on the island. However, it would appear that they had little success in this endeavour (Rodríguez García, 1988). In this respect, the work performed in Majorca was not isolated. To the contrary, the techniques used and the types of pieces manufactured were influenced by the workshops that developed in the surrounding area.

In this historical context, the main objective of the present study on the Sa Gerreria glass furnaces' materials is to provide more in-depth knowledge about regional production that revolved around Barcelona. This study begins with an initial archaeometric characterization of the materials (glass lumps, technological elements, and pieces) that were recovered from one of the few glass furnaces from the modern period archeologically documented in Spain. The analysis of these materials continues the work of previous studies that analysed the raw materials used in this furnace and some of the techniques used by 17th century glassmakers (Capellà and Albero, 2015). The archaeometric analysis performed using the materials from the Sa Gerreria workshop has been developed with several objectives in mind. On the one hand, the aim is to determine the chemical composition of the products manufactured by this furnace and to define a control group associated with the same, in addition to determining the degree of variability of the products. Doing so would allow us to identify what types of pieces were manufactured on the island and in this centre, which in turn would provide us with a much more complex understanding of the role that local production had within the general context described above. Finally, this study allows us to identify the possible existence of objects that follow differential production strategies and that could have been imported to the island. This is an important issue, since the pieces produced in the Western Mediterranean area have a noticeable typological similarity. We attempt to provide a more in-depth perspective on the typology of pieces and their possible relation with the recycling processes performed by local workshops and contrasted to the written documentation of the era (Capellà, 2015: 55). The information generated by this study is of great relevance because it will allow us to confirm, refute, or explain the data obtained from historical texts and from the typological analysis of objects held in private collections. Furthermore, it provides us with more solid knowledge concerning the networks that connected the islands with the continent. This knowledge forms not only part of the written documentation but also part of the material-based analysis itself.

2. MATERIALS AND METHODS

2.1. *The glass furnace of Sa Gerreria*

The glass materials analysed in this study were conserved in a ceramic container that was recovered during the archaeological excavations performed in the Sa Gerreria district, which is situated in the historic centre of the city of Palma (Figure 1). The archaeological campaign documented numerous industrial structures, which began to be installed in this sector of the city in the Middle Ages. In particular, structures related to pottery production were documented (Estarellas and Merino, 2006: 147-148). The clay vessel found appears to correspond to a structure associated with a glass furnace that gave the *Calle del Vídrio* (literally "Street of the Glass") its name, that disappeared during this urban reform, and that was previously referred to as the *Forn del Vidre Vell* (Zaforteza 1987). Documentary sources showing the urban layout in 1729-30 refer to block 151 as the *horno del vidrio viejo* (literally "old glass furnace") in, exactly where the studied workshop was located (Muntaner, 1977-78: 5-53). This urban toponymy was used in several occasions throughout the history of the city to refer to the place where a workshop, which was no longer active at the time that the document was written, was situated.

The container was buried underground in a zone with limited sediment potency and natural rock lying just below parts of the contemporary pavement. In some of the sectors, the first floors of the current buildings had been cut from the rock, destroying the remainder of the workshop's architectonic structures. Multiple indicators of this artisan activity appeared inside this deposit, in addition to some ceramic fragments produced in Pisa that had speckled and incised decoration. These vessels allowed us to perform a relative dating of the group of remains that linked them with the mid-17th century (Estarellas and Merino, 2006). There was also a highly deteriorated copper coin that had been minted in Majorca in the era of Felipe IV (1621-1665). This coin confirmed the chronological framework proposed for the use of the infrastructure. The conjecture that this workshop may have functioned beyond the first third of the 18th century can be discarded, given that no crystal fragments were identified amongst the recovered materials. Crystal is frequently found in the archaeological contexts and houses of this era, as can be inferred from the archival documents from the mid-18th century (Capellà, 2015: 216-217).

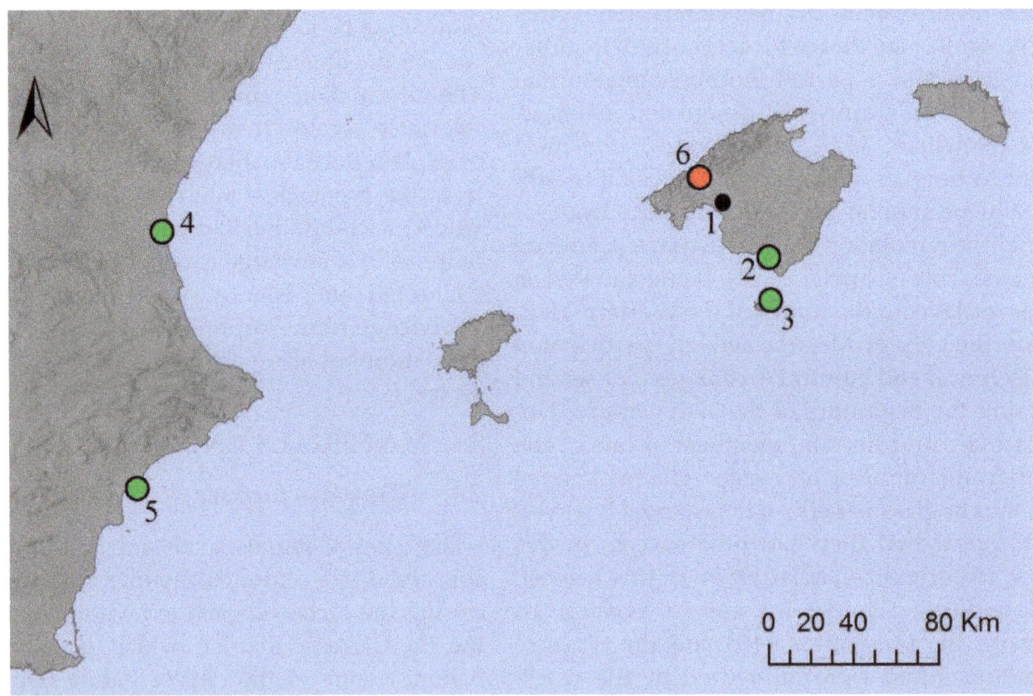

Figure 1. Map of the Balearic Islands and the area of "Levante" in the southeast of the Iberian Peninsula showing the location of the glass workshop of Sa Gerreria (1), the barilla plant production areas cited in the text (2 = Campos, 3 = Cabrera, 4 = Valencia, 5= Alicante) and the sand outcrops exploited according to the written sources (6).

The numerous remains associated with glass production are very well preserved because they have not come into direct contact with sediment and therefore show no signs of deterioration. The function of this deposit within the workshop's structure is not clear. The disparity of its contents indicates that it was a depository in which waste from the diverse labours of master glassmakers was accumulated. Another difficulty that presents itself in the interpretation of the deposit's function concerns the discernment of the length of time with which these materials are associated. They may be the product of a short period of activity, for example, an annual period, or they may be the result of a more prolonged period of production.

We have selected a total of 104 samples from the clay vessel to analyse their chemical composition by means of SEM-EDS. On the one hand, five glass lump fragments of diverse hues of green, honey-coloured, violet, and blue have been analysed. These glass lumps are the most important remains of the vessel's materials (3.808 g)[1]. The great majority respond to a standardized pattern of breakage, presenting similar dimensions of between 2 and 5 cm in length. The presence of direct impact on them suggests that they were broken with a metallic club (Figure 2A). The macroscopic analysis determines the existence of a conchoidal fracture that is characteristic of the impact and breakage patterns of glass. This finding shows the desire of the artisans to obtain fragments of regular dimensions that are then deposited in the crucibles to polish the glass lumps, preceding the blowing of objects. Additionally selected is a fragment that presents a more heterogeneous external aspect with defects from the fusion process (1.417 g) and that should be related to

[1] The weight in parentheses refers to the total number of samples recovered in the workshop.

the frits remains (Figure 2B).

On the other hand, we have selected 48 technological elements derived from the technical process of the production of pieces (Figures 2C and D). The most notable of these are flat pieces with one end folded over the other, flux-cored wires, flat elongated wires with a convex interior and a concave exterior that are most likely the result of scissor cuttings, and other remains identified by tong marks. Similarly, three flat glass fragments have been analysed (1.938 g). Seven samples that correspond to dark and light green, violet, honey-coloured, and colourless drops or teardrops that are also related to the production process have also been studied (2.324 g).

Finally, 50 fragments of glass pieces that had been conserved in the clay vessel have been selected. Everything suggests that these were gathered and stored so that they may be recycled. We suppose that the majority of these fragments are remains of pieces associated with the work of the glassmakers who used furnaces.

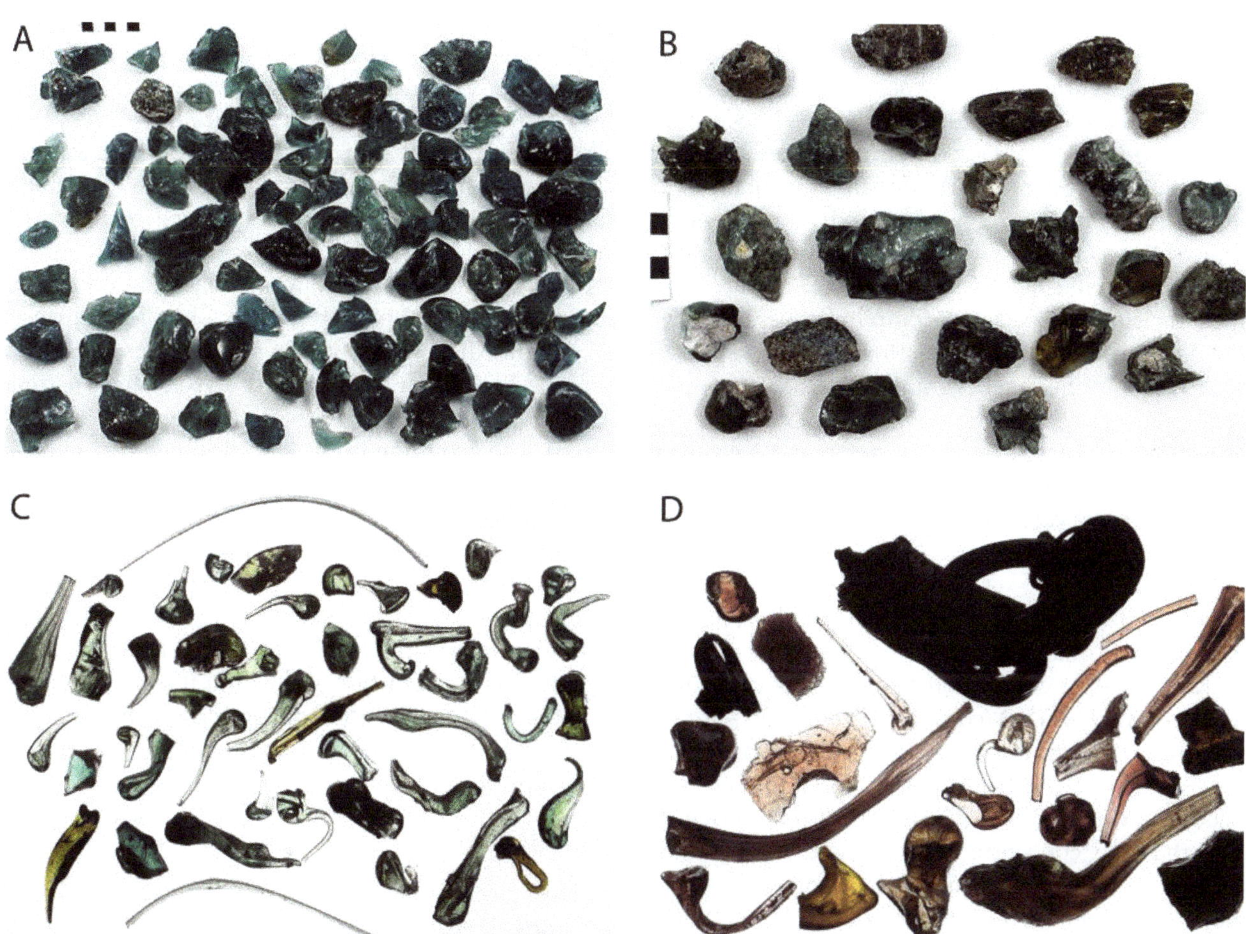

Figure 2. Photographs showing a selection of the materials recovered in the glass workshop of Sa Gerreria. A) Fragments of green glass lumps with the same standardized breakage pattern. B) Irregular frits fragments that present fusion defects. C and D) Production remains of green, violet, and diverse hues.

2.2. *Methodology*

The characterization of the chemical composition of the furnace's materials has fundamentally centred on the analysis of their major and minor elements using SEM-EDS. To that end, the concentrations of Na_2O, MgO, SiO_2, P_2O_5, K_2O, CaO, MnO, Fe_2O_3, Al_2O_3, and Cl^- of the 104 selected samples have been determined (Table I) through X-ray energy dispersion using a RX-EDS Bruker AXS XFlash 4010 microanalysis system connected to a scanning electron microscope Hitachi S-3400-N, using a 15kV operating voltage and Quantax 400 software to perform the quantification. This method of analysis has allowed us to characterize the major and minor elements of the materials. Thus, it should be noted that we have not been able to register trace elements using this technique. The instrument only makes it possible to detect those elements that have a weight greater than 0.3% of the total sample. Thus, this technique provided semi-quantitative data related to major components of the glass (vitrifying and stabilizing components) and the fluxes. Quantitative analysis related to the minor and trace elements will be conducted in future works. Even though we are aware that SEM-EDS has certain limitations for glass analysis, we hold that the chemical characterization conducted has been useful to carry out a first approach to the glass objects of this workshop and to establish certain assumptions that can be further developed in future studies.

All quantitative results are reported as weight per cent oxides with oxygen determined by stoichiometry. Between two and three measurements per specimen were collected on clean cuts in order to avoid potentially weathered points near the surfaces of the glass and their average calculated (Table I). Since the outside area of the glass is commonly subjected to lixiviation processes of virtually all elements (except silicon and aluminum), we avoided to analyze this area of the samples with the aim to promote replicate analysis and more reliable results. The accuracy and precision of the systems employed were checked against Corning B, C and D reference glasses. In order to explain the major variations in the set of compositional data, bivariate and multivariate approaches using Principal Component Analysis (PCA) and Cluster Analysis (CA) were performed using SPSS software package.

3. RESULTS

Our first observation in the statistical analysis of the chemical data obtained is the existence of a significant positive correlation between the concentrations of CaO and K_2O (correlation r Pearson = 0.725). However, a significant negative correlation is observed between the quantities of CaO and SiO_2 (correlation r Pearson = -0.77). These correlations indicate that the concentrations of these three oxides have a strong relationship to each other and that they are fundamental to understanding the data performance.

A factor analysis through principle components analysis (PCA) performed with the sub-composition Na_2O, MgO, SiO_2, K_2O, CaO, Fe_2O_3, and Al_2O_3 (MnO, P_2O_5, and Cl^- have not been considered because they presented missing values and because the latter two elements may have been contaminated) allowed us to establish three factors that accumulate a total of 84% of the variance in the data. In the first factor, accounting for 45.8% of the data variance, the oxides that had a significant positive correlation (r Pearson > 0.7) were CaO, SiO_2, and Al_2O_3. The last two oxides showed a negative correlation with the first. This finding indicates a clear differentiation of the samples as a function of the quantity of aluminosilicates and stabilizers present in the mixtures. Considering that the glassmakers of the era were not aware of the stabilizing effect of calcium oxide, found in its natural form in the selected sands (Capellà and Albero, 2015) or in the plant ashes used as flux (Freestone and Gorin-Rosen, 1999), we can suppose that the differential concentrations in these oxides may be closely related to the composition of the raw materials used to manufacture the pieces.

The second component represents 24.7% of the data variance, with an accumulated variance of 70.5%. The oxides that contribute the most to explaining the variance (> 0.67) are K_2O and Na_2O, which show a negative correlation to each other. The changes in both oxides allow us to propose that clear differences exist in the register analysed as a function of the fluxes used in the preparation of the glass. Thus, the analyses performed suggest that a classification of the register as a function of the use of different raw materials and fluxes can be performed *a priori*.

To classify the samples, we have generated a bivariate plot with the two factors obtained through PCA. The dispersion of the samples in the graph (Figure 3) allows us to establish diverse groups that are compositionally divergent from each other (Table II). The grouping of the samples included in each group was made according to the results obtained from a cluster analysis conducted using the squared Euclidean distance and the centroid agglomerative method. The level of similarity of the samples within each cluster is > 94%. In the next sections, we generate a description of the compositional traits of each - of the groups identified and of the types of samples that they included to then perform a specific analysis of the types of pieces and productions with which these are associated.

3.1. *Group 1*

This group is the best represented, given that it includes 71 samples that are characterized by concentrations that match with the use of soda-lime-silica glass (Melcher and Schreiner, 2005), that is, by the mixture of sand and sodium as a flux. The sodium is related to Na-rich plant ash that were used as flux to decrease the melting temperature of the quartz raw material used as a source of silica. The use of Na-rich plant ashes is suggested by both concentrations of K_2O > wt. 2% (Verità and Toninato, 1990) and the written sources available. These plants grow commonly in the island on saline marshes in marine coastal sedimentary environments. Thus, the documentary sources available demonstrate that the barilla plants (*Salsola soda*) located in the archipelago of Cabrera, the salty coastal area of Campos and its closest islets, in southern Mallorca (Figure 1), had been exploited since the Middle Age. Moreover, some historical sources of the period under study point out that the production of barilla plant aimed for the production of glass and soap significantly increased in Mallorca during the 17th Century. In this sense, it is documented in 1639 the existence of a glass furnace that used barilla produced in this area of the island. In addition to the locally produced fluxes, it is also well-known the import to the island of fluxes from Alicante and Valencia (Capellà, 2015: 49-51). Such areas of the Iberian Peninsula (Figure 1) produced fluxes of high quality (Amouric and Foy, 1981, 1991).

The soda-lime nature of the glass of this group is evident and constitutes the one with the highest concentrations of Na_2O (average = 10.3%) of the entire register analysed. Furthermore, SiO_2, CaO, and Na_2O are the three principle components of the samples. Taken together, these components constitute more than 85% of the weight of the samples. This group includes samples of a varied range of colours: green, dark green, colourless, honey-coloured, violet, and blue. A clear divergence in the composition as a function of colour could not be observed with the methodology used in this study. This majority group includes all the samples associated with technological elements and remains of drippings derived from the production process, in addition to frits remains and glass lumps. These are practically all (89.6%) of the sample materials that are directly and undoubtedly related to the glass production developed in this workshop. For this reason, we note that this group of artefacts, rich in sodium and MgO (Table I; Figure 4), composes the reference groups of this furnace, that is, the type of products that were produced the most.

However, despite these general trends, it should be noted that there is a great variation within this group regarding basic major oxides such as SiO_2 (wt. 53-74%), Na_2O (wt. 4-18%) and CaO (wt. 5-15%). This variation suggests the use of different raw materials or certain intra-deposit variability in the raw material used in this workshop. On the one hand, there can be a high variation in plant ash compositions, even of the same species. On the other hand, we suggested in previous works that these products were most likely manufactured with local raw materials and limited recycling processes (Capellà and Albero, 2015). Thus, there are written sources that confirm the exploitation of local sands located in the Serra de Tramuntana from the Middle Age to XIX century to produce glass (Capellà, 2015: 45). Unfortunately, compositional analyses of these raw materials have not been conducted yet in order to shed light on the internal variability of these deposits.

The high variability observed can be also associated with the archaeological context of the samples under study. As we have been noted above, we do not know if the glass samples analyzed recovered from the ceramic container are synchronic or related to diverse batches. In this sense, it must be considered that the samples analyzed had been stored to be recycled and they can be related to a long period of activity.

In addition, other postdepositional and analytical factors have to be considered to explain this wider variability. First, even though the samples were relatively well-preserved inside a vessel, the variations can result from the presence of potentially corroded surfaces in some samples. The detection of low concentrations of Na_2O, K_2O and CaO in some samples of the assemblage analysed may point to some alteration processes. Second, we have to consider also that the variations observed in Na_2O concentrations can be related, in some cases, to the migration phenomenon of the alkalis when they are irradiated with an electron beam (Gedeon et al., 1999, 2000).

The macroscopic and archaeometric study of the workshop allows us to confirm that the majority of the pieces fabricated in it were differing tonalities of green and honey-coloured glass. This type of glass should be associated with an industrial and simple production process that was commonly executed and low-cost. Among the samples of Group 1 we identify a fragment of the neck of a small bottle and two handles that were most likely attached to bowls (Figure 4, MO-88, MO-52, and MO-57). Furthermore, there is the base of an indeterminate object and a fragment of the stem of a cup with a simple ring knot (Figure 4, MO-86 and MO-47), which is similar to that of other cups found in other archaeological sites in Palma and dated to the end of the 16th century and the duration of the 17th century (Capellà, 2015: 190-191).

Additionally, amongst the studied samples that were assigned to the majority group associated with the workshop, there are a few pieces that stand out from the rest because they are related to productions of a more prestigious nature. This is the case with a small blue block (MO-14) used to make pieces and to decorate colourless objects. Such cases show that higher-quality works of art were produced in this workshop. Amongst the remains studied, the base of a cup (Figure 4, MO-45) crafted from colourless glass with a drop of colour at its centre as decoration was preserved. These ornamentations are associated with Catalan production of the modern era. Amongst the different parallels found, we can cite another cup, dated to the first half of the 17th century, which has a stem in the shape of a baluster and the aforementioned decoration on its base (Philippart, 2011: 142).

This statement can be also applied for the violet-coloured glass, which is another chromatic range related to Catalan production of quality sumptuary glass between the 16th and 17th centuries (Domènech, 2004: 97). The large number of elements of this lump and its evident grouping with the pieces in the control group leave no doubt that the workshop blew objects of this hue. This assertion is also corroborated by the large amount of waste generated during formal production that also shows tool marks (Figure 2D). This fact lends even more consistency to the evidence supporting the hypothesis that these pieces must be associated with this workshop's production. Amongst the recovered objects, there is a violet piece of a base (Figure 4, MO-22) and a bit of what appears to be a ribbon handle (MO-73). This glass can be associated with the objects described as "leonart" (*lleonat* or *lleonart* in Catalan) in the notarized inventories of the era. Leonart refers to a colour of paste that includes the hues honey-coloured, reddish yellow, and violet.

This hue, which is associated with Catalan production, is linked to a significant number of objects preserved in different collections, both European and Spanish. In the majority of cases, these objects are high-quality specimens with high decorative values. One of the oldest pieces is a footed bowl from the Prats-Sedó collection (Amatller Institute of Hispanic Art, Barcelona), dated to the beginning or first half of the 16th century and produced in Venice or Catalonia, with a ribbed decoration, *mezza-stampatura*, and *lattimo* glass thread (Carreras and Pastor, 2010: 122). In addition to this specimen, we can add a blow-moulded spouted jug that is decorated with white lines and dated to the first half of the 16th century, in addition to another jug of the same century. Both jugs are of Catalan manufacture, with a ribbed neck that is decorated with a chord with stamping and *lattimo* white lines. They belong to private collections that were displayed in an exhibit on Spanish glass in the Grand Curtius Museum of Lieja (Philippart, 2011: 113, 138). Another specimen of this colour with a painted gold decoration, dated to the second half of the 16th century or beginning of the 17th century, belongs to the Museum of Decorative Arts of Paris *(Musée des arts décoratifs de París)* (Baumgartner and Olivié, 2003: 116). We can also associate a few fragments, most likely of a bottle and with *lattimo a penne* thread ornaments, preserved in the Majorca Museum of Palma *(Museo de Mallorca)*. These fragments have been dated to the 17th century by the remainder of the excavation's archaeological materials (Capellà, 2015). Finally, due to the similarity of its form with the base that was recovered in this container, we should cite a table service preserved in the Museum of Glass and Ceramics of the Peralada Castle *(Museu del Vidre del Castell de Peralada)*, of Catalan manufacture and dated to between 1650 and 1750. In this regard, the existence of this material base, the production remains, and the two fragments of objects confirm that works of this range were made in Majorca. This is an unequivocal sign that techniques for the production of pastes of a certain quality, more sophisticated than common glass, had disseminated to the different territories that composed the Crown of Aragon.

3.2. *Group 2*

This small group of only eight samples is closely related to the former group with regard to its composition, given that it has a soda-lime-silica base. It includes six fragments, all of which are colourless glass, a portion of glass lumps, and a portion of green colour frits. These pieces are separate from those of Group 1 because they present concentrations of Na_2O (4.1-6%) that are significantly lower and concentrations of SiO_2 (71-78%) that are significantly higher. In previous studies (Capellà and Albero, 2015), we could observe that the samples of raw materials from this group differ notably from the rest of the glass lumps documented in this workshop particularly with regard to the quantities of MgO and Na_2O. As proven by written sources, this aspect is associated with the diverse origins of the soda used by glass makers in this period. The fact that a workshop can produce glass with a differential composition if it uses raw materials that come from different suppliers should be considered. Regarding this question, other archaeometric studies (Henderson, 2000; Freestone et al., 2002) have noted that the divergences in the concentrations of these elements can also be explained by the use of ash from different plants as fluxes.

Group 2, which is limited in size, is composed of four piece fragments, two more fragments with indeterminate forms and the two aforementioned glass lumps. Amongst these objects stands out a fragment of the wall of a drinking-glass (Figure 5, MO-48), which has a fluted decoration formed by blowing into a mould and subsequently twisting the piece while it is still hot to achieve the spiral effect. Furthermore, there are two bottleneck fragments with common glass (Figure 5, MO-90 and MO-54). Finally and perhaps the most significant of the remaining material, there is a wall fragment of an indeterminate object with a *latticinio* decoration that is undoubtedly of a higher-quality production than the rest of the objects described in this group.

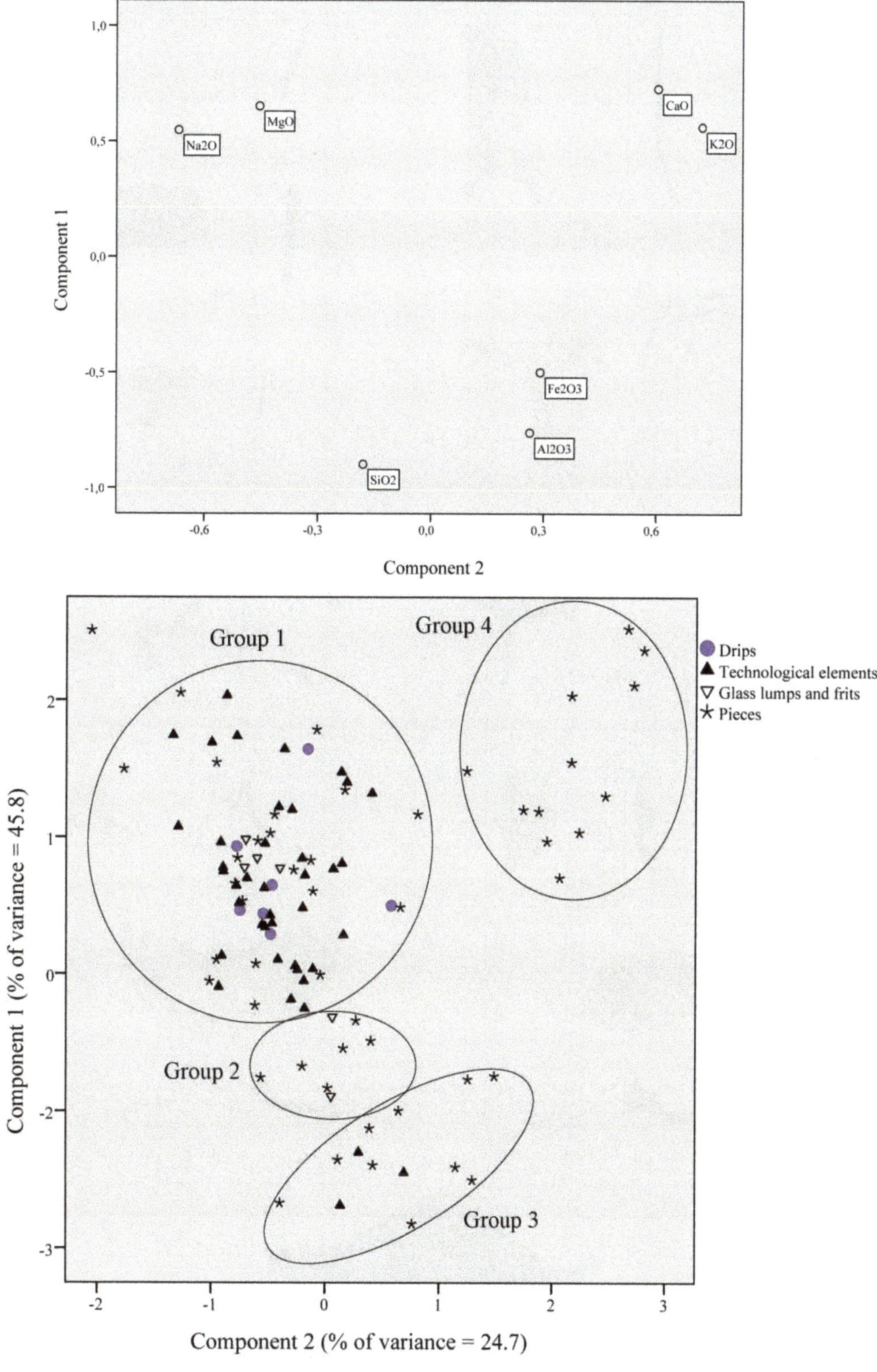

Figure 3. A) Bivariate plot generated with the first two factors obtained from principal components analysis (PCA) showing the dispersion of the different quantified oxides. B) Bivariate plot generated with the first two factors obtained from PCA showing the dispersion and grouping of the samples according to the type of artefact analysed.

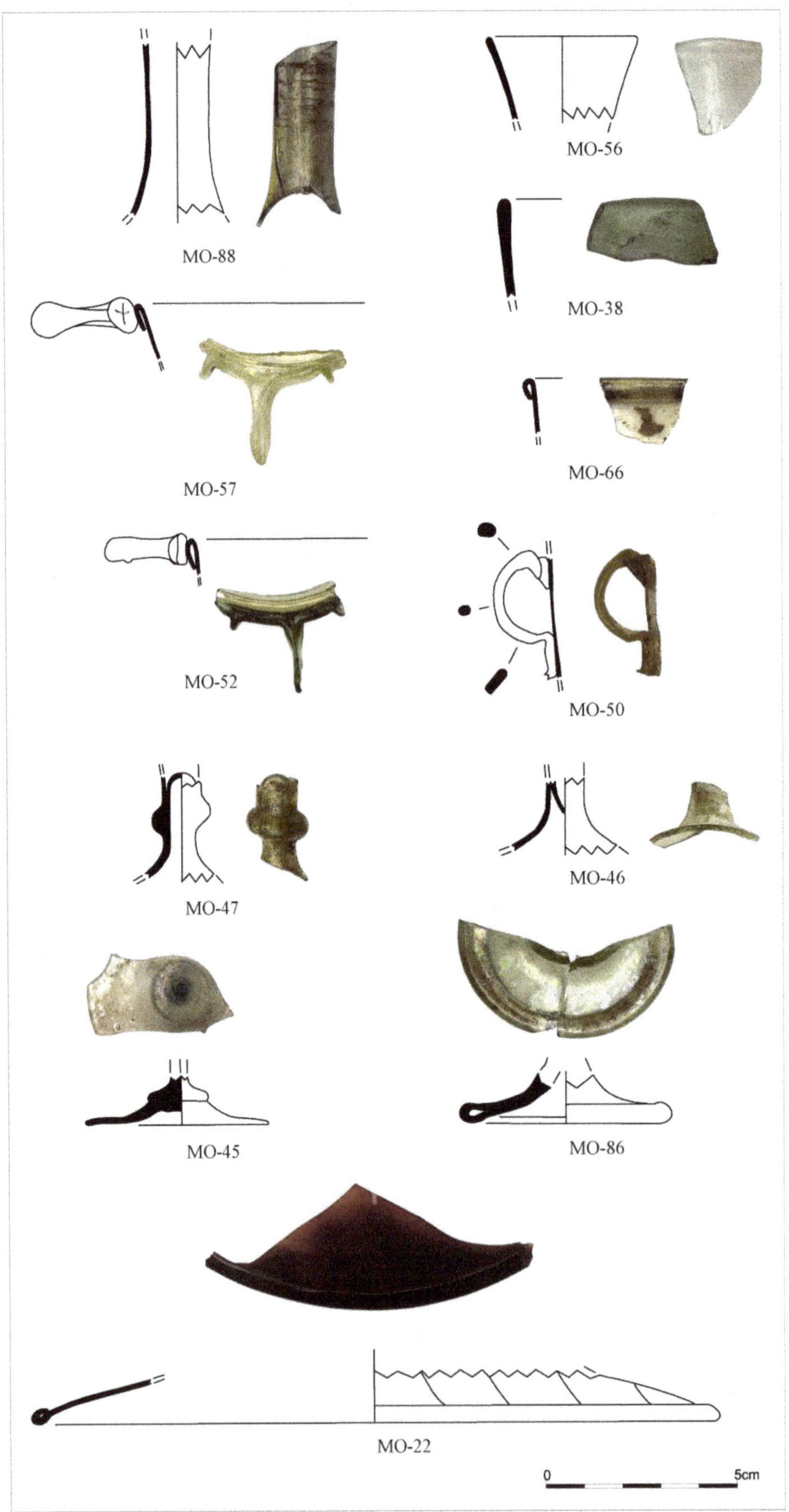

Figure 4. Group 1. Glass fragments: handle (MO-50), bases (MO-86 and MO-22), cup bases (MO-45), rims of indeterminate containers (MO-38 and MO-66), bottles (MO-88 and MO-56), handles of bowls (MO-57 and MO-52), and cup stems (MO-47 and MO-46).

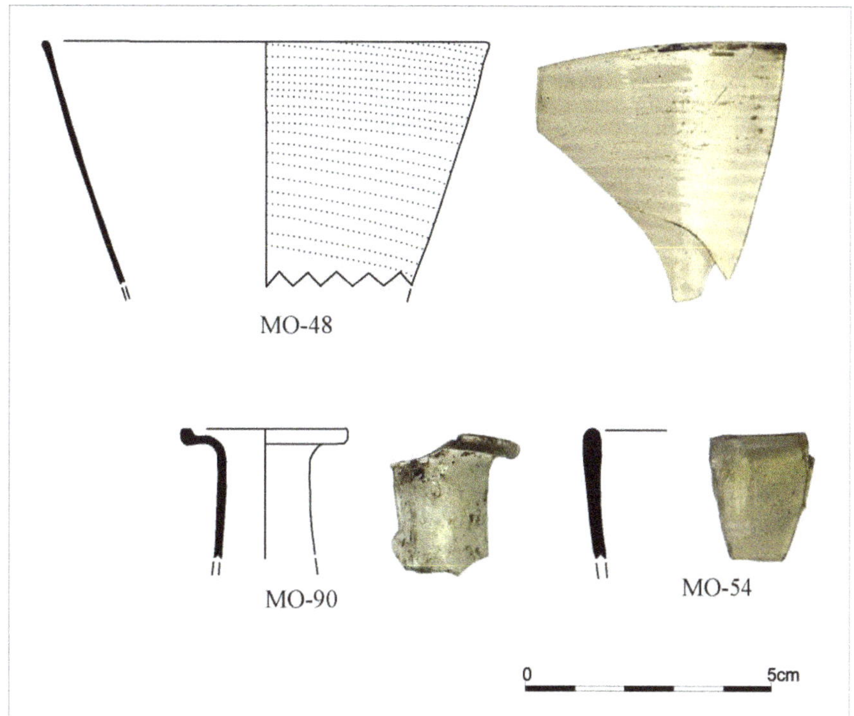

Figure 5. Group 2. Glass fragments: bottle (MO-90), rim of an indeterminate container (MO-54), and drinking-glass (MO-48).

3.3. *Group 3*

Group 3 contains 13 samples that include 10 pieces and three technological elements of colourless or green glass. This group stands out due to its high degree of compositional variability. That said, all of the samples present both low and similar concentrations of K_2O (1.5-4%) and Na_2O (1-5.2%). These samples present the highest concentrations of SiO_2 (average = 76%) and Al_2O_3 (4.2-9.5%), showing a composition in which the aluminosilicates weigh more and therefore have a higher concentration of sand. One hypothesis that allows us to explain the high variability and the characteristics of this group is that these are the result of recycling processes in which pieces of potassium carbonate and sodium carbonate have been mixed together - in addition to fragments of glass lumps - to produce new pieces. The absence of glass lumps associated with this group and the existence of technological evidence of mould blowing support this interpretation, which is based on the recycling activities developed in the workshop.

The majority of the forms associated with this group are objects of common use. The small bottle MO-89 (Figure 6) is a relatively frequent form in island archaeological contexts and was most likely used to store medicines, amongst other things (Capellà, 2015: 181). We also identify a fragment of a base, a handle, and a dark-green lid (Figure 6, MO-87, MO-51, and MO-53). A bit of dark-green wall (Figure 6, MO-49), belonging to an object that we cannot identify due to the lack of parallels, has a geometric decoration of raised diamond patterns formed by blowing into a mould. Finally, a fragment with a *latticinio* decoration (Figure 6, MO-80) is conserved. As explained above in reference to the previous group, this treatment is characteristic of higher-quality pieces.

3.4. *Group 4*

This group is of a limited size and is composed of 12 samples, the majority being of dark-green glass (*n* = 8) and, to a lesser extent, colourless glass. They are associated with eight objects and four flat pieces of glass characterized by a preferential use of Ca-K glass. Therefore, the main elements in the composition of these pieces (> 85%) are K_2O, CaO, and SiO_2, with potassium being related to the type of flux used. This fact determines that they are the samples in the analysed register that present the greatest quantity of K_2O (average = 5.5%). Indeed, the concentrations of K_2O (3.6-7.3%) in this group are always greater than those of Na_2O (0.8-5.7%). There is a notably large quantity of calcium oxide in this group (average = 24%), which must be related to the stabilizer present in the mixture. These glass pieces are associated with the use of raw materials, possibly ashes of caducifolian trees (Freestone et al., 2002; Gimeno et al., 2008), and recipes that are completely different from those that were typically used in this workshop. Such CaO concentrations are quite unusual, but they are documented in 16th century workshops located in northern Germany which were centered on the production of stained glass windows. In such Ca-K-glass productions, the concentrations of CaO can reach up to 23% (Basso et al., 2009; Orlando et al., 1996). Furthermore, there are French glass workshops dated in the 18th century that also produced glass pieces with similar CaO concentrations (Losier, 2012). In these cases, it can be suggested that high amounts of CaO were intentionally added in order to decrease the melting temperature of the quartz introduced as a source of silica.

Considering the different composition of these samples and the total absence of technological elements and lumps associated with this group, it must be assumed that these objects were most likely not manufactured in this workshop but rather imported to the island. Therefore, the fact that the clay vessel contains these objects must be connected with the processes used to collect waste that was stored in the workshop for the purpose of recycling. The imported objects that compose Group 4 are eight bottle bases and four flat pieces of glass that were most likely intended to be placed in leaded windows (MO-28, MO-30, and MO-31). The bottles, which were crafted by blowing into a mould, are characterized by a square sectioned base and body and also by an outward flaying neck with a simple semi-circular lip (Figure 7). The bottles present the pontil mark on their bases. The paste used is a common paste, generally of a dark-green colour. This type of bottle was used to store not only gin but also cognac, brandy, and other liquors. It originated in Germany and Bohemia at the end of the 16th century (Hollingworth, 1980: 41). Preserved in European collections are specimens with pictorial decorations in the glaze used in table services and simpler specimens that were used for transport. This form was also produced in Holland and Belgium from the beginning of the 17th century, whereas in England it did not appear until 1750. The German origin of the model is evident due to a reference made by the Belgian manufacturer Colinet, which refers to them as *"boutelle quarrée diste Allemande"* (Bossche, 2001: 136-137). This is the reason for the great difficulty presented in determining the models' origins based on the remarkable similarities of form that exist between specimens preserved in different collections, many of which are dated to the 18th century, a period when these liquors became widely popular. The form's square format facilitated its transport in wooden boxes that could hold 4, 6, or 12 specimens (Bellanger, 1988: 289). The rest of the eight specimens that were studied can be considered precursors of the 18th century forms. In other European sites, squared bottles also appear in archaeological contexts of the second half of the 17th century, as is the case with those found in the excavation in Santa Clara-a-Velha (Coimbra, Portugal) (Medici, 2009: 395).

In Majorca, the written documents of the era identify these forms as existing since the first third of the 17th century and becoming more frequent towards the middle of the same century. In Catalan, this form is referred to as *flascó*, which can also be used to refer to other forms. A documentary reference of 1658 and another of 1661 describe these forms as squared. Furthermore, they appear to be inevitably associated with wooden boxes and decanters, carved from more or less fine materials and possessing locks with which to close them. The importation of products in these containers that come from diverse European cities is also well documented. For example, in 1678, the ship "Ntª Srª de Europa", which was travelling to Majorca, bought "two bottles of distilled spirits" in the port of Messina (López, 1986: 555). Nonetheless, although the analysis of the materials and the context of their removal indicate that these types of forms were imported to the island and stored for recycling upon being thrown out, we cannot rule out the possibility that the local workshops may have blown their own version of these simple squared forms of German origin and European dissemination. An indication of this is provided to us by a well-known document of 1655 that contains a record of a *flascó de vidre mallorquí* (literally *flascó* made of Majorcan glass) (Capellà, 2015: 182-184).

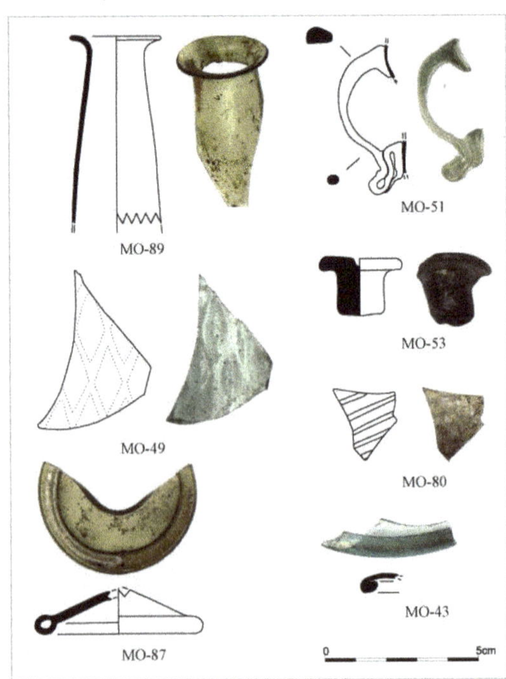

***Figure 6.** Group 3. Glass fragments: handle (MO-51), bases (MO-87 and MO-43), bottle (MO-89), tap (MO-53), wall fragment with decoration blown using an open mould (MO-49), and wall fragment with lattimo thread decoration (MO-80).*

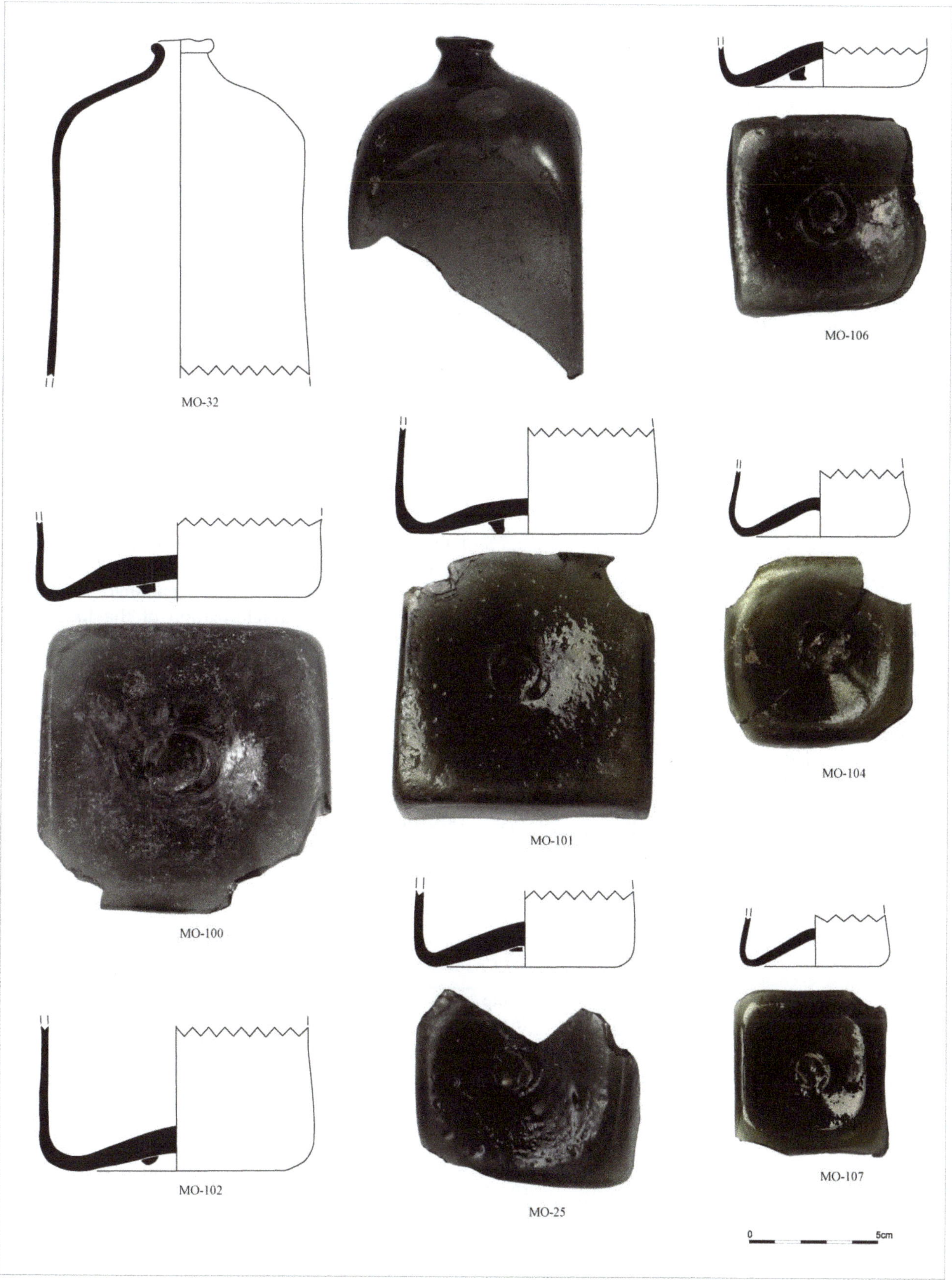

Figure 7. Group 4. Glass fragments: Square sectioned bottles (MO-32, MO-100, MO-101, MO-102, MO-106, MO-107, MO-85 and MO-88).

4. CONCLUSIONS

The archaeometric study of the glass materials of Sa Gerreria has allowed us to approach the chemical composition of the remains of the raw materials, technological elements, and pieces present in this 17th-century workshop and to establish groups of different natures. Even though the methodology applied in this research has certain limitations, we consider that the chemical characterization of the samples from this workshop by means of SEM-EDS allowed us to shed light on some interesting aspects regarding glass production and distribution that can be further developed in future works. On the one hand, we have been able to record the existence of a group with high concentrations of Na_2O that encompasses a large number of samples associated with the productions developed in the workshop, presumably using local raw materials. The types of pieces placed within this group are linked with an artisan activity primarily centred on utilitarian and low-cost products. However, this study has also allowed us to propose that several more sophisticated pieces were crafted in this workshop with finer-quality pastes and fashionable forms and were sold to more demanding clients. We refer here to the production of pieces of prestige such as those that present blue decorations or the violet pieces. The manufacture of these pieces on the island reveals a link with the Catalan region insofar as the taste and technical knowledge of Majorcan production are concerned. Similarly, the manufacture of these pieces in Palma reveals the dissemination of techniques associated with the production of pieces of a certain quality, more sophisticated than common glass, throughout the different territories of the Crown of Aragon. The diversification of production and the development of different types of products can be explained in part by the characteristics of the island market. This market, especially with regard to high-end pieces, was very much determined by glass imports from Barcelona and other zones of Catalonia as well as Venice.

On the other hand, we have recorded the existence of a group exclusively composed of pieces that differ significantly from the other groups due to its greater K_2O and calcium oxide content. These objects were manufactured using technological choices that have nothing to do with local production and therefore should be considered imported. We can associate them with very particular types - liquor bottles and flat pieces of glass, the origins of which most likely should be determined and as a function of typological parallels with Northern European cities. Everything points to the fact that upon falling into disuse, these products were deposited in the Sa Gerreria workshop so that they may subsequently be recycled. During this process, they were fused with the remains of local productions.

Ultimately, this study has generated significant advances in the characterization of the local glass production of Majorca in the modern era and in the identification of regional products linked to the Crown of Aragon and the Italian market. These analyses provide us with more detailed knowledge about the technical choices put into practice by the Sa Gerreria workshop and the dissemination of some techniques between different interconnected territories, in addition to importation of certain types of glass to the island.

Table II. Statistical summaries (average and standard deviation (σ)) for each of the groups obtained in the PCA analysis[2].

	Group 1 (n = 71)	Group 2 (n = 8)	Group 3 (n = 12)	Group 4 (n = 12)
Na_2O	10.2 ± 3.4	5 ± 0.7	2.5 ± 1.2	2.3 ± 1.6
MgO	3.4 ± 0.6	2.5 ± 0.6	1.6 ± 0.6	3 ± 0.5
SiO_2	64.4 ± 5.4	74 ± 2.2	76.3 ± 5.7	56.6 ± 2.2
P_2O_5	0.5 ± 0.2	0.2 ± 0.3	n.d.	1.3 ± 0.7
Cl^-	1 ± 0.3	0.8 ± 0.4	0.6 ± 0.2	0.5 ± 0.2
K_2O	3.3 ± 0.7	3 ± 0.4	3 ± 0.7	5.5 ± 1.2
CaO	10.6 ± 2.3	6.6 ± 1.6	5.9 ± 3	24 ± 2.8
MnO	1.6 ± 0.7	0.3 ± 0.6	3 ± 1.5	1.6 ± 0.5
Fe_2O_3	1.9 ± 0.6	2.2 ± 0.4	2.5 ± 0.8	1.8 ± 0.6
Al_2O_3	3.8 ± 1	5.4 ± 0.7	6.6 ± 1.5	4.1 ± 1.2

[2] Regarding P_2O_5, there have been multiple cases in Group 1 of missing values in which we have not been able to identify the quantities $wt\% > 0.3\%$. Therefore, the displayed mean represents only n = 52. Regarding MgO, the displayed mean represents only n = 54 for Group 1, n = 4 for Group 3, and n = 8 for Group 4. Finally, regarding Fe_2O_3, the displayed mean represents n = 66 for Group 1.

REFERENCES

Amouric, H. and Foy, D. (1981) Notes sur la production et la commercialisation de la soude dans le midi méditerranéen du XIIIe au XVIIIe siècle. *Histoire des techniques et sources documentaires, Méthodes d'approche et expérimentation en région méditerranéenne.* Aix-en-Provence, pp. 157-172.

Amouric, H, Foy D (1991) De la salicorne aux soudes factices; mutations techniques et variation de la demande. L'évolution des techniques est-elle autonome? Aix-en-Provence, *Publications de l'Université de Provence Marseille-Aix 1*, pp. 39-75.

Basso, E., Riccardi, M.P., Messiga, B., Menderab, M., Gimeno, D., Garcia-Valles, M., Fernandez-Turiel, J.L., Bazzocchi, F., Aulinas, M. and Tarozzi, C. (2009) Composition of the base glass used to realize the stained glass windows by Duccio di Buoninsegna (Siena Cathedral, 1288–1289 AD): A geochemical approach. *Materials Characterization,* Vol. 60, pp. 1545-1554.

Baumgartner, E. and Olivié, J.L. (2003) *Venise et Façon de Venise. Verres renaissance du Musée des Arts Décoratifs.* Paris, Union centrale des arts décoratifs.

Bellanger, J. (1988) *Verre d'usage et de prestige: France, 1500-1800.* Paris, Editions de l'Amateur.

Bossche, W.V. (2001) *Antique Glass Bottles. Their History and Evolution (1500-1850).* Antique Collectors' Club.

Camiade, M. and Fontaine, D. (2006) *Verreries et verriers catalans.* Perpignan, Sources.

Capellà, M.À. (2015) *Ars Vitraria: Mallorca (1300-1700).*Palma, Edicions UIB.

Capellà, M.À. and Albero, D. (2015) El horno de vidrio del siglo XVII de Sa Gerreria (Palma, Mallorca): contextualización histórica y análisis preliminar de los materiales. *Boletín de la Sociedad Española de Cerámica y Vidrio,* Vol. 54-4, pp. 142-152.

Carreras, T. and Pastor, P. (2010) *Catàleg. Ànimes de vidre. Les col·leccions Amatller.* Barcelona, Museu d'Arqueologia de Catalunya.

Domènech, I. (2004) Spanish Façon de Venise Glass. In *Beyond Venice. Glass in Venetian Style, 1500-1750,* J.A. Page JA (ed.), Corning, New York, The Corning Museum of Glass, pp. 84-113.

Domènech, I. (1999) El vidrio. In *Las Artes Decorativas en España,* B. Arraiza (ed.), Madrid, Espasa-Calpe XLV 1.

Domènech, I. (2011) El vidrio español de los siglos XVI a XVIII. In *Frágil Transparencia. Vidrios españoles de los siglos XVI a XVIII,* J.P. Philippart and M. Mergenthaler M (eds.), Dettelbach, Verlag J.H. Röll GmbH, pp. 19-61.

Estarellas, M.M. and Merino, J. (2004) Excavacions a Sa Gerreria de Palma. *Revista del Col·legi de Doctors i Llicenciats en Filosofia i Lletres i en Ciències de les Illes Balears,* Vol. 14, pp. 27-28.

Estarellas, M.M. and Merino, J. (2006) Instal·lacions artesanes i industrials a Sa Gerreria de Palma (Segles XV-XX). *I Jornades de Patrimoni Industrial a les Illes Balears,* Fundació Endesa, Amics del Museu de Mallorca, Palma de Mallorca, pp. 144-153.

Freestone, I. and Gorin-Rosen, Y. (1999) The great glass slab at Bet She'Arim, Israel: an early Islamic glassmaking experiment? *Journal of Glass Studies,* Vol. 41, pp. 105-116.

Freestone, I., Pointing, M. and Hughes, M. (2002) The origins of Byzantine glass from Maroni Petrera, Cyprus. *Archaeometry,* Vol. 44, pp. 257–272.

Gedeon, O., Jurek, K. and Hulínsky, V. (1999) Fast migration of alkali ions in glass irradiated by electrons. *Journal of Non-Crystalline Solids,* Vol. 246, pp. 1-8.

Gedeon, O., Hulínsky, V. and Jurek, K. (2000) Microanalysis of glass containing alkali ions. *Mikcrochimica Acta,* Vol. 132, pp. 505–510.

Gimeno, D., Garcia-Valles, M., Fernandez-Turiel, J.L., Bazzocchi, F., Aulinas, M., Pugès, M., Tarozzi, C., Riccardi, M.P., Basso, E., Fortina, C., Mendera, M. and Messiga, B. (2008) From Siena to Barcelona: Deciphering colour recipes of Na-rich Mediterranean stained glass windows at the XIII-XIV century transition. *Journal of Cultural Heritage,* Vol. 9, pp. e10-e15.

Henderson, J. (2000) *The Science and Archaeology of Materials. An investigation of inorganic materials.* London-New York, Routledge.

Hollingworth, J. (1980) *Collecting Decanters.* London, Studio Vista - Christie's South Kensington Collectors Series.

López, G. (1986) *El corsarisme mallorquí: a la Mediterrània occidental, 1652-1698. Un comerç forçat.* Palma, Conselleria d'Educació i Cultura.

Losier, C. (2012) Bouteilles et flacons: Les Contenants utilitaires français du début du XVIIIe siècle au début du XIXe siècle. Aspects techniques et sociaux. *Journal of Glass Studies,* Vol. 54, pp. 151-179.

Medici, T., Lopes, F.M., Lima, A.M., Larsson, M.A. and Pires de Matos, A. (2009) Glass Bottles and Jugs frons the Monastery of Sta. Clara-a-Velha, Coimbra, Portugal. In *Annales du 17e Congrès de l'Association Internationale pour l'Histoire du Verre*, K. Janssens, P. Degryse, P. Cosyns, J. Caen, and L. Van't'T Dack (eds.), Brussels, University Press Antwerp, pp. 391-400.

Melcher, M. and Schreiner, M. (2005) Evaluation procedure for leaching studies on naturally weathered potash–lime–silica glasses with medieval composition by scanning electron microscopy. *Journal of Non-Crystalline Solids*, Vol. 351, pp. 1210–1225.

Moretti, C. (2002) *Glossario del vetro veneziano, dal Trecento al Novecento*. Venezia, Marsilio editori.

Muntaner, L. (1977-1978) Un model de ciutat preindustrial. La Ciutat de Mallorca al segle XVIII. *Trabajos de Geografía*, Vol. 34, pp. 5-54.

Newman, H. (1977) *An Illustrated Dictionary of Glass*. London, Thames and Hudson.

Orlando, A., Olmi, F., Vaggelli, G. and Bacci, M. (1996) Mediaeval stained glasses of Pisa cathedral (Italy): their composition and alteration products. *Analyst*, Vol. 121, pp. 553-558.

Philippart, J.P. (2011) Catálogo. In *Frágil Transparencia. Vidrios españoles de los siglos XVI a XVIII*, J.P. Philippart and M. Mergenthaler M (eds.), Dettelbach, Verlag J.H. Röll GmbH, pp. 101-206.

Rodríguez García, J. (1985) La influencia del vidrio de Venecia en Cataluña. *Annales du 10e Congrès de l'Association Internationale pour l'Histoire du Verre*, Madrid-Segovia, Fundación Centro Nacional del Vidrio, pp. 421-433.

Rodríguez García, J. (1988) Domingo Barovier, vidriero veneciano en España (1600-1608). *Espacio, tiempo y forma. Serie IV: Historia moderna*, Vol. 1, pp. 467-500.

Verità, M. and Toninato, T.A. (1990) Comparative analytical investigation on the origins of the Venetian glassmaking. *Rivista della Stazione Sperimentale del Vetro*, Vol. 20, pp. 169–175.

Zaforteza, D. (1987) *La Ciudad de Mallorca: ensayo histórico-toponímico*. Palma de Mallorca, Ajuntament de Palma.

Table I. Chemical composition (wt%) of the samples analysed from the Sa Gerreria workshop determined through SEM-EDS (n. d. = not detected).

Sample	Type of artefact	Colour	Group	Na_2O	K_2O	MgO	SiO_2	P_2O_5	Cl	CaO	MnO	Fe_2O_3	Al_2O_3
MO-10	Technological element	Dark green	1	16.6	4	3.8	56	0.4	1	12.1	1.2	1.5	3.4
MO-33	Technological element	Colourless	1	8.6	2.6	3.1	66.3	0.5	0.9	9.8	2.2	2	4
MO-34	Technological element	Colourless	1	14.5	4.1	3.5	56.4	0.3	0.8	13.6	1.9	1.6	3.3
MO-35	Technological element	Colourless	1	10	2.6	3.2	64.9	0.4	0.9	11.1	n. d.	2.1	4.8
MO-36	Technological element	Colourless	1	5.6	3.1	2.8	72.1	0.4	1	6.7	1.5	1.9	4.9
MO-37	Technological element	Green	1	6.7	2.7	2.7	70.1	0.8	1.4	9.6	n. d.	2.2	3.8
MO-82	Technological element	Dark green	1	11.3	2.9	2.9	61.6	n. d.	1.7	13.4	n. d.	2.8	3.4
MO-83	Technological element	Dark green	1	11.4	2.8	3.4	63.3	0.8	0.7	10.2	n. d.	2.8	4.6
MO-38	Piece	Dark green	1	11.3	3	3.5	59.7	0.7	0.8	12.9	2.3	1.8	4
MO-58	Technological element	Colourless	1	3.7	2.6	3	72.6	n. d.	1	10.3	1.6	1.6	3.6
MO-11	Technological element	Green	1	17.8	3.4	4.1	56.3	0.8	0.9	11	1	1.2	3.5
MO-60	Technological element	Violet	1	6.3	3.3	3.1	67.8	0.5	1.1	10	2.8	1.7	3.4
MO-61	Technological element	Yellow	1	6.8	2.1	3.7	70.1	0.6	1	6	3	2.4	4.3
MO-62	Technological element	Violet	1	10.6	3.3	3.9	68.9	n. d.	1.3	8.6	n. d.	n. d.	3.4
MO-84	Technological element	Colourless	1	10.1	2.5	3.5	63	1	1	12.4	n. d.	2.2	4.3
MO-63	Piece	Green	1	10.4	5.1	3	64.1	0.4	n. d.	9.1	n. d.	3.4	4.5
MO-99	Piece	Colourless	1	9.9	3.8	3.2	63.7	n. d.	0.8	11.3	1.6	1.8	3.9
MO-64	Piece	Colourless	1	9.1	3.1	3.1	68.1	n. d.	1.8	11	n. d.	n. d.	3.8
MO-12	Technological element	Yellow	1	16.5	3.8	3.7	57.3	0.5	1.2	11	1.7	1.2	3.1
MO-66	Piece	Colourless	1	4.1	2.5	2	73.9	n. d.	0.8	6	n. d.	2.7	8
MO-14	Lump	Blue	1	13	3.1	4	59.1	0.6	0.8	11.1	1.4	2.2	4.7
MO-15	Drip	Green	1	7.3	3	3.5	67.9	0.7	0.7	8.4	2.2	1.9	4.4
MO-16	Drip	Green	1	8.2	3	3.4	66.5	0.5	0.7	11.2	1.2	1.6	3.7
MO-17	Technological element	Yellow	1	8	2.8	2.9	67.6	0.4	0.6	8.7	1.6	2.8	4.6
MO-18	Drip	Violet	1	9.8	3.3	3.7	65.4	0.4	1.1	8	1.3	2	5
MO-19	Drip	Green	1	8.7	2.8	3.6	67.7	0.5	0.8	9.1	1	1.6	4.2

MO-2	Lump	Dark green	1	11	3.3	3.6	65.1	n. d.	0.7	10.8	n. d.	2	3.5
MO-20	Technological element	Dark green	1	10.8	4.9	2.3	61.4	0.4	1.6	13.2	1.6	1.3	2.5
MO-21	Drip	Yellow	1	9.1	3.1	3.6	67.4	n. d.	0.9	10.9	1	1.3	2.7
MO-22	Piece	Violet	1	11.7	4.9	2.1	55.9	0.5	1.1	13.6	4.4	2.2	3.6
MO-23	Piece	Colourless	1	12.1	4.7	2.8	60.4	0.4	1	12.6	1.5	1.9	2.6
MO-27	Drip	Violet	1	15.1	4.4	3.2	55	0.5	1.7	13.3	1.7	1.8	3.3
MO-3	Lump	Green	1	10.6	3.9	4.1	64	0.6	0.5	9.3	n. d.	2.1	4.9
MO-98	Technological element	Green	1	9.4	3	3.4	66.5	0.5	0.9	8.7	1	1.9	4.7
MO-40	Technological element	Colourless	1	12.4	4.4	2.9	57.8	n. d.	1.1	14	2.4	2	3
MO-67	Technological element	Colourless	1	9.6	3.8	2.5	66.6	n. d.	1.3	13.6	n. d.	n. d.	2.6
MO-68	Technological element	Dark green	1	8.4	3.9	2.8	64.5	0.3	1.1	12.3	1.6	1.7	3.4
MO-4	Lump	Violet	1	9.9	2.8	3.6	65	0.4	0.6	11.4	0.9	1.6	3.8
MO-79	Technological element	Dark green	1	8.3	3.9	2.9	65.4	0.5	0.9	11.7	1.3	1.7	3.4
MO-69	Technological element	Colourless	1	6.9	2.8	2.8	72.4	n. d.	1.4	10.9	n. d.	n. d.	2.8
MO-85	Technological element	Colourless	1	17.3	4	4.4	52.7	0.4	0.8	13.3	1.9	1.6	3.6
MO-70	Technological element	Green	1	9.1	2.9	3.5	67.6	0.4	0.8	8.9	1.3	1.6	3.9
MO-86	Piece	Colourless	1	16.6	3.4	2.9	58.9	0.2	1.1	12.2	1.1	0.9	2.7
MO-45	Piece	Colourless	1	0.9	1.8	3.7	71.7	n. d.	0.4	15	n. d.	2.2	4.3
MO-88	Piece	Colourless	1	18.4	2.1	4.4	54.2	0.8	1.3	11.1	1.8	1.7	4.2
MO-46	Piece	Colourless	1	7.1	2.9	3.5	70.1	0.5	1.2	7	1.1	1.7	4.9
MO-47	Piece	Colourless	1	13.4	4.8	3.2	58.7	n. d.	1	13.7	1.6	1.5	2.1
MO-91	Piece	Colourless	1	5	1.9	3.5	75.9	n. d.	0.8	8	n. d.	1.8	3.1
MO-50	Piece	Colourless	1	11.6	2.9	3.4	63.8	0.4	1	9.3	1.6	1.7	4.3
MO-6	Drip	Green	1	10.7	3.5	3.1	59.1	n. d.	0.8	14.1	n. d.	4.6	4.1
MO-57	Piece	Dark green	1	13	3	3.7	58.5	1.2	0.6	12	1.2	2.1	4.7
MO-52	Piece	Colourless	1	5.3	2.6	3.1	73.8	0.5	1.2	6.1	1.3	1.6	4.5
MO-55	Piece	Colourless	1	10	3.3	3.9	60.2	0.5	1.4	11.3	2	2.2	5.2
MO-56	Piece	Colourless	1	4.2	3	4.9	74.3	n. d.	0.9	5.3	0.8	1.6	5
MO-92	Piece	Colourless	1	7.7	3.9	3.1	67.7	0.3	0.8	9.6	1.7	1.6	3.6

MO-7	Technological element	Yellow	1	6.1	3.1	2.8	70.2	n. d.	1	8.7	2	2.3	3.8
MO-103	Piece	Colourless	1	16.6	2.6	5.2	57.2	n. d.	1	15.5	n. d.	n. d.	1.9
MO-8	Technological element	Yellow	1	12.9	4.7	2.8	58.9	n. d.	1.6	13.2	1.5	1.8	2.6
MO-108	Piece	Colourless	1	13.8	3.2	3.9	61.3	n. d.	1	15.2	n. d.	n. d.	1.6
MO-109	Piece	Green	1	12.6	3.7	3	61	0.7	0.8	11.3	2.3	1.5	3.1
MO-73	Piece	Violet	1	9.8	3	3.5	66.3	0.5	0.8	8.7	1.5	1.6	4.3
MO-9	Technological element	Green	1	13.6	3.8	3	59.7	0.7	1	11.5	1.8	1.7	3.2
MO-74	Technological element	Colourless	1	6.9	2.4	3.8	70.2	0.6	0.8	7.2	1.9	1.8	4.4
MO-75	Technological element	Colourless	1	10	3	3.5	64.6	0.7	1	9.7	1.9	1.6	4
MO-93	Technological element	Green	1	8.6	3	3.3	67.3	0.5	0.8	7.8	1.4	2.2	5.1
MO-94	Technological element	Green	1	8.8	3.4	3.5	63.4	0.3	0.8	12.5	1.5	1.7	4.1
MO-76	Technological element	Colourless	1	6.8	3.7	2.7	67.6	0.6	1	10	1.4	1.6	4.6
MO-95	Technological element	Colourless	1	11.4	3	4.1	62.5	0.4	0.8	10.1	1.9	1.7	4.1
MO-96	Technological element	Colourless	1	12.4	2.3	3.1	62.1	0.5	1.2	11.8	0.9	1.2	4.5
MO-77	Technological element	Colourless	1	6.6	3.6	3.3	71	0.1	0.9	11.6	n. d.	n. d.	2.9
MO-78	Technological element	Colourless	1	6.4	2.6	3.4	71.1	n. d.	1.2	8	n. d.	3.8	3.5
MO-97	Technological element	Colourless	1	10	2.5	3.6	65.2	0.5	1	11.3	0.8	1.4	3.7
MO-13	Lump	Dark green	2	4.7	3	1.4	78.5	n. d.	0.9	5.1	n. d.	1.7	4.7
MO-44	Piece	Colourless	2	4.1	2.6	3.1	73.2	n. d.	1	6.6	n. d.	2.9	6.5
MO-5	Lump	Green	2	5.6	3.1	2.5	71.6	0.5	0.3	8.2	1	1.9	5.3
MO-90	Piece	Colourless	2	4.3	3.3	2.3	74.4	n. d.	0.7	6.5	1.4	1.9	5.2
MO-48	Piece	Colourless	2	4.5	3.3	2	74	n. d.	0.8	8.5	n. d.	2.4	4.5
MO-54	Piece	Colourless	2	5.2	3.4	2.7	71.7	n. d.	0.8	8.4	n. d.	2.3	5.5
MO-72	Piece	Colourless	2	6	3	2.4	75.1	n. d.	1.6	4.5	n. d.	2.3	5.1
MO-81	Piece	Colourless	2	5.4	2.1	3.3	73.7	0.9	0.6	5.3	n. d.	2.4	6.3
MO-59	Technological element	Green	3	1	2.3	1.4	83.1	n. d.	0.7	3.4	n. d.	1.9	6.2
MO-39	Technological element	Green	3	2.1	2.8	1.3	81.1	n. d.	0.6	5	n. d.	1.7	5.5
MO-26	Piece	Green	3	5.2	4	1.8	67.2	n. d.	0.9	10.3	n. d.	4.3	6.3
MO-41	Technological element	Colourless	3	1.6	2.9	1.4	78.7	n. d.	0.5	5.9	n. d.	2.6	6.3

MO-87	Piece	Colourless	3	3.5	2.6	2.3	73.1	n. d.	0.7	5.7	2.6	3.9	5.6
MO-43	Piece	Green	3	1.7	3.2	3	66.6	n. d.	0.4	13.1	n. d.	2.5	9.5
MO-89	Piece	Colourless	3	2.1	2.9	1.4	77.5	n. d.	0.3	3.7	1.2	2.7	8.2
MO-71	Piece	Dark green	3	2.2	2.3	1.1	79.2	n. d.	n. d.	4.3	3.8	1.7	5.4
MO-49	Piece	Green	3	2.1	3.6	1.5	75.7	n. d.	0.5	6.3	n. d.	2.9	7.4
MO-51	Piece	Dark green	3	4.3	3.4	1.5	74.7	n. d.	0.7	6.7	n. d.	2	6.7
MO-53	Piece	Dark green	3	2	4	1	73.6	n. d.	0.6	3.8	4.6	2.3	8.1
MO-80	Piece	Colourless	3	2.1	1.5	1.1	85.3	n. d.	0.7	2.9	n. d.	2.2	4.2
MO-65	Piece	Colourless	4	4.3	4.7	3.2	55.5	1.5	0.6	22.5	n. d.	1.7	6
MO-25	Piece	Dark green	4	1.5	6.4	3.8	56.9	1	0.2	23.9	1.5	1.4	3.4
MO-28	Piece	Colourless	4	3.3	5.6	2.5	56.1	0.8	0.7	24.1	n. d.	2.3	4.6
MO-30	Piece	Colourless	4	2.5	5	2.3	58.4	1	0.6	23.4	n. d.	1.8	5
MO-31	Piece	Colourless	4	3.2	4.5	2.7	57.2	1.4	0.7	21.6	n. d.	2.8	5.9
MO-32	Piece	Dark green	4	1.8	5.5	3	60.6	2	0.5	19.5	1.3	1.9	3.9
MO-100	Piece	Dark green	4	1.2	6.4	3.6	57.9	2.1	0.5	20.1	2.1	1.6	4.5
MO-101	Piece	Dark green	4	0.8	7.3	3	55.7	1.4	0.4	26.6	1.4	0.8	2.6
MO-102	Piece	Dark green	4	0.8	6.5	3.2	52	2.2	0.3	29	2.6	1.1	2.3
MO-104	Piece	Dark green	4	1.1	6.9	3.5	55.4	n. d.	n. d.	26.3	1.6	1.5	3.7
MO-106	Piece	Dark green	4	1	3.6	2.1	58.7	1.6	0.4	25.8	1.1	2.2	3.5
MO-107	Piece	Dark green	4	5.7	3.6	3.1	55	n. d.	0.9	24.9	1	2.3	3.5

10

ARCHAEOMETRIC CONTRIBUTION TO THE INTERPRETATION OF THE LATE BRONZE AGE "HOARD" FROM PORTO DO CONCELHO (MAÇÃO, CENTRAL PORTUGAL)

Carlo Bottaini*[1,2], Raquel Vilaça[3], Ignacio Montero-Ruiz[4], José Mirão[1], António Candeias[1]

[1]HERCULES Lab, University of Evora, Portugal.
[2] CIDEHUS, University of Evora, Portugal.
[3]Institute of Archaeology, CEAACP, University of Coimbra, Portugal.
[4]Instituto de Historia-CSIC, Spain.

Corresponding author: Carlo Bottaini (carlo@uevora.pt)

ABSTRACT

This paper presents and discusses the results of the multi-analytical study carried out on a group of 39 Late Bronze Age artefacts from the site of Porto do Concelho, Central Portugal. The chemical composition of the objects was determined by Energy Dispersive X-ray Fluorescence (EDXRF) and their microstructural features were identified by Optical Microscopy (OM) and Scanning Electron Microscopy with Energy Dispersive X-ray Spectroscopy (SEM-EDS). The results show that metals are binary alloys (Cu+Sn) and leaded bronzes (Cu+Sn+>2.0 wt.% Pb), with a variable content of impurities, such as Pb (when lower than 2.0 wt.%), Fe, As, Ag, Sb and Ni. The microstructural characterization carried out on 21 artefacts allowed the identification of two main operational sequences: 10 objects show a dendritic microstructure suggesting that metals have not undergone any post-casting treatment; 11 artefacts display the presence of annealing twins with, in some cases, slip bands, resulting from the application of thermal and mechanical treatments.
The analytical results are compared to those of other metal collections from regional LBA, and together with the bibliographic information available become an opportunity to question and rediscuss the real nature of a collection of metals that most of archaeologists consider as a typical LBA founder's hoard.

KEYWORDS: Hoards, Late Bronze Age, Central Portugal, EDXRF, SEM-EDS, OM.

1. INTRODUCTION

The study of metal hoards belonging to the Late Bronze Age (LBA) from Western Iberia has been a subject of interest for the Portuguese archaeologists since the second half of the 19th century (Sarmento 1888; Veiga 1891; Azevedo 1895; Pereira 1898). Ever since, this topic has been irregularly regarded, generally in the occasion of new findings (Fortes 1905/ 1908a; Fortes 1905/ 1908b; Fortes 1905/1908c; Viana 1938; Cortez 1951; Costa 1963; Júnior 1968; Pereira 1971; Cardoso et al. 1992), while it was only in recent years that this phenomenon has been studied in a more comprehensive and systematic way, also through multidisciplinary approaches (Vilaça 2006; Gutiérrez Neira et al. 2011; Bottaini 2012; Bottaini et al. 2016).

The steady constraints to be faced in the study of this archaeological evidence are well known by the researchers and reside mainly in the antiquity of most of the findings and in the fortuitous nature of the discoveries published to date. In fact, most of the hoards from Western Iberia were found by chance between the late nineteenth century and the last quarter of the last century, usually by individuals engaged in rural activities.

In this scenario, after having been discovered, the objects were generally recovered in a precipitous way and then dispersed among the finders, sold to antiquarians or remelted in order to check the nature of the metal, with no major concerns about the record of the objects' contexts of provenance. Thus, information about the archaeological contexts, the circumstances of the findings and the exact content of the hoard are almost always incomplete and often divergent, if not irretrievably lost (Vilaça 2006: 29-37). Furthermore, it is not rare to have more or less arbitrary interpretations of contents and contexts perpetuating uncritically in the scientific community, acknowledging hoards that have never actually existed in the way they are described in literature. For all these reasons, the study of bronze deposits from Portuguese territory requires working with partial information whose authenticity is frequently hard to check.

Unlike this framework, the way the metals from Porto do Concelho were uncovered and the exact location of the finding place have been described in some detail in a paper published shortly after the discovery of the artefacts (Jalhay 1944). Despite this group of metals being considered one of the most significant evidences of the LBA metallurgy from Central Portugal, the artefacts have never been properly characterized from an analytical point of view, usually being valued for their typological features (Pereira 1970; Coffyn 1985) and for the relationship between the place of hoarding and other elements of the cultural landscape, i.e. nearby settlements and hoards (Delfino 2016).

In this paper, the application of chemical and micro-structural techniques has been used as a tool to better understand the nature of the metals from Porto do Concelho. For this purpose, a portable Energy Dispersive X-ray Fluorescence (EDXRF) spectrometer was adopted to determine the chemical composition of the objects; Optical Microscopy (OM) and Scanning Electron Microscopy with Energy Dispersive X-ray Spectroscopy (SEM-EDS) was used to characterize the microstructure of the metals, in order to define the operational sequences that the ancient metalworker applied in the manufacture of the artefacts and to identify the presence of inclusions, casting defects and phases.

The aim of this paper is to understand the technological choices that the ancient metalworker made during the metal production process, allowing to answer to some specific questions: which alloys were employed for the production of these objects? How were they manufactured? How many operational sequences may we recognize within this group of metals? Is the metallurgy from Porto do Concelho coherent with that from LBA Central Portugal?

Moreover, through the discussion of the archaeometric data, preliminarily presented in Bottaini (2012) and Bottaini et al. (2015), and the critical reading of the information available in the bibliography, a new interpretation of Porto do Concelho is proposed.

2. PORTO DO CONCELHO METALS

The group of metals presented in this paper was discovered between March and July 1943 at the Porto do Concelho site, in Central Portugal (Fig. 1).

Figure 1: Location of Porto do Concelho and other sites mentioned in the text, namely: 1. Vila Cova de Perrinho; 2. Travasso: 3. Moura da Serra; 4. Coles de Samuel; 5. Castro de Argemela; 6. Quinta de Ervedal; 7. Gruta da Nascente do Algarinho; 8. Cabeço de Maria Candal (or Freixianda); 9. Senhora da Moita; 10. Castelo Velho do Caratão; 11. Casais de Fiéis de Deus; 12. Casais da Pedreira; 13. Moinho do Raposo.

The collection of metals, currently stored in the Museu de Arte Pré-Histórica e do Sagrado no Vale do Tejo, consists of tools, weapons, ornamental objects and artefacts with unknown function/functionality, being composed by 41 items, belonging to 40 artefacts, namely: two looped palstaves (PC127 and PC128); two Rocanes-type talon sickles (PC129 and PC130); three spearheads (PC131, PC132 and PC133); five swords (PC134, PC135, PC136, PC137 and PC138); four daggers (PC140, PC141, PC144 and PC150); two bracelets (PC143+PC 146 and PC145); one fibula (PC148); eleven entire ring-shaped objects (both closed and opened) (PC157; PC152; PC155; PC156; PC153; PC159; PC158; PC162; PC160; PC154 and PC163); two blades (PC139 and PC142); one conical-shape object (PC149); seven fragments (PC164; PC151; PC147; PC161; PC166; PC 168 and PC167). A sword is currently lost. The metal reaches a total weight of about 1.5 kg (Fig. 2).

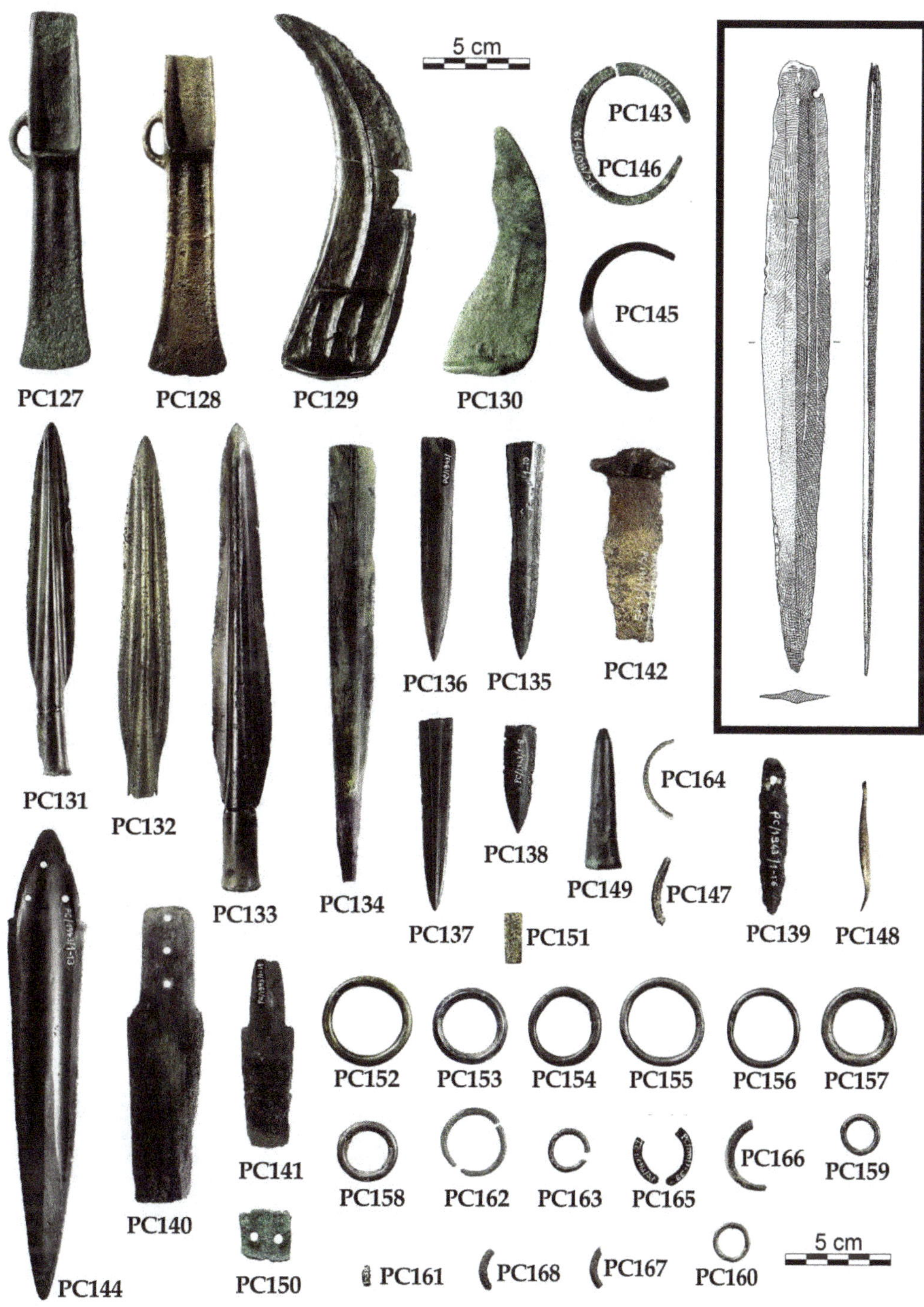

Figure 2: Artefact collection from Porto do Concelho, including the lost sword (upper right box, according with Pereira 1970).

According to E. Jalhay, these objects were not all discovered at the same time, resulting instead from the assemblage of artefacts found in three different occasions: a first group composed by 35 objects was found under a stone slab by Joaquim Pires Caratão and a group of workers while building a country road, on March 6th 1943 (Fig. 3).

Figure 3: The founders of the first group of metals discovered on March 6th 1943 (Jalhay 1944) (upper). The site where the metals would be found, with a commemorative plaque of the finding (photograph of Museu de Arte Pré-Histórica e do Sagrado no Vale do Tejo) (lower).

Immediately after the discovery, the metals were dispersed among the finders, being recovered two days later by João Calado Rodrigues, the one who, during a survey carried out on March 9th 1943 in the site of Porto do Concelho, also proceeded to the discovery of four more artefacts. Finally, on July 8th 1943, Eugénio Jalhay, in the occasion of a new prospection, found the last group of metals, composed by two ring-shaped objects and one fibula (Jalhay 1944).

In a recent paper, the number of items assigned to this metal collection rose to 45 units (Delfino 2016: 94), although no further information has been provided about the typology and the circumstances in which these other artefacts would have been collected. Thus, in the absence of new and duly justified data, the artefacts to be attributed to the site of Porto do Concelho are the 42 described by E. Jalhay.

Within the traditional stigma of classification and categorization of hoards, the artefacts found in these three occasions have been interpreted as part of a single founder's hoard, i.e. as a group of materials temporarily stored to be recovered within the recycling and the consumption processes of metal (Jalhay 1944; Pereira 1970; Coffyn 1985; Ruiz-Gálvez Priego 1995; Melo 2000; Vilaça 2006: Cardoso 2007; Delfino 2016).

The seeming lack of logic in the composition of the collection, both at a typological and functional level, the physical state of the materials, with whole and fragmented objects, and the localization of the site where the artefacts were uncovered, i.e. in a strategic zone which would have apparently served as a crossing point, played a crucial role for this kind of interpretation.

From a typological point of view, the artefacts denote a strong regional character: in fact, although with a Mediterranean dissemination (Giardino 1995), the single-looped palstaves (Monteagudo 1977), the Rocanes-type sickles (Coffyn 1985), the Porto de Mós type of daggers (Fernández-García 1997), the socketed spearheads (Cardoso et al. 1992) and the swords (Meijide Cameselle 1988; Brandherm 2007) fall into the typical LBA productions documented in several settlements and hoards from Central Portugal (Coffyn 1985; Vilaça 2006; Bottaini 2012).

Only PC 148, corresponding to one fibula, and PC142 differ from that indigenous matrix. In the latter case, the function of the artefact, unique in the Portuguese LBA panorama, is unknown. Taking into account its elongated conical shape and its longitudinal drilling, this object has been interpreted as a metallic tuyères (Pereira 1970: 204), i.e. an object used to blow air in the forge, although the reduced size of the diameter of the hole makes this interpretation unlikely (Fig. 4).

Fig. 4: Two different views of the conical-shape object PC142.

Most of the artefacts are fragmented: palstaves, sickles, spearheads, swords, daggers, as well as some of the rings have fractures that clearly make them useless for the tasks for which they have been produced, although the antiquity of these fractures is, in some cases, questionable.

Indeed, and according to M. H. Pereira (1970: 184), one of the two sickles was broken at the time of the finding, which could also have happened with other artefacts, possibly damaged by the finders while verifying the nature of the alloy. Thus, it is hardly possible to distinguish the ancient fractures from the recent ones, also because in the meantime the objects were treated and preserved.

In any case, it must be noted that both tools and weapons are fractured. The main difference lies in the fact that the former, i.e. palstaves and sickles, despite fractured, are complete, while the latter, namely swords (except the lost specimen) and daggers (except PC144), appear to be limited to a single part of the artefact: the lower part of the blade for the swords, the handle for the daggers.

3. EXPERIMENTAL

According to the morphology and the state of conservation of the objects, different preparation methodologies were adopted: in order to avoid contamination from superficial corrosion patinas, the most fragile and deteriorated metals were mechanically cleaned in a small area to obtain the chemical composition of the bulk alloy. In the material studied by optical and electron microscopies, the analyses were performed on cross-sections of samples of about 3mm^2, manually removed from the artefacts with a jeweler's saw and mounted in resin.

Chemical analyses were performed by EDXRF with a portable spectrometer INNOV-X Alpha of the National Archaeological Museum of Madrid, equipped with a silver anode X-ray tube. Working conditions: 35kV, 2μA. The acquisition time was set at 40 s and the quantitative values were calculated from a calibration validated by certified standards. In the case of silver and antimony the detection limit is 0.15 wt.%, while for the remaining elements it is set to 0.02 wt.%.

Principal component analysis (PCA) has been used to correlate X-ray fluorescence data from Porto do Concelho with those from other Central Portugal LBA hoards. PCA was carried out on Sn, Pb and Fe, in order to understand compositional differences among the considered groups of metals.

The microstructural observation was carried out on samples mounted in epoxy resin and polished with silicon carbide papers (220-1200 μm) and diamond pastes (up to 1μm). The metallographic study was made with a Leica optical microscope, model DMLM, equipped with a DFC480 digital camera. In order to reveal the microstructure of the metal, the samples were etched with a ferric chloride acid solution ($FeCl_3$+HCl+H_2O) (Scott 1991).

Analyses by SEM-EDS were performed with an Hiachi S-3700N interfaced with a Quanta EDS microanalysis system with a Bruker AXS Xflash Silicon Drift Detector (129 eV Spectral Resolution at FWHM/Mn Kα). Data processing has been carried out with the Bruker ESPRIT 1.9 software.

4. RESULTS

4.1. *Alloy composition*

Some of the metals from Porto do Concelho were analysed in the past, although the results have never been published or discussed in detail. A group of objects, whose typology is not referred, was analysed by X-ray Diffraction (XRD) in the sixties of the last century. The results obtained are manifestly incompatible with the LBA metallurgy, since it was determined that metals were made with copper and zinc as main constituents (Pereira 1970: 24).

Some years later, A. Coffyn reports to have analysed four objects, without mentioning neither which objects were studied nor the analytical technique used. The results were summarily published, leading the author to state that the artefacts were made with alloys of copper and tin, with an average of 13.26 wt.% Sn, and low levels of lead (Coffyn 1998: 175).

In the present occasion, the whole collection from Porto do Concelho has been analysed, with the exception of three artefacts: PC161 and PC168 for being very small fragments and bearing a thick patina; and a sword for being lost. Chemical analysis by EDXRF was carried out on 40 items (corresponding to 39 objects since PC 143 and PC1466 belongs to the same bracelet).

The EDXRF elemental composition results are shown in the table 1. According to the data, copper is present in variable percentages between 64.6 wt.% (PC155) and 92.2 wt.% (PC132), with a major concentration in the range between 84.0 wt.% and 86.0 wt.% (fig. 5A). Tin also presents a very remarkable variability, ranging from 7.3 wt.% (PC132) to 29.1 wt.% (PC153), being the most recurrent range from 14.0 wt.% to 16.0 wt.% (fig. 5B).

The high tin content suggests that metals from Porto do Concelho were produced with fresh tin and not with scrap bronzes. In fact, experimental studies have shown how in bronze alloys produced from scraps without the addition of fresh tin, the tin content decreases significantly already from the first re-castings, resulting in alloys poorer in tin (Sarabia-Herrero 1992).

It is worth to be recalled that the control over the tin content is an essential condition in order to produce objects with good mechanical properties, since an excessive amount of tin (above 14.0 - 15.0 wt.% Sn) led to the formation of the α+δ eutectoid phase that makes the alloy increasingly brittle and difficult to deform without causing a crack.

Table 1: Results from EDXRF and OM. EDXRF elemental composition (wt.%); n.d.: not detected. Manufacture column: C: Casting; A: Annealing; F: Forging; FF: Final Forging. N.A.: not analyzed.

Object	Ref.	Cu	Sn	Pb	Fe	As	Ag	Sb	Ni	Manufacture
Palstave	PC127	85.4	14.3	0.18	n.d.	0.12	n.d.	n.d.	n.d.	C+(F+A)
Palstave	PC128	90.7	9.11	0.21	n.d.	n.d.	n.d.	n.d.	n.d.	C+(F+A)+FF
Sickle	PC129	81.7	15.1	0.18	n.d.	2.97	n.d.	n.d.	n.d.	C
Sickle	PC130	84.7	14.8	0.2	n.d.	0.26	n.d.	n.d.	0.34	C
Spearhead	PC131	86.5	12.6	0.57	n.d.	n.d.	n.d.	n.d.	0.16	C
Spearhead	PC132	92.2	7.3	0.46	n.d.	n.d.	n.d.	n.d.	n.d.	C+(F+A)
Spearhead	PC133	85.0	14.2	0.33	n.d.	n.d.	n.d.	n.d.	n.d.	C+(F+A)
Sword	PC134	88.3	10.8	0.91	n.d.	n.d.	n.d.	n.d.	0.21	C
Sword	PC135	88.5	11.2	0.29	n.d.	n.d.	n.d.	n.d.	n.d.	C
Sword	PC136	80.7	18.3	0.23	n.d.	n.d.	n.d.	n.d.	n.d.	C
Sword	PC137	87.7	11.9	0.39	n.d.	n.d.	n.d.	n.d.	n.d.	C
Sword	PC138	82.1	17.6	0.25	n.d.	n.d.	n.d.	n.d.	n.d.	C
Blade	PC139	80.5	18.6	0.35	n.d.	n.d.	n.d.	n.d.	0.54	C
Dagger	PC140	85.4	14.2	0.37	n.d.	n.d.	n.d.	n.d.	n.d.	C+(F+A)
Dagger	PC141	84.0	15.6	0.3	n.d.	n.d.	n.d.	n.d.	n.d.	C+(F+A)
Undefined object	PC142	90.0	8.72	1.09	0.13	n.d.	n.d.	n.d.	0.09	C+(F+A)
Bracelet shaped object	PC143	90.0	9.92	0.1	n.d.	n.d.	n.d.	n.d.	1.14	C+(F+A)
	PC146	88.6	11.2	0.15	n.d.	n.d.	n.d.	n.d.	1.06	N.A.
Dagger	PC144	86.7	12.9	0.4	n.d.	n.d.	n.d.	n.d.	n.d.	C
Bracelet shaped object	PC145	85.7	14.0	0.24	n.d.	n.d.	n.d.	n.d.	n.d.	C+(F+A)+FF
Ring shaped object	PC147	89.1	10.5	0.33	0.09	n.d.	n.d.	n.d.	n.d.	N.A.
Fibulae	PC148	91.8	7.89	0.24	n.d.	0.08	n.d.	n.d.	n.d.	N.A
Undefined object	PC149	75.6	22.5	0.08	n.d.	0.98	0.17	0.41	0.14	N.A.
Dagger	PC150	88.2	11.3	0.27	n.d.	n.d.	n.d.	n.d.	0.18	C+(F+A)+FF
Undefined object	PC151	88.9	10.9	0.16	n.d.	n.d.	n.d.	n.d.	n.d.	C+(F+A)
Ring shaped object	PC152	82.3	14.0	3.67	n.d.	n.d.	n.d.	n.d.	n.d.	N.A.
Ring shaped object	PC153	69.1	29.1	0.51	n.d.	1.31	n.d.	n.d.	n.d.	N.A.
Ring shaped object	PC154	84.8	14.7	0.25	n.d.	0.12	n.d.	n.d.	n.d.	N.A.
Ring shaped object	PC155	64.6	20.9	14.5	n.d.	n.d.	n.d.	n.d.	n.d.	N.A.
Ring shaped object	PC156	75.6	23.1	0.83	n.d.	0.43	n.d.	n.d.	n.d.	N.A.
Ring shaped object	PC157	74.3	23.7	1.62	n.d.	0.25	n.d.	n.d.	n.d.	N.A.
Ring shaped object	PC158	76.6	22.3	0.26	n.d.	0.84	n.d.	n.d.	n.d.	N.A.
Ring shaped object	PC159	72.2	26.1	0.61	0.48	0.57	n.d.	n.d.	n.d.	N.A.
Ring shaped object	PC160	80.4	19.3	0.28	n.d.	n.d.	n.d.	n.d.	n.d.	N.A.
Ring shaped object	PC162	85.74	9.16	5.0	0.11	n.d.	n.d.	n.d.	n.d.	N.A.
Ring shaped object	PC163	77.4	20.90	0.63	0.63	0.46	n.d.	n.d.	n.d.	N.A.
Ring shaped object	PC164	85.8	12.2	1.98	n.d.	n.d.	n.d.	n.d.	n.d.	N.A.
Ring shaped object	PC165	77.6	20.6	1.33	0.1	0.29	n.d.	n.d.	n.d.	N.A.
Ring shaped object	PC166	85.5	12.0	2.53	n.d.	n.d.	n.d.	n.d.	n.d.	N.A.
Ring shaped object	PC167	87.4	8.42	4.14	n.d.	n.d.	n.d.	n.d.	0.07	N.A.

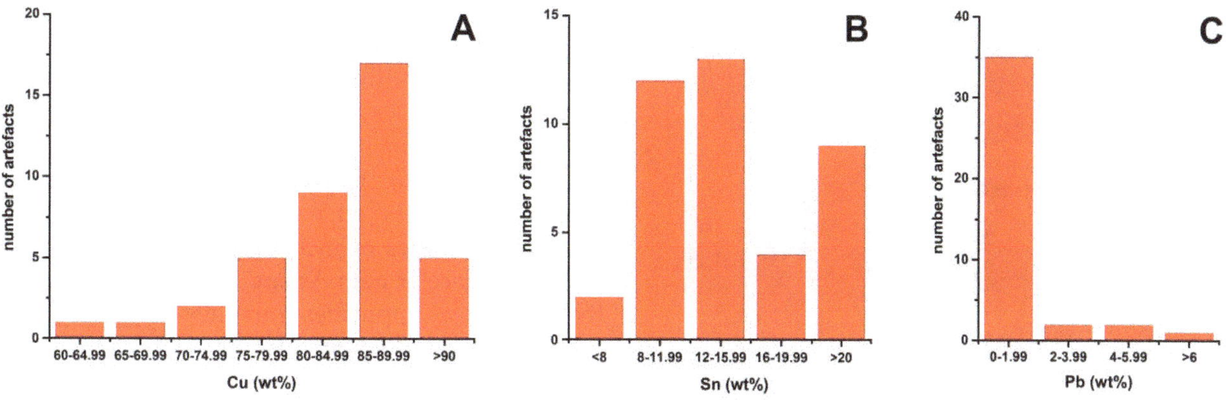

Figure 5: Histograms with the distribution of Cu (A), Sn (B) and Pb (C).

The results from Porto do Concelho show that in the objects that supposedly required higher mechanical strengths, such as palstaves, sickles and most of the weapons, tin is kept below the limit of 15.0 wt.%, whilst it is higher in most of the ring-shaped objects, wherein half of the specimens have a content above 20.0 wt.% Sn, with a global average of ~18.0 wt.% Sn.

Metals with high tin content are not an absolute novelty in regional terms, as already demonstrated by a ring from the LBA settlement of Castro de Argemela (27.6 wt. % Sn) (Vilaça et al. 2012b).

Since alloys with tin content between 20.0 and 30.0 wt.% produce a characteristic silver colour (Giardino 1998: 142), more suitable for ornamental objects, it may be admitted that high tin content could be an intentional technological choice in the production of certain type of artefacts.

Lead is systematically identified in all the artefacts, ranging from 0.1 wt.% (PC143) to 14.5 wt.% (PC155) (Fig. 5C). Most of the analysed objects (35 out 39) contain a low amount of lead (< 2.0 wt.%), also visible by SEM-EDS images (Fig. 6), suggesting that its occurrence is not the result of an intentional addition, instead resulting from presence of this element in the ores used within the fabrication of the alloys or providing a clue for the use of recycled metals.

Conversely, the higher lead content in four ring-shaped objects (from 2.53 up to 14.5 wt.% Pb) probably results by a clear technological option. Although the function of ring-shaped objects is rather ambiguous, the high lead content may confirm that these type of artefacts were used for tasks that did not require high mechanical strength. In fact, the low miscibility of Pb in Cu+Sn alloys leads to the formation of unalloyed segregations that increases brittleness and reduces the strength of the alloy.

Besides the major elements, impurities were identified as well, namely Ag, Sb, Fe, As, Ni and Pb (<2.0 wt.%). PC149 is the only artefact containing small amounts of both Ag and Sb, respectively, 0.17 wt.% and 0.41 wt.%, demonstrating the uniqueness of this artefact not only from the morphological point of view, as well as in terms of chemical composition.

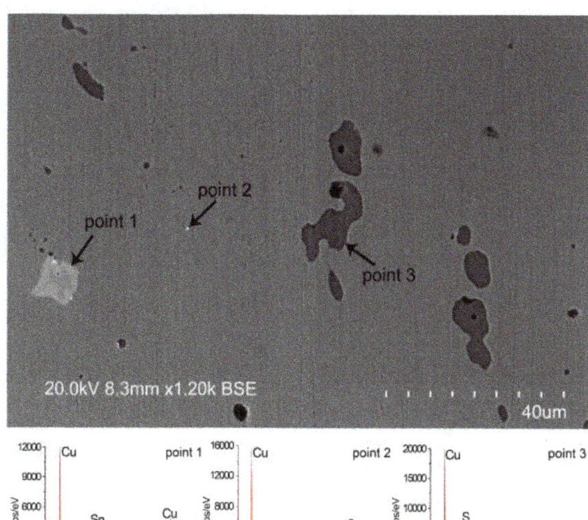

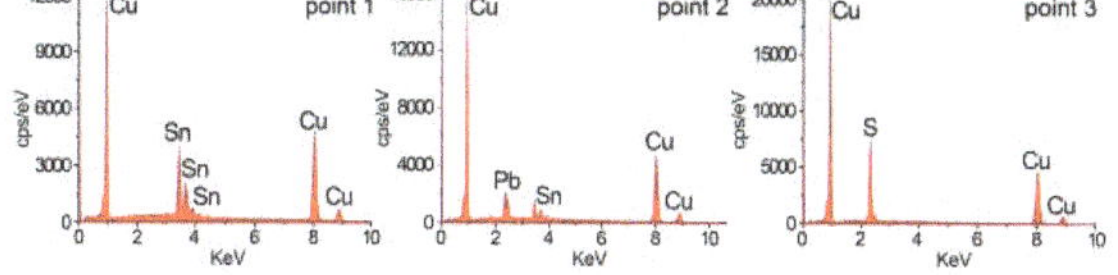

Figure 6: Backscattered electron image with EDS spectra of the bracelet PC145, showing the α+δ eutectoid phase (27.0 wt.%) (point 1); Pb-rich inclusion (point 2); Cu-S inclusion (point 3).

The occurrence of Ag and Sb is a common feature of the LBA metallurgy from Central Portugal, although with values generally below 0.1 wt.%, as the analyses by Particle-induced X-ray emission (PIXE) on the metals from Cabeço de Maria Candal (also known as Freixianda) hoard proved (Gutiérrez Neira et al. 2011). In the case of Porto do Concelho, the high detection limits for both Ag and Sb (0.15 wt.%) did not allow to properly quantify their presence.

To overcome this limitation, SEM-EDS analysis was performed which allowed the identification in several pieces of small inclusions enriched in Ag, such as in PC130, PC137, PC139, PC141 and PC143 (Fig. 7).

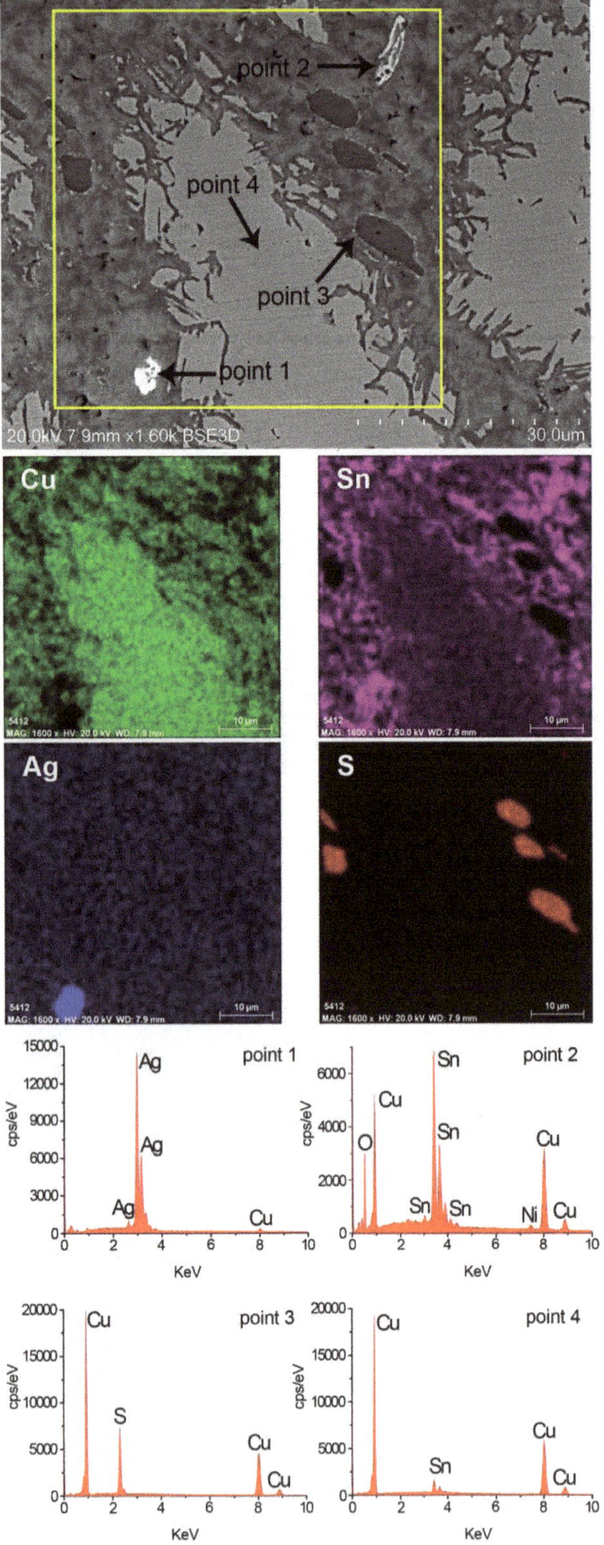

Figure 7: Backscattered electron image with EDS elemental distribution maps and EDS spectra of the blade PC139, showing the presence of the an Ag-rich inclusion (point 1); a+δ eutectoid phase (49.5 wt.% Sn) (point 2); S-rich inclusion (point 3); a-phase (10.4 wt.% Sn) (point 4).

One undefined object (PC142) and five rings (PC147, PC159, PC162, PC163, PC165) contain iron, with amounts ranging from 0.09 and 0.63 wt.%, suggesting the use of copper smelting furnaces able to achieve temperatures sufficiently high to reduce the iron impurities present in the ores, much more efficient than the traditional furnace vessels (Craddock and Meeks 1987; Rovira and Ambert 2002), probably used for the production of the rest of the objects. Arsenic is present in 13 objects with values between 0.08 wt.% and 2.97 wt.%., whilst 10 objects contain variable quantities of nickel (to 0.07 up 1.14 wt.%). The occurrence of both As and Ni is probably due to the presence of impurities contained in the ores used within the production process and carried out through to the finished artefact.

Thus, the artefacts from Porto do Concelho appear to have a more heterogeneous elemental composition when compared with binary bronzes with few impurities typical of the LBA metallurgy from Central Portugal.

Fig. 8 displays a statistical multivariate analysis (PCA) carried out on a matrix dataset in which XRF data from Porto do Concelho and from LBA hoards from Central Portugal are compared. The data confirms that within a group of metals from Porto do Concelho, tin, iron and lead achieves a slightly higher average content with respect to the metals found in the rest of the regional collections. Finally, it should be highlighted that the total impurities amount (Fe, As, Ag, Sb, Ni and <2.0 wt.% Pb) identified in 13 objects from Porto do Concelho reaches higher values (> 1.0 wt.% of the alloy composition) than those expected for the region.

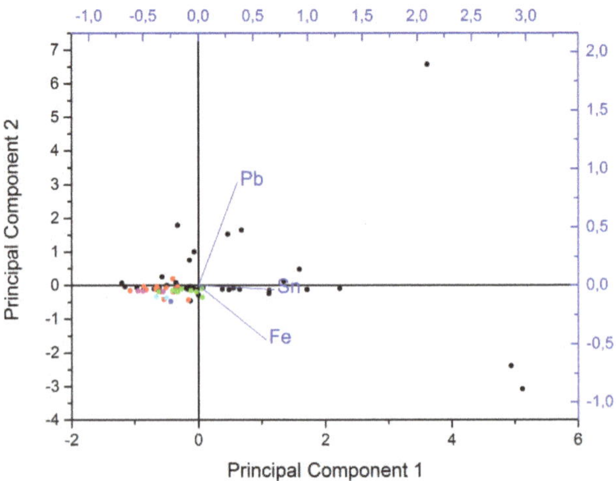

Figure 8: PCA discriminating among the Sn, Pb and Fe amount in Cu-based artefacts which shows the deviation of the elemental composition of the Porto do Concelho metals relative to other metal sets in the LBA of Central Portugal. Porto do Concelho (black dots); Coles de Samuel (red dots); Cabeço de Maria Candal (green dots); Moinho do Raposo (dark blue dots); Casais da Pedreira (light blue dots); Travasso (purple dots).

4.2. Microstructure

The metallographic study focused on 21 artefacts, namely: two one-looped palstaves (PC127 and PC 128), two sickles (PC129 and PC130), three spearheads (PC131, PC132 and PC133), five swords (PC 134, PC135, PC136, PC137 and PC138), two blades (PC139 and PC142), four daggers (PC140, PC141, PC 144 and PC150), two bracelets (PC145 and PC146+ PC143) and one undefined object (PC151).

Based on the data, two different manufacturing techniques were identified. Two sickles (PC129 and PC 130), one spearhead (PC131), five swords (PC134, PC 135, PC136, PC137 and PC138), one blade (PC139) and one dagger (PC144) show a dendritic micro-structure (Fig. 9), which suggests that after being removed from the mould, the ancient metal-worker did not apply any thermomechanical treatment to the artefacts.

As for the rest of the objects, two palstaves (PC127 and PC128), two spearheads (PC132 and PC133), three daggers (PC140, PC141 and PC150), two bracelets (PC145 and PC143) and two undefined objects (PC142 and PC151) show the presence of recrystallized twinned grains with, in some cases, slip bands (PC128, PC145 and PC150). This kind of microstructure suggests that after being removed from the moulds, artefacts were heated under the melting point to make it more ductile and more suitable to be plastically deformed through forging. This way, cycles of hot/cold working were repeated until the objects had the desired shape and hardness. The presence of slip bands indicates a finishing treatment through the application of a more intense forging cycle (Fig. 10).

The observation by SEM allowed to identify several inclusions dispersed in the microstructures of the alloys: in addition to those mentioned above ($\alpha+\delta$ eutectoidc and Ag), segregations of Cu-S, nickel-rich inclusions (Fig. 11A) and unalloyed copper inclusions (Fig. 11B) were also detected. The presence of the latter could be explained as a remnant of incomplete mixing or as the result of a copper redeposition process resulting from corrosion phenomena (Bosi et al. 2002; Emami et al. 2013).

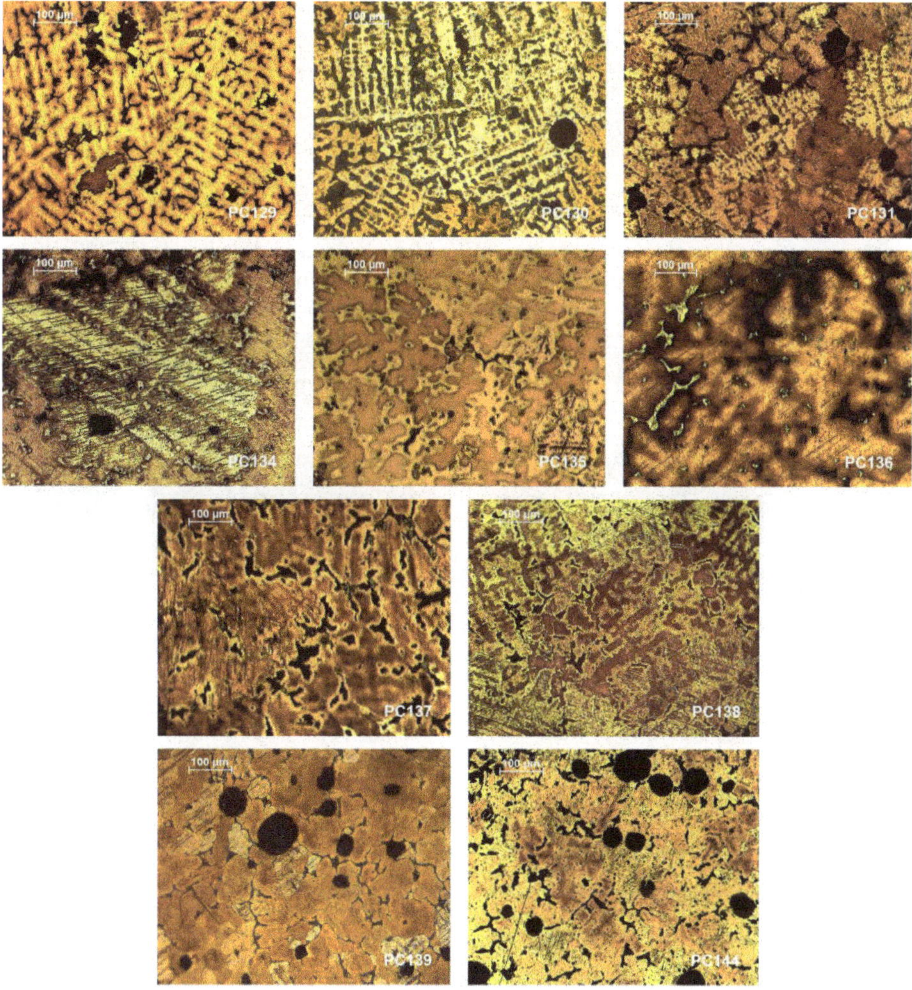

Figure 9: Microstructures of artefacts showing the dendritic microstructure typical of metals that did not undergone to any post casting treatment.

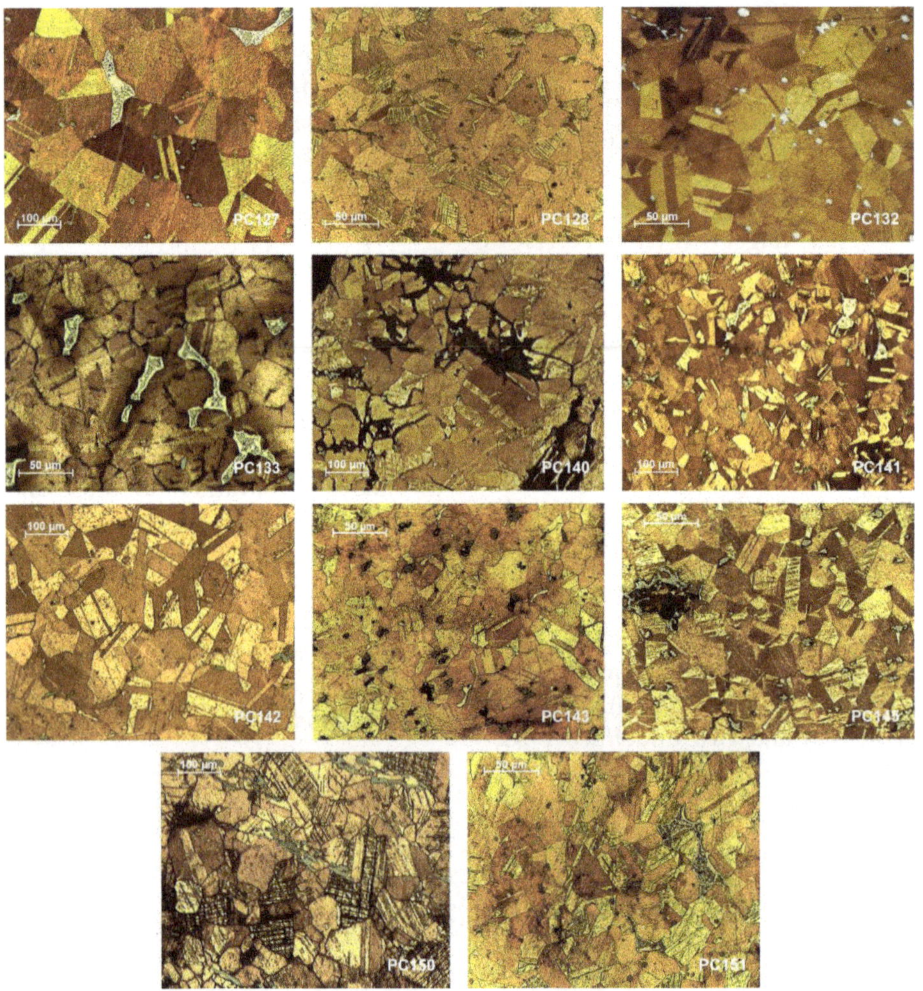

Figure 10: Microstructures of artefacts showing recrystallized grains and sliding bands (PC128, PC145 and PC150), which suggests the applying of post-casting treatment (forging+annealing).

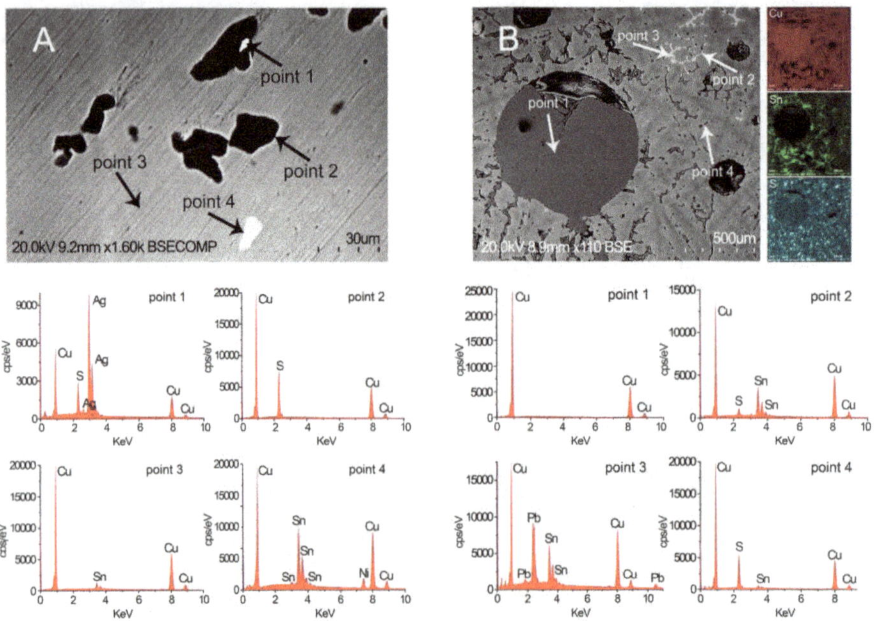

Figure 11: A) Backscattered electron image with EDS spectra of the bracelet PC143 showing an Ag-rich inclusion (point 1); S-Cu inclusion (point 2); a-phase (7.8 wt.% Sn) (point 3); Ni-rich inclusion (point 4). B) Backscattered electron image with EDS elemental distribution maps and EDS spectra of the sickle PC130 with a globular unalloyed Cu-inclusion (point 1); a+δ eutectoid phase (24.15 wt.% Sn) (point 2); Pb rich-inclusion (point 3); Cu-S inclusion (point 4).

5. DISCUSSION

The description of the circumstances in which the metals from Porto do Concelho were found has been used to support the interpretation of this collection as a founder's hoard. However, the paper published in 1944 does not provide suitable information on the real composition of the collection and leads one to wonder about its real archaeological nature.

In fact, the artefacts were found in at least three circumstances and by different people in an area generically designated with the toponym of Porto do Concelho. The spatial relationship between the exact location where each single group of metals stood is not referred and there is not any effective control over the type and the number of artefacts assigned to the first finding. In respect of the latter, the 1944 paper informs that it was composed by 35 artefacts, among which rings, daggers, bracelets and axes. But are these artefacts those that were discovered in that occasion or are just those that J.C. Rodrigues was able to recover two days later? It stands to reason that the artefacts recovered might not correspond to those actually found under the stone slab.

In fact, it is worth mentioning that other sites with LBA metallurgy are known close to Porto do Concelho, namely Senhora da Moita and Castelo Velho do Caratão, and that metals from these sites were found casually at about the same time of those from Porto do Concelho, being dispersed among local people as well (Pereira 1970). Given the lack of more detailed information on the objects found at Porto do Concelho on March 6th 1943 and those recovered from the hands of the finders two days later, it is admissible that other artefacts coming from nearby sites could also have been mixed and arbitrarily attributed to the collection from Porto do Concelho.

Thus, the strict reading of the information presented by E. Jalhay would eventually open up the possibility of being faced with a different reality than the one that has been perpetrated until now in the bibliography. In fact, the widespread of different groups of metals within an area where neither settlement nor grave have been apparently found, suggests that we are not dealing with a single hoard but rather with different hoards that ancient local communities buried in an evocative space possibly devoted to the deposition of artefacts with culturally shared values (Fontijn 2002-2003; Vilaça 2006: 39). This is a well-known reality in other European regions, such as in the Armorican region, in the Northwest of France (Verron 1983; Gabillot 2003), where single or multiple depositions, not necessarily with chronological relation, occurred in areas with clearly defined borders, possibly chosen for meanings reflecting the perception that ancient societies had of such a place.

In fact, the group of metals from Porto do Concelho shows internal elements that are distinctive of the hoarding practices from Central Portugal and that seem to point out the existence of selective deposition processes, especially at the level of combinations of certain metal types. The association between palstaves, sickles, bracelets, daggers, swords and spearheads, for example, appears to be documented in several LBA regional hoards, such as Cabeço de Maria Candal (palstave + dagger) (Gutiérrez Neira et al. 2011; Vilaça et al. 2012a), Coles de Samuel (palstave + bracelet + sickle) (Bottaini et al. 2016), Travasso (palstave + sickle) (Leitão e Lopes 1984), Moura da Serra (palstave + sickle) (Nunes 1957) and Casal de Fiéis de Deus (bracelet + dagger + sword + spearhead) (Vasconcelos 1919-1920; Melo 2000).

At the same time, certain other types of metals present at Porto do Concelho, such as the fibula (PC 148), the object interpreted as a "tuyères" (PC149) and the ring-shaped objects, seem to be deliberately avoided within the hoarding practices known for Central Portugal.

From an analytical point of view, the comparison between the elemental composition of the metals from Porto do Concelho and others from LBA Central Portugal hoards also highlights a contrasting situation. Unlike the Late Bronze Age / Early Iron Age metallurgy from Northwestern Iberia, where the addition of lead to copper-based artefacts was a common practice (Montero et al. 2003), LBA metals from Central Portugal are generally composed of binary Cu-Sn alloys (with 8.0-15.0 wt.% Sn in most of cases), with a reduced amount of impurities (Vilaça 1997; Figueiredo et al. 2010). The analysis carried out on Cabeço de Maria Candal hoard show that artefacts were made of bronze with a slightly higher average of tin contents (~14.0 wt.% Sn) and reduced amount of impurities (<1.0 wt%) (Gutiérrez Neira et al. 2011); similarly, the 18 artefacts from the Coles de Samuel hoard are composed by binary bronzes (~11.0 wt% Sn) with impurities not exceeding 1.1 wt.% (Bottaini et al. 2016).

These data are not entirely consistent with the results obtained at Porto do Concelho, where different groups of copper-based alloys may be identified. Most of the artefacts are composed by bronze alloys, with tin not exceeding 15.0 wt.% and generally reduced impurities (<1.0 wt.%). Fifteen artefacts can be classified as high tin bronzes (>15.0 wt.%), while five rings are leaded bronzes (Cu + Sn + >2.0 wt.% Pb). Ring-shaped objects show a clearly different chemical composition when compared with the rest of the material. Five rings contain more than 2.0 wt.% of lead, whilst five have more than 0.05 wt.% of iron, not being possible to establish any relationship between the occurrence of these two elements.

The observation of the artefacts' microstructure provides information very useful from an interpretative point of view. At a first glance, it can be observed that both ascast metals and artefacts which suffered post casting treatments coexist in the same context, being these results coherent with metallographic studies carried out on bronze artefacts from Cabeço de Maria Candal (Vilaça et al. 2012a), Coles de Samuel (Bottaini et al. 2016), Gruta da Nascente do Algarinho (Figueiredo et al. 2011), Vila Cova de Perrinho, Casais da Pedreira and Moinho do Raposo (Bottaini 2012). In a broader perspective, the data from these hoards suggest that metals had distinct biographical trajectories, some retrieved from circulation without being adequately prepared for practical purposes, others presumably thrown out after being used.

According to a visual and a microscopic observation of the artefacts, five swords (PC134, PC135, PC136, PC137 and PC138) and three daggers (PC140, PC141 and PC150) seem to stand out from the rest of the artefacts from Porto do Concelho, revealing a situation probably more complex than that accepted for their interpretation as scrap metals. As already high-lighted, the five swords are reduced to the lower part of the blade and the tip, with the only exception of PC134; they have a dendritic microstructure, whilst the blades show irregularities (i.e. asymmetrical blades and presence of nicks) that suggest some kind of impact. The three daggers are limited to the handle and, in the cases of PC140 and PC141, to the upper part of the blade; the microstructure suggest that these artefacts were subjected to a plastic deformation by annealing and forging.

The deposition of fragmented weapons, often with signs of deliberate destruction, damage and breaking, is recurrent in the LBA hoards from the European Atlantic façade (Bradley 1990; York 2002; Quilliec 2008), being also documented in Central Portugal, namely in the deposits from Quinta do Ervedal (Villas-Bôas 1947), Casais de Fiéis de Deus (Vasconcelos 1919-1920; Melo 2000) and Cabeço de Maria Candal (Vilaça et al. 2012a).

The repetitiveness of this depositional pattern over a wide geographical area, as well as the physical conditions and the microstructural features observed in the swords and in the daggers from Porto do Concelho, would allow one to consider these two groups of artefacts not as a simply accumulation of metal arbitrarily stored to be later recycled (i.e. as part of a founder's hoard), rather as the materialization of codified and structured depositional practices in which weapons (as well as others types of artefacts) could be ritually broken before being deposited (Nebelsick 2000; Fontijn 2002-2003). In this way, and according to an understanding of the hoarding phenomenon that goes beyond the dichotomy between profane and ritual hoards, the act of fragmentation itself would be part of the biography of object identities, being a crucial event able to legitimate the voluntary deposition of a certain object (Chapman and Gaydarska 2007).

Thus, the analyses carried out on the Porto do Concelho collection show a quite heterogeneous situation in terms of both chemical composition and microstructural characterization, partially in agreement with the characteristics of the LBA metallurgy from Central Portugal. According to these data, metals from Porto do Concelho could have been made by craftsman with different levels of technological know-how and technical skills, able to produce binary bronzes, leaded alloys as well as metals with higher iron amount (which could indicate a different smelting technology) and to give these objects the desired shape through casting or forging and annealing cycles. Hence, it is possible that the artefacts from Porto do Concelho were produced at different times, being hoarded at the same time or, in a vision of "open hoard", over several times. But none of the analytical data confirms that the objects have been imported from other regions, as has been recently suggested (Delfino 2014).

6. CONCLUSIONS

The study of the metal hoards from the Portuguese territory requires working with very partial and sometimes equivocal information, which makes the interpretation of each single hoard, as well as of the hoarding phenomenon in general, even more difficult. In the historiography on this topic, the collection from Porto do Concelho represents a very paradigmatic case: resulting of fortuitous findings discovered in three different circumstances, this group of artefacts was immediately regarded as an example of a typical LBA founder's hoard.

The lack of control over the findings and over the recovery of the artefacts dispersed among the finders after the unearthing of the first group of objects, raise questions on the authentic nature of the metals from Porto do Concelho. The analytical results seem to strengthen these doubts: while the LBA hoards from Central Portugal show a fairly homogeneous chemical composition, i.e. pure bronze alloys with reduced impurities, the metals from Porto do Concelho are characterized by a more diverse composition, coexisting binary Cu-Sn alloys and leaded bronzes (Cu+Sn+>2.0 wt.% Pb), containing amounts of impurities, namely Fe, that in some cases appear to be very significant. Furthermore, the high Sn content is a relevant issue, since if we consider the metals of Porto do Concelho as a founder's hoard whose existence is justified within the metal recycling practices, a lower Sn content might be expected.

Metallographic observations enable to describe the microstructure of the alloys, thus providing additional information about technological aspects. In particular, this technique made possible the identification of two main different microstructures: a group of artefacts presents a dendritic microstructure typical of objects that have not been subjected to any post-casting treatment; a second one shows the presence of recrystallized grains, sometimes with slip bands, which suggests the use of alternate cycles of annealing and forging applied in order to obtain metals with higher resistance.

In conclusion, based on archaeological information and on the analytical data, and unlike the interpretation generally accepted in the bibliography, the idea that metals from Porto do Concelho were part of a single hoard temporarily stored by an ancient founder does not seem plausible. Anyway, at the same time, the presence of recurring elements within the phenomenon of selective deposition from Central Portugal, i.e. the occurrence of characteristic typological combinations of certain objects, the physical features of the swords and daggers, etc., does not exclude the existence, within the whole collection from Porto do Concelho, of smaller groups of artefacts that may have been voluntarily removed from circulation and separately hoarded in an area specially designed for this purpose.

ACKNOWLEDGEMENTS

This work has been financed by national funds by FCT – Foundation for Science and Technology under the UID project UID/HIS/00057/2013 (POCI-01-0145-FEDER-007702) and UID/Multi/04449/2013 (POCI-01-0145-FEDER-007649), COMPETE, FEDER, Portugal2020. The contribution of IMR and RV is part of the I+D+i project HAR2014-52981-R funded by the Spanish Ministerio de Economía y Competitividad. The authors would like to acknowledge Dr. Luiz Oosterbeek (Instituto Politécnico de Tomar and Director of the Prehistoric Art Museum of Mação) for allowing the study of the metal artefacts and the Museu Dom Diogo de Sousa (Braga) for the restoration of the objects. The first author also thanks the FCT for the SFRH/BPD/111039/2015 grant and Neil Young for the support during the preparation of this paper.

REFERENCES

Azevedo, M. (1895) Notícias archeologicas de Trás-os-Montes. *O Archeologo Português*, s. I, Vol. 1, pp. 130-136.

Bosi, C., Garagnani, G.L., Imbeni, V., Martini, C., Mazzeo, R. and Poli, G. (2002) Unalloyed copper inclusions in ancient bronze artifacts. *Journal of Materials Science*, Vol. 37, pp. 4285-4298.

Bottaini, C. (2012) Depósitos metálicos no Bronze Final (XIII-VII A.C.) do Centro e Norte de Portugal. Aspectos sociais e arqueometalúrgicos. Umpublished PhD Dissertation, University of Coimbra, Portugal.

Bottaini, C., Mirão, J., Candeias, A., Vilaça, R. and Montero-Ruiz, I. (2015) A multi-analytical approach for the study of Late Bronze Age metals from Central Portugal. *Microscopy and Microanalysis*, Vol. 21, S6, pp. 134-135.

Bottaini, C., Vilaça, R., Schiavon, N., Mirão, J., Candeias, A., Bordalo, R., Paternoster, G. and Montero-Ruiz, I. (2016), New insights on Late Bronze Age Cu-metallurgy from Coles de Samuel. *Journal of Archaeological Science: Reports*, Vol. 7, pp. 344-357.

Bradley, R. (1990) *The passage of arms: an archaeological analysis of prehistoric hoards and votive deposits*, Cambridge University Press.

Brandherm, D. (2007) *Las Espadas del Bronce Final en la Península Ibérica y Baleares*. Prähistorische Bronzefunde, Abteilung IV, 16. Band, Stuttgart: Franz Steiner Verlag.

Cardoso, J.L. (2007) *Pré-História de Portugal*, Universidade Aberta, Lisboa.

Cardoso, J.L., Guerra, M.F. and Bragança, F. (1992) O depósito do Bronze fnal de Alqueva e a tipologia das lanças do Bronze Final português. *Mediterrâneo. Revista de Estudos Pluridisciplinares sobre as Sociedades Mediterrânicas*, Vol. 1, pp. 231-250.

Chapman, J. and Gaydarska, B.I. (2007) *Parts and wholes: fragmentation in prehistoric context*. Oxbow Books, Oxford.

Coffyn, A. (1985) *Le Bronze Final Atlantique das la Péninsule Ibérique*. Diffusion de Boccard, Paris.

Coffyn, A. (1998) Une entité contestée: le Bronze Atlantique. In *Existe uma Idade do Bronze Atlântico?*, S.O. Jorge (ed.), Trabalhos de Arqueologia, Vol. 10, pp. 166-178.

Cortez, F.R. (1951) O Esconderijo de Moreira (Monção). *Trabalhos de Antropologia e de Etnografa*, Vol. XIII, No 1-2, pp. 155-161.

Costa, J.G. (1963), Achado arqueológico encontrado em Solveira, concelho de Montalegre, em abril de 1961. *Lucerna, Cadernos de Arqueologia do Centro de Estudos Humanísticos*, Vol. 3, pp. 119-125.

Craddock, P.T. and Meeks, N.D. (1987) Iron in Ancient Copper. *Archaeometry*, Vol. 29, No 2, pp. 187-204.

Delfino, D. (2014) Bronze recycling during the Bronze Age: some consideration about two metallurgical regions. *Antrope*, Vol. 1, pp. 121-143.

Delfino, D. (2016) Model of metalwork and scrap's bronze circulation during the Late Bronze Age in the Middle Tagus. In Late Prehistory and Protohistory: Bronze Age and Iron Age. In *The emergence of warrior societies and its economic, social and environmental consequences*, F. Coimbra and D. Delfino (eds.), Proceedings of the XVII UISPP World Congress, Vol. 9, pp. 91-102.

Emami, M.A. and Bigham, M. (2013) Mechanism of corrosion due to unalloyed copper inclusion in ancient bronzes. *Surface Engineering*, Vol. 29, No 2, pp. 128-133.

Fernández-García, S. (1997) Los puñales tipo Porto de Mós en el Bronce Final de la Península Ibérica. *Complutum*, Vol. 8, pp. 97-124.

Figueiredo, E., Araujo, M.F. and Silva, R.J.C. (2011) A ponta de lança da gruta da nascente do Algarinho (Penela) no contexto da metalurgia do Bronze Final. In *Actas do Encontro Internacional sobre Ciência e Novas Tecnologias aplicadas à Arqueologia na Villa Romana do Rabaçal*, pp. 41-49.

Figueiredo, E., Silva R.J.C., Senna-Martínez J.C., Araújo M.F., Fernándes, F.M.B. and Vaz, J.L.I. (2010) Smelting and recycling evidences from the Late Bronze Age habitat siteof Baiões (Viseu, Portugal). *Journal of Archaeological Science*, Vol. 37, pp. 1623-1634.

Fontijn, D.R. (2001/2002) *Sacrifcial Landscape. Cultural biographies of persons, objects and natural places in the Bronze Age of the Southern Netherlands, c. 2300-600 BC*. Analecta Praehistorica Leidensia, Vol. 33/34.

Fortes, J. (1905-1908a) Esconderijo morgeano da Carpinteira (Melgaço). *Portugalia*, Vol. 2, No 3, p. 475.

Fortes, J. (1905-1908b) Esconderijo morgeano de Ganfei (Valença). *Portugalia*, Vol. 2, No 4, p. 661.

Fortes, J. (1905-1908c) Thesouro de Viatodos. Da idade do Bronze. *Portugalia*, Vol. 2, No 1, pp. 110-111.

Gabillot, M. (2003) *Dépôts et production métallique du Bronze Moyen en France Nord-Occidentale*, BAR International Series 1174, Oxford.

Giardino, C. (1995) *West Mediterranean between 14th and 8th century B.C. Mining and metallurgical spheres*, BAR International Series 612, Oxford.

Giardino, C. (1998) *I metalli nel mondo antico: introduzione all'archeometallurgia*, Ed. Laterza, Roma.

Gutiérrez Neira, P.C., Zucchiatti, A., Montero-Ruiz, I., Vilaça, R., Bottaini, C., Gener, M. and Climent-Font, A. (2011) Late Bronze Age hoard studied by PIXE. *Nuclear Instruments and Methods in Physics Research B*, Vol. 269, pp. 3082-3086.

Jalhay, E. (1944) O esconderijo pré-histórico de Pôrto do Concelho (Mação, Beira Baixa). *Brotéria*, Vol. 38, pp. 263-277.

Júnior, J.R.S. (1968) Quatro lanças de bronze de Lama Chã (Montalegre). *Trabalhos de Antrologia e Etnologia*, Vol. 20, No 3-4, pp. 339-347.

Leitão, N.M. and Lopes, J.M. (1984) Nótula sobre um achado arqueológico no lugar do Travasso, concelho da Mealhada. Instrumentos do Bronze. *Pampilhosa. Uma Terra e um Povo*, Vol. 3, pp. 29-36.

Meijide Cameselle, G. (1988) *Las espadas del Bronce Final en la Península Ibérica*. Arqueohistórica, Vol. 1.

Melo, Á.A. (2000) Armas, utensílios e esconderijos. Alguns aspectos da metalurgia do Bronze Final: o depósito do Casal dos Fiéis de Deus. *Revista Portuguesa de Arqueologia*, Vol. 3, No 1, pp. 15-120.

Monteagudo, L. (1977) *Die Beile auf der Iberischen Halbinsel*. Prahistorische Bronzefunde IX, Vol. Band 6, Munchen.

Montero, I., Rovira Llorens, S., Delibes De Castro, G., Fernández Manzano, J., Fernández-Posse, M.D., Herrán, J.I., Martín, C. and Maicas, R. (2003) High leaded bronze in the Late Bronze Age metallurgy of the Iberian Peninsula. In *Archaeometallurgy in Europe*, Associazione Italiana di Metallurgia, Milan.

Nebelsick, L. (2000) Rent asunder: ritual violence in Late Bronze Age Hoards. In *Metals make the world go round: the supply and circulation of metals in Bronze Age Europe*, C. Pare (ed.), Proceedings of a Conference held at the University of Birmingham in June 1997, 160-175.

Nunes, J.C. (1957) Un importante hallazgo del Bronce en Portugal. *Zephyrus*, Vol. 8, pp. 135-145.

Pereira, F.A. (1898) Dois machados de bronze. *O Archeologo Português*, s. I, Vol. 4, pp. 88-93.

Pereira, M.A.H. (1970) *Monumentos históricos do concelho de Mação*. Câmara Municipal de Mação.

Pereira, M.A.H. (1971) O esconderijo do bronze fnal de Coles de Samuel (Soure). *Arqueologia e História*, s. 9, vol. 3, pp. 165-174.

Quilliec, B. (2008) Use, wear and damage: treatment of bronze swords before deposition. In *Hoards from the Neolithic to the metal ages: technical and codifed practices*, C. Hamon and B. Quilliec (eds.), Session of the XIth Annual Meeting of the European Association of Archaeologists, BAR International Series 1758, pp. 67-78.

Rovira Llorens, S. and Ambert, P. (2002) Vasijas cerámicas para reducir minerales de cobre en la Península Ibérica y en la Francia meridional. *Trabajos de Prehistoria*, Vol. 59, No 1, pp. 89-105.

Ruiz-Gálvez Priego, M. (1995) *Ritos de paso y puntos de paso: la Ría de Huelva en el mundo del Bronce Final Europeo*. Universidade Complutense, Madrid.

Sarabia-Herrero, F.J. (1992) Arqueología experimental. La fundición de bronce en la Prehistoria Reciente. *Revista de Arqueología*, Vol. 130, pp. 12-22.

Sarmento, F.M. (1888) Antigualhas. *Revista de Guimarães*, Vol. 5, No 4, pp. 157-163.

Scott, D.A. (1991) *Metallography and Microstructure in Ancient and Historic Metals*. The J. Paul Getty Trust.

Vasconcelos, J.L. (1919-1920) Estudos sobre a época do Bronze em Portugal. VIII - Tesouro do Casal dos Fiéis-de-Deus. *O Archeologo Português*, s. I, Vol. 24, pp. 193-195.

Veiga, S.P.M.E. da (1891) *Antiguidades monumentaes do Algarve: tempos prehistoricos*. Imprensa nacional, Lisboa, Vol. IV.

Verron, G. (1973) Méthodes statistiqueset étude des cachettes complexes de l' Age du Bronze. In *L' Homme d' Hier et Aujourd' hui. Recueil d' Études en Hommage à André Leroi-Gourhan*, pp. 609-624.

Viana, T.S. (1938) Um esconderijo de fundidor. *Revista Alto Minho*, Vol. 1, pp. 7-9.

Vilaça, R., Almeida, S., Bottaini, C., Marques, J.N. and Montero-Ruiz, I. (2012b) Metalurgia do castro do Cabeço da Argemela (Fundão): formas, conteúdos, produções e contextos. In *Povoamento e Exploração de Recursos Mineiros na Europa Atlântica Ocidental*, C.M.B. Martins, A.M. Bettencourt, J.I. Martins and J. Carvalho (eds.), Actas do 1° Congresso Internacional, CITCEM, Braga, pp. 427-452.

Vilaça, R. (1997) Metalurgia do Bronze fnal da Beira Interior. Revisão dos dados à luz de novos resultados. *Estudos Pré- históricos*, Vol. 5, pp. 123-154.

Vilaça, R. (2006) Depósitos de Bronze do Território Português. Um debate em aberto. *O Arqueólogo Português*, s. III, Vol. 24, pp. 9-150.

Vilaça, R., Bottaini, C. and Montero-Ruiz, I. (2012a) O depósito do Cabeço de Maria Candal, Freixianda (Ourém, Portugal). *O Arqueólogo Portugês*, s. V, Vol. 2, pp. 297-353.

Villas-Bôas, J.S. (1947) Nuevos elementos del Bronce Atlántico en Portugal. In *Crónica del II Congreso Arqueológico del Sudeste Español* (Albacete 1946), Imp. Provincial.

York, J. (2002) The life cycle of Bronze Age metalwork from Thames. *Oxford Journal of Archaeology*, Vol. 21, No 1, pp. 77-92.

11

INTEGRATED DYNAMIC AND THERMOGRAPHY INVESTIGATION OF MALLORCA CATHEDRAL

Ahmed Elyamani[1], Oriol Caselles[2], Pere Roca[2] and Jaime Clapes[2]

[1]*Archaeological Conservation Department, Cairo University, Giza, Egypt*
[2]*Department of Civil and Environmental Engineering, Technical University of Catalonia, Barcelona, Spain*

Corresponding author: Ahmed Elyamani (a_elyamani@cu.edu.eg)

ABSTRACT

An integrated investigation of engineering archaeometry was carried out using dynamic identification, dynamic monitoring and Infra-Red (IR) thermography for the study of the dynamic behavior of Mallorca cathedral in Spain. The cathedral is a large historical masonry structure built during 14-16th c. Dynamic identification and monitoring allowed the capturing of eight natural frequencies of the cathedral. IR thermography was used as a complementary inspection technique in the context of a continuous monitoring. Usually, IR thermography is used punctually for the inspection of a part of an inspected structure. Here an alternative was tried as the IR camera was installed for two two-weeks periods in the winter and in the summer of 2011 to monitor the stone surface temperature of a large portion of the cathedral. The correlation between the cathedral natural frequencies and the stone surface temperature of some selected structural elements was investigated and compared with the correlation with the external and the internal temperatures. It was found that the correlation with stone surface temperature was lower than that with external temperature. The study allowed a better understanding of the influence of temperature changes on the structure's dynamic behavior.

KEYWORDS: Mallorca Cathedral, Historical Structures, In-situ Investigation, Dynamic Identification, Dynamic Monitoring, IR Thermography, Air Temperature, Stone Temperature

1. INTRODUCTION

Historical structures are very important assets of the world heritage as cultural resources involving important artistic, spiritual, technical and scientific merits. They contribute to the identity of cultures and countries and provide valuable documents on the great achievements from the past. Moreover, they represent important economic resources. For these reasons and many others, modern societies allocate great technical and economical effort to the conservation of their architectural heritage. European researchers, in particular, have carried out a number of research projects on the subject (PERPETUATE, 2010-2012, SEVERES, 2010-2012, PROHITECH, 2004-2008, EU-INDIA, 2004-2006, RISK-UE, 2001-2004, CHIME, 2000-2003).

In fact, the preservation of the architectural heritage faces significant challenges ranging from the difficulty in understanding the historical construction materials to the complexity of possible actions influencing on it. Due to these difficulties, often faced when assessing the structural safety of a historic structure, the assessment of heritage structures requires combining different approaches such as historical investigation, inspection, experiments, static monitoring, dynamic monitoring and structural analysis. The aim is to respect the authenticity of the historic structure, to the extent possible, by designing an efficient solution which, while attaining the required safety level, minimizes the impact in terms of material and structural alteration. In the study here presented, dynamic identification, dynamic monitoring and Infra-Red (IR) thermography were employed for studying the dynamic behavior of Mallorca cathedral, one of the largest worldwide masonry historical structures, and its dependency on external temperature, internal temperature and stone surface temperature.

Two different but interconnected activities, namely dynamic identification and dynamic monitoring, can be envisaged for the study of the dynamic response of historical structures. While dynamic identification is based on punctual measurements of the dynamic response by means of tests performed in a discrete way, dynamic monitoring involves the continuous measurement of the dynamic properties.

Dynamic identification is carried out to obtain information on the global dynamic behavior of the structure, including natural frequencies, mode shapes and damping coefficients. It is also an efficient tool to validate and update structural numerical models by comparing experimental and numerical natural frequencies and mode shapes (Elyamani and Roca, 2018a,b). Some of the early applications of dynamic identification in studying historic structures can be found in (Chiostrini et al., 1992; Erdik et al., 1993; Modena et al., 1997). For recent applications, the reader is referred to (Diaferio et al., 2015; Foti et al., 2014; Ceroni et al., 2014; Cagnan et al., 2015; Votsis et al., 2015; Votsis et al., 2012).

Dynamic monitoring can be carried out to confirm the obtained information from the dynamic identification. Additionally, it aims at studying the evolution of modal parameters in time, studying the influence of environmental climatic effects (temperature, humidity, etc.) on the dynamic parameters and capturing the dynamic response in the occasion of possible seismic events, among other possible purposes (Elyamani and Roca, 2018a,b). Some recent applications have been presented by (Masciotta et al., 2016; Basto et al., 2016; Lorenzoni et al., 2013; Rivera et al., 2008; Cabboi et al., 2014).

Most materials absorb Infrared Radiation (IR) over a wide range of wavelengths which results in an increase in their temperature. When an object has a temperature greater than absolute zero it emits IR energy. IR thermography is a nondestructive inspection technique which converts the emitted IR radiation pattern into a visual image by the usage of an IR camera. An IR camera measures, calculates and displays the emitted IR radiation from an object (Clark et al., 2003).

IR thermography has been applied to several emblematic historical structures for inspection purposes. For instance, the IR thermography was used extensively in the inspection activities carried out on the church of Nativity in Bethlehem (Faella et al., 2012). The IR thermography showed: 1) moisture problems due to rainwater seepage and re-climbing moisture presence in several masonry walls; 2) the plugging of some openings; 3) nearly homogenous materials used in the roof except one area in which different materials were used; and 4) great seepages of rainwater in the narthex roof caused by the lack of an efficient waste disposal system for drainage. Binda et al. (Binda et al., 2011) used IR thermography as one of the inspection techniques applied to the Spanish Fortress damaged by L'Aquila earthquake. Because the masonry was hidden by thick plaster, the IR thermography was used to reveal its texture, which helped in identifying the most representative areas where to execute minor destructive tests like flat-jack. Tavukçuoğlu et al. (2010) used the IR thermography in the inspection of a 16th century historical mosque. The aim was to discover the activeness of observed structural cracks. Other studies involving the use of thermography in ancient structures can be found in (Jo and Lee, 2014; Alves et al., 2014; Bagavathiappan et al., 2013; Martinez et al., 2013).

This research was carried out within the research project NIKER (NIKER, 2010-2012) aimed at investigating the effects of earthquakes on historical constructions via extensive experimental and numerical studies applied to several case studies. Mallorca cathedral was chosen as one of the selected case studies. A comprehensive review on the restoration of the cathedral is given in Elyamani and Roca (2018c).

The experimental investigation activities employed for the study of the cathedral included Ambient Vibration Testing (AVT) and dynamic monitoring. An IR thermography was used as a complementary system for the measurement of temperature. Usually, the IR thermography is used punctually for inspecting a certain part of a structure. Here, an alternative application was tried. The IR camera was used to continuously monitor the temperature during two two-weeks periods within summer and winter of 2011. This allowed a detailed investigation of the correlation between the natural frequencies of the cathedral and the stone surface temperature of different structural elements of the cathedral like columns, vaults and arches.

2. MALLORCA CATHEDRAL

Mallorca cathedral is a Cultural Heritage of National Interest in Spain since 1931 (Figs.1 and 2). It is located in the city of Palma, in Mallorca Island. When compared with other worldwide Gothic cathedrals, it is found that its piers show an unusually large slenderness ratio, while its main nave span is the second longest span among Gothic cathedrals after Girona cathedral. Its main nave is among the highest ones after those of Beauvais and Milan cathedrals.

The construction started in the beginning of the 14th century and continued to the beginning of the 17th century. The first built part was the Trinity Chapel (part I in Figure 3) in year 1311. About 60 years later the Royal Chapel (part II in Figure 3) was finished. It was then decided to modify the design from that of a single nave building to a three-nave one. No documented justifications behind this decision were revealed by any historical research carried so far about the cathedral construction. The imposing main large nave and the west facade (part III in Figure 3) were completed by the year 1601.

Figure 1. Mallorca Cathedral from outside: apse area (left), south façade (centre) and main façade (right).

Regarding the geometrical configuration of the cathedral (Figure 3), it is found that the main nave has a length of 77 m distributed over eight bays and the width covered by the naves is 35.3 m. The lateral nave and the central nave spans are 8.75 m and 17.8 m, respectively. The lateral naves are covered by pointed vaults of simple square plan. The central nave is covered by vaults of double square plan. This scheme is repeated in all the bays of the naves except in the 5th one (from the choir), due to the presence of lateral doors. In this bay, the longitudinal span of the vaults is slightly longer. The height reached by the vaults at their highest point (the key of the transverse arches) is about 44 m. The cathedral is also unique in being the Gothic cathedral with the highest lateral naves (29.4 m). All of the octagonal columns have a circumscribed diameter of 1.7 m except those of the first three bays from the choir that have a slightly lesser value of 1.6 m. More information on the cathedral can be found at (Caselles et al., 2012; Elyamani et al., 2017a; Gonzalez et al., 2008; Elyamani et al., 2017b; Pela et al., 2014; Elyamani, 2015; Caselles et al., 2015; Elyamani et al., 2012; Roca et al., 2013).

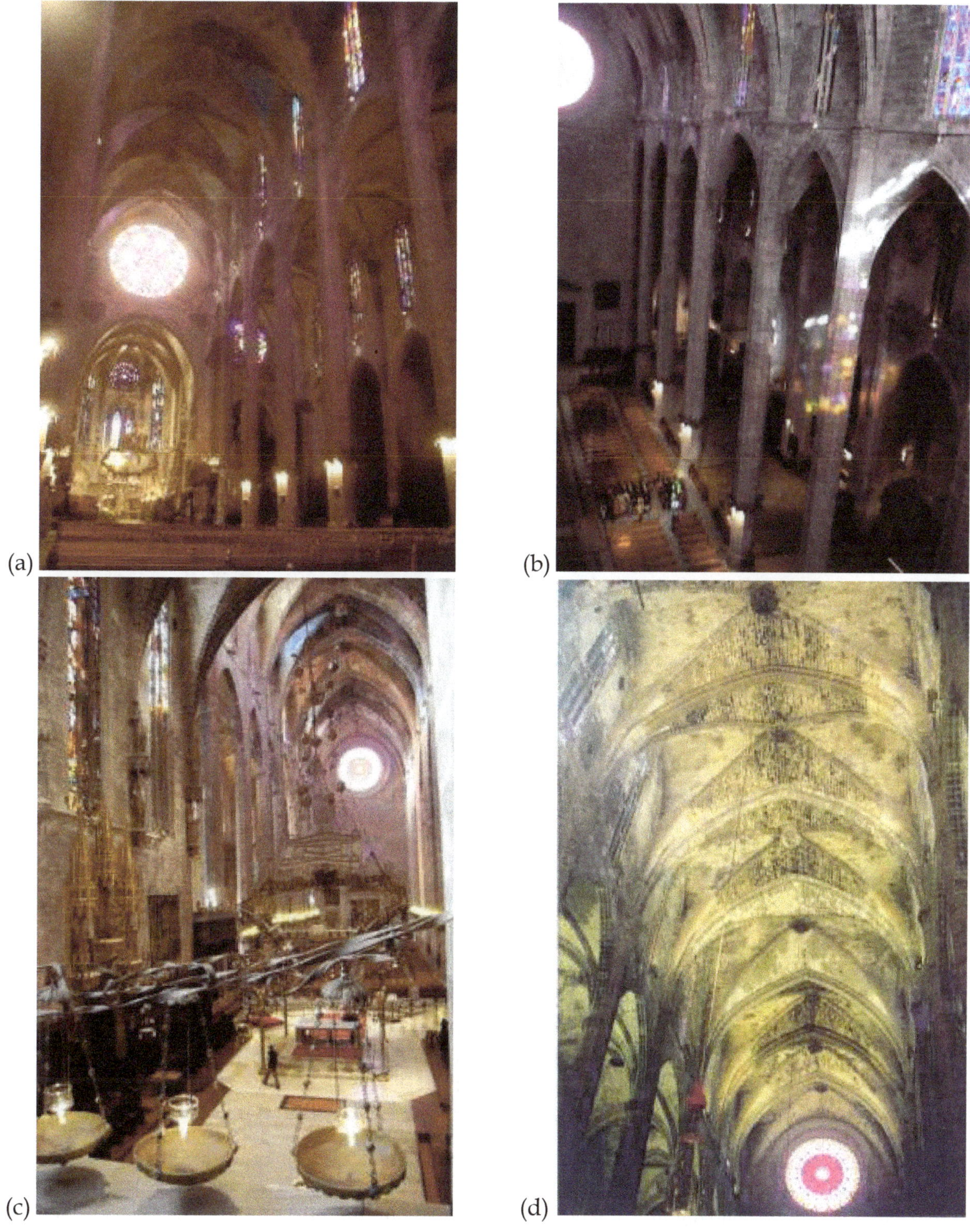

Figure 2. Internal views of Mallorca cathedral: (a) view of the choir, central nave and south lateral nave; (b) view of the west façade and north nave showing the slenderness of columns and the upper and lower clerestory walls; (c) view of the central nave from the choir; and (d) central nave vaults .

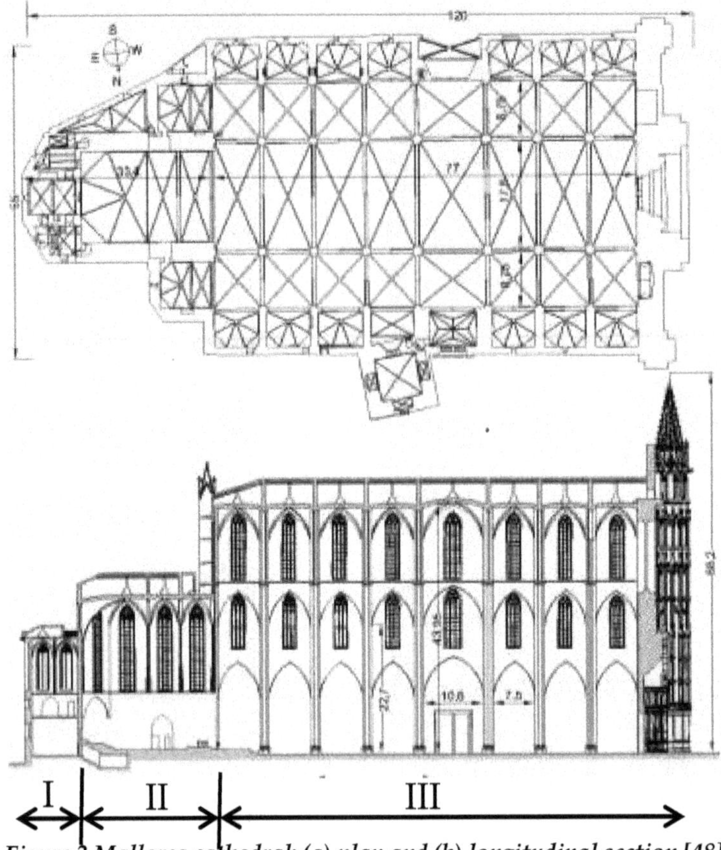

Figure 3.Mallorca cathedral: (a) plan and (b) longitudinal section [48].

2. DYNAMIC INVESTIGATION OF THE CATHEDRAL

2.1 *Ambient vibration testing (AVT)*

The objective of AVT was to identify the natural frequencies, mode shapes and damping ratios of the cathedral. The natural frequencies and modes shapes were used to update the numerical model of the cathedral which was then used in the seismic analysis of it (Elyamani et al., 2017a). A brief about AVT is given here and full details can be consulted at (Elyamani et al., 2017b; Elyamani, 2015).

The tests configuration was based on a preliminary modal analysis carried out using an initial FE model of the cathedral. It was noticed that only the first and the second modes were global ones with considerable mass participation and characterized by predominant movement of the main and lateral naves of the cathedral. Consequently, the used accelerometers were organized in different setups so that capturing these two modes would be achievable. Three tri-axial force balance accelerometers were used in AVT and the sampling rate was 100 samples per second.

The obtained signals during AVT were processed for dynamic identification using MACEC software (MACEC, 2011). Four different methods were employed: the Frequency Domain Decomposition (FDD) (Brincker et al., 2001); reference-based covariance-driven Stochastic Subspace Identification (SSI-cov/ref) (Peeters and De Roeck, 1999); reference-based data-driven Stochastic Subspace Identification (SSI-data/ref) (Peetres and De Roeck, 1999) and poly-reference Least Squares Complex Frequency domain identification (pLSCF) (Peetres and Van der Auweraer, 2005). Eight modes were identified. The natural frequencies of all of them were satisfactory identified (Table 1), whereas, the mode shapes and the damping ratios of only three of them were satisfactory identified.

Table 1. Identified natural frequencies (Hz) using different methods.

Identification method	Mode ID.							
	1	2	3	4	5	6	7	8
FDD	1.143	1.431	1.503	1.569	1.942	2.232	2.406	2.649
SSI-cov/ref	1.162	1.433	1.511	1.576	1.939	2.214	2.421	2.656
SSI-data/ref	1.166	1.445	1.514	1.576	1.942	2.241	2.434	2.662
pLSCF	1.145	1.430	1.509	1.576	1.943	2.234	2.432	2.666

2.2 Dynamic monitoring

The use of AVT was followed by a continuous dynamic monitoring system. A brief is given here and more details can be referred to at (Elyamani et al., 2017b; Elyamani, 2015). The system was composed of a digitizer, a Data Acquisition system (DAQ), a Global Positioning System (GPS) antenna, an internet router and the three tri-axial accelerometers previously used in the dynamic identification tests, Figure 4. The system worked properly for two periods: from 17/12/2010 to 13/9/2011and from 18/5/2012 to 29/12/2012. Within this second period, the system was interrupted from 30/7/2012 to 4/9/2012. The system was programmed to continuously measure, record, and wirelessly transfer the records of the accelerations on a 24 h basis. The natural frequencies were determined manually using the Peak Picking (PP) method four times per day: at 6 a.m. (06:00), 2 p.m. (14:00), 8 p.m. (20:00) and 12 a.m. (24:00) during the entire monitored periods.

The eight natural frequencies identified from AVT were identified continuously by the system. The identified natural frequencies were plotted versus the time as presented in Figure 5. The gap in the second period corresponds to the dates previously mentioned during which the system was out of service due to technical problems.

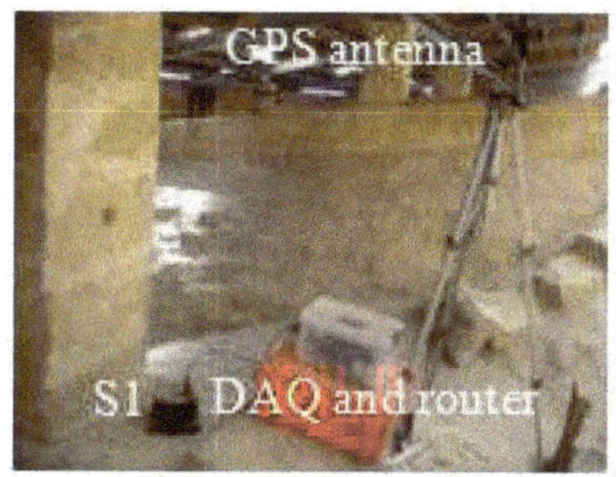

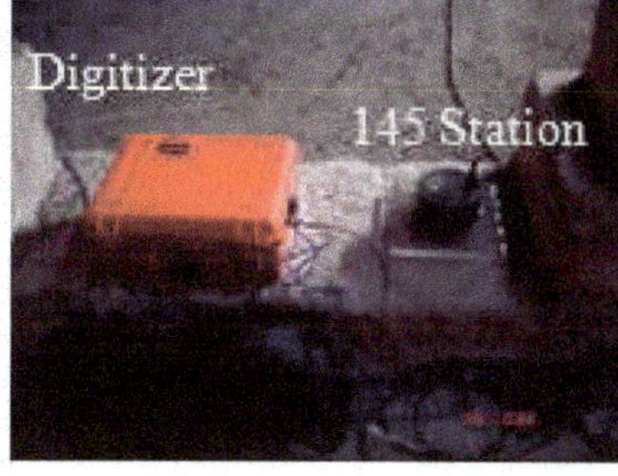

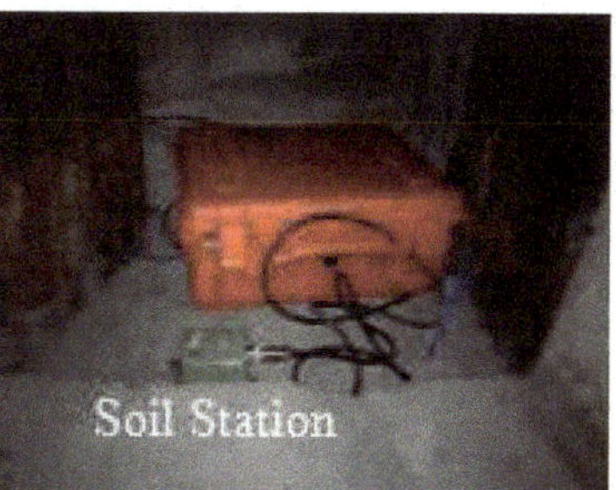

Figure 4.The dynamic system in operation: accelerometer S1, DAQ, router and GPS antenna (left); accelerometer 145-Station and digitizer (middle); and accelerometer Soil-station (right).

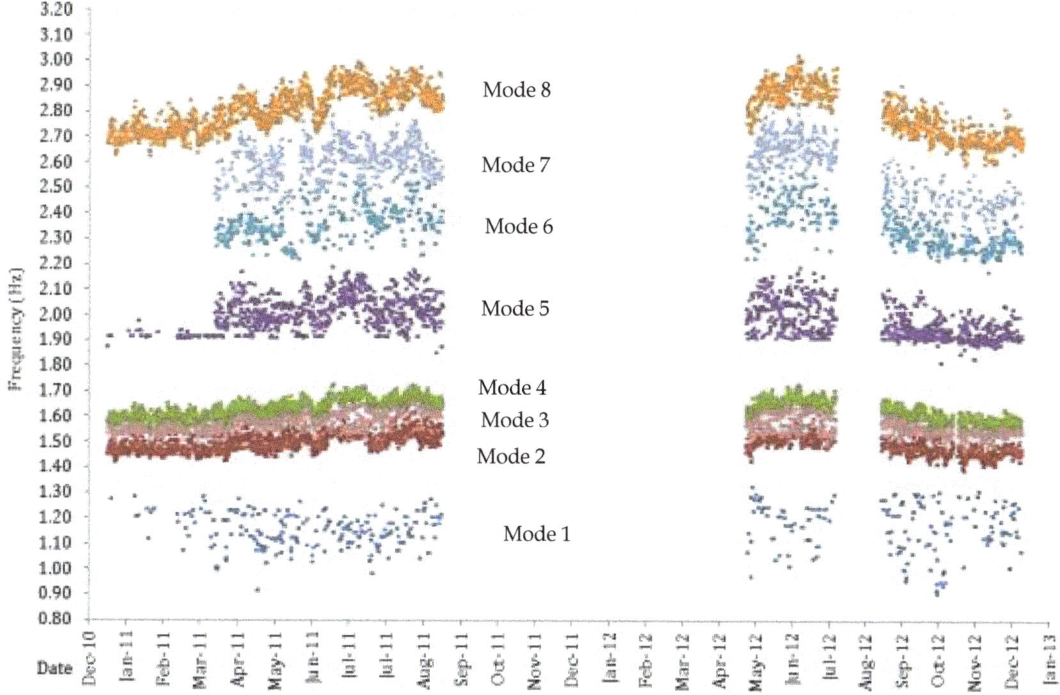

Figure 5. Evolution of the natural frequencies of the cathedral over time.

In the first monitoring period, the cathedral natural frequencies showed an increasing trend that can be attributed to the raising of the temperature, since the monitoring started in winter and ended in summer. The contrary was found for the second monitoring period during which a decreasing trend was noticed, also attributed to the temperature variations as the monitoring started in summer and ended in winter.

Table 2. Comparing natural frequencies (Hz) from AVT and dynamic monitoring, and amount of changes of the natural frequencies over the monitoring period.

Mode number	1	2	3	4	5	6	7	8
AVT (SSI-cov/ref)	1.162	1.433	1.511	1.576	1.939	2.214	2.421	2.656
Dynamic monitoring	1.158	1.496	1.576	1.631	1.988	2.353	2.593	2.797
Coefficient of Variation (CV) (%)	7.1	2.57	2.49	2.29	3.51	3.48	3.74	3.18
(Max.-Min.)/Max. (%)	31.8	14.9	13.9	10.4	17.0	16.6	18.5	14.3

Table 3. Correlation coefficients between temperature and cathedral frequencies.

	Mode ID.							
Regression model	1	2	3	4	5	6	7	8
Linear	0.197	0.766	0.544	0.834	0.618	0.640	0.602	0.806
Quadratic	0.241	0.802	0.544	0.854	0.643	0.660	0.603	0.819

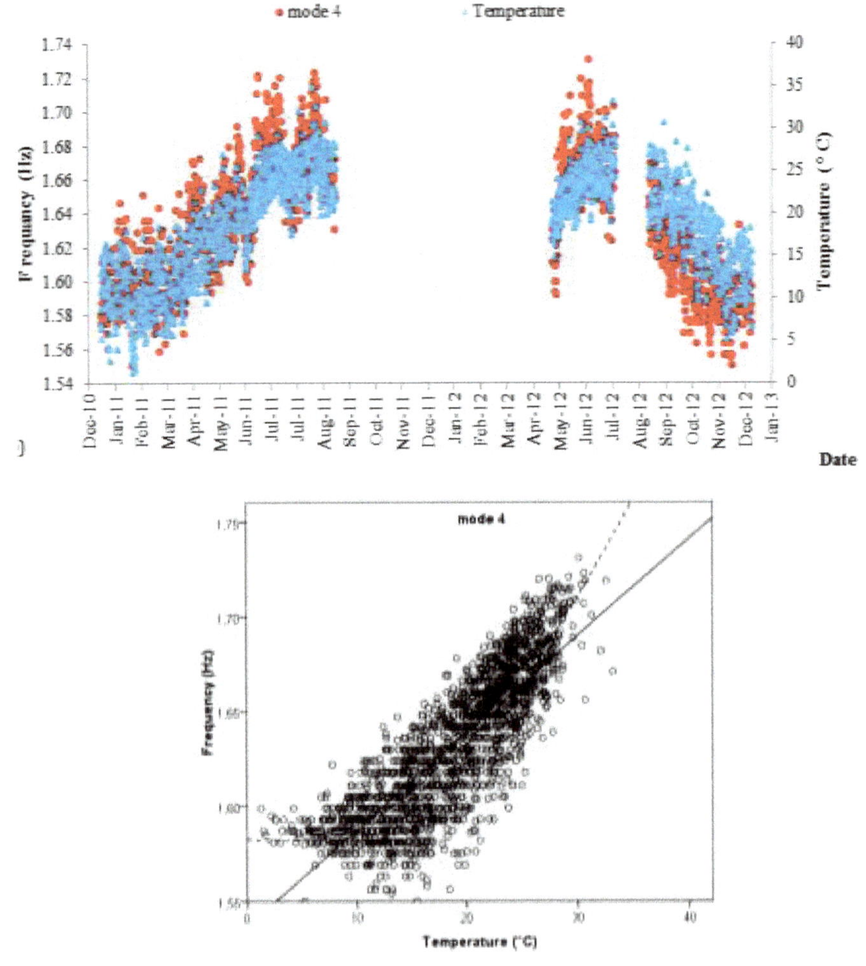

Figure 6. Changes of the natural frequency of mode 4 with external temperature (top) and correlation with external temperature (bottom). Linear and quadratic regression models are in solid and dashed lines, respectively.

It can be observed that modes 2, 3, 4 and 8 showed curves characterized by more continuous and intensive readings when compared to the curves of the other modes 1, 5, 6 and 7, that showed less continuity and intensity of readings. In addition, the curves of modes 2, 3, 4 and 8 showed a lesser scattering in comparison with the curves of other modes. The increasing and decreasing trends observed over time were clearer in the case of the continuously detected modes 2, 3, 4 and 8, whereas no distinguishable trends were observed for the remaining modes.

The frequencies detected in the dynamic tests were lesser than the mean values found by the dynamic monitoring system, Table 2. This difference can be attributed to the fact that the tests were performed in winter, whereas the monitoring system covered several summer months. The months from May to July and also half of the month of September were repeated two times in the entire monitoring period, thus resulting in an average temperature about 18.4 °C, whereas in the tests it was about 7.4 °C.

Table 2 also reports the changes of the natural frequencies over the whole monitoring period. In terms of coefficient of variation (CV), the modes 2, 3, 4, and 8 showed the lowest values. These modes were more centralized and manifested less variability when compared with the rest of the modes which had higher CV values. The same note can be stated when relating the range (maximum–minimum) with the maximum value as shown in the last row of the table. The Modes 2, 3, 4, and 8 had less variability than other modes. The very high value of Mode 1 could be related to the difficulty of detection rather than to changes in environmental conditions.

The change of the frequencies with temperature was plotted for the eight detected modes (Figure 6 for mode 4 as an example). It was noticed that the relation was clearer and the in-phase oscillation was more evident for modes 2, 4 and 8 than for modes 3, 5, 6 and 7. The frequency variations under changes of exterior temperature were investigated and both the correlation and the regression were studied, Figure 6. It can be noticed in Figure 6 that the trend is not exactly linear. Therefore, both of linear regression and quadratic regression were considered to investigate into more detail the type of the relation between temperature and frequencies. The obtained correlation coefficients are summarized in Table 3. As can be seen from the comparison among all models, a linear relation between temperature and natural frequencies provided a good approximation. No significant increase in the coefficients of correlation was obtained when considering a higher degree model. The correlation coefficient of the quadratic model was only slightly higher than that of the linear one. The highest correlation value was around 0.80 to 0.86 for modes 2, 4 and 8, followed by the correlation coefficients ranging from 0.55 to 0.66 for modes 3, 5, 6, and 7.

3. THERMOGRAPHIC INVESTIGATION

3.1 Description of the thermographic monitoring System

An infrared (IR) camera of type "Thermo GEAR G120" produced by NEC Company was used. Its main characteristics are: 1) measuring range from -40° C to 500° C with accuracy of ±2°C or ±2% of reading, whichever is greater; 2) thermal image of 320 pixels (horizontal) X 240 pixels (vertical); 3) spectral range from 8 to 14 μm; 4) frame rate of 60 frames/sec; 5) automatic focusing with focal distance from 10 cm to infinity; and 6) automatic recording of images with interval from 3s to 60 min.

It worked at the same location in two periods: 1) in the winter of 2011 for 14 days from 27/1 (at 11:15) to 9/2 (at 23:45), and 2) in the summer of the same year for 16 days from 28/6 (at 8:16) to 13/7 (at 22:46).

The IR camera position and its coverage area are shown in Figure 7. As shown, it was located inside the north pulpit and directed to the arches, the vaults, the upper clerestory and the columns of the main nave. This place allowed the IR camera to cover a large portion of the first five bays of the main nave. The IR camera recorded photos each half an hour. A sample of the monitoring photos in the summer and the winter periods is shown in Figure 8.

(a)

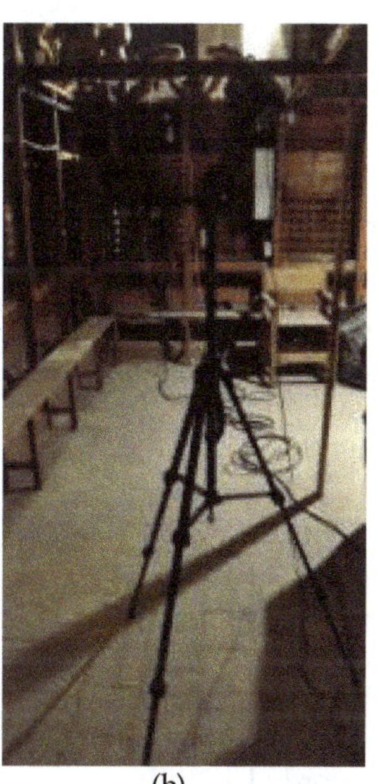

(b)

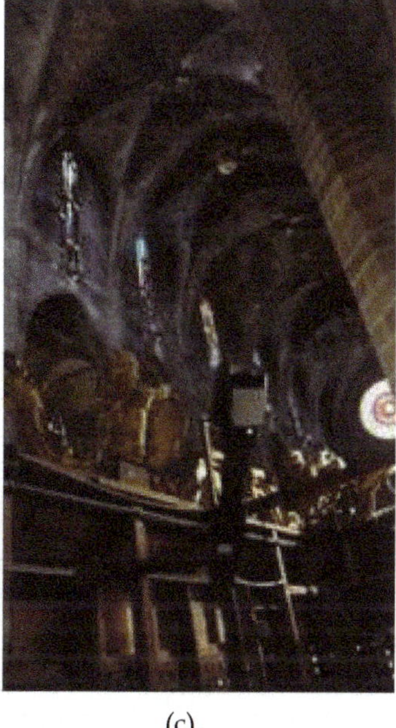

(c)

Figure 7. Mallorca cathedral thermography monitoring: (a) the red circle shows the IR camera position; (b) the IR camera during operation (inside the pulpit); and (c) the area covered by the IR camera.

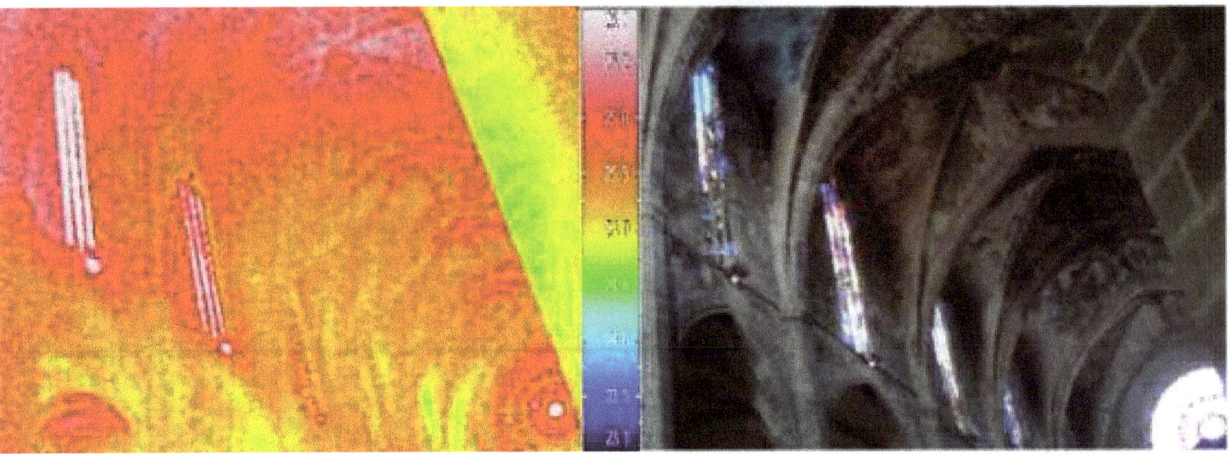

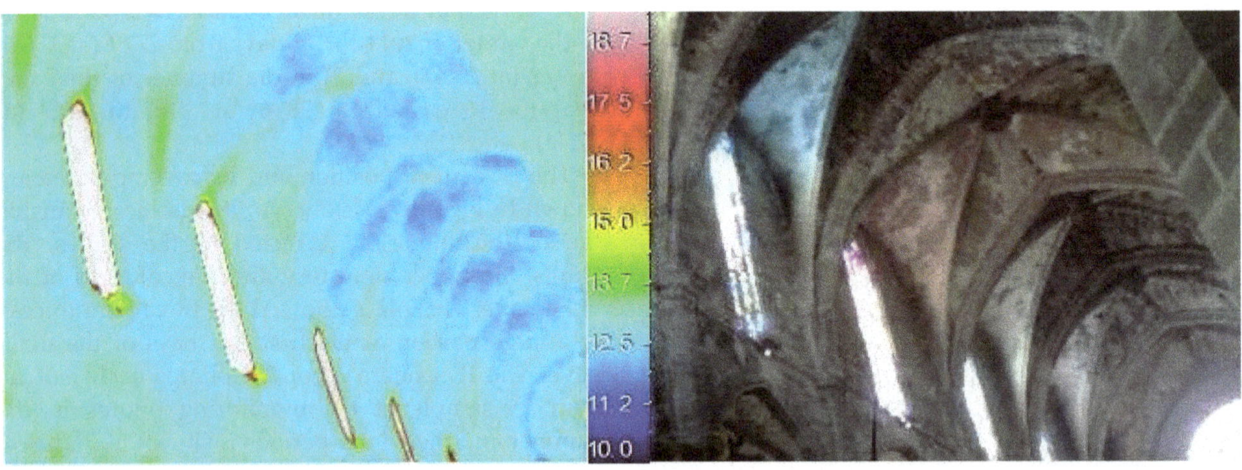

Figure 8. Two examples of the thermography monitoring: 1) summer period on 2nd of July 2011 at 9:46 a.m. (top); and 2) winter period on 2nd of February 2011 at 13:15 (bottom). Temperature scale in (°C).

3.2 Comparisons between different temperatures

For each day of the two monitoring periods, four IR photos were processed at the same times of the dynamic monitoring data, i.e., at 6 a.m., 2 p.m., 8 p.m. and 12 a.m. Using the software "Inf ReC Analyzer NS9500 Standard" which was provided with the IR camera, the stone surface temperature was determined for two samples from the considered structural elements (the columns, the clerestory walls, the arches and the vaults) as shown in Figure 9. In the figure also the places of the three temperature sensors used in the summer period are shown.

The stone surface temperature recorded is influenced by the distance from the IR camera, the ambient relative humidity, the ambient temperature and the stone emissivity. The available geometrical survey of the cathedral provided the distance from the IR camera to each of the considered structural elements samples. An average ambient relative humidity and temperature of 65% and 27.9 °c, respectively, were used for the summer period and 83% and 13.5 °c for the winter period. These approximate values were estimated from the previous static monitoring system that worked for five years (from 2003 to 2008) and showed clearly the repeated cycles experienced by these parameters. More details about this monitoring are available in (Gonzalez et al., 2008). Regarding, the stone emissivity, the cathedral was built mainly from limestone which has an emissivity of 0.95 according to the references on the subject (Gosse, 1986; Adler, 1969).

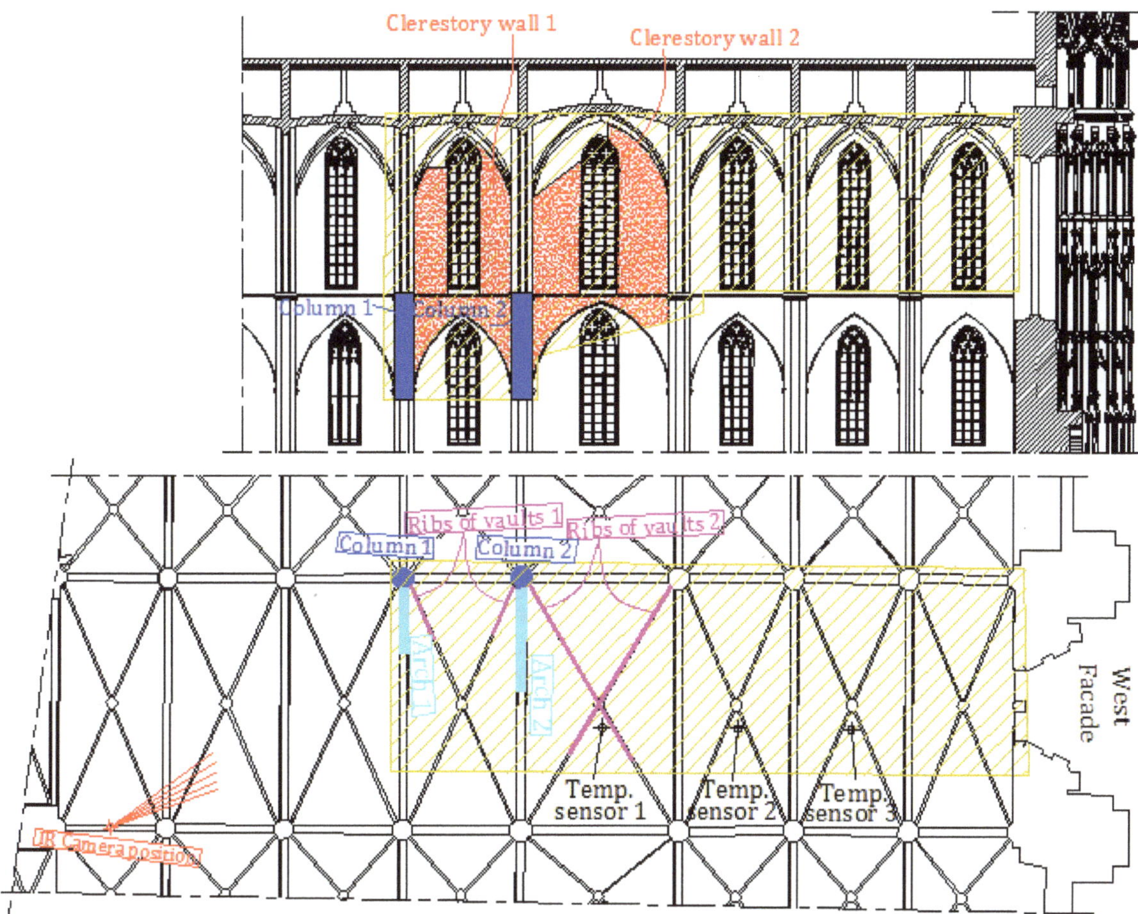

Figure 9. Selected samples from structural elements within the IR camera coverage area: clerestory walls and columns (top), arches, columns and vaults (bottom). Coverage area hatched in light brown.

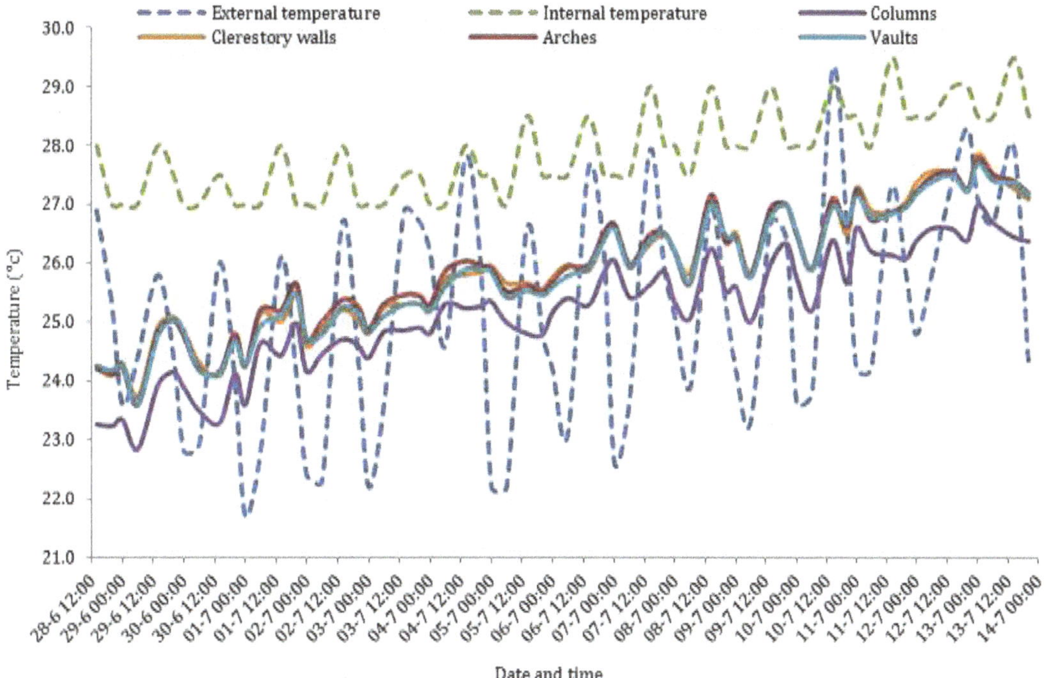

Figure 10. Comparison between external, internal and stone surface temperatures in the summer period from 28/6/2011 to 13/7/2011.

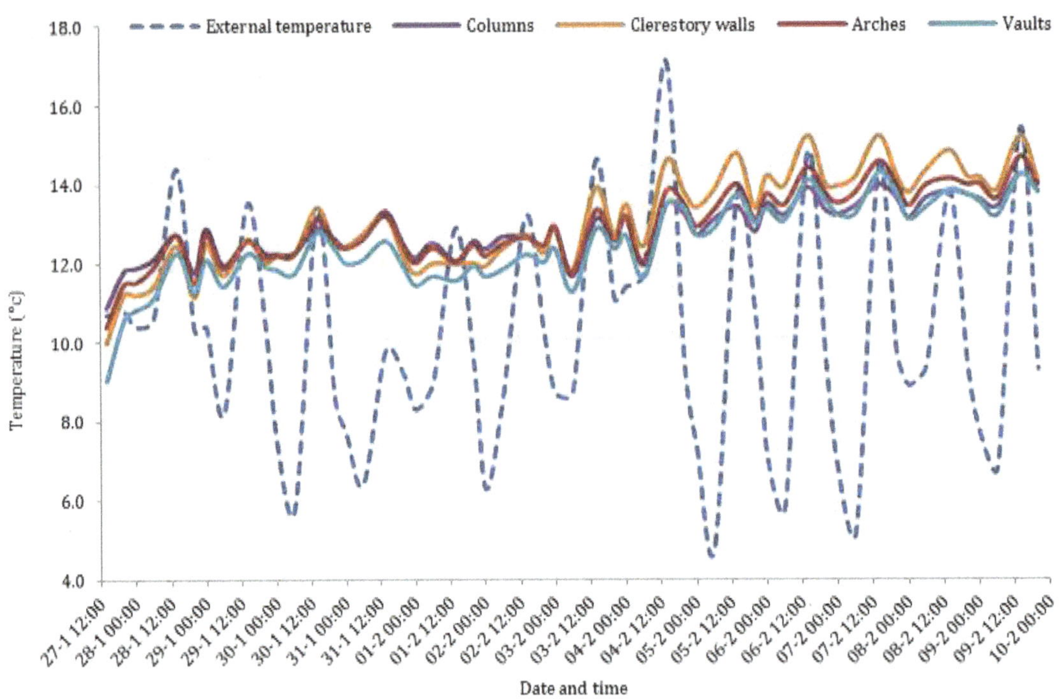

Figure 11. Comparison between external and stone surface temperatures in the winter period from 27/1/2011 to 9/2/2011.

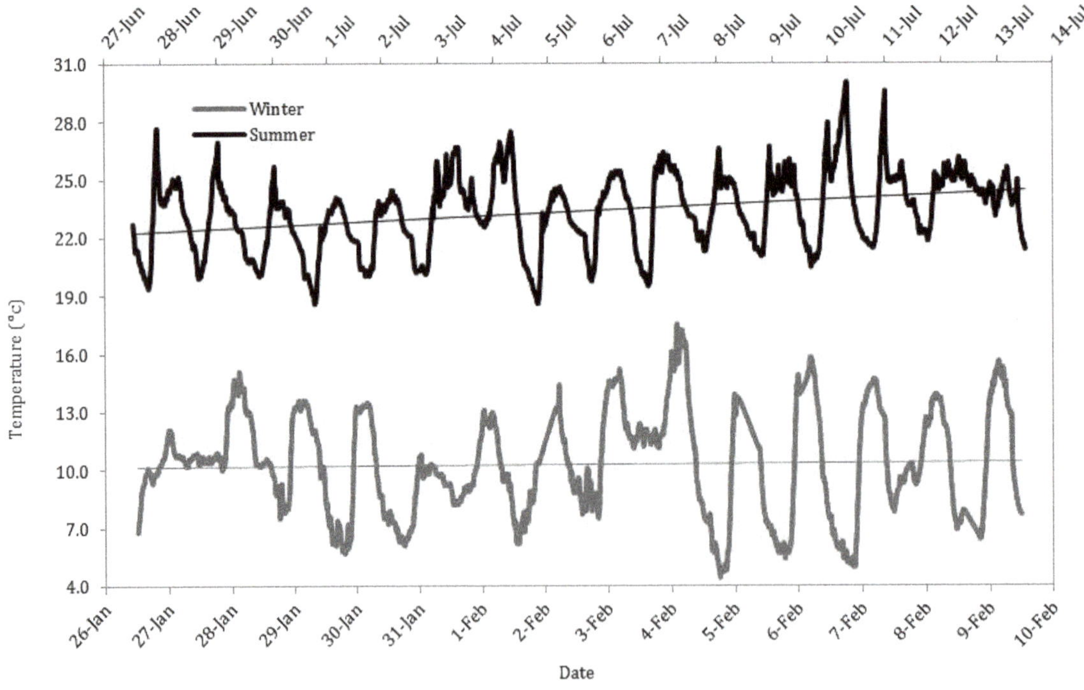

Figure 12. Comparison between external temperatures for the summer and winter periods. The trend lines are also shown.

A comparison was made between the external temperature (measured from a near meteorological station), the internal temperature (measured in summer only using temperature sensors) and the stone surface temperature of the considered structural elements for the summer period (Figure 10) and the winter period (Figure 11). It can be seen that the stone surface temperatures of the different structural elements were in phase and very near to each other for the two monitoring periods. For the summer period, the internal and the external temperatures were in phase, whereas, the stone surface temperature was sometimes delayed with respect to the external and the internal temperatures. In the winter period, the stone surface temperature was in phase with the external temperature.

To explain the reason of the delay of the stone surface temperature in the summer period, a comparison between the external temperature of the summer and the winter periods is shown in Figure 12. It can be noticed that an increasing trend was observed during the summer period, whereas a constant trend was obtained during winter. It can be assumed that, in the summer period, the stone was not able to radiate the stored heat as fast as the rapidly increasing external temperature, therefore producing a delay in the variation of surface temperature with respect to the external one. This phenomenon disappeared in the winter period during which the stone could radiate the heat in phase with the almost constant rate of change of the external temperature.

3.3 Correlation between natural frequencies and different temperatures

An acceptable qualitative correlation was found between the natural frequencies of the cathedral and the stone temperature changes. Figure 13 shows this correlation for mode 4 as an example. The stone surface temperature indicated in Figure 13 corresponds to the average temperature of the columns, the vaults, the arches and the clerestory walls.

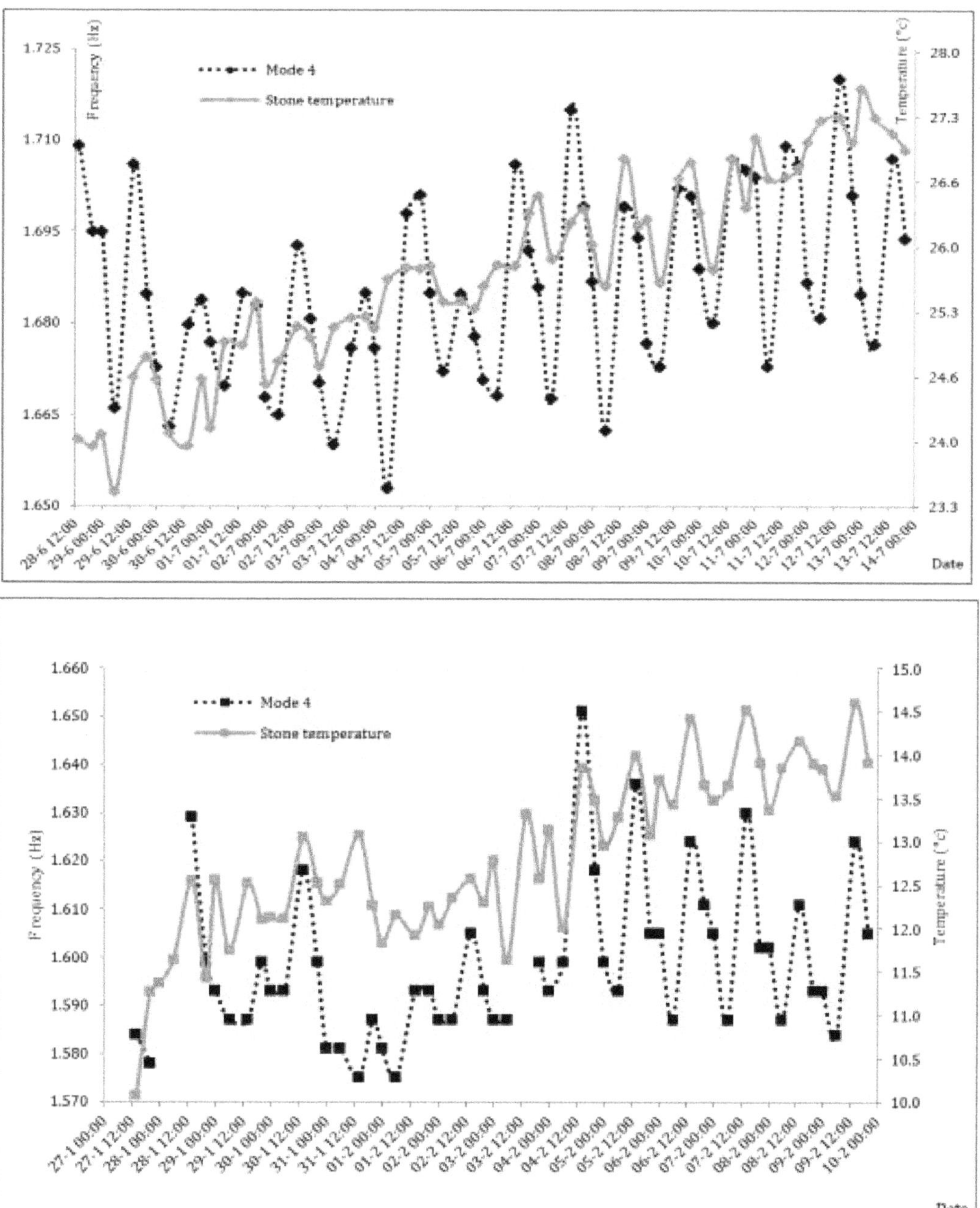

Figure 13. Changes of mode 4 with stone temperature: summer period (top); and winter period (bottom).

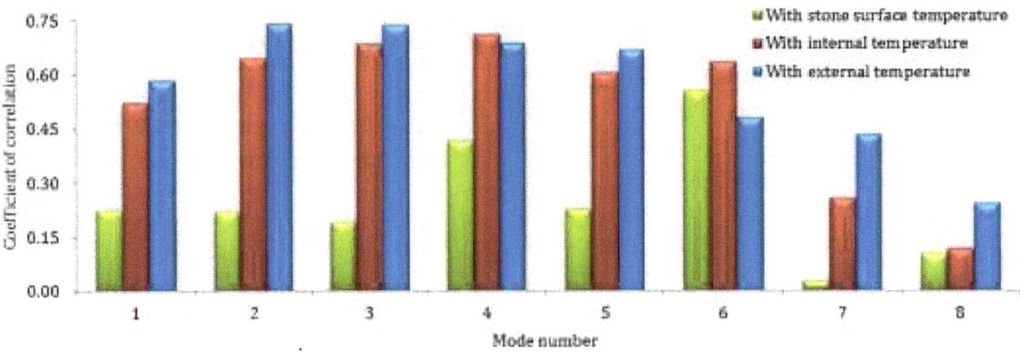

Figure 14. Summer period: comparison between coefficients of correlation of different temperatures with the first eight modes of the cathedral.

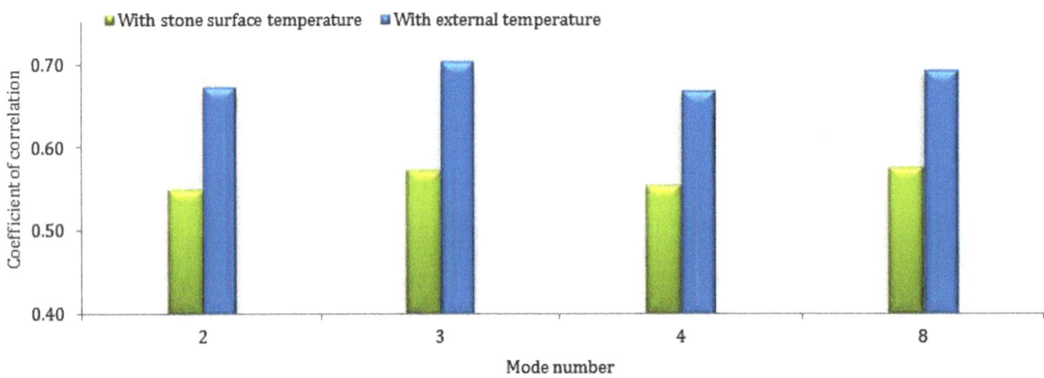

Figure 15. Winter period: comparison between coefficients of correlation of different temperatures with four of the cathedral modes.

Table 4. Statistical variations in the cathedral frequencies in the summer and winter periods.

Monitored period	Parameter	Mode no.							
		1	2	3	4	5	6	7	8
Summer 28/6-13/7/2011	CV (%)	2,79	1,59	2,38	0,91	2,19	3,49	2,42	1,21
	$\frac{(\text{Max.}-\text{Min.})\%}{\text{Max.}}$	9,2	6,1	8,5	3,9	9,1	10,5	9,9	5,7
Winter 27/1-9/2/2011	CV (%)	–	1,59	1,68	1,02	–	–	–	1,48
	$\frac{(\text{Max.}-\text{Min.})\%}{\text{Max.}}$	–	6,4	7,1	4,6	–	–	–	6,0

In Figures 14 and 15 the coefficients of correlation between the natural frequencies of the cathedral and the different temperatures are presented. For the summer period and during the period of thermography monitoring, the eight modes were identified, whereas, for the winter period only the modes number 2, 3, 4 and 8 were identified. The other modes were local ones; therefore, their identification was not always attainable as can be noticed in Figure 5. It can be noticed for the summer and the winter periods that the coefficients of correlation with the stone surface temperature were less than those with the external and the internal temperature. In the summer period, the coefficients of correlation with the external temperature were in average 0.57 and were clearly higher than those with the stone surface temperature which were in average 0.25.

On the contrary, in the winter period the coefficients of correlation with the stone surface temperature were in average 0.56 and were not so far from those with the external temperature which were 0.68 in average. The discussion given in the previous section (3.2) may explain this finding. The statistical variations in the identified modes during the summer and winter monitored periods are reported in Table 4.

For modes 2, 4 and 8 slightly higher changes could be noticed in winter period than in summer period. For mode 3 the contrary was found.

Table 4. Statistical variations in the cathedral frequencies in the summer and winter periods.

Monitored period	Parameter	Mode no.							
		1	2	3	4	5	6	7	8
Summer 28/6-13/7/2011	CV (%)	2,79	1,59	2,38	0,91	2,19	3,49	2,42	1,21
	$\frac{(\text{Max.}-\text{Min.})\%}{\text{Max.}}$	9,2	6,1	8,5	3,9	9,1	10,5	9,9	5,7
Winter 27/1-9/2/2011	CV (%)	–	1,59	1,68	1,02	–	–	–	1,48
	$\frac{(\text{Max.}-\text{Min.})\%}{\text{Max.}}$	–	6,4	7,1	4,6	–	–	–	6,0

4. CONCLUSIONS

An integrated inspection and monitoring program, encompassing different activities, has been applied to Mallorca cathedral a large masonry historical structure built during the 14th - 16th c. The AVT allowed for a good identification of the natural frequencies of eight modes. The AVT was followed by a continuous dynamic monitoring that worked for about 15 months on a 24 h base. It confirmed the results of the AVT by allowing the monitoring of the evolution of the eight natural frequencies over time. It was found that the changes in the natural frequencies of the cathedral, in terms of CV, were between 2.3 and 3.7%, and their percentual variation was between 10.4 and 18.5%.

A seasonal thermography monitoring (as a complementary study for the dynamic monitoring) was used. An IR camera was installed in the winter and the summer of 2011 for two weeks to monitor the internal stone surface temperature of a large portion of the cathedral. The correlation between the cathedral natural frequencies and the internal stone surface temperature of some selected structural elements was investigated. The correlation of the natural frequencies with the external and internal temperatures was also analyzed.

Concerning the correlation among the different temperatures measure, the main conclusions are: I) The internal stone surface temperature of the columns, vaults, arches and walls was in phase and very near to each other; II) In summer, it was observed that the internal stone surface temperature did not always vary according to the external temperature because the stone was not able to radiate the stored heat as fast as the rapidly increasing external temperature; III) in winter, the stone surface temperature was in phase with the external temperature.

Regarding the correlation between the natural frequencies and the different measured temperatures, the thermography monitoring revealed an acceptable correlation between the stone internal surface temperature and the cathedral frequencies. In the winter period higher correlation coefficients than in the summer period were found. It was observed also that the natural frequencies were more correlated with the external temperature then the internal temperature and finally with the internal stone surface temperature.

ACKNOWLEDGMENT

This research has been carried out within the project "New Integrated Knowledge based approaches to the protection of cultural heritage from Earthquake-induced Risk-NIKER" funded by the European Commission (Grant Agreement n° 244123), whose assistance is gratefully acknowledged. The authors also wish to express their gratitude to the Chapter of Mallorca cathedral for the possibility of carrying out the present study and the assistance received.

REFERENCES

Adler, D. (1969). Metric Handbook: Planning and Design Data. Second edition. Architectural press, Oxford, UK.

Alves, C., Vasconcelos, G., Fernandes, F. M., & Silva, S. M. (2014). Deterioration of the granitic stone at Misericórdia chapel in Murça (northern Portugal). In Amoeda, R., Lira, S. & Pinheiro, C. (c) *Proc. of the International Confer-enece on Preservation, Maintenance and Rehabilitation of Hisotircal Buildings and Structrues (REHAB 2014).*

Bagavathiappan, S., Lahiri, B. B., Saravanan, T., Philip, J., & Jayakumar, T. (2013). Infrared thermography for condition monitoring–a review. Infrared Physics & Technology, 60, 35-55.

Binda, L., Cantini, L. and Cucchi, M. (2011). Thermovision: Applications in conservation field to detect hidden characteristics of building structures. *11th North American Masonry Conference,* 5-8 June, Minneapolis, USA.

Basto, C., Pelà, L. and Chacón, R. (2017). Open-source digital technologies for low-cost monitoring of historical constructions. Journal of Cultural Heritage, 25, pp.31-40.

Brincker, R., Zhang, L., Andersen, P. (2001). Modal identification of output-only systems using frequency domain decomposition. Smart materials and structures, 10(3):441- 445.

Cabboi, A. (2014) Automatic operational modal analysis: challenges and applications to historic structures and infrastructures. PhD Thesis, University of Cagliari, Italy.

Cagnan, Z, Chrysostomou, C Z, Kyriakides, N, and Votsis, R. (2015) Dynamic response of a Gothic cathedral in Cyprus. Proceedings COMPDYN 2015, Paper 677, 25-27 May 2015, Crete, Greece.

Caselles, O, Martínez, G, Clapes, J, Roca, P., and Pérez-Gracia M.D.L.V. (2015). Application of particle motion technique to struc-tural modal identification of heritage buildings. International Journal of Architectural Heritage, 9(3):310-323.

Caselles, O., Clapes, J., Roca, P. and Elyamani, A. (2012). Approach to seismic behavior of Mallorca cathedral. *15th World Conference of Earthquake Engineering*, Lisbon, Portugal, 24-28 September 2012.

Ceroni F, Sica S, Pecce M.R. and Garofano A. (2014). Evaluation of the natural vibration frequencies of a historical masonry building accounting for SSI. *Soil Dynamics and Earthquake Engineering*, 64:95-101.

CHIME, Conservation of historical Mediterranean sites by innovative seismic protection techniques. Funded by EC under the 5th Framework program, (2000-2003).

Chiostrini S, Foraboschi P. and Vignoli A. (1992) Structural analysis and damage evaluation of existing masonry buildings by dynamic experimentation and numerical modelling. *Proc. of the 10th World Conference on Earthquake Engineering*.

Clark, M. R., McCann, D. M. and Forde, M. C. (2003). Application of infrared thermography to the non-destructive testing of concrete and masonry bridges. *NDT and E International*, 36(4), 265-275.

Diaferio, M., Foti, D. and Giannoccaro, N. I. (2015) Identification of the modal properties of a building of the Greek heritage. *Key Engineering Materials*, 628:150-159.

Elyamani, A. and Roca, P. (2018a). A review on the study of historical structures using integrated investigation activities for seismic safety assessment. Part I: dynamic investigation, *Scientific Culture,* Vol. 4, No. I, pp. 1-27. DOI: 10.5281/zenodo.1048241.

Elyamani, A. and Roca, P. (2018b). A review on the study of historical structures using integrated investigation activities for seismic safety assessment. Part II: model updating and seismic analysis, *Scientific Culture,* Vol. 4, No. I, pp. 29-51. DOI: 10.5281/zenodo.1048243.

Elyamani, A. and Roca, P. (2018c) One Century of Studies for the Preservation of one of the largest cathedrals worldwide: A review. *SCIENTIFIC CULTURE*, Vol. 4, No.2, 1-24.

Elyamani, A. (2015) Integrated monitoring and structural analysis strategies for the study of large historical construction. Application to Mallorca cathedral. PhD thesis, Technical University of Catalonia, Spain.

Elyamani, A., Caselles, J.O., Roca, P. and Clapes, J. (2017b) Dynamic investigation of a large historical cathedral. *Structural Control and Health Monitoring*, 24, e1885. DOI: 10.1002/stc.1885.

Elyamani, A., J. O. Caselles, J. Clapes, and P. Roca, (2012). Assessment of Dynamic Behavior of Mallorca Cathedral, *8th International Conference of Structural Analysis of Historical Construction*, Wroclaw, Poland, 15-17 Oct. 2012.

Elyamani, A., Roca, P., Caselles, O. and Clapes, J. (2017a). Seismic safety assessment of historical structures using updated numerical models: The case of Mallorca cathedral in Spain. Engineering Failure Analysis 74, 54-79.

Erdik, M., Durukal, E., Yuzugullu, B., Beyen, K., Kadakal, U. (1993). Strong-motion instrumentation of Aya Sofya and the analysis of response to an earthquake of 4.8 magnitude. Proc. of the 3rd Conference: Structural Repair and Maintenance of Historical Buildings III, Bath, UK.

EU-INDIA, Improving the seismic resistance of cultural heritage buildings. Funded by EU-INDIA Economic Cross Cultural Programme, contract n. ALA/95/23/2003/077-122, (2004-2006).

Faella, G., Frunzio, G., Guadagnuolo, M., Donadio, A. and Ferri, L. (2012). The church of the nativity in Bethlehem: Non-destructive tests for the structural knowledge. *Journal of Cultural Heritage*, 13(4), 27-41.

Foti D., Gattulli V. and Potenza F. (2014). Output only identification and model updating by dynamic testing in unfavorable condi-tions of a seismically damaged building. *Computer Aided Civil and Infrastructure Engineering* 2014, 29(9), 659-675.

González, R., Caballé, F., Domenge, J., Vendrell, M., Giráldez, P., Roca, P. and González J. L. (2008). Construction process, damage and structural analysis. Two case studies. In D'Ayala, D. and Fodde, E. (Eds.) *Structural Analysis of Historical Construction*. CRC Press Balkema, pp. 643–651.

Gosse, J. (1986). Technical guide to thermal processes. Cambridge university press, UK.

Jo, Y. H. and Lee, C. H. (2014). Quantitative modeling of blistering zones by active thermography for deterioration evaluation of stone monuments. *Journal of Cultural Heritage*, 15(6), 621-627.

Lorenzoni, F., Casarin, F., Modena, C., Caldon, M., Islami, K, and da Porto, F. (2013). Structural health monitoring of the Roman Arena of Verona, Italy. *Journal of Civil Structural Health Monitoring*, 3(4), 227-246.

MACEC 3.2 (2011). a MATLAB Toolbox for Experimental and Operational Modal Analysis, 2011. Developed by Reynders E, De Roeck G, Copyright © KU Leuven, Belgium.

Martínez, E., Castillo, A., Martínez, I. and Castellote, M. (2013). Methodology for intervention in historical elements: the case of the belfry of the convent of Nuestra Señora de la Consolación, (Alcalá de Henares-Madrid-Spain). *Informes de la Construcción*, 65(531), 359-366.

Masciotta, M. G., Roque, J. C., Ramos, L. F. and Lourenço, P. B. (2016). A multidisciplinary approach to assess the health state of heritage structures: The case study of the Church of Monastery of Jerónimos in Lisbon. *Construction and Building Materials*, 116, 169-187.

Modena C, Rossi PP, Zonta D. Static and dynamic investigation on the roman amphitheatre (Arena) in Verona. *Proc., IABSE Int. Colloquium, Inspection and Monitoring of the Architectural Heritage*, 1997, pp. 73-80.

NIKER, New Integrated Knowledge-based approaches to the protection of cultural heritage from Earthquake-induced Risk. Funded by EC under the 7th Framework program, contract n. ENV2009-1-GA244123. (2010-2012), www.niker.eu.

Peeters, B., De Roeck, G. (1999). Reference-based stochastic subspace identification for output-only modal analysis. Mechanical Systems and Signal Processing, 13(6):855-878.

Peeters, B., Van der Auweraer, H. (2005). PolyMAX: a revolution in operational modal analysis. 1st International Operational Modal Analysis Conference (IOMAC), 2005, 26-27 April, Copenhagen, Denmark.

Pelà L, Bourgeois J., Roca P., Cervera M. and Chiumenti M. (2014). Analysis of the Effect of Provisional Ties on the Construc-tion and Current Deformation of Mallorca Cathedral. *International Journal of Architectural Heritage*, 10(3), 418-437.

PERPETUATE, Performance-based approach to the earthquake protection of cultural heritage in European and Mediterranean countries. Funded by EC under the 7th Framework program, grant agreement n° 244229. www. perpetuate.eu, (2010-2012).

PROHITECH, Earthquake PROtection of HIstorical Buildings by Reversible Mixed TECHnologies, Funded by EC under the 6th Framework program grant No. INCO-CT-2004- 509119, (2004-2008).

RISK-UE. An advanced approach to earthquake risk scenarios with applications to different European towns. Funded by EC, contract n. EVK4-CT-2000-00014m (2001-2004).

Rivera, D., Meli, R., Sánchez, R. and Orozco, B. (2008). Evaluation of the measured seismic response of the Mexico City Cathedral. *Earthquake Engineering and Structural Dynamics*, 37(10), 1249-1268.

Roca P., Cervera M., Pelà L., Clemente R. and Chiumenti M. (2013). Continuum FE models for the analysis of Mallorca Cathedral. *Engineering Structures*, 46, 653–670.

SEVERES, Seismic vulnerability of old masony buildings. Funded by Portuguese Foundation for Science and Technology, contract n. PTDC/ECM/100872/2008, www.severes.org, (2010-2012).

Tavukçuoğlu, A., Akevren, S. and Grinzato, E. (2010). In situ examination of structural cracks at historic masonry struc-tures by quantitative infrared thermography and ultrasonic testing. *Journal of Modern Optics*, 57(18), 1779.

Votsis, R. A., Kyriakides, N., Chrysostomou, C. Z., Tantele, E. A. and Demetriou, T. (2012). Ambient vibration testing of two masonry monuments in Cyprus. *Soil Dynamics and Earthquake Engineering*, 43:58–68.

Votsis, R. A., Kyriakides, N., Tantele, E. A. and Chrysostomou, C. Z. (2015). Effect of damage on the dynamic characteristics of St. Nicholas cathedral in Cyprus. In Psycharis I N, Pantazopoulou S J, Papadrakakis M (Eds.) Seismic Assessment, Behavior and Retrofit of Heritage Buildings and Monuments (pp. 281-295). *Computational Methods in Applied Sciences*, V. 37, Springer International Publishing.

12

A COMPARATIVE STUDY TO EVALUATE CONVENTIONAL AND NONCONVENTIONAL CLEANING TREATMENTS OF CELLULOSIC PAPER SUPPORTS

Yasin Zidan[1], Ahmed El-Shafei[2], Wafika Noshy[1] and Eman Salim[1]

[1]*Conservation Departement, Faculty of Archaeology, Cairo University, Egypt*
[2]*Polymer and Color Chemistry, College of Textile, North Carolina State University, USA*

Corresponding author: Eman Salim (emantheflower@gmail.com)

ABSTRACT

Aqueous cleaning of ancient paper samples is a common treatment for the removal of degradation products, external contaminants and salts, which can cause degradation of cellulose by hydrolysis or oxidation processes. The present study examined the influence of selected cleaning treatments on chemical properties of some historical paper samples and studying the efficiency of cleaning methods in removing of degradation products. It also investigated the effects of five different cleaning treatments, namely immersion in deionized water, akapad paper sponge, hydro gellan gum, Cellulose nano Crystal gel and cleaning with wolbers solvent gels on ancient cellulosic paper supports. In particular, the effect of the cleaning treatments on different properties of cellulosic paper supports, namely colorimetric properties (CIE L*a*b* coordinates), crystallinity index (X-Ray diffraction), Fourier transform infrared spectroscopy(FTIR), scanning electron microscopy (SEM) and pH (cold-extraction method), were investigated. The study concluded that all cleaning treatments affected the colorimetric properties of the selected paper samples.

KEYWORDS: Cellulosic paper supports, akapad paper, deionized water, cleaning, gellan gum, solvent gels, Cellulose Nano Gel

1. INTRODUCTION

Conservation treatment is performed in order to preserve or restore artifacts. Therefore, only trained conservators who have experience in the appropriate material (such as paper, books art of works on paper, textiles, furniture, photographs, archeological objects, ethnographic objects and natural history specimens) should perform conservation treatments on ancient artifacts.

The preservation of cultural heritage to future generations is one of the main duties of humanity. Unfortunately natural, archaeological, historical and artistic materials are constantly subject to the action of many detrimental actions due to environmental pollutants, wrong handling practices, natural disasters, accidental damage, or simply to neglect. Thus, in order to ensure the durability of the whole human cultural heritage, any further decay shall be minimized (DeI, 2013).

Conservation treatments must ensure the most appropriate treatments for their continued preservation and use for objects, archives, and specimens and take into consideration an object's condition, history, significance, and use, treatments to be performed by skilled, experienced conservators and properly documented.

The preservation and conservation of paper documents are a necessary operation which applied in order to prolong the life time of artifacts by reducing chemical and physical deterioration in order to prevent and reverse further decay. There are several aqueous and non aqueous conservation treatments for paper artifacts, e.g. cleaning, consolidation, deacidification, neutralization, and aqueous methods for the ink fixatives. The effectiveness of these processes has been mainly studied by analysing changes in paper properties.

For example, wet cleaning of ancient papers is one of the most critical steps during a conservation treatment. It is used to improve the optical qualities of a graphic work and to remove dust and by-products resulting from cellulose degradation. Nevertheless, washing treatment usually involves a substantial impact on the original morphological structure of paper and can sometimes be dangerous for water sensitive inks and pigments. The use of rigid hydrogel of Gellan gum as an alternative paper cleaning treatment is developed. It was reported that the application of a rigid hydrogel minimizes damages caused by water. Therefore, it is much more respectful for the original integrity of ancient paper (Mazzuca et al. 2014).

The aqueous, non-aqueous and mechanical surface cleaning of cellulosic paper supports are long held techniques in the conservation treatments of paper manuscripts. In the twentieth century, paper conservation practice often involved the washing of degraded or discoloured paper artefacts. After bathing, paper artefacts were often perceived to be whiter, stronger, and healthier (Vitale, 1992).

Washing and deacidification processes are intended to convert the paper from an acidic to an alkaline condition by removing soluble discoloration at the same time. Therefore, it is necessary to begin by listing sources of the paper's acidity so that these could be properly counteracted and the deacidification treatments could have the required long-term benefit. Hence, knowledge of cellulose chemistry and paper making technology is essential when investigating paper conservation procedures (Hey, 2014).

aqueous treatments of cellulosic supports currently outweigh the risks. Among their potential benefits: (1) aqueous surface cleaning is a quick and effective means to remove dirt and discoloration; (2) immersion in deionized water is often a reliable method for removing manuscripts from degraded and damaged mounts; and (3) the washing of cellulosic manuscripts reduces the presence of degradation products in the paper support and may decrease the yellow/brown discoloration (Fench et al., 2011).

Solvent Cleaning used in removed types of spots or stains such as stains penetrate in to paper fibres and cannot be easily removed .The basis of stain removal with solvent its solubility in the selected chemical, their efficacy will depend on the nature of the stains and nature of the paper. (Rabee, 2015).

Akapad sponge has been designed for the cleaning of sensitive surfaces. It is used to carry out the convenient and safe dry cleaning of surface soiling on dry, non-staining nor chalking walls, ceilings, pictures, frescos, mural paintings, wallpaper, paper, textiles, coats of paint etc. The composition of the akapad white sponge has been especially formulated to provide excellent results in cleaning the works of art on paper (PH neutral). It leaves no residue and it is safe for use on sensitive surfaces. The wishab paper sponge consists of a blue grip and an attached cleaning sponge. The sponge works by absorbing dirt particles, then crumbling of to avoid polishing the treated surface (Scbotte et al., 2012).

Recently, gellan gum hydrogels have been proposed as effective tools to remove contaminant from paper supports due to the controlled water release and adhesive properties of gellan gum. Several polymers have been used by conservators for the formulation of gels and viscous polymeric dispersions either with organic solvents or water-based cleaning systems. The captive of a given cleaning (e.g. water, organic solvent, enzymes solutions, chelating agents, etc.) is fluid (Bonelli et al., 2016).

The use of hydrogels as a new tool in the conservation of cultural heritage or cleaning and diagenostic is important because it does not require liquid treatments that could induce damage on artworks, while electrochemical biosensors are not only easy to prepare, but they can also be selective for a specific compound. Therefore, they are suitable for monitoring the cleaning process. In the field of restoration of paper artworks, more efforts have to be done in order to know how to perform the best way for an effective restoration. Rigid Gellan gel, made up of Gellan gum and calcium acetate, was proposed as a paper cleaning treatment (Micheli et al., 2014).

The present research aimed to evaluate the effect of the various cleaning treatments chemical and mechanical stability of cellulosic paper supports, the benefits of immersion in deionized water cleaning, akapad paper sponge and hydro gel gum cleaning the paper supports were treated by aqueous and non aqueous surface cleaning. Colour, as well as mechanical properties measurements were applied after this surface cleaning procedure.

2. MATERIALS AND METHODS

2.1. Materials

Archaeological unsized cellulosic paper support (cotton pulp paper) was selected for the study.

- Akapad Paper Sponge soft, White, Size: 90 x 67 x 42 mm (length, width, height) pH-Wert: Neutral. Purchased from Kremer pigments247 west 29th Street New York, NY1001.
- Deionized water and water from which dissolved ions have been removed by passing the water through cationic and anionic ion exchange resin, prepared in the chemistry lab at NCSU.
- Hydrogel gellan gum prepared in the lab, Gellan gum (Gelzan CM Geletric) and calcium acetate was delivered from Sigma (Sigma-Aldrich,Mo, St. Louis, USA.) To prepare the hydrogel an aqueous solution of Gelzanpowder 20 g (conc. 1-4%) and calcium acetate (0.40 g/ L) was put for a minute in the microwave at 600 W until complete hydration. (According to Casoli et al. 2013)
- Cellulose Nano Crystal gel. Cellulose Nanocrystal (CNC) purchased from The University of Maine a public research university in Orono, Maine, United States (process Development Center) 1-3 wt% of Cellulose Nanocrystals (CNC) (Freeze dried solid, Grade CNC 0.85 wt% sulfur on dry CNC Sodium form).
- Wolbers solvent gels (acetone gel, 2-propanol gel) Purchased from Kremer pigments247 west 29th Street New York, NY100.

2.1. Cleaning procedures

The paper supports were divided into five samples depending on the type of cleaning procedure. While the first sample was cleaned by immersion in de ionized water, the second sample was cleaned with akapad paper sponge, the third sample was cleaned by hydro gellan gum, the forth sample was cleaned with Cellulose Nano Gel and the last sample was cleaned with Wolbers solvent gel.

2.2. Accelerated aging of paper after cleaning

In order to evaluate the long-term of cleaning treatments, the selected paper samples were exposed to heat accelerated-aging procedures. The samples were exposed to 105 ± 2°C in a laboratory oven for 28 days. The samples were analyzed for surface pH, CIE L*a*b*, tensile strength (TS). Previous to and immediately after the tests, samples were equilibrated at 23°C and 50% RH for 24 hours. (Wang et al, 2013)

2.3. Scanning electron microscope (SEM)

Scanning electron Microscopic examinations of the samples was carried out using an Electron Microscope Survey Nanoscience instrument FEI Company MVE00001162, FP 3950/00 at NCSU. All the samples examined were prepared according to the standard procedures. The samples were coated with gold using EMITECH K450X sputter coater to avoid charging. The SEM has a scan area of 50 mm x 50 mm as standard. Optionally, the motorized scan area can be upgraded to 100 mm x 100 mm. The examination of samples was performed at the SEM Laboratory, Department of Polymer and Color Science, the University of North Carolina.

2.4. Fourier Transform Infrared Spectroscopy (FTIR)

FTIR spectroscopy was used to study the functional groups present in paper and the changes that have occurred due to treatments compared to the control paper sample. FTIR spectra of paper samples were measured on a thermo scientific FTIR Nicolet IS10 GE Crystal 64 scans, 4 resolution, in the frequency range of 4000 - 500 cm^{-1}, in reflectance mode.

2.5. *CIELab color variations measured with Color iMatch Spectrophotometer*

The colorimetric coordinates L*, a*, and b*of the CIE L*a*b* color space were used to express color change.

The colour change resulted from cleaning was registered by measuring the L*a*b* parameters which define the colour in CIE L*a*b* colour space. The total changes of the L*a* b* value was described as the colour change (ΔE), which is calculated according to the given formula (Jeżewskaetal, 2016):

$$\Delta E = [(\Delta L^*)^2 + (\Delta a^*)^2 + (\Delta b^*)\ 2]^{1/2}$$

In which: ΔL*, Δa*, Δb* stand for – in our studies – changes of the values resulted from the deacidification. Measuring the color difference was performed on the Color iMatch spectrophotometer manufactured by X-rite Michigan USA. This instrument enables the direct read out of the ΔE value.

2.6. *Evaluation of pH values before and after cleaning treatments*

Determinations of pH were performed with an Oakton pH/mv/c Meter737850 manufactured by Eutech instruments, thermo fisher scientific Measurement of pH was performed on samples according to. The paper is mixed with water, and after letting it stand for 1 hour in the cold, the pH is determined in the unfiltered mixture, using a glass electrode (Launer, 1939).

2.7. *Determination of paper crystallinity with X-ray Diffraction*

This technique was employed to study the crystallinity degree of cellulose for the treated samples compared to the control samples.

The cellulose crystallinity for the measured samples control sample and the treated samples with consolidants were calculated according to the following equation:

$$Cr.I\% = \frac{I(002) + I\ 18^{\circ} * 100}{I\ (002)}$$

Where I (002) and I 18° are the maximum scattering intensities of the diffraction from the (002) plane at 2θ = 2.26° and the diffraction intensity of the background scatter measured at 2θ = 18°, respectively, and the latter value being attributed to the non-crystalline cellulose form (Zidan et al., 2016).

$$Crystallinity\ (\%) = \frac{Area\ under\ crystalline\ peaks\ * 100}{Total\ area\ under\ all\ peaks}$$

XRD of the treated and untreated paper samples before and after cleaning treatments was carried out on a Philips XLF diffractometer, ATPS XRD 1000 with OMNI instruments, Luc customized Auto mount with cupper tube.

2.7. *Physical Testing (Tensile strength and elongation for paper samples after Cleaning treatments)*

Mechanical behaviour of the samples (tensile strength, elongation % and breaking factor) were studied using the MTS Q-Test/5 Universal Testing Machine, according to ASTM_D828-Modified-250-load.msm.

The samples were cut in the machine direction to strips of 2 cm × 10 cm. All measurements were made before and after treatment and compared to that of the control sample. The procedure was carried out in aging ovens at the physical testing lab at college of textile North Carolina State University.

3. RESULTS AN DISCUSSION

3.1. *Scanning Electron Microscopic analysis*

SEM of the samples was carried out using an Electron Microscope Survey Nanoscience instrument FEI Company MVE00001162, FP 3950/00 at NCSU. All the samples examined were prepared according to the standard procedures. The samples were coated with gold using EMITECH K450X sputter coater to avoid charging. The SEM has a scan area of 50 mm x 50 mm as standard. Optionally, the motorized scan area can be upgraded to 100 mm x 100 mm.

The scanning electron microscope (SEM) produces detailed images at a higher magnification than a light microscope. In our study we used the SEM to study the surface of paper support, and the effects of different cleaning treatments. SEM is particularly useful for looking for subtle signs of deterioration in paper, such as the initial stages of defibrillation of plant fibers; the morphology of fracture surface.

SEM examination of paper support revealed the source of cellulose fiber which has been identified as cotton pulp paper. The SEM examination also showed a high degradation degree with the cellulose fibers broken (Fig. 1). SEM observation also revealed mechanical damage.

SEM photos of examined paper samples before cleaning treatments are illustrated in Fig.1. These photos show that the paper support is extremely degraded. Comparing all the obtain SEM photos it can be noticed that CNC gel and hydro gellan gum were most effective treatments in removing of degradation products, soils and dust.

SEM examination also revealed a superficial coating on the treated paper samples hydro gellan gum (Fig. 4).

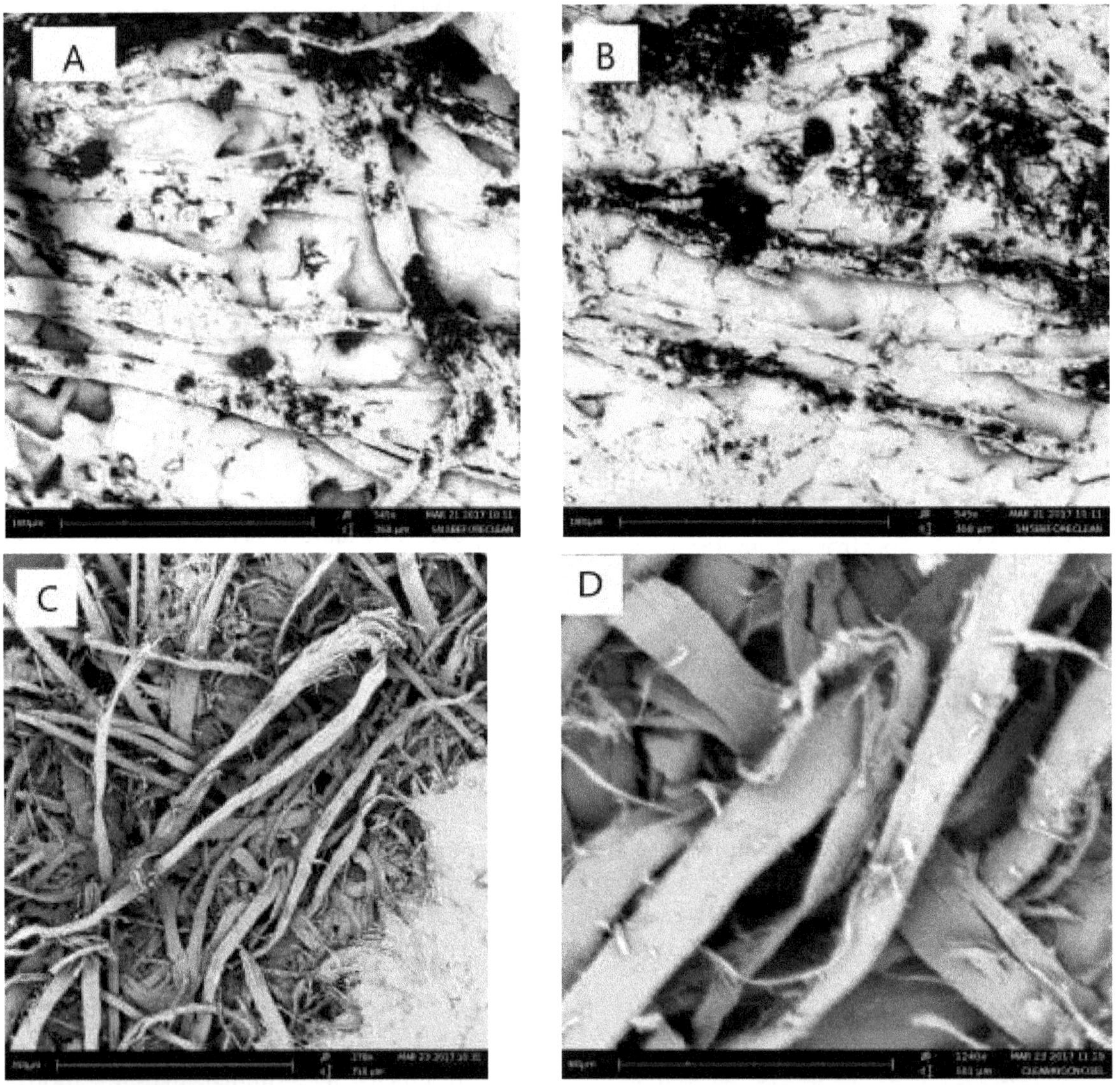

Figure 1. SEM micrographs of historical sample before and after cleaning methods.; Photo A and B show critical damage of paper support while C,D show SEM image of cotton fibres used to make the paper support.

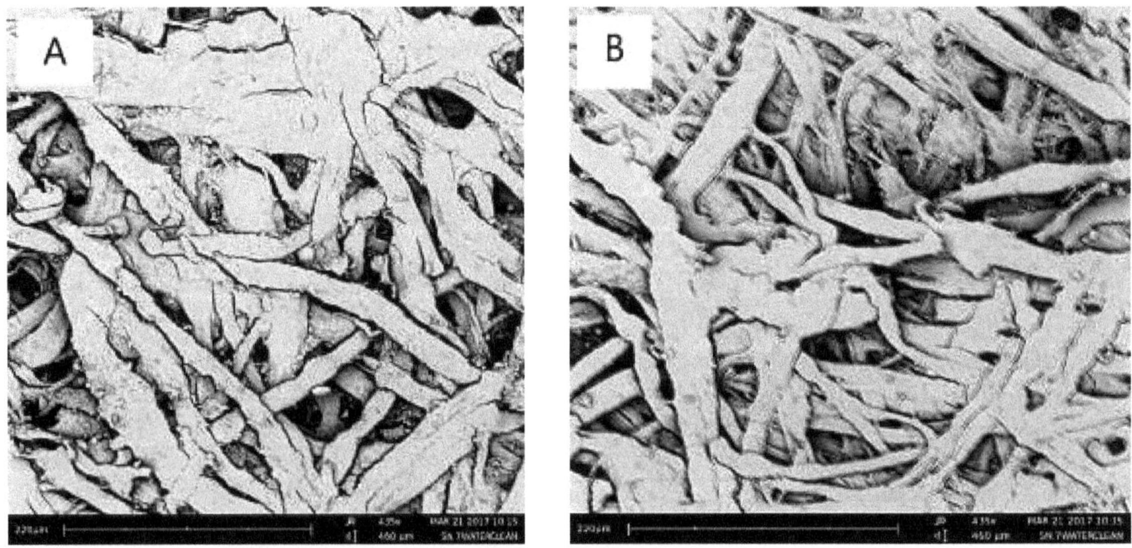

Figure 2. SEM micrographs of paper sample after cleaning with deionized water; photo A show the paper surface after cleaning treatment while B show the paper Surface after aging. (wet cleaning)

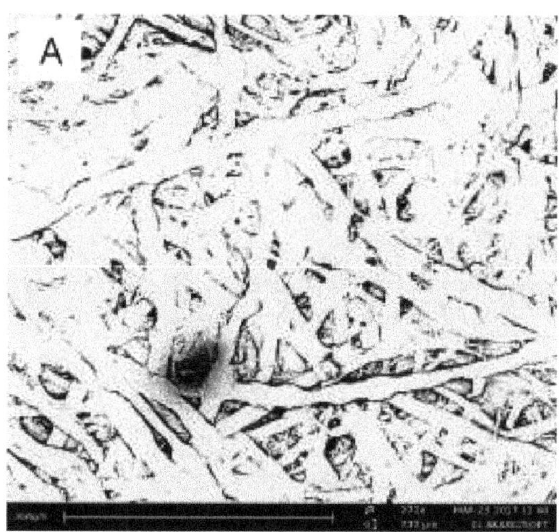

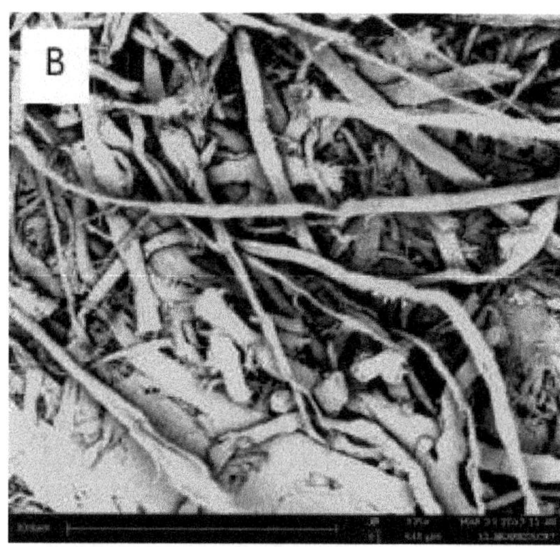

Figure 3. SEM micrographs of paper sample ;Photo A shows the paper surface after cleaning with akapad soft sponge the sponge works by absorbing dirt particles, then crumbling of to avoid polishing the treated surface while B shows the cellulose fibre after ageing . (Mechanical cleaning)

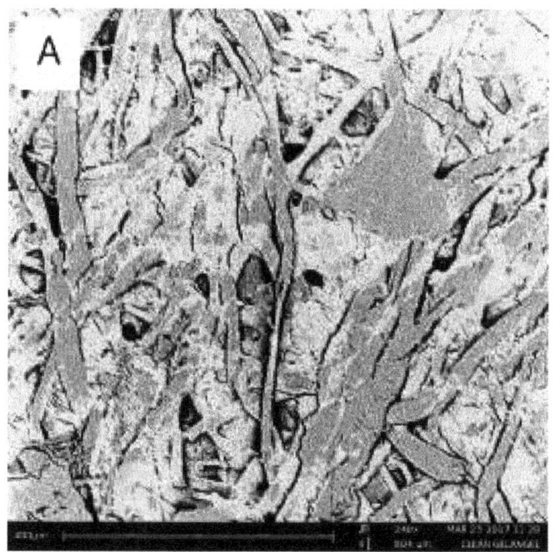

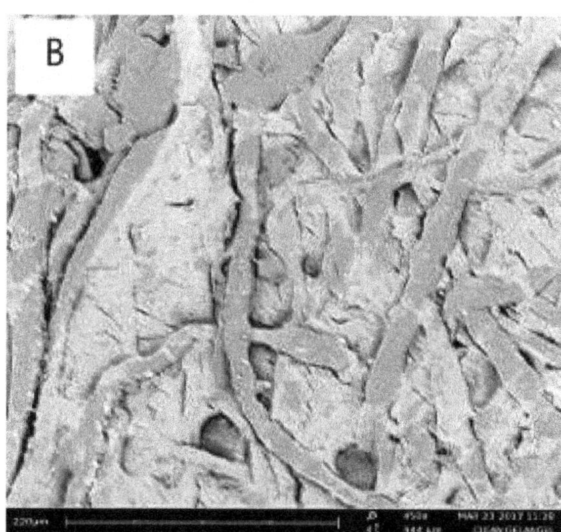

Figure 4. SEM micrographs of paper sample; Photo A shows the paper support after cleaning with hydro gellan gel prepared in the lab. B shows the paper support after aging.

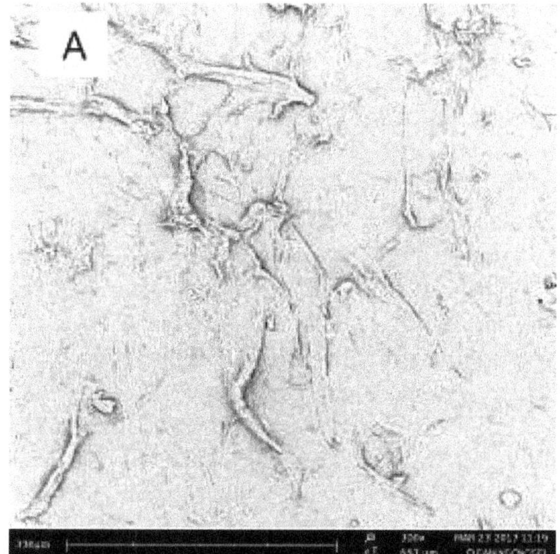

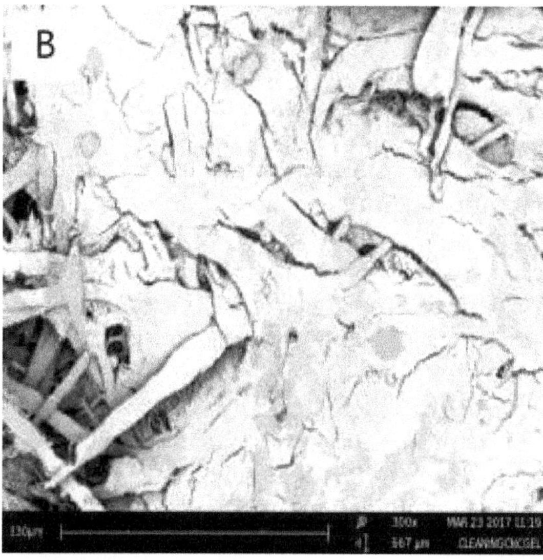

Figure 5. SEM micrographs of paper sample; Photo A shows the paper support after cleaning with Cellulose Nano Crystal gel prepared in the lab, this method was performed in order to clean and consolidate paper while B shows the surface after accelerated thermal ageing.

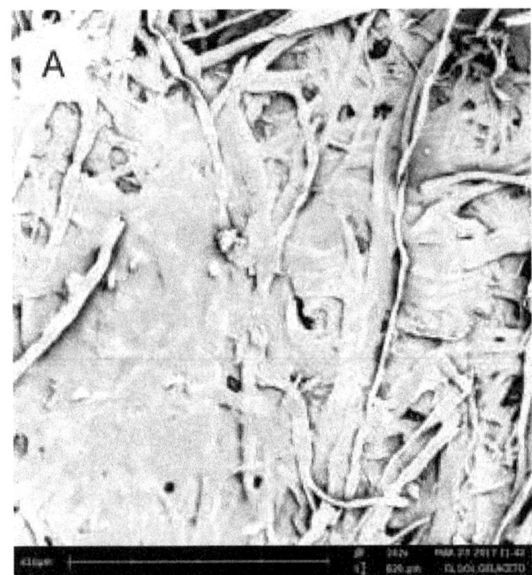
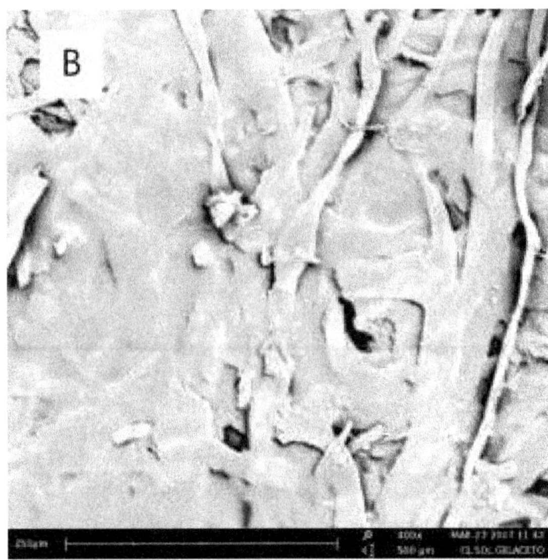

Figure 6. SEM micrographs of paper sample; Photo A shows the paper support after cleaning with Wolbers solvent gel acetone while B shows the surface after accelerated thermal ageing.

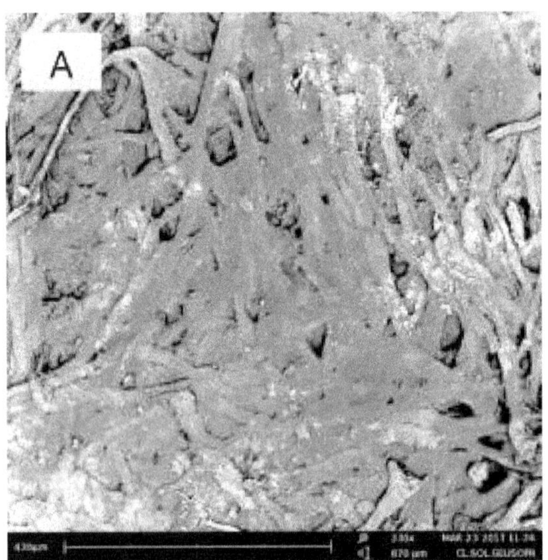
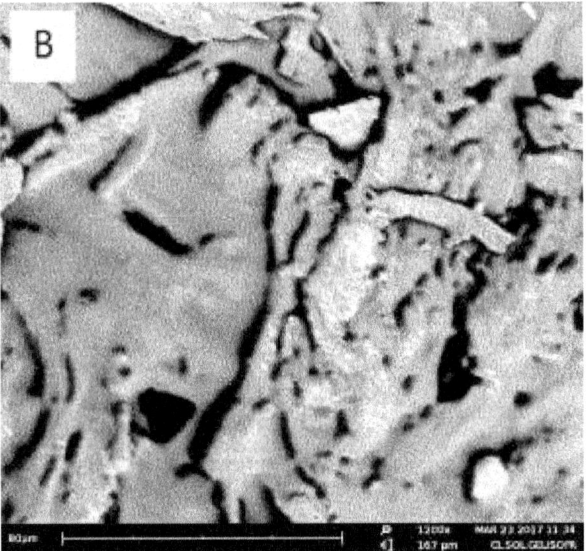

Figure 7. SEM micrographs of paper sample Photo A shows the paper support after cleaning with Wolbers Solvent gel isopropanol while B shows the surface after accelerated thermal ageing.

3.2. Fourier Transform Infrared Spectroscopy (FTIR)

Fourier-transform infrared (FTIR) spectroscopy is an important analytical tool used in the examination of historical materials. The technique produces a spectrum that provides intrinsic details about bonding features between atoms or characteristic functional groups in a molecule. It also provides information regarding chemical changes due to chemical treatment or aging, based on appearance of a new band, band shift, or intensity change of individual bands. One of the important advantages of using this technique is the ability to perform non-destructive analysis on historical objects.

Since the FTIR is very useful for examining the variation of hydrogen-bonds due to various defects. The structure of cellulose has a remarkable and complex influence on the course of chemical reactions of the polymer (cellulosic materials). Generally, the structure of cellulose consists of three structural levels: namely (i) the molecular level of the single macromolecule; (ii) the supramolecular level of packing and mutual ordering of the macromolecules; (iii) the morphological level concerning the architecture of already rather complex structural entities, as well as the corresponding pore system. (Fan et al, 2012)

The (FTIR) spectroscopy is very important tool for detecting the functional groups. The paper samples were identified by the interpretation of the absorption spectra from IR spectrometric analysis. It was noticed from the FTIR chart in Fig. 8 that the broad peak at 3320cm^{-1} is due to OH stretching vibration it is assigned to the hydroxyl groups in cellulose, and the band at 2900 cm^{-1} is related to CH_2 stretching vibration of CH3 group and it is assigned to the hydrocarbon group in cellulose, hemicellulose and lignin. The band at 1642 cm^{-1} is assigned to stretching vibration of -C=O and it is due to cellulose oxidation and formation of carbonyl and carboxyl groups. (Rabee 2015)

The paper support has been slightly hydrolyzed, showing an in-crease in the OH stretching band region at around 3320cm^{-1}, the presence of the C-O stretching band, and the presence of the H_2O band at 1642 cm^{-1} (figure 8, 9). The spectrum of the treated sample with akapad sponge peak at around 1650cm^{-1} which indicates the presence of carbonyl groups (C=O) which are due to cellulose oxidation. The increase in the OH stretching band is due to the hydrolysis of the cellulose and formation of hydroxyl groups. In addition, the very broad OH stretching band indicates more hydrogen bonding.

The FTIR absorption band at 1426 cm^{-1}, assigned to the CH_2 band, which is known as the "crystallinity band", decreaces in its intensity; this reflects reduction in the degree of crystallinity of cellulose. (Ferrer and Sistach, 2007).

A comparison of results for treated samples with different cleaning procedures shows spectra with relevant differences depending on the internal acidity of paper support. These differences are most evident the efficiency of cleaning methods in removing of degradation products; therefore, the most acidic samples are those which show the most important changes in the carbonyl band depending on the cleaning procedure.

After cleaning treatment, dried samples were analyzed to assess treatment efficiency. FTIR analysis shows that hydro gellan gel applications do not leave residues on paper material. The hydrogel displays a very characteristic IR spectrum, whose peaks are not present in every spectrum of the treated samples, as shown in Fig. 11. The spectra obtained before and after treatment, are indeed comparable, also suggesting that no detectable chemical degradation of cellulose takes place as a result of the hydrogel treatment. SEM images (Fig. 2, 4) confirm these results as both samples after immersion in deionized water and hydrogel treatment, seem cleaner and no swelling are present.

The spectrum of the treated sample with deionized water has no changes are observed in the functional groups characteristic of cellulose, an increase in the OH group at around 3332cm^{-1} is observed and this indicates the hydrolysis process, an increase is also noticed in the C=O absorption band at 1648 cm^{-1} indicating the oxidation process of cellulose molecule. A decrease is also noticed at the band of -CH stretching (2917-2900) due to the reduction of the hydrocarbon group in cellulose, hemicellulose and lignin. Peak at around 1650 cm^{-1} which indicates the presence of carbonyl groups (C=O) which are due to cellulose oxidation. The increase in the OH stretching band is due to the hydrolysis of the cellulose and formation of hydroxyl groups. In addition, the very broad OH stretching band indicates more hydrogen bonding (Fig. 10).

Similar case was observed in the treated sample with cellulose nano crystal gel (Fig. 12). FTIR spectrum no changes are observed in the functional groups characteristic of cellulose, a slight increase in the OH group at around 3331cm^{-1} is observed, an increase is also noticed in the C=O absorption band at 1649 cm^{-1} indicates to the oxidation process of cellulose molecule. A decrease also noticed at the band of –CH stretching at around 2917-2899. (Batterham and Rai, 2008)

FTIR spectrum of paper treated with wolbers solvent gels reveals the presence of the carbonyl groups at around 1650 cm^{-1} indicating the occurrence of slight oxidation. The presence of the C=C stretching of the aromatic ring at around 1506 cm^{-1} indicates the presence of lignin which explains the embrittlement and yellowing of paper support. A slight increase of carbonyl vibrations at around 1644 cm^{-1} and carboxyl vibrations at around 3466 cm^{-1} Oxidation of the cellulose molecule. Changes are also observed in the functional groups characteristic of cellulose, a slight increase in the OH group at around 3333cm^{-1} this indicates the hydrolysis process (Fig. 13, 14)

Table 1: shows the function groups for the historical paper sample.

Wave number cm^{-1}	Functional group
3320 cm^{-1}	-OH Stretching
2917 cm^{-1}	-CH Stretching
1642 cm^{-1}	-C=O Stretching
1426 - 1315 cm^{-1}	-C=C Stretching
1103- 1128 cm^{-1}	C-O Stretching
556-435 cm^{-1}	-C=C-H

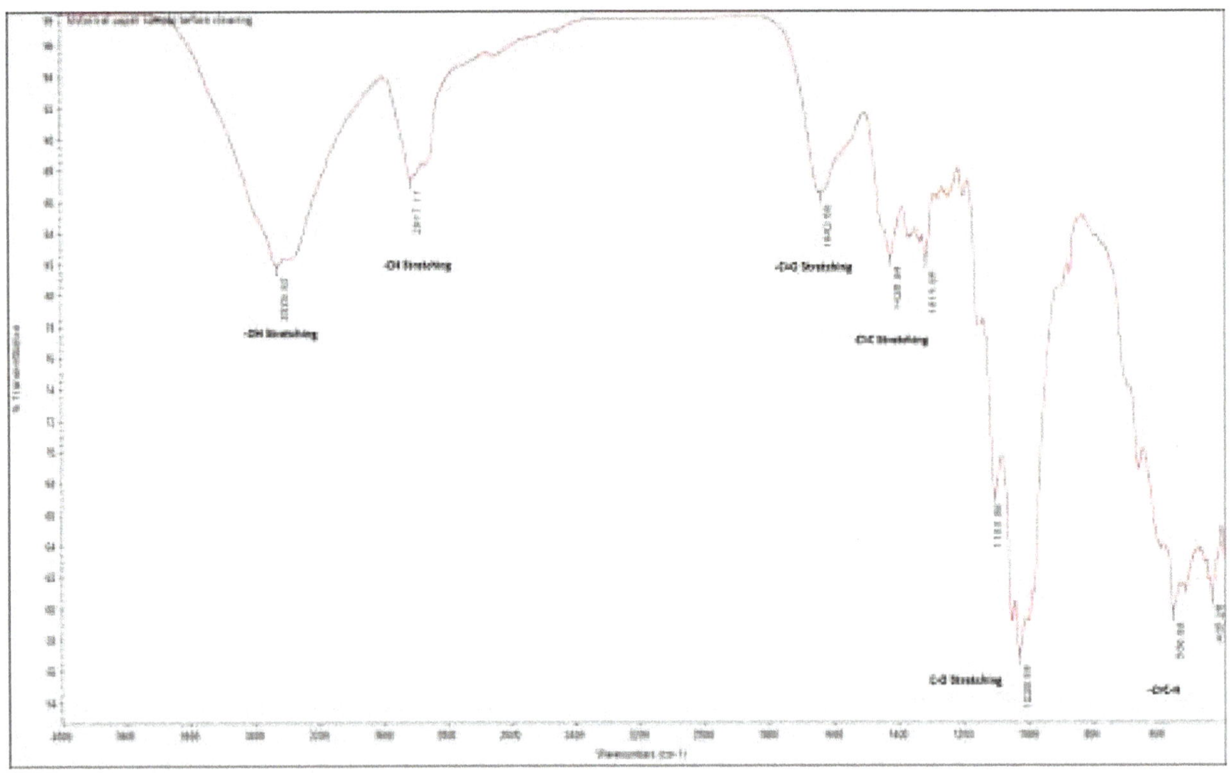

Figure 8. FTIR spectrum of historical paper sample before cleaning The broad peak at 3320cm^{-1} is due to OH stretching vibration it is assigned to the hydroxyl groups in cellulose, and the band at 2900 cm^{-1} is related to CH_2 stretching vibration of CH_3 group and it is assigned to the hydrocarbon group in cellulose, hemicellulose and lignin. The band at 1642 cm^{-1} is assigned to stretching vibration of -C=O and it is due to cellulose oxidation and formation of carbonyl and carboxyl groups.

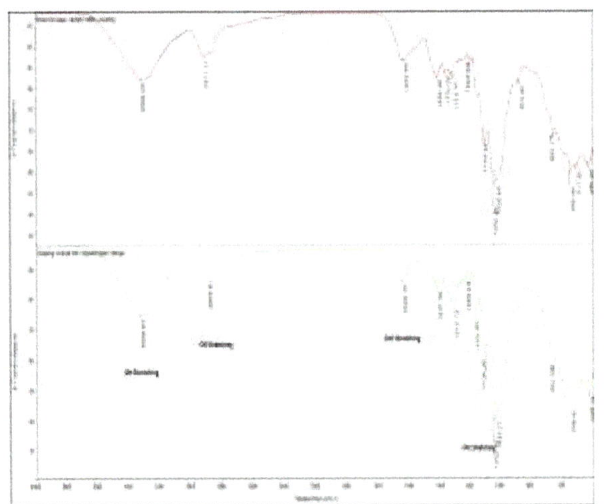

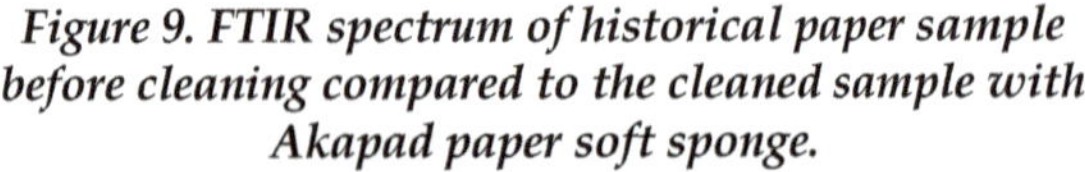

Figure 9. FTIR spectrum of historical paper sample before cleaning compared to the cleaned sample with Akapad paper soft sponge.

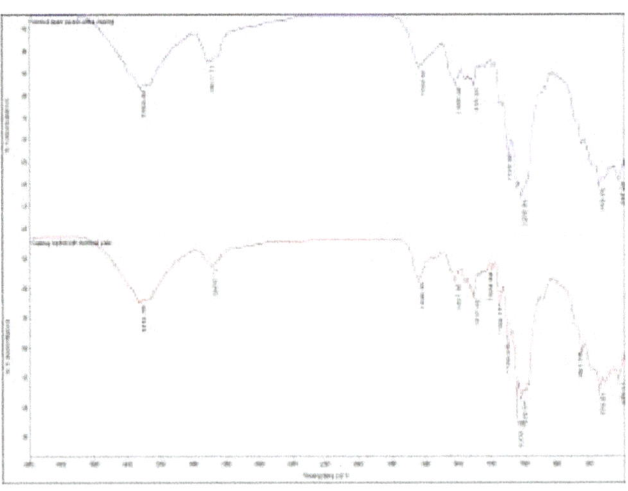

Figure10. FTIR spectrum of historical paper sample compared to the cleaned sample with deionized water.

There is no changes are observed in the functional groups characteristic of cellulose, an increase in the OH group at around 3332cm^{-1} is observed and this indicates the hydrolysis process, an increase is also noticed in the C=O absorption band at 1650 cm^{-1} which indicates the oxidation process of cellulose molecule. A decrease is also noticed at the band of –CH stretching (2917-2899) due to the reduction of the hydrocarbon group in cellulose, hemicellulose and lignin.

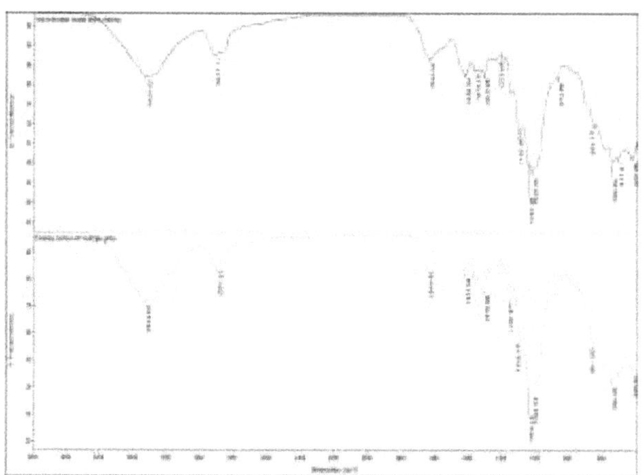

Figure 11. FTIR spectrum of historical paper sample before cleaning compared to cleaned sample with hydro gellan gel.

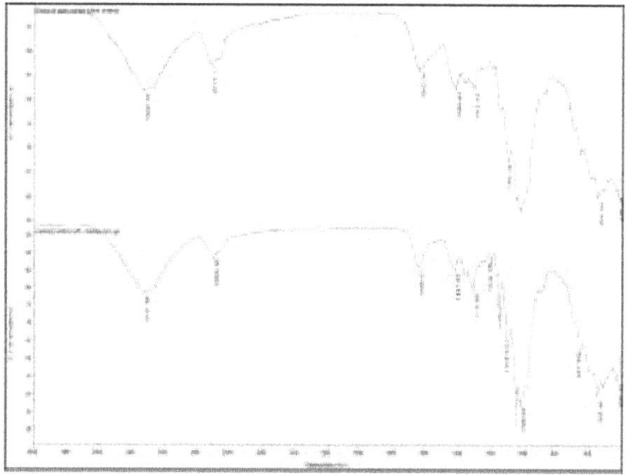

Figure 12 . FTIR spectrum of historical paper sample before cleaning compared to cleaned sample with cellulose nanocrystal gel

There is no changes are observed in the functional groups characteristic of cellulose, a slight increase in the OH group at around 3331cm^{-1} is observed and this indicates to hydrolysis process, an increase is also noticed in the C=O absorption band at 1649 cm^{-1} indicates to the oxidation process of cellulose molecule. A decrease also noticed at the band of -CH stretching at (2917-2899) it is assigned to reduce the hydrocarbon group in cellulose, hemicellulose and lignin.

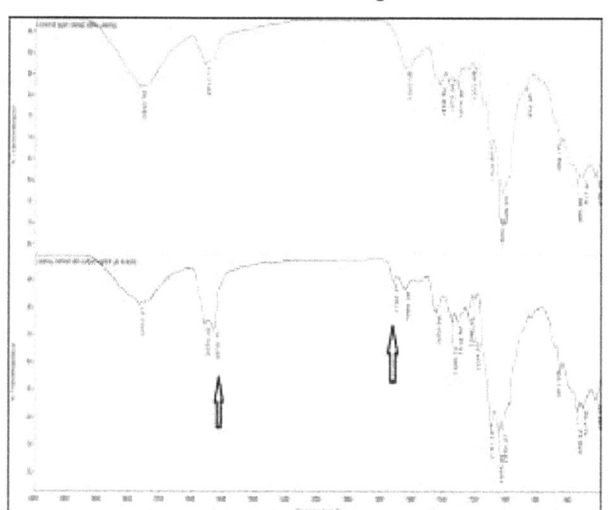

Figure 13. FTIR spectrum of historical paper sample before cleaning compared the cleaned sample with acetone Wolbers solvent gel.

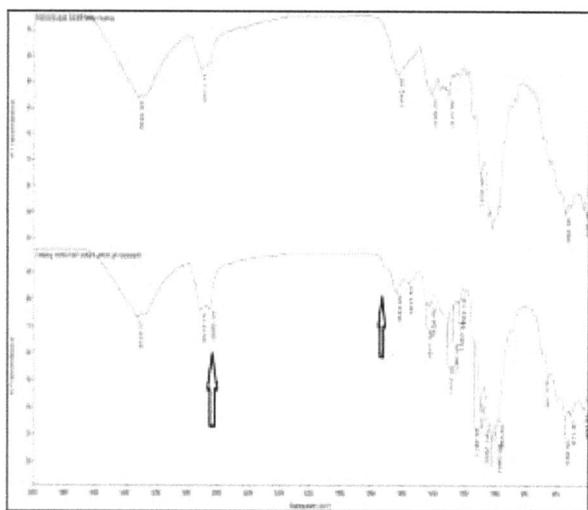

Figure14. FTIR spectrum of historical paper sample before cleaning compared the cleaned sample with isopropanol Wolbers solvent gel

Changes are observed in the functional groups characteristic of cellulose, a slight increase in the OH group at around 3333cm^{-1} is observed and this indicates the hydrolysis process, an increase is also noticed in the C=O absorption band at 1650cm^{-1} indicates to the oxidation process of cellulose molecule. An increase also noticed at the band of -CH stretching (2917-2920cm^{-1}) due to the hydrocarbon group in cellulose, hemicellulose and lignin.

3.3. *CIELab color variations measured with Color iMatch Spectrophotometer*

Colorimetric measurements were carried out on untreated, treated samples to assess chromatic variations. Chromatic values are expressed in the CIE L*a*b* space, where L* is the lightness/darkness coordinate, a* the red/green coordinate (+a* indicating red and −a* green) and b* the yellow/blue coordinate (+b* indicating yellow and −b* blue).

CIELab b* values Test results are provided in Table 2. Lower (more negative) CIELab b* values and higher positive values indicate that more blueing, or whitening effect .The data showed that the total color change ΔE for the sample treated with wolbers solvent gel were lower than the treated with akapad sponge . It was observed also that ΔE value in samples treated with cellulose nano crystal gel higher as compared to the control sample, with all values still in the acceptable range.

Slight color changes were measured in the aqueous treatment (immersion in deionized water) these changes are primarily due to the removal of dirt. A layer of dirt behaves much like a neutral-density filter; each wavelength in the visible spectrum receives a slight boost in reflectance when it is removed. The slight increases in all three of the CIE L*a*b* parameters, L* lightness, a* redness and b*yellowness, should be interpreted as an increase resulting from a slight increase in reflectance for all wavelengths. One can't observe an increase in yellowness and redness while ignoring the increase in lightness. The increases in both spectral reflectance and CIE L*a*b* are favourable. The CIE L*a*b* data for some of the historical paper samples (summarized in Table 3) immersion in deionized water treatment increased lightness, and decreased yellowness and redness for the paper support. (Messier & Vitale, 1994)

Table 2. Presents all colorimetric results for the historical paper support measured before cleaning treatments, and after cleaning treatments. Note the relatively large gains for the L value for paper support after cleaning with cellulose nano gel.*

Samples	L	a	b	ΔE	ΔL*	Δa*	Δb*	ΔE*
Control sample before cleaning	73.06	7.23	26.55	0	0	0	0	0
akapad Paper Sponge soft	81.73	2.99	17.32	6.89	10.51	-4.24	-9.22	11.82
Immersion in deionized water	78.90	4.48	20.67	4.20	5.83	-2.75	-5.88	8.37
Hydrogel gellan gum	83.57	3.90	19.23	5.51	8.67	-3.33	-7.32	14.61
cellulose nano crystal gel	84.10	2.79	15.99	7.50	11.04	-4.44	-10.56	15.91
Wolbers solvent acetone gel	77.42	5.53	24.16	2.45	4.35	-1.70	-2.38	5.24
Wolbers solvent 2-propanol gel	77.45	5.54	24.07	2.47	4.39	-1.69	-2.48	5.31

3.4. *Measurement of pH values before and after cleaning treatments:-*

pH measurements (Table 3) give information on the amount of acidity present in the paper and so to the preservation state of the historical samples. pH value detected in the paper sample is probably due to the presence of lignin. The increase of pH values obtained after cleaning procedures indicates that acidic components, involved in degradation processes are removed; anyhow it should be noted that the pH values are acidity is lightly higher after Gellan hydro gel cleaning procedure. These results indicate that hydro gel treatment is an efficient cleaning method and does not cause change in the morphology of paper (Fig. 14). It can be observed that there is an increase in the pH values of the treated samples with both Cellulose Nano Crystal gel and hydro gellan gel compared to the control sample before cleaning. The samples treated with akapad paper sponge showing no change in the pH values.

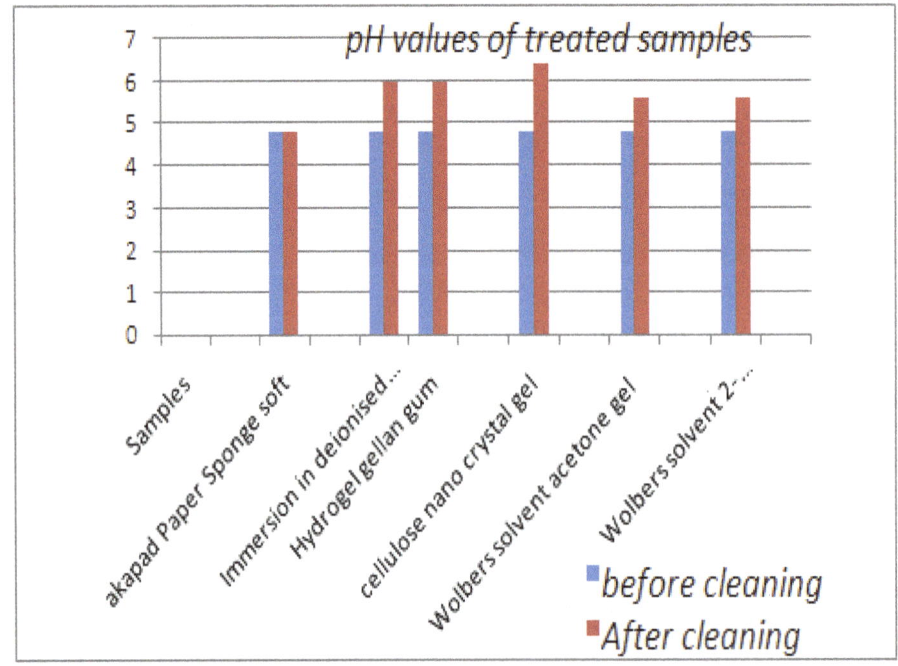

Figure 14. pH values of untreated & treated paper samples.

Table 3 shows pH values before and after cleaning procedures

Samples	pH values before cleaning	pH values after cleaning
Akapad Paper Sponge soft	4.8	4.8
Immersion in deionised water	4.8	6
Hydrogel gellan gum	4.8	6
Cellulose nano crystal gel	4.8	6.4
Wolbers solvent acetone gel	4.8	5.6
Wolbers solvent 2-propanol gel	4.8	5.6

3.5. *X-ray Diffraction Analysis (XRD)*

X-ray diffraction was also used to measure crystallinity index of cellulose according to Segal equation. Where: (Cr) expresses the crystallinity of cellulose (I002) express the maximum intensity of the crystallinity peak at (2θ = 22-24°) and (Iam) represents the intensity of diffraction of the non-crystalline cellulose at (2θ = 18°) Comparison between the cellulose crystallinity of the historical paper sample and the sample after cleaning with selected cleaning procedures indicated a decrease in the crystalline index of the treated samples.

The results of XRD show that there are noticeable differences in the crystalline & amorphous areas in the paper before and after cleaning treatments (see Fig. 15, 16, 17, 18, 19 and 20). They illustrate that the paper samples were affected by the selected cleaning procedures. Also, the results show that there was a change in the XRD pattern of the untreated and treated paper samples after cleaning treatments. Crystalline regions of the treated paper samples were slightly decreased. By comparing the results of x ray diffractograms of treated samples (with deionized water, akapad sponge, and wolbers solvent gels) and untreated sample, the data shows that a large decrease in the crystallinity index of cellulose, indicating that a significant change has occurred in the chemical and mechanical properties of cellulose molecule.

Cellulose Nano Crystal treatment showing a slight increase in the crystallinity index in the cellulose crystallinity compared to the control sample, which means that a moderate change has occurred in the chemical and mechanical properties of cellulose molecule (Fig. 20).

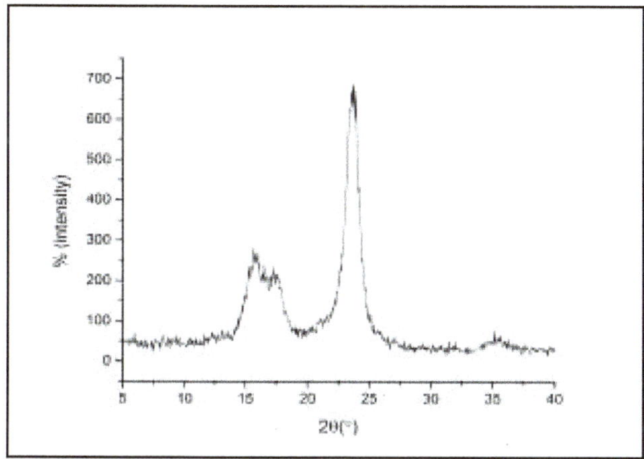

Figure 15. XRD pattern for the control sample before cleaning Crystallinity index=61

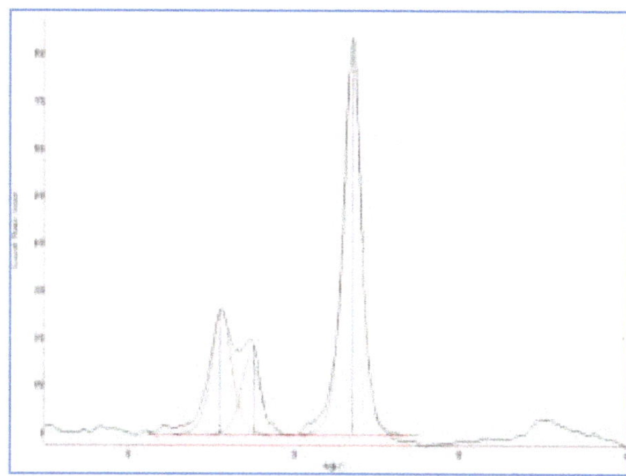

Figure 16. X-ray diffraction pattern of historical paper sample explaining how the crystallinity peaks of cellulose are measured

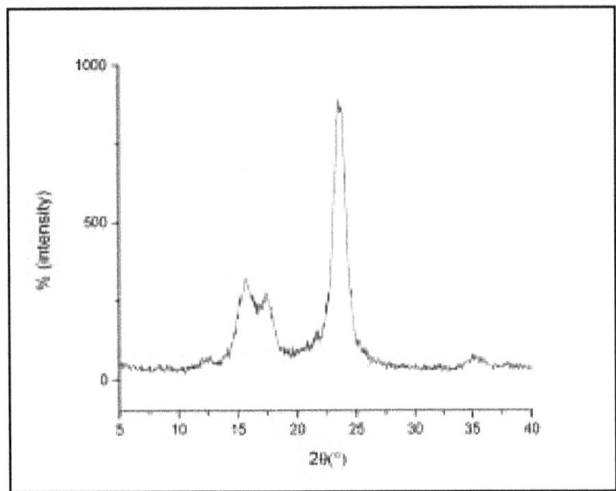

Figure 17. XRD pattern for the cleaning method with deionized water crystallinity index=11 showing a large decrease in the crystallinity index of cellulose indicating that a significant change has occurred in the chemical and mechanical properties of cellulose molecule.

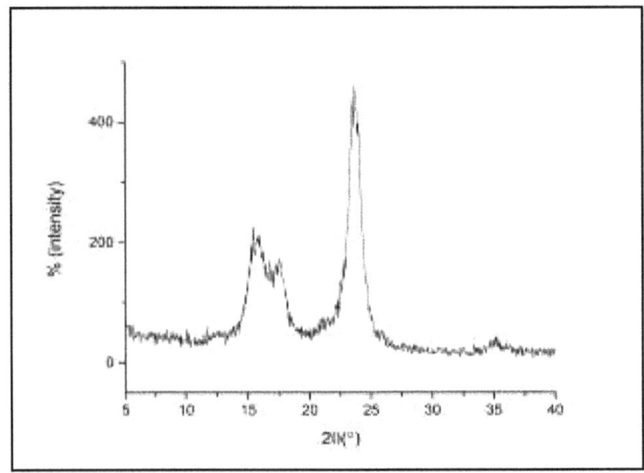

Figure 18. XRD pattern for the cleaning method with akapad paper sponge Crystallinity index=11.16 showing a large decrease in the crystallinity index of cellulose, indicating that a significant change has occurred in the chemical and mechanical Properties of cellulose molecule.

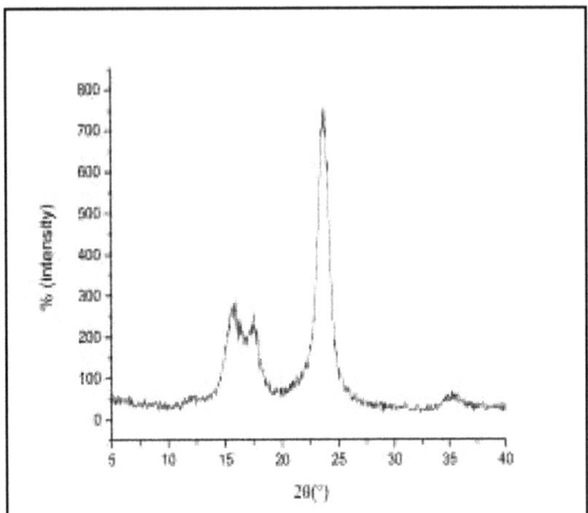

Figure 19. XRD pattern for the cleaning method with hydro Gellan gum crystallinity index=58.3 showing a slight decrease in the crystallinity index of cellulose indicating that only a less change has occur the chemical and mechanical properties of cellulose molecule.

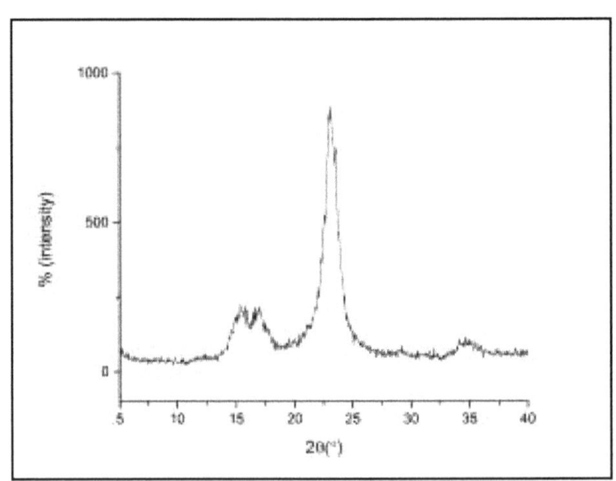

Figure 20. XRD pattern for the cleaning method with Cellulose Nano Crystal gel crystallinity index=17.00 showing a large decrease in the crystallinity index of cellulose, indicating that a significant change has occurred in the chemical and mechanical properties of cellulose molecule at the crystalline regions.

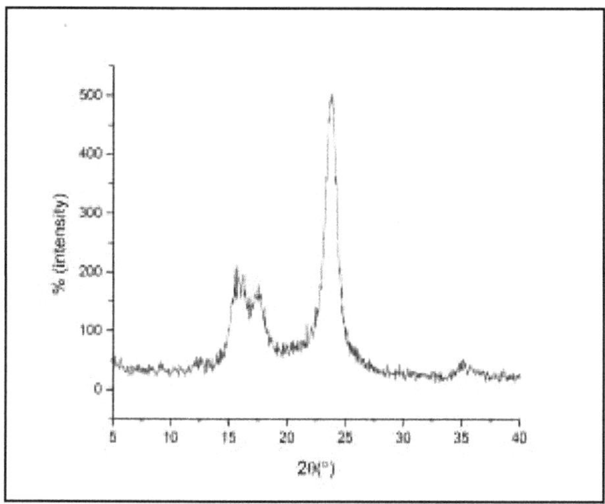

Figure 21. XRD pattern for the cleaning method with Wolbers solvent acetone gel crystallinity index=61.4 showing a slight increase in the crystallinity index in the cellulose crystallinity compared to the control sample which means that a moderate change has occurred in the chemical and mechanical properties of cellulose molecule

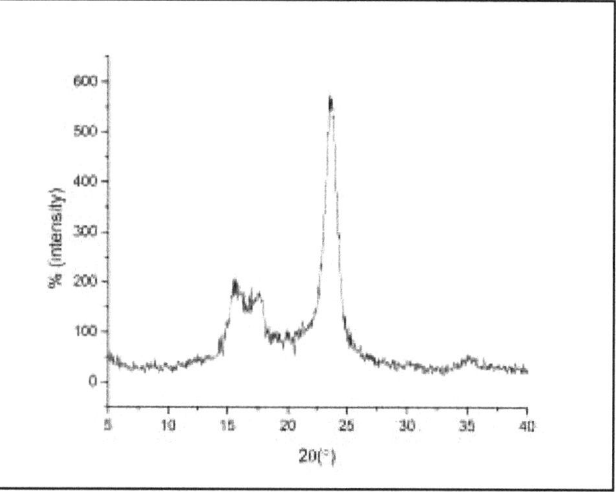

Figure 22. XRD pattern for the cleaning method with Wolbers solvent 2-propanol gel crystallinity index=18.5 showing a large decrease in the crystallinity index of cellulose, indicating that a significant change has occurred in the chemical and mechanical properties of cellulose molecule at the crystalline regions

3.6. *Mechanical behaviour of the samples (tensile strength, elongation % and breaking factor)*

The values of tensile strength and elongation (%) are shown in Table 4. The results reported are the average of five measurements with standard deviation. The Values of tensile strength reflect the detailed structure of the paper and the properties of its individual fibers, i.e., the dimension and strength of fibres, their arrangements, and inter fibre bonding Values of tensile strength reflect the detailed structure of the paper and the properties of its individual fibers, i.e., the dimension and strength of fibers, their arrangements, and inter fiber bonding (Caulfield& Gunderson, 2008). The percent loss in tensile strength of treated paper samples with akapad paper and wolbers solvent gels revealed a high sensitivity of tensile strength to the effects of cleaning procedures. (Rabee, 2015). Treated papers with acetone and isopropanol solvent gel caused a noticeable decrease of tensile strength while in the case of wet cleaning procedure (deionizied water treatment) treated samples exhibited a statistically significant decrease in tensile strength From these results, it can also be concluded that preconditioning can satisfactorily bring the moisture content of the treated paper to levels that do not affect tensile strength.Which is capable of swelling the carbohydrate components of celluloses and may accelerate further degradation, and can also dissolve and extract the starch and decayed hemicelluloses (Zervo, 2013).

Treated sample with CNC Gel gave the highest increase in tensile strength and elongation compared to the other samples, while treated sample with deionized water gave the lowest values for tensile strength and elongation. The results for Hydro gellan gum indicate average values.

Table 4. All Physical Testing results; Tensile strength and elongation for paper samples after cleaning treatments - According to ASTM_D828-Modified-250-load.msm.

Samples	Elongation @ pkLd mm	Tensile Strn @ pk %	Breaking Factor N/mm
Control sample	2.6	3.42	1.36
Akapad Paper Sponge soft	1.7	2.24	0.83
Immersion in deionized water	2.4	2.19	0.89
Hydrogel gellan gum	2.5	3.30	0.85
Cellulose nano crystal gel	4.1	5.37	1.07
Wolbers solvent acetone gel	2.2	2.91	0.60
Wolbers solvent 2-propanol gel	2.1	2.79	1.77

4. CONCLUSION

Conventional and nonconventional cleaning treatments of cellulosic manuscripts were evaluated using different experimental techniques including the mechanical properties, pH measurements, FTIR spectroscopy, measurement of color change and XRD after thermal accelerated aging. The study concludes that:

CNC gel & hydro gellan gum appeared to be more effective in removing of surface soils and dust. Additionally, an improvement was noticed in the mechanical properties of paper samples. Thus, it can be used safely in the conservation treatments of cellulosic supports, but water treatment should be used in the case of uncoloured paper to avoid bleeding of dyes or pigments. Although the data obtained from both mechanical properties and pH were completely compatible, it is useful to evaluate the chemical composition of treated samples using FTIR. It appeared that the all treatments were relatively safe to use on cellulosic paper samples.

Color changes occurred in treated samples, and these generally increased with post-treatment ageing time. The color changes, which were documented by colori Match, may be due to: 1) a loss of brightness resulting from the action of the akapad paper, and 2) deposition of akapad powder on the surface and within the fibres of the paper. The papers cleaned with the akapad Paper Sponge soft lost their brightness.

On comparing the effective method in cleaning and removal of ageing products (soils &dust) the most effective methods followed in order: Cellulose Nano Crystal Gel> Hydrogel gellan gum > akapad Paper Sponge soft > Immersion in deionised water> Wolbers solvent 2-propanol gel> Wolbers solvent acetone gel.

Washing treatments usually involves significant effects on the original morphological structure of paper and can sometimes be dangerous for water sensitive inks and pigments. The use of hydro gel of Gellan gum & CNC gel as an alternative paper cleaning treatment is developed. The application of hydrogels in conservation treatments minimizes damages caused by the use of water.

ACKNOWLEDGEMENTS

We thank the reviewers for their constructive comments. I would like to express my gratitude to Judy Elson Chemistry Lab and Birgit Anderson Research assistant and Lab Manager, TECS College of textile, polymer and colour chemistry in North Carolina University. I would like to thank Egyptian Government for funding this project and for its support.

REFERENCES

Adam W. (2015) Washing, spraying and brushing. A comparison of paper deacidification by magnesium hydroxide nanoparticles. *Restaurator: International Journal for the Preservation of Library and Archival Materials*, Vol .36, N.1, 3-23.

Angel M. et al. (2014) First experiments for the use of microblasting technique with powdered cellulose as a new tool for dry cleaning artworks on paper. *Journal of Cultural Heritage*, Vol. 15, No. 4, 365–372.

Antonella, C., Paolo, C., Clelia, I., Roberto, G., Stefano, P. and Nicola, S. (2013) Evaluation of the effect of cleaning on the morphological properties of ancient paper surface. *Springer Link*, Vol. 20, No. 4, 2027–2043.

Ardelean, E., Bobu, E., Niculesu, G. and Groza, C. (2011) Effect of different consolidation additives on ageing behaviour of archived document paper. *Cellulose Chem.Technol.*, Vol. 45, No. 1-2, 97-103.

Bansa, H. (1998) Aqueous deacidification – with calcium or with magnesium?". *Restaurator*, Vol. 19, PP.1–40.

Batterham, I., Rai, R. (2008) A Comparison of Artificial Ageing with 27 Years of Natural Aging. *AICCM Book, Paper and Photographic Materials Symposium.*

Bogaard, J. and Paual, W. (2001) Effect of dilute calcium washing treatments on paper. *The American Institute for Conservation of Historic & Artistic Works*, 105-123.

Calvini, P., Grosso, V., Hey, M., Rossi, L. and Santucci, L. (1988) Deacidification of paper-A more fundamental approach. *The Paper Conservator*,35-39.

Cannoletta, D., Lionetto, F., Del Sole, R., Vasapollo, Maffezzoli, A. (2012) Monitoring Wood Degradation during Weathering by Cellulose Crystallinity. *Materials*, Vol. 5.

Caulfield, D.F. and Gunderson, D.E. (1988) Paper testing and strength characteristics. *Proceedings of the Paper Preservation Symposium, Paper Preservation*, 31–40.

Giorgi, R., Dei, L., Schettino, C. and Baglioni, P. (2002) A new method for paper deacidification based on calcium hydroxide dispersed in nonaqueous media. *Works of art on paper: books, documents and photographs: techniques and conservation: contributions to the Baltimore Congress*, 69-73

Darwish, S., El Hadidi, N., & Mansour, M. (2013). The Effect of Fungal Decay on Ficus sycomorus wood. *International Journal for Conservation Science*, 271-282

Fenech , A., Schiro ,J., Farrugia ,C., and Baluci, C.(2011)A Comparative Study of the Effects of Cleaning Treatments on Two Historic Papers: A Preliminary Study" in Varella, E.A. and Caponetti E. In: Proceedings of the 2nd *Chemistry and Conservation Science Residential Summer School* (Societa Chimica Italiana & ECTN).

Ferrer, N., Sistach, C. (2007) FTIR Technique Used to Study Acidic Paper Manuscripts Dating from the Thirteenth to the Sixteenth Century from the Archive of the Crown of Aragón, *The Book and Paper Group Annual*, Vol. 26, 21-25.

Herbert F. (1939) Determination of the pH value of papers. *Journal of Research of the National Bureau of Standards*, Vol. 22, 553-564.

Heyun, W., Gang, L., Jinping, Z. and Dongqing, Z. (2013) Multifunctional nanocomposites for paper conservation. *The International Institute for Conservation of Historic and Artistic Works, Studies in Conservation*, Vol. 58, No. 1, 23-29.

Kolar J. et al. (2003) Laser cleaning of paper using Nd: YAG laser running at 532 nm. *Journal of Cultural Heritage*, Vol. 4, 185–187.

Kwiatowska, A., Wojech, R. and Wojciak, A. (2014) Paper deacidification with the use of magnesium oxide nanoparticles. *Annals of Warsaw University of Life Sciences – SGGW, Forestry and Wood Technology*, No. 85, 144-148.

Li-Ming, Z., Lu-E, S., Zhi-Liang, Z., Jian-Min, C., Dong-Dong, S., Jie, Y. and Zhen-Xing, T. (2011) Preparation and application of chitosan nanoparticles and nanofibrers. *Brazilian Journal of Chemical Engineering*, Vol. 28, No. 03, 353 – 362.

Maryam, A., Saleh, I. and Shahrzad, A. (2011) Zno nanocomposites: Control of environmental effects for preservation of old manuscripts. *International Journal of Chemical, Molecular, Nuclear, Materials and Metallurgical Engineering*, Vol:5, No.4, 298-300.

Maryam, A., Fereshteh, T. and Hamid, M. (2011) New cellulosic titanium dioxide nanocomposite as a protective coating for preserving paper art works. *Journal of Cultural Heritage*, Vol. 12, Np. 4, PP.380-383.

Mazzuca, C., Micheli, L. and Carbone, M. (2014) Gellan hydrogel as a powerful tool in paper cleaning process: A detailed study. *Journal of Colloid and Interface Science*, Vol. 416, 205–211.

Moropoulou, A. and Zervos, S. (2003) The immediate impact of aqueous treatments on the strength properties of paper. *Restaurator. International Journal for the Preservation of Library and Archival Material*, Vol. 24, No. 3, 160–177.

Nicole, B., David, C., Michele, B., Rodorico, G. and Piero, B. (2016) Confined aqueous media for the cleaning of cultural heritage: Innovative gels and amphiphile-based nanofluids. *Nanoscience and Cultural Heritage*, 283-311.

Paolo, C. (2012) *Rigid gels and enzyme cleaning*. The Centre for the Study of Materials for Restoration, Via Lombardia Saonara, Italy, 180-183.

Peter, D.V. (1989) Basic paper treatments for printed book materials. *Proceedings of the Guild of Book Worker' 9th Anniversary Seminar on the Standards of Excellence*, Portland, Oregon.

Piero, B., David, C., Rodorico, G. and Giovonna, P. (2015) *Cultural heritage conservation: Paper and Wood Nanoparticles, Encyclopaedia of Surface and Colloid Science*, Third Edition DOI: 10.1081/E-ESCS3-120047373, 1597-1612.

Piero, B., Luigi, D., Emiliano, C. and Rodorico, G. (2009) Gels for the conservation of cultural heritage. *American Chemical Society*, 8373–8374.

Poggi, G., Giorgi, R., Toccafondi, N., Katzur, V. and Baglioni, P. (2010) Hydroxide nanoparticles for deacidification and concomitant inhibition of iron-gall ink corrosion of paper, *Langmuir*, 21;26 .

Rabee, R. (2015) Behavior of archaeological paper after cleaning by organic solvents under heat accelerated ageing, *Mediterranean Archaeology and Archaeometry*, Vol. 15, No. 3, 141-150.

Rodorico, G., Luigi, D., Massimo, C., Claudius, S. and Piero, B. (2002) Nanotechnologies for conservation of cultural heritage: Paper and canvas deacidification. *American Chemical Society*, 8198-8203.

Rodorico, G., Claudio, B., Luigi, D., Chiara, G., Barry, N. and Piero, B. (2005) Nanoparticles of Mg(OH)2: Synthesis and application to paper conservation. *Langmuir*, Vol. 21, 8495-8501.

Sequeiraa, S., Casanovab, C. and Cabrita, E. J. (2006) Deacidification of paper using dispersions of Ca(OH)2 nanoparticles in isopropanol: Study of efficiency. *Journal of Cultural Heritage*, Vol. 7, 264–272.

Tella, B., Delia, F., Chillura, M., Vincenzo, R., Maria, L. S., Giovanna, P. and Eugenio, C. (2016) Alcoholic nanolime dispersion obtained by the insolubilisation-precipitation method and its application for the deacidification of ancient paper. *Colloids and Surfaces A: Physicochemical and Engineering Aspects*, Vol. 513, 241-249.

Ulla, K., Istvan, K., Ilkka, H. and Tuomo, R. (2012) Control *of aqueous paper treatments with ion chromatography*. EVTEK Institute of Art and Design, Vantaa, Finland.

Viera, J., Eva, B., Zuzana, M. and Bohuslava, H. (2015) Influence of deacidification on Arylmethane dyes on paper. *Restaur*, Vol. 36, No. 3, 211–228.

Zervos, S. (2013) Revising established tenets in paper conservation. *Procedia - Social and Behavioral Sciences*, Vol. 73, 35 - 42.

Zidan, Y.,El Hadidi ,N.,Mohamed ,M.,(2016)Examination and analysis of a wooden face at the museum storage at the faculty of archaeology, Cairo University. *Mediterranean Archaeology and Archaeometry*, Vol. 16, No 2, 1-11.

Zou, X., Gurnagul, N., Uesaka, T. and Bouchard, J. (1994) Accelerated aging of papers of pure cellulose: mechanism of cellulose degradation and paper embrittlement. *Polymer Degradation and Stability*, 393–402.

13

BIOARCHAEOLOGY, CONSERVATION AND DISPLAY OF A 16K-HUMAN SKELETON, JORDAN

Ahmad Y. Abu Dalou[1], Abdelrahman M. ElSerogy[2,3], Abdulla A. Al-Shorman[1], Mohammad Alrousan[1], Ali Khwaileh[1]

[1]*Department of Anthropology, Faculty of Archaeology and Anthropology, Yarmouk University, Irbid, Jordan*
[2]*Department of Restoration Faculty of Archaeology, Fayoum University, Fayoum, Egypt*
[3]*Department of Conservation and Management of Cultural Resources, Faculty of Archaeology and Anthropology, Yarmouk University, Irbid, Jordan*

Corresponding author: Abdelrahman ElSerogy (xserogy@yahoo.com)

ABSTRACT

The Jordanian Museum of Cultural Heritage houses the oldest human skeleton unearthed in Jordan; Radiocarbon analysis revealed a date of approximately 16000 years BP. The purpose of the study is to reconstruct the biology and way of life of an individual who lived in an era that is still ignored by archaeologists in the region. The methods of the reconstruction include bioarchaeological investigation, XRD, XRF, FTIR, pH meter, and microbiology. The reults indicate a 31-years-old male with an estimated height of about 172.4-175.2 cm. The bone pathology on the vertebrae and long bones suggests that the individual endured hard daily life activites. His teeth showed oblique dental wear that is attributed to using them as tools. The cause of death was probably due to a blunt force trauma to the left side of the skull. The bone analyses using XRD, XRF, FTIR, and pH meter ruled out bone diagenesis, which nominate the skeleton for further chemical analyses. The microbiological tests revealed the presence of a wide range of microorganisms: *Aspergillus viger, Pencillium chryogenum, Penicillum digitatum, yeasts, Corynebacterium equantium, Corynebacterium pyogemes, Escherichia coli, Pseudomonas pseudoaclingenes, Staphylcococus aureus, Salmonella enterica,* and *Corynebacterium pseudodiphthriticum.* For the purpose of exhibiting the skeleton at the Museum and ensuring longer survival, the previous conservation materials (P.V.A) were replaced by new ones (Paraloid B 72).

KEYWORDS: Bioarchaeology, Conservation, Skeleton, Jordan, XRD, XRF, FTIR.

1. INTRODUCTION

The archaeological skeletal remains are one of the most abundant findings at the Jordanian archaeological sites and probably the most useful. Studying them adds to the understanding of the health, growth, diet, environment, and migrations of past human societies (Larsen, 2015; Al-Shorman, 2007), especially when archaeolohgical records stand effete in reconstructuing the past history as triggered by the absence or scarcity of other archaeological materials. An example of such an archaeological period in Jordan is the period when there was a shift from hunting and gathering to agriculture (Rolston, 1982). Archaeologists agreed that there was a decline in the overall health for the generations of people who lived during this shift (Latham, 2013). This deterioration was triggered by greater physiological stress due to under nutrition and infectious diseases (Ulijaszek et al., 1991:271). However the period before 15000 BP has received little if any archaeological studies. In this period, the cold and harsh environment possessed extra demand on the human adaptation (Olszewski, 2008), especially in arid and semi arid regions of the Near East. Al-Kharaneh, eastof Jordan, is one of these areas were fortunately an Epipaleolithic human skeleton was recoved in 1982. Studying this skeleton adds to the general archaeological picture of this ingnored period. Consequently, a special attention should be directed toward the preservation and conservation of recovered skeletal materials from this period since discovery because they are sensitive and fragile (Plenderletih and Werner, 1971; Muller and Reiche, 2006).

Studying archaeological bone materials icludes a wide array of chemical and analytical methods. For example, Fourier Transform Infrared Spectroscopy (FTIR) has been used extensively to examine the bone organic material and its crystallinity (Wright and schwarcz, 1996; Lee-Throp and Sponheimer, 2003; Alvarez-Lioret et al., 2006; Brock et al., 2010), where the FTIR peaks at $565\ cm^{-1}$ and 605^{-1} increased while the peak at 595^{-1} decreased (Stiner et al., 2001). On the other hand, XRD uses X-rays of known wavelengths to determine the lattice spacing in the bone crystal lattice and therefore identifies chemical compounds of the sampled bones (Al-Shorman, 2013). An example of one of the earliest use of XRD in archaeological bones analysis is the study by Hassan et al. (1977) who evaluated the chemical composition of bones for radiocarbon dating. Another study was conducted on four archaeological sites from Jordan to examine the crystallinity index using XRD (Al-Shorman, 2010) and found that the burial environment is a major factor in bone digenesis. Another technique is X-ray Fluorescence (XRF), which measures the elements of bone samples. For example, Todd and Landriagan (1993) and Little et al. (2014) measured the heavy metal content in archaeological bone using XRF. This technique was used also to examine the ionic exchange between soil solutions and bone (Pate et al., 1989). The burial environment has also received the archaeologists attention (Nord et al., 2005), where the soil acidity is a major factor in skeletal preservation (Gordon and Buikstra, 1981). The microbial attack of archaeological bones has also received a significant consideration especially during the early stages of digenesis (Muller et al. 2011). Such studies were able to visualize the microstructural damage cause by the bacteria (Nielsen-Marsh and Hedges, 2000; Jans et al., 2004), identify the various microbial species colonizing bones (White and Booth, 2014) and then inferring the biological burial context (Child, 1995).

However, the inclusion of modern chemical analyses in the field of archaeological skeletal analysis has contributed to the advancement of knowledge regarding the biological and social contexts of buried human remains. There are several factors that need to be considered in studying bone diagenesis: microbial attack, collagen loss, crystallinity increase, dissolution, and uptake of groundwater solutes (Hedges, 2002), porosity, bulk density, carbonate to phosphate ratio, and cracking (Smith et al., 2007). The current case study is an example, but one, that elucidates on the intertwined methods in extracting information from skeletal materials.

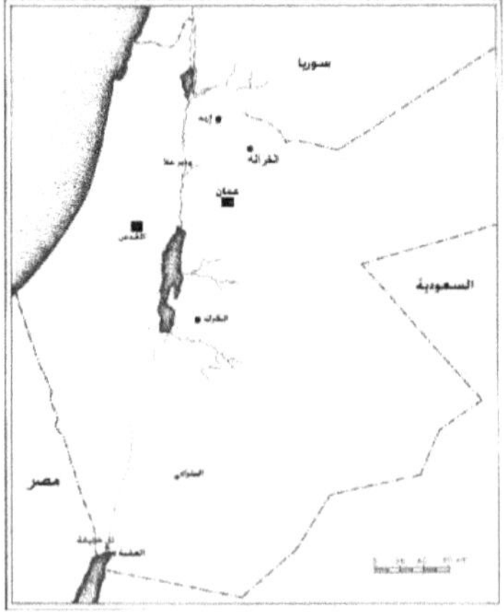

Figure 1. A Map of Jordan that shows Al-Kharaneh archaeological site.

The studied skeleton is displayed at the Jordanian Museum of Cultural Heritage/Yarmouk University, Jordan. It was recovered from a pit at the archaeological site of Al-Kharaneh, Al Azraq desert, 70 Km east of Amman (Fig. 1). The individual was buried in an extended position, where the head and legs were covered by large boulders and two antlers (Fig. 2). However, the common burial practices during this period (Epipaleolithic) was a flexed position in a small pit (Al-Shorman, 2007), which questions the manner of death as the study clarifies later.

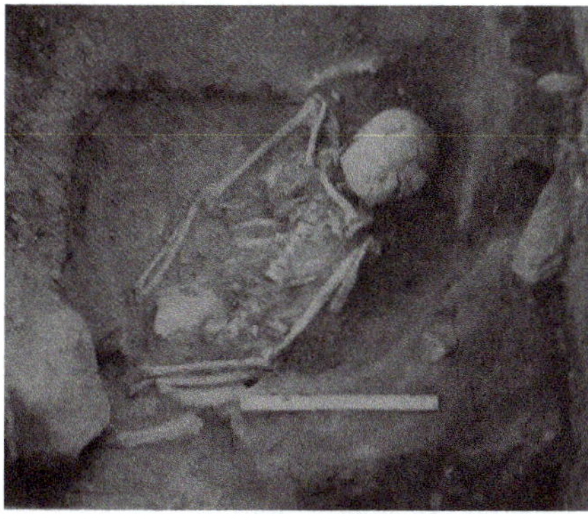

Figure 2. The human skeleton during its discovery in 1982 (Muheisen, 1988).

Radiocarbon analysis revealed a date of approximately 16000 years BP (Rolston, 1982), which puts the skeleton on top of the oldest skeletal collections in Jordan. This skeleton tells the story of a vague period in the history of the transition from hunting and gathering to agriculture. The previous conservation has technical problems; the conservation materials were inappropriate and contributed to further deterioration. and the method of application did not follow 'thin film' techniques. In addition, the skeleton was displayed on dirt with the presence of insects (Silverfish). The temperature and humidity of the showcase are not appropriate for preserving organic materials. The average humidity is about 74% during summer days and 34% during nights; this fluctuation contributes to the deterioration of the organic matter of the skeletal materials at the museum (Khasawneh, 2006). In summer, the temperature may reach 30°C during the day, and the difference in temperature between day and night may reach 10°C, which enhances further deterioration especially by insects and microbes (Caple, 2000). The skeleton was not exhibited in an anatomical position.

2. MATERIAL AND METHODS

This study comprised one human skeleton that was recovered during a field excavation in the year of 1982. Radiocarbon dating revealed a date of about 16000 years BP- the Epipaleolithic Period (22500-10500 BP). Accordingly, the individual lived in a period just before humans were semi sedentary living in larger and organized groups (Al-Shorman and Khwaileh, 2011). The methods of the study include anthroposcopic examination of the human skeleton after Buikstra and Ubelaker (1991) while the stature was estimated after (Bass, 1987). The other method is analytical chemistry techniques (XRD, XRF, and FTIR). The sample size for analytical chemistry is 1 mg each (after grinding to a fine powder) and obtained from bone fragments (total number is 3). For the X-ray diffraction (XRD, Schimatzo 6000), the results were calibrated to a synthetic hydroxyapatite curve, where the used voltage is 40 Kv at 2 theta with a continuous speed of 1 deg/min. The other technique is X-ray fluorescence (XRF, Philips Minipal PW4025), which was standardless as the results do not aim to quantify the concentrations but to characterize the presence of elements. Fourier Transform Infrared Spectroscopy (FTIR, Bruker-Tensor 27) was also performed after mixing the grinded samples with 30 mg of KBr to ensure noise elimination of the peaks. The pH meter (PH315i/set) was used to measure the acidity of soil sample after calibration with known standards. The methods of conservation include cleaning, sterilization, consolidation, and coating to protect the skeleton from the surrounding environment using Paraloid B72 (Ambrose and Paine, 2007). For microbial testing, sterilized swabs were taken from the skeleton and cultivated in nutrient agars after Barrow and Feltham (2003). Fungi Complete media was also used to obtain pure cultures of them. After 3 days of growth at 37 °C, fungal colonies were observed. Morphological identification of fungal isolates was performed microscopically after Elserogy et al. (2016). (Fig. 3).

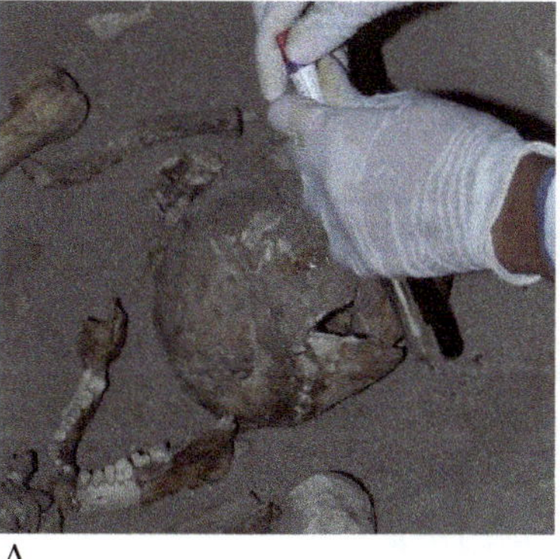

A

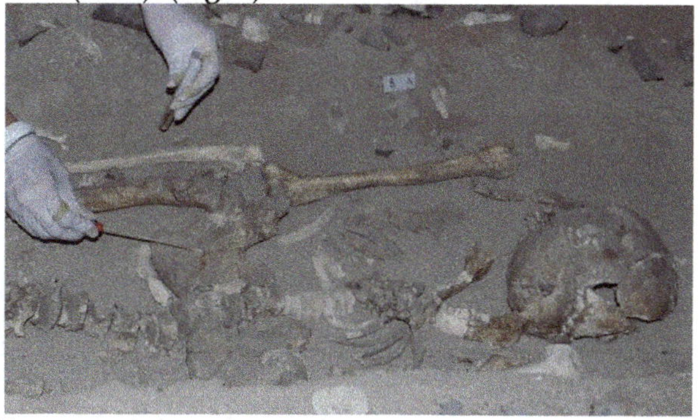

B

Figure: 3. The method of taking swabs for microbial culture from (A) the skull and (B) the spine.

3. RESULTS AND DISCUSSION

3.1. *Bioarchaeological assessment*

The skeleton displays a poor preservation condition, where most of the bones were fragmented, bleached, and fragile. The bioarchaeological assessment extracts the demographic elements of the individual as well as the health status. Based on the shape of the Greater Sciatic Notch of the pelvis, Sacrum, Supra Orbital Ridge, and Mastoid process, the sex of the individual was male. The age of the individual was determined based on teeth, bone fusion, and the morphology of the auricular surface to be 30-31 years old (Table 1).

Table 1: The age estimation based on teeth, bone fusion, and the morphology of the auricular surface.

Feature	Description	Estimated age
Teeth	All of the teeth were fully erupted	+18 years
Bone fusion of the clavicle	Medial and lateral epiphyses are fused	+30 years
Morphology of Auricular surface of the pelvis	No apical activity, slight retroauricular activity, coarse granulity on superior demiface and significant striae on inferior demiface	31 years

There is myositis ossificans on the medial side of the left tibial midshaft (Fig. 4). This type of pathology is usually occurred at the insertion of muscles due to traumatic origin (Vargova et al., 2016), where after prolonged inflammation calcification starts to accumulate. Rolston (1982) in his report on the skeleton to the Jordanian Department of Antiquities mentioned that the left tibia is 9mm shorter than the right one. However, the right tibia is currently missing. The left fibula shows a healed fracture at its distal end (Fig. 5). Both of the clavicles show bone lesions on their inferior medial surfaces (rhomboid fossa), the site at which costaclavicuar ligament is attached. When prominent, the rhomboid fossa may be mistaken for an osteolytic lesion (Kumar et al., 1989) (Fig. 6). Osteoarthritis is apparent at the synovial joints and severe osteophytes mostly on the lumbar vertebrae (Fig. 7), which could be attributed to carrying heavy loads on the back (Kim et al., 2012; Alrousan and Abu Dalou, 2013). Although osteoarthritis advances with aging, the current case as being young is a clear indicator of living in a very harsh environment and at the same time enduring a tough daily living activity. The skull exhibits multiple fractures that probably happened perimortem as each fracture did not extend beyond the previous one. Accordingly, the sequence of the fractures can be reconstructed as shown in figure 8 below. The fracture labeled 1 occurred first followed by 2 and then 3. This type of fracture is caused by a blunt force trauma to the left side of the skull. This trauma explains the manner of death, where the individual was found buried in extended not flexed position and at the same time not in a cemetery.

Unfortunately, the bones of the face are missing where nothing can be said about the maxillary teeth. The mandible shows that the left lower second incisor was lost long time before death as the tooth socked was completely healed. The rest of the teeth were still in occlusion at the time of death. Periodontal disease is substantial as there were extensive alveolar bone resorption of the lower jaw. The left and right premolars and molars show extensive oblique dental wear caused by using teeth as tools (Al-Shorman, 2003; Al-Shorman and Khalil, 2006; Alrousan, 2009; 2016) (Fig. 9). The left side shows more oblique wear compared to the right one, which concludes a person who wasprobably left-sided.

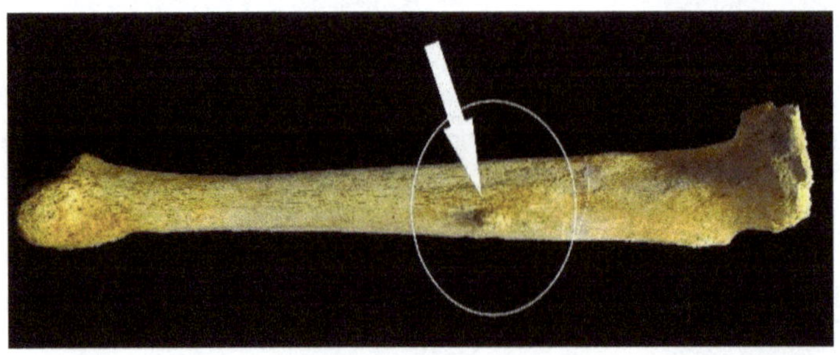

Figure 4: Myositis ossificans of the midshaft of the left Tibia.

Figure 5: Healed fracture of the left fibula.

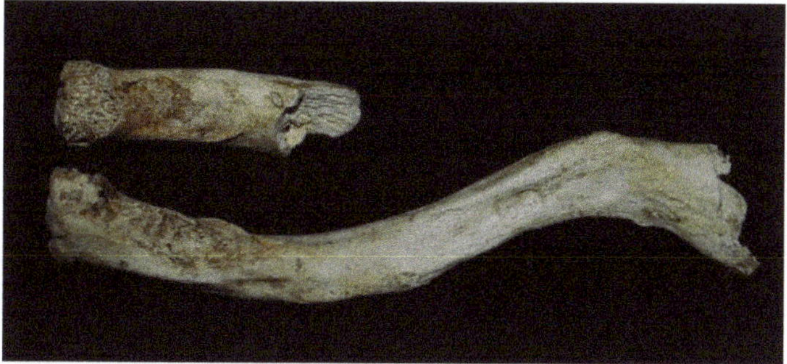

Figure 6: Right and left clavicle lesions at the rhomboid fossa.

The stature of the individual was estimated using the maximum lengths of the humerus and tibia (31.1 cm and 36.9 cm respectively). The stature based on the humerus is 172.4-181.4 cm and 167.2-175.2 cm based on tibia. The final estimate would be 172.4-175.2 cm. This value falls within the range of the male living population in the country of Jordan (Abu Dalou, 2016).

Figure 7: Osteophytosis of the lumbar vertebrae.

Figure 8: The pattern of skull fracture.

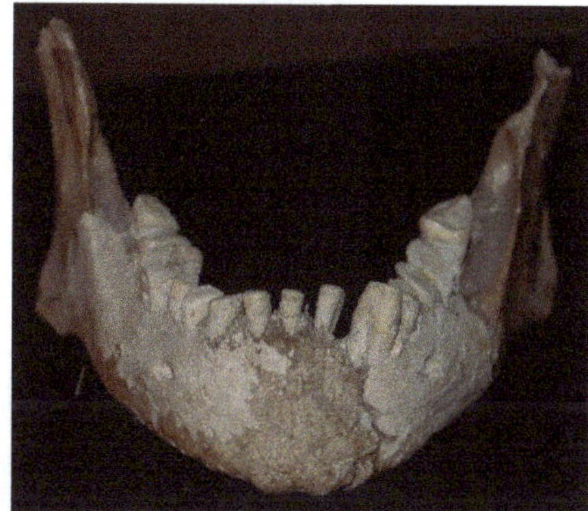

Figure 9: the oblique dental wear of the lower jaw.

3.2. The previous conservation of the skeleton

Unfortunately, the previous conservation method and procedures were not documented, which required extra examination and evaluation of the preservation condition of the skeleton. For example, the previous consolidation depended on the use of a regular glue without prior cleaning, and the application method was not thin films. Furthermore, the vertebrae were glued together using the same material without cleaning. Some of these vertebrae glued together using a paste that resembles gums (Figs. 10, 11, and 12). In addition, a piece of newspaper was found glued to some vertebrae.

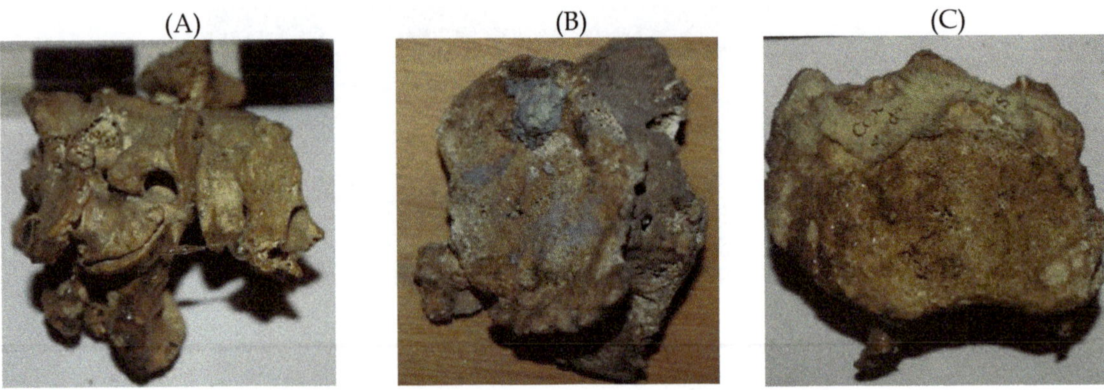

Figure 10: (A) The previous conservation in which the adhesive material was used excessively (B) the use of a gum to glue vertebra broken parts together, (C) A piece of a newspaper was placed on one of the vertebrae.

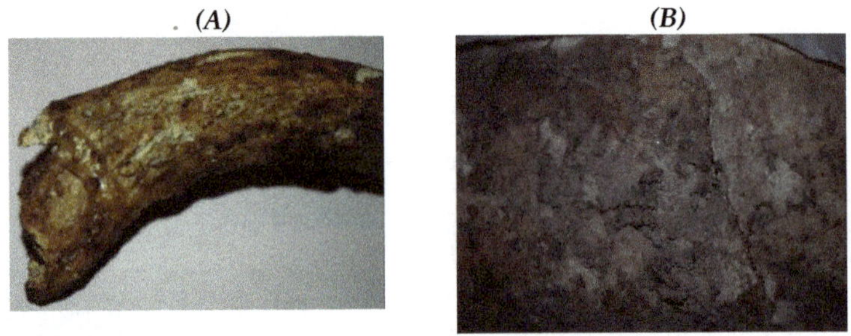

Figure 11: (A and B) The adhesive material was placed over the dirt.

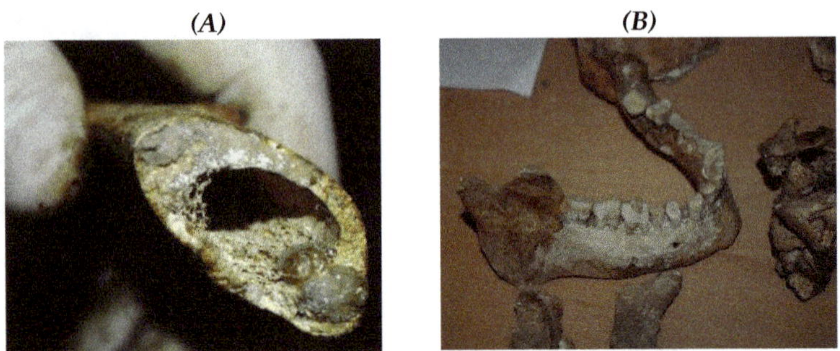

Figure 12: (A) The excessive adhesive material inside a bone. (B) The mandible was partially cleaned and it appears with multiple colors.

The length of the display area was 95 cm; not convenient to the stature of the skeleton. The presence of the skeleton in a pit of dirt helps gather insects and fungi (Fig. 13), where they have the ability to digest bone collagen (Metcalf et al., 2016). In addition, these insects can digest calcium and phosphorus of the bones (Brady et al., 2008); a recovered example is silverfish bugs (*Lepisma saccharina*). Humidity plays an important role in the biological deteriorations as a chemical reaction between bone elements and SO_2 or CO_2. Humidity also enhances further microbial attack (Collins et al., 2002). The microbes consume a huge amount of phosphorus for their growth: an element that constitute about 18% of bone weight. In addition, anaerobic microbes produce a number of organic acids (Metcalf et al., 2016), which convert phosphorus insoluble compounds to soluble ones and dissolve the inorganic lattice of bone (Hydroxyapatite: $Ca_{10}(PO_4)_6(OH)_2$). In addition, fungi are among the agents that are responsible for the deterioration of organic materials and produce a number of enzymes that contribute to collagen autolysis (Hiller et al., 2004).

Figure 13: The method of old display, the bones were placed incorrectly.

3.3. *pH value*

The pH was measured for soil samples that were attached to the surface of the bones using pH mater in order to control further diagenesis. Three readings were taken at different time intervals. The results show an average pH of 5.9, which means an acidic environment. Some bacterial species are able to live in such an environment (Gerardi, 2006). Furthermore, the acidic soil dissolves the hydroxyapatite of bones (Abdel-Maksoud and Abdel-Hady, 2011) and soften collagen (Al-Shorman, 2013).

3.4. *The microbiological test*

The method isolates, identifies, and treats the microbes that are responsible for the deterioration of the archaeological bone. The results revealed the presence of *Aspergillus niger*, *Penicillium chryso-genum*, *Penicillium digitatum*, and yeasts. The bacterial species are *Corynebacterium aquatium*, *Corynebacaterium pyogemes*, *Escherichia coli*, *Pseudomonas pseudoaclingenes*, *Staphylococcus aureus*, *Salmonella enterica*, and *Corynebacterium pseudodiphthriticum*. The study also shows that the concentration of the bacteria (Colony-Forming Units/ml: CFU/ml) on the sampled bones is very high compared to the other displayed artifacts (Fig. 14).

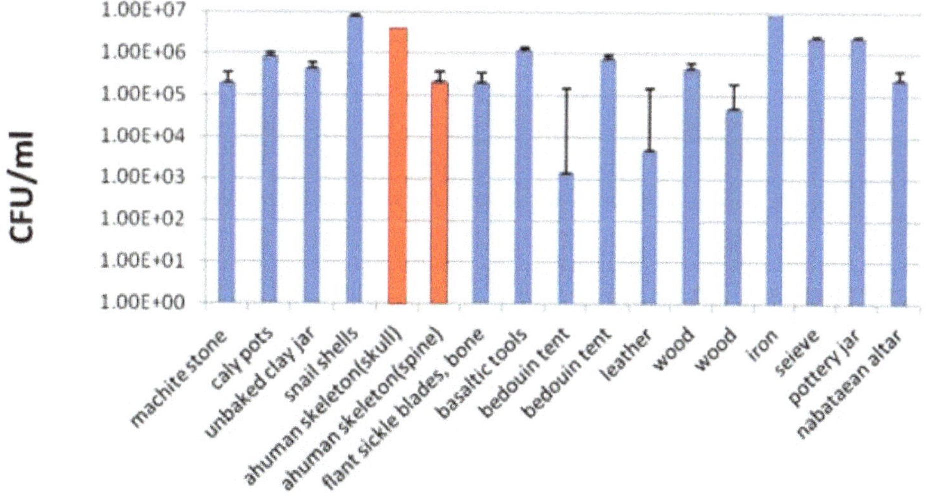

Figure 14: The percentages of bacteria in the skeleton and the other materials in the museum.

3.5. *X-Ray diffraction*

This technique characterizes the various crystal compounds attached to the bone surface or incorporated into its lattice structure due to soil bone exchange. Samples for XRD analysis were taken from the broken parts of the skeleton. The results showed the presence of fluoroapatite (Fig. 15). The fluorine enters the bones after they are buried as fluorides and/or dissolved fluorine, where it replaces the

(OH) group in the hydroxyapatite forming fluroapatite ($Ca_{10}(PO_4)_6F_2$). The percentage of fluorine increases in bones as along as the burying period increases. The formation of fluoroapatite took place while the skeleton had been buried not during exhibition.

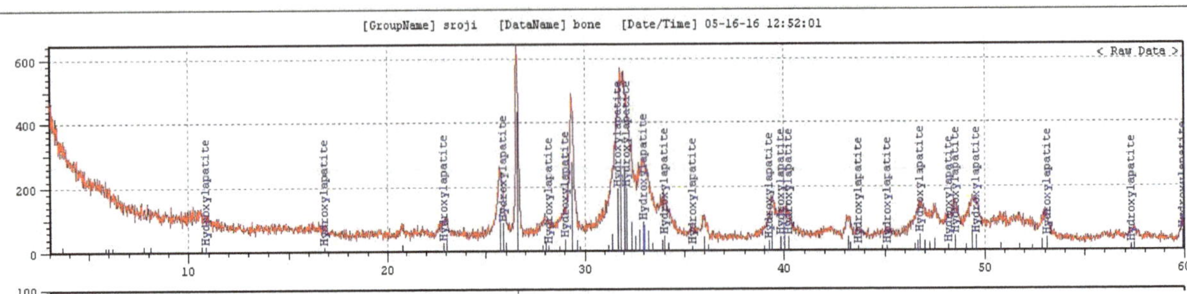

Figure 15. XRD results for a sample from the skeleton

3.6. X-Ray fluorecence

X-ray fluorescence is a technique that evaluates the presence of exogenous elements in the sampled bones to evaluate the preservation condition of the skeleton. The XRF analysis of the sampled bones (Fig. 15) showed no exogenous minerals attached either to the surface of the samples or the chemical structure except for fluoroapatite. This means that there is no chemical damage to the samples.

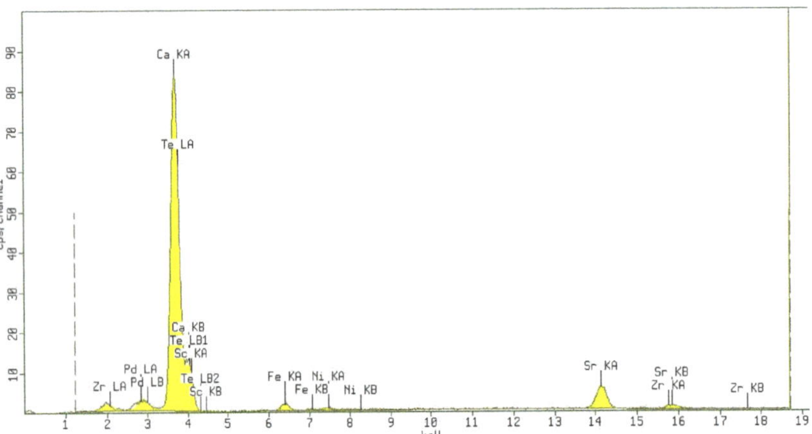

Figure 16: XRF results for a sample from the skeleton (a fragment from Tibia).

3.7. Fourier transform infrared spectroscopy

Although FTIR has the potential to characterize the organic component of the sampled bones, it is used here to evaluate digenesis through examining the crystallinity of bones. The results of the FTIR analysis showed a peak of absorption at 571 cm^{-1} and 608 cm^{-1} (Fig. 17). The heights of these peaks were used to calculate the Crystallinity Index (CI) of the sampled bone after Holland et al. (2013) and Al-Shorman (2013). A baseline correction then was drawn between 750-495 cm^{-1}. The CI is calculated to be 3.1 and thus indicating no digenesis (Cruz Baltazar, 2001), and thus supporting the previous XRF results. In addition, the FTIR analysis supports the XRD one regarding the presence of fluoroapatite in the samples, where a peak at 1096 cm^{-1} is noticed.

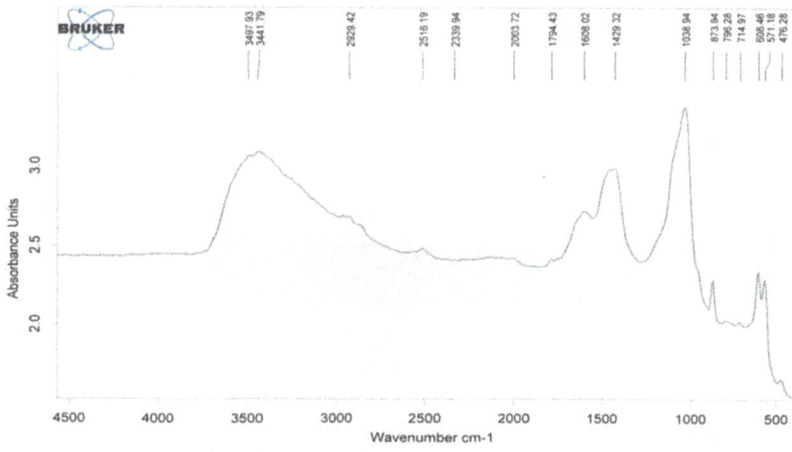

Figure 17. FTIR results for a sample from the skeleton (A fragment from a rib as it's the most vulnerable to digenesis due to its thin cortical bone).

4. *Removal of the previous conservation materials*

The skeleton was cleaned mechanically by the use different types of paint brushes in order to remove the accumulated dirt (Fig. 18). Then the cleaning process continued using a wood spatula, a medical scalpel, and dentist's tools in order to remove the calcified mud on the bones. Chemical cleaning was then used to remove old consolidants using organic diluted solutions (Ethyle Alcohol: C_2H_5OH) with a concentration of 80% after Johnson (1994).

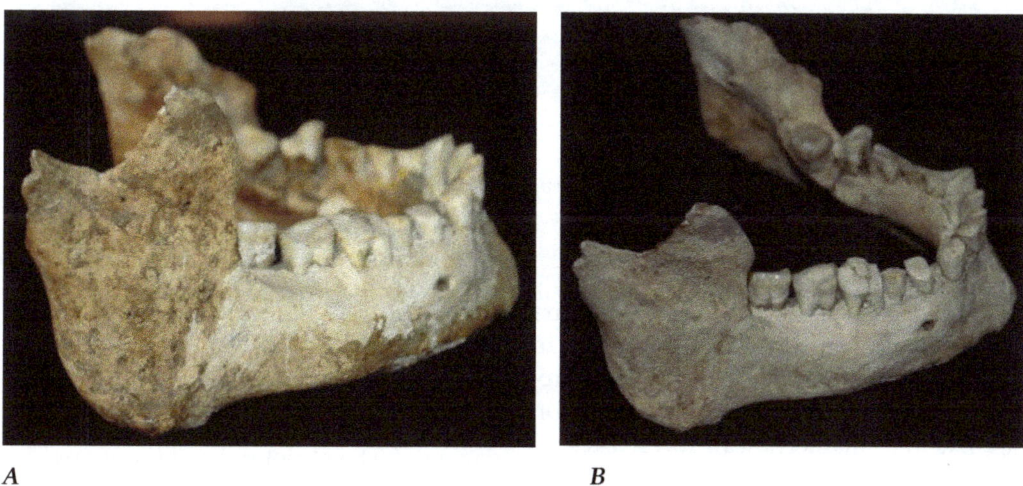

A B

Figure 18. The mandible (A) before and (B) after the cleaning and conservation processes.

Gluing the broken parts

After the application of the mechanical and chemical cleaning, several broken bones were carefully identified and glued using Paraloid B 72 with a concentration of 10%(Podany et al., 2001). Previous studies revealed that Paraloid B 72 is considered as one of the best adhesive materials in bone conservation and can be used under room temperature. Paraloid B 72 is a reversible adhesive material, transparent, and its color is temperature resistant (Brielery, 2010).

Consolidation and coating of the skeleton

The consolidation and coating is one of the most important steps in conservation of archaeological bones. A thin film of Paraloid B 72 w/aceton (5% concentration) was applied for consolidation (Podany et al., 2001). The consolidation procedure was applied under room temperature (Turner, 2007).

The display of the skeleton

The skeleton was displayed in a showcase (Fig. 19). It was laid according to the anatomical position taking into consideration the stature of the skeleton. Light-Emitting Diode was used in the showcase, which is not harmful compared to previous ultraviolet or infrared lights. Ultraviolet and infrared lights generate heat that degrade the organic materials in bones. Furthermore, the glass showcase ensures a clean environment with no dirt, dust, or pollutants that may affect the archaeological bones negatively (Ambrose and Paine, 2007).

A

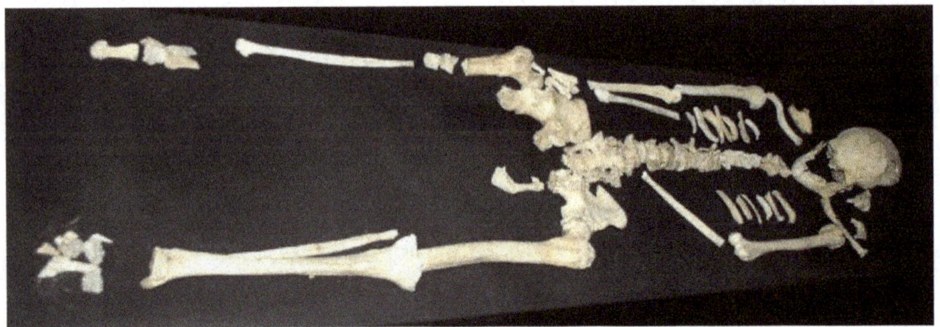

B

Figure 19: (A) before conservation and (B) after conservation.

5. CONCLUSIONS

The individual of this study had lived 1000 years before the climate began to ameliorate as glaciers in the northern latitudes began a relatively rapid retreat (Olszewski, 2008). Around 15000 BP vegetation communities like the Mediterranean forest became much broader in distribution, as temperatures became somewhat warmer and humidity increased (Baruch and Bottema 1991: 16). In other words, the individual lived in a very harsh environment with limited food resources that impacted his health. His death was tragic as he died of a blunt force trauma to the head. The previous preservation, conservation and display that were performed after its recovery in 1982 were scientifically incorrect and could have been attributed to further physical and chemical damages. The skeleton has little if any diagenesis as reported by the results of FTIR, XRD and XRF. However, there is considerable microbial attack that could lead to further degradation of the bones.

REFERENCES

Abdel-Maksoud, G., Abdel-Hady, M. (2011) Effect of Burial Environment on Crocodile Bones from Hawara Excavation. *Journal of Cultural Heritage, 12*, 180–189.

Abu Dalou, A. (2016) Height of Northern Jordanian Middle-Class Adults, Born 1960-1990 in the Response to Improving Socio-economic Conditions. *Economics and Human Biology*, 22: 155-160.

Alrousan, M. (2009) *The Mesolithic-Neolithic Transition in the Near East: Biological implications of the shift in subsistence strategies through the analysis of dental morphology and dietary habits of human populations in the Mediterranean area 12,000-5,000 B.P.* PhD Dissertation, University of Barcelona, Spain.

Alrousan, M. (2016) Human Dental Buccal Microwear and Paleodiet Reconstruction. *Anthropologie*. 54(3): 305-315.

Alrousan, M. , Abu Dalou, A. (2013) *Reflections on Human Skeletons from Tall Abu Al-Kharaz. Pp: 333-338. in P. M. Fischer and T. Bürge, The* Swedish Jordan Expedition 2011 and 2012 at Tall Abu al-Kharaz. Fourteenth and Fifteenth Seasons: Preliminary Results. *Opuscula. Annual of the Swedish Institutes in Athens and Rome*, 6: 307-338.

Al-Shorman, A. (2003) A Byzantine tomb from Khirbat Yajuz, Jordan. *Journal of Paleopathology, 15*(3), 177-186.

Al-Shorman, A., Khalil, L. (2006) The Evidence of Weaving at Khirbit Yajuz. *International Journal of Dental Anthropology.8:1-9.*

Al-Shorman, A. (2007) *The arcaheothanatology of Jordan.* Irbid: Yarmouk University Press.

Al-Shorman, A. (2010) Diagenesis of the Skeletal Remains in Four Archaeological Sites in Northern Jordan. *Jordan Journal for History and Archaeology* 4(1): 202-217.

Al-Shorman, A. (2013) *The Chemistry of Archaeological Human Bone.* Irbid: Yarmouk University Press.

Al-Shorman, A., Khwaileh, A. (2011) Burial practices in Jordan from the Natufians to the Persians . *Estonian Journal of Archaeology, 18*, 88-108.

Alvarez-Lioret, P., Navarro, A., Romanek, C., Gaines, K., & Congdon, Y. (2006) Quantitative analysis of bone mineral using FTIR. *MCLA , 6*, 45-47.

Ambrose, A., Paine, G. (2007) *Museum basics* . London: Taylor and Francis .

Barrow, G., Feltham, R. (2003) *Cowan's and Steel's manual for the identification of medical bacteria.* Cambridge: Cambridge University Press.

Bass, W. (1987). *Human Osteology: A laboratory and field manual* (3rd ed.). Columbia: Missouri Archaeological Society.

Baruch, U. Bottema, S (1991) Palynological Evidence for Climatic Changes in the Levant ca. 17,000-9,000 B.P. In Bar-Yosef, O. and Valla, F. (eds.), *The Natufan Culture in the Levant*, 11-20. Ann Arbor: International Monographs in Prehistory.

Brielery, L. (2010). Conservation of a Neolithic plaster statue from ain Ghazal, Jordan IIC . *Istanbul congress for conservation in the Eastern Mediterranean.* Istanbul.

Brock, F., Higham, T., & Bronk Ramsey, C. (2010) Pre-screening techniques for identification of samples suitable for radiocarbon dating of poorly preserved bones. *Journal of Archaeological Science , 37*, 855-865.

Buikstra, J., Ubelaker, D. (1994) *Standards: For data collection from human skeletal remains.* Fayetteville: Arkansas Archaeological Survey Research Series No. 44.

Caple, C. (2000) *Conservation skills, judgment, methods and making.* London: Routledge.

Child, A. (1995) Microbial taphonomy of archaeological bone. Studies inn Conservation 40: 19-30.

Collins, M., Nielsen, C., Hiller, J., Smith, C., Prijodich, R., Wess, T., & Turner-Walker, G. (2002). The survival of organic matter in bone: a review. *Archaeometry, 44*, 383-394.

Cruz Baltazar, V. (2001) Studies on the state of preservation of archaeological bone. *Unpublished PhD thesis.* University of Bradford.

Elserogy, A., Kanan, G., Hussein, E & Khreis, S. (2016) characterization and treatment of microbial agents responsible for the deterioration of archaeological objects in three Jordanian museums. *Mediterranean Archaeology and Archaeometry, 16*(1), 117-126.

Gordon, C., Buikstra, J. (1981) Soil pH, bone preservation, and sampling bias at mortuary site. *American Antiquity* 46: 566-571.

Gerardi, M. (2006) *Waste water Bacteria.* New Jersey: John Wily and Sons Ltd.

Hassan, A. (1977) Mineralogical studies of bone apatite and their implications for radiocarbon dating. *Radiocarbon , 19* (3), 364-374.

Hedges,R. (2002) Bone diagnosis: an overview processes. Archaeometry 44 (3): 319 – 328.

Hollund, H., Ariese, F., Fernandes, R., Jans, M., Kars, H. (2013) Testing an alternative high throughput tool for investigating bone diagenesis: FTIR in attenuated total reflection (ATR) mode. *Archaeometry* 55 (3): 505-532.

Hiller, J., Collins, M. J., Chamberlain, A., & Wess, T. (2004) Small-angle X-ray scattering: a high-throughput technique for investigating archaeological bone preservation. *Journal of Archaeological Science, 31*, 1349–1359.

Janes, M., Nielsen-Marsh, C., Smith, C., Collins, M., & Kars, H. (2004) Characterisation of microbial attack on archaeological bone. *Journal of Archaeological Science* 31:87-95.

Johnson, J. (1994) Consolidation of Archaeological Bone from a Conservation perspective. *Journal of Field Archaeology, 21*, 221-233.

Khasawneh, T. (2006) Museum Environmental Control as a Tool for Preventive Conservation Museum of Jordanian Heritage as Case Study. Unpublished Master's Thesis- Department of Conservation and Cultural Heritage Managment- Yarmouk University, Irbid - Jordan. *Unpublished MA Thesis*. Irbid, Jordan.

Kim, D., Kim, M., Kim, S, Oh, C., & Shin, D. (2012). Kim, D.K., Kim, M.J., KiVertebral osteophytes of pre-modern Korean skeletons from Joseon tombs. *Anatomy and Cell Biology, 45*(4), 274 - 281.

Kumar, R.; Madewell, J.; Swischuk, L.; Lindel, M.; & David, R. (1989). The Clavicle: Normal and Abnormal. Radiographics, 9(4): 677-706.

Larsen, C. (2015) Bioarchaeology: interpreting behavior from the human skeleton (2nd. ed.). *Cambridge*: Cambridge University Press.

Latham, K. (2013) Human Health and the Neolithic Revolution: an Overview of Impacts of the Agricultural Transition on Oral Health, Epidemiology, and the Human Body. *Nebraska Anthropologist*. Paper 187.

Lee-Thorp, J., Sponheimer, M. (2003) Three case studies used to reassess the reliability of fossil bone and enamel isotope signals for paleodietary studies. *Journal of Anthropological Archaeology , 22*, 208-216.

Little, C., Florey, V., Molina, I., Owsley, D., Speakman, R. (2014). Measuring heavy metal content in bone using portable X-ray fluorescence. *Open Journal of Archaeometry* 2: 5257

Metcalf, J., Carter, D., & Knight, R. (2016) Microbiology of death*: Current Biology* 26 (13):561-563.

Muheisen, M. (1988) The Epipaleolithic Phases of IV. In: A. Garrard and Gebel. H (ed.) The Prehistory of Jordan, The State of Research in 1986 :353-367. Oxford, BAR International Series 396.

Müller, K., Chadefaux, C., Thomas, N., & Reiche, I. (2011) Microbial attack of archaeological bone versus high concentrations of heavy metals in the burial environment. A case study of animal bones from a mediaeval copper workshop in Paris. *Palaeogeography, Palaeoclimatology, Palaeocology* 310 (1-2): 39-51.

Muller, K., Reiche, H. (2006) *Archaeological bone and ivory in the of synchrotron light*. Paris, France.

Olszewski, D. (2008) 'Ihe Palaeolithic Period, including the Epipalaeolithic, in *Jordan, an Archaeological Reader*, Adams, R. (ed.), London: Equinox.

Nielsen- Marsh, R., Hedges, C. (2000) Patterns of diagenesis in bone I: the effects site environment. Journal of Archaeological Science 27: 1139-1150.

Nord, A., Kars, H., Ullén, I., Tronner, K., & Kars, E. (2005) Deterioration of archaeological bone – a statistical approach. Journal of Nordic Archaeological Science 15: 77-86.

Pate, F.; Hutton, J.& Norrish, J. (1989) Ionic exchange between soil solution and bone: toward a predictive model. Applied Geochemistry 4: 303-316.

Plenderletih, H., & Werner, A. (1971) *The conservation of antiquities and works of arts*. London: Oxford University Press.

Podany, J., Garland, K., Freeman, W., & Rogers, J. (2001) Paraloid B-72 as a structural adhesive and as a barrier within structural adhesive bonds: evaluations of strength and reversibility. Journal of the American Institute *for Conservation* 40 (1): 15-33

Roston, S. (1982) Two Prehistoric Burials from Qasr Kharaneh. Annual of the Department of Antiquities, 26: 221-229.

Smith, C., Nielsen-Marsh, C., Jans, M., & Collins, M. (2007) Bone diagenesis in the European Holocene I: Patterns and mechanisms. *Journal of Archaeological Science* 34 (9): 1485-1493.

Stiner, M., Kuhn, S., Surovell, T., Goldberg, P., meignen, L., Weiner, S., et al. (2001) Bone preservation in Hayonim Cave (Israel): a macroscopic and mineralogical study. *Journal of Archaeological Science , 28*, 643-659.

Todd, A., Landrigan, P. (1993). X-ray fluorescence analysis of Lead in bone. Environmental Health Prespectives 10(6): 494-495.

Turner – Walker, G. (2007) Degradation pathways and conservation strategies for ancient bone from wet anoxic sites. The 10th Triennial Meeting of the ICOM-CC Working Group for Wet Organic Archaeological Materials - 10-15th September 2007.

Ulijaszek, J., Hillman, G., Boldsen, L., & Henry, J. (1991) Human Dietary Change. *Philosophical Transactions: Biological Sciences*, 334 (1270):271-279.

Vargová, L.; Horáčková. L.; Horákováb, M.; Eliášovác, H.; Myškovád, E. & Ditrichd, O. (2016) Paleopathological, Trichological and Paleoparasitological Analysis of Human Skeletal Remains from the Migration Period Cemetery Prague-Zličín. *Interdisciplinaria Archaeologica Natural Sciences in Archaeology* 7(1): 13-32.

14

VIRTUAL AGORA: REPRESENTATION OF AN ANCIENT GREEK AGORA IN VIRTUAL WORLDS USING BIOLOGICALLY-INSPIRED MOTIVATIONAL AGENTS

Spyros Vosinakis[1] and Nikos Avradinis[2]

[1]*Department of Product & Systems Design Eng, University of the Aegean, Greece*
[2]*Department of Informatics, University of Piraeus, Greece*

Corresponding author: Spyros Vosinakis (spyrosv@aegean.gr)

ABSTRACT

Populating virtual worlds with computer controlled characters is a key issue in virtual heritage applications, an argument that can also be held as valid for the majority of virtual world applications. Virtual heritage worlds usually tend to be either devoid of people, or include computer-controlled characters that function as animated props, demonstrating pre-scripted and repetitive behaviour. In more advanced approaches, digital characters in special roles, such as virtual guides, may also be situated in the virtual world. Recent virtual heritage reconstruction works seem to acknowledge the necessity of incorporating non-human controlled characters that include intelligence in order to enhance presence and provide the user with an engaging experience. This paper presents the design and development of Virtual Agora, a virtual heritage application in the Open Simulator environment aiming to replicate daily life in an ancient Greek agora using biologically-inspired motivational agents. The application follows a multi-layered motivational model for agents that includes biological, as well as psychosocial needs. Every agent possesses a set of basic attributes that relate to its biological and physical characteristics, as well as its personality. Furthermore, agents are endowed with a set of behaviours that satisfy particular goals and consist of a sequence of actions towards achieving this goal. In addition to this generic action set, every agent possesses an extra set of actions, based on its assignment of a role or profession. The roles and the respective behaviours have been designed and selected based on available resources regarding life in the ancient agora of classical Athens. In the current implementation visitors can walk around the environment observing daily activities performed by the digital characters and interact with them by asking questions about aspects of their profession.

KEYWORDS: virtual worlds, virtual heritage, intelligent agents, virtual humans, ancient Greece

1. INTRODUCTION

Interactive 3D environments such as Virtual Worlds (VWs), in the form of serious games applications, have the capacity to serve as dissemination and learning platforms for history, culture and archaeology (Anderson et al., 2010; Gaitatzes et al., 2001). They incorporate a number of distinguishing characteristics, including high-quality visualization of digital content, real-time simulation of realistic or imaginary environments, natural and intuitive user interactions, and single- or multi-user embodiment in the 3D space through animated avatars. These characteristics enable interactive 3D environments to represent existing or reconstructed cultural artifacts and places in high detail, enhanced by features such as the superimposition of associated descriptions and media. Added interactivity allows users to freely navigate and explore the content, as well as provide engaging features such as interactive digital stories or mini-games related to the historical and cultural context of the subject. Applications of this kind not only allow people to closely observe cultural heritage artifacts that may be difficult for them to physically approach, for reasons of distance, cost or accessibility but can also serve as a motivating means to supplement people's knowledge and increase their interest in culture.

While high-quality 3D visualization of spaces and artifacts is a desired element in virtual heritage applications, it is not alone adequate to ensure that the user experience will be as engaging and fruitful as expected. There are plenty of 3D applications developed in the last two decades that provide static representations of cultural or historical content and let users freely navigate around and observe the artifacts. The problem with such approaches is that they lack any additional interactive and social features that would further engage and motivate users. On the contrary, in these environments users quickly feel a sense of void and lose interest. After all, understanding the form of constructed objects or buildings is only one aspect of history and cultural heritage; these reconstructions need to be experienced together with a number of other, intangible aspects of the related historic period and culture in order to be immersed in the cultural context (Pujol & Champion, 2012). E.g. visitors might be interested in observing aspects of daily life, activities and rituals taking place in the buildings, typical usage of the artifacts being presented, related stories and events, etc. Even more, they would like to be part of the story themselves, to be able to participate in the environment and interact with the content.

Demonstrating daily life situations and narrating short stories that aim to present social aspects of culture and life in antiquity requires the introduction of digital characters that can act these stories out in the virtual world. These characters can either be human controlled, in the form of human avatars, or computer controlled, with varying levels of adaptability to the environment or human user input (Lombardo & Damiano, 2012; Papagiannakis et al., 2005). The advancement of real-time 3D graphics and animation technology in the past fifteen years or so has allowed for the creation of realistic-looking digital characters that have the ability to move around, communicate and act in the environment, utilizing multiple means of expression, such as gestures, facial expressions or advanced locomotion. Virtual heritage applications have recently started to take advantage of the affordances of digital characters, and have incorporated them in the representation environment.

In the case of computer controlled characters, however high the quality of the visual representation or the detail of animation and other means of expression, there is often failure to achieve the expected results, in terms of user engagement. This is largely due to the fact that the agents' behavior patterns are limited, often predictable, and mainly not always in context, seeming incompatible with the high level of visual quality. This is an inhibiting factor for the acceptance of the virtual character on the part of the user and undermines the whole experience of the virtual world. Due to this fact, it has been argued that computer controlled virtual characters should be totally abolished from virtual heritage applications and any roles in the world should be played by human avatars (Morgan, 2009).

However, the behavior of digital characters can be enriched by adopting approaches stemming from the fields of Artificial Intelligence and Intelligent Agents. Instead of performing pre-scripted behavior, virtual characters can be designed as intelligent agents that possess knowledge about their environment and are endowed with a degree of autonomy that allows them to make decisions, in accordance with their perceived physical, mental and psychological profile as well as their role in the virtual world. Work towards this direction has been introduced to VWs and interactive 3D environments since the early 2000s (Luck & Aylett, 2000), and currently there are a few virtual heritage applications that incorporate digital characters based on intelligent agent architectures in their environment (Bogdanovych et al., 2010).

Adopting this approach, we are presenting a biologically-inspired intelligent agent approach for digital characters, and we are examining its suitability for virtual heritage applications from both the designer's and the final user's point of view. We have developed a platform based on VWs for creating multi-user virtual heritage applications that include multiple intelligent virtual human agents. Each agent can have its own appearance and personality traits, and may adopt one or more typical patterns of behavior (roles) according to his profession and identity in the environment. Their behavior is, however, not repetitive and predictive; they decide about their actions based on their needs and generate suitable plans in order to fulfil them. The implemented platform has been tested in a prototype edutainment application that demonstrates daily life and rituals in an ancient Greek agora. The environment includes typical buildings and roles based on available information about the Agora of Athens. Visitors can walk around, observe daily activities performed by the digital characters, interact with them by asking questions about aspects of their profession, and participate in some of the activities using their avatars.

2. ADDING LIFE TO VIRTUAL RECONSTRUCTIONS

An important element in adding storytelling capabilities and creating rich, interactive content in virtual heritage applications is the addition of computer-controlled characters. These characters can adopt a variety of roles in virtual heritage applications: they may populate virtual cities, demonstrate typical activities, present stories, or communicate with the visitors and offer them guidance to the visitors, to name a few of their potential functions. As such, they can tackle the problem of empty and inanimate places by transforming cultural representations into 'living' spaces and enhancing their interactivity.

In most cases, however, digital characters act using pre-scripted, repetitive patterns. In some cases they simply execute repetitive behavioral patterns based on scripts predefined by the designer, whilst in others they adopt shallow reactive behavior, where incoming stimuli are directly associated to corresponding reactions or short action sequences. In any interaction exceeding a few seconds, this produces repetitive behavior. This mechanistic and predictive behavior of virtual human characters makes them far from believable in the long term. Visitors expect from digital characters to contain at least some of the qualities found in human behavior, such as rationality, decision making, personality traits, emotions, etc.

2.1. Digital characters in virtual heritage applications

Examining the various modes of operation in digital characters, one can distinguish three general approaches. The most obvious approach to introduce digital characters in virtual reconstructions is to have them operate as *'animated props'*. Such characters usually execute pre-scripted animation sequences that are sometimes parameterized for greater diversity, and their operation is independent from any changes in the environment or user activity. Their main functionality is to augment the scenery with their presence and to make the digital environment feel livelier for the human visitor. As such, their primary contribution in cultural heritage applications is to have the user observe the appearance and typical activities of indicative people in the place and time of reference. In some cases they may be also used to play back stories, anecdotes or historical events related to the place. Nevertheless, pre-scripted characters can only produce linear, non-interactive narratives, thus leaving no room for user participation or intervention.

More interesting and dynamic character behavior can be achieved with the use of *virtual crowds*. In this case, characters move and act collectively imitating the behavior of real human crowds. The actions of each individual agent depend on the presence and motion of other agents or users nearby, and in some cases it is also affected by locations or elements of the environment that apply positive or negative attraction to them. In most virtual crowd systems, individual agents are automatically generated based on generic rules that define their appearance and properties, and they are assigned a role from a predefined set. E.g., in the work of Maïm et al (2007) a real-time simulation environment presenting a reconstructed district of ancient Pompeii has been populated with a crowd of virtual Romans. A number of human templates has been used to instantiate the crowd members with variations in clothes and body parts. The agents walked around the environment and followed simple behavioral patterns triggered by semantic labels associated with places and objects of the environment, e.g. buy bread from the bakery store, look at the window of a building, etc.

A different utilization of digital characters with more essential contribution to the user experience is to have them operate as *virtual guides*. In that case, the characters have the additional ability to communicate with the users, and their goal is make the experience more lively and pleasant for the visitors by presenting places, objects or related stories to them. There are plenty of virtual guide implementations in virtual museums and reconstructed cultural sites, which vary in terms of the means of communication and the adaptability of the presentation. A simple solution is to have the visitor choose from a list of pre-defined options regarding the content and type of presentation, whilst more sophisticated agent implementations involve communication in natural language using text or speech. Furthermore, some applications include digital characters that can take into account user preferences and context to personalize their presentations. The museum gallery presented by Oberlander et al (2008) included an agent that could communicate with visitors in natural language and adapt the presentation based on the preferences and the visiting history of users.

Finally, digital character implementations based on *intelligent agent* approaches can have a long-term, autonomous, goal-oriented operation in cultural heritage applications. Intelligent agent architectures such as the well-known *BDI (Beliefs – Desires – Intentions)* approach can be used to implement digital characters with the ability to accumulate new knowledge about the environment using the input received by their sensors, to prioritize their next tasks according to their long-term goals, and to plan a sequence of actions to achieve the desired results. This approach leads to a more elaborate behavior that is not as predictive and repeatable as in the case of following pre-scripted orders. Furthermore, such characters can expand the affordances of virtual heritage applications by demonstrating daily life aspects of ancient cultures and letting users not only observe but also interact with them. Given that the characters have an autonomous operation, any changes in the environment, e.g. due to user presence and interventions, do not distort their behavior; rather, they adapt to the new situation by re-planning their actions in order to reach their goals effectively.

The City of Uruk (Bogdanovych et al., 2010) is a virtual heritage application that uses intelligent agents in a VW to present daily life in an ancient city. The characters have been built based on a BDI architecture and follow a daily routine that involves movement, interaction with objects and communication with other characters. The agents' actions are shaped by their beliefs about the environment. They can follow pre-scripted plans in order to perform some standard activities, and they can also update their goals and generate dynamic plans as a result of certain changes in the environment. Finally, they have the ability to communicate with human visitors using natural language. They can talk about their current goal and planned actions, and they can also present information about the surrounding objects and environment. In a study aimed to validate its learning effectiveness (Bogdanovych et al., 2012) the application yielded positive results regarding student performance.

Table I. A categorization of digital characters based on their characteristics and their respective function in virtual heritage applications

Category	Characteristics	Function
virtual props	pre-scripted, repeating behavior	demonstrate appearance and typical actions
virtual crowd	dynamic locomotion, behavioral patterns	populate reconstructions, present daily activities
virtual guides	communication, adaptivity	dialogs with users, present content, provide information
living agents	autonomous, goal-oriented behavior	long-term simulation of daily life, user participation

The four categories of digital characters in cultural heritage applications presented above are summarized in Table 1.

2.2. Believability of digital characters

A key requirement for virtual worlds is *believability*, a rather complex concept that involves diverse aspects of virtual worlds and has led to equally diverse approaches of the matter. Before attempting to provide a definition for believability, it is important to distinguish the concept from realism, a close term that is, however distinct from believability. Realism refers to creating high fidelity reconstructions of the physical world. On the other hand, believability has to do with a synthetic character being consistent to essence of the entity it is supposed to embody as well the coherence of this character within the world it is situated in.

An obvious and important aspect of believability is the presentation of the virtual world (Magnenat-Thalmann et al., 2005). Common sense would dictate that the more realistic the presentation of the virtual world, the higher the degree of believability. However, this is not necessarily the case. Very high fidelity reconstructions of the physical world have a high degree of realism, but not necessarily believability, especially if the virtual world is devoid of people. As argued by Loyall & Bates (1997), realism is neither adequate, nor required to ensure believability. It is rather the consistency of the presentation in relation to the thematic context of the virtual world that leads to a greater degree of believability.

In regard to realism, what holds true for the unpopulated virtual world, also holds true for the characters situated within. As Mori (1970) has suggested in the well-known uncanny valley hypothesis, certain levels of realism may seriously undermine the acceptance of the character as real by the audience and produce awkward responses, especially if other constituents of the total experience such as gaze or locomotion are missing.

Believability, in the context of synthetic characters, has been defined by Bates (1994) as the ability on the part of the system to suspend the users' disbelief, by providing an illusion of life. Plainly put, believability in virtual agents is about making the human user accept they are interacting with a living character, whose existence is consistent and coherent in the context of the virtual world it is situated in.

Extending beyond the strictly physical properties of the virtual world and the agents, it has been widely discussed that believability equally involves the agent's behavior (Lester & Stone, 1997; Prendinger & Ishizuka, 2001; Ortony, 2003). Works on behavioral believability are diverse in approach, depending on what aspect of emotion one has is focusing on. A most common approach examines behavior as expressing a synthetic agent's internal state through gaze, facial expression, gesture or posture (Bevacqua et al., 2007). Believability also demonstrates a narrative aspect, both in terms of plot coherence and character expression (Ho & Dautenhahn, 2008; Riedl & Young, 2003). In terms of affect, the importance of emotion and personality has been widely discussed (Becker-Asano, 2005; Lim & Aylett, 2007).

The focus of the current work is on the generation as well as the expression of believable behavior. As argued by Ortony (2003), believability in the behavior of an intelligent virtual agent consists in demonstrating coherence in the agent's reactions and its motivational states and consistency among similar kinds of situations. Adopting a viewpoint on behavior as decision making, we aim to achieve believability in terms of producing behavior that is consistent to virtual characters' goals, state of mind and personality (De Rosis et al., 2003). We are viewing behavior as a process of making decisions and determining the appropriate course of action, taking into account the agent's role and function, as well as its physical, emotional and mental status at the moment. The outcome of this decision making process is a series of corresponding physical or communicative actions that implement the decisions made, in a way consistent to the agent's physical and affective state and traits as well as the holding conditions in the environment at the time of execution. As Dautenhahn (1998) argues, it is a matter of enabling the virtual character to produce behavior that matches what would be expected of the user, and this is something that can be accomplished by blending together various contributing elements, such as rationality, reactivity, personality and emotion.

2.3. *Needs, wants and obligations – a balancing act*

Necessary prerequisites for the development of intelligent virtual characters that demonstrate believable behavior is the incorporation of affective features (Bailey et al., 2012) and elements of autonomy (de Sevin et al., 2005). As already mentioned in the previous section, computer controlled virtual characters can be classified into four generic categories, depending on their role within the virtual world but also the level of autonomy they can demonstrate. Virtual props and crowds show relatively low autonomy or none at all and follow mainly pre-scripted behaviors with limited flexibility, whereas living agents are self-driven and can demonstrate adaptability to the environment and user actions.

As has been argued by de Sevin et al. (2005), in order to achieve high levels of believability, digital characters should be developed as autonomous agents, in the sense that they possess their own set of goals, that they proactively pursue, rather than only follow a set of given instructions. This will allow them to maintain the capacity to demonstrate purposeful behavior and continue acting even where there is no particular extrinsic goal, whereas a prescripted character in a similar case would exhaust its repertoire of behaviors, resulting in repetitive sequences of actions or purposeless trivial behavior, reducing itself to an animated prop. This is of particular importance in persistent open virtual worlds, where the user is allowed to freely explore and is not limited to specific pathways, while also the world continues to exist even after the user exits. In order to achieve autonomy, virtual agents need a mechanism to produce and select their own goals, that is, a motivational subsystem that drives the agent towards particular courses of action, aimed towards satisfying its self-interests. This motivational subsystem acts as a source of intrinsic motivation and complements any directly provided goals or other extrinsic goals resulting from social norms and obligations as well as agent and human avatar interactions within the world.

Since the agent is embodied and situated within a virtual environment where other agents co-exist, the specific driving forces incorporated in the motivational subsystem should include low level, biological factors, along with affective and social factors. Mixing the three and balancing the agent's personal goal agenda with external goals is a hard task; virtual characters should act autonomously and function as if they were living their own lives, but also possess the ability to adapt their behavior when human users interact with them or when external events occur that require their attention. Goal generation has to be complemented with a differentiation of behavior among individual agents, consistent with their particular physical, social, metal or emotional characteristics, which constitute their virtual persona.

3. A MULTI-AGENT PLATFORM FOR VIRTUAL HERITAGE APPLICATIONS

We have developed a platform for cultural heritage applications in VWs that include multiple autonomous agents moving and interacting with the users and the environment. The platform allows the execution of complex virtual heritage scenarios that may include features such as:

- demonstration of activities, habits and rituals of ancient cultures,
- agents communicating with users and presenting locations, elements or activities of interest, and
- scenarios requiring user participation, such as interactive stories and quests

The platform provides a set of high-level tools and reusable components that aim to assist developers in creating new applications and programming the interactive behavior of virtual agents. It includes a *plan definition language* to design and test static agent plans, a *planning engine* to dynamically produce plan sequences in order to achieve a desired goal, a *dialog engine* for the agent-user communication, and a *programmable perception mechanism* to identify elements of interest. A prototype environment of an Ancient Greek Agora with multiple virtual agents demonstrating typical roles has been developed using this platform.

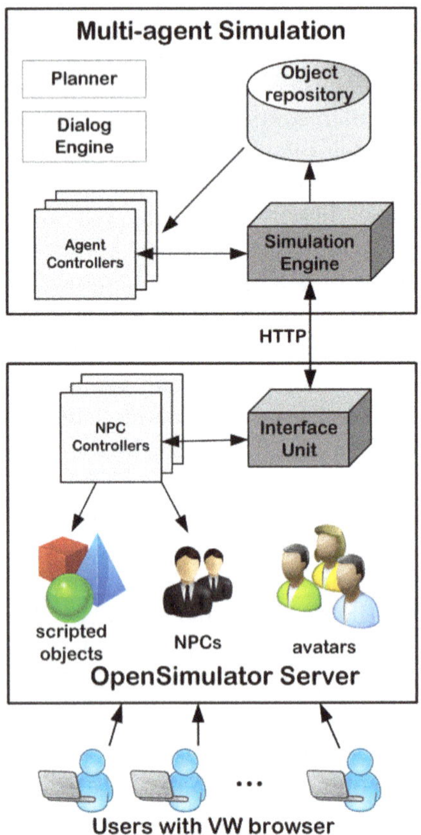

Figure 1. System architecture of the multi-agent platform.

Our platform is based on OpenSimulator, an open source alternative to the VW of Second Life. Users connect to an environment running in an OpenSimulator server using specific VW browser software and have the ability to personalize their appearance, navigate around, meet and communicate with other users, interact with the objects of the environment, and even to construct new content provided that they have the appropriate rights to do so. The environment provides simple and usable tools for in-world building, allows complex geometry models (meshes) to be imported, and produces a good quality rendering of the environment. As such, it is suitable for the collaborative reconstruction, exploration and visualization of cultural heritage sites. Furthermore, it is equipped with a powerful scripting language named LSL, which can be used to program the interactive behavior of the 3D elements contained in the environment. Finally, it allows the introduction and control of multiple digital characters (termed NPCs - Non Player Characters) in the environment.

The architecture of our platform follows a three-tier client-server model based on the OpenSimulator server (Figure 1). Users join the application using a compatible browser that connects to the OpenSimulator server, and they are embodied as avatars in the representation space. The interactive behavior of the environment is orchestrated by a special object named *Interface Unit* that mediates between the objects and NPCs of the VW, and a *multi-agent simulation environment*. The latter is an external application implemented in Java, which handles the agents' perception, decision making, dialogs and high-level actions using an abstraction of the actual VW and its contents. Thus, the agent operation takes place in two parallel layers: the low-level execution layer of the VW, in which the NPCs move and interact with the objects and users of the environment, and the high-level layer of the multi-agent simulation, in which the agents update their beliefs, prioritize their goals, and decide about their next actions.

The elements of the VW that have an active role in the application are three: the Interface Unit, the *NPC Controllers* and the *scripted objects*. The functionality of the Interface Unit is twofold: it constantly updates the multi-agent simulation with any changes happening in the VW, i.e. users and NPCs moving, communicating and interacting, and it also triggers and controls the action execution of individual NPCs. For the first function, it makes use of a specially built extension to the OpenSim server (Region Module), which monitors the placement of all entities of the environment and identifies any changes. For the second function, it makes use of the NPC Controllers. Each NPC created in the environment is attached a scripted object, the NPC Controller, which initiates and controls the execution of the supported actions. When the execution of an action by a specific NPC is requested, the Interface Unit communicates with the respective NPC Controller and transmits the request using the action name and any additional parameters, e.g. lookAt user1. When the NPC completes the action, the controller notifies the Interface Unit that the action execution has finished, and the latter forwards the message to the multi-agent simulation environment. Finally, there are agent actions that involve some interaction between the NPC and an object of the environment, e.g. to grasp an object, or to leave it in a specific position. The objects that support these interactions include a specific script that receives requests from the NPC Controllers and triggers the respective responses.

The multi-agent simulation environment controls and monitors the behavior of the agents that participate as NPCs in the application. The operation of each agent is driven by a respective *Agent Controller*, which updates its beliefs, takes any required decisions and executes the current plan. The agents' sensory input is based on an *object repository* that stores basic geometric information (size, position and rotation) of all elements that actively participate in the simulation, i.e. agents, users and selected objects. The repository is constantly updated by the Interface Object to reflect the active status of the VW. The multi-agent environment is equipped with two additional components to support the agent operations: a *planner* based on PyHOP (Nau, 2013) that can generate dynamic plans according to the status of the environment, and a dialog engine based on AIML (Wallace, 2009) for the agent-user communication.

3.1. A biologically-inspired agent model with needs and personality traits

The agent implementation in our platform follows a multi-layered motivational model that includes biological, as well as psychosocial needs (Figure 2). Every agent possesses a set of basic attributes that relate to its biological and physical characteristics, as well as its personality. Following a needs hierarchy, needs arising at the lowest motivational level are assigned greater priority than needs on a higher level, therefore the corresponding goals are queued first for satisfaction. Need priority is also determined by the intensity of each corresponding motivation, as well as an internal priority index corresponding to the relative urgency of needs within the same level.

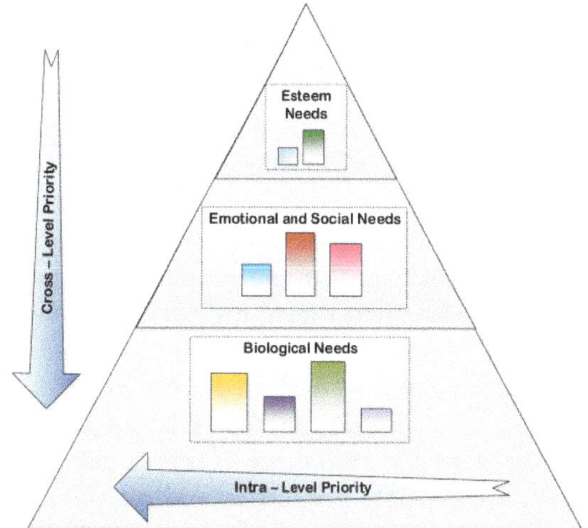

Figure 2. Motivational hierarchy model.

At the lowest level, a biologically inspired model (Avradinis et al., 2013) monitors and regulates the thirst, hunger, hygiene and sleep needs based on the value of corresponding reserve variables. Reserve variables are regulated by means of a homeostatic mechanism that is based on human physiology and tries to maintain the agent in a well-being state. When the value of a reserve variable moves outside a defined comfort zone, a corresponding need rises, in turn activating a behavior aiming to satisfy the particular need.

Every agent is endowed with a set of behaviors that satisfy particular goals. These behaviors are described as task networks that are evaluated to a sequence of actions towards achieving the goal based on the actual status of the environment. In addition to a generic behavior set that is assigned to all agents, selected characters with an assigned role or profession possess an additional set of behaviors to fulfil goals related to their specialization. The agent architecture is presented in Figure 3.

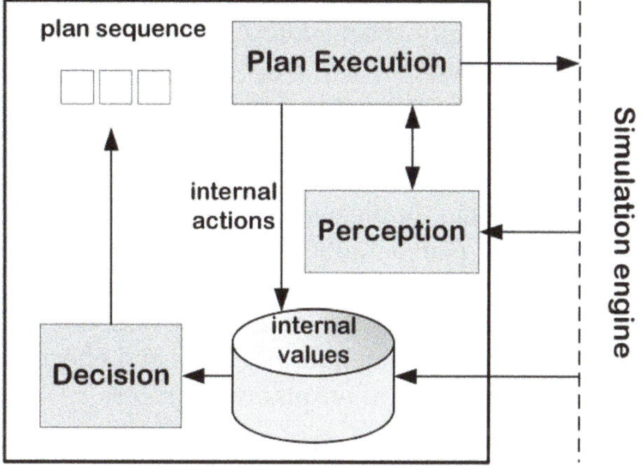

Figure 3. Agent architecture.

3.2. Planning and Action Execution

The execution of a new action sequence is triggered when a certain need fires. In that case, the agent sets as a goal to fulfil the need and decides about its next steps based on the actual status of the environment. An HTN planner (Erol et al., 1994) is being utilized to reach that decision. All possible agent goals, e.g. to drink water in order to quench its thirst, are described as hierarchical task networks, where higher level tasks trigger the execution of lower-level ones based on the properties of the environment. At the lowest level are the primitive tasks which have a direct mapping to the scripted plans that the agent executes in the VW. Whenever a planning operation is requested, the HTN planner is given an appropriate initial state representation that includes appropriate properties and relations of objects of interest based on their representation in the Object Repository. The planner tries to detect an appropriate task sequence based on the initial status and the preconditions and effects of each possible sub-task. The result is a sequence of primitive tasks with respective arguments that are executed by the agent and lead to a number of NPC actions.

The plans that the agent can execute in the environment are described using a dedicated high-level scripting language, the *Plan Definition Language (PDL)*. Each plan defined in this language has a unique name and an arbitrary number of argument variables. The plan implementation is encoded in an imperative programming manner that allows sequential, conditional and iterative execution of commands, based on the definition of PDL. The supported commands fall into the following categories:

- actions that are executed by the NPC in the VW,
- "internal" actions that affect the internal values of the agent,
- message passing between agents,
- dialogs with users,
- memory processes (store / retrieve temporary information),
- perception of specific elements based on criteria

Finally, the execution of a new plan can be called during the plan implementation, thus leading to more complex plan definitions.

Each plan that is defined using PDL must be described as a primitive task in the task network and be assigned appropriate preconditions and effects to be able to participate in the planning process.

3.3. *NPC actions in the 3D environment*

The NPCs can perform a variety of actions in the VW. They can walk to certain targets, animate their body, interact with objects, and communicate with users. All actions are triggered and controlled by the NPC Controller that is attached to them.

There are four distinct actions for NPC walking. The first is to have the NPC wander around in a given location, i.e. a part of the environment defined by the designer with a unique name. E.g. a number of citizens wander around in the agora when they have no urgent needs to fulfil. The second action is to ask the NPC to walk to an entity (object, agent or user) up to a specific distance from its center. E.g. if the agent decides to talk to a user, the NPC walks to the user's avatar keeping a 2m distance. The third action makes the NPC walk to a specific position related to an existing object. The designer can add an arbitrary number of named spots to the scripted objects of the environment. These spots are useful for having the NPC take correct position when performing an action, e.g. to perform the action of drinking water from the fountain, the NPC has to be in an appropriate position with respect to the fountain before animating its body. Finally, the 'look at' action makes the NPC orient its body towards a target entity.

An NPC can start or stop playing animation sequences using respective actions. The OpenSimulator environment has already a large number of animation sequences, and new animations can also be created and uploaded in the environment. Using these two actions, the NPCs can demonstrate a variety of activities in the VW.

Two NPC actions are provided for communicating with users. The first one causes the agent to say a message in public using the chat channel of the VW. The second triggers a dialog with a specific user. In that case the NPC not only sends the message to the public channel, but also listens for replies from the specific user. The replies are forwarded to the Dialog manager of the multi-agent simulation environment to proceed with the dialog.

Finally, NPCs can attach or detach objects to specific body parts based on respective actions. When an NPC decides to hold an object, e.g. take an apple from the tree, the NPC Controller sends a message to the target object, and it attaches to the requested body part of the NPC, e.g. the right hand. OpenSimulator allows designers to adjust the attachment point of the object with respect to the NPC body part, and thus the objects that participate in the environment can be designed to be correctly attached to the characters. An NPC can also detach an object from its body and leave it in a specified spot.

3.4. *Internal Actions*

Besides actions that have a direct visual effect in the VW, there are also actions that affect the agents' internal values. E.g. an agent eating an apple is performed as an animation of her holding the apple and bringing it to her mouth, but it also has an effect on her food reserves. The latter is an 'internal' action, which is not executed in the VW but in the multi-agent simulation environment. We have currently implemented a number of internal actions that affect the agents' reserves, such as eating, drinking, resting, working, etc. The final effect of these actions on the agents' internal value is determined by the argument values and also by other relevant attributes of the agent, e.g. sex, weight, age, etc. An example internal action is the 'bite <food>' action, where the type of food determines the calorie increase per bite.

3.5. Inter-agent communication

The implemented multi-agent platform includes a simple message-passing mechanism for the communication between agents. An agent can send a message to any other agent using a designated action, and the message will be instantly submitted to the receiver. Messages are formed as subject-predicate-object triples and are not restricted to a specific vocabulary. It is thus the responsibility of the designer to ensure that messages are properly interpreted. A second action allows an agent to read incoming messages from other agents. When a message is received, the sender id and the message triple are stored in selected variables for further processing. An example of message passing between agents is the following. A citizen meets the pottery seller and wishes to buy an amphora. The message would be 'me wantsToBuy amphora'. The seller identifies that the citizen wants to buy something, checks the product price and replies with a message 'amphora priceIs 5'. The citizen learns the price, checks if she has the required amount of money or an object of equivalent price to trade, and proceeds with the transaction or cancels it accordingly.

3.6. Dialogs with users

Agents can start dialogs with users using the dialog engine, which is based on the Artificial Intelligence Markup Language (AIML). Designers can create a number of AIML bots, each of which is based on its own collection of AIML files that define how it responds to user input. In our platform we use the bots as dialog patterns that can be chosen depending on the type of dialog that the agent decides to start. E.g. some agents might serve as virtual guides and present the various places of the environment, whilst others might wish to present their own profession, or even to assign a quest to the user. The action that initiates a dialog takes as argument the name of the user and the name of the bot to be used as pattern. It is, therefore, possible to have the same agent use more than one patterns during its lifetime, or to use the same pattern for multiple agents.

We have extended the AIML language with custom tags in order to embed dynamic information in the dialog and to trigger new agent actions during the discussion. There are tags that can dynamically insert information from the object repository and from the agents' internal status, like the name of the user with whom the agent is discussing, the current activity and needs of the agent, etc. Furthermore, we have created another tag that can trigger the execution of a scripted plan. When this tag is called, the agent executes the plan and then continues with the dialog. This feature is important, as it can lead to a more natural and human-like behavior that blends dialogs and activities. A simple example would be to look and point at a building while discussing about it. In a more complicated example, the agent could ask the user to follow her, walk to a place of interest and present the activities taking place.

3.7. Memory Processes

Designers can define and use new variables in PDL to store intermediate data while executing a plan. However, there may be cases where long-term storage of information may be needed. Sometimes important knowledge may need to be stored during the execution of one plan and retrieved later on, during another. E.g. an agent whose role is to guide users might need to remember whether he has spoken to a specific user before, or not. Having such information will allow her to direct her attention towards newcomers. A repository for managing such information is included in the platform, and respective actions for storing and retrieving data to and from the memory are provided. Memory clauses follow the same conventions as agent messages: they are formed as subject-predicate-object triples.

3.8. Perception Mechanism

A simple perception mechanism enables agents to identify specific objects of interest in the region in order to execute their actions. The process of perceiving the environment in virtual agent platforms is based on the idea of 'filtering' the surrounding entities based on specific criteria, in order to generate usable information that will facilitate action execution (Bordeux et al., 1999; Vosinakis & Panayiotopoulos, 2003). E.g. if an agent decides to eat an apple to satisfy her hunger, she has to find the nearest apple tree and select a reachable apple from that tree before performing the action of grasping it. Both these decisions can be supported by a perception mechanism that searches for entities matching the required properties.

The perception mechanism can be triggered using a specific command in PDL. It combines custom filters regarding the properties of entities in the environment and returns a single entity that matches the filters, if any. The returned entity is stored in a variable for further processing. The available filters can be about:

- the type of entities (e.g. objects, users, NPCs)
- their description, if any (e.g. apple, basket, temple, etc), applicable only to objects
- their role, if any, applicable only to NPCs (e.g. worker, priest, etc).
- a statement about them in the agent's memory (e.g. me spokenTo).

Filters such as the above can be combined using logical operators (and, or, not) and create more complex filtering mechanism. Finally, the user has to provide the criterion to select a single entity from the list of entities that pass the perception filters, and the variable in which the result will be stored. The implemented selection criteria are two: nearest and any. In the first case, the mechanism selects the entity with the shortest distance from the agent.

4. VIRTUAL AGORA: DAILY CITY LIFE IN CLASSICAL ANTIQUITY

The Virtual Agora is an experimental interactive edutainment environment, aiming to present life in ancient Greece and educate users about common daily activities and important religious rituals. The setting of the Virtual Agora is inspired by actual Ancient Agora sites and includes buildings typically contained in a classical ancient forum. The main focal point of the Agora is the Temple of Hephaestus, along with a sacrificial altar, modeled according to measurements from Hepahestus' Temple in Athens' Agora (Dinsmoor, 1941). The Temple is where commoners gather to satisfy their religious needs. A public water source, modeled after the Enneakrounos source in Athens' Agora, is located nearby the Temple and is where citizens could get water as well as bathe themselves (Figure 4). The setting also contains workshops and stands, where craftsmen and salesmen could create and sell their goods.

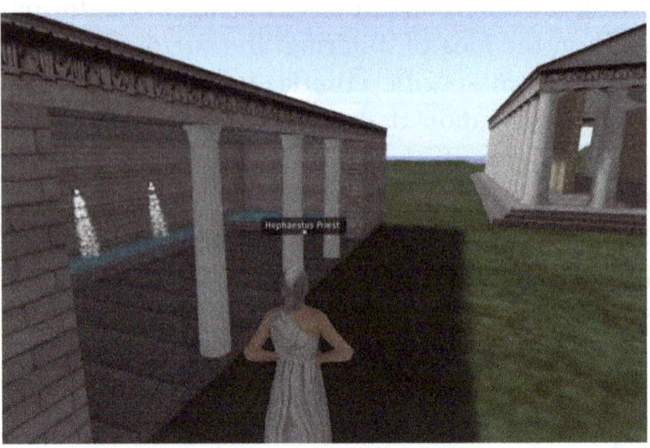

Figure 4. The water source alongside the temple of Hephaestus.

Virtual characters in the Agora have appearances that conform to their distinct roles. A priest, a potter, a fruit seller as well as a few commoners inhabit the Agora, each performing their own duties and acting according to their own roles. All characters are free to wander around the place, however, particular installations or buildings can only be used by the corresponding professional. Commoners can interact with the craftsmen and priest and buy goods or otherwise request their services.

A craftsman's typical behavior is working, which involves the use of a raw material (clay, metal or straw), to be processed into pottery, ornament or basket. These items are then put on display, to be sold to prospective clients. A food vendor typically engages in a gathering behavior, picking fruit from nearby trees as well as a selling behavior, selling fruit to clients. The food vendor also sells wine to interested clients, stored in small size amphorae. Food and wine purchased by the food vendor can either be used as an offering in the temple, or directly consumed by the virtual agent, to satisfy its hunger or thirst. Priests stand by the temple, performing their own religious duties, until a worshipper requesting a religious service approaches. The priest can perform libations and food sacrifices, as well as pray on behalf of the worshipper. Figure 5 shows a typical scene in front of the altar.

Characters can interact with human users, in the form of simple AIML dialogue interactions that provide information on the place and the daily activities of each character, as well as directions towards key points of interest.

Figure 5. NPCs in front of the altar waiting for priest to perform libation.

All characters have a set of biological needs that have to be satisfied as the characters get hungry, thirsty, sleepy or tired. The rise of a need generates goals that are satisfied through a series of actions. In addition to these needs, the characters also lose their interest and get bored when they have nothing particular to do, which motivates them to engage in any sort of active behavior. They also have a need of spirituality, which causes them to visit the temple. All these needs are satisfied by a set of behaviors. These are compound plans, with alternative implementations through sequences of actions. Some behaviors and actions are common among all Agora dwellers, however some are specific and linked to each agent's profession. Such is, for example the behavior of performing a libation, for the priest, or the crafting of an item, for the potter.

Table II. Professions and common behaviors of Virtual Agents

Profession	*Sub-role*	Profession Behaviours	Common behaviours	Actions
Priest		-Perform offering -Perform libation	-Acquire offering -Visit temple -Offer item -Request libation ritual -Buy item -Satisfy hunger -Satisfy thirst -Satisfy hygiene -Rest	-pick up item -drop item -put on table/put in place -give item to other agent -take item from other agent -eat -drink -wash -sit -sleep
Craftsman	Metal Worker Basket Weaver Potter	-gather materials -create (craft) item -sell item		
Food Vendor		-pickup food -sell food/wine		

All citizens, craftsmen and commoners alike, have a need of spirituality. When this spirituality need exceeds a predefined threshold, dependent on the agent's personality, the agent initiates the "perform_religious_duty" behaviour, which causes the agent to first cleanse itself by visiting the fountain and then visit a shrine or a temple. At a shrine, the agent can satisfy the spirituality need by praying to the god the shrine is devoted to. At the temple, in addition to praying, the agent can also interact with the priest and worship the god either by offering wine and requesting a libation or by giving the priest a votive offering, such as food, pottery or a metal ornament, to be acquired at the corresponding vendor or craftsman.

For example, let us consider a complex task for a character assigned the role of a potter, which is creating a pottery artifact. The potter first needs to acquire the materials required for the artifact and then actually start making the object itself. The top level tasks (acquire clay, acquire water, make pottery) are further decomposed hierarchically into subtasks, that are implemented by operators, corresponding to actions executed by the agent. A plain language task breakdown into subtasks for the potter scenario is as follows.

```
create Pottery
    acquire clay
        go to clay pit
        pickup clay
        go near potter's wheel
        drop clay on potter's wheel
    acquire water
        acquire jug
        go to nearest fountain
        hold jug near water
        go near potter's wheel
        drop jug on potter's wheel
    make pottery
        pickup jug
        pour jug on clay
        turn wheel
        pickup clay
        put clay on potter's table
end (create Pottery)
```

Gathering the materials requires several trips within the virtual world on behalf of the potter, which causes the consumption of energy, water as well as the fall of its levels of hygiene. This triggers further goals that will have to be satisfied after the pottery artifact has been created. The intertwining of goals regarding biological needs as well as emotional or social needs with obligations such as work or other externally given goals allows for rich and believable behavior, that is largely self-driven rather than mostly dictated.

5. CONCLUSIONS

In this paper we have described the design and early development of Virtual Agora, a virtual heritage application for demonstrating daily life activities and rituals in ancient Greece. Our implementation has been based on a generic platform for multi-agent applications in virtual worlds, which focuses on believable, long term, dynamic behavior of digital characters. The platform allows designers to easily extend and adjust existing scenarios, or even to create new ones and extend the functionality of the application. Furthermore, the platform is not linked in any way to specific objects, appearances or customs of ancient Greece, and, as such, it can be further used in alternative cultural heritage applications. The implemented environment currently supports only a few user activities, but we are planning to extend it with further affordances, such as quests and mini-games.

From our experience with the implemented prototype and the early test scenarios, it seems that the adoption of a generic multi-agent architecture for virtual heritage applications has both prospects and pitfalls. On the positive side is the fact that it gives freedom to the designers to define the functionality and behavior of digital characters that suits the application. An agent can demonstrate an action, simulate daily life, present places of interest to the users, communicate with them, participate in common activities with users, etc. All these possibilities may be a useful starting point to create novel approaches to demonstrating intangible culture. On the other hand, designers have little control on the final outcome, as agent behaviors are a result of complicated planning procedures, and a lot of fine-tuning is needed to achieve the desired effect. It seems that further research is needed regarding the needs of virtual heritage applications and the appropriateness of current agent architectures.

In the future we are planning to conduct a number of user evaluations of the Virtual Agora environment and assess its effectiveness as an edutainment environment.

ACKNOWLEDGEMENTS

We would like to thank Ms Grigoria Dimitrellou for her kind assistance in 3D modeling work.

REFERENCES

Anderson, E. F., McLoughlin, L., Liarokapis, F., Peters, C., Petridis, P. and de Freitas, S. (2010). Developing serious games for cultural heritage: a state-of-the-art review. *Virtual Reality*, Vol. 14(4), 255–275.

Avradinis, N., Panayiotopoulos, T. and Anastassakis, G. (2013) Behavior believability in virtual worlds: agents acting when they need to. *Springerplus 2013*, Vol 2:246

Bailey, C., You, J., Acton, G., Rankin, A. and Katchabaw, M. (2012) Believability Through Psychosocial Behaviour: Creating Bots That Are More Engaging and Entertaining, in Hingston P. (Ed), *Believable Bots*, Springer Berlin, 2012, 29-68.

Bates, J. (1994) The role of emotion in believable agents. *Communications of the ACM*, Vol. 37(7), 122-125.

Becker-Asano C., Prendinger H., Ishizuka, M. and Wachsmuth, I. (2005) Evaluating Affective Feedback of the 3D Agent Max in a Competitive Cards Game, *Proceedings of Affective Computing and Intelligent Interaction*, LNCS 3784, 466–473.

Bevacqua, E., Mancini, M., Niewiadomski, R. and Pelachaud, C. (2007) An expressive ECA showing complex emotions. *Proceedings of the AISB Annual convention, Workshop on Language, Speech and Gesture for Expressive Characters*, Newcastle UK, 208-216.

Bogdanovych, A., Rodriguez-Aguilar, J. A., Simoff, S. and Cohen, A. (2010). Authentic Interactive Reenactment of Cultural Heritage With 3D Virtual Worlds and Artificial Intelligence. *Applied Artificial Intelligence*, Vol. 24(6), 617–647.

Bogdanovych, A., Ijaz, K. and Simoff, S. (2012). The city of Uruk: Teaching ancient history in a virtual world. *Lecture Notes in Computer Science*, Vol. 7502, 28–35.

Bordeux, C., Boulic, R. and Thalmann, D. An efficient and flexible perception pipeline for autonomous agents. *Computer Graphics Forum*, Vol. 18(3).

Dautenhahn, K. (1998) The Art of Designing Socially Intelligent Agents - Science, Fiction, and the Human in the Loop. *Applied Artificial Intelligence*, Vol. 12, 573-617.

De Rosis, F., Pelachaud, C. and Poggi, I. (2003) Transcultural Believability in Embodied Agents: A Matter of Consistent Adaptation. In Payr, S. & Trappl, R. (Eds.), *Agent Culture: Designing Human-Agent Interaction in a Multicultural World*, Lawrence Erlbaum Associates.

De Sevin, E. and Thalmann, D. (2005) A motivational Model of Action Selection for Virtual Humans. *Proceedings of Computer Graphics International 2005 (CGI)*, New York, USA: IEEE Computer Society Press.

Dinsmoor, W.B. (1941) Observations of the Hephaesteion. *Hesperia: Journal of the American School of Classical Studies at Athens, Suppl. 5*, Swets-Zeitlinger Amsterdam (repr. 1975), 1-164

Erol, K., Hendler, J. and Nau, D. S. (1994). HTN planning: Complexity and expressivity. *Proceedings of AAAI*, 1123-1128.

Gaitatzes, A., Christopoulos, D. and Roussou, M. (2001) Reviving the past : Cultural Heritage meets Virtual Reality. *Proceedings of the 2001 Conference on Virtual Reality, Archeology, and Cultural Heritage*, 103–110.

Ho, W.C. and Dautenhahn K. (2008) Towards a Narrative Mind: The Creation of Coherent Life Stories for Believable Virtual Agents. In: Prendinger, H, Lester, J, Ishizuka, M (Eds) *Lecture Notes in Computer Science 5208*, Springer Berlin-Heidelberg, 59-72.

Lester, J.C. and Stone, B.A. (1997) Increasing believability in animated pedagogical agents. *Proceedings of the first international conference on Autonomous agents (AGENTS '97)* New York, USA, 16–21.

Lim M.Y. and Aylett R.S. (2007) Feel the difference: A Guide with Attitude! *Proceedings of Intelligent Virtual Agents 2007*, 317–330.

Lombardo, V. and Damiano, R. (2012) Storytelling on mobile devices for cultural heritage. *New Review of Hypermedia and Multimedia*, Vol. 18, 11–35.

Loyall, A.B. and Bates, J. (1997) Personality-rich believable agents that use language. *Proceedings of the First International Conference on Autonomous Agents*. ACM Press, NY USA, 106–113.

Luck, M. and Aylett, R. (2000) Applying artificial intelligence to virtual reality: Intelligent virtual environments. *Applied Artificial Intelligence*, Vol. 14(1), 3–32.

Maïm, J., Haegler, S., Yersin, B., Mueller, P., Thalmann, D. and Gool, L. Van. (2007) Populating Ancient Pompeii with Crowds of Virtual Romans. *Proceedings of VAST: International Symposium on Virtual Reality, Archaeology and Intelligent Cultural Heritage*.

Magnenat-Thalmann, N., Kim, H.S., Egges, A. and Garchery, S. (2005) Believability and Interaction in Virtual Worlds. *Proceedings of the 11th Intl. Multimedia Modelling Conference (MMM'05)*. IEEE Computer Society, Washington, DC

Morgan, C. (2009) (Re)Building Catalhoyuk: Changing Virtual Reality in Archaeology. *Archaeologies: Journal of the World Archaeological Congress*, Vol. 5(3), 468-487.

Mori, M. (1970) The Uncanny Valley, *Energy*, Vol. 7(4), 33–5.

Nau, D. (2013) Game applications of HTN planning with state variables. *Proceedings of ICAPS Workshop on Planning in Games*.

Oberlander, J., Karakatsiotis, G., Isard, A. and Androutsopoulos, I. (2008) Building an adaptive museum gallery in Second Life. *Proceedings of Museums and the Web*, Montreal, Quebec, Canada.

Ortony, A. (2003) On making believable emotional agents believable. In: Trappl, R., Petta, P., Payr, S., (Eds) *Emotions in humans and artifacts*. Cambridge, MA: MIT Press.

Papagiannakis, G., Schertenleib, S., O'Kennedy, B., Arevalo-Poizat, M., Magnenat-Thalmann, N., Stoddart, A. and Thalmann, D. (2005) Mixing virtual and real scenes in the site of ancient Pompeii. *Computer Animation and Virtual Worlds*, Vol. 16(1), 11–24.

Prendinger, H. and Ishizuka, M. (2001) Let's talk! Socially intelligent agents for language conversation training. *IEEE Transactions on Systems, Man and Cybernetics, Part A: Systems and Humans*, Vol. 31(5), 465–471.

Pujol, L. and Champion, E. (2012) Evaluating presence in cultural heritage projects. *International Journal of Heritage Studies*, Vol. 18(1), 83–102.

Riedl, M.O. and Young R.M. (2003) An objective character believability evaluation procedure for multi-agent story generation systems. *Proceedings of Intelligent Virtual Agents*, 278–291.

Vosinakis, S., & Panayiotopoulos, T. (2003) Programmable agent perception in intelligent virtual environments. *Proceedings of Intelligent Virtual Agents 2003 Conference*.

Wallace, R. S. (2009) The anatomy of ALICE. In Epstein, R., Roberts, G., Beber, G. (Eds) *Parsing the Turing Test*, Springer Netherlands

15

AUTHENTICATION OF ROMAN CORRODED LEAD ARTEFACTS FROM ARCHAEOLOGICAL SITES IN CALCAREOUS ENVIRONMENT IN JORDAN BY ELECTROCHEMICAL ANALYSIS

Wassef Al Sekheneh[1,2], Antonio Doménech-Carbó[2], Firas Alawneh[1,3], Atef Al Shiyab[1], and Ziad Al Saad[1]

[1]Faculty of Archaeology and Anthropology-Yarmouk University, Irbid, Jordan.
[2]Department of Analytical Chemistry, University of Valencia, Spain.
[3]Department of Conservation Science, Queen Rania Faculty of Tourism & Heritage, Hashemite University, P.O. Box 330127 Postal Code 13115 Zarqa, Jordan

Corresponding author: sekhaneh@yahoo.de

ABSTRACT

The process of authentication involves a wide variety of steps that are intimately linked and completely interdependent. In this research voltammetry of micro-particles (VMP) is used to date and authenticate a five late Roman lead balance weights. The chronology of the archaeological finds together with lead balance weights was estimated to be 4th century AD. A set of independent experiments: square wave voltammetry and electrochemical impedance spectroscopy (EIS) with the corresponding calibration curves obtained from several archaeological samples, which have been done in our laboratory. The collected sample were corroded under burial conditions in calcareous soils, are consistent with an attribution of the age of both studied lead samples. The ratio of PbO_2 and the porous PbO which formed during the process of led corrosion in the calcareous environment reflects the date of corrosion. These attribution, however, must be taken with caution because of the differences in the aging process for the studied samples and the lead materials used for calibration purposes corresponding to the reduction of the PbO 'continuous' patina formed under the ordinary exposure of the lead piece to the atmospheric environment. The ratio between peaks resulted from the corrosion process of Ancient led and reference one revealed the date of corrosion. Assuming the 4th century AD chronology of the lead samples erection to be correct, it was found that the applied method provide the same result which is consistent with archaeological estimations.

KEYWORDS: Authenticity, Dating, Corrosion, Voltammetry, Weight lead, Impedance Spectroscopy

1. INTRODUCTION

Authenticity is a vital process in archaeology and is extremely important to the archaeological context especially for the less developed techniques for metals (Ali & Abd-Allah, 2015; Holtorf & Schadla-Hall, 1999; Miller, Sayre, & Keisch, 1970; Nambi, 1981; Odegaard & Cassman, 2014; Cruz et al., 2015; Liritzis 2006). The more that is known about the artifacts and its relation to the surrounding environment the more that can be interpreted on boarder issues. A methodology for dating archeological lead artifacts based on the voltammetry of microparticles is described. This methodology is based on the comparison of the height of specific voltammetric features from PbO_2 and PbO corrosion products formed under long-term alteration conditions (Brusic, Dimilia, & MacInnes, 1991). Two basic requests must be met for the electrochemical instrumental technique when it is applied in conservation of cultural heritage research: sensitivity, for attaining significant data from very small quantity of nano, micro or miligramscale; and specificity, for definitely identifying compounds and quantifying the analytes from the complex combinations of substances that form the materials present in the monument, sarcophagus or other artifacts (Rocca, Mirambet, & Steinmetz, 2004; Taylor, 1993). Other requirements are also required for analytical method when it is applied to archaeological objects. Electrochemical voltammetry of microparticles technique were used for the authenticity of lead samples. This methodology is based on the comparison of the height of specific voltammetric peaks from PbO_2 and PbO corrosion products formed (Doménech, 2011). This attribution, however, must be taken with caution because of the differences in the aging process for the studied samples and the lead materials used for calibration purposes corresponding to the reduction of the PbO 'continuous' patina formed under the ordinary exposure of the lead piece to the atmospheric environment. The proposed electrochemical technique enables the dating of lead artifacts with a time-dependent (Antonio Doménech-Carbó, Doménech-Carbó, & Costa, 2009; A Doménech-Carbó et al., 2017; Lahanier, 1991).

According to Lahanier et al. (1991) the electrochemical techniques are non-intrusive, non-destructive, fast, allowing the analysis of single artifacts as well as large collections of them. This method are able to deal with various shapes and sizes as well as providing information on both average or bulk composition of the artifact. Another advantage of this multi-element analysis, it's capability of allowing qualitative information on multiple elements or compounds present in the artifact by means of a single measurement (Lahanier,1991).

Materials authentication could help in our understanding not only to their functions but about other matters, such as trade and economy (Burtenshaw, 2013). In fact, the material remains of the past that conform to contemporary aesthetics are often the most valuable. It gives artifacts their legal authenticity and archaeological significance (Lovata, 2016).

Qasr Al-rabah temple is located in Al-Qasr town, approximately 5 km to the north of Al-rabah town, about 5 km to the north of Karak city and 18 km to south of Wadi Al-Mujib (Fig.1). During the Roman period, Qasr Al -rabah was one of the important cites of the ancient world. It was first excavated in 1993 by Al-Shiyab followed in the period 1995-2002. Early excavation which was conducted by Al-Shiyab, (1993), revealed that the site was extensively settled during the Roman and Byzantine periods. This site comprises a collection of ruins of various buildings and structural remains (Fig. 2). Considerable collections of glass, lead-based scale weights were uncovered, together with plenty of ceramic sherds from different structures (A. Al-Shiyab, 1993). Archaeological studies at the site were very rare and limited. Waterhouse (1998) studied the construction style of the tombs (Waterhouse, 1998). Abu-Baker et al. (Abu-Baker et al., 2014) studied the composition and corrosion behaviour of five archaeological lead scale weights. In a study conducted by Al-Shorman and Shiyab (2015) several ceramic sherds have been chemically and mineralogical analyzed to see the effect of function on selecting raw materials and technology.

The current article describes the analytical studies performed on five lead samples, one of the samples correspond to a fragment of a lead sarcophagus and the second weight sample from roman period. The data estimated from archaeological context was late Roman period (al-Āmmah, 1997; Al-Shiyab, 1993; Al-Shorman & Shiyab, 2015).

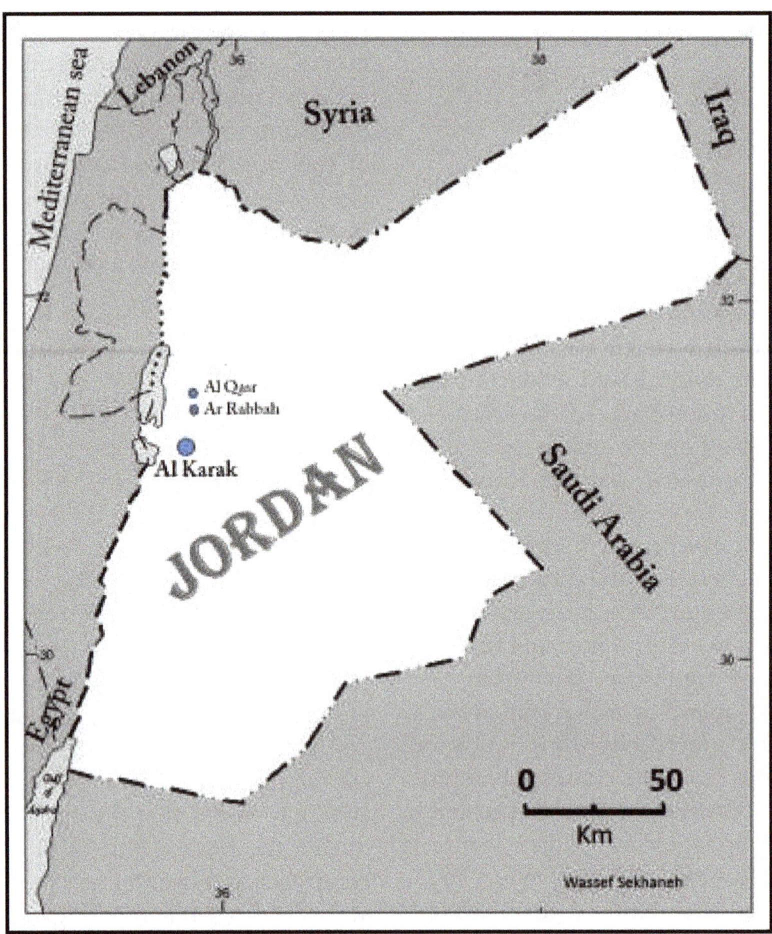

Figure 1. The location of archaeological site of Qasr Al -rabah

Figure 2. Temple remains in the study area

The study is primarily aimed to authenticate and to date the samples (Fig. 3). For this purpose, a series of electrochemical methods developed in our laboratory at Valencia university (Antonio Doménech-Carbó, Doménech-Carbó, & Peiró-Ronda, 2011; Antonio Doménech-Carbó, Doménech-Carbó, Peiró-Ronda, Martínez-Lázaro, & Barrio-Martín, 2012; A Doménech-Carbó et al., 2016; Antonio Doménech-Carbó, Doménech-Carbó, Capelo, Pasíes, & Martínez-Lázaro, 2014) have been used. These methods, based in the voltammetry of microparticles methodology for analyzing solid materials developed by Scholz et al. (Scholz, Schröder, & Gulaboski, 2005), involve non-destructive sampling and permits to obtain relevant information for archaeometry, conservation and restoration (Antonio Doménech-Carbó, 2010; Antonio Doménech-Carbó, et al., 2009; A Doménech-Carbó, et al., 2016), in particular, for authentication (A Doménech-Carbó, Doménech-Carbó, Peiró-Ronda, & Osete-Cortina, 2011; Doménech, 2011).

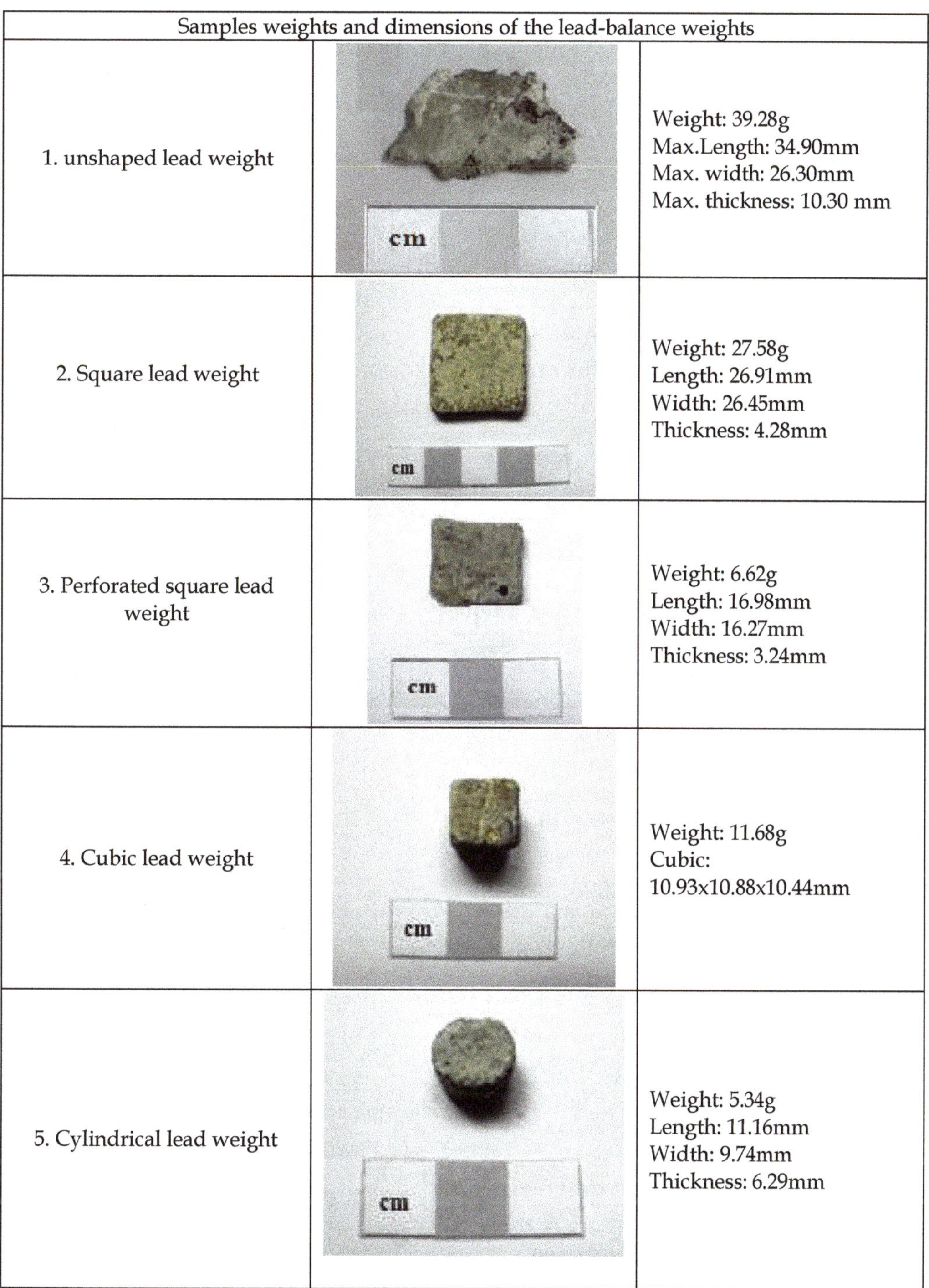

Samples weights and dimensions of the lead-balance weights		
1. unshaped lead weight		Weight: 39.28g Max.Length: 34.90mm Max. width: 26.30mm Max. thickness: 10.30 mm
2. Square lead weight		Weight: 27.58g Length: 26.91mm Width: 26.45mm Thickness: 4.28mm
3. Perforated square lead weight		Weight: 6.62g Length: 16.98mm Width: 16.27mm Thickness: 3.24mm
4. Cubic lead weight		Weight: 11.68g Cubic: 10.93x10.88x10.44mm
5. Cylindrical lead weight		Weight: 5.34g Length: 11.16mm Width: 9.74mm Thickness: 6.29mm

Figure 3. The studied lead samples from the temple of Qasr Al-rabah

It should be noted, however, that dating is obtained upon comparison of electrochemical data for samples with those for reference archaeological lead of known age which has been aged under identical calcareous environmental of burials conditions Table 1.

Table 1. reference lead samples After Doménech-Carbó (A Doménech-Carbó, et al., 2017)

Sample	Description of the Artifacts	Provenance
MP-1-1 to MP-1-3	Votive figurine; dark green surface, apparently homogeneous with greenish localized regions in corners	Iberian site (Despeñaperros, Jaén), fourth to second century BC
MP-2-1 to MP-2-3	Buckle, black surfaces with high homogeneity but with several localized greenish pits	San Cristóbal church (Picassent), 18th–19th century AD
UPV-1	*Gades, la dança*, dark grey surface apparently homogeneous	Sculpture by Antonio Miró, 2001
UPV-2	*Crónica del viento*, dark grey surface apparently homogeneous	Sculpture by Martín Chirino, 1991
UPV-3	*Unidad yunta*, dark grey surface apparently homogeneous	Sculpture by Pablo Serrano, 1970
V-122–1 to V-122–3	Fragment 1 of sculpture, dark grey surface with greenish localized regions	*Valeria* site, second half of the first century AD
V-390-1 to V-390-3	Fragment 2 of sculpture, dark grey surface with greenish localized regions	*Valeria* site, second half of the first century AD
VI-1-1 and VI-1-2	Fibulae, dark green surface, apparently homogeneous, with greenish pitting and localized regions in corners	El Viveret site, first to second century AD
G-1-1 to G-1-4	Pieces 1–4 of a set of weights, black surfaces with high homogeneity	*Gadara* site, fourth century AD
X-1	Fragment of spur (Caliphal period), dark green surface with greenish localized regions in corners	Xàtiva (Valencia), AD 950

The study is based on disposable data for calibration corresponding to samples corroded under burial conditions in calcareous soils all from the Mediterranean region of Spain Doménech-Carbó, A., et al., (2017).

2. MATERIALS

Sampling was performed by means of the one-touch technique already described (Doménech-Carbó et al. 2011) using 0.1 mm diameter graphite bars (Staedtler HB). One touch method means: the minimum amount (im microe or nano scale) of corrosion products that one could get once electrode touch the materials. Sample 1 consisted of a lead plate ca. 1.5 × 1.5 × 0.3 cm. Fig. 4 shows an apparently recent cut in one of its corners and one circular hole (ca. 1 mm diameter) in the vicinity of other of the corners. Except in the cut region, the piece is covered by a gross, continuous white-grey patina. Sampling was performed in the center of the piece and in the cut region (labeled in the following as S1corr and S1cut). Sample 2 consisted of an irregular lead plate covered by a gross white crust (see Fig. 4). Sampling was performed in two regions where the patinated lead appeared exposed with grey (S2grey) and reddish (S2red) hues. As a control, a lead sample from the buildings at the University of Valencia (30 years old) was used. Architect used these lead nails in the construction of the building, and they used it as decoration features. The lead nails were the same age of the construction and uses as reference to measure the time of corrosion process. This consisted of a grey button 1 cm diameter with no traces of gross corrosion processes.

Table 1. Description of the studied samples in this study.

Sample	Piece	Description
S1corr	Piece 1	Corroded zone of white-grey hue
S1cut	Piece 1	Cut region, dark grey hue
S2grey	Piece 2	Grey region exposed under the white crust
S2red	Piece 2	Reddish region exposed under the white crust

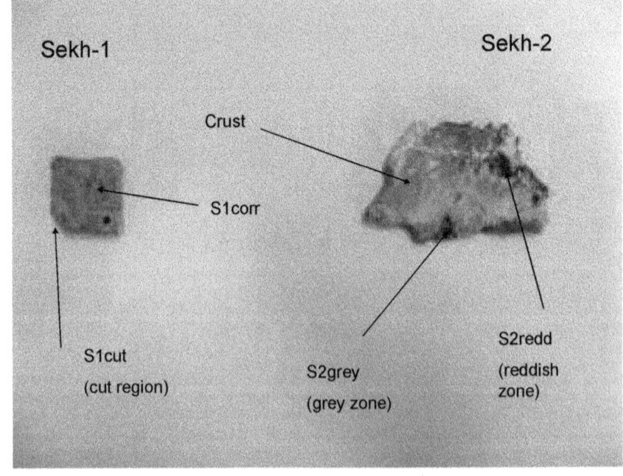

Figure 4. Image of the lead fragments in this study with indication of regions where the sampling was carried out.

3. METHODS AND EXPERIEMENTS

The advantage of using the electrochemical method are non-intrusive, non-destructive, fast and allowing the analysis of single artifacts as well as large collections of them. This method could use various shapes and sizes to provide information on both average or bulk composition of the artifact and the exact and localized composition of areas. Multielement analysis capability, allowing qualitative information on multiple elements or compounds present in the artifact by means of a single measurement. Electrochemical experiments were performed using a CH I660C potentiostat according to the manufacturing product. Measurements were performed in 0.25 M acetic acid/sodium acetate Buffer (Panreac), pH 4.75, in a thermostated three-electrode cell under argon atmosphere using a AgCl (3M NaCl)/Ag as reference electrode and a platinum-wire auxiliary electrode. Voltammetry of micro-particles (VMP) experiments were performed at sample-modified at paraffin impregnated graphite electrodes (PIGEs).

Five independent measurements were performed for each sample; reported numerical values for the different electrochemical parameters involved in this study correspond to average values from each series of measurements. Electrochemical impedance spectroscopy (EIS) was carried out using a ±10 mV perturbation signal within a frequency range from 100 kHz to 0.10 Hz at different potentials. Sampling for electrochemical measurements was performed by means of the 'one-touch' procedure by pressing the edge of the graphite electrode on the desired point of the lead sample as described in literature (Antonio Doménech-Carbó, et al., 2012; Scholz, et al., 2005). Sampling was performed on two of the fragments whose surfaces appeared as no submitted to recent scratching. Sample S1cut, immersed into 0.25 M HAc/NaAc, pH 4.75. Potential scan initiated at +1.25 V in the negative direction. Potential step increment 4 mV; square wave amplitude 25 mV; frequency 5 Hz.

4. RESULTS AND DISCUSSION

The authenticity result compares the square wave voltammograms recorded for for : a) recent lead fragment (30 years old); b) sample S1cut, immersed into 0.25 M HAc/ NaAc, pH 4.75. Potential scan initiated at +1.25 V in the negative direction. Potential step increments 4 mV; square wave amplitude 25 mV; frequency 5 Hz.

The authenticity tests measurements (VMP) for (30 years old) lead piece shows no sign of detectable corrosion layer and very low intensity peak, which is related to the short time span of the sample S1cut in contact with aqueous acetate buffer (Fig 5a,b). The voltammogram of the S1cut sample shows the characteristic features of archaeological lead. As you can see from the figure and if compared with Fig.5a one defines the define and the sharp cathodic peaks at +0.80 V, assigned to the reduction of PbO_2-type species, and-1.00 V, which correspond to the reduction of 'porous' layers of PbO formed on the metal surface. Such peaks accompany the ubiquitous peak at -0.70 V corresponding to the reduction of the PbO 'continuous' patina formed under the ordinary exposure of the lead piece to the atmospheric environment (A Doménech-Carbó, et al., 2017) .

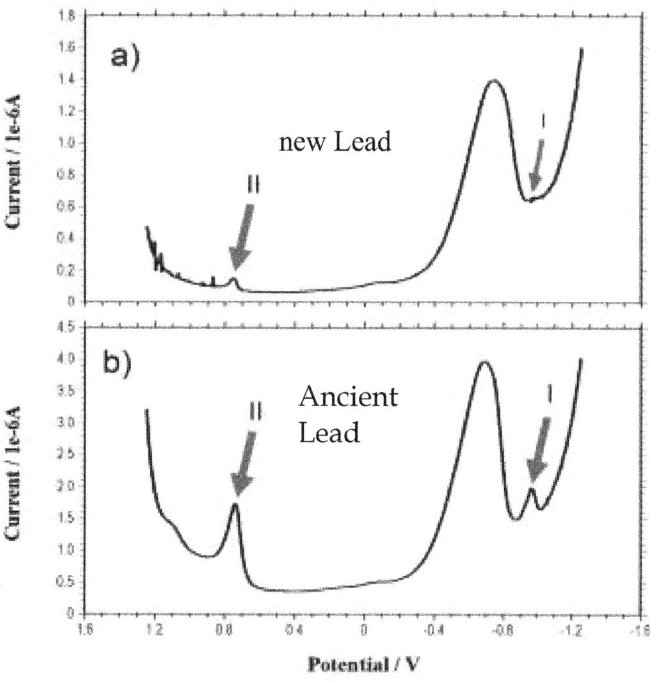

Figure 5. Square wave voltammograms for graphite electrodes modified by means of 'one-touch' methodology

As can be seen in Fig. 6 the cyclic voltametric responses recorded at graphite electrodes modified by means of 'one-touch' methodology for: a) modern lead fragment (30 years old), b) sample S1corr, c) sample S2grey; d) sample S2red.The samples exhibit the profiles characteristic of aged lead, with enhanced cathodic signals at ca. -1.0 V (marked by arrows) and oxidative dissolutions signals at ca. -0.50 V (dotted arrows). These last signals correspond to the oxidation of lead metal previously generated in the reduction of lead corrosion products at more negative potentials. Pb metal is oxidized to Pb2+ (aq) ions in solution giving rise to characteristic tall (stripping) peaks. .As seen in figure 5 the voltammetry measurements : a) recent lead fragment (30 years old), b) sample S1corr, c) sample S2grey; d)sample S2red, immersed into 0.25 M HAc/NaAc, pH 4.75. Potential scan rate 50 mV/s.

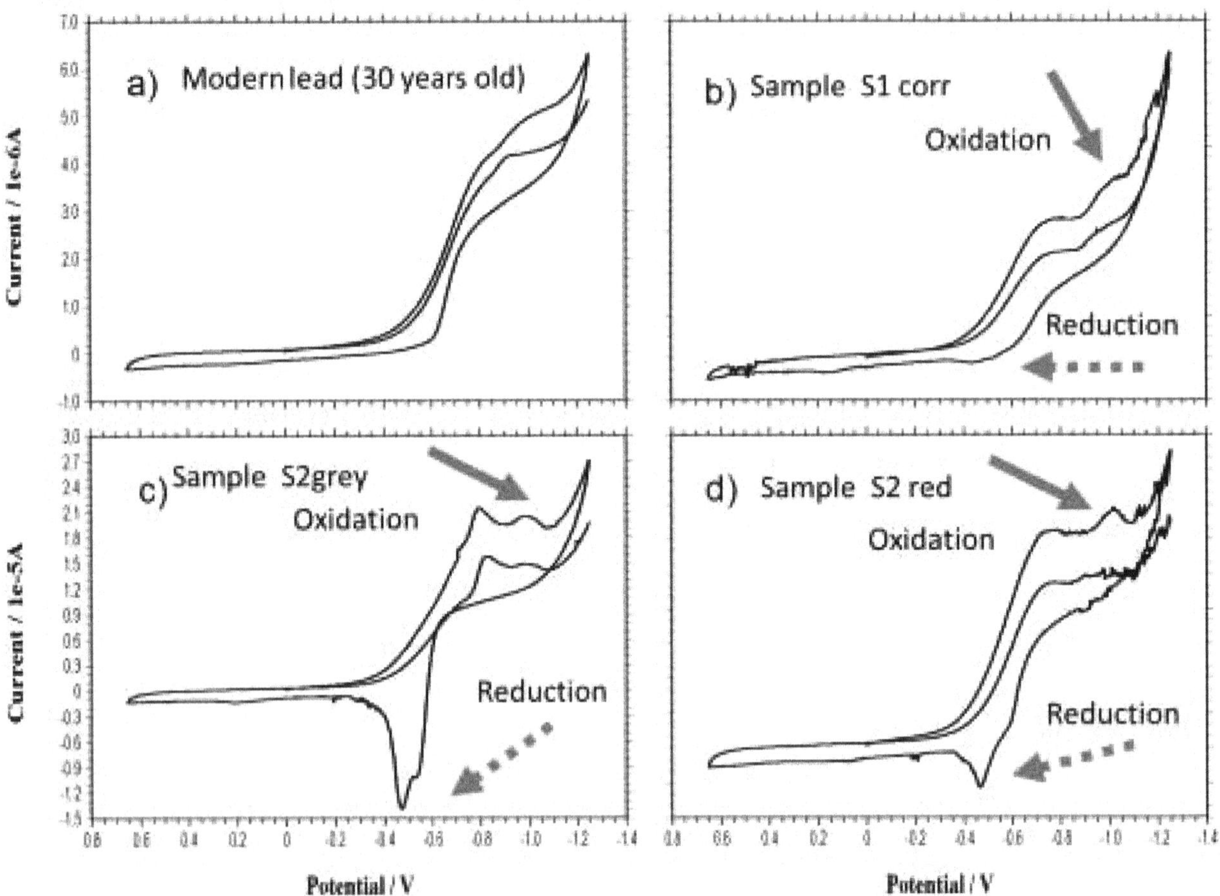

Figure 6. Cyclic voltammetry measurments for graphite electrodes (Oxidation –Reduction) modified by means of 'one-touch' method for the lead samples

Such stripping peaks can be clearly seen in square wave voltammograms obtained upon scanning the potential in the positive direction, as can be seen in Fig. 4. Here, the lead stripping signals at ca. -0.50 V are accompanied by minor signals attributable to copper (oxidative dissolution peak at ca. 0 V). Other weak signals could denote the presence of antimony (ca. -0.20 V) and arsenic (ca. +0.20 V).

In order to confirm the result in Fig. 4, and for double checking that our result is consistent with the estimation, the square wave stripping method was used. Through this method stripping peaks can be clearly seen in square wave voltammograms obtained upon scanning the potential in the positive direction, as can be seen in Fig. 7 Here, the lead stripping signals at ca. -0.50 V are accompanied by minor signals attributable to copper (oxidative dissolution peak at ca. 0 V). Other weak signals could denote the presence of antimony (ca. -0.20 V) and arsenic (ca. +0.20 V) as a minority accompanying elements. The presence of minor components accompanying lead can be considered as demonstrating of the 'ancient' origin of the metallic material, as far as the signals of minority components are absent in 'modern' and contemporary lead (Antonio Doménech-Carbó, et al., 2011; Doménech, 2011).

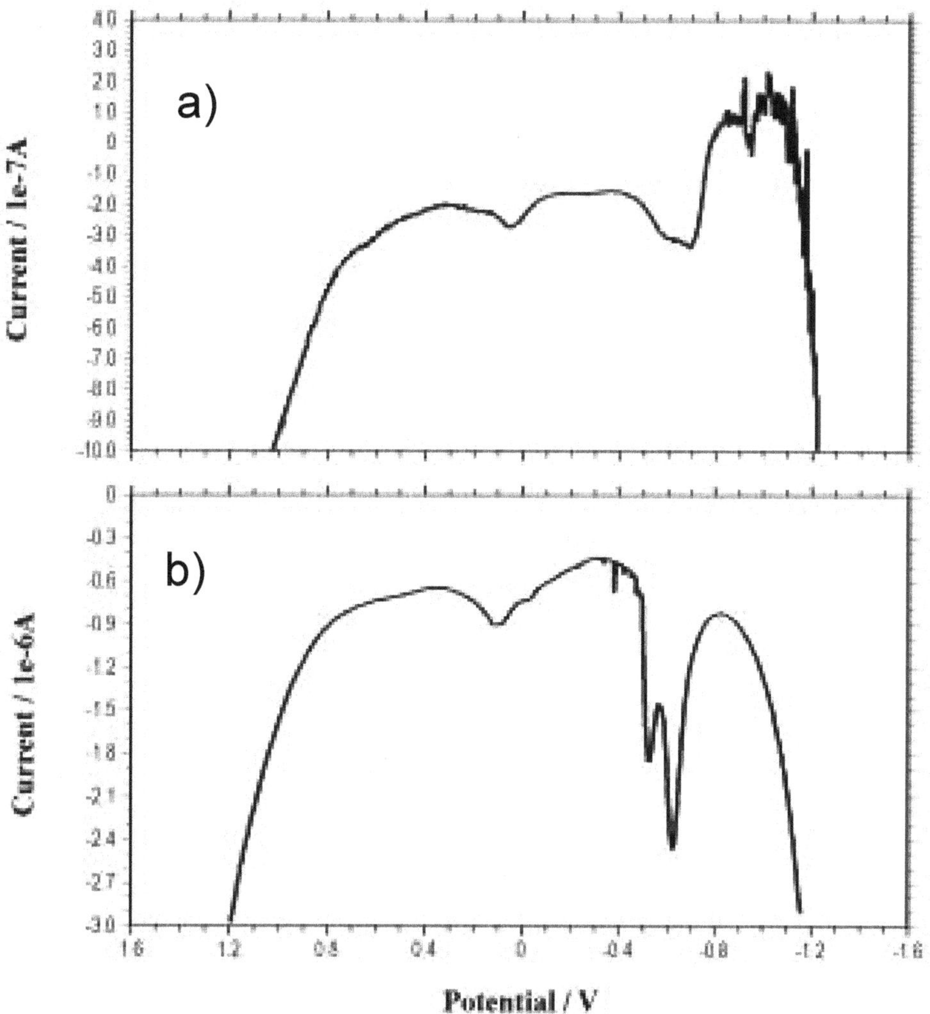

Figure 7. Square wave voltammograms for graphite electrodes modified by means of 'one-touch' methodology for samples a) S1corr and b) S2grey immersed into 0.25 M

The dating method of the studied samples was performed using the procedures described in detail in (Antonio Doménech-Carbó, et al., 2009; Antonio Doménech-Carbó, et al., 2012; Scholz, et al., 2005), as described in the following.

The method is based on the determination of the peak ratio for signals corresponding to the reduction of continuous and porous PbO layers recorded, as recommended in (Scholz, et al., 2005), in voltammograms such as in Fig.7. The peak current (ip(II)/ip(I)) and peak area (A(II)/A(I)) ratios for the studied samples (see Table 1) was compared with the calibration curve obtained for Spanish archaeological samples. This comparison can be seen in Fig. 6, where the variation of the peak area ratio vs. the estimated age is depicted. In this figure, A(II)/A(I) is plotted against $(age)^{0.935}$, a representation resulting from the fit of calibration data to a potential law as previously described (Antonio Doménech-Carbó, et al., 2009; Scholz, et al., 2005). As can be seen in Fig. 7 that data points for samples S1corr, S2grey and S2red are located close, but separated, from the calibration line, whereas sample S1cut falls clearly separated from the calibration line. These data suggest that both samples S1 and S2 are contemporary and their age can be estimated within a time range of ca. 1500 ± 150 years. Sample S1cut separates clearly from the above, but this separation can be attributed to the different time in which this region was probably submitted to corrosion. Squares correspond to calibration data from Spanish samples Purple squares denote the measured samples in this study, which have an age of 1600 years BP (Fig. 9).

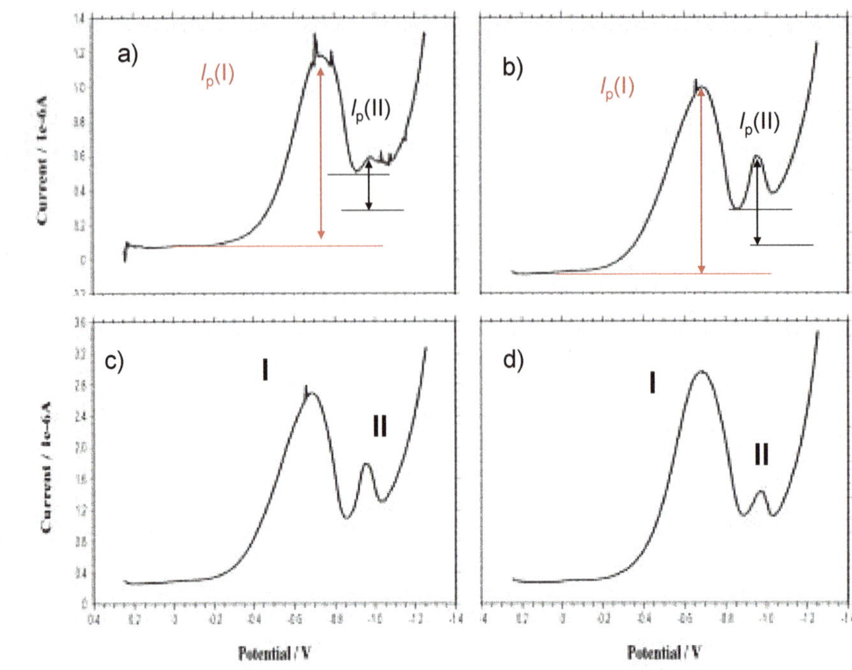

Figure 8. Square wave voltamograms for graphite electrodes modified by means of 'one-touch' methodology.

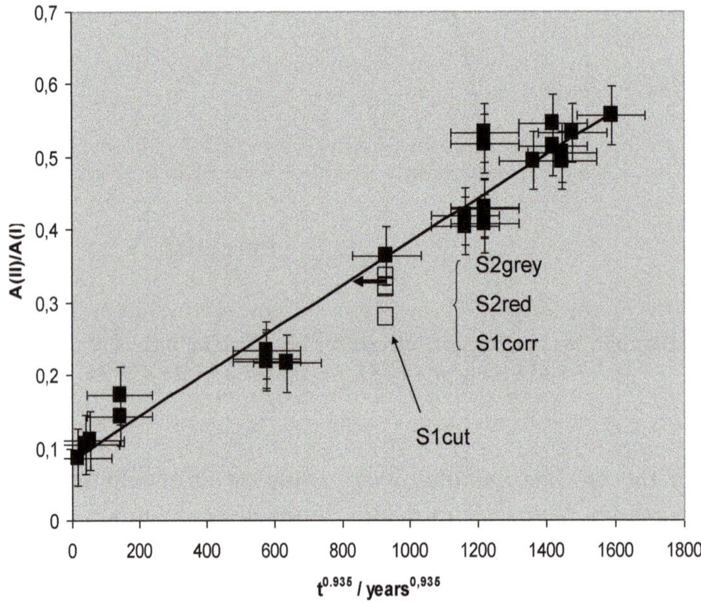

Figure 9. Peak area ratio vs. estimated age representation for archaeological lead.

As previously described, the Litharge PbO to Plattnerite PbO_2 ratio, expected from the intensity of peak current ratio between the signals(II) and (I), ip(II)/ip(I), is used to calculate the age of a lead artifacts. Figure 8 shows the position of the ancient samples in our study, corrosion products were extracted from lead weight balances from the site of Qasr Al-rabaha (4th century AC, Jordan) (see Fig. 3), in the calibration curve constructed from already reported table 1.

Using Electrochemical impedance spectroscopy measurements (EIS) to confirm the authenticity by comparing the series of samples in Table 1 with our measured samples. EIS experiments produced results comparable to those reported in Doménech-Carbó, A., et al., (2017). The Fig. 10 compares the (phase angle) vs. log(frequency) plots for recent lead and S2grey sample, both in contact with aqueous acetate buffer. Here the high frequency region for both samples is similar while the phase angle clearly differs in the low frequency region. This feature can be attributed to the different charge transfer properties associated to the different thickness of the corrosion layers. Comparison of the measured phase angles at a frequency of 0.10 Hz, taken as age-representative quantity (Antonio Doménech-Carbó, et al., 2012; Scholz, et al., 2005), permits a calibration plot depicted in Fig. 10. As can be seen in this figure, here once again data for the studied samples are consistent with the attribution to an aging time of ca. 1600 years. Bode (phase angle) vs. log(frequency) plots for a recent lead fragment (30 years old, black data points), and sample S2grey (red data points), immersed into 0.25 M HAc/NaAc, pH 4.75, aqueous solution. Bias potential -0.95 V.

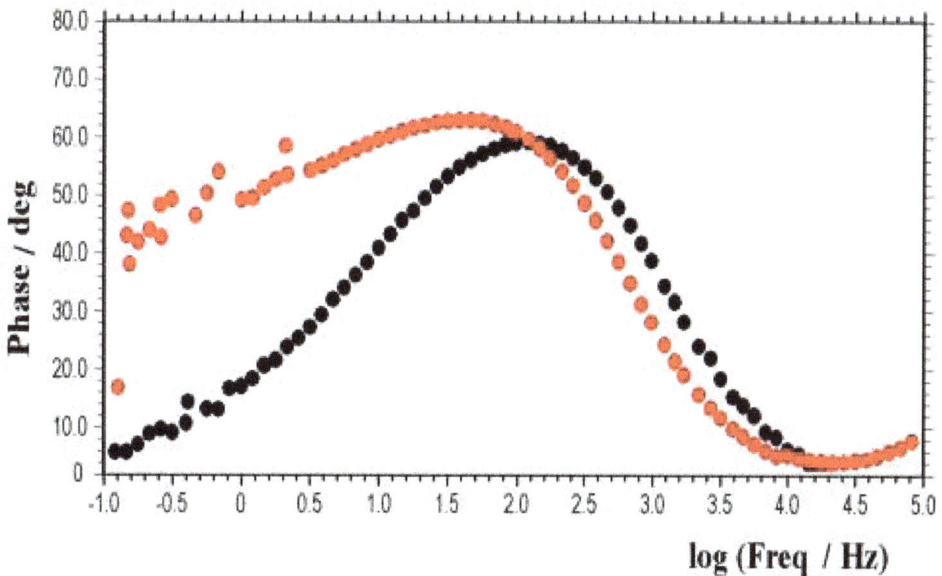

Figure 10. Bode (phase angle) vs. log(frequency) plots for a recent lead fragment (30 years old, black data points), and sample S2grey (red data points), immersed into 0.25 M HAc/NaAc, pH 4.75, aqueous solution. Bias potential -0.95 V.

EIS experiments are achieved in this study for samples that were used different bias potentials and electrolyte media, including 0.25 M aqueous of acetic acid / sodium acetate buffer at pH 4.75. After equilibration for 10 min, the EIS curves showed excellent good repeatability for replicate experiments performed for a fixed set of conditions. However, experiments varying the level of the immersion and the location of the connected clamp, although maintaining the profile of Bode plots and Nyquist, produced major variations in the numerical values of the impedance variables. These features can be seen in Fig. 9, where the Bode plots and the Nyquist of repeated experiments for a sample in two different immersion plus clamp configurations are shown.

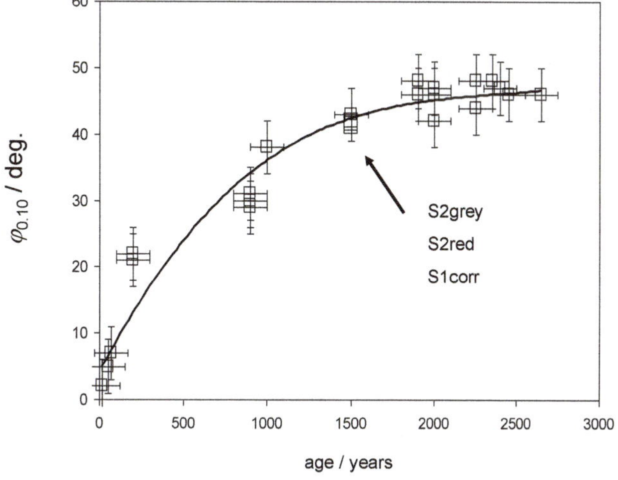

Figure 11. Calibration plots showing the variation of phase angle at a frequency of 0.10 Hz, $\varphi_{0.10}$, with the corrosion time for samples in this study. Data from EIS experiments for sample-modified graphite electrodes immersed into 0.25 M HAc/NaAc. Bias potential -0.95 V.

As can be seen in Fig. 8, insertion of data points for S1corr, S2grey and S2red samples in this study falls in the calibration curve obtained from a set of archaeological lead samples from Spain (Doménech-Carbó et al. 2009, 2012) for an age of 1500 ± 100 years, thus agreeing square wave voltammetric data from independent experiments. Fig.11 shows the variation of the maximum phase angle at intermediate frequencies with the nominal age of several artifacts in the study. From five replicate EIS measurements for each sample that were immersed in mineral water. The continuous curve corresponds to the fit of the data to a potential equation. In calibration plots resulted (Fig.11), the variation of the phase angle φ frequencies with respect to the age of several samples is shown.

5. CONCLUSION

Assuming the 5th century AD chronology of the lead samples erection to be correct, it was found that the applied method provide the same result which is consistent with archaeological estimations. The voltammetry of microparticle–nanoparticle is an excellent non-destructive method, used in authenticity and dating archaeological materials.

The electrochemical methods which have been used in this study are easy, cheap and convenient. VMP could help in a absolute chronology for archaeological metals.

At the expense of a re-calibration using additional archaeological samples, the electrochemical analysis performed on samples in this study permits to conclude:

1) The studied samples exhibit the voltametric features characteristic of lead of archaeological origin, namely, stripping peaks for minority components accompanying lead and well-developed signals for PbO_2 and porous PbO patinas.

2) Comparison of electrochemical parameters using two sets of independent experiments: square wave voltametry and electrochemical impedance spectroscopy with the corresponding calibration curves obtained from Spanish archaeological samples corroded under burial conditions in calcareous soils, are consistent with an attribution of the age of both studied lead samples to 1450 ± 150 years. This attribution, however, must be taken with caution because of the differences in the aging process for the studied samples and the lead materials used for calibration purposes.

ACKNOWLEDGEMENTS

We are grateful to Prof. Dr. Antonio Doménech-Carbó from Department de Química Analítica, Universitat de València in Spain for the laboratory support.

REFERENCES

Abu-Baker, A., Al Sekhaneh, W., Shiyab, A., Dellith, J., Scheffel, A., Alebrahim, M. A., et al. (2014). Analytical Invistigation of Five Roman PB-based Scale Wieght (Qasr Ar-Rabbah, Jordan): A case study. *Mediterranean Archaeology and Archaeometry, 14*(1,), 181-190.

al-ʿĀmmah, J. D. a.-Ā. (1997). *Annual of the Department of Antiquities*: Department of Antiquities, Hashemite Kingdom of Jordan.

Al-Shiyab, A. (1993). *Excavation at Al-Qasr and Ar-Rabba unpublished excavation report at Faculty of Archaeology.* Yarmouk University in Jordan..

Al-Shorman, A., & Shiyab, A. (2015). The effect of function on the selection of raw materials and manufacturing technology of Byzantine pottery: A case study from Qasr Ar-Rabbah, South Jordan. *Mediterranean Archaeology & Archaeometry, 15*(2).

Brusic, V., Dimilia, D. D., & MacInnes, R. (1991). Corrosion of lead, tin, and their alloys. *Corrosion, 47*(7), 509-518.

Burtenshaw, P. (2013). *The Economic Capital of Archaeology: Measurement and Management.* UCL (University College London).

Cruz,J, Figueiredo,E, Corregidor, V, Girginova, P.I, Alves, L.C,ׅ Cruz, C Silva, R.J.C, and Liritzis, I (2015) First Results on Radiometric Dating of Metals by Alpha Spectrometry. Microchemical Journal, *124, 608-614,* doi:10.1016/j.microc.2015.10.001

Doménech-Carbó, A. (2010). Voltammetric methods applied to identification, speciation, and quantification of analytes from works of art: an overview. *Journal of Solid State Electrochemistry, 14*(3), 363-379.

Doménech-Carbó, A., Doménech-Carbó, M., Peiró-Ronda, M., & Osete-Cortina, L. (2011). Authentication of archaeological lead artifacts using voltammetry of microparticles: the case of the Tossal de Sant Miquel Iberian plate. *Archaeometry, 53*, 1193-1211.

Doménech-Carbó, A., Doménech-Carbó, M. T., & Costa, V. (2009). *Electrochemical methods in archaeometry, conservation and restoration*: Springer Science & Business Media.

Doménech-Carbó, A., Doménech-Carbó, M. T., & Peiró-Ronda, M. A. (2011). Dating archeological lead artifacts from measurement of the corrosion content using the voltammetry of microparticles. *Analytical Chemistry, 83*(14), 5639-5644.

Doménech-Carbó, A., Doménech-Carbó, M. T., Peiró-Ronda, M. A., Martínez-Lázaro, I., & Barrio-Martín, J. (2012). Application of the voltammetry of microparticles for dating archaeological lead using polarization curves and electrochemical impedance spectroscopy. *Journal of Solid State Electrochemistry, 16*(7), 2349-2356.

Doménech-Carbó, A., Capelo, S., Piquero, J., Doménech-Carbó, M., Barrio, J., Fuentes, A., et al. (2016). Dating archaeological copper using electrochemical impedance spectroscopy. Comparison with voltammetry of microparticles dating. *Materials and Corrosion, 67*(2), 120-129.

Doménech-Carbó, A., Doménech-Carbó, M., Redondo-Marugán, J., Osete-Cortina, L., Barrio, J., Fuentes, A., et al. (2017). Electrochemical Characterization and Dating of Archaeological Leaded Bronze Objects Using the Voltammetry of Immobilized Particles. *Archaeometry, in press,* DOI: 10.1111/arcm.12308.

Doménech-Carbó, A., Doménech-Carbó, M. T., Capelo, S., Pasíes, T., & Martínez-Lázaro, I. (2014). Dating archaeological copper/bronze artifacts by using the voltammetry of microparticles. *Angewandte Chemie International Edition, 53*(35), 9262-9266.

Doménech, A. (2011). Tracing, authenticating and dating archaeological metal using the voltammetry of microparticles. *Analytical Methods, 3*(10), 2181-2188.

Holtorf, C., & Schadla-Hall, T. (1999). Age as artefact: on archaeological authenticity. *European journal of archaeology, 2*(2), 229-247.

Lahanier, C. (1991). Scientific methods applied to the study of art objects. *Microchimica Acta, 104*(1), 245-254.

Lovata, T. R. (2016). *Inauthentic archaeologies: public uses and abuses of the past*: Routledge.

Liritzis, I (2006) The dating of ancient metals: review and a possible application of the ^{226}Ra/ ^{230}Th method: (a tutorial). *Mediterranean Archaeology & Archaeometry,* 6, 2, 81-95.

Miller, F., Sayre, E. V., & Keisch, B. (1970). Isotopic methods of examination and authentication in art and archaeology.

Nambi, K. (1981). Thermoluminescence as a tool for dating and authenticating in archaeology. *Nuclear India, 19*(6), 1-8.

Odegaard, N., & Cassman, V. (2014). Authentication and Conservation in Archaeological Science *Encyclopedia of Global Archaeology* (pp. 702-711): Springer.

Rocca, E., Mirambet, F., & Steinmetz, J. (2004). Study of ancient lead materials: A gallo-roman sarcophagus—contribution of the electrolytic treatment to its restoration. *Journal of materials science, 39*(8), 2767-2774.

Scholz, F., Schröder, U., & Gulaboski, R. (2005). *Electrochemistry of immobilized particles and droplets*: Springer.

Taylor, A. (1993). A Roman lead coffin with pipeclay figurines from Arrington, Cambridgeshire. *Britannia, 24*, 191-225.

Waterhouse, S. (1998). Tomb Type I: Chamber tombs with loculi radiating from the chamber (pp. 21-44): Andrews Univ. Press, Berrien Springs, MI.

Permissions

All chapters in this book were first published in MAA, by University of the Aegean; hereby published with permission under the Creative Commons Attribution License or equivalent. Every chapter published in this book has been scrutinized by our experts. Their significance has been extensively debated. The topics covered herein carry significant findings which will fuel the growth of the discipline. They may even be implemented as practical applications or may be referred to as a beginning point for another development.

The contributors of this book come from diverse backgrounds, making this book a truly international effort. This book will bring forth new frontiers with its revolutionizing research information and detailed analysis of the nascent developments around the world.

We would like to thank all the contributing authors for lending their expertise to make the book truly unique. They have played a crucial role in the development of this book. Without their invaluable contributions this book wouldn't have been possible. They have made vital efforts to compile up to date information on the varied aspects of this subject to make this book a valuable addition to the collection of many professionals and students.

This book was conceptualized with the vision of imparting up-to-date information and advanced data in this field. To ensure the same, a matchless editorial board was set up. Every individual on the board went through rigorous rounds of assessment to prove their worth. After which they invested a large part of their time researching and compiling the most relevant data for our readers.

The editorial board has been involved in producing this book since its inception. They have spent rigorous hours researching and exploring the diverse topics which have resulted in the successful publishing of this book. They have passed on their knowledge of decades through this book. To expedite this challenging task, the publisher supported the team at every step. A small team of assistant editors was also appointed to further simplify the editing procedure and attain best results for the readers.

Apart from the editorial board, the designing team has also invested a significant amount of their time in understanding the subject and creating the most relevant covers. They scrutinized every image to scout for the most suitable representation of the subject and create an appropriate cover for the book.

The publishing team has been an ardent support to the editorial, designing and production team. Their endless efforts to recruit the best for this project, has resulted in the accomplishment of this book. They are a veteran in the field of academics and their pool of knowledge is as vast as their experience in printing. Their expertise and guidance has proved useful at every step. Their uncompromising quality standards have made this book an exceptional effort. Their encouragement from time to time has been an inspiration for everyone.

The publisher and the editorial board hope that this book will prove to be a valuable piece of knowledge for researchers, students, practitioners and scholars across the globe.

List of Contributors

Derya Atamtürk and İzzet Duyar
İstanbul University, Faculty of Letters, Department of Anthropology, Ordu Caddesi 6, 34134 Laleli/İstanbul, Turkey

Rana Özbal
Koç University, Department of Archaeology and History of Art, Rumelifeneri Yolu, 34450 Sarıyer/İstanbul, Turkey

Fokke Gerritsen
Netherlands Institute in Turkey, İstiklal Caddesi 181, Merkez Han, 34433 Beyoğlu/İstanbul, Turkey

Vahid Pourzarghan
Department of Restoration, Faculty of Art and Architecture, University of Zabol, Iran

Hossein Sarhaddi-Dadian
Archaeological Research Center, University of Zabol, Iran

Zuliskandar Ramli
Institute of the Malay World and Civilization, the National University of Malaysia

Atilla Batmaz
Ege University, Department of Archaeology, 35100, Bornova, Izmir, Turkey

İlker Özkan
Dokuz Eylül University, Torbalı Vocational School, Industrial Glass and Ceramics Department, Torbalı, Izmir, Turkey

G. Barone, P. Mazzoleni, L. Mirabella and S. Raneri
University of Catania, Department of Biological, Geological and Environmental Sciences, C.so Italia 57, 95129 Catania, Italy

R. Chowaniec and M. Fituła
University of Warsaw, Institute of Archeology, Krakowskie Przedmiescie 26/28, PL 00-927, Warsaw, Poland

Zisan Kaplan, Basak Ipekoglu and Hasan Boke
Department of Architectural Restoration, İzmir Institute of Technology

Álvaro Sánchez-Climent and María L. Cerdeño
Departamento de Prehistoria. Facultad de Geografía e Historia. Universidad Complutense de Madrid. 28040. Madrid. Spain

Carlos J. Sánchez-Jiménez
Área de Mineralogía y Cristalografía. Departamento de Química-Física. Facultad de Ciencias y Tecnologías Químicas. Universidad de Castilla-La Mancha. 13071. Ciudad Real. Spain

Francisco J. Poblete
Departamento de Química-Física. Facultad de Ciencias y Tecnologías Químicas. Universidad de Castilla-La Mancha. 13071. Ciudad Real. Spain

Javier Rodriguez-Corral
School of Archaeology, University of Oxford, UK

Kalaitzaki, A, Vafiadou, A and Frony, A.
Dept. of Mediterranean Studies, University of the Aegean, Rhodes, Greece

Reese, D.S.
Peabody Museum of Natural History, Yale University, New Haven, U.S.A.

Drivaliari, A
Lab of Environmental Archaeology, Dept. of Mediterranean Studies, University of the Aegean, Rhodes, Greece

Liritzis, I
Collaborative Innovation Center on Yellow River Civilization of Henan Province & Key Research Institute of Yellow River Civilization and Sustainable Development, Henan University, China
Dept. of Mediterranean Studies, Lab of Archaeometry, University of the Aegean, 1 Demokratias Str., Rhodes 85132, Greece

D. Albero Santacreu and M. À. Capellà Galmés
Department of Historical Sciences and Arts Theory, University of the Balearic Islands (Spain), Ramon Llull, Campus UIB, Ctra. Valldemossa km 7.5 s/n 07122 Palma, Spain

José Mirão and António Candeias
HERCULES Lab, University of Evora, Portugal

Carlo Bottaini
HERCULES Lab, University of Evora, Portugal
CIDEHUS, University of Evora, Portugal

Raquel Vilaça
Institute of Archaeology, CEAACP, University of Coimbra, Portugal

Ignacio Montero-Ruiz
Instituto de Historia-CSIC, Spain

Ahmed Elyamani
Archaeological Conservation Department, Cairo University, Giza, Egypt

Oriol Caselles, Pere Roca and Jaime Clapes
Department of Civil and Environmental Engineering, Technical University of Catalonia, Barcelona, Spain

Yasin Zidan, Wafika Noshy and Eman Salim
Conservation Departement, Faculty of Archaeology, Cairo University, Egypt

Ahmed El-Shafei
Polymer and Color Chemistry, College of Textile, North Carolina State University, USA

Index

R

S

T

U

X

Lightning Source UK Ltd.
Milton Keynes UK
UKHW052033220922
409258UK00002B/53